CONFESSING AND COMMENDING THE FAITH

CONFESSING AND COMMENDING THE FAITH

HISTORIC WITNESS AND APOLOGETIC METHOD

Alan P. F. Sell

Wipf & Stock
PUBLISHERS
Eugene, Oregon

Wipf and Stock Publishers
199 W 8th Ave, Suite 3
Eugene, OR 97401

Confessing and Commending the Faith
By Sell, Alan P. F.

ISBN: 1-59752-872-2
Publication date 8/11/2006
Previously published by University of Wales Press, 2002

This edition of Confessing and Commending the Faith: Historic Witness and Apologetic Method is published by arrangement with University of Wales Press.

To our grandchildren:
Andrew and Christopher,
Lisa, Nicola and Olivia,
Alejandro and Elisabeth,
and in memory of
Rachel

May [God's] Providence guard, and his Grace sanctify and save you! May you continue to bear the ark of Christian testimony when our heads are no longer able to uphold the sacred cause! May you tell to the generation that we shall never behold, that there is no peace but in virtue, no assurance of the pardon of sin but in the mercy of God, and no hope of the life to come but in the Gospel of our Lord and Saviour Jesus Christ! May God's merciful presence be with you and yours until that joyful, solemn day, when we shall meet, if we be worthy followers of the Son of Man, to celebrate the warfare of earthly virtue accomplished and the victory over death and the grave achieved, and to wear and triumph in the crown of life everlasting! Amen.

(Robert Aspland, *The Beauty and Excellence of Christian Morality. A Sermon for the Young*, 1838)

Contents

Preface

With this volume I complete a trilogy concerned with the approach to Christian apologetics. In the first two volumes, *John Locke and the Eighteenth-Century Divines* and *Philosophical Idealism and Christian Belief*, I took historical soundings with a view to showing how starting points and methods are of critical importance in the attempt to commend the Christian faith. I presumed to find certain difficulties in the approaches of Locke and his successors, and in those of the British post-Hegelian Christian idealists to whom I paid attention. I must now directly address the question: is there a more satisfactory approach, or is the apologetic aspiration for ever doomed? I attempt to answer this question with reference both to the Christian testimony of the ages and to those within and without the Church who have queried, and in some cases denied, the possibility of viable Christian apologetics. My concern is thus with the prolegomena to Christian apologetics. Since I have sought fully to explain my objectives in the following Introduction, I shall say no more about them here. Two general observations may, however, be made.

First, it may become evident that this is the work of one who has sought, with greater or lesser degrees of success, to occupy more than one frontier: most obviously that between theology and philosophy; but also that between Christian thought and actual church life at various periods. In this latter connection, while by no means uninterested in the broad swathe of Christian thought, I have over a number of years focused upon Reformed thought in general and English Dissenting thought in particular, with a view to seeing what happens on the ground when, for whatever reasons, Christians embrace certain ideas or espouse particular interpretations of doctrine. But this activity opens up a further frontier: that between the Reformed and other Christian traditions. Hence my ecumenical interests, my concern for the manifestation of genuine catholicity by those who are, by grace, one in Christ, and my abhorrence of sectarian impediments to this. Finally there is the frontier between Christianity and the many other faiths by which people live. In this connection above all I believe that it is possible and desirable to be committed in faith and eirenic in spirit; and while I have not had the opportunity of occupying this frontier so regularly or for such long periods as many other writers, I trust that my passing references to it in this book will sufficiently indicate the importance I attach to it.

Secondly, in my attempts to expound and assess the views of others, I shall from time to time find it necessary to discuss the earlier writings of some (among them some of the Death of God theologians of the 1960s, for example) whose literary endeavours continue unabated. I do this because of the interest of positions they once adopted, without in any way implying that they would necessarily speak in identical terms today. Incidentally, I have noticed an unfortunate tendency in some quarters to be so 'instant' or to do such obeisance to the god Relevance that ideas of the recent past are dismissed as 'old hat', passé – an attitude which is never more incongruous than when it is adopted by writers who seem to have no qualms about exploring the more obscure nooks and crannies of medieval or patristic thought.

As other duties have permitted, this trilogy has occupied me for the past fifteen years, though some of the ideas in it have been circulating in my mind since student days. I have earlier sought to test some of these ideas in articles in a variety of journals, and have reworked a few paragraphs from these for present purposes. I have even drawn some thoughts from hitherto unpublished portions of my Nottingham doctoral thesis of 1967. For the initial testing of these ideas by editors and examiners alike I am grateful.

In relation to this third volume I express thanks to the staff of the following libraries: The British Library; Dr Williams's Library, London; the Hugh Owen Library, University of Wales, Aberystwyth; the National Library of Wales; and Princeton Theological Seminary Library. It is a testimony to the comprehensiveness of the library of the United Theological College, Aberystwyth, and to its particular strengths in modern Christian thought, that I have not had to stray from home as much as I expected in order to locate the books and journals needed for this task. Since an extensive bibliography was reduced first to a list of works referred to in the text and notes, and then only to a selection of these, I ought to explain that for translations of patristic and medieval texts I have turned to such standard series as the *Ante-Nicene Christian Library* (Edinburgh: T. & T. Clark) and *The Library of Christian Classics* (London: SCM Press).

I am most grateful for the sabbatical year which was granted by the authorities of the United Theological College. This enabled me to complete a number of writing tasks, and to make headway with this one.

My association with the University of Wales Press has from the outset been most cordial. When I embarked upon this project Ned Thomas was the Director, and his place has now been taken by Susan Jenkins. For their commitment to the trilogy, and for the promptness and expertise of my editors, Ceinwen Jones and Jane Robson, I am grateful.

My sense of relief that I have been able to bring this series to completion is as nothing compared with that of Karen, my wife, whose support is never-failing, despite the fact that on this occasion books overflowed from my study not only into the dining room, but even into her studio.

It will seem strange not to be living with this trilogy any longer. My thoughts on dispatching this final volume are summed up by words taken out of context from Byron's *Childe Harold's Pilgrimage,* IV.clxxxv:

> The torch shall be extinguish'd which hath lit
> My midnight lamp – and what is writ is writ;
> Would it were worthier!

Alan P. F. Sell
Aberystwyth

1

Introduction

> If it be the cause of God which we handle in our writings, then let us handle it like the prophets of God, with quietness and moderation, and not in the violence of passion, as if we were possessed rather than inspired.
>
> (*Golden Remains of the Ever Memorable Mr John Hales*, 1659)

> If the materials collected together in this volume have any lesson to teach, it is that of the many-sidedness involved in serious theological work.
>
> (Donald M. MacKinnon, of his *Explorations in Theology*, 5, 1979)

On 18 September 1745 the Presbyterian divine, Samuel Bourn of Coseley and Birmingham, addressed these words to Job Orton at the latter's ordination in Shrewsbury:

> Be just to the Truths of God, and to the Gospel of Christ. Spare no Pains to be Master of the Evidences of Christianity and a Scripture Religion, in an Age wherein both serious and ludicrous Attacks are made upon it . . . [W]e are not to expect that our People will blindly receive what we say is Truth, or practise what we affirm is Duty, unless we make them appear to be so. It is no time of Day for such fond and unjust Hopes.[1]

Such 'fond and unjust hopes' would be even more out of place today; but, in the wake of the widespread loss of confidence in the classical theistic arguments as copper-bottomed demonstrations, in view of the problematic nature of the biblical 'evidences' of miracle and prophecy, and in face of the demise of Christendom, and of the availability of numerous alternative faith options and non-religious world-views, how is the Christian faith to be commended?

In this book an attempt is made to discuss some of the issues which those who wish to devise a Christian apologetic in the early decades of Christianity's third millennium may wish to consider. It is the final volume of a trilogy, and it is necessary to set the scene by reference to its two predecessors. In *John Locke and the Eighteenth-Century Divines* and *Philosophical Idealism and Christian Belief* I took two detailed soundings in Enlightenment and post-Enlightenment thought with a view to raising the question of apologetic starting points and methods. The question left on the table in *John Locke* was: how far is it viable to set out from the epistemological question, what can we know? The question discussed in *Philosophical Idealism* was: how far may Christian thought be articulated in relation to, or in terms of, a particular philosophical 'ism'? None of those who have been kind enough to review these two volumes have queried the legitimacy of these questions, to which I shall return shortly. I here seek to build upon what I have done; to take stock and to propose a way of proceeding with Christian apologetics in the twenty-first century; and to do this in conversation with Christians and others, ancient and modern, and with an eye to the circumstances in which the Church is called to confess the faith today.

In one of his many perceptive editorials Cyril S. Rodd has declared that 'What is needed is not a reinterpretation of the meaning of God which accommodates religion to the current situation, but an apologetic which takes the present culture with all seriousness and then offers a satisfying defence of religion . . .'[2] Quite so; but the desired apologetic, I am convinced, must also take with equal seriousness the heritage of Christian witness. In making this grand-sounding claim I do not suppose that any apologist is, or could be, familiar with all the literature of the Christian centuries. On the contrary, I am daunted by the amount of extant relevant texts and almost (but not quite) reduced to silence by my ignorance of so many of them. I do, however, think it of great importance that scholars in all branches of theology, but especially, perhaps, in apologetics, shun the arrogance which suggests (despite the Christian doctrines of providence and the Holy Spirit) that everything which came before us is passé and hence valueless.

It is also necessary to counter any theological amnesia which some might be tempted to excuse by appealing to theology's need to be relevant to the immediate context.[3] My conversing with past witnesses does not self-indulgently arise from the pleasure I take in hearing them in their own words and in inviting others to hear them too. It originates in my belief that to deal with arguments or trains of thought in abstraction from their intellectual contexts – as if Augustine, Locke or Kant were sitting across the table from us in the Senior Common Room – can be to miss the point of the arguments as originally articulated. The danger is especially acute when semantic changes over time go unrecognized. Moreover, if we focus our attention exclusively on the 'big names', and have no regard for their 'hinterland' contemporaries who variously stimulated and responded to them, and on occasion cut them down to size, our understanding of what the 'stars' were about will be so far impoverished.

While acknowledging and benefiting from the heritage of Christian witness, it is not the case that in apologetics we simply apply a collection of received truths to our times as if from without. Rather, we learn to speak the faith where we are, or not at all. In saying this I think I am endorsing what the African theologian John Mbiti has more poetically expressed thus: 'We can add nothing to the Gospel, for this is an eternal gift of God; but Christianity is aways a beggar seeking food and drink, cover and shelter from the cultures and times it encounters in its never ending journeys and wanderings.'[4] Or, to pass from Mbiti the poetic to Forsyth the pungent: 'An up-to-date Gospel is a nauseous expression, but if apologetics are not up-to-date they are of little value.'[5] A viable Christian apologetic must be rooted in the heritage without being antiquarian;[6] and it must be relevant without being 'instant' – as if it were preceded by an intellectual void.

These are not easy days for Christian apologetics. On the one hand there is the nagging question of the propriety, in what are now widely deemed to be pluralistic Western societies, of seeming to suggest that one religion has the intellectual advantage over all others – is even the 'best'; on the other hand there is the embarrassment of those apologetic works to be found in some Christian bookshops which do not rise above wanton cult-bashing. And there are more sophisticated voices from both theological and philosophical circles whose owners query, and sometimes deny, the possibility of apologetics. To these last I shall turn in some detail in due course. Suffice it to say now that it was not ever thus. One hundred years ago the theological world was, one might say, awash with systems, manuals, handbooks of apologetics. Among significant contributors to this industry were Scots – John Tulloch, Robert Flint, A. B. Bruce, James Iverach, James Orr, Robert Mackintosh among them. I shall have cause to refer to the contributions of some of these, and others, as we proceed. They did not by any means agree on all points; their emphases differed;[7] and they were all writing in the post-Hume, post-Kant period of the 'decline of the evidences' – that is to say, at a time when the traditional appeals to miracle, prophecy and the like were, by many, repudiated or at least viewed askance, and that not only by the 'enemies' of the faith.[8] Robert Flint, for example, Scotland's most learned Christian apologist, declared in a lecture delivered on 22 March 1899 that

> The evidentialist view . . . did great injustice to such a revelation as the Christian, and was, in fact, neither reasonable nor Christian. A revelation which presents mysteries as its substantive and distinctive message is a revelation which does not reveal, and belief in which is not belief in truth as such.[9]

Attention increasingly turned to developments in historical method, especially as these provoked scepticism concerning the reliability of the biblical texts; such novelties as positivism and scientific evolutionism required to be dealt with, while repristinations of such venerable foes as naturalism and materialism also clamoured for attention.

That not all theologians – even all Scottish theologians – were vastly impressed by apologetic activity is clear from the gnomic utterance of John 'Rabbi' Duncan (1796–1870), Free Church professor of Hebrew: 'We have been acting too long the part of God's apologists, rather than his heralds. We have been trying to show that God's word is consistent with the best philosophy. Our business is to "herald" the good news.'[10] Again, William Garden Blaikie, professor of apologetical and pastoral theology at New College, Edinburgh, from 1868 to 1897, queried whether apologetics was of much use to those training to be preachers and, for himself, confessed, 'My mind and my method were so thoroughly in favour of a basis of facts, as to be uncongenial to those who could see no value in any foundation save the abstract';[11] and, while some philosophically competent young men rightly refrained from philosophizing in the pulpit, Blaikie lamented the fact that the weight of philosophical difficulties had been more responsible than any other single cause for propelling many out of the ministry.

To return to Duncan's first two sentences: they epitomize the protest of faith against rationalism (though not against reason) which, in different ways, was articulated by Kierkegaard in Denmark and, later, by P. T. Forsyth in Britain:

> Do we start from the world or the Word? Are we to demand that Christ shall submit to the standard of certain principles or ideals which we bring to him from our human nature at its heart's highest and its thought's best? Or as our new creator is he his own standard, and not only so, but both judge and king, and redeemer of human nature, and the fountain of a new life, autonomous in him, and for all the rest derived?[12]

We shall meet this question again (and may well wish to modify it) when we consider embargoes against Christian apologetic activity. For the present, and returning to Duncan: his three sentences taken together imply a disjunction which Robert Mackintosh, in another context, repudiated. Writing of one aspect of the role of the apologist he notes that, no less than the evangelist, 'the apologist, too, in his own way, offers the message of God's love to every heart when he seeks to deliver faith from overwhelming distresses'.[13]

Forsyth's remark raises the question of starting points in Christian apologetics, and with this I shall be greatly occupied in this study. As noted, an important question which came to the fore in *John Locke and the Eighteenth-Century Divines* was: how far was Locke well advised to set out from the epistemological starting point – especially since, as he proceeded, he found it necessary to appeal to scripture, the example of Christ and revelation? The 'cliff-hanger' question which I left for future consideration was:

> Can the epistemological starting-point be redeemed for Christian apologetic use, or is it not viable at all – in which event, is there a more satisfactory point of departure, or combination of approaches, which will permit Christians to give a reasoned testimony to and defence of the faith over against those who in our time declare that the apologetic enterprise is doomed?[14]

We shall have occasion to review some of the candidates which have been proposed as apologetic starting points: reason, revelation, faith, and moral, aesthetic and religious experience. By way of offering a preliminary clue to my own position I would recall Alexander Campbell Fraser's judgement that

> Perhaps exclusive regard for the *lumen siccum* made [Locke] apt unduly to disparage emotion and imagination, faith and will, as factors in the final interpretation of human existence, and to forget that all that is highest in man must be in response to all that is highest in existence, in order to a true insight of the realities.[15]

As I remarked in the second volume of this trilogy, 'In Fraser's words lie the seeds of an apologetic method'.[16] The danger of overlooking Fraser's point was clearly expressed by W. H. V. Reade:

> No sooner are we convinced that in one realm of experience – be it religious, artistic, or scientific – the vision of absolute truth is ours than we press on to one or other of two further conclusions. Either we insist that the whole of reality can be interpreted in like manner or, if driven to confess that this is impossible, we then protest that only through one window does the light of heaven stream into us, while elsewhere all is dark.[17]

What I had positively in mind when quoting Fraser, and what I shall here seek to show, is that all of the aforementioned starting points, none of which is to be despised and all of which are to be accounted for in any rounded apologetic, best serve Christian apologetics when they are viewed in the light of what I take to be the only satisfactory starting point: the confession of what God in Christ has done (a question here begged, but to be discussed in detail in Chapter 5 below). It is not that, taken together, the results of setting out from the several starting points somehow combine to yield a knockdown demonstration of Christianity's truth – any more than do the several classical theistic arguments yield a cumulative demonstrative proof of the theistic claim. Nevertheless, rational reflection and personal experience may be channels through which the apprehension of God may come – or, as a Christian may wish to say, they can be means which God uses in his approach to human beings; but their deliverances need to be viewed in relation to, and tempered by, God's redemptive activity in Christ. In the words of an able minister of the Gospel who came to serve the little church which I had left in quest of ministerial education, 'When all is said, all apologetic, all Christian theology, starts from what is given, from what is done.'[18] I thus seek a hospitable – even an eclectic – apologetic which takes due account of the deepest insights, sensitivities and experiences of human beings – through which, surely, God the Holy Spirit can and does address us; but not a freewheeling, wanton or random apologetic; for all is alive and responsive to the prevailing culture, and brought to the bar of the Cross. In saying this I am well aware of the problems which may crudely be stated thus: if we set out from God's action in Christ, how shall we avoid an 'unapologetic' circle of revelation? If, on the other hand, we begin elsewhere, how shall we subsequently work in all that Christians wish to assert?[19] Are systematic or constructive theologians necessarily restricted to making assertions designed for the ears of the faithful alone? Are Christian apologists doomed to reducing Christian affirmations to those which are allegedly demonstrable in the (possibly vain) hope of enticing non-believers?[20] And what are we to make of the claim typified by Robert Flint's remark that 'neither the head nor the heart is a competent witness . . . when the one is dissociated from the other'?[21] Such questions as these will regularly tease – even haunt – us as we proceed, and it will become clear that 'a change of starting-points is not necessarily a cure-all'.[22]

It is also necessary to point out that, unless otherwise made clear by the context, what I have in mind is the logical, rather than the temporal, starting point of Christian apologetics. That is to say, whereas in an actual situation in which apology is called for one might proceed in accordance with the educationalist's maxim, 'Begin where the other person is' (a maxim, incidentally which presupposes common epistemological ground, the availability of which some Christian apologists would deny), the logical starting point is that which ensures that the resulting apologetic is Christian – rather than, for example, theistic. The question of how far Christian claims presuppose, or depend for their force, upon theistic claims is yet another to be raised in what follows.

Inextricably interwoven with the question of starting points is that of apologetic method. In the conclusion of the volume on philosophical idealism I ventured the opinion that 'Since the terrain to be traversed by Christian testimony is wide, involving a texture of historical, existential, theological, metaphysical, ethical, aesthetic, liturgical assertions, its method must be correspondingly hospitable.'[23] Clearly, to a considerable extent, the apologetic method should be compatible with, and will be influenced by, the point of departure. As Robert Barclay, the seventeenth-century Quaker apologist, well understood,

> he that errs in the entrance is not so easily brought back again into the right way; he that misseth his road from the beginning of his journey, and is deceived in his first marks, at his first setting forth, the greater his mistake is, the more difficult will be his entrance into the right way.[24]

From his vantage point at the opposite ecclesial pole from that of Barclay, Maurice Blondel observed that 'there is a wrong way of defending the truth and that, in spite of apparent results, a false method can never give genuine and solid support to religious doctrine'.[25] Thus, if we set out from Locke's psychological question – how do we come to know what we know? – or from his epistemological question – what counts as knowledge? – our enquiry, if it is to be satisfactory, will follow a direction likely to yield the answers we seek. If we pursue the route of classical natural theology, regarding deliverances of rational enquiry as in some sense paving the way for divine revelation, our method is set from the outset. If we begin from moral, aesthetic or religious experience we shall require a method which will accord due place to personal considerations and judgements. If we are guided by a particular philosophical 'ism', and seek to adumbrate our apologetic by reference to or in the light of it, we may find that our method becomes unduly intellectualist, and even that certain Christian claims are put at risk. This was the conclusion of my study of British post-Hegelian idealism. I found that those idealists who were closest to Christianity – especially the absolutists among them – had difficulty in maintaining the Creator-creature distinction; in taking the full force of evil which, for them, could be but a stage on the way to a greater good; and in dealing with the scandal of particularity which Christianity poses to all who seriously examine the historical claims integral to it. I therefore made bold to conclude that 'A Christian philosophy, or world-and-life view, cannot, I judge, bypass the historic act of redemption wrought once for all by God-in-Christ. Time and again this criterion has emerged as the rock on which idealism founders.'[26] Indeed, concerning both the Christian idealists and Locke, I presumed to suggest, and attempted to show, that their philosophical methods could not accommodate all that they wished to believe.[27] I shall hope to show that there is a way between the undifferentiated divine being of theism, whom no Christian actually worships, and the God replete with biblical attributes who is enclosed within his own revelation; and that if we set out from what is at the heart of the Christian confession – namely, God's free, gracious, saving act in Christ – we can accommodate God's approach through human thinking and experience without landing in the methodological difficulties which Locke and the idealists, in their differing ways, exemplify. In brief, mine is an attempt to delineate the contours of a Christian apologetic which sets out from the central, distinctive, claims of the Christian confession. What else do Christians wish to commend?

Does this imply that there can be no commerce between Christianity and a prevailing philosophy? In a discussion of Platonism Reade declared, 'Whenever the Church has adopted or patronised a philosophy of secular origin, the result, sooner or later, has been disastrous.'[28] Certainly, when Augustine wrote that for all their worth the writings of the Platonists were silent on the fact that 'the Word was made flesh and came to dwell among us',[29] he had detected an Incarnation-shaped blank of crucial importance to Christian thought. But I should not wish to endorse Reade's disjunction just as it stands. Its overall implication is that, where ideas are concerned, Christianity is in its box, and idealism is in its, and that one may dip into either box and extract the ideas one needs and then proceed to mix them together. But the Christianity we know is already influenced by the intellectual environment in which we find it, and 'alien' world views are not uninfluenced – positively or negatively – by the Christianity they encounter. This makes it all the more important that, when in conversation with those who espouse views other than our own, we should remember that if we utilize terms drawn from elsewhere we are engaging in an analogical activity, and that analogies may be both positive and negative. It is not so much that Christians borrowed the term 'Logos' from the Greeks: they rebaptized it when associating it with the words 'made flesh' – which is one way of developing Augustine's point.[30]

Clearly, my findings on the Christian idealists were influenced by my understanding of what is at Christianity's heart; for one can hardly specify alleged attenuations of, or divergences from, the faith without having some notion of what is being reduced or forsaken. I admitted as much in my book, and promised a consideration of my own vantage point in this.[31] I have already alluded to my starting point, and, after much reflection, I have decided to expound and discuss it in some detail it in the next chapter. This decision signals the fact that, as well as the major question of the starting point of Christian apologetics, I have had to confront the question of the starting point for this book. Ought I to set out in turn from a number of rival starting points, seek to show how they do not assist our arrival, and then introduce what I believe Christianity would have us say? Or ought I to begin from a consideration of the nature and content of Christian confessing, and then discuss the apologetic implications of this in relation to the several starting points? I have chosen the latter course, not least because the Christian confession has been implied in my earlier work, and it is time I addressed it directly.

For the present I make the general point that, assuming that an apologist is proceeding with integrity, the method adopted will reflect, or presuppose, a particular way of looking at the world. We shall in due course have to examine the nature and logic of world-views – not least because Christians claim that theirs offers the most satisfactory account of the world's creation, course and end. If this is to be publicly witnessed to (as distinct from remaining the gnosis of a coterie), it is vulnerable to adverse criticism; for others clearly have alternative, opposing, views of the meaning and purpose of life, and some may even doubt whether it makes sense to speak of such things.

But if Christians, like Locke and the idealists whose work I discussed, can operate with a method which strictly precludes the articulation of some of their cherished convictions, it is also the case – and twentieth-century intellectual history is particularly full of such examples – that when the faith's opponents (whose manner may vary from the genial to the hostile) seek to set the parameters concerning, for example, what counts as a 'fact', or which assertions can be meaningful, they are, from the Christian's point of view, in the position of one who attempts to pick up soup on a fork – some always falls through the prongs. More technically, the criteria sometimes brought to Christian claims are ill-adapted in so far as they rule out Christian testimony from the start. How far such testimony is justifiable is yet another question to which we shall attend as this work proceeds.[32]

It will not have gone unnoticed that I have come thus far without hazarding a definition of 'apologetics'. How has the apologetic task been understood by some of its practitioners? In his *Apologetics and Catholic Doctrine*, 428,000 copies of which had been printed by 1955, M. Sheehan nails his colours to the mast in no uncertain terms: 'Apologetics is the science concerned with the defence of the Catholic religion . . . [I]t concludes that the one and only guide of faith on earth is the Catholic Church, Holy and Infallible.' In a footnote he adds, '"Catholic Apologetics" . . . is not a mere appeal for the acceptance of Catholicism or a plea for its toleration but a solid demonstration that it is the one and only true religion.'[33] It is hard to believe that these words, which seem more sectarian than catholic, were being reprinted within ten years of the convening of the Second Vatican Council. Interestingly, from the extensive index of a substantial collection of Vatican II documents the term 'apologetics' is absent, and the emphasis of the documents overall is upon 'dialogue with the world' rather than the aggressive assertion and the defence of one brand of the Christian faith against it.[34] For his part, William C. Placher explains that '"Apologetics" traditionally constitutes the part of Christian theology devoted to defending Christian faith to a non-Christian audience'.[35] On the other hand, in his oft-reprinted work of the middle of the twentieth century Alan Richardson informs us that

> apologetics is primarily a study undertaken by Christians for Christians; and in this respect it is to be distinguished from the task of apology, since an apology is addressed to non-Christians . . . Christian apologetics . . . is concerned with the implications of the Christian revelation for the rational understanding of the world and of our existence in it.[36]

Now, while it is true that some church polities – notably the congregational – turn upon the distinction to be drawn between the saints[37] and everybody else – a distinction grounded in God's gracious call on the one hand and the response of personal allegiance on the other, and traditionally maintained by godly discipline (invoked with varying degrees of success), where intellectual matters are concerned it does not seem to me to be so easy to distinguish between the saints (who are also sinners) and everybody else. The faith may well have to be defended against doubting Christians, sincere heretics and 'outside' opponents alike. Robert Flint is in agreement when he writes,

> By a Christian Apologetics I mean a vindication of Christianity which aims at being thorough and comprehensive; one which includes the theory as well as the practice of the vindication, and which seeks not merely to defend some particular portion of Christianity, but to justify it as a whole.[38]

Moreover, Flint does not restrict the apologetic vocation to those who combat external foes. On the contrary, while the preacher and pastor 'may seldom be called to be apologists against the avowed foes of the Christian faith . . . they must have constant need to be apologists for that faith in the forum of the hearts of their hearers and people, and perhaps even of their own hearts'.[39] This latter consideration was elevated to primary status by A. B. Bruce, of whose 1892 work, *Apologetics; or, Christianity Defensively Stated,* no fewer than 10,000 copies had been printed by 1927:

> Apologetic, then, as I conceive it, is a preparer of the way of faith, an aid to faith against doubts whencesoever arising, especially such as are engendered by philosophy and science . . . It addresses itself to such as are drawn in two directions, towards and away from Christ, as distinct from such as are confirmed either in unbelief or in faith. Defence presupposes a foe, but the foe is not the dogmatic infidel who has usually made up his mind that Christianity is a delusion, but anti-Christian thought in the believing man's own heart . . . The wise apologist instinctively shuns conflict with dogmatic unbelief as futile.[40]

Although Bruce's one-sided understanding of the apologetic task is open to question (and not altogether in accord with his practice, for he challenges a number of 'dogmatic infidels' in the course of his work), he does well to elevate the apologist's pastoral role within the Church. Indeed, it is a disturbing thought that there may be many church members who agonize in silence over difficulties in believing – especially, perhaps, over those thrown up by unmerited suffering – but who feel either that there is no one able to help them, or even in some cases to understand their plight; or else that if they were to articulate their concerns they would be slapped down by the godly for their lack of faith.

P. T. Forsyth's apologetic focus was decidedly upon the Church.

While he did not diminish the importance of defending Christian truth against attack from without, he did relatively little of it himself, because, with reductionist liberal theology swirling all around him, he was convinced that 'The greatest issue for the moment is within the Christian pale; it is not between Christianity and the world. It is the issue between theological liberalism (which is practically unitarian) and a free but positive theology, which is essentially evangelical.'[41]

It seems quite clear to me that since the Church comprises saints/sinners, probably all of whom are doubters at least occasionally, and some of whom are fairly consistent doubters, and since intellectual challenges arise both within and without the Church, Christian apologetics may properly look in both directions, though it may be granted that at some periods the predominant clamant challenge may come from the one direction or the other. I cannot therefore endorse William Robertson Smith's remark: 'Apologetic theology, though practical in its bearing on those who are without the Church, has, for those who are within the Church, either no value at all, or a value purely speculative.'[42] No doubt it makes a strategic difference that 'insiders' who doubt or who are heretical are differently placed from 'outsiders' who owe no allegiance whatever to Christ. The former are united with their critics in a common allegiance, however much they may differ in doctrinal interpretation, and in their understanding of the authority – Bible, Church, tradition, conscience – to which deference is variously held to be due.

Richardson proceeds to introduce a distinction additional to that between 'outsiders' and 'insiders'. He urges that, while apologies are defences of Christian truth, 'apologetics . . . is the study of the ways and means of defending Christian truth' – and this in relation to the wider sphere of 'secular' knowledge.[43] It seems to me that, while in urgent situations – such as when the flames encircle his or her fastened body – the most an apologist may be able to do is to bear witness that Jesus Christ is Lord, very frequently it is in the interest of the apologist (in Richardson's sense of the term) to consider, though not necessarily to spell out, the appropriate ways of responding to the challenge at hand. Indeed, the more carefully this is done, the more like the apology is to succeed. Thus what Richardson calls apologizing and what he calls apologetics can be, and perhaps most frequently are, part and parcel of the same activity, which I shall call the act of confessing – hence the first word in the title of this book. Accordingly, I express my agreement with Robert Mackintosh in thinking that while 'Any *single* effort in apologetics may be termed "an apology"', and while 'more elaborate contrasts have been proposed' between 'apology' and 'apologetics', these 'are of little practical importance'.[44]

A number of writers have sought to distinguish between the roles of the apologist and the philosopher. For example, J. V. L. Casserley declares that 'the apologist sets out to show [contemporaries] how they can see God from their own existing point of view, whereas the philosopher often attempts the more ambitious task of persuading them to try a new point of view altogether'.[45] This prompts three questions. Why may not a Christian apologist challenge others to change their views by proposing reasons why they should? Are there not, rather, numerous contemporary philosophers who maintain that it is no part of their purpose to change anyone's mind about anything, but simply to analyse claims which are made? Where 'point of view' is synonymous with 'world-view', will not the apologist gather such evidence as is available, marshall such philosophical arguments as may seem appropriate, and undertake such linguistic analysis as may seem necessary, in order to confess the faith in intellectual terms (which are not the only terms – or even the most important, given that Christianity is primarily a way, not an ideological system)? Along this line the apologist–philosopher distinction is properly blurred. Indeed, on the next page, Casserley himself blurs it in a cumbersome way, now from the side of the Christian philosopher:

> the work of the Christian philosopher may indirectly subserve an apologetic purpose, in so far as he is successful not merely in attaining his purposes, but also in making his attainment of them clear to others, in so far that is, as he succeeds in showing that it is possible to think one's way through the problems of human existence with the aid of Christian analogies and hypotheses, and to compose a satisfying and stimulating metaphysical interpretation of life out of such raw materials, he will be drawing attention to the illuminative power and intellectual stimulus which Christianity is capable of communicating. He will commend his point of view by indicating the range and steadiness of the vision enjoyed by those who look out from it upon life.[46]

He proceeds to argue that, whereas the apologist is primarily concerned with the cosmological argument for God's existence (because people are interested in the cosmos, if not in God), the Christian philosopher begins by vindicating 'the native bias of his interest' along ontological lines. But since Christian apologists and philosophers alike may and in some cases do begin elsewhere, Casserley's observations constitute implied recommendations only. And when he avers that it is 'the high prophetic office' of the Christian philosopher 'To interpret the world to the Church and the Church to the world',[47] I cannot suppress the question, what, then, does the Christian philosopher do which the Christian apologist does not? And, who is sufficient for these things? The force of the latter question is increased by Casserley's expectation that the Christian philosopher will propose 'a genuinely creative synthesis' of the diverse points of view of Church and world. But (*a*) how could any one person accomplish this, and how would he or she know when the task was done? And (*b*) how can possible Church–world contradictions (most basically: there is a god/there is not a god) be harmonized within one system? It is difficult not to feel that Casserley is here in homiletic-rhetorical mode.

The Church is called to confess the faith and to commend it by faithful witness. (I am well aware that I am begging huge questions here, but patience.) This commendation is by word and life, and it is not the business of individual Christians only; it is an ecclesial task: 'What Christ founded was not an order of preachers, nor the institution of preaching, but a community, a Church, whose first charge His preaching should be. It is Church and preacher together that reach the world'[48] – or not, as the case may be. Within the general task of commendation there is a variety of tasks – preaching, praxis – one of which is that of responding to intellectual challenges to the faith from within or without the Christian fold. We might say that, in its broadest sense, confession includes commendation, while the intellectual task of apologetics is a variety of commendation. Not all Christians are called to, or are able to, undertake the task of apologetics in this sense, and they are none the worse for that: there are diversities of gifts, each needs the other, and there should be no elitism here. In an address on 'Christian learning and Christian living' delivered on 12 May 1936 from the chair of the Congregational Union of England and Wales, Principal A. J. Grieve of Lancashire Independent College said, 'At once the fullest and the acutest mind with which I was ever brought into close contact was that of my late colleague Robert

Mackintosh. Yet he had the heart of a little child.'[49] Grieve went on to recount Mackintosh's experience of a prayer meeting at Douglas, Lanarkshire, at which George Wilson, a Scottish peasant, 'went right home to the heart of truth in a way which I could not then achieve – and now I feel I can hardly hope ever to compass it . . . He knew the permanent things of the Gospel.' I take this point very seriously indeed, and while my chosen method here is to enter into conversation not only with contemporaries but with many thinkers of former years, I should be very distressed if anything in this book were taken as patronizing, or still worse pouring scorn upon, the witness of those – including some of my own folk – who have no written memorial, but whose confession was secure, and who commended the faith by their lives. This breadth of commendation is all to the good, not least because by no means all of the Church's problems now or at any time are exclusively intellectual: hypocrisy and failures in love take their toll, as does that sectarian spirit which forbids 'eucharistic hospitality'. More effective apologetics in the technical sense will not by itself cure these ills which involve every Christian, for wills must be won over as well as minds convinced.

With this reference to the will we come to a further introductory point. Those who are called to commend the faith intellectually need to remember their place. While, as I believe, the major claims of Christianity are open to rational scrutiny and defence, Christian apologists are not the producers of what the Quakers call an individual's 'convincement'. It is integral to the Christian confession that the 'God of all grace' is Lord of the harvest; that he alone removes the scales from a person's eyes, and that his being is so great that no apologist, however accomplished, could plumb its depths. We may therefore suppose that the God who is no respecter of persons refuses to give apologists an unfair advantage, and calls out a household of faith rather than a postgraduate seminar. A corollary of this is that those called to commend the faith as apologists – whether in churchly circles or outside – must understand that the hard work involved is not only the intellectual sort. It is a Johannine principle that those who do the truth know the doctrine. At this point the relationship between apologetics and spirituality comes into view, and we begin to see that, as any *bona fide* mystic will testify, the latter has at least as much to do with resolution and discipline as it has with languid baskings and cosy glows. That it has even less to do with presumptuous swaggering is the contention of Irenaeus against 'spiritual persons' of the Valentinian gnostic sort.[50] As C. S. Lewis pointed out, 'If you want joy, peace, power, eternal life, you must get close to, or even into, the thing that has them . . . If you are close to it, the spray will wet you; if you're not, you will remain dry.'[51] Moreover, those who heed this injunction may well be able to endorse Augustine's testimony to the effect that his thoughts 'were multiplied by His grace . . . [and] I shall be made to rejoice in a marvellous increase of wealth'.[52]

So to the plan: in Part I we shall ask what it is to confess the faith; what is to be confessed; and who are the confessors. This will entail a consideration of the context in which the confession has currently to be made and its intellectual puzzles and opponents tackled. This will bring into view the fact of societal pluralism, the question of how far there is or can be identity of Christian confession through the ages and around the world, and the vexed question of epistemological common ground as between Christians and others. In Part II we shall consider some of the presuppositions of confessing – such as that Christians legitimately use language to refer to God, that God acts in history, and that it makes sense to speak of the supernatural. As we proceed we shall have to examine some of the challenges – even in some cases embargoes – which have, in our time, been imposed against Christian apologetics. In Part III we shall consider two major traditional apologetic starting points: reason and experience (aesthetic, moral and religious). These will be viewed in relation to the basic Christian confession, and to those who would raise objections to Christian apologetics on rationalist, anti-rationalist or fideistic grounds. In the course of the enquiry I shall make bold to challenge philosophers of a sectarian bent, and theologians who too swiftly retreat into a theological ghetto.

In speaking of the 'basic Christian confession' I am aware that I am implying a distinction between apologetics and systematic theology. This distinction is analogous to Forsyth's distinction between 'the deep motive of the Church' and 'the first method of the missionary'.[53] That is, I wish to distinguish between such a basic confession as 'Jesus is Lord and Saviour', or 'Christ is risen', and the fuller articulation of the scope of these claims which fall within the systematician's purview. The latter is, in my opinion, best developed along trinitarian lines, and this possibiity will be alluded to in Chapter 8 where world-views will be in question. But the main thrust of the present work is in the direction of asking what is involved in making the basic Christian claim, and how far can the claim reasonably be commended to others.

As we proceed through the territory thus sketchily (perhaps even elusively) marked out, we shall find that older ways of prosecuting the apologetic task cannot be ours. No more than the early apologists – and unlike Augustine, Aquinas and Calvin – can we make the assumption of Christendom. In the wake of the Enlightenment (which, as I shall hope to show is by no means the 'bogeyman' that some contemporary theologians and others take it to be) we cannot make an unsophisticated appeal to proofs or to miracles – still less to the credulity of our hearers. Standing on our side of modern biblical criticism, we cannot with integrity construe all biblical propositions as literal truth, still less allegorize them after the fashion of Origen. As for the appeal to the authority of the Church: however such an appeal is currently to be made, it clearly will not suffice to persuade the unconverted while there is ample evidence that 'the faithful' have more than a little difficulty with, and various avoidance strategies for drawing the sting of, deliverances from a magisterium, whether official, as in Rome, or unofficial or pretended elsewhere. All of these factors and others have contributed to the creation of an intellectual environment hospitable to interpretations of Christianity of the most diverse kind – espoused, we might be tempted sardonically to think, by people who present a continuum at one end of which are found those who are all at sea on the sea of faith, and at the other, those who have all but concussed themselves on what W. E. Gladstone called in a book title, *The Impregnable Rock of Holy Scripture* (1890). In such a climate the words of W. P. Paterson return to haunt us:

> It is doubtful if apologetic treatises are much read outside of theological circles; but if they do penetrate to the world of unbelief, that world might forcibly retort that apologists should come to an understanding among themselves as to what the Christian religion is before they undertake to prove to non-Christians that it is true.[54]

I cannot, of course, pretend that I shall speak for all Christians in what follows. Even if some agree with me that the venture of beginning Christian apologetics from Christian confession is worthwhile, they may well understand and expound the content of the confession differently from myself. But the risk is worth taking of enquiring what it would be like to commend the faith from the basis that in Christ God has acted once and for all for the redemption of the world. The very proposal constitutes a gigantic hostage to fortune but, undeterred, let us proceed.

As to the manner of our proceeding, I have already mentioned the apologists' need of humility, but there is charity too. If, as I shall propose, everything the Church and the Christian does is, for good or ill, an apology after its fashion, I must be alive to the exhortation of Aquinas, and to Locke's dying words, with which I closed the second volume of this trilogy. Declared Aquinas, 'We must love them both, those whose opinions we share and those whose opinions we reject. For both have laboured in the search for truth and both have helped us in the finding of it.'[55] And Locke's aspiration was to be 'in perfect charity with all men and in sincere communion with the whole church of Christ, by whatever names Christ's followers call themselves'.[56]

I thus find myself able to agree almost entirely with Charles Raven:

> To reduce an opponent to silence by dialectic, to overwhelm him with paradoxes or ridicule, is neither Christian nor conclusive: indeed, it only hardens his dislike of the faith and obstructs his approach to it. It is our business not to defend but to commend the faith; and the devil's weapons of sarcasm and superciliousness will not help us.[57]

It is the first half of Raven's second sentence here which, I think, contains too strong a disjunction; for gracious, thoughtful commendation which is alive to the other's situation is, surely, the best defence possible – always remembering that not even the apologist (or the bishop, moderator or creed) is charged with the final responsibility of guarding the ark, for God the Holy Spirit is *the* defender of the faith.

I

THE CONFESSION AND THE CONFESSORS

He that desireth to acquire any art or science, seeketh first those means by which that art or science is obtained. If we ought to do so in things natural and earthly, how much more then in spiritual? In this affair, then, should our enquiry be the more diligent, because he that errs in the entrance is not so easily brought back again into the right way; he that misseth his road from the beginning of his journey, and is deceived in his first marks, at his first setting forth, the greater his mistake is, the more difficult will be his entrance into the right way.

(Robert Barclay, *An Apology for the True Christian Divinity*, 1678)

2

Confession and Church

During the first decade of the twentieth century the Congregational theologian, P. T. Forsyth, declared, 'Our first business with the Gospel is to understand it.'[1] Shortly before the last decade of the same century the Roman Catholic theologian, Hans Küng, advised that when the biblical witness and our present experiences collide, our ultimate recourse is to 'the Christian message, the Gospel, Jesus Christ himself'.[2] But what is to be understood? To what are we to have recourse? Christians claim to have good news to tell, and we may suppose that this good news is at the heart of the Church's confession. If this is so, it must be possible for the Gospel to be articulated in words – however inadequate human words may finally be – and commended by word and life. But the question presses: is there an unchanging 'essence' of the Gospel, or have those who have gone in quest of such been chasing a will-o'-the-wisp? Some are quite convinced that there is no such thing as an isolable essence of the Gospel, if what is envisaged is a verbally formulated unalterable dictum of eternal validity and adequacy. They properly note that within the New Testament itself there are various formulations of the Gospel, and they rejoice to think that the good news is translatable through changing centuries and in widely differing geographical locations and cultural contexts. Their motto might be, 'One person's essence is another person's millstone.' They would welcome the realism of H. R. Mackintosh's remark, 'No pretence of scientific rigour can hide the plain fact that we all decide that the essence of Christianity shall mean for us by a judgement of value formed through personal insight or intuition';[3] and, by way of pointing out that the opinion was not exclusive to Presbyterians they might seek the confirmation of the Anglican, C. C. J. Webb: 'An appeal to the evidence of the intuitive moral consciousness has seldom been wholly absent from Christian apologetic, even when it has not been stressed or perhaps acknowledged.'[4] But neither Mackintosh nor Webb would have wished to license a wanton subjectivism, and both would have agreed with Forsyth that 'There must surely be in every positive religion some point where it may so change as to lose its identity and become another religion [or, we might add, no religion at all].'[5] Bishop John Jewel (1522–71) knew where the centre of gravity lay: 'We would seek no other foundation than the same which we knew was long ago laid by the apostles, that is to wit our Saviour Jesus Christ.'[6] But insofar as we are inclined to take his point concerning continuity, we must also be cautioned by what other Christians say concerning the dynamism of the Gospel, its ever-freshness, lest we are tempted to externalize or fossilize it.

I

It goes without saying that many true or false statements may be made concerning Christianity – its history, its worship, its architecture, its global spread – without touching the core of its confession. But if some, like Jewel and many others, have sought an indispensable minimum of belief, others have been content with nothing less than a full-blown system of doctrine. Let us suppose for the moment that the Gospel has something to do with the Cross of Christ. If this is so the implications cry out for systematic expression. If the Cross is in any sense redemptive, who needs to die upon it for it to be so? From what do people need to be redeemed? How is the conviction that the Cross is redemptive reached? Thus doctrine leads into doctrine, and we can at least understand why Gordon Clark once expostulated, 'The whole Gospel is not just a few disjointed truths. It is an ordered and logical system . . . God does not ramble his message to us. His thoughts are not desultory and disconnected. On the contrary, God speaks with logical consistency.'[7] Thus (Clark's biblical inerrancy apart) a twentieth-century conservative Reformed philosopher seems to be in the line of Alan of Lille (d. 1203) who, in his *Regulae caelestis iuris*, sought to deduce an entire system of Christian theology from a set of fundamental axioms. We need not, however, opt for such a deductive scheme, but nor need we endorse Forsyth's unduly disjunctive approach. With deductive schemes of theology – which he brands theosophy – in mind, and writing of the theologian, he declares,

> Our theological capital is not ideas we arrive at but experience we go through . . . The theologian is not a syllogist but an experient, an observer . . . The order of treatment is not a process of proof so much as a piece of orderly testimony . . . It is less deductive than descriptive. The order is not a law of logic but the suggestion of a travelled experience as to contiguous provinces.[8]

Undeniably, if theologians are to testify, they cannot keep themselves out of their work; but can testimony be innocent of ideas – at least those we formulate as we interpret our experience? And if the testimony is to be orderly, have logic and careful reasoning no place?

The fact remains, however, that while the Gospel may imply a system, it is not a system – least of all mine. Systems are constructed by people who, however clearly and logically God may speak, can be notoriously hard of hearing. Moreover, the Gospel is both more and less than any system. It is more in that it represents a claim upon a person's entire life, not just upon the intellect (which is not to revive the old liberal heresy that Christianity is not creed but life);[9] it is less, because a system may be so full, even complicated, and require such experience and sophistication both in its construction and its reception, that the majority of the childlike, for whom the Gospel is, would choke upon it. It may be that the foundation of the Christian system – or, rather, of a Christian system – is the doctrine of the Trinity, or of the Holy Spirit, or of the authority of scripture, but the ranks of the redeemed include many who could not adequately articulate, and only imperfectly grasp, these doctrines. Erasmus' word of consolation is highly appropriate: 'You will not be damned for not knowing whether the Spirit proceeds from one origin only, or from both the Father and the Son';[10] and James Denney implicitly put systematicians in their place by reminding them that 'Arianism and Athanasianism both give answers to a question which multitudes of genuine Christians never ask.'[11] As P. Carnegie Simpson insisted, Christ's first question does not concern dogma; it is, 'What is your attitude to me? . . . Whatever else may be said of the building, there is the authentic site.'[12]

The upshot is that, while there is much to be said for James Orr's view that

> Christianity is not something utterly formless and vague, but has an ascertainable, stateable content, which it is the business of the Church to find out, to declare, to defend, and ever more perfectly to seek to unfold in the connection of its parts, and in relation to advancing knowledge,[13]

to suppose that any given system is the Gospel is to have failed to understand that some of Christianity's saddest times have been when that view has been widely held by believers. Hence, for example, Joseph Butler's lament, 'It is come . . . to be taken for granted by many persons that Christianity is not so much a subject for enquiry, but that it is now at length discovered to be fictitious.'[14] Furthermore, there is something arrogant, 'Pelagian' and divisive in the supposition that acceptance of our favoured system is the criterion of the *bona-fide* Christian; and to unchurch those who do not see things our way is inherently sectarian. Not for nothing did some of the eighteenth-century divines accuse their more hard-line Calvinist counterparts of peddling Protestant popery. For example, John Taylor of Norwich vowed that 'A popish, anti-christian Spirit, I will ever oppose, as God shall enable me';[15] and such a spirit he found in the high Calvinist James Sloss, a *Congregationalist*. There is thus something eerie in B. B. Warfield's blandly confident assertion of 1904 that 'Calvinism is just religion in its purity. We have only, therefore, to conceive of religion in its purity, and that is Calvinism.'[16] It is difficult not to believe that as well as overlooking the many varieties of Calvinism, of which he was thoroughly aware, Warfield here basks in the false security of circularity. By contrast, the obituarist of Thomas Elford Poynting (1813–78), a Unitarian minister and philosopher, wrote,

> In one of his letters to me he said, 'Alas, the religion that begins in dogma is compelled to look on false doctrine as a crime'; thus indicating his dislike to the attempt to get a mere dogmatic basis for religion, and, at the same time, in his kindly way, trying to find an excuse for the conduct of those who were carried by dogma into bigotry.[17]

At the opposite end of the Christain scale from the system-builders we find almost all of the Quakers – the most prominent exception being Robert Barclay (1648–90). None have more vociferously opposed 'notions' than Friends; and insofar as their plea has been for inwardness in the sense of an experimental as opposed to an external, purely formal, profession of faith, all Christians may learn from them and be challenged by them. But 'inward' can also mean 'innate', and perhaps in those heady Cartesian days it did mean that to Barclay. Then it is not a long step to 'private', or 'detached from the world', or 'unhistorical' or even 'anti-historical'; and along any of these paths an undifferentiated mysticism can be reached from which, at the extreme, the Gospel is evacuated.[18] It would seem that a truly experimental Christian faith is a faith in someone about whom certain things are believed to be true – supremely, that he has done the decisively redemptive deed.

II

What, then, of creeds and confessions of faith? Do they encapsulate the Church's confession? The straight answer is: yes and no. Certainly there is much to be said for the several churches' setting down the faith commonly held in their midst. Whether the primary motive in a given case is doxological, explanatory, defensive or missionary, there is something to be conserved and passed on; and those who would churlishly dispense with such statements on the ground of their antiquity should be warned by Forsyth that the iconoclasts do not always appear to understand that 'it takes a great deal of theology to revolutionise theology'.[19] Yet there are undeniable difficulties surrounding corporate Christian affirmations. Such documents are inevitably and properly the products of their time. Thus the so-called Apostles' Creed makes strong, crisp historical affirmations concerning Jesus with a view to countering docetism. But not all have thought that it drives to the heart of the Christian confession. With the doctrine of the atonement in mind the Scottish theologian W. M. Clow bluntly declared, 'A creed which leaves out the Cross is not a Christian creed. One reason why the massive and noble Apostles' Creed has never won wide acceptance with simple Christian folk is because it allows us to grope among its clauses for this master truth.'[20] John Macpherson, that doughty defender of the Westminster Confession of Faith, concurred, adding a long list of additional credal deficiencies;[21] but in turn his favoured statement – originally designed to make good weaknesses in family instruction and thereby to overthrow ignorance and error, 'The two great pillars upon which the kingdon of Satan is erected'[22] – was severely criticized by Robert Mackintosh: 'We have found Confessionalism barren in apologetics, wrong in its scientific inferences from Scripture, very dubious in its critical assumptions, quite mistaken in its ways of handling history.'[23] With reference to the same Confession T. F. Torrance lamented the absence of a trinitarian or christological structure, and concluded that 'Apart from being methodologically erroneous and inadequate, the doctrine of God . . . is strictly not a fully *Christian* doctrine of God, that is, of God the Father made known to us definitively through Christ and his Spirit in the Gospel.'[24]

My own more general view of the sixteenth- and seventeenth-century Reformed confessions is that they take the colour of their times – understandably, but to the point of expatiating on justification by grace through faith at the expense of the doctrine of creation, for example; and some of them would commit us to views of Anabaptists and the Pope which are unscriptural, ecumenically unhelpful and wrong.[25] Standing as one in the line of John Wesley, Geoffrey Wainwright writes of the ancient creeds (though what he says applies also to their later, often fuller, confessional counterparts), that they 'must, theologically, be seen as summaries of the scriptures before they can be seen, as it were independently, as their hermeneutical key'.[26] No doubt, but this begs the question of their adequacy as summaries.

Useful as they may be for certain purposes, creeds and confessions of faith cannot by themselves guarantee orthodoxy: 'Experience has shown that it passes man's wit to devise a form of words which can be guaranteed to exclude the possibility of unorthodoxy.'[27] What they can do – and it is sad – is constrict: 'Where you fix a creed you flatten faith.'[28] An unfortunately aristocratic impression may be conveyed that Christianity is primarily a matter of intellectual assent to authoritatively prescribed formulae.[29] Frequently the posited authority has been the Church, as appears in Newman's hymn, 'Firmly I believe and truly':

> And I hold in veneration,
> For the love of him [the Son] alone,
> Holy Church as his creation,
> And her teachings as his own.[30]

There is a world of difference (in fact, a Reformation) between Newman's words and those of Robert Mackintosh:

> Let the Church, then, exclude all blasphemy on the part of clergy or of laity; let the Church exclude what is incompatible with good order; let the Church make sure that her preachers are not hindered by habitual doubt from bearing witness to the whole circle of rudimentary Christian and spiritual truths; but do not let her go beyond this. Let her remember that she is herself a learner – that her creed is only a broken light, that free discussion, of essentials with those outside, of non-essentials with brethren as well, is one indispensable precondition of a growing knowledge of the truth.[31]

Again, creeds and confessions may be the means of fostering or justifying the schismatic tendency, so that instead of being a last, reluctant, resort, schism becomes to its promoters a badge of purity of faith and fidelity to the Gospel. It would therefore seem that, far from being the Gospel, formal affirmations of faith do not necessarily give an adequate account of it; still less do they by themselves guard the faith or unite Christian believers. They have their proper but subordinate place. But to what are they subordinate? The answer can only be, to the Gospel as witnessed to in Scripture; and yet again the question arises: what is the Gospel?

III

Some have suggested that the heart of the Christian Gospel is Christ. Clearly, by definition, there would be no Christian gospel apart from him, and it is not difficult to find numerous examples through Christian history of those who have affirmed Christ's centrality unequivocally. The earliest gospel opens, 'Here begins the gospel of Jesus Christ the Son of God'; and we may take 'gospel' here to mean not simply the message which Jesus proclaimed, but 'the good news about Jesus'. Again, Calvin writes, 'By the Gospel, I understand the clear manifestation of the mystery of Christ.'[32] To Thomas Watson, the English Puritan divine, 'Jesus Christ is the sum and quintessence of the gospel; the wonder of angels, the joy and triumph of saints. The name of Christ is sweet, it is as music in the ear, honey in the mouth, and a cordial at the heart.'[33] 'Eventually,' wrote H. R. Mackintosh, 'the distinctive fact in Christianity is Christ.'[34]

Admittedly, these sentences have been removed from their contexts, but the point to be made is that crisp testimonies to the centrality of Christ do not tell us very much. We need to know with what kind of Christ we have to do. Is he master, leader, example, the first Christian, elder brother, Lord, saviour – behind these descriptions lie theologies ranging from the most orthodox to the most liberal. To take one example: P. T. Forsyth was in no doubt that 'A Christ that differs from the rest of men only in saintly degree and not in redeeming kind is not the Christ of the New Testament nor of a Gospel Church.'[35] Not all theologians agree, however, and some of them positively assert a degree christology. Others leave us in some doubt as to their position. Thus Stephen Sykes has said, 'I wish to speak of the "character of Christ" as the essence of Christianity.'[36] On hearing this out of context a Forsyth might suspect a return of the 'liberal-aesthetic' Christ, and there is little in Sykes's article to suggest that Christ's character needs to be of a kind to redeem. The matter is further complicated when he declares that 'identifiably continuous with' Christ's character is 'the character of Christ in the cooperative activity of individuals outside the date span of Jesus' historical experience'.[37] But again Forsyth would say, 'Christ is more precious to us by what distinguishes Him from us than by what identifies Him with us',[38] and he would be wary of the possible implication that the Church is a continuation of the Incarnation on the ground that 'That [namely, the Church] which owes itself to a rebirth cannot be a prolongation of the ever sinless'.[39]

Over and above its usefulness as a modest example of what may be called internal apologetics, the example just given makes it clear that 'The essence of Christianity is not in the bare fact, but in the fact and its interpretation'.[40] This would, indeed, seem to be but a particular application of the general principle that there are no such things as bare facts: interpretation and judgement enter into the pronoucement that '*x*' is a fact. Indeed,

> a fact is only available for knowledge if we construct theories of its meaning – always imperfect, but always capable of correction and growth. Accordingly, fact is never exhausted in theory or lost in theory; at the same time, it can never be divorced from theory. To adapt a well-known formula: theories without facts are 'empty,' and facts without theory are 'blind.'[41]

But the question presses: what are the interpreted facts which lie at the heart of the Christian confession? Some, not least many Anglican theologians who are heirs of the nineteenth-century rediscovery of Alexandrian theology, would say that first among them is the Incarnation – and here we stumble into another fertile field of internal apologetics.[42] Prominent among those who elevated the Incarnation was J. R. Illingworth, in whose work, as I showed in *Philosophical Idealism*, ideas of Incarnation and post-Hegelian immanentism are blended in such a way that he can exult that '[S]ecular civilization is . . . nothing less than the providential correlative and counterpart of the Incarnation'[43] – 'naïve optimism', declared A. M. Ramsey,[44] who further explained:

> Bent upon the recovery of the incarnation as the central principle in theology, [Illingworth] wrote in deprecation of those who gave centrality to the Atonement . . . This was incautious, inasmuch as the formulation of the doctrine of the Incarnation had sprung, alike in the apostolic age and in the patristic period, from out of the experience of Redemption: the saving act had been the key to the Church's faith in the divine Christ.[45]

Earlier, though not in relation to Illingworth, James Denney had made the same point with characteristic conciseness: 'the rationale of the incarnation is in the atonement.'[46] In entire accord, Forsyth declared,

> The centre of the Incarnation is where Christ placed the focus of His work – not at the beginning of His life, but at its end; not in the manger, but in the cross. The key to the Incarnation is not in the cradle, but in the cross. The light on Bethlehem falls from Calvary. The virtue lies in some act done by Christ; and He Himself did no act at His birth, but in His death he did *the* act of the universe . . . God was in Christ as reconciler, not as prodigy.[47]

More recently another Anglican, J. A. Baker, began an interesting article on 'The essence of Christianity' by claiming that 'Part at least of the essence of Christanity as such . . . must be whatever central tenet it does not share with any other faith; and that is one thing only, the classical doctrine of the Incarnation.'[48] Leaving on one side the claim concerning 'one thing only', it is significant that when Baker wishes to counter those Christians who prefer a God who is 'like' Jesus to the classical doctrine of the Incarnation, he declares, 'The thing which gave Christianity its wide-ranging appeal was that it offered not a revelation of what God was like but a salvation through what God had done'.[49] He properly adds that the truth hidden in the crucified Jesus 'would have remained hidden but for one thing: that the crucified Jesus is also the Risen Lord'.[50] This, I believe, is to place the emphasis in the right place. Here we approach the heart of the Christian confession. Here are those interpreted facts which are so vulnerable in the hands of 'Pelagian' and immanentist alike. It is not that one wishes to endorse cruder evangelical statements that 'Jesus came to die' – as if this were all: his coming and the whole course of his life are of the highest importance. But there seems little doubt that the christological question and the outworking of incarnational doctrine were stimulated by the saving experience of those who, after the resurrection and against all their Jewish upbringing, ascribed the title 'Lord' to Jesus:

> The early Christians were sure of two things, that through Christ they had found God and that Christ was living: I believe it was fundamentally for those two things that the affirmation 'Jesus is Lord' (*kurios*) stood, the tense as well as the predicate being stressed. As their conviction, those two things were the interpreted facts of their experience, and I think that to be a Christian means that one interprets one's own experience similarly. So much is necessary: it is not enough simply to believe that the Apostles were right in interpreting their experience as they did; but it is more than is necessary (if, indeed, it be possible) to go on to accept the thought-forms in which their thus interpreted experience of the revelation of God in Christ was elaborated by them in the New Testament or by the Fathers in the Creeds.[51]

It may therefore be that those currently known as the exponents of radical orthodoxy are not radical enough. Their leaders, John Milbank, Graham Ward and Catherine Pickstock correctly understand that 'radical' is derived from the Latin *radix*, a root, but it may be questioned whether their roots are deep enough. Among other things they claim to be radical 'in the sense of a return to patristic and medieval roots, and especially to the Augustinian vision of all knowledge as divine illumination – a notion which transcends the modern bastard dualisms of faith and reason, grace and nature'.[52] This sentence typifies their style, which both suggests scholarly concern and leaves one feeling taken by the throat. But the main point is that whether we turn to Acts, Paul,

Hebrews or other epistles, the root of the faith is in the Bible, and the Gospel on the early Christians' lips was not about the cradle, but the Cross, for he who had been crucified was now raised. Here is the root of Christian faith, hope, life and theology, and it is to be feared that the radical orthodox theologians pay insufficient attention to this fact, and further that in offering their wares as a 'new theology' they overlook its almost uncanny likeness at certain points to the incarnationalism of J. R. Illingworth and other writers of the Anglo-Catholic *Lux Mundi* school of the later nineteenth century.[53]

With commendable reticence the Church has never formally defined the doctrine of the atonement, and this is not the place to expound the many formulations of it which individuals have offered. I must, however, record my conviction that any even remotely satisfactory account of God's saving work in Christ must make it plain that God has done something in Christ, and not merely shown something: 'The scriptural testimony is that the Cross is not only a visual aid – even a divine one.'[54] Again, the Gospel is not simply that God in Christ has taught us something of which we should otherwise have been ignorant: 'The gospel is no mere proclamation of "eternal truths", but the discovery of a saving purpose of God for mankind, executed in time.'[55] No doubt, Christianity

> assumed that there were sin and misery in the world, that redemption was needed by man. Its chief characteristic was that it was a message of salvation to sinners. It was a proclamation of mercy, an authoritative command to sinners to repent, and an authoritative statement that in Jesus Christ and in Him alone salvation was to be found by men . . . [But nevertheless] it must always be remembered that Christianity is in the first place a religion of redemption. Its aim and purpose are mainly practical.[56]

In attempting to explicate the meaning of Christ's saving deed the New Testament writers work with more than one model – Christ as priest, Christ as victim[57] – but Paul's realization that '*God* was *in Christ* reconciling the world to himself' (2 Corinthians 5: 19) makes the former more than a humanitarian act, and should (but does not always) make it impossible for theologians to turn the latter into the grotesque view rightly condemned long ago by Benjamin Jowett: 'God is represented as angry with us for what we never did; He is ready to inflict disproportionate punishment upon us for what we are; He is satisfied by the sufferings of His Son in our stead.'[58] This immoral doctrine drives a wedge between Father and Son, and turns the Gospel on its head; for, far from procuring grace, the atonement is the gift of holy, condescending grace.[59] Throughout, the saving initiative is God's, and the human response is enabled by God the Holy Spirit, for 'Christ's was a death on behalf of people within whom the power of responding had to be created'.[60]

In a grand phrase Luther spoke of God as 'a glowing furnace full of love'.[61] But if Luther was anxious to guard against what he took to be Erasmus's coldness in speaking of God's love, we may surmise that he would have approved still less the sentimentality with which some nineteenth- and twentieth-century liberal popularizers have shrouded it. After all, the fire of a glowing furnace refines. It fell to Forsyth to emphasize as few others have done that God's love is holy love. It is not a genial, amoral benignity. Moreover, 'Love is not holy without judgement. It is the love of the holy God that is the consuming fire.'[62] The grace of the holy God is his overflowing love to those who not only do not merit it, but deserve its opposite: 'It was while we were still helpless that, at the appointed time, Christ died for the wicked . . . Christ died for us while we were yet sinners, and that is God's own proof of his love towards us' (Romans 5: 6, 8). As William Jay put it in his ordination confession of faith,

> I think no man can rationally hope for pardon unless he can see a way in which God can do it *as God*, and be '*faithful* and *just* to forgive us our sins, and to cleanse us from all unrighteousness'. Such a scheme is the Gospel; it reveals a free, rich, righteous salvation through Jesus Christ . . . Hence it answers its name: it is good news, glad tidings.[63]

In his now quaint-sounding way the Puritan Thomas Willcox (1621–87) brought out the novelty of the Gospel as he reflected upon the very different gospel which human nature might have concocted: 'Let nature but make a gospel and it would make it quite contrary to Christ: it would be to the just, the innocent and the holy; Christ made the gospel for you; that is, for needy sinners, the ungodly, the unrighteous, the accursed. Nature cannot endure to think the gospel is only for sinners; it will rather choose to despair than to go to Christ upon such terrible terms.'[64] As Paul put it, '[I]t is by grace you are saved through faith; it is not your own doing. It is God's gift, not a reward for work done.' However we attempt to construe it, Christianity's central piece of good news is that in Christ's death and resurrection God has done for us that which we could never have done for ourselves. A broken relationship is restored, the penitent are forgiven and a new quality of life is bestowed. Accordingly, while there is much to be thankful for, 'There is nothing for anyone to boast of' (Ephesians 2: 8–9).

IV

It is by now clear how far we have departed from the view that the complete definition of 'Christians' is that they are people who have verbally assented to a creed, or added their signatures to a confession or covenant. Indeed, 'Where saving faith is identified with the believer's assent to a body of doctrine we are at the furthest remove from anything that can be regarded as a personal encounter of the believer with his Saviour and a personal assurance of forgiveness.'[65] However desirable official formulae may be, something more existential is required: the Christian is one who has been claimed by Christ as his own, and has begun to live what Paul calls a new life in the power of the Spirit. For this reason I find Stephen Sykes's definition somewhat over-intellectualist: 'The term "Christian" stands for a position in which a positive response is offered to the truth claims of the gospel of Jesus Christ.'[66] I entirely agree, however, that while 'Christianity certainly is more than its truth . . . there is no Christianity apart from its truth'.[67] I repeat that our understanding of what God in Christ has done may be – indeed, will be – inadequate, but those who have by grace responded to grace are *in via*, and that is enough.

But they are not *in via* as isolated individuals. The Cross does not concern the individual's life alone. The New Testament scholar, William Manson, concluded that 'We are . . . on firm ground when we assert that in the two things, the Cross of Christ and the transcendent principle of the Holy Spirit, there lie the distinctive marks of Christianity and the foundations on which the Christian Church is built.'[68] In more distinctly trinitarian terms one might say that on the ground of the Son's finished work the Father, by his Holy Spirit, graciously calls individuals to himself and at the same time gives them to one another in love so that united as branches to the vine they are inescapably united in fellowship one with another. Thus is the Church catholic constituted. The inescapability of the Church is underlined in different accents from many traditions. Said Calvin of Christians, 'If they are truly persuaded that God is the common Father of them all, and Christ their common Head, they cannot but be united in brotherly love, and mutually impart their blessings to each other.'[69] To the early Quakers 'truth' was 'a comprehensive term that embraced publishing truth, receiving truth and being gathered into a fellowship of Friends in the truth'.[70] The Presbyterian H. R. Mackintosh declared that 'The Christian life is nothing without the mutual giving and receiving of the brethren',[71] while Forsyth was his usual, pungent self: 'Salvation is personal, but it is not individual.'[72] As John Owen had exhorted his hearers in the seventeenth century, 'Let none . . . pretend that they love the brethren in general, and love the people of God, and love the saints, while their love is not fervently exercised towards those who are in the same church society with them.'[73] That this communal understanding is part of Christianity's inheritance from Judaism, and that to be saved as an individual is at the same time to be incorporated into the community of faith, was strongly emphasized by the Roman Catholic theologian Henri de Lubac.[74]

The common life of Christians must continually be nourished by the same Gospel which called it into being. In 1881, as he weighed the gains and losses of fifty years of churchly life, the venerable John Stoughton ruefully observed,

> when instead of a full exhibition of the redeeming love of God in the gospel of Christ, only 'a faint shadow of Christian sentiment' and graphic sketches 'touched with Christian tints' appear, there must be loss – grievous loss . . . New Testament facts and doctrines . . . are so essential to the production of the experience and practice of a truly Christian life, that if the former are overlooked or thrown into the background, the latter are impossible . . . Christian life must have something to live upon. It cannot support itself. It dies without the bread of God that came down from Heaven. And therefore when we miss that there must be terrible loss.[75]

The times have changed, but the caution stands; indeed, it is underlined for us who live in the wake of decades of ecumenical dialogue: 'in striving to reach the heart of the Atonement', wrote Robert Paul, 'we find ourselves worshiping at the same place, eating the same Bread, and drinking from the same Cup.'[76] Well, many, but sadly not yet all, of us do.[77]

V

I must now address more thoroughly three issues to which passing reference has already been made: confessing and commending the faith as an ecclesial task; the context in which the faith is to be confessed and commended; and the question of divergent statements of Christian truth.

Those who are 'saints by calling' (Romans 1: 7) – that is, Christians, believers – are challenged to confess and commend the faith individually and corporately, by word and deed. It will hardly be denied that the public worship constitutes the primary sphere of corporate confessing. No doubt the motives of worshippers and those who lead them are always mixed. Ignatius of Antioch (*c.*35–*c.*107), for example, exhorted the Christians of Ephesus to be regular in giving praise and thanks to God on the ground that this was the way to destroy Satan's powers.[78] The Puritan Robert Traill (1642–1716) prophesied:

> As long as God hath a mind to give mercy and grace, as long as any of the children of men are sensibly needy of grace and mercy, and askers and receivers thereof from the Lord (and that will be till the heavens be no more), this throne of grace will be plied and praised.[79]

In our own time some have complained that in some circles people attend worship because of its entertainment value – its amplified musical groups and the like. But before looking down on such from too great a height let us recall that some of the old 'princes of the pulpit' – especially those still fondly recalled as 'characters' – managed without much difficulty to entertain, and, furthermore, that their lack of any need of amplification was frequently among the qualifications sought by those who called them. On balance, it is perhaps preferable that people go to church hoping to be entertained rather than expecting to be bored. The fact remains that, whatever the mixed motives of those who attend and conduct services of worship, the primary objective is to praise God and confess the faith. Ideally, in this task the entire fellowship is sincerely engaged.

Properly conceived, a service of worship, though its Bible readings and sermons may intellectually stimulate and challenge the hearers, is a bulwark against undue intellectualism. God is to be praised, the Gospel to be told; and as, by God the Holy Spirit, the Word becomes clamant to those who hear, they are drawn into ever closer fellowship with God and with their fellow believers. Sometimes, however, as John Whale remarked,

> Instead of putting off our shoes from our feet because the place whereon we stand is holy ground, we are taking nice photographs of the burning Bush, from suitable angles: we are chatting about theories of Atonement with our feet on the mantlepiece, instead of kneeling down before the wounds of Christ.[80]

On the other hand, the peril of anti-intellectualism is to be avoided too: it patronizes and disturbs the thoughtful, it cheats the 'babes in Christ'. The Bible is a difficult enough book for people to understand without causing them to think that they have to imbibe its mythological aspects as if they were historical – or, what is worse – 'deal with' difficulties by avoiding them. Such thoughts seem to have been in the mind of A. S. Pringle-Pattison when he delivered his presidential address to the Theological Society of New College, Edinburgh:

> It is because I believe that there is a real danger of your relapsing insensibly into the old grooves that I wish to remind you to-day of the great multitude outside the Churches, sympathetic to Christian ideals but alienated from official Christianity by the incredibilities which are mingled with its teaching. It is upon them that your gaze should be fixed, and not upon the unlettered occupants of the pews whose simple faith you might disturb . . . Simple piety may be trusted to recover soon from the initial disturbance caused by new views of truth, while embittered orthodoxy may be left to its own evil passions: there is nothing more un-Christlike on this sinful earth.[81]

An echo of this view is heard in the outburst of Dean Inge:

> The worst enemies of Christianity are Christians. A religion will never be destroyed by worldliness, sensuality or malicious wickedness. The world, the flesh and the devil are the natural enemies of the Church, which thrives on the struggle against them. But when traditional ortho-

> doxy provokes the moral indignation of the enlightened conscience, and when it outrages our sense of truth and honesty by demanding our assent to scientific errors which were exploded centuries ago, then indeed the Church is in danger . . . If our leaders were wise in their generation . . . [t]hey would have the courage to disregard the prejudices of the church-going public, and would appeal to the conscience and intelligence of a wider circle.[82]

It is no defence to say that, despite the evidence, people believe all kinds of non-religious falsehoods – such as that Oklahoma is the Dust Bowl. Psycho-geographers tell us that, although there was a long period of drought in the 1930s (which affected neighbouring states as well as Oklahoma itself), the lingering myth of Oklahoma as a parched, arid state (which nowadays proclaims itself as an 'aquatic vacationland') has more to do with John Steinbeck's novel, *The Grapes of Wrath* (1939), and the film of it starring Henry Fonda (1940) than with reality; yet the falsehood remains powerfully present in many minds.[83] Be that as it may, Christian confessors should be more interested in proclaiming truth than allowing misconceptions concerning the Bible or the Christian faith to stand – especially when these needlessly alienate those to whom they are called to witness. But such misconceptions are most likely to be dispelled when the Bible is read eagerly, humbly, reverently and intelligently within the *ecclesia* which is its natural home:

> The Bible can become a dangerous book to put into the hands of people unless they clearly realize that it is the book of the Church and needs the life and order of the Church for its interpretation, not in the formal sense of giving a correct meaning to a particular passage through an authoritative teaching organ but in the deep inward sense of providing the right environment for its true understanding.[84]

Worship as a corporate act enables both personal testimony and communal confession, while at the same time eschewing individualism. As Bernard Lord Manning pointed out, eighteenth- and nineteenth-century Christians had the deepest fellowship with one another 'when they sang the most individual hymns:

> Jesu, lover of *my* soul;
> Rock of Ages, cleft for *me*.
> When *I* survey the wondrous cross . . .

At such moments they had most communion with one another and most impact on the world.'[85] But this balance of the personal and the corporate is all too easily disturbed in an individualistic direction. Among many accounts of the inroads of individualism is one by Timothy George. It concerns Baptists in America, whose traditional theology, grounded in the covenant idea, was 'inherently communitarian': 'They shared fellowship with other believers of like precious faith through a common confession, and they were intentional about passing on the faith to a rising generation through a shared catechism . . . Today "Baptist catechism" sounds like an oxymoron.'[86] The perceived decline is the result of the privatization of religion; and George quotes Winthrop S. Hudson to the effect that by the twentieth century Baptists were developing an apologetic grounded in the individualistic general and religious culture of the day rather than in the Bible, and that 'the practical effect of the stress upon "soul competency" as the cardinal doctrine of Baptists was to make every man's hat his own church'.[87]

The Mennonite theologian, J. Denny Weaver, throws the net wider: 'For too much of American Protestantism, the existence of the church is not integral to salvation, but is a group of persons *already saved*, who in recognition of their salvation gather for mutual encouragement and inspiration.' He argues that 'The Anabaptist tradition has the potential to remind Western thought of the social component of biblical religion . . . Since Jesus, acceptance of Christ inaugurates one into God's people, and experience of Christ means to experience the reconciliation among persons which Christ brings.'[88]

That Baptists in America are not alone in being prey to individualism emerges in a review by A. E. Taylor of J. M. E. McTaggart's book of 1906, *Some Dogmas of Religion*. According to Taylor, McTaggart understands religion as 'a form of emotion arising from a conviction of harmony between ourselves and the nature of ultimate reality'. To which Taylor replies, 'Every great historical religion, so far as I am aware, has departed from Dr. McTaggart's definition by attaching fundamental importance to something which has to be *done*, an end to be attained by the co-operation of the religious community.'[89]

The first cooperative end is, to come full circle, the worship of God. In this activity, as an Orthodox theologian has suggested, we may find the remedy for excessive individualism:

> Europe [but the words have a wider application] needs an appropriate liturgical model not only to heal the wounds of its individualism and free-market economy, but also to offer the occasion for people to celebrate together, to listen to each other, to look into each other's face in order to find a common mind for common action. The dominant model of individualism, verbal and formal, is only interested in private commodities, and leads to careless attitudes, to cynical self-serving participation. The liturgical model intends to deepen communion, to recover unity and foster co-operation and common activity. The liturgy provides the possibility for God to act in recapitulating the whole creation in Christ (Eph. 1: 10). Nobody is independent or disconnected within the Liturgy. It has a mechanism (*oikonomia*) which does not allow for discrimination between people (*laos*), between rich and poor.[90]

These things may be so, though we must beware of an instrumentalism which would 'use' worship to achieve extraneous ends, and of implying that if we do not worship God has no possibility of acting. None of which is to deny that the Church's worship, entailing as it does the confessors' openness to God's gift and demand, should equip and encourage them for confession in deed and life.

It is a sobering thought that, whatever they do, Christians and churches make a confession, for good or ill. It is well known that some of Jesus's most stern denunciations were addressed to those hypocrites who professed with their lips that to which their lives gave the lie. The condition is familiar, and one example will sufficiently illustrate it. On 7 January 1900 the *Observer* published a review of J. E. C. Welldon's book, *I Believe*, in which the bishop of Calcutta writes:

> Let us not be narrow or unchristian in our conception of the Church. Let us not consent to the meagre spirit of Roman Catholics, who look upon the Easter and Reformed Churches which form more than half of Christendom, or to the equally meagre spirit of Protestants, who look upon the Roman Catholic Church, which is the largest of the Churches, as utterly heretic and alien . . .

The anonymous reviewer then asks: 'has Dr. Welldon himself acted entirely in the spirit of this exposition in the action he has taken to close the garrison churches in India to Presbyterian and Wesleyan religious services?'[91]

But if individual Christians can thus be challenged to eat their words, so can churches conceived as corporate bodies. Here, however, matters are more complicated because even when a church formally endorses what to many, within and without the Church, appears to be a policy alien to the Gospel – apartheid in South Africa, for example – there are generally those within the offending church who stoutly oppose its stance. We might therefore have to say that in such cases the Christian confession is officially undermined but is empirically ambiguous. This argument should be employed with care, however, if the charge of special pleading is to be repudiated. Having taken full account of the dire record of Christian political-ecclesiastical history – the very thing so often hurled at Christians by everyone from sophisticated atheists to saloon bar pundits – Herbert Butterfield alluded to 'the spiritual work done by humble men over the face of the continent [of Europe] for fifteen hundred years', and concluded that this 'moving spectacle' reveals that 'the spread of piety does mean a growth in charity'.[92] To John Kent this was 'special pleading', because 'The spirit of piety . . . is as closely linked to intolerance, cruelty and warfare as it is to any growth of charity, and charity will grow as vigorously from humanist as from Christian soil.'[93] It would seem that, if Butterfield overlooked Kent's proper point concerning humanist charity, Kent fails to distinguish between true and false piety: there is no necessary connection between the former and 'intolerance, cruelty and warfare'.[94]

This exchange reminds us that churches can connive at untoward practices and policies even when they do not officially endorse them. To take one example from many around the world which might have been cited: according to a report on church life in the Cook Islands,

> Cook Islanders are avid churchgoers, and church leaders wield considerable power, so a priority for politicians is to co-opt and corrupt the churches. It is surprisingly easy. When any religious organization builds a church, Sunday School, or other project, the government provides workers (paid by the government), equipment, and sometimes material and cash . . . No cash is paid for government services. The understood price is collusion.[95]

Amidst calls in June 1996 for the prime minister and government to resign, most of the churches rallied to their aid.

It would seem that, its worship and doctrinal confession apart, the Church makes a confession, for good or ill, by the face it presents to the world, and by the attitudes and activities, collective and individual, of its members. What Larry Rasmussen has said in relation to social ethics applies to the Church's confession at large:

> The church will form – or malform – those whose lives are shaped by liturgy, cathechesis [*sic*], moral witness, church order, or any other expression in its life. Its very structure and the manner in which its members relate to one another and the wider society constitute a social ethic.[96]

We saw at the outset that the way in which the Church confesses the Gospel is varied; it is now clear that the broader confession of the Church is equally varied. 'The Christian way of life' means different things to different individuals and groups. One prominent way in which the difference has been manifested has concerned relations between the Church and the 'world' (understood here, in one of its New Testament senses, as sinful and liable to drag believers down). In particular, Christians have fretted over the question: how far, and in connection with which issues, should we, who are 'separated unto the Lord' (to use the language of Canaan), withhold ourselves from the wicked world around us lest our witness be compromised and we ourselves be sullied? How Peter Cartwright, the nineteenth-century American backwoods preacher, agonized over things which would scarcely disturb most Methodists today. He looks back with nostalgia to former times, and is convinced that things are now going from bad to worse:

> Parents did not allow their children to go to balls or plays; they did not send them to dancing-schools; they generally fasted once a week . . . But O, how things have changed for the worse, in this educational age of the world! . . . The moment we saw members begin to trim in dress after the fashionable world, we all knew they would not hold out.[97]

It would be easy to catalogue a considerable number of similar views – not least that of an English Primitive Methodist for whom the milieu of the football field was so 'impure and degrading' that he assumed the stance of a sixteenth-century Separatist: 'Let us take the advice of the Word of God, "And come out from among the ungodly, and be separate from sinners."'[98]

Whether they knew it or not, Cartwright and the Primitive Methodist were wrestling in their day with dilemmas which have haunted Christians in every age, and which derive from the fact that Christians are supposed to be in the world, but not of it. As the author of the second-century *Letter to Diognetus* wrote of Christians:

> although they live in Greek and barbarian cities alike, as each man's lot has been cast, and follow the customs of the country in clothing and other matters of daily living, at the same time they give proof of the remarkable and admittedly extraordinary constitution of their own commonwealth. They live in their own countries, but only as aliens . . .[99]

With regard to the entertainments of his day, Tertullian, towards the end of the same century, famously declared:

> We renounce all your spectacles as strongly as we renounce the matters originating them, which we know were conceived of superstition; when we give up the very things which are the basis of their representations. Among us nothing is ever said, or seen, or heard, which has anything in common with the madness of the circus, the immodesty of the theatre, the atrocities of the arena, the useless exercises of the wrestling-ground.[100]

Here are early examples of the Church as an alternative society, and in a very different context the early Anabaptists sought to embody this principle. Of them it has been said that, wary of individualism, relativism and anti-historicism, they gathered in Bible Schools not only in order to ponder God's word, but to train themselves for active discipleship in response to it: theirs

> was a costly obedience which did not arise out of a desire to be heroic but out of the recognition that to know God's will is to do it. This, rather than an adherence to literalistic or legalistic ways of reading the Scriptures, is the reason for their emphasis upon discipleship.[101]

At the present time powerful voices are seeking to recall us to this understanding. Among them are Stanley Hauerwas and William Willimon, who advocate a 'confessing church' rather than a Constantinian or privatized model of the Church. The Church is to be a 'community of the cross', and, as if to echo the early Anabaptists, they aver that 'the main political task of the church is the formation of people who see clearly the cost of discipleship and are willing to pay the price'. Such people, they say, as if updating

Diognetus, are 'resident aliens, an adventurous colony in a society of unbelief'.[102] Christians comprise a community of people who have seen something which cannot be seen without Christ, and their calling is not to defend a set of beliefs, but to live in obedience to what they have seen.

Not surprisingly, some have accused the advocates of intentional churchly formation of adopting an incipiently sectarian stance.[103] But, while this – whether in vociferously polemical or quietist mode – is an ever present danger, if the concepts of discipleship and mission are to the fore in the community of faith, sectarian ghettoization will not be a necessary result; and insofar as Christians seek to articulate what they have seen, they are engaged in constructing a belief system, however informal. The extent to which they may then commend their beliefs to others depends in part upon whether they endorse Hauerwas's view (which, as we shall see later, bears a family resemblance to that of George Lindbeck, in turn a debtor to Wittgenstein) that Christian discourse is meaningful only within the Christian circle. A further point to note is that no communal nurturing of the saints should overlook the point which the Mercersburg theologian, John Williamson Nevin, was so eager to emphasize, namely, that by the Incarnation and in his risen life, Christ is present by his Spirit in the world (not naughty in this context), and not only in the Church. Christ is 'continually present and active in all the forms of outward material existence'.[104] In a very different context Nevin's sentiments were in a broad sense echoed by Bonhoeffer: 'It is in Jesus Christ that God's relation to the world is defined. We know of no relation of God to the world other than through Jesus Christ.'[105] The danger of the opposite position, in which intentional community formation is played down in the interests of openness and non-judgementalism, is that the Church may become so identified with its host society in everything from ethical attitudes and genial belief to management styles that any distinctive witness it might have had to make is under threat.

Endorsement of the 'resident aliens' idea, construed in non-sectarian terms, comes from a variety of theological directions. Thus, Walter Brueggemann makes the point in language appropriate to an Old Testament scholar: we exiles are each day 'in the presence of those who preside over the exile, that is, in the presence of "Babylonians."'[106] Far from withdrawing from the surrounding society, however, the exiles are to engage with it 'with a sense of subversiveness that gives unnerving freedom'.[107] A similar point is made using different language by the conservative evangelical scholar David F. Wells: 'Only those who are counter-cultural by way of being other-worldly have what modern culture most needs to hear – a Word from God that can cut through the deceits of modernity to reach the hearts that lie within.'[108]

At least one further pitfall presents itself to those who are eager to confess the faith by their deeds: it is the temptation to 'use' (and thereby to abuse) Christianity as a means of toning up the moral muscles of society – a policy reminiscent of school speech day exhortations at their worst, and one trounced by A. B. Bruce, who refers to eighteenth-century apologetics, which was marked by a 'prominent defect', namely,

> The low view it took of the chief end of revealed religion, as intended to serve the purpose of a moral police to restrain vice and keep men within the bounds of decency. It was strongly insisted on, as a great recommendation of Christianity, that its doctrines had a powerful tendency to reform men's lives and correct their manners. This truth was emphasised very specially in connection with the doctrine of a future life, and its certified solemnities of bliss and woe. The fear of a future hell, it was gravely pointed out, helped sinners to behave themselves here. What a degradation of religion to convert it into a mere purveyor of motives to morality, and hold it up as a bugbear to frighten evil livers into sobriety and righteousness . . . The aim was mean, and the success, had it been as great as its promoters wished, would have been a gain to the State rather than to the kingdom of God. But the success was by all accounts small. The age of the 'Evidences' appears to have been an age of dissolute morals.[109]

While it would not be difficult to adduce eighteenth-century exemplars of the kind of apologetics to which Bruce here takes exception – John Tillotson comes to mind – there is an element of caricature in Bruce's description of eighteenth-century apologetics – moral earnestness in dissolute times is not a bad fault. It must, however, be granted that the argument of which he complains is invoked to this day, and has, as Christianity's third millennium opens, been restated in general terms by at least one very prominent clergyman of the Church of England as a ground for opening more church schools.

Enough has been said to justify my contention that confessing and commending the faith is the task of the whole Church, and that it entails both worship and verbal profession and witness in the broadest sense.[110] It has further become clear that both the content of what is professed and the witnessing stances which are and have been adopted, are context- and time-related. Into this latter aspect we must now enquire more closely. In the next section, by taking soundings from the first 250 years of the Christan era and then from the 250 years to 1900, I shall illustrate the way in which the articulation of God's saving work in Christ has been influenced by its cultural, and especially its intellectual, environment; and in the following chapter I shall focus upon those to whom the Gospel is directed – that is, I shall review diverse strands of Christian anthropology with special reference to their epistemological significance.

VI

As long ago as 1647 Jeremy Taylor declared that 'men do not learn their doctrines from Scripture, but come to the understanding of Scripture with preconceptions and ideas of doctrines of their own'.[111] It was ever thus and, what is more, the New Testament writers themselves were not innocent of presuppositions or unindebted to their religious and intellectual heritage and socio-political context. For this reason, as, for example, we have already seen in relation to Christ's roles as Priest and Victim, the New Testament 'lends its sanction impartially to many varieties of thought'.[112] Even greater latitude in modes of expression is detectable as the Christian centuries unfold, and as a missionary religion found its way to many parts of the world.[113] It would therefore seem that, far from being simply permissible or desirable, a certain liberty of interpretation is necessary and inevitable if the Gospel is to be communicated beyond its original cultural cradle. But the phrase 'a certain liberty' begs the question which affords ample scope for that 'internal apologetics' to which reference has been made, whereby those with antennae sensitive to Gospel reductionism have indulged in defences ranging in style from the most alarmist Ark-guarding pamphleteering to the most highly sophisticated theorizing.

In seeking to illustrate the way in which the articulation of the

Gospel has been influenced by the context of the confessing, we may set out from the *Epistle to Diognetus*, where in chapter 9 there is a strong statement of the view that, when humanity had sunk in sin and could not save itself, God took pity on us, and 'Himself in mercy took on Him our sins, Himself gave up His own Son as a ransom for us . . . For what else could cover our sins but his righteousness?'[114] This affirmation appears to be more of an amalgam of biblical ideas than an apology tailored to those whose own intellectual presuppositions would have to be considered. The same may be said of the contribution of Ignatius of Antioch who, although concerned to answer the docetics, nevertheless remains largely within the field of biblical imagery, some of which he develops in striking ways, as when he speaks of Christians being pulled up to God on Jesus's crane, the Cross, by the rope of the Holy Spirit.[115] Above all, as E. F. Osborn has said, 'Ignatius sees the climax of saving history in the new humanity of Jesus Christ'.[116]

While Justin Martyr holds Christ in very high esteem, his Platonic understanding of the ineffable God inhibits him from believing that God can have close dealings with mere mortals. Hence L. W. Barnard's judgement that 'this philosophic idea of God remained uppermost in [Justin's] mind and threatened, at times, to overwhelm the more biblical and Christian idea which Justin knew as a fact of experience'.[117] Thus, for example, Justin holds that it was the Logos-Son and not the eternal One who appeared to the Hebrew patriarchs: 'neither Abraham, nor Isaac, nor Jacob, nor any other man, saw the Father and ineffable Lord of all, and also of Christ, but [saw] Him who was according to His will His Son'.[118] After all, he continues, 'that that which is begotten is numerically distinct from that which begets, any one will admit'.[119] The role of the Logos is to impart to human beings that true knowledge of God which leads to salvation, and this task is brought to completion in his incarnation. But if Justin's idea of the Logos leaves him at some distance from the fourth evangelist, his identification of sin with ignorance which, because it is the work of demons, is non-culpable, leaves him far removed from Paul.[120] There is an incipient doctrine of recapitulation in his writings, as when he says of Christ that 'He became man by the Virgin, in order that the disobedience which proceeded from the serpent might receive its destruction in the same manner in which it derived its origin';[121] he speaks of Christ as suffering to save the inhabitants of all the earth;[122] he says that 'our Christ, by being crucified on the tree, and by purifying [us] with water, has redeemed us';[123] and his entire position is grounded in a typological analysis of biblical texts.[124] But if this, together with the fact that 'The description of God as Father has no discernible significance in Justin's soteriology',[125] makes Justin's position appear inadequate to us, we should not overlook the fact that, surrounded by idol-worship, he was, as Harnack pointed out, pleading 'the cause of spiritual monotheism . . . in the manner most easily understood'.[126]

Where the Logos doctrine is concerned, Irenaeus, keen to offer no concessions to the Gnostics, is more cautious than Justin. Christ is the enfleshed Logos; and while Irenaeus sometimes suggests that the Son is subordinate to the Father, and the Holy Spirit to both Father and Son,[127] his main emphasis is upon the full God-manhood of the Son, and this not only for ontological reasons but for soteriological ones too. For he elevates the doctrine of *recapitulatio*,[128] stoutly maintaining that Jesus must be God-man if he is, as second Adam, to reverse the calamity by which humanity fell in the first Adam, and restore us to God. The Son of God was with the Father from the beginning,

> But when He became incarnate, and was made man, He commenced afresh the long line of human beings, and furnished us, in a brief, comprehensive manner, with salvation; so that what we had lost in Adam – namely, to be according to the image and likeness of God – that we might recover in Christ Jesus.[129]

Far from being a mode of, or an emanation from, the divine, the Son is 'the Word of God, our Lord Jesus Christ, who did, through His transcendent love, become what we are, that He might bring us to be even what He is Himself'.[130] In this way, Irenaeus 'tries to make of the Logos not a buffer between the ingenerate God and the generate world, but the presence within the world of the Godhead itself'.[131] The Gnostics, with their claim to know the truth already, make the Incarnation and redemption redundant.[132] In fact, however, Christ has

> redeemed us through His own blood, giving His soul for our souls, and His flesh for our flesh, and had also poured out the Spirit of the Father for the union and communion of God and man, imparting indeed God

> to men by means of the Spirit, and, on the other hand, attaching man to God by his own incarnation, and bestowing at His coming immortality durably and truly, by means of communion with God.

Hence, 'all the doctrines of the heretics fall to ruin'.[133]

For an accurate statement of Tertullian's view of Christ's work we may turn to Maurice Wiles: 'Man is not just a spirit but flesh and spirit. If the Word did not become flesh, then flesh has been left outside the sphere of redemption. The possibility of full salvation depends upon the reality of the incarnation.'[134] As to what the incarnate Word did, Tertullian says that 'God held converse with man, that man might learn to act as God. God dealt on equal terms with man, that man might be able to deal on equal terms with God. God was found little, that man might become very great.'[135] It would seem, then, that human beings need to be enabled by Christ, but when Tertullian speaks of Christ the mediator who 'shall reconcile both God to man and man to God',[136] he seems less firm than Irenaeus on Christ's finished work of redemption. On the other hand, against docetism he emphasizes the actual sufferings of Christ:

> He suffered nothing who did not truly suffer; and a phantom could not truly suffer. God's entire work, therefore, is subverted. Christ's death, wherein lies the whole weight and fruit of the Christian name, is denied . . . No, if His death be denied, because of the denial of His flesh, there will be no certainty of His resurrection . . . if Christ's resurrection be nullified, ours also is destroyed.[137]

To Clement of Alexandria, as to Philo and other Platonists, the Logos is the mind of God, who becomes an immanent principle, somewhat as in Stoicism.[138] This immanent principle is the power of God, the creative principle, and the source of such wisdom as the ancients possessed. The Logos became incarnate in Christ, the Son, who is the Tutor, the Instructor, the Educator – three descriptions used in *Paedogogus* I. i, where the function of the Logos is summed up thus: 'Eagerly desiring, then, to perfect us by a gradation conducive to salvation, suited for efficacious discipline, a beautiful arrangement is observed by the all-benignant Word, who first exhorts, then trains, and finally teaches.'[139] Clement's struggle to relate the historic Jesus to the Philonic Logos emerges in many ways, not least when he declares that the human Jesus did not eat because he needed to, but because he wished to demonstrate his humanity to his followers.[140] As to Christ's work: sin is the irrational abuse by human beings of the freedom in which they were created; it is everything that is contrary to right reason.[141] By the pathway of education, immortality is restored. As Lilla has remarked, 'The idea of Christ as redeemer of the whole of mankind by means of his sacrifice is replaced, in Clement's philosophical system, by the esoteric idea of *gnosis*.'[142] On the other hand, against Gnostics who deemed their esoteric knowledge superior to faith, Clement insists that 'knowledge is a sure and certain demonstration of the things received through faith'.[143] This is compatible with what we might call the more evangelical side of Clement: 'Receive Christ, receive sight, receive thy light . . . I urge you to be saved', he cries, for 'This Christ desires. In one word, he freely bestows life on you.'[144] Small wonder that an older commentator wrote:

> Clement's theology is composite rather than organic – a structure of materials old and new, hardly fit for the open air, the wind and the rain. But his faith is another thing – it rests upon the living personality of the Saviour, the love of God and the significance of the individual soul, and it has the stamp of such faith in all ages – joy and peace in believing. It has lasted because it lived.[145]

Origen conceives of the Fall in terms of the Greek chain of being. Souls sinned in a pre-existent state – hence, for example, some babies are born blind. In an apparently unreconciled way he also teaches that people do not sin until they are born as rational human beings having freedom of choice. Be that as it may, one spirit did not fall in the pre-existent state, and in due course this one, united with the Logos, was fit to become the human soul of Jesus. Whereas the Monarchians identified the Father and the Son, Origen sometimes, when deferring to Plato's incorporeal Monad, taught that the Son is subordinate to the Father, though in his homilies he prayed directly to Christ.[146] In opposition to Gnostic emmanationist doctrine, Origen maintains that the Son was eternally generate and, like Justin Martyr and others, he finds it difficult to find a role for the Holy Spirit which he has not already allocated to the Logos. The work of Christ is viewed variously as a ransom to Satan, a vicarious sin-offering, and a propitiation; and there is a Hellenistic undertow in his work which pulls him in the direction of sitting loose to the historical Jesus in the interests of the Logos who, to the true Christian gnostic, is all-sufficient.[147] To Origen, redemption is, above all, the reunion of fallen spirits with God, and 'It is in our power to stretch out our hand, to do good works, and to lay hold on life and deposit it in our soul'[148] – in which assertion some have seen incipient 'Pelagianism'. Redemption is an ongoing process, and, with more than a nod in the direction of Neoplatonic eschatology, Origen can envisage the creation of successive worlds as theatres of restoration, and even contemplate the possibility that Satan may finally be restored – a view which prompted his denunciation as a heretic at the Fifth General Council of 553.

For our second illustration we leap forward to England in the second half of the seventeenth century. Here we find a significantly different set of circumstances, but an equal concern to communicate the Gospel in a contemporary way. In the aftermath of the Civil War, with the antics of radical sects fresh in the mind, and with religious toleration looming and eventually granted to Protestant orthodox Dissenters in 1689, some sought an indispensable minimum of belief which would foster the unity of all who embraced it. This was Locke's motivation when, in *The Reasonableness of Christianity* (1695) and its sequels, he posited 'Jesus is the Messiah, our King' as his favoured fundamental belief.[149] He was appalled by the attitude of the high Calvinist Anglican, John Edwards, who will 'boldly affirm, you have no christianity, if you will not swallow it just as it is of his cooking';[150] and he found entire Christian traditions guilty of the same tendency:

> [H]owever clearly we may think this or the other doctrine to be deduced from scripture, we ought not therefore to impose it upon others, as a necessary article of faith, because we believe it to be agreeable to the rule of faith; unless we would be content also that other doctrines should be imposed upon us in the same manner; and that we should be compelled to receive and profess all the different and contradictory opinions of lutherans, calvinists, remonstrants, anabaptists, and pother sects which the contrivers of symbols, systems, and confessions, are accustomed to deliver unto their followers as genuine and necessary deductions from the Holy Scripture. I cannot but wonder at the extravagant arrogance of those men who think that they themselves can explain things necessary to salvation more clearly than the Holy Ghost, the eternal and infinite wisdom of God.[151]

Although, as I have suggested elsewhere in this trilogy, Locke's indispensable minimum of belief is, at least on some occasions, a portmanteau confession in which the term 'Messiah' covers Christ's death, resurrection, ascension and second coming,[152] it is not on all fours with that of his contemporary, Richard Baxter, himself a tireless worker for Christian unity. Although Baxter exhorted his friend Peter Ince to 'bottom upon Christ and the great fundamentals. Unite in those with men of holiness & righteousness',[153] he knew better than most 'how ticklish a Business the Enumeration of fundamentals was',[154] and therefore urged the making of 'no larger a Profession necessary than the creed and the Scriptures'[155] – a considerably more comprehensive 'minimum' than Locke's. In 1654 Baxter attended a conference in London convened to determine the fundamentals of religion. When he specified the Apostles' Creed, the Lord's Prayer and the Decalogue as the desired fundamentals some commissioners complained that 'A Socinian or a Papist will Subscribe all this, I answered them, So much the better.'[156] Baxter consistently urged union in necessary truths, and warned his contemporaries 'not to make a larger creed and more necessaries than God hath done'.[157] For 'all over-doing is undoing!'[158]

During the eighteenth century, with the eddies of deism, rationalistic Arminianism and Arianism swirling around them, some divines gave themselves to ever further refinements of their doctrinal systems. That such precision was not the preserve of professionals alone is clear from the distress caused by an early sermon of Francis Hutcheson. On completing his studies at Glasgow University he returned to Armagh, and was invited to preach for his father on a certain Sunday. The expressions on the faces of the members of the congregation as they came out of church clearly indicated that they had not heard 'the language of Canaan' to which they were accustomed, and which they thought they had a right to expect. An elder, a native of Scotland, spoke for them all to Hutcheson's father:

> We a' feel muckle wae for you mishap, reverend sir, but it canna be concealed. Your silly loon, Frank, has fashed a' the congregation wi' his idle cackle; for he has been babbling for this hour about a gude and benevolent God, and that the sauls of the heathens themsels will gang to heaven if they follow the light o' their ain consciences. Not a word does the daft boy ken, speer, or say about the gude auld comfortable

doctrines of election, reprobation, original sin, and faith. Hoot, mon, awa' wi' sic a fellow!'[159]

From the opposite end of the theological spectrum Howell Harris, the Welsh Calvinistic Methodist, found that ringing the changes upon evangelical certainties was not necessarily a certain road to success. He confides to his diary on 11 December 1751:

> The first 4 years the Lord sent me to thunder the Law, and to bring people to leave outward sin and perform duties. The next 4 years I was sent to preach the Gospel and faith, assurance and free/grace, then Dissenters stayed behind as the clergy, gents, etc. were offended before, and now these last 6 or 7 years since I have preached the Person and Death of Christ, the Methodists have stumbled and stayed behind.[160]

In face of such opposed doctrinal attitudes there were, not surprisingly, some who cried, 'a plague on both your houses!' Among these was the Baptist Thomas Crosby, himself shunned by his high Calvinist fellow Baptist John Gill:[161]

> It is Christ that must be followed, and not Calvin or Arminius . . . Are the peculiar distinguishing doctrines of Calvin or Arminius, essential to a Christian? If not, why are they made essential to communion with one another? . . . What praise can they expect from Christ their divine master, who make the door to a profession of his religion straiter than he has left it?[162]

Lest it be thought that Britain alone suffered from differently accented presentations of the Gospel, we may cite one instance from the American frontier in the early nineteenth century. In 1810 the Cumberland Presbytery was formed in Kentucky as an offshoot from established Presbyterianism in that region. The issue was the desire of the seceders to modify the Westminster Confession in such a way as to remove what they perceived as its fatalism. They devised their own Confession, which 'teaches on the one hand conditional election and unlimited atonement, and on the other, the final perseverance of the saints. It is an eclectic compromise between Calvinism and Arminianism . . . and makes no attempt to harmonize these antagonistic elements.'[163] Eighty years on the Cumberland Presbyterian Church's application for membership of the World Alliance of Reformed Churches was declined because of lack of evidence that 'the Cumberland Church now accept the doctrinal basis of the Alliance'.[164] Among many expressions of concern at this decision was one to the effect that, since the Alliance was a fellowship of autonomous churches, each of which was responsible for its own Confession, and since the Alliance as such did not have a Confession, no aspiring member church could be guilty of breeching it. The Cumberland Church was received four years later.[165]

Underlying the concern of the Cumberland Presbyterians was the conviction that certain aspects of Calvinism as currently received would not preach. They did not sound like good news. This conviction increasingly dawned upon some in Britain, so that, for example, the newly constituted Congregational Union of England and Wales (1832) devised a Declaration of Faith, prepared by George Redford and only slightly amended, which was approved in the following year, albeit not as a document to be taken on churchly authority. Indeed, on 4 June 1832, in a covering letter sent with the Declaration to all churches, Joseph Turnbull, one of three co-secretaries of the infant Union, said that the Congregationalists hardly needed the document for their own information, but it was necessary for the information of others – not least for those who mistakenly 'take us to be either Socinians or Methodists'; and also because the Savoy Declaration of Faith and Order (1658) was now scarce and, in any case, too long.[166] That the Declaration exemplifies moderate Calvinism is clear from the fact that it mentions the covenant of grace, but not that of works; and at certain points what is left unsaid is significant, as when clause VII makes no reference to preterition: '[Congregationalists] believe that God having, before the foundation of the world, designed to redeem fallen man, made disclosures of his mercy, which were the grounds of faith and hope from earliest ages.'[167] Here we have an example of the beneficial effect of that moral critique of doctrine – especially of the notion of the sovereign God of inscrutable will – which was initiated by more liberal divines of the eighteenth century, and is, in the opinion of some, a positive result of an Enlightenment so frequently trounced by theologians then as now.[168] It hardly needs to be said that there were some for whom the Declaration (which was not intended as a full statement of all Christian doctrines) was too anodyne. Among them was Richard Winter Hamilton: 'I am no accuser', he wrote to another of the secretaries, Algernon Wells,

> but I do fear that there is creeping among us a refining method as to the great propoundings of the gospel. The full-blooded dogma of the old school must be revived. Popery, Methodism, etc., can speak of Divine sacrifice, 'the blood of God'; our own hymns abound in the expressions, 'God the mighty Maker died'; but there is a modern shrinking from them . . . Our Congregational Union symbol of faith is to me unsatisfactory and lamentable.[169]

In the middle of the nineteenth century doctrinal tensions were still in evidence. In 1859 John H. Godwin, professor at New (Congregational) College, London, delivered his Congregational Lecture on *Christian Faith: Its Nature, Object, Causes and Effects*. The following words encapsulate his case:

> If Jesus Christ be the object of the Christian Faith, those representations must be erroneous, which assign this place to any particular facts or propositions. Not the birth of Christ, nor His death, nor His resurrection, can be the object of this faith; though these and many other facts will be included in the knowledge of Christ, which is possessed by those who have faith in Him. The proposition, that Jesus is the Christ the Son of God, is not the object of this faith; though this must be believed, that there may be faith in Him . . .[170]

To the ears of the Baptist Brewin Grant this sounded damagingly reductionist. He came forth as a defender of the evangelical faith against Godwin's 'evasions', and regretted that in New College, 'instead of the citadel of truth, we should find the receptacle and stronghold of such doctrines and their emissaries!'[171] At the heart of Grant's complaint is Godwin's lack of emphasis upon the juridical element in Christ's work. He charges Godwin (not altogether fairly) with adopting an anti-propositional stance which makes faith in Christ nothing other than blind trust; and he regrets that Godwin's idea of Christ's work rises no higher than that Christ suffered for the truth – in which respect Godwin does not follow Christ, 'or he would long ago have "sacrificed" the emoluments of his office by telling the truth – that he is opposed to the doctrines for the teaching of which that office was established'.[172]

But the knock-about jibes of Grant could not halt the erosion of the received Calvinist way of confessing the faith. In his address of autumn 1873 to the Congregational Union of England and Wales, Eustace R. Conder specified the cause of the change of doctrinal stance in the following terms:

> The old Theology was not overthrown by argument. Calvinism is an iron ring of logic, which the hammer has not yet been forged that can break. It was burst asunder by the expansive force of love. The breaking point of the strain was the restriction it laid on the honest offer of salvation to all. Men began to suspect that if their theory of the Gospel hindered the Gospel, they were paying too dear a price for logic. It was possible there might be a hidden flaw in their reasoning; it was impossible God should be insincere . . . Possibly, also, they were taking hold of the wrong end of the great problem of human salvation, in beginning with the eternal decrees of God, and the eternal covenant between the Father and the Son, instead of busying themselves with the end put into their hands by the Saviour's command – 'Go ye into all the world and preach the Gospel to every creature'.[173]

Conder was well aware that he was speaking in the wake of Methodist revival which, in both its Calvinist and Arminian forms, had been influential in modifying older Calvinistic doctrine; that modern missionary zeal had underlined the change; that writers such as Coleridge, Carlyle and Maurice (and he might have added Erskine of Linlathen and McLeod Campbell) had made their powerful contribution; and there was an

> indefinite but immense modification of the general national mind which shows itself in philanthropic enterprises, in efforts for reform of criminals, mitigation of punishment, suppression of drunkenness, provision for popular amusement, lightening of the burdens of labour, and a thousand indications of a general softening of public opinion . . . The wonder is, not that the change wrought by all these causes on Theological thought has been so great, but that it has not been greater.[174]

Dr R. Vaughan Pryce, principal of New College, London, gave some specific illustrations of doctrinal modifications. He pointed out that it was only after the Reformation that 'For the first time in history the death of Christ was viewed as a vicarious punishment, inflicted by the Father on Him instead of on us. He, our substitute, was punished and accursed of God for us. Luther does not hesitate to say this.'[175] If such teaching is unacceptable, how are we to understand Galatians 3: 13, which asserts that by reason of sin we are accursed under the law? How are we delivered by Christ's death? 'Not', replies Pryce,

> by His becoming accurst of God in our place and stead, as some have dared to say, but by His dying as our Representative, Sponsor, Surety, in the covenant of grace; by His so identifying Himself with us that He

> might 'die unto sin once for all' for us. Here is the vicariousness of His death.[176]

In his account of the progress of theology through the nineteenth century W. F. Adeney, who became principal of Lancashire Independent College in 1902, described the way in which 'The disintegration of the granite mountain [of Calvinism] has been a gradual process'.[177] Commenting upon George Payne's Congregational Lectures of 1836 he notes that Payne devoted 'six lectures of his not very bulky volume to the doctrine of election. Can we imagine any influential theological writer proceeding on these lines today? In point of fact, we have ceased to be interested in the doctrine of election at all.'[178] He goes on to argue that the spirit of the times is against Calvinism which, 'While prostrating itself before the awful Majesty of God . . . had no pity for man. The elect were to be grateful for their favours, but the rest might perish like flies in autumn.'[179] Such views can no longer stand, for '"Liberty, equality, fraternity," sound the death-knell of Calvinism as well as of feudalism.'[180] Prominent among the solvents of Calvinism was the idea of the Fatherhood of God which

> entirely demolished the notion that He was an implacable Being who required to be appeased by the blood of His innocent Son before He would consent to forgive a guilty world. This dreadful calumny on the Divine character was not sanctioned by the great theological teachers, although their language had sometimes come dangerously near it. But undoubtedly, though unconfessed, it lurked in the background of popular conceptions of the Atonement; and some of Dr. Watts's hymns are responsible for giving it substantial support.[181]

To Adeney's colleague from 1902, Robert Mackintosh, 'Calvinism, in its naked reality, is anything but Christian', and his own summary of the heart of the Christian confession was: 'Belief in God as our Father, and in Christ as the Saviour of the world, is Christian faith. Whatever obscures this is leaven of the Scribes and Pharisees.'[182]

The critique of Calvinism continued until well into the twentieth century, and while it was never without its supporters, it was increasingly on the defensive. Even some of those who had no desire to turn the doctrinal clock back could, however, express certain reservations concerning the dilution of the Christian confession. Consider, for example, the remarks of the judicious

Caleb Scott, Adeney's immediate predecessor at Lancashire College:

> I cannot understand how any man can occupy the position of a Congregational minister devoid of a conviction, which is becoming ever stronger, of the reality of the incarnation, the life, the death, the resurrection, of the Word who was with God, who was God, the eternal Son of the Great Father. If we are in doubt about any of these truths, what is the message of good news we have to deliver to our fellow-men?[183]

These are the words of one who is rightly disturbed by certain trends and fashions of his time. If, on the positive side, the more angular aspects of Calvinism were being smoothed away, on the negative side, some, repudiating all authority in the interests of liberty of conscience, were embracing a genial humanism grounded in the idea of God's Fatherhood on the one hand and evolutionary progress on the other, from which the Cross – except as an example of obedient suffering – was evacuated; and they were feeding their scepticism concerning the credibility of biblical texts on the newer historical method as embraced by more liberal exponents of higher criticism.[184] All of which led to attempts in some circles to 'prune' the faith of doubtful assertions, and to seek a minimum of belief which would stand the test of modern scholarship – a very different motivation from that which prompted Locke and Baxter to seek an indispensable minimum of belief. Small wonder that P. T. Forsyth, after his conversion from theological liberalism (not that he became a fundamentalist!) complained of his erstwhile friends that 'Too many are occupied in throwing over precious cargo; they are lightening the ship even of its fuel.'[185] Thus, while convinced of the need to reduce the burden of belief, he distinguished between distilling and distorting the Gospel. As he looked back on the period in question C. H. Dodd ruefully remarked,

> We tried to believe that criticism could prune away from the New Testament those elements in it which seemed to us fantastic, and leave us with an original 'essence of Christianity', to which modern man could say, 'That is what I have always thought.' But the attempt has failed.[186]

Among other challenges to the confession of the faith were those from the philosophical direction. I leave on one side for the moment positivism, naturalism, materialism and agnosticism, and refer only and briefly to philosophical idealism in its several forms. As I sought to show in the first volume of this trilogy to appear, even those idealists most inclined to Christian belief had difficulty in squaring their Christian convictions with a philosophical method which, among other things, invited them to skirt the scandal of particularity and to construe evil as a stage on the way to a greater good. Indeed, *Philosophical Idealism and Christian Belief* was intended as an extended illustration of this point. No doubt the motive of some of them was to spare the Christian faith from the destructive effects of modern historical criticism. Of T. H. Green, for example, it was said that he tried 'to provide a sort of lowest common denominator of belief for those who were looking in those days of attack upon religion for moral principles upon which to base their daily lives'.[187] While, as I believe, there was more to Green than this, it is difficult to deny that this was one element in his thinking.

Sufficient illustrations have now been given from two temporally separated periods of Christian history to show that the Christian faith is confessed in different accents in different times, places and intellectual environments. We may therefore endorse Calvin's remark that 'according to the diversities of the times, [Christians] have divers ways of learning'.[188] This is not the most surprising of conclusions, but since believers of the bolder sort have on occasion found it surprisingly easy to overlook it – with disastrous sectarian consequences – it has been worthwhile to substantiate it in some detail.

3

Confessors and Continuity

Having discussed the nature of the Christian confession, its ecclesial rootedness and liturgical articulation, the way in which it involves the whole of a believer's life and the variety of contexts in which it has to be articulated, we must now pay closer attention to the recipients of the Gospel, who are called to be its confessors. Our question is not by which routes – Bible reading, preaching, conversation – do people actually come by the Gospel. It is not the psychological question: what is the constitution of the human mind which receives knowledge, sense impressions, revelation? It is not the epistemological question: what may we know? To some of these questions we shall return; but our present question is the anthropological one: who are they who know, receive revelation, make commitments, confess the faith? This question has been answered in a diversity of ways in the Christian tradition: indeed it is a question of some ecumenical significance between the Eastern Orthodox churches and those whose roots lie in the West, for among the former the doctrine of humanity is of great importance to their understanding of the Gospel. But the reason for treating the issue here is with a view to preparing the ground for later discussions of religious language, reason, truth, faith and knowledge, and experience – moral, aesthetic and religious. It is, after all, quite remarkable how many discussions of these topics have proceeded without asking who they are who speak, make knowledge or faith claims, or advert to experiences of one kind or another.

I

In developing their understanding of humanity, the Eastern theologians (though not they alone) made much of the declaration in Genesis 1: 26, 27:

> Then God said, 'Let us make human beings in our own image, after our likeness, to rule the fish in the sea, the birds of the air, the cattle, all wild animals on land, and everything that creeps on the earth.' God created human beings in his own image; in the image of God he created them; male and female he created them.

What did the theologians understand by 'image' and 'likeness', and did they all agree on the matter?

Clement of Alexandria, for example, draws a distinction between 'image' and 'likeness'. The pious Christian alone is said to be 'God's image, and *also* his likeness'.[1] The supreme image of God is

> the divine and royal Word [that is, Christ] . . . the image of the image is the human mind. And if you wish to apprehend the likeness by another name, you will find it named in Moses, a divine correspondence. For he says, 'Walk after the Lord your God, and keep his commandments.'[2]

For Clement, our creation in God's image means that we have the power of reason; we have freedom of will; and (as the Genesis context makes plain) we are superior to all other animals. All of this is literally the fact of our life, and none of this can be taken from us. But we grow into God's likeness by the right exercise of our will.

Origen agreed, and put the matter in a nutshell thus:

> Now the expression 'In the image of God created He him,' without any mention of the word 'likeness', conveys no other meaning than this, that man received the dignity of God's image at his first creation; but that the perfection of his likeness has been reserved for the consummation.[3]

More than a hundred years later, Gregory of Nyssa thought of the image as a perfect artist's model, and of virtues as the paints we use to reproduce the image in our lives.[4] This entire line of thought was summed up by John of Damascus in the eighth century: 'the "according to His image" means the intellect and free will, while the "according to His likeness" means such likeness in virtue as is possible'.[5]

Although Eastern theologians emphasized this line of thought, it was by no means exclusive to them. In a succinct statement, Peter Lombard distinguishes between 'image' and 'likeness' thus: 'the image consists in the cognition of truth; the similitude in the love of virtue'.[6] But not all – even of the Eastern writers – accepted the distinction. Cyril of Alexandria was among those who remained unpersuaded by the exegesis.[7] Equally unconvinced were many in the West, not least some of the Reformers. Calvin speaks for many when he declares that

> there is no slight quarrel over 'image' and 'likeness' when interpreters seek a non-existent difference between these two words, except that 'likeness' has been added by way of explanation. First, we know that repetitions were common among the Hebrews, in which they express one thing twice; then in the thing itself there is no ambiguity, simply man is called God's image because he is like God. Accordingly, those who thus philosophize more subtly over these terms appear to be ridiculous.[8]

Calvin goes on to speak of God's image as engraved upon us – the analogy is with a king's image stamped upon a coin of the realm. But this, though illuminating as far as it goes, is not the sum of Calvin's position. Overall, he construes 'image' in the context of a covenant relationship with God into which believers are brought by grace. 'The Word itself', he elsewhere writes, 'is like a mirror in which faith may contemplate God.'[9] Those who respond to God in faith reflect, or image, God's 'wisdom, righteousness and goodness'.[10] To Calvin the image is supremely a spiritual gift, not a natural property. Human beings are not manufactured replicas, they are adopted into the covenant of grace. This line of thought recurs, for example, in the writings of the eighteenth-century Baptist theologian Andrew Fuller, who understands the image to be partly natural – that which equips us to exercise dominion over all other creatures – and partly moral – that righteousness and true holiness which fits us for communion with God.[11]

In our own time Karl Barth emphasized the relational connotation of 'image', and the English theologian H. F. Lovell Cocks was in the same line when he succinctly wrote:

> When this covenant relation is taken as the central truth of the doctrine of the *imago Dei* we are saved from the difficulties that beset the older orthodoxy. We have no need to make a forced distinction between *imago*

> and *similitudo*, or to ask how far man's rational nature is impaired by the Fall, or how much of the *imago Dei* survives it. Man is what he is only by virtue of the *relation* in which he stands to God, the relation pictured in the Old Testament conception of the covenant.[12]

This would seem to take us to the heart of the matter, and one feels obliged to stand with Cyril of Alexandria and all who have found the proposed distinction between 'image' and 'likeness' exegetically untenable. In commenting on Genesis 1: 26 W. H. Bennett speaks for most of his Old Testament colleagues: 'No distinction can be drawn here between "image" and "likeness"; they are not intended to express two distinct ideas, but are a pair of synonyms setting forth one idea with special emphasis and some variety in language.'[13] This granted, we are relieved of the necessity of associating the image of God with special faculties – reason, freedom – which we possess. We have rather the familiar Hebrew device of parallelism; and in any case, as Vriezen has reminded us, the Old Testament regards persons as wholes, and not as admixtures of spiritual and corporeal components.[14]

The case against the image/likeness distinction receives further support from Westermann. He points out that, whereas the phrase concerning our creation in the image of God occurs once only in the rest of the Old Testament (Psalm 8), and although it has been prominent in theology from Irenaeus to Barth, it was not treated seriously by biblical scholars until the nineteenth cenutry.[15] His own view is that the Genesis text is not primarily concerned with the composition of human beings, but with the creative activity of God. He goes so far as to say that 'There can be no question that the text is describing an action, and not the nature of human beings. A false start has been made here which could have been avoided.'[16] Perhaps, however, this is to go too far. We may agree that God's action is paramount, and that 'image' and 'likeness' are not distinct entities. But Genesis 1: 26 does make the profound claim that human beings are related to God as his image-bearers; the entire context concerns their accountability to God, their superiority to the rest of the animal creation, and their stewardship of the created order. Indeed, Westermann himself can say that 'it is humanity created in this way that is the image of God'.[17] He concludes his discussion thus: 'the uniqueness of human beings consists in their being God's counterparts. The relationship to God is not something which is added to human existence; humans are created in such a way that their very existence is intended to be their relationship to God.'[18]

Further support for the view that where the image of God is concerned the key notion is that of relationship is forthcoming from Genesis 3. There, in the narrative of the Fall, we see, above all else, the profound moral disturbance – even rupture – of our relationship with God. But let us see what the Eastern theologians made of the Fall. The unanimous answer to the question 'Who fell?' is 'Adam'. But as between East and West there are differing views as to the sort of person Adam was; and as with 'image' and 'likeness', there are varying emphases among the Eastern Fathers. To Irenaeus, Adam and Eve were children and, like all children, they had to grow and mature. Their very innocence made Adam an easy target for the devil, and Adam disobeyed God's command.[19] Clement of Alexandria makes much of Adam's original freedom. He 'was free as a child at play', but having made the wrong choice, he became enslaved to sin.[20] Similarly, Gregory of Nyssa strongly denies that Adam was a slave of necessity, an automaton. On the contrary, because he was the image and likeness of that power which rules all things, he was able freely to make his choice. His disastrously wrong choice has consequences which plague humanity to this day.[21]

What was Adam's condition after the Fall? It appears (though it is difficult to be absolutely certain) that Irenaeus believes that fallen human beings retain souls and bodies; they can reason, and their freedom of will is unimpaired. In other words, from Irenaeus's point of view, the 'image' is intact. But we have lost the spirit, which was embryonically present in the immature Adam and Eve, by which alone they could be conformed to God's likeness (note the exegetically untenable distinction once again).[22] The spirit can be restored only by God, and Christ is the agent and exemplar of this reassimilation of humanity to God.[23]

For reasons to be offered shortly, Irenaeus seems to be on secure ground in suggesting that something is left to sinful humanity, but his way of apportioning what is left is prompted by his failure to regard 'image' and 'likeness' as synonyms. Furthermore, he thinks in terms of violated constituents of humanity rather than in terms of a broken relationship with God. This will become clearer as we explore some Western responses to the question of what happened at the Fall.

In Augustine's view, for example, the Fall is much more dramatic than in Irenaeus and Clement. Adam fell from a great height – indeed, from the height of wisdom and knowledge. He was no novice, no child. His wisdom and knowledge were not merely potential, they were actual, as was his original moral perfection. To Augustine, what was lost at the Fall was immortality. Humanity became mortal, and from mortality we can be rescued only by the grace of God:

> God was not ignorant that man would sin, and so incur mortality both for himself and his progeny . . . But God foresaw withal that His grace should adopt the godly, justify them by the Holy Spirit, pardon their sins, and rank them in eternal peace with the angels, the last and most dangerous death being destroyed.[24]

For their part the Reformers had no hesitation in ascribing the Fall to humanity's sin. Thus in the Heidelberg Catechism, largely the work of the third generation Reformer, Ursinus, we read:

> Q: Did God create man evil and perverse like this?
> A: No. On the contrary, God created man good and in his image . . .
> Q: Where then, does this corruption of human nature come from?
> A: From the fall and disobedience of our first parents, Adam and Eve, in the Garden of Eden; whereby our human life is so poisoned that we are all conceived and born in the state of sin.
> Q: But are we so perverted that we are altogether unable to do good and prone to do evil?
> A: Yes, unless we are born again through the Spirit of God.[25]

Here we come to the troublesome doctrine of total depravity. Those who, on biblical and exegetical grounds, dissent from those Eastern (and Western) theologians who classify human attributes under the allegedly distinct categories of 'image' and 'likeness' cannot hold that the sinful disruption of humanity's relationship with God entails that, while human reason and freedom remain intact, moral conformity to God is destroyed. The effects of the Fall (however that is conceived) must be 'total' in the sense of extending through the whole person. Natural gifts remain, though the use of them is impaired; the relationship with God, which should be 'natural' to us, is broken, and is seen as it should be only in Christ, Luther's Proper Man. Along this line we come in the seventeenth century to the following assertion of John Owen:

> By the entrance of sin, this image of God, so far as it was our righteousness and holiness before him, was utterly defaced and lost . . . It did not depart from any one power, part, or faculty of our souls, but from our whole nature . . . All the original first actings of the powers of our souls, in or about things rational and moral, are always evil.[26]

Owen is here faithful to Calvin, who declared that 'the substance of our bodies and souls is [not] evil, for we are God's creatures'. However, 'every part of us is saturated in evil'.[27]

What is required here is a careful analysis of 'total' in 'total depravity'. A person as saturated in evil as Owen and Calvin suppose us all to be would not be a moral agent: no choice of the good would be possible. It is one thing to say that alienation from God prevents us from truly pleasing him; that we are separated from him by a moral gulf. It is quite another to say that we can do no good at all. Nevertheless, Calvin declares in a sermon that God's image in us has been lost – 'disfigured and all but obliterated by Adam's transgression'.[28] He reiterates the point when preaching from Deuteronomy,[29] and the undeniable difficulty in all of this is not lost upon the Orthodox theologian, Timothy Ware.[30]

It may well be that Calvin's mode of expression is influenced by the polemical context in which he writes: he does not wish to admit the Roman Catholic notion that we can cooperate with God in the matter of our salvation. We can do nothing: all is of grace. Yet for God to have anything in us to appeal to, on the basis of which he can prompt our faith response, we can only conclude that while our corruption is total in extent – there is nothing unaffected by sin – it is not corrupted in depth. The image is defaced, not utterly obliterated.[31] For testimony on this point we may turn to the Scot, Thomas Chalmers, who, against 'injudicious defenders of orthodoxy' who trumpeted utter depravity in such a way as 'to render it not merely obnoxious to the taste but obnoxious to the understanding', declared, 'Let the nature of man be a ruin, as it certainly is; it is obvious to the most common discernment that it does not offer one unvaried and unalleviated mass of deformity.'[32] Or as John Whale more recently put it,

> Total Corruption does not and never did mean that the stream of human history, instead of being crystal clear, is solid mud; but that it is impure, corrupted in every part of its course: that even the purest ideals

> and the most disinterested achievements of individuals and societies are . . . tainted by sinful self-interest and pride.[33]

What emerges strongly from the post-Reformation West is the conviction that what is required in view of human moral and spiritual ruin is rescue. Hence the urgent prayer of the Puritan Thomas Watson: 'Lord! thou hast once made me, make me anew; sin has defaced thy image in me, oh draw it again by the pencil of the Holy Ghost.'[34] Consistently with this, Lovell Cocks writes:

> the Fall destroys the image of God in man and yet leaves it standing. Were the image really lost by the Fall man would cease to be a sinner, for he would cease to be a man . . . even in his sin man bears witness to the divine image within him. For it is precisely *his sin* that is the image of God, now distorted beyond recognition.[35]

What is to be done about this? One way of putting things is to say that, because the Eastern theologians, characteristically, did not think that humanity fell as far as did Augustine and his followers, they were more optimistic regarding humanity as it is; and that, consequently, their understanding of what needs to be done to restore us is less dramatic and radical. Whereas from the East we hear much of humanity's education and gradual, grace-assisted development, from the West the accent is much more upon the need of dramatic rescue, whether this be tricked out with evangelical references to 'miry clay', or with Tillich's Heideggerian-existentialist terminology (overlaid upon an idealistic philosophical basis) concerning humanity's loss of 'authentic being' – the kind of being recoverable only as Christ, the 'new being', overcomes humanity's estrangement, of which the Fall is the enduring symbol.[36]

In both East and West theologians differed when facing the question: would God have become incarnate if Adam had not sinned? From the standpoint of modern historical method this is a question which admits of no answer. All we can say (if we think that the evidence warrants it) is that God did, as it happens, become incarnate in Christ. But both Eastern and Western theologians were less inhibited. Some, like Maximus the Confessor, the arch-opponent of monophysitism and monothelitism, held that, because of his love for humanity, God would have become incarnate even if the Fall had not occurred. This view was later echoed in the West – by Rupert of Deutz, for example, who argued that God's creative purpose, far from being thwarted by human sin, was thrown into relief by it. The Fall made God's loving purpose shine more brightly, for 'when sin was thus multiplied, grace immeasurably exceeded it'.[37] The Franciscans, in oppositon to the Thomists, ploughed the same furrow. The composite *Summa Theologiae*, traditionally ascribed to Alexander of Hales, and partly his, advances the argument that the supreme good cannot but diffuse itself;[38] to which Duns Scotus added the consideration that so great a work as the Incarnation could not be merely contingent, but must have been willed by God prior to his foreknowledge of sin.[39] Aquinas, on the other hand, held on biblical grounds that the Incarnation was most properly regarded as the remedy for sin and, hence, that it was contingent upon the Fall. However, he did not altogether rule out the possibility that, had there been no sin, God might still have become incarnate.[40]

Our main question, however, is, given the Incarnation, what did it achieve? Irenaeus returns a clear, characteristically Eastern, answer:

> [God's] Word was manifested when the Word of God was made man, assimilating himself to man and man to himself, that by means of his resemblance to the Son, man might become precious to the Father. For in times long past, it was said that man was created after the image of God. Wherefore also he did easily lose the similitude. When, however, the Word of God became flesh, he confirmed both these, for he showed forth the image truly, since he became himself what was his image, and he re-established the similitude after a sure manner, by assimilating man to the invisible Father through means of the invisible Word.[41]

Christ depicts, is and restores the image of God in humanity. Irenaeus's emphasis upon the flesh, and upon the visibility of the entire action, is an implicit protest against Gnostic ideas, current in his day, according to which only a few specially enlightened intellects could grasp the intention of the Incarnation. Irenaeus's Christ has his feet very much on the ground.

Athanasius summed the matter up thus: 'we men could not have profited had the Logos not been true flesh any more than if he had not been truly and by nature Son of God'.[42] He elaborated upon this theme in his *De Incarnatione*.

II

In declaring that the Son is *the* image of the Father, the early theologians are clearly in the wake of Paul, for whom the Son is 'the image of the invisible God'.[43] Again, it is equally Pauline teaching that believers have discarded the old nature and put on the new, which is being 'constantly renewed in the image of its creator and brought to know God'.[44] Nor is this a matter of the restoration of isolated atoms: there is a corporate, an ecclesial, dimension here which constitutes the standing objection to adverse discrimination on grounds of race, sex and class as between the Church's members, and sectarianism as between its several branches; for Paul immediately explains that, where renewal in the divine image is concerned, 'There is no question . . . of Greek and Jew, circumcised and uncircumcised, barbarian, Scythian, slave and freeman; but Christ is all, and in all.'[45]

It is precisely at the point of what happens to human beings that many Eastern theologians have traditionally caused many in the West to be on their guard, though here, as elsewhere, there are differences of emphasis among the Eastern writers. Irenaeus,[46] for example, seems to think more in terms of deification than does Clement of Alexandria.[47] Clement conceives of our likeness to God in terms of our self-constraint and control of the passions. By exercising such control, he says, we become 'assimilated to the Lord *as far as is possible for us* being mortal in nature'.[48] Later, John of Damascus seeks to resist a divine–human fusion of natures by explaining that, while we do become divine, this is 'not by being transformed into the divine substance, but by participation in the divine illumination'.[49] Such variations notwithstanding, the Eastern theologians characteristically think of the restoration of the image of God in humanity, effected by the Incarnation, in terms of *theosis* – divinization or deification. On this matter the Methodist scholar, Benjamin Drewery, was clear, if a trifle blunt, in saying that 'deification is, in my view, the most serious aberration to be found not only in Origen but in the whole tradition to which he contributes . . . here lies the disastrous flaw in Greek Christian thought';[50] but it has to be admitted that there are ways of talking about deification and the mystical union with Christ which appear to deny the Creator–creature distinction to the point that in some writers pantheism threatens, and humanity's redemption comes to be understood as an ongoing process with which the Cross of Christ has little to do.[51]

Clearly, Paul's so-called 'Christ-mysticism', that is, his convictions concerning the Christian's status as being 'in Christ', are of great importance. It is those who are 'in Christ' who are new creatures: 'For anyone united to Christ there is a new creation: the old order has gone; the new order has already begun.'[52] The Johannine way of making the same point is in terms of our union with, or abiding in, or dwelling with, Christ: 'Dwell in me, as I in you.'[53] Moreover, all of the teaching concerning sanctification – that progressive growing up into Christ by the Spirit – which culminates in our being 'like him, because we shall see him as he is',[54] is unmistakably biblical. It is at the heart of Christ's prayer to the Father that his disciples may be at one with him as he and his Father are one;[55] and it informs the writings of the Church's theologians – not least Reformed theologians. Thus, for example, Farel speaks of the Church as the 'holy congregation of the faithful who through real faith are united and incorporated into Christ';[56] and Calvin says that we receive the benefits of Christ only as we possess him, that is, 'when he is one with us – when we are members of his flesh (Eph. 5: 20) – in fine, when we are incorporated with him (so to speak) into one life and substance'.[57] Not surprisingly, in view of his desire to recover the classical theological heritage for nineteenth-century American Christians, J. W. Nevin has much to say on this subject – not least that

> The union of Christ with believers is wrought by the power of the Holy Spirit. The new birth is from the Spirit. It is by the Spirit, the divine life is sustained and advanced in us, at every point, from its commencement to its close. There is no other medium by which it is possible for us to be in Christ, or to have Christ in ourselves.[58]

For all the biblical assertions and allusions, it remains the case that human beings are never deified in the sense of becoming God, or becoming one in essence with God. God remains God, beside him there is no other; and when in 2 Peter 1: 4 we are envisaged as coming 'to share in the very being of God', this participation cannot, consistently with the overall biblical witness, be taken as identity of essence. The statement of Athanasius, echoing that of Irenaeus, that 'God became man that we might be made God'[59] requires qualification; and it has been qualified by the Orthodox theologian, Archimandrite Sofrony, among others. He writes:

> The saints, fully deified by the gift of grace, are so introduced into the Divine Act that all the attributes of Divinity are imparted to them, even to identity – but identity of Act only, never of Nature. By His Nature God eternally and immutably remains God for created beings, even when they arrive at perfect identity.[60]

R. G. Stephanopulos is equally clear:

> The Scriptures proclaim and witness to the primacy and absolute sovereignty of God who is the origin and source of all creation. The distinction between the Creator and His creation is absolute and unbridgeable . . . In no sense must *theosis* be understood in pantheistic terms, as the mystical return of the divine to the Divine or the ontological commingling of the divine with human nature . . . *Theosis* is union with God, but a proper union as between two completely distinct orders of being, a relative union on the moral and spiritual level between God and man made possible by faith and grace . . . *Theosis* can in no sense be seen as a compromise or a reduction of God to the created order of being . . . At best, deified man is still of the created order, not to be confused with the uncreated divine order. Deified man is man renewed, re-created and transfigured into the son of God by grace, whereas God remains inviolate, sovereign and inaccessible in His unknowable and unapproachable essence . . . The Orthodox doctrine of *theosis* emphasizes that the work of Christ has established the objective conditions for the believer's participation in the divine life.[61]

Not all Orthodox theologians are as careful in their writing, however, and when they are not Western perplexity can result. Thus, V. Lossky writes, 'We remain creatures while *becoming God* by grace, as Christ remained God in becoming Man by Incarnation.'[62] Despite Lossky's important qualification that we do not, by deification, achieve identity of nature with God, the words 'becoming God' do not assist in making this clear. Understanding is further threatened by such an explanation as the following: 'Man is thus to reunite by grace two natures in his created hypostasis, to become a "created god", a "god by grace", in contrast to Christ who being a divine person assumed human nature.'[63] As for Gregory Palamas, his expositor advises us that he

> totally rejects the idea that created things can participate in the divine essense . . . Deified man is united with [God] only in grace and energy; yet inasmuch as this grace and energy are the natural radiance of the divine nature, we may say that through them God's nature is partici-

> pable by man, even though in itself it is not participable. So the divine nature is paradoxically both participable and nonparticipable, or else it is participable in a nonparticipable way; that is to say, as superessential essence it remains beyond all participation, but it becomes capable of participation through its natural energies.[64]

In the *Anglican–Orthodox Dialogue* the distinction between the divine essence and the divine energies which underlies the quotations just given was brought out into the open. It was represented by Orthodox representatives as being grounded not in metaphysics but in Christian experience. With one exception the Anglicans preferred the Augustinian line that, while God's nature or essence will never fully be comprehended by human beings, it is not for ever unavailable to human knowledge; and that in the state of glory humanity will see and know God as he is. Richard Hanson opined that the Orthodox and the Augustinians seek to express the same convictions in different terms.[65]

Be that as it may, until we come to the last sentence we are on less problematic ground with the following Orthodox assertion concerning humanity as made in the image of God:

> The image, of course, has been distorted through a mysterious tragedy which happened in creation and which is described through the story of Genesis 3, but it has also been restored through the death and resurrection of Jesus. In Christ, the fulness of Divinity abides 'bodily' and can be seen, accepted and participated in again. *Therefore*, it is also in Jesus that one discovers what man authentically is – for Jesus is fully God and fully man, and the one is ('hypostatically') inherent in the other.[66]

Is it implied that man is fully God? While it is reassuring that modern Orthodox theologians do not intend to advocate our mystical absorption into God, the Scottish theologian, D. S. Cairns, has a cautionary word for any whose language might be taken as implying otherwise: 'God is God, and man is man, and only in the Incarnation do we find One who is both God and man.'[67] As a Latin American commentator on the international Orthodox–Reformed dialogue remarked, 'The mystery of the incarnation leads us to understand the God did not become incarnate so that man should become divine, but rather so that true humanity might be realized to the full in Christ.'[68] The same writer observes that the Chalcedonian inheritance bypasses the emphasis of Philippians 2, which he deems so important in Third World christology, namely, that the exaltation of Christ is inextricably interwoven with his humiliation.[69]

It is not only that some ways of speaking about deification may blur the Creator–creature distinction; such talk may almost suggest that gracious salvation is transmuted into automatic process. An analogous problem arises in the West in connection with the views of Erskine of Linlathen and F. D. Maurice, who advocated the idea of Christ's union with the human race. H. R. Mackintosh quotes Maurice as saying, 'The truth is that every man is in Christ . . . except He [*sic*] were joined to Christ he could not think, breathe, live a single hour', and remarks:

> One can understand what is meant by a Christ who is vitally one with believers; for this is interpreted to us by first-hand acquaintance with the Christian life, and the psychological coefficients involved in it can be pointed out. But if we refuse to depersonalise Christ, or to think away the ethical qualities revealed in His career on earth, the statement that He is vitally one with all men, even a Caesar Borgia, becomes, I submit, quite unintelligible. The tendency of such a view, in short, is to bring salvation down to the level of a natural process.[70]

He further points out that believers are 'in Christ' as a result of the second, not the first, birth; and he rightly adds the important qualification, which is consistent with the doctrine of the *imago dei*, that 'to deny that all men are in Christ is not the same thing as saying that they have no relation to Him at all'.[71]

No doubt Christ has already won his victory; of course believers have, by grace, the principle of new life in them. But given the radical moral breach between humanity and God, there can be no bypassing the route to that new life which is grounded in Christ's finished work at the Cross, the benefits of which become ours only by grace through faith – faith which is itself a gift of the Spirit, so that we shall not become boastful.[72] The atoning work is in danger of being minimized in some theologies – Orthodox and Western alike. The tendency is detectable in some passages in the writings of J. W. Nevin, as when he says that, by the Incarnation, 'our nature as a whole was lifted from its fallen state, and brought into union with God'.[73] By contrast, R. Vaughan Pryce holds together the theme of union with Christ and the atoning work in what appears to be a satisfactory manner:

> the doctrine of the incarnation is not that Christ became *a* man, but it is that Christ became *the* man, the second Adam, humanity recapitulated in one, the second head of the race, the Representative of humanity as a whole, and not of this or that man in particular. By faith we become incorporated with Christ . . . Paul's theology cannot be understood unless this spiritual union between the redeemed and the Redeemer is recognised. In order to apprehend the meaning of Christ's dying unto sin, we must apprehend the meaning of Christ's incorporation of humanity, of all mankind, into Himself. That was His offering to God. The sinless head of the race died unto sin for the race, in covenant, promising that through Him men should die unto sin, and pledging them to do so. The early Fathers make frequent allusion to this idea of incorporation. They knew nothing of the later doctrine of imputation, and of the imputed righteousness of Christ, – a fiction invented by men who had departed from the simplicity of earlier times.[74]

Interestingly, however, when addressing the issue of evangelism an Orthodox report can declare that 'Evangelistic Witness is a call to salvation, which means the restoration of the relationship of God and man, as understood in the Orthodox Christian teaching of Theosis.'[75] The reference to a call to salvation, and to restoration of a relationship, suggests, against some Orthodox ways of speaking, that *theosis* is not an automatic process in the lives of human beings as such, but is the privilege and experience of the converted. In this connection the following Orthodox statement on mission is significant:

> This mission of Christ takes place in a 'fallen' world and is met by the resistance of the 'powers and principalities' of evil and sin. This has made the cross the inevitable passage of Christ's mission. Mission, therefore, takes place in the context of struggle and implies a conversion, a paschal and baptismal passage of the world into a 'new creation'.[76]

The upshot is that we need to hold together the prominent New Testament teaching concerning union with God in Christ, justification by grace through faith, and, above all, the redemption wrought at the Cross–resurrection, which is the ground of the union and of justification, and hence of our eternal hope. It is noticeable that John of Damascus can say, 'Even though we be *creatures*, faith is capable of making us to be adopted through the Spirit and brought to our former state of blessedness.'[77] He can also say of Christ that 'by His own birth, or incarnation, and by

His baptism and passion and resurrection, He freed our nature from the sin of our first parent, from death, and corruption. And he became the first-fruit of the resurrection . . . '[78] Again, Palamas emphasizes the soteriological importance of the Son's human–divine nature, and regards entry into the Church as affording the opportunity of beginning a new life.[79] But warning lights flash when we turn to the writings of the Pseudo-Dionysius. He has much to say concerning redemption, but he says it in the context of confrontation with Manichaean dualism. Perhaps for this reason he seems to downplay the reality of evil: to him it has no true being at all. His sympathetic commentator, C. E. Rolt, is forced to admit that Dionysius fails to grasp the ugliness of things: 'The fault of Dionysius is the natural failure of his mental type to grasp the mere fact of the actual world as mere facts.'[80] Incarnation as incorporating the whole life, death, resurrection and ascension of Christ – with all that that means in terms of God's holy love, humanity's sin and Christ's once-for-all victory – must be our key, and our defence against any notion of *quasi*-automatic deification or divinization. We may not forget that, according to Paul, being in Christ is not simply a matter of union, it is a matter of aquittal and adoption. As Nevin's opponent, J. H. A. Bomberger, thundered,

> Christ is *not* our life in any pantheistic sense. Nay, the mystical union established between the regenerated soul and him is not even a hypostatical union of their two natures. Man is not deified by regeneration. In it men become Christians, but are not made Christs.[81]

Alongside this we may set the explanation of the Orthodox theologian, Nicholas Lossky:

> This participation of human beings in the divine life of the Holy Trinity, their incorporation in Christ as adopted sons and daughters through the Spirit of the Son who in their hearts cries 'Abba, Father' (Gal. 4: 6; cf. Rom. 8: 15), is what the Orthodox often express in the famous patristic adage, 'God became man that man may become God' (Irenaeus et al.). It is also the meaning of the term 'deification' (*theosis*).[82]

It is the emphasis upon adoption which stands as a bulwark against untoward constructions of *theosis*. One may still, however, wonder whether much that is positively intended by *theosis* is not better, and less problematically, expressed by the doctrine of sanctification.

A further puzzle to some in the West is the quasi-Pelagian ring of some of the Eastern theologians' modes of expression. Thus, Origen declares that we may attain God's likeness

> by the exercise of [our] own diligence in the imitation of God, the possibility of perfection being granted [us] at the beginning through the dignity of the divine image, and the perfect realization of the divine likeness being reached in the end by the fulfilment of the [requisite] works.[83]

As a protest against antinomianism, and as an encouragement to Christian fruit-bearing, and with reference to the challenge that we be God's 'fellow workers',[84] this is salutary enough. But unless it is made clear that all of this is a consequence of God's prevenient, enabling grace, such talk can have an unduly 'worksy' flavour. This concern should not be pressed too far, for even Irenaeus, who believes that our likeness to God is achieved only by striving,[85] balances his moralism with a strong conviction of the objectivity of Christ's recapitulatory work. At the same time, the comment of R. S. Franks, following Werner, is not altogether unjust. Irenaeus, he writes,

> has not the Pauline conception of justification as an abiding state of communion with God in which the believer rejoices in the forgiveness of sins and faith works by love . . . [O]n the whole the practical Christianity of Irenaeus, like that of the Apologists, is a moralism very different from the Pauline Christianity.[86]

For his part, however, Maximus the Confessor declares that human beings have been created to partake of God's eternity, and to appear like him 'according to the deification which is from grace'.[87]

More disconcerting is Anthony of Egypt's almost casual assertion that virtue is within us, and that we can easily be virtuous if only we have the will for it.[88] This was too big an 'if' for most Eastern, not to mention Western, theologians. Moreover, the quasi-Pelagianism sometimes takes a mystical turn, as when the Pseudo-Dionysius's ways of purgation, illumination and union are expounded as steps towards deification;[89] sometimes it takes a more this-worldly, ecclesiastical turn, as when Timothy Ware offers the following advice:

> If a man asks, 'How can I become god?' the answer is very simple: go to church, receive the sacraments regularly, pray to God 'in spirit and in truth', read the Gospels, follow the commandments . . . Church and sacraments are the means appointed by God whereby *man may acquire* the sanctifying Spirit and be transformed into the divine likeness.[90]

To which one might reply: Word and sacraments are means of grace, but they and the sanctifying Spirit are always the gift of grace. Christians are undeniably called to obedience, and to participation in the life of the Church; but their obedience and participation are their Spirit-enabled grateful response to God's gift in the Gospel; they are not bartering counters deployed to achieve the divine likeness. I do not think that most present-day Orthodox theologians would wish to disagree with this, but the language sometimes used fails to make their agreement crystal clear.

There is currently widespread agreement that the distinction between 'image' and 'likeness', which some of the early theologians posited, is untenable on exegetical grounds, and hence that attempts to apportion human faculties in relation to the two supposed entities are doomed to failure. The Genesis text witnesses to the covenant relationship in which human beings stand before God. The Fall proclaims the rupture of that relationship, the defacement of God's image; but careful analysis of 'total' in 'total depravity' is required if we are to accommodate biblical exhortations to virtue. The plight of human alienation from God may not be minimized, but nor may the emphasis upon the believer's present and final union with Christ. Nevertheless, the Creator–creature distinction must be maintained and pantheism avoided; and because entry into the covenant is by God's gracious call and not by natural right, unguarded talk of humanity's deification should be avoided. Since the union which Christians partially enjoy now, and to which they are called, is achieved by grace alone and entails living the new life, there is no place for either antinomianism or Pelagianism. As Luther wrote, putting Paul and James nicely together, 'We are not saved by works, but if there be no works there must be something amiss with faith.'[91]

Happily, the differences of emphasis between East and West on the doctrine of humanity have not been Church-dividing. Indeed, as we have seen, there is a good deal of each on either side.

Taking the measure of the whole we have a tremendous affirmation of human dignity: made in God's image; and of human need: saved by grace. The ethical implications of human dignity are manifold, and pressing in our time, as are the implications for dialogue in a pluralist world. Concerning the latter, Schleiermacher's reference to 'the unenlightened man' in whom 'we may indeed trace many a Christian feature, which nevertheless is not in him a thing of living power, but merely the reflection of what is present as a reality in others', seems to presuppose a doctrine of the *imago dei*. If this is so, the last clause quoted would more accurately refer to an aspect of 'the unenlightened man's' own creaturehood; and, by the same token, the whole would apply to all human beings, and not only to those who have 'only an outward connection with Christianity'.[92] In all of this the epistemological significance of the defaced-yet-not-obliterated *imago dei* is underscored, not least in connection with that common ground which must be supposed if witness to, and dialogue with, those who do not share the Christian faith is to be possible at all. This point will recur as our study proceeds. As for the soteriological aspects of human need, they are not to be minimized. The salvation which is freely given in Christ is salvation into a restored, covenantal relationship with God and with his people. Eternal fellowship is assured by the Cross–Resurrection event, but it begins with an earthly, ecclesial fellowship which is as encouraging as it is challenging. Christians are called to run the race with others, humbly confident that with them we shall be 'partakers in the splendour that is to be revealed'.[93]

III

In this chapter and the last an attempt has been made to discover what it is that Christians confess; to make it clear that confession is by word and life, and that, since Christians are called into fellowship, it is an ecclesial task; to show how the context of confessing influences the articulation of the confession in different times and places; and to illustrate the variety of ways in which the nature of the confessors as human beings has been understood through the Christian ages.

One further question arises. Having regard to the differing

socio-politico-intellectual environments in which the Gospel has been, and needs to be, confessed, how far is it appropriate or even meaningful to speak of the 'same' faith throughout the ages? In his classic statement on the matter, Vincent of Lérins sought to allow both for an unchanging faith and for varied expressions of it:

> Is there to be no growth within the Church? Nay, let there be growth to the greatest extent . . . but yet let it be such that it be growth, not change of faith . . . As time goes on, it is right that the old truths should be elaborated, polished, filed down: it is wrong that they should be changed, maimed or mutilated. They should be made clear, have light thrown on them, be marked off from each other; but they must not lose their fullness, their entirety, their essential character.[94]

Vincent's criterion of catholicity, the so-called Vincentian Canon, was *quod ubique, quod semper, quod ab omnibus creditum est.*[95] Even if what is believed everywhere, always and by all could be determined, this would not, logically, make it true. But our more immediate concern is to ask: given the wide variety of expression employed in Christian confessing, does it make sense to speak of the 'same' faith running through the ages?

One way of approaching an answer to this question is to ask another: can a person or a group of persons so 'elaborate, polish or file down' Christian doctrines as to have placed themselves outside of Christianity? At this point we may recall the assertions Forsyth made in two different books: 'Where you fix a creed you flatten faith'; and 'There must surely be in every positive religion some point where it may so change as to lose its identity and become another religion.'[96] These remarks seem to represent two poles between which the variety of Christian confessional affirmations actually oscillate. The first warns against the danger of elevating our favoured formulae into laws of Medes and Persians to be wielded over the heads of dissenters. They thereby become badges of sectarianism – all of this in denial of the need of Christians to hear God's word anew in different times and places. The latter raises the question: are there no limits to freedom to believe as one pleases? How are we to answer this question?

Striking out in a very different direction from that of Vincent of Lérins, the Unitarian Joseph Priestley, declared:

> The wisdom of one generation will ever be folly in the next. And yet . . . we persist in the absurd maxim of making a preceding generation dictate to a succeeding one . . . [C]an we think that wisdom will die with us? No: our creeds, could we be so inconsistent with ourselves to draw up any, would, I make no doubt, be rejected with equal disdain by our posterity.[97]

Priestley, of course, regarded himself as a Christian, but he stands in his tradition midway between those who drew up the Westminster Confession of Faith and those today who worship – or at least gather (I do not speak pejoratively) – in Unitarian chapels as atheists, agnostics, humanists and even trinitarians, on the basis that 'Unitarianism is a faith without a creed'.[98] Between Priestley and these last we find such a typical late nineteenth-century Unitarian observation as the following:

> Ours is the only church to-day in America or England which bases itself distinctly on the religious capacities in the soul of man and not on traditions and dogmas; which uses the method of a free reason to arrive at truth, and which makes not opinions but personal character the arbiter of man's earthly welfare and heavenly hopes.[99]

A contemporary declares that 'The saving faith in Jesus Christ is to believe as he believed, trust in God as he trusted, hope as he hoped, and love as he loved'[100] – a remarkable way of ensuring the emptiness of heaven! With the liberal Christian adjustments to intellectual change the secularist magazine, *The Freethinker*, made merry, frequently quoting Erasmus Darwin's verdict that Unitarianism was 'a feather-bed to catch a falling Christian'.[101] There remain, of course – in Britain, North America, Romania and elsewhere – those whose self-description is 'Unitarian Christian'; and a journal which serves some of these quoted the following description of a Unitarian service in Washington DC without comment:

> It was Easter Day, but nothing so improbable as the Resurrection was mentioned. Indeed, Christ did not get a look in at all. Outside, it was a gloriously sunny day and it was made quite clear that we were really celebrating the arrival of spring, not some weird, paranormal event which might or might not have happened 2000 years ago to someone who may or may not have existed.

> The Minister announced, with vague embarrassment, that 'some of our fellow Unitarians, up in New England mostly, still incorporated Christ in their worship', but this was evidently regarded as a curious throw-back.
>
> He took as his text the scene from Moby Dick when a small boat is overwhelmed and Starbuck holds up a candle in the darkness. His message was, 'We're on our own out there. No power is looking after us, so we have to look after each other.'[102]

It would seem from the evidence thus presented that some members of Unitarian churches are not, by their own decision, theists, while others regard themselves as Christians. It is equally clear that such members do not share the 'same' faith. It is not that they all believe in Christianity and interpret it in slightly or radically different ways (though the Christians among them may well do this); some of them disclaim the name Christian – as is their right – and remain in fellowship with others as their creedless polity permits. It does, however, appear to a friendly outsider that the breadth in which they rejoice prohibits a churchly, corporate Christian confession – except in those local churches where all are Unitarian Christians, or where these are tolerated by everyone else as they make such a confession. But if ideologically diverse Unitarian churches are held together by a commitment to freedom and tolerance, and if some members of Unitarian churches have moved outside of Christianity, what holds together the generality of Christians in such a way that it makes sense to speak of the 'same' faith through the Christian ages?[103]

In approaching an answer to this question we do well to remember that continuity and change are not experienced by the Christian tradition alone. Nations, political parties, schools and universities – many human institutions exemplify this fact. Consider, for example, the Hampshire Regiment. Its roots go back to Thomas Meredith's regiment (the 37th Regiment of Foot) raised in 1702. In 1881 it united with the 67th Regiment of Foot to form the Hampshire Regiment. In 1946 George V conferred the title 'Royal' upon it. But through all of these changes of nomenclature there was continuity, as there was in the regiment's insignia, so important in regimental identity. Following an extended period of twenty-one years' service in India, George IV, in 1826, granted the regiment the right to add the Bengal tiger to its Hampshire Rose badge. From 1946 a king's crown was added, superseded in

1953 by a queen's crown. Other changes over time included those concerning uniforms, weapons, modes of transport and the like. Throughout, however, the objective remained the defence of the realm and, according to the regiment's historian, 'personal friendships often begun grudgingly, build up the character of each regiment. And battles, and the way men acquit themselves in them, build up its traditions.'[104] From 1958 onwards, however, army reorganization occurred in various phases until, in 1992, the Royal Hampshire Regiment finally lost its separate identity. On the basis of this information it might be said that, like Christianity, the Hampshires changed through time in response to changing circumstances; that their symbols and methods changed accordingly; but that their objective remained constant, and their sense of fellowship and loyalty, however imperfect, was a feature of their continuing life. The analogy is partial only, however, because, unlike a nation's regiment – and even apart from theological considerations concerning its divine origin – Christianity cannot be closed down by the decision of a particular government (though religious toleration is not universal and is never to be taken for granted). Above all, however, the objectives differ radically. Whereas the regiment's primary objective is the containment or defeat of alien aggression through what the regimental historian calls the 'ignoble enterprise' of war,[105] Christianity's is the proclamation of a Gospel of salvation designed to affect individuals and communities universally. It is a way of life grounded in a message which is capable of being articulated at various levels. Is it, then, more like a philosophy than a regiment?

Let us examine a further partial analogy, the 'perennial philosophy'. John Laird has cast doubt upon the idea that there is such a philosophy. Considering philosophy in its global expressions, he finds more than one claimant to the title. But even if the term were restricted to a dynasty including Plato, Aristotle, Descartes, Spinoza, Leibniz, Kant and Hegel,

> it is far from certain that the royal blood in their veins belongs to the same group (especially in the case of Kant), and there are serious difficulties about people like Hume who did not belong to the dynasty, and devoutly thanked the originating principles of things (if there were any) for the circumstance.[106]

He goes on to suggest that 'many philosophies of to-day treat other philosophies not as brothers or even as enemies, but as untouchables'.[107]

We have seen that within the Christianity of the ages there have been many emphases in the verbal confession of the Gospel, and a variety of views as to who the confessors are (granting that every Christian is supposed to be a confessor). This underlines our finding in our opening discussion of theological systems, creeds and confessions. Because of the nature of the Gospel, differences in times and places, and the varied presuppositions and temperaments and experiences which Christians bring to the matter, statements, though necessary, will never finally satisfy, and will always be variously composed and construed. For the same reason we do not today preach the sermons of John Chrysostom or Calvin just as they stand; nor do we feel at ease singing some older hymns, many of which have been dropped from current hymnals not necessarily on account of archaisms, but because we no longer understand things as the writers did – concerning 'the heathen', for example, or death as the bogeyman to bring little children to heel. Again, it is not surprising that in the cultural environment of which they were a part, in which slavery was a feature, some early Christian theologians had recourse to the image of 'ransom' when explicating Christ's saving work. In justification of this they could appeal to Paul's word to the Corinthians: 'you were bought at a price';[108] and certainly the idea of the costliness of redemption can never be excluded from any satisfactory account of the atonement. But when the ransom image was pressed, as it was by some, to the extent of claiming that the ransom was paid to the devil, others protested on the ground that the devil had no rights in the matter. In later times the concepts of satisfaction, penal substitution and moral influence were invoked in expositions of Christ's saving work. Nor is variety of expression exclusively a matter of changes over time. In view of cruel injustice and gross inequality it is not surprising that the liberation theologians of our own time have frequently emphasized 'God's preferential option for the poor'. But in the relatively few cases when the concerns underlying this use of language have led to the view that the needed liberation is political only, entailing revolution, others have entered qualifying caveats concerning sin and moral redemption. Certainly the attempt to demonstrate one's theological 'soundness' by parroting

'God's preferential option for the poor' does as little to help those in need as does the analogous reiteration of 'the blood of the Lamb' (which also still goes on) assist sinners. By their slogans ye shall know them.

This variety of expression through time and in our own time suggests that thus far we seem to be in much the same case as the seeker after a perennial philosophy – even, sadly, to the extent that some Christians may regard others as untouchables, to use Laird's word. But at this point the analogy breaks down, for Christianity is, as we have seen, a religion, a way, and not simply an intellectual construction. Even from this point of view, however, Christians have not been slow to find reasons for disagreement over what counts as following the way. We thus have new legalisms, some of which turn upon the denunciation of those sins which the particular legalist is not particularly inclined to commit ('Don't go to the dance hall because it is a sink of iniquity' – as uttered by one who secretly harbours racist thoughts which others are, happily from the legalist's point of view, quite unable to detect). Not without good reason did Robert Mackintosh lament the way in which some in the Puritan tradition confused the moral order with their own favoured legal order, with the consequence that 'doctrinally and emotionally [the Christian] was to live by grace; but his conduct was to be exactly the same as if he expected to be justified by works'.[109] Small wonder that Bernard Lord Manning declared that the empirical Church, composed as it is of saints who are sinners, is an earthen vessel. It is, however, 'the earthen vessel which carries the real presence of the saviour'.[110]

The attitude repudiated by Mackintosh could and did lead to legalistic preaching in which the first matters driven home were human sinfulness and guilt. Hence John McLeod Campbell's pastoral experience of a doleful, introspective congregation, whose members were for ever wondering whether they displayed the evidence of God's gracious dealings with them. Hence also his determination to make it plain that the first word of the Gospel is not sin, but grace.[111] Such are the time lags in these matters that, as Christianity's third millennium proceeds, a contribution to the magazine of the Associate Reformed Presbyterian Church – a body stoutly committed to the Westminster standards – pleads for 'A kinder, gentler Calvinism'. The author relates how he went to his first pastorate proclaiming the 'five points' of the Synod of Dort, and was nonplussed when, after his eloquent disquisition on sin, an elder asked him, 'Son, don't you have any good news?' Later he learned of a colleague who had been rebuked because in his preaching he set out from the love of God and not from the law of God.[112]

For all the differences of doctrinal emphasis, for all the varieties of linguistic expression, Christianity is something into which people are called by grace, and held by grace, and it entails fellowship with others. It is not non-credal, for the basic confession is that Jesus Christ is the crucified and risen Lord and Saviour, but there are many ways of construing this, and in the corporate life of the Church the individual's grasp of it all expands as his or her experience deepens. But this brings us back to the central way of confessing the faith: in worship. For this, more than formulaic intellectual construction, is what has united people in the same faith through the ages. From earliest Christian times to the present believers have gathered in worship, they have offered their praise, confessed Christ as risen Lord and Saviour, heard God's Word, responded in thanksgiving, known the Lord in the breaking of the bread and gone forth in mission. These things have happened no matter how banal the liturgy, unsingable the hymns, sinful the worshippers, varied the context. Those called and gathered are, humanly speaking, the continuity, which is why A. B. Bruce drew the following contrast: 'Orthodoxy will not save the church any more than ecclesiastical dignitaries – priests, bishops, cardinals, popes. The temple which endures for ever is founded on Christ, the Rock of Ages, and built up of "lively stones".'[113] Or, in the words of Bernard Lord Manning, who had the Fundamentalist–Modernist controversy in mind,

> This hideous legalistic controversy about what is the indispensable minimum of belief offends the conscience of all Christians . . . The grace of God, we affirm, needs no legal machinery to protect it. The Church animated by this grace has the resources of a healthy body. It grows . . . It drives out of itself, by spontaneous unnoticed action, whatever is irreconcilable with the grace that is its creative and sustaining principle. In a word it combines fullness of faith and fullness of liberty.[114]

In such an environment, however much they may differ over this or that dogma, and even if they seldom think in terms of dogma at all,[115] however far apart their cultures, politics, ethical opinions, however unusual a particular act of worship may be to them, Christians – among whom are all sorts and conditions of people – hear God's voice and respond to it, and they recognize one another as belonging to the same household of faith.[116] As Alexander Raleigh told the Assembly of the Congregational Union of England and Wales in 1868:

> I am not going to enter here upon any argumentative statement of the atonement as manifesting and upholding the righteousness of God in the salvation of man. It is sufficient to note the fact that this has been the uninterrupted, and we may say, universal faith of the Church from the beginning until now. All believers have, in one form or another, believed this . . . [Similarly, there has been] a conviction that has never wavered that God is just and holy in forgiving the sin and renewing the nature of man, and that, in some way or other, the life and death and resurrection of Christ embodies and conciliates all Divine attributes; while, at the same time, they form the object, desire, and satisfying goal of all human affections and hopes.[117]

The Quaker apologist may sum up this point for us: 'the object of the saints' faith is the same in all ages, though held forth under divers administrations'.[118]

But it is time to opt out of confessional mode in the interests of the intellectual commendation of the faith. It must be quite plain that in this chapter and the last, on confessing and confessors, a large number of assumptions have gone unremarked and unchallenged. To some of these we must now turn, though offering in defence of the route thus far taken the reiterated claim that, if we wish to apologize for the faith in the sense of investigating and explicating its intellectual basis (which is, as we have seen, to undertake a task of abstraction), it is well that we have some idea of what Christians confess, and who the confessors think they are. A. E. Taylor said of theologians, 'What we have a right to demand of the theologian . . . is that the matter upon which his thought works shall be something genuinely *given*, and that in his reflective elaboration of it he shall be true to *it*. I do not see that we have a right to demand more.'[119] If we substitute 'commendation and defence' for 'elaboration' we have sentiments which apply to the Christian apologist. The Christian given not only provides the starting point for Christian apologetics, it suggests the method also. Because Christianity is a way, it involves a persons's thought, practice, values, experiences – and all of these in relation to others. It will not therefore be surprising if the intellectual commendation of Christian claims takes the form of a hospitable reasoned eclecticism in which reference is made to this range of considerations. Equally, it will not be surprising if a prominent line of defence against alternative positions consists in charging them with having overlooked, or ruled out *ab initio*, factors of significance, with the result that their accounts of Christianity are partial and inadequate because, to invoke a culinary image, they have been trying to pick up soup on a fork: there is always some which will not stay on. Less cryptically, the opponents' starting points imply the inadmissability from the outset of certain Christian claims – especially those concerning what God has done in Christ, and who human beings made in God's image are – and so they cannot deal with Christianity as it is. Hence, for example, Nevin's hysterical, and not entirely fair, outburst against Locke, Bacon and the common-sense philosophy: 'The general character of this bastard philosophy is, that it affects to measure all things, both on earth and in heaven, by the categories of the common abstract understanding, as it stands related simply to the world of time and sense.'[120] Charles B. Upton expressed the same point more graciously, and with other thinkers in view, in his Hibbert Lectures of 1893:

> The Mystic may, as Schleiermacher sometimes does, exclusively insist on the soul's immediate feeling of the Universal and Divine; the Rational Idealist, on Thought as the ultimate reality; and the Ethical Theist on the Moral Imperative which commands the Will; but whenever any one of these ignores the other two, he is dealing with an unreal abstraction, and not with the concrete fact of the actual self-revelation of the Eternal to the human soul.[121]

From a very different perspective, Gadamer made a similar point in criticism of Descartes's reductionism, namely, his attempt to achieve 'the total reconstruction of all truths by reason';[122] while Moltmann has observed that the 'process of abstracting our own individual subjectivity from all relationships to the world in endless reflection is a modern phenomenon'.[123]

Conversely, as we shall see, some Christian apologists, by setting out from the opponents' reduced ground, find it impossible subsequently to accommodate all that they wish to confess. To them, no less than to their intellectual opponents, the godly defiant words of Robert Mackintosh comprise a salutary caution:

> Our little systems, when they have had their day, cease to be. It is Christ who does not cease: he is more than they. With that caution, this is how one has learned Christ: We believe not only that 'perfection is eternal' not only (in Bible language) that God's will is done already in heaven by his holy angels; not merely, again, with the moralising people, that God's will may come to be done upon earth; but that the battle has already been fought and won. Thus in Christ we have not merely the possibility but the certainty of redemption, and not forgiveness alone but the new life . . . And so we still preach Jesus as Lord and Saviour; to the Pragmatist a stumbling block, to the Idealist foolishness; but to them who are called, whether from the one camp or the other, Christ the power and wisdom of God. This is more than our theology; it is our gospel. Woe be unto us if we desert it, because this or that school of philosophy, or, if it be so, all philosophy finds it anomalous! The foolishness of God is wiser than men . . . Christian theology is not yet mediatized, or retired upon a pension, or a suppliant for the crumbs from the philosophical banquet . . . Philosophy, however well disposed, and however competent in its own sphere, must not lay down the law to Christian doctrine; which strives to anwer the other, the immense question, *What thinkest thou of Christ?*[124]

II

PRESUPPOSITIONS OF THE CONFESSION

[A] rule of thinking which would absolutely prevent one from acknowledging certain kinds of truth were really there, would be an irrational rule.

(William James, *The Will to Believe*, 1897)

No theory can be adequate which concludes that what happens cannot take place.

(G. F. Woods, *Soundings*, 1963)

4

The Meaning, Use and Reference of Religious Language

We may set out from an incredible set of assertions made by Herbert Kohl towards the end of his generally helpful book of 1965, *The Age of Complexity*:

> Throughout my text there has been no mention of God or religion. This is not because contemporary philosophers are necessarily atheists, or because I believe modern philosophy refutes religion. Rather it is because contemporary philosophers, with few exceptions, have faced the fact that religion is no longer an active part of the everyday life of men in the Western world . . . [H]ence philosophy insofar as it is modern does not consider religion as an issue.[1]

Kohl first prompts a general consideration to which we shall return, namely, the importance of context when seeking to understand or interpret written or spoken discourse. For he writes from the United States, where religion influences the daily life of many, and one wonders how he could have failed to notice this. More particularly, he writes in 1965, and reprints J. L. Austin's notable paper on 'Other minds', which is a discussion of John Wisdom's unfinished series of papers on that topic[2] – the very John Wisdom whose seminal paper, 'Gods', was already ten years old when it was reprinted in *New Essays in Philosophical Theology* (1955). This latter paper stimulated a good deal of philosophizing – and storytelling; and among other catalysts of the period before Kohl wrote was Norman Malcolm's paper of 1960 on 'Anselm's ontological arguments', which did as much as anything to prompt a proliferation of reappraisals of that subject. More generally, Frederick

Ferré published *Language, Logic and God* in 1962 – something he would have been quite incapable of doing had there not by then been considerable philosophical analytical activity relating to religious discourse. Indeed, as early as 1958 H. J. Paton wrote with considerable justification, 'The most surprising development of philosophy in recent years has been the sudden interest, friendly or hostile, in theology – or at least in the philosophy of religion.'[3] It would be quite impossible here to rehearse the tale of this activity in detail; nor is it necessary.[4] But a few remarks may be offered by way of setting the ensuing discussion in context.

To G. E. Moore must go much of the credit for the linguistic turn in twentieth-century British philosophy. In the name of common sense, he urged philosophers to analyse the meaning of propositions, and to pay particular attention to ordinary language which, he was convinced, provided many traps into which the unwary could fall.[5] Moore's objective was the correct formulation of questions and the making of necessary distinctions. He was not in principle opposed to metaphysics (though to some forms of it he took exception[6]), but it was not his primary interest. Interestingly from our point of view, he did not think that belief in God and in life after death contradicted common sense.

For a time Moore's contemporary, Bertrand Russell, a convert from idealism, sought to bring ideas of mathematical precision to bear upon the construction of an ideal language. Even after he had forsaken that objective, Russell continued to believe that philosophy's primary task was analytical rather than synthetic, and that it should be modelled upon logic.[7] During his first sojourn in England, Wittgenstein, Russell's pupil turned master, added grist to the analytical mill with his insistence upon the need for propositional clarity.

Not all went with the tide, however. R. G. Collingwood, for example, believing that philosophy's task was to enunciate propositions which are 'in essence and fundamental intention categorical',[8] warned that metaphysical scepticism could all too easily become covert dogmatism, and declared that 'Analytic philosophy does indeed involve a constructive philosophical doctrine, but, true to its character as a form of scepticism, declines the task of stating it.'[9] That C. D. Broad was more than a little inclined to take certain developments in philosophy with a pinch of salt is clear from his delightful remark, 'I shall watch with a fatherly eye the philosophical gambols of my younger friends as they dance to the highly syncopated pipings of Herr Wittgenstein's flute.'[10] The very title of an article of 1926 by W. G. De Burgh, 'Faith and logic', was a harbinger of things to come. His point was that philosophy and religion alike require both faith and logic if they are to be fully developed, and that faith, which 'for all its certainty of conviction, fails to prove',[11] is not confined to belief in propositions. It includes trust in God – an experience of a relationship which precedes the beliefs and is 'an immediate awareness of the given reality'.[12]

The analytical tendency was soon to be numerically strengthened. R. B. Braithwaite welcomed the fact that 'Implicitly in Russell and explicitly in Moore, philosophy demands the answers to the question "What is the analysis of what we all agree to be true?"'[13] While not thinking that the time was ripe for metaphysical construction, L. S. Stebbing nevertheless defined that discipline as 'a systematic study concerned to show what is the structure of the facts in the world to which reference is made with varying degrees of indirectness, whenever a true statement is made',[14] and raised such questions as: what are we believing when we believe that there is a table in the room? She had earlier found some of A. N. Whitehead's 'indefensible' language 'nothing short of scandalous',[15] and was later to remind all who would listen that 'the purpose of analysis as practised by philosophers is to enable us to learn how to avoid asking misleading questions – to which we are only too likely to find senseless answers – and to encourage us to ask sensible questions'.[16] J. Wisdom gave an affirmative answer to his question, 'Is analysis a useful method in philosophy?'[17] and in a series of articles entitled 'Logical constructions' he sought to show how analytical techniques can delineate the logical structure of ordinary propositions.[18] A. J. Ayer, under the inspiration of the Vienna Circle, sought a criterion of meaning, found it in the verification principle, published his positivistic 'manifesto', *Language, Truth and Logic*, in 1936, and consigned moral, aesthetic and religious language to the realm of the meaningless. To him we shall return.

Gilbert Ryle hove into view, bringing his instruments (or weapons?) of analysis to bear upon ordinary language, his informal logical antennae sensitive to the slightest suspicion of a category mistake, his humour and fluent style making *The Concept of Mind*

(1949) one of the most enjoyable philosophical books of the twentieth century. But was it serious enough? Iris Murdoch, in a paper on Sartre in which she welcomed the way in which continental philosophy took the human condition seriously, rebuked Ryle thus: 'The "world" of *The Concept of Mind* is the world in which people play cricket, cook cakes, make simple decisions, remember their childhood and go to the circus; not the world in which they commit sins, fall in love, say prayers or join the Communist Party.'[19] Undeterred, Ryle remained true to his conviction, expressed as early as 1932, that the role of the philosopher was to display the logical structure of facts with which we are familiar, and to pursue the therapeutic mission of eradicating puzzlement caused by the ill-advised use of ordinary language.[20]

During the first half of the twentieth century very few theologians responded to the analytical challenges laid at their door. It was left to philosophers such as H. H. Price and Karl Britton to consider the kind of reponses Christians might make. Price tentatively suggested that a defence of theism might be mounted on the basis of 'evidence of the existence and activities of a non-human intelligence' yielded up by ordinary perception and introspection; but 'whether there really are such events, and whether (if there are) the intelligence whose existence they give evidence of has the characteristics which Theists would wish to attribute to God, I do not know.'[21] Britton adopted a quite different approach. He conceded that religious propositions cannot properly be called 'true' or 'false', but declared nevertheless that, irrespective of this, they have a value to the believer. Hence, 'The Lord is my shepherd' is true if the feelings and actions it arouses in me, and perhaps in others, are accompanied by feelings of moral approval. He described this as a pragmatic approach to religious truth, noted that 'good' and 'useful' had to be defined in relation to a community of believers, and declared that 'The membership of such groups will be vague: there will be conversions from one group to another. A conversion is not a change of opinion but a change of heart.'[22] As far as I know, not even Britton's bracketing of the question of religious truth claims provoked any theologians into a response. Twenty years later, however, when R. B. Braithwaite published his Eddington Memorial Lecture, *An Empiricist's View of the Nature of Religious Belief*, which in some respects mirrored Britton's proposal, a wider discussion ensued. Denying that religious statements were meaningful in the way that statements of empirical fact and scientific hypotheses are, Braithwaite granted that they were meaningful if construed as declaring a person's decision to act in certain ways. In distinction from purely ethical propositions, however, religious assertions are linked to stories or sets of stories which have the psychological effect of undergirding the will; and this they may do whether or not the propositions contained in them are true or false. A. C. Ewing could not see how one's power to act could be undergirded by stories unless they were believed to be true;[23] R. M. Hare pointed out that, far from constituting religious belief, moral judgement arises from it;[24] and R. W. Hepburn wondered why, on Braithwaite's terms, one should prefer Christian stories to any others.[25]

The analytical pace increased (though such philosophers as H. J. Paton,[26] T. M. Knox,[27] A. C. Ewing,[28] John Laird, H. D. Lewis, J. D. Mabbott, W. D. Ross and others busied themselves in other ways, in some cases dispatching an occasional torpedo in the direction of perceived philosophical trivializers), but as early as 1945 H. H. Price found it necessary to correct, on the one hand, those who spoke as if analysis was the invention of the twentieth century and, on the other hand, those who, from whatever motive, were tempted to dismiss analysis as being so much triviality.[29] He did, however, point out that there was a synoptic as well as an analytical clarity, and he exhorted philosophers to strive after both.[30]

Fresh energy was imparted to the analytical quest by the later writings of Wittgenstein, as we shall see, as well as by the patient, stimulating and attractively presented analytical findings of J. L. Austin who, in his paper, 'Other minds', introduced the concept of the performative utterance. A performative utterance involves a commitment. Thus, 'I promise' betokens my promising. The application of this insight to religious discourse – especially to credal and prayer language, though it was rather late in coming – is clear. Stuart Hampshire distinguished a strong and a weak thesis that may plausibly be attributed to Austin. The former is that

> For every distinction of word and idiom that we find in common speech, there is a reason to be found, if we look far enough, to explain why this distinction exists . . . If, as philosophers, we try to introduce an altogether new distinction, we shall find that we are disturbing the economy of the language by blurring elsewhere some useful distinctions that are already recognised.[31]

The weaker thesis is that before we construct a theory we must be certain that we are in possession of all relevant facts.[32] Elsewhere Hampshire pointed out that to date no criterion had been proposed for distinguishing between a question of language and a question which was not one of language. He noted that, when saying that all philosophical questions are questions of language, some philosophers wish to imply that 'no philosophical questions are empirical questions', or 'all philosophical questions are questions of definition'. However, 'Probably no philosophical questions are *purely* empirical questions, and some philosophical questions are *purely* questions of definition, but certainly some philosophical questions are partly one, and partly the other.'[33]

During the fifteen years from the mid-1950s it became possible to gather together numerous papers all of which, in one way or another, were presenting, or responding to, challenges posed by analytical philosophers.[34] I shall have occasion to refer to some of these later, but I sum up my findings thus far by saying that, to different degrees in different writers, there has been a concern for the verification of propositions, for clarity of utterance, for the uses to which language is put, and for the logic of language – that informal logic which disallows any preconceptions as to which varieties of language are 'legitimate', and seeks to give an account of the ways in which the several types of discourse attain meaning (if that is what they do).

Sufficient information has by now been supplied to indicate the context out of which two challenges of continuing importance have emerged: those of logical empiricism and 'Wittgensteinianism'. [35] In rather different ways these pose a significant challenge to one of the assumptions underlying the previous two chapters, namely, that Christian discourse, though its uses are manifold, is at heart cognitive: it makes a claim to knowledge – supremely to knowledge of the God who makes himself known in Christ; it is not simply an emotivist or subjectivist ploy, and it is not meaningless. A further challenge to the same general effect has more recently been issued by that amorphous collocation of writers who are often known (to the distress of some of them) as postmodernists.[36] Let us consider each tendency in turn.

I

In a review of 1956, and with reference to A. J. Ayer, A. N. Prior declared that 'there's no one so completely and hopelessly out of date as the conductor of the bandwaggon that's just gone past'.[37] It rather depends upon whether the band on the waggon was playing, 'The song is ended, but the melody lingers on';[38] for although hard-line positivists may be more scarce than once they were, their criterion of meaning, namely, that those propositions only are meaningful which are either analytic or empirically verifiable (in principle if not in practice), though modified in certain ways, and rebaptized as Anthony Flew's falsification challenge (of which more anon), lingers in a continuum at one end of which we find determined atheists, unreconstructed scientists and many a 'person in the street'; then more sensitive but no less persistent atheists such as Kai Nielsen;[39] to the other end where stand such Christian philosophers as Ian Ramsey, who deliberately conceded as much as he could to empiricism whilst hoping to generate more-than-empirically-circumscribed disclosures of the divine.

Relatively fresh from his encounter with members of the Vienna Circle, among whom Rudolf Carnap was a particularly strong influence upon him, Ayer signalled his intentions in a paper published two years before *Language, Truth and Logic*:

> My purpose is to prove that any attempt to describe the nature or even to assert the existence of something lying beyond the reach of empirical observation must consist in the enunciation of pseudo-propositions, a pseudo-proposition being a series of words that may seem to have the structure of a sentence, but is in fact meaningless. I call this a demonstration of the impossibility of metaphysics because I define a metaphysical enquiry as an enquiry into the nature of reality underlying or transcending the phenomena which the special sciences are content to study . . . [I]t will be shown in this paper not that the metaphysician ought to use scientific methods to attain his end, but that the end itself is vain. Whatever form of reasoning he employs, he succeeds in saying nothing.[40]

This position was elaborated with gusto in his celebrated book of 1936. Out with metaphysics went ethical, aesthetic and religious discourse. These could only be, strictly, nonsensical: 'to say that "God exists" is to make a metaphysical utterence which cannot be either true or false'.[41] Nor may recourse be had to religious experience, for, while we cannot deny that a person is experiencing a particular emotion, we have no grounds for positing the existence of a transcendent being who is its object. Hence 'we offer the theist the same comfort as we gave to the moralist. His assertions cannot possibly be valid, but they cannot be invalid either.'[42] What purported to be religious assertions could be expressions of emotion only.

For the rest of his life Ayer pondered the verification principle, and was never satisfied that he had stated it with sufficient precision. On the appearance of the second edition of *Language, Truth and Logic*, which he admitted was a young man's book, he qualified the principle to the extent of saying that a 'weak' version of it only was required for his theory. Whereas in the strong sense a proposition was verifiable 'if and only if its truth could be conclusively verified in experience', in the weak sense it was verifiable 'if it is possible for experience to render it probable'.[43] He went on to point out that these were not, however, genuine alternatives – a point which he confessed he had overlooked – because

> all empirical propositions are hypotheses which are continually subject to the test of further experience; and from this it would follow not merely that the truth of any such proposition never was conclusively established but that it never could be; for however strong the evidence in its favour, there would never be a point at which it was impossible for further experience to go against it.[44]

He did not, however, rest with this conclusion, because he had come to think that 'there is a class of empirical propositions of which it is permissible to say that they can be conclusively verified . . . they refer solely to the content of a single experience.'[45]

Such softenings notwithstanding, the positivist stance drew fire from many quarters, as the following illustrations will demonstrate. R. G. Collingwood, for example, agreed with Ayer that metaphysical propositions cannot be verified empirically, but argued that this was not because they were nonsense, but because they were not propositions which could be true or false; nor could they be nonsensical. They were non-experientially derived absolute presuppositions – 'catalytic agents which the mind must bring out of its own resources to the manipulation of what is called "experience" and the conversion of it into science and civilization'.[46] From quite another standpoint, and though in considerable sympathy with positivist objectives, W. V. O. Quine regretted that by concentrating upon single propositions the positivists overlooked the fact that 'The totality of our so-called knowledge or beliefs . . . is a man-made fabric which impinges on experience only along the edges.' As if to echo Austin, he pointed out that statements are logically related to one another in such a way that adjustment here entails adjustment there. Accordingly, 'it is misleading to speak of the empirical content of an individual statement – especially if it is a statement at all remote from the experiential periphery of the field'.[47] His advocacy of regard for the totality of language accompanied his conviction that language was ever revisable in the light of pragmatic considerations as to its efficiency or non-efficiency. From another direction, as the philosopher of science, David Papineau, has reminded us, Quine cast doubt upon other convictions cherished by hard-line positivists: 'Working closely with the now-emigrated Carnap, he showed that logic and mathematics cannot be reduced to mere definition, and that the scientific description of the world cannot be decomposed into a substantial synthetic component and a conceptual analytic component.'[48]

Other critics sought more directly to overturn the verification principle. Among these, E. L. Mascall had a particular interest in religious assertions, and I shall therefore summarize his four adversely critical comments. In the first place, Mascall is suspicious of the fact that the verification principle had to be modified. This leads him to think that further modifications might be permissible which would admit ethical, metaphysical and theological statements. Secondly, he offers a *tu quoque* argument to show that while Ayer deems his verification principle meaningful, the proposition enshrining it is neither empirically verifiable nor analytic. Thirdly, when comparing Ayer's more temperate assertions in his second edition of *Language, Truth and Logic* with the bolder claims of the first edition, we find that in the former case he oscillates between regarding the verification principle as a definition, a truth of logic, and an empirically verified generalization. Fourthly, the experience to which, on Ayer's view, all meaningful assertions are to be referred is arbitrarily restricted to the bodily senses, and this is a grossly circumscribed understanding of experience.[49]

Numerous other critics, some gentler than others, weighed in. Price was prepared to concede that, in the case of propositions claiming to state particular matters of fact, the positivists' view is obviously correct, for 'If we do *not* know what sort of entities we must be acquainted with in order to verify a given statement, then it seems to me obvious that we are *not* talking sense when we utter the statement.'[50] I. M. Crombie, considering the implications of the verification principle for theological statements, argued that if we specify the reference-range of such statements, lay down the rules for their use and show how they are to be understood,

> we are justified in claiming that they are meaningful. For, in order that an utterance be meaningful, what more is necessary than that speaker and hearer know, or can find out, what it is being made about and how to determine the extent of the claim which is being made about it?[51]

Profound dissatisfaction was also expressed regarding the emotivist fate to which religious language was consigned by the positivists. A. C. Ewing, for example, contended that to regard religious assertions as expressions of emotion was not only to falsify their character, but also, by extruding the factor of belief from them, it was to ensure that the emotion itself would not long survive.[52] Errol E. Harris developed the point in the direction of religious truth claims thus:

> We have argued that religion is not and cannot be simply a matter of feeling, for without belief the feeling (unless it were spurious) would evaporate. But the belief must be rationally grounded; it must have some acceptable claim to truth, which mere feeling cannot substantiate. Theology, therefore, cannot renounce reasoning and proof, and if such reasoning as is used is esoteric to those who claim to have had certain identifiable experiences, it remains subjective and is no valid reasoning. Belief that is thus incommunicable degenerates into superstition.[53]

When A. G. N. Flew posed his falsification challenge he provoked a number of celebrated responses. The nub of his case was that those making religious assertions will not allow anything to count against their truth; when confronted by such a question as 'How can God be a God of love if unmerited calamities strike people?' the believer qualifies the original assertion – 'But God's love is not exactly like ours', and when pressed retracts further, until the original assertion suffers 'death by a thousand qualifications'. Such a death is 'the peculiar danger, the endemic evil, of theological utterance'.[54] If nothing could possibly count against an assertion, that assertion has no meaning. His challenge therefore was: 'What would have to occur or to have occurred to constitute for you a disproof of the love of, or of the existence of, God?'[55]

We need not review the replies offered by Hare, Mitchell and Crombie,[56] but we ought to note Flew's subsequent refinement of his position, namely, the recognition that 'counting against' was not equivalent to 'being incompatible with'. But even if believers are able at least in some cases to specify considerations which count against their beliefs (but are not incompatible with them), the main question remains: how far may they go along this line before they land in irrationalism or plain silliness?[57]

It remains only to add that Flew has never bowed before criticism or significantly modified his challenge to religious believers. On the contrary, in *God and Philosophy* (1966) he returned to the fray and earned a swingeing review by H. P. Owen, one of whose many adverse criticisms is directly relevant to our present discussion: Flew

> nowhere even attempts to prove (what cannot be proved) that empirical verifiability or falsifiability is a condition of either the meaningfulness or the validity of the truth-claims inherent in religious experience. Yet on the last page he rests his case against theism on its empirical non-falsifiability.[58]

More temperately, P. R. Clifford discussed the positions of both Flew and Nielsen in a paper on 'The factual reference of theological assertions'. He here pointed out the error in thinking that 'verification and falsification are precise counterparts of one another', for 'When an assertion is falsified by the evidence, it has to be discarded, but supporting evidence can at best only point to its provisional adequacy.'[59] He further makes it quite clear that believers do agree that certain circumstances count against the truth of such a proposition as 'God is love'; but, he adds,

> within the Christian tradition there is the experience of redemption, focused in the cross of Christ and worked out in the crucible of human travail; and while this does not explain the problem of suffering, it appears to me to be much more powerful positive evidence for the divine love and mercy than the counter-evidence of suffering itself.[60]

As one who is seeking to understand what is involved in commending the Christian confession to which I (who am, like all other human beings, made in God's image) subscribe, I find myself in broad general sympathy with the opponents of logical positivism. Indeed, if the positivists are right and Christian discourse is literally nonsensical, then Christian apologists would be foolish to continue their endeavours, for to admit to the vocation of commending nonsense would, to say the least, cause the eyebrows of others to rise in incredulity or derision. It would seem that, quite apart from the fact that the statement of the verification principle seems not to meet their own criteria of meaningfulness, the positivists are working with an untenable distinction between fact and value, as is shown by their division of propositions into those which are empirically verifiable and those which are emotive. But if, as many have argued, every fact is an interpreted fact, and if this is shown by the intricacies of language (as Austin's work reveals),[61] then evaluative and emotive assertions cannot be held to be noncognitive.

Again, the positivists subscribe to an unduly narrow assertion (I speak advisedly) of what counts as a fact – an assertion, incidentally, which many scientists would nowadays question. Only phenomena which are actually or in principle open to empirical investigation and experimentation are to be dignified as facts. But this is to rule out by definition, and not by any empirical procedures, all facts and assertions about them which do not meet the criteria; and this move raises the suspicion of ungrounded prejudice. There are the facts of aesthetic, moral and religious experience. From a more specifically Christian standpoint there are the facts of forgiveness, new life in Christ and what may variously be described as growth in grace or the gradual restoration of the divine image – and all of these as related to the facts of Christ's life, death, resurrection and ascension. The question of how far propositions asserting these facts are rationally defensible will occupy us later. For the present it is enough to declare that they are there for consideration (a claim which is no more 'dogmatic' than the downright denial of it), and that any verifiability/falsifiability policies which preclude them from consideration *ab initio* are ill advised. As Ferré rightly said,

> There remain many problems confronting language which hopes to speak meaningfully about supernatural 'facts', . . . but we shall not advance our understanding of theological language by making it

analytically impossible – as does verificational analysis – for language to refer to any but scientific facts. Such victories are too cheap to be convincing.[62]

In this connection, T. M. Knox was puzzled by Basil Mitchell's assertion in one place that 'If statements about the divine activity are not even *in principle* open to scientific test they are not to be regarded as statements of fact', while later he writes that the requirement that this in principle condition be met 'is one we have no *a priori* ground for accepting and as yet very little empirical evidence for'.[63] Knox remarks, 'I welcome this admission that we are dealing here with a dogma, but I would have thought that we had no empirical evidence for it at all and in the nature of the case could not have.'[64]

All of which endorses the main thrust of my objection to the verification principle, namely, that, to recall my earlier somewhat crude image, it is a fork which will not pick up all of the soup of religious assertions. To change the image, it is an arbitrarily imposed straitjacket which will not permit meaning to certain important classes of statements, and which relies upon too strong a disjunction between fact and value. It is encouraging to have the support of H. J. Paton at this point:

> When the principle of verification is used to dispose of all theological statements and arguments at a single blow, this method of attack appears to many to be quite unanswerable. Yet there is a risk that a purely linguistic approach may conceal from us what we are doing and so make the argument seem more shattering than it really is . . . [I]f we choose to confine our beliefs within the limits of common-sense statements and scientific hypotheses, we can have no room for belief . . . Yet a personal decision of this kind would not be regarded as a serious argument for refusing to examine the possibility that religious beliefs – not to mention aesthetic and moral judgements – may have grounds other than sense perception or scientific discovery.[65]

Even more encouraging are some remarks of A. J. Ayer himself, for they tempt us to launch a *tu quoque* argument in his direction. As early as 1946 he made the following important statement:

> a person who affirms the existence of a deity may try to support his contention by appealing to the facts of religious experience; but it does not follow from this that the factual meaning of his statement is wholly contained in the propositions by which these religious experiences are

> described. For there may be other empirical facts that he would also consider to be relevant; and it is possible that the descriptions of these other empirical facts can more properly be regarded as containing the factual meaning of his statement than the descriptions of his religious experiences. At the same time, if one accepts the principle of verification, one must hold that his statement does not have any other factual meaning than what is contained in at least some of the relevant empirical propositions; and that if it is so interpreted that no possible experience could go on to verify it, it does not have any factual meaning at all.[66]

Here is a clear recognition of the truth that facts are theory-laden, and this became the basis of a criticism he levelled against others. Thus, on more than one occasion he weighed the ordinary language philosophy and found it wanting. In 1960 he accused ordinary language philosophers of too often forgetting that there is no strong disjunction between facts and their interpretation, and that 'even at the level of common sense our ordinary language will be found to carry a considerable load of theory'.[67] And when, six years later, he said that 'In philosophy, nothing should be absolutely sacrosanct: not even common sense',[68] it is not simply wickedness which inclines us to add, 'nor yet the verification principle'.

In the light of the foregoing discussion it may reasonably be claimed that we have removed one boulder – the verification principle – from the path of the would-be utterer of Christian assertions. We have yet to show the ways in which the claims integral to the Christian confession acquire meaning, and we shall in due course view them in context and consider their appropriateness or otherwise. Proceeding one step at a time, our next task is to discuss the use and reference of Christian discourse, and our approach to this will be through a consideration of Wittgenstein and his legacy.

II

In lively fashion, and with evident glee, Anthony Quinton disposes of the Wittgenstein of the *Tractatus* thus:

> To the extent that he was a positivist, Wittgenstein was a positivist at the top of his voice. Vanity and hysteria seem to have co-operated in making

> him repress the thought that he could possibly be wrong. Wittgenstein's exaggerations include the view that everything except the 'propositions of natural science' is literally senseless, not in the manner of logical truths as being void of factual content, but in the fullest possible fashion, as altogether without meaning, mere nonsense. At first this version of antimetaphysics was an agreeably iconoclastic way of securing attention for the Circle's ideas. Eventually it became an embarrassment, a nihilistic tin-can tied to the tail of a respectably liberal and enlightened bandwaggon.[69]

It is not to our purpose to enquire further into the relations between Wittgenstein and the members of the Vienna Circle. Suffice it to say that Wittgenstein's view that 'The right method of philosophy would be this. To say nothing except what can be said, i.e. the propositions of natural science . . .'[70] commended itself to members of the Circle, though they cooled towards him at the point at which Wittgenstein, in what they regarded as a distinctly anti-anti-metaphysical manner, invoked the mystical, and pronounced that 'There is indeed the inexpressible. This *shows* itself; it is the mystical.'[71] As Carnap reported, Wittgenstein

> had recognised that many statements in the field of religion and metaphysics did not, strictly speaking, say anything . . . I had erroneously believed that his attitude towards metaphysics was similar to ours [that is, to Carnap's and Schlick's]. I had not paid sufficient attention to the statements in his book about the mystical, because his feelings and thoughts in this area were too divergent from mine.[72]

Even so, Wittgenstein's appeal to the inexpressible relates directly to the positivistic restriction of experience to sense perception – a restriction which takes its cue from a prominent aspect of Locke's epistemology – and is the ground of the numerous charges of reductionism which have been levelled against many who have, to a greater or lesser degree, swum philosophically (some would say drowned) in Wittgenstein's wake.[73]

As to Wittgenstein's primary objective in the *Tractatus*, D. F. Pears has well said that 'the task which Kant set himself was the demarcation of the limits of thought, and the parallel task which Wittgenstein set himself was the demarcation of the limits of language'.[74] Like Russell, he was influenced and impressed by Frege's work in mathematics, and in his early years he sought comparable precision in language. He summarized his aim thus:

> The right method of philosophy would be this. To say nothing except what can be said, *i.e.* the propositions of natural science, *i.e.* something that has nothing to do with philosophy: and then always, when someone else wished to say something metaphysical, to demonstrate to him that he had given no meaning to certain signs in his propositions. This method would be unsatisfying to the other – he would not have the feeling that we were teaching him philosophy – but it would be the only strictly correct method.[75]

The Wittgenstein of the *Tractatus* is not concerned only with the meaningfulness or otherwise of discourse; he is interested in the ontological conditions which make linguistic usage appropriate. His question is: what must reality be like if language is properly used? In this context he develops his picture theory of meaning, in which the steps are:

> The total reality is the world.
> We make to ourselves pictures of facts.
> The picture presents the facts in logical space,
> the existence and non-existence of states of affairs.
> The picture is a model of reality.
> It is like a scale applied to reality.[76]

Thus, for every fact, or possible state of affairs, there is a proposition which is a literal picture of it: the proposition shows its sense to us as a picture shows itself to us; and if it is a true picture, it shows us how things are in reality: 'The proposition *shows* how things stand, *if* it is true. And *says*, that they do so stand.'[77] If it should seem that many of our propositions do not fulfil this requirement, this is because they are complex and are thus candidates for analysis.

As is well known, following the publication of the *Tractatus*, Wittgenstein, feeling that his contribution to philosophy was over, left Cambridge and went school teaching and gardening in Austria. In 1929 he returned to Cambridge and began to criticize his former work, though how seriously his criticisms should be taken is one of many puzzles which teases scholars to this day. Certainly any view that there is an 'early' Wittgenstein who is utterly distinct from a 'later' one is now seen to be untenable, not least because of the industry of those who, by gradually making available the many thousands of notes left by Wittgenstein, have made it quite clear that he was constantly revising his earlier thoughts.[78] So malleable were his thoughts that, in the light of the evidence now available, it appears too straightforward to say that the *Blue Book*, circulated from 1933, and the *Brown Book* with which it was published in 1958 were studies preliminary to the *Philosophical Investigations* of 1953.

Wittgenstein's own repudiation of the *Tractatus* notwithstanding, there are links between his early and later work.[79] His interest in the relation of language to the world never left him, though he forsook that quest of an ideal language the possibility of which he had earlier granted; he did not cease to posit the mystical; and he remained hostile to what he regarded as the pseudo-problems of speculative metaphysics (the metaphysical implications of his early atomistic view notwithstanding). But he turned away from logical atomism, made much less of the picture theory of meaning (though he never formally repudiated it),[80] and, instead of confining himself to the investigation of the meaning of an expression in the context of 'the forms of all propositions in which it can occur', as in the *Tractatus*,[81] he now proceeded to investigate the variety of uses, arising in the context of social communication, to which language is put – though, as we shall see, he drew the line at the possibility that language might have an ontological reference to God. The force of the celebrated epigram with which he ended the *Tractatus* never left him: 'Whereof one cannot speak, thereof one must be silent';[82] and the echo of Descartes's clear and distinct ideas in such a claim as the following can still be heard: 'Everything that can be thought at all can be thought clearly. Everything that can be said can be said clearly.'[83] Notwithstanding this, Wittgenstein henceforth analysed discourse in accordance with the understanding he had by now reached, namely, that 'For a *large* class of cases – though not for all – in which we employ the word "meaning" it can be defined thus: the meaning of a word is its use in the language.'[84] Referring to the period from 1930 onwards, he said:

> If I had to say what is the main mistake made by philosophers of the present generation, including Moore, I would say that it is that when language is looked at, what is looked at is a form of words and not the use made of the form of words.[85]

When usage is confused needless puzzlement is the result, and Wittgenstein now sought to remedy this by the therapy of careful analysis illuminated by illustrations of the way in which language properly works. The description 'therapist' is important – Wittgenstein was not a surgeon cutting away diseased language: that would be unwarrantably to interfere. On the contrary, of crucial and continuing importance was his conviction that 'Philosophy may in no way interfere with the actual use of language; it can in the end only describe it. For it cannot give it any foundation either. It leaves everything as it is.'[86] As he elsewhere said, 'My ideal is a certain coolness. A temple providing a setting for the passions without meddling with them.'[87] He never departed from his view that expressions such as 'I believe that so and so will happen' are used in one way in science and in another in religion, and he dissents from the view of Fr. O'Hara and others that the alleged historical basis of Christainity is open to scientific investigation. To Wittgenstein this is an unreasonable position to adopt, because religious faith is not, and does not pretend to be, and could not be shown to be, reasonable in that sense.[88]

Against this background we may further specify Wittgenstein's view of language, by noting his view of language games, forms of life and the reference of religious language. No disrespect is intended to Wittgenstein by pointing out that he was not the first to lay emphasis upon the use of language. For example, in addition to the customary view, inherited from Locke, that ideas bestow content upon words which on their own are empty, Berkeley held that, as well as communicating ideas, words have 'other ends, as the raising of some passion, the exciting to or deterring from an action, the putting the mind in some particular disposition'; and he elsewhere surmised that words

> have other uses besides barely standing for and exhibiting ideas – such as raising proper emotions, producing certain dispositions or habits of mind, and directing our actions in pursuit of that happiness which is the ultimate end and design, the primary spring and motive, that sets rational agents at work . . .[89]

Here we have a harbinger in one sense of Wittgenstein's concern for the use of language, and, in another, of Braithwaite's empiricist (as distinct from Berkeley's spiritual realist) recourse to words as morality-boosting stimulants.[90]

My particular interest is in Wittgenstein's view of the use of religious language. First, however, we must attempt to discern his attitude towards religion as such. Here, as so often with

Wittgenstein, there is an elusiveness which renders any absolute pronouncements foolhardy. Norman Malcolm concluded that there was in Wittgenstein the possibility of religion; indeed, 'he looked on religion as a "form of life" . . . in which he did not participate, but with which he was sympathetic and which greatly interested him'.[91] Insofar as he had a theory of religion it appears to have been of a behaviourist kind, for he described religious speech to Friedrich Waismann as 'a component of religious behaviour and not a theory. Therefore nothing turns on whether the words are true, false, or nonsensical.'[92] This is consistent with his already quoted assertions that language use in religious discourse differs from that in scientific discourse, and that, where such terms as 'dogma' and 'faith' are concerned, 'We don't talk about hypothesis, or about high probability. Nor about knowing.'[93] Positively, religious discourse finds its home and use within a religious 'form of life'. A 'form of life', contrary to the impression which some have received, is not a 'way of life' in the sense in which I have called Christianity a way of life; rather, it is a social activity part of which is speaking a language, or playing a 'language game'. As Wittgenstein says, a '*language-game* is behaviour';[94] and again, '*practice* gives words their sense'.[95] It is not easy to square this emphasis upon the social functions of, and way of learning the use of, language with Wittgenstein's earlier view of the metaphysical subject as 'the limit – not part of the world';[96] or with the solitariness of his continuing belief that 'at the end of it all *he himself*, the human being, is the one who has to die'.[97]

There are, we are informed, multiple language games, and in a list of them which is not intended to be exhaustive Wittgenstein includes, among others, 'Giving orders, and obeying them . . . Reporting an event . . . Forming and testing a hypothesis . . . Making up a story, and reading it . . . Guessing riddles . . . Asking, thanking, cursing, greeting, praying.'[98] Contrary to what some have thought, Wittgenstein did not suppose that there were separate language games, each with it own rules, for science, ethics, aesthetics, law, theology and other disciplines.[99] Language games overlap, they are played in particular human situations, their content changes and they may become obsolete. He contends that the multiplicity of kinds of use 'is not something fixed, given once for all; but new types of language, new language-games, as we may say, come into existence, and others become obsolete and get forgotten. (We can get a *rough picture* of this from the changes in mathematics).'[100] I am not aware that Wittgenstein makes it clear how language games come to be or change or cease – especially since, though overlapping and to this extent in contact, one such game may not judge another and hence possibly provoke change. Moreover, if the number of overlapping language games is vast, do not the concepts 'language game' and 'form of life' become ever less significant as indicative of linguistic difference?

Be all this as it may, of actual games Wittgenstein wrote:

> [W]e see a complicated network of similarities overlapping and criss-crossing: sometimes overall similarities, sometimes similarities of detail. I can think of no better expression to characterize these similarities than 'family resemblances'; for the various resemblances between members of a family: build, features, colour of eyes, gait, temperament, etc. etc. overlap and criss-cross in the same way. – And I shall say: 'games' form a family.[101]

In any game, rules are crucial. To know how to play the game properly is to have mastered the rules, and the rules of games can be stated. But where a language game is concerned we learn to judge what are the right rules by using the language in a social context.[102] Here we are concerned not so much with what Wittgenstein calls the 'surface grammar' of words – that is, the way they are used in the construction of sentences as heard by the ear, but with the 'depth grammar' of the words used.[103] In *On Certainty* Wittgenstein pursues this theme further. He distinguishes between propositions concerning states of affairs in the world, and propositions which are 'unmoving foundations' of language games.[104] The latter specify appropriate tests and, accordingly, are not themselves testable. They belong to a language game's 'depth grammar', and they regulate it.

We have already noted some of the constant features as between the 'early' and the 'later' Wittgenstein. Another, which survives the forsaking of his 'ideal language' atomism, is his view that, while we may name and indicate the phenomena in the world, we cannot define them: 'The name cannot be analysed further by any definition. It is a primitive sign.'[105] In *Philosophical Investigations*, where he sets out from what he deems to be Augustine's over-simple view that every word has a meaning and that the meaning is the object with which the word is correlated,[106] he exhorts his readers thus:

> We must do away with all *explanation*, and description alone must take its place. And this description gets its light, that is to say its purpose, from the philosophical problems. These are, of course, not empirical problems; they are solved, rather, by looking into the workings of our language, and that in such a way as to make us recognize those workings: *in despite of* an urge to misunderstand them. The problems are solved, not by giving new information, but by arranging what we have always known. Philosophy is a battle against the bewitchment of our intelligence by means of language.[107]

What may be said of Wittgenstein's approach as thus briefly sketched? In the first place, just as the logical positivists ruled out religious (and therefore Christian) assertions as, in accordance with their verificationist principle of exclusion, meaningless, so Wittgenstein, for all his concern to investigate language as it is used and as it is useful (for there is ambiguity in 'Don't ask for the meaning, ask for the use'), seems intent upon blocking off certain usages which, for his own reasons, do not suit him. To take the distinction between naming and defining: why may language not be used in appropriate contexts to define as precisely as possible? While in many contexts the general family resemblances within language games may suffice to prompt the appropriate use of words, where insurance policies or courts of law or title deeds are concerned precise definition of terms is required, and it is simply untrue to pronounce that this is not how language is *used*. If the point is that language ought not to be used in this way, then we have an implicit, arbitrary, prohibition which undermines the professed objective of description only. We have instead the recommendation that language be used in a certain way; we have prescription.[108]

In the work of some philosophers, prescription is no offence. Indeed, their objective may well be to recommend certain usage as correct: their therapy may entail surgery – cutting away 'diseased' language, not simply dissolving linguistic puzzles. In other words, they do not restrict themselves to describing how language is used; they make evaluative judgements and declare how it ought to be used. R. G. Collingwood, for example, did this when he spoke of the 'proper version' of the concept of art. Collingwood's philosophy thus has not simply a descriptive function, but a revisionary one: the way to discover the proper meaning is to ask not, 'What do we mean?' but, 'What are we trying to mean?' And this involves the question 'What is preventing us from meaning what we are trying to mean?'[109]

The movement from 'how language is used' to 'how language ought to be used' is, in the light of Wittgenstein's objectives, illicit. But it frequently occurs in his own work and that of those influenced by him. Thus, we have already seen that, against Fr. O'Hara, Wittgenstein propounded an alternative theory, grounded in the thesis carried forward from the *Tractatus*, namely that there is a distinction to be drawn between religious and scientific discourse. On this basis he felt able to pronounce: 'I would definitely call O'Hara [who seeks evidence for the truth of religious claims] unreasonable. I would say, if this is religious belief, then it's all superstition.'[110] This is more than simply a recommendation, grounded in an undefended theory, concerning how we should speak; and even if we take Wittgenstein's concluding phrase as being a literal description, it is difficult, in the context of refuting a priest, to eradicate altogether the pejorative connotation of 'superstition'; and this gives the remark an unfortunately *ad hominem* flavour. Again, in elucidating the proposition 'God's eye sees everything', Wittgenstein says, 'I want to say of this that it uses a picture.' When Smythies sugests that the speaker might do more than associate language use with a picture, Wittgenstein expostulates, 'Rubbish. I meant: what conclusions are you going to draw? Etc. Are eyebrows going to be talked of, in connection with the Eye of God?'[111] Here, clearly, is something more than a description of how language is used; Wittgenstein's use of 'picture' hides a theory concerning the nature of religious belief which rules out anything more – a transcendent reference, for example – which a believer might intend, and which, on Wittgenstein's own terms, would be perfectly legitimate within the religious language game in question.

Similar criticisms have been levelled against D. Z. Phillips by a number of writers. In approaching Phillips's ever-expanding *corpus* we should observe that, as well as owing a considerable debt to Wittgenstein, especially in his quest of the 'depth grammar' of religious discourse, he has been greatly influenced by Kierkegaard and his Christian existentialist successors in the direction of defending the unique nature of religious commitment. Consider his oft-discussed remarks on prayer. Fortifying himself with a reference to remarks by Peter Winch, he writes:

> One can say *within* any . . . context, whether it be science or religion, 'This is the rule which *must* be observed, this is the meaning which a word *must* have if it is to belong to this conceptual family.' But when philosophers say, 'This is the meaning which a word *must have*', without specifying any context, they are guilty of arbitrary linguistic legislation. The 'must' is not a logical '*must*', but simply the 'must' of their own preferences, or the 'must' of one context which they have elevated, consciously or unconsciously, to be a standard for all others.[112]

As to prayer, Phillips says, 'I want to try to say what people *are* doing when they pray.' What does he think they are doing?

> When deep religious believers pray *for* something, they are not so much asking God to bring this about, but in a way telling Him the strength of their desires. They realise that things may not go as they wish, but they are asking to be able to go on living whatever happens. In prayers of confession and in prayers of petition, the believer is trying to find a meaning and a hope that will deliver him from the elements in his life which threaten to destroy it.[113]

As I have elsewhere remarked,

> Many have felt that the assertion in the first sentence here is false; that that in the second is true; and that that in the third provides only an attenuated account of what most believers understand to be going on when they confess their sins and pray for forgiveness.[114]

Above all, it disallows the ontological reference apart from which many believers would deem prayer to be an unreal activity.[115] Time and again in Phillips's writings – when he is considering language concerning God as creator, Christ as Saviour, for example – we meet doctrinal statements construed not as referring to facts or attitudes, but as pictures in which believers repose their confidence, and which sustain and regulate their lives. The question of the absence of this reference is, as far as Christian apologetic is concerned, the single most disquieting feature of Wittgenstein's position and of that of those fairly thoroughly indebted to him.

Not surprisingly, Phillips has been dubbed a reductionist and a 'Wittgensteinian fideist'.[116] Both labels he refuses, contending that the true reductionists are those who suppose that religious pictures refer to objects, thereby reducing the significance of religious belief. Consistently with this he elsewhere says that 'Religious language is not an interpretation of how things are, but determines how things are for the believer. The saint and the atheist do not interpret the same world in different ways. They see different worlds.'[117] It is not clear how religious language determines anything for believers; rather, it is used by them because it enables them to interpret their experience, praise God, say their prayers, make their testimony and commend their faith. But the second and third sentences are still more problematic. For it is as if Phillips implies that the believer is in one form of life, the atheist in another (the very thing which Phillips repudiates when his opponents charge him with recourse to autonomous language games),[118] and this, we were led to believe, is precisely a thought which we are not supposed to entertain regarding Wittgensteinian forms of life or language games: they criss-cross, we were told; they overlap, they are plastic according to context and circumstances, and hence to speak of their 'borders' would be open to question. Moreover, Wittgenstein (unlike Phillips's posited atheist and believer) was able to understand those in the habit of playing a different language game from himself, and this suggests at least that he and they shared an epistemological form of life (something denied by Cornelius Van Til and his followers, as we shall see later), and to that extent the same 'world'.

In fairness to Phillips we must point out that in 1970 he described himself as 'one who has talked of religious beliefs as distinctive language-games, but also as one who has come to feel misgivings in some respects about doing so'.[119] He came to see that the reason why people should cherish their religious beliefs in the way they do 'cannot be shown simply by *distinguishing between* religious beliefs and other features of human existence'.[120] He works towards his newer position that

> So far from it [*sic*] being true that religious beliefs can be thought of as isolated language-games, cut off from all other forms of life, the fact is that religious beliefs cannot be understood at all unless their relation to other forms of life is taken into account.[121]

But later in his paper he wishes still to claim that 'religious beliefs are distinctive language games'.[122] That this is not the contradiction it appears to be is shown by the fact that the context of the last utterance quoted is that of the justification of religious beliefs. That is, if I understand him aright, such beliefs arise out of commerce with the world, but there is no means of justifying them from outside the religious language game, and no point in attempting the task within it.[123] We seem to be back with the tension we detected in Wittgenstein's (admittedly elusive) thought about religion, namely, that between the believer as the replica of Kierkegaard's lonely knight of faith on the one hand, and as societally-rooted-and-influenced player of language games on the other.

To the traditional user of Christian language what is most disquieting about the linguistic proposals of Wittgenstein and his successors is that religious assertions are deemed by them not to have an objective reference, and the question of the truth or otherwise of religious claims is foreclosed. Let us examine each point in turn.

N. H. G. Robinson threw down the gauntlet before Wittgensteinians in these terms: '[R]eligious language has always[124] been ontologically, not just logically, oriented, that is to say, oriented towards a distinctive reality, not simply towards a word which behaves peculiarly; and to minimise or to eliminate this objective reference would break the nerve of religion.'[125] With this challenge I find myself in broad sympathy, except that, in deference to the language of some non-Christian faiths, for example, and with reference to my quest of a Christian apologetic method, I should prefer to substitute 'Christian' for 'religious'.

D. Z. Phillips has not been slow to take up the challenge. He finds different criteria of rationality operative in different contexts, and hence 'the distinction between the real and the unreal does not come to the same thing in every context. If this were observed, one would no longer wish to construe God's reality as being that of an existent among existents, an object among objects.'[126] Later in the same book he underlines the point:

> The objector who accuses me of denying the objective reality of God may have in mind a statement which I should support – namely, the statement that God is not an object. That is a statement of grammar. Those who deny it, I suggest, speak of God in a way which is a logical extension of ways in which we speak of human beings. If God is a thing He is finite; and a finite God satisfies the needs neither of religion nor of theology.[127]

To this we may reply that of course the Christian God is not an object in the sense in which a material object or 'thing' occupying a given space in the world is an object; and we may also agree that those relatively few philosophers who have posited a finite God have been unrepresentative of Christian thought at large, and have generally been regarded as endorsing a position which is at least as reductionist as some say that of Phillips is.[128] But 'object' is ambiguous. It is consistent with a long tradition of Christian thought and experience (which does not, of course, by itself make it true) that God has objective reality without being a quasi-material object. Furthermore, he is not one 'object' among many others; he is the one who is at the same time transcendent over all yet immanent in the world. In the next chapter I shall have more to say about this claim. The point at the moment is that if we are genuinely interested in the linguistic usage of Christians, this is what most of them seem to be intending when they speak of God.[129] They are concerned with the existence of one who has made himself known in Christ (a notion to be unpacked later), and not with the way in which a concept, 'God', behaves. More than thirty years on, a statement which John Hick made in reply to Phillips stands (indeed, given the subsequent flurry of postmodernist activity, its message is underscored): 'The debate which Phillips here enters between cognitive and non-cognitive analyses of religious language constitutes, I believe, the central issue in the philosophy of religion today.'[130] In Hick's view at that time, 'Christian language, as the actual speech of a living community, presupposes the extra-linguistic reality of God.'[131] Phillips makes two points in reply. First, that it is '*within* religious discourse that we find what is meant by God'.[132] But Hick need not deny this, though he may wonder why what Phillips has discovered as to how the religious language game is played differs so markedly from what other equally sincere players have found. Secondly, Phillips counters that '*the same* believers who say that the existence of God is a fact would, if pressed, admit that the discovery of God is not like the discovery of a matter of fact, and that there is no question of God ceasing to exist, of having existed for a certain length of time, or of having come into existence'.[133] At this point Phillips is tacitly operating with a theory which is dangerously close to the positivist one entailing the restriction of facticity to empirical matters; and we have already had occasion to query this limitation. Not indeed that Phillips wishes to deprive himself of language referring to the reality of God. Elsewhere, in the context of a denial of our ability to prove the existence of God, he says, 'In learning by contemplation, attention, renunciation, what forgiving, thanking, loving, etc. mean . . . the believer is participating in the reality of God; *this is what we mean by God's reality*.'[134] Apart, however, from the objective reality of God, this is but a stipulation that we learn the meaning of the specified terms by relating them to the concept 'God'. It all seems somewhat less demanding than actually confessing to, thanking or loving anybody, and it brings to mind the observation of Stuart Hampshire:

> It is not possible consistently to maintain both of the following two propositions: (1) that to understand an expression is to be able to use the expression correctly, and to recognise the standard occasions of its use: and (2) that existential statements have no place among philosophical conclusions, philosophy being solely concerned to analyse the actual meanings of terms in use.[135]

Among the most radical non-cognitivist accounts of religious language was that of Thomas McPherson. At the heart of his case is the claim that

> There are some things that just cannot be said. As long as no-one tries to say them there is no trouble. But if anyone does try to say them he must take the consequences. We ought not to try to express the inexpressible. The things that theologians try to say (or some of them) belong to the class of things that just cannot be said. The way out of the worry is to retreat into silence.[136]

McPherson does not regard his stance as necessarily irreligious; rather, impressed by Rudolf Otto's expositon of the numinous, he suggests that the essence of religion is its non-rational side.

It did not take long for the fur to fly. Many of the adverse criticisms of McPherson's position were summarized by Ferré: McPherson bracketed the question of religious truth; he left no place for public worship, which uses language, or for the proclamation of a Gospel; and not even a private non-linguistic religion would be viable. We should be left with 'the formless "rosy glow" of "positive thinking" – without even the thought to think positively!'[137] It remains only to add that McPherson's position was too much for Dewi Phillips, who quoted John Passmore against it: 'One difficulty with this line of reasoning, considered as a defence of religion, is that it "saves" religion only at the cost of leaving the door open to any sort of transcendental metaphysics – and indeed to superstition and nonsense of the most arrant sort.'[138]

It should be pointed out that the cognitive–non-cognitive debate has taken many forms, and has not been confined to Britain. To take one example only, Paul Ricoeur, a debtor to existentialism, phenomenology and analytical philosophy, has insisted on the 'aboutness' of religious language, as well as on the assumption that religious discourse claims not only to be meaningful, but to be true.[139]

William Alston's rhetorical questions underline the point I am concerned to make:

> Why should I express a feeling of security by saying 'God made the heavens and the earth' unless I believe, or at least have a tendency to believe, that as a matter of objective fact the physical universe owes its existence to the creative activity of a supernatural personal deity? Still more, why should I take on the complex of attitudes and activities that goes along with this assertion unless I believed it to be true?[140]

It would therefore seem that if we are seriously concerned to examine how religious believers use their language (which is what 'Wittgensteinians' are supposed, on their own account, to do), we must be doubly careful not to permit our tacit evaluations or undeclared theories imperialistically to render them dumb by prohibition, or distorted by prescription. It has been said that 'the worst philosophical sin in Wittgensteinian terms' is 'that of not attending to the actual use of, and our natural expertise in using, language'.[141] It has further been pointed out that the upshot of the later Wittgenstein's endeavours is that 'there is no way of getting between language and the world and finding out if there is a general fit between them'.[142]

To caution oneself against a positivistic, constricted understanding of 'fact', and a 'Wittgensteinian' disinclination to allow for the objective reference of religious language, is in no way to despise the contribution which analytical philosophy can offer to Christian apologetics. On the contrary, it is to open the way to analysis which is true to the discourse under review. I have every sympathy with those who regret that some theologians are slow to practise the analytical art,[143] and I shall attempt an analysis of my own which focuses upon what I have claimed to be the primary locus of Christian corporate confession: public worship. But first a few general remarks on 'religious language' are in order.[144]

III

It might be suggested that discourse is 'religious' if it employs special 'religious' vocabulary. It is true that every religion has its technical terms, and that Christianity is replete with them in both the theological and the ecclesiastical fields. We have to learn both the meanings of these terms and the contexts in which it is appropriate to use them. We learn the meaning of 'alb' in much the same way as we learn the meaning of 'table'. But it is not the use of special terms which makes discourse religious. 'An alb is a white vestment worn by the priest at the celebration of the eucharist' is a definitive assertion of the same kind as 'A table is an article of furniture consisting of a flat smooth board furnished with legs'. On the other hand, when Isaiah of Jerusalem lamented, 'Woe is me, I am doomed',[145] although he used no technical religious terms he was nevertheless uttering a religious statement. This claim is justified by reference to the context of his words: he, the sinner, is confronted by the holy One of Israel. But this reference to context leads us to the second possible understanding of the question, what is religious discourse?

The question may be taken to mean: 'Is there a class of statements which may properly be designated religious?' At first sight this may appear to be the case. 'I believe in the Holy Ghost' seems to be a very different kind of assertion from 'I believe in Arthur'. Arthur differs considerably from the Holy Ghost, and not just in the way that he differs from Charles or even from Mary. Moreover, the contexts in which it would normally be customary to make these assertions differ also. I say 'normally' because while the credal assertion's natural home is public worship, the assertion could be recited in a classroom where the lesson or lecture concerns Christian belief. In such a context, on the lips of a teacher or lecturer who was not a Christian, the assertion would be purely informative rather than (following J. L. Austin) performative. The teacher or lecturer would be describing what Christians believe, not articulating a personal belief, just as a Christian might provide an account of Hindu beliefs, for example.

But what of the assertion, 'Jesus suffered under Pontius Pilate'? Is this a religious statement, or is it merely historical (assuming that it is at least historical)? As it stands it purports to be historical; it is of the same order as, 'John Bunyan suffered under the

Royalists', and its method of verification is the same. But when the statement about Jesus becomes a statement about Jesus *Christ our Lord*, and appears in a creed – that is, in an affirmation-*cum*-definition principally designed to be used performatively in worship – everything points to the fact that we have a more-than-merely-historical use of language here. The context in which the assertion is made, together with its manifold associations, makes it clear that we have here a use of language in which the reference is not merely, or even primarily, to history, but to certain transcendental facts such as that this Jesus, who did indeed suffer under Pontius Pilate, is not significant simply because of that, but because he who thus suffered was none other than the Son of God. But the fact that religion is, as I have argued, a matter of the whole of life, leads to a third possible understanding of the question, what is religious discourse?

The question may be taken to mean: does something happen to language when it is used by religious believers? Or, to be more specific: does language become religious when Christians use it? The outstanding difficulty with this notion is that it makes it very difficult for Christians to sound irreligious, which they sometimes are. It is difficult to see how it could be maintained, on any unforced interpretation of language, that Christians who drop bricks on their toes and blaspheme are using religious language religiously. Clearly, not any use of language by Christians, nor even any use of religious terminology or jargon, ensures that the act of utterance in question is a religious act. Conversely, many philosophers of religion who are not Christians use Christian language regularly, but not, presumably, religiously (though the best of them have acute imaginative sympathy which helps them to understand what it would be like so to use it). We come here upon the element of purpose in the use of language. We are concerned not merely with context, but with intention. But if for the believer all life is in some sense religion, does it follow that even the most mundane assertions a Christian makes qualify for the designation 'religious'? When a Christian says, 'I'm going to the sweet shop to buy an Easter egg', does he or she mean what everybody else means; or does the Christian mean something like this:

> I'm going to trust in the providence of God, and in the ability he has given me to walk and to remember the way, and I am going to the sweet shop; and when I get there I shall buy a symbol of the heart of my faith,

> having first exercised prayer and thought in the matter of my stewardship of money, and my duty not to put excessive weight on the temple of the Holy Spirit.

No doubt the Christian normally means the same as everybody else. But can we altogether rule out a theology of shopping (even if it should sound rather strained), while we admit a theology of war (do bombs drop on enemies or on brothers and sisters for whom Christ died?), of industry (do charge hands work for money, for their employers, or for the glory of God?)? Clearly, any such applied theologies emerge because the language of every day is brought, more or less crudely, into relation to an overall Christian view of the world. At this point some would invoke the notion of 'levels' of language, pointing out that many otherwise ordinary statements may be intended by their speakers to be given a religious interpretation, and that we can usually determine without great difficulty the occasions when this is so. The context of the utterance, the speaker's manner, any knowledge we may have, or acquire, concerning the speaker's religious allegiance or lack of it, will help us here.

It is at this point that, over against the verificationists' prohibition, we benefit from Wittgenstein's emphasis upon the uses of language, though we shall not restrict that use in the way he and his followers do. Nor shall we take the most mundane 'levels' of language to be paradigmatic of all language use – an unjustified assumption which lay at the root of much 'ordinary language' philosophy.[146]

The idea of levels of language may be of some assistance to the informal logician, though it is not entirely unproblematic. If the slogan 'Every statement has its own logic' were taken to mean that, by dint of searching, a level of language may be found whereon even the most irrational assertion will emerge as the epitome of reasonableness, we should have a notable abuse of what is, after all, a metaphor. Again, if the idea of 'levels' were to tempt us to construe statements hierarchically and to smuggle in evaluations such that 'higher' uses of language are somehow 'better', we may find ourselves fostering quite unnecessary confusions. But if 'levels' simply reminds us that language has many uses, that contexts of language use are manifold, and that speakers have many intentions, little harm may be done. With the cautions in mind, let us now consider the following statements about the cuckoo.

> (*a*) [T]he character of the bird is not admirable, and it causes destruction to many innocent and useful young birds each season.[147]

Leaving on one side the question of the innocence or otherwise of young birds, we note that the opening evaluative statement is based upon empirical observation of the cuckoo's habits, and no doubt it would be possible to obtain supportive photographic evidence of the cuckoo ousting the eggs of other birds from their nests if such were required. Concerning this first-order 'level' of language there are fairly definite and widely known evaluative rules and procedures.

> (*b*) O blithe New-comer! I have heard,
> I hear thee and rejoice.
> O Cuckoo! Shall I call thee Bird,
> Or but a wandering Voice?

It is clear that language is being used very differently here. It is used evocatively, and it is not Wordsworth's primary intention to provide information about the cuckoo. Rather, he wishes to fire the imagination by reference to the haunting notes of the bird coming from several directions. Hence, in the last two lines he is not raising a question of definition concerning which it would be appropriate to seek an ornithologist's advice. And an ornithologist who argued with the poet because to him the cuckoo is a pest, whilst to Wordsworth it is the thrice welcome 'darling of the Spring', would merely show that he had failed to grasp what the poet is about.

> (*c*) The cuckoo is one of the creatures God has made.

This statement is not designed to provide us with scientific information over and above that which an ornithologist could provide. Nor is it intended to be merely evocative. It is conceivable that it may stimulate the mood of adoration or worship in some, though there is no guarantee of this, for the darker side of the cuckoo's character might be said to focus a number of aspects of the problem of evil – shades of John Stuart Mill and nature's 'red-in-tooth-and-claw-ness'. The distinguishing feature of this assertion (*pace* Thomas McPherson) is its transcendent reference. It is the assertion of one who interprets what is seen religiously, fully aware, presumably, that the statement 'This is a cuckoo God has made', is of a very different order, or is on a different level, from the statement, 'This is the house that Jack built'.

It is not difficult to fall into logical traps caused by the jumbling up of levels of language. From our cuckoo examples it is easy to construct an 'assertion' which manifestly bears the marks of the preposterous, thus: 'The cuckoo is a God-created wandering Voice which destroys other birds' eggs each season.'[148] But not all mixtures are so obviously absurd, especially to those to whom they have a degree of familiarity, and particularly if they partake of the nature of the language of an 'in group'. Consider the following examples.

(*i*) On the record sleeve of Saint-Saëns's *Carnival of the Animals*[149] Jack Wood writes of 'The Aquarium', 'The *trickling* pianos are accompanied by muted strings while, towards the end, the harmonica *makes occasional flurries through the water.*' I have italicized the word and phrase which suggest that this is a piece of poetic prose designed to match the music and stimulate the imagination. We know that pianos cannot literally be said to trickle, and that if harmonicas were subjected to water they would not flurry, but eventually rust away. But Wood also uses the technical term, 'muted strings'. 'Muted' is not of the same order as 'trickling' and 'flurrying'. It is not that we do not know what he means to convey, but he is speaking on two levels at once. We could watch violinists, viola players, cellists and double bassists place mutes on their strings if we were in the recording studio; this is a matter open to empirical investigation. But the question whether 'trickling' and 'flurrying' are appropriate terms is a matter of aesthetic judgement.

(*ii*) A report in the magazine of a conservative evangelical missionary society refers to a journey of two of the society's officers to various parts of Africa. It continues, 'And to cap it all, their homeward route lay through the Holy land, where the dear Son of God was "made flesh and dwelt among us . . . full of grace and truth."'[150] This is all recounted in a matter-of-fact way, and it appears in the report of an actual itinerary. Moreover, the writer's inverted commas indicate a quotation from John's Gospel, and not an odd use of language. We may compare the phrase, 'Where the dear Son of God was "made flesh . . . "' with a phrase in the preceding sentence of the report. We are there informed that the Mission's representatives went to Ethiopia, 'where, for over thirty-five years His Imperial Majesty Haile Selassie I has been on the throne'. If we were to replace 'Son of God' with 'Jesus of Nazareth' in the first phrase we should have comparable statements here. But into what at first sight appears to be recorded as a statement of historic fact, a religious – even a confessional – judgement has been introduced concerning who this Jesus is: a judgement, moreover, which incorporates a transcendent reference.

Already we see something of the wide variety of language uses which are commonly found in Christian discourse. As David Pailin has pointed out, linguistic analysis has shown that

> religious statements have metaphysical, empirical, performative, moral, perspectival, attitudinal, and convictional elements, intricately interrelated and expressed by means of myths, symbols, models, metaphors, analogies, stories, parables, historical reports, exclamations of worship and supposedly literal assertions. When the analyses started, those making them may have thought that the task of identifying the nature of religious statements was comparable to that of the chemical analysis of a substance which identifies it as being composed of one or two elements. As they have progressed, however, the analyses have shown that what is to be identified is more like a complex molecule with many constituents and intricate internal bondings.[151]

Nowhere is this variety more concentrated than in a service of public worship, as the following illustrations will show. (Incidentally, the ease with which I can offer examples of Christian discourse which I have some confidence in supposing to be ecumenically understandable should caution any who would suggest that Christian discourse is not sufficiently homogeneous to be capable of general analysis. Certainly no advocate of multifarious 'ordinary language' should hold such a view.)

It would be impossible to comment upon every kind of language that might be used in a Christian service; the following examples are representative only. Let us consider first

A hymn

Were it not for diligent editors, Christians might still be invited to sing, 'Here every bowel of our God / With soft compassion rolls'

(Isaac Watts). To the modern ear this would sound odd, primarily because of the archaism of 'bowel' as here used, and its association with compassion. The following, again by Watts and not currently sung, is odd in a different way:

> He spoke, and straight our hearts and brains
> In all their motions rose;
> 'Let blood,' said he, 'flow round the veins,'
> And round the veins it flows.

This has the oddity of doggerel, and it is difficult not to agree with the distinguished hymnologist who said, 'there is always something solemnly and arrestingly remarkable about a puritan slipping on a banana skin'.[152] But neither the oddity of archaism nor that of doggerel principally concern us. Consider, however, the following stanza, again from Watts:

> Eternal power, whose high abode
> Becomes the grandeur of a God;
> Infinite length beyond the bounds
> Where stars revolve their finite rounds.

Is Watts saying that God lives in a skyscraper? Or that his house is suspended above all other houses? And how does he know enough about God's house to know that it is in keeping with God's grandeur? To frame the questions is to realize how out of place they are – yet, as I recall, back in the 1960s questions of this kind concerning the image of height caused the then bishop of Woolwich no little anguish.[153] He thought that such images made God remote from people, and that they depended upon a three-tier conception of the universe which we moderns have long since outgrown. However, it is by no means certain that people of Old Testament times were as literalistically minded as some would have us suppose, and certainly Watts would have been astounded if anyone in his lifetime (1674–1748) had construed his words as empirical descriptions. He is clearly using images, selected in accordance with his understanding of God's nature, suggestive of authority, dignity and moral loftiness, as distinct from serfdom, slovenliness and moral degradation. The contrast is underlined in a further stanza from the same hymn:

> Lord, what shall earth and ashes do?
> We would adore our maker too;

From sin and dust to Thee we cry,
 The Great, the Holy, and the High.

Here we have the telling conjunction of high and lowly images, but in his concluding stanza Watts realizes that even these are inadequate. What can we say of, or to, God?

God is in heaven, and men below;
 Be short our tunes, our words be few;
A sacred reverence checks our songs,
 And praise sits silent on our tongues.

In his hymn Watts uses a number of models which serve to suggest the otherness of God, and in juxtaposition with these he places images denoting human unworthiness. He then expresses the paradoxical human state of desiring to praise God, yet finds words more or less inadequate to their task. That the last line is a graphic description of the Christian's wondering adoration of God and not a quasi-Wittgensteinian recommendation is clear from the fact that Watts wrote another 453 hymns and paraphrases. As far as the worshipper is concerned, the use of Watts's words is performative. As far as Watts is concerned, he is using language to refer to God, the high and holy One, who nevertheless deigns to come into the midst of humanity with saving intent – as Watts's greatest hymn, 'When I survey the wondrous Cross', makes abundantly clear.

The lection

There may well be more than one Bible reading in the service, but let us suppose that one of them is a parable. I select this form because it constitutes an important type of Christian discourse. A parable is a story or a metaphor which is not literally true, but which is employed to make at least one point, sometimes more than one point. Hence, if someone were to consult a medical textbook with a view to seeing whether Jesus's description of the eye as the lamp of the body[154] is accurate, a failure to grasp the meaning of the parable – indeed, a failure to grasp that the saying was a parable – would be revealed. Again, our service might include the reading of such an extended parable as one of the creation narratives. These are sometimes termed 'myths' – not in the sense of legends which do not purport to deal in truth, but in the technical sense of 'truth-conveying narratives'. But what if the reading concerned the Second Coming of Christ? Is this a myth, or an event expected to occur literally in due course? Philosophers may feel relieved that this is a question which falls largely into the lap of the biblical scholar, but they are entitled to suggest that some methods of interpretation are more unfortunate for logical reasons than others. Consider the assertion of the South African New Testament professor, Dr J. J. Müller: '[A]ccording to the scripture the truth stands undisputed that an actual and visible coming or appearing of Christ on the clouds will take place.'[155] This would seem to be an assertion after the manner of what T. R. Miles called 'simple literal theism'.[156] It is intended literally, and is in principle verifiable by empirical means. That is, if Christ were to appear on the clouds as suggested, we could take steps to ensure that our eyes were not deceiving us, that the figure was actually Christ, and so on. Müller proceeds to inform us that Christ will be everywhere visible in the same instant, though he does not, he says, presume to surmise whether television will aid us in this (though this would explain the delay of the Parousia until the twentieth-first century: perhaps we should now read 'internet' for 'televison'?). Suppose, then, we ask, 'Will the cloud bear the weight of a man?' The literalist might reply either that 'This is to be a divine act and it is not appropriate to ask such mundane questions – God will take care of everything and make it work', or he might claim that the cloud will be a special cloud, or Christ's body a special body, or both. But in either case the original literalism has seriously been qualified, and we are bound to ask whether a genuinely historical event is envisaged at all. As if to repudiate the view of his South African colleague, J. A. T. Robinson wrote of the Second Coming:

> What went wrong was when this picture, this myth, was taken for a literal event, a second advent parallel with the first, lying on the same temporal line, and separated from it by an interval, whose length could be measured, 'if not now, then immediately after the second has happened'.[157]

We thus have one person who, on hearing a passage concerning the Second Coming read in church, would construe it literally; another who would interpret it mythologically. But both may regard the narrative as encompassing a truth-claim concerning God's winding up of history. The more radical Robinson is not necessarily committed to the view that such narratives are simply morality-boosting stories of a Braithwaiteian kind.

A response

At various points in the service performative language may be used. I have already referred to credal statements wherein in saying 'I believe . . . ' the Christian is doing the believing. But this may not be a sufficiently broad way of stating what is happening. N. H. G. Robinson saw this, and the implicit truth-claim, when he wrote:

> When in using the name of God we say 'We acknowledge thee to be the Lord', of course we are *doing* something, of course we are taking a stand; but am I not right in thinking that in doing so we are also coming into line? And coming into line, not with the establishment, but with something like ultimate reality? . . . When Luther said, 'Here I stand, I can do no other' it is possible indeed to try to understand the compulsion as that of self-consistency, but that would be to misunderstand him. It seems plain that it was loyalty to his apprehension of objective truth that was the governing factor.[158]

The sermon

Needless to say, the linguistic analyst is not professionally interested in the principles of homiletics. It suffices to know that the sermon is intended primarily as a declaration of Christian truth, and that it frequently includes the attempt to apply such truth to the lives of the hearers. Any given sermon may include a variety of language uses. There may be historical assertions such as 'Jesus was born in Bethlehem'; analytic or definitive assertions, such as, 'the Church is the body of Christ'; evaluative judgements, exhortations and condemnations; parabolic utterances of the kinds already considered; and assertions which at first sight appear to be empirically grounded, but which turn out upon examination to have a clear transcendent reference. Some such assertions are paradoxical, such as 'Christ is present at his table' (well, if he is, he is and he is not); and 'The life I now live is not my life, but the life which Christ lives in me.'[159] We may hope that our preacher will not fall for the maxim, when in doubt invoke a paradox! But we should not be as eager as some philosophers have been to assume that 'paradox' is synonymous with 'logical contradiction'.[160]

Time and again, when considering the variety of uses of language in the context of Christian worship, we have seen that the ultimate reference of the language is to God as objectively conceived, and the intention from the side of the worshippers is to praise God and adjust themselves in his presence; to make claims about him and his ways which are true; and to respond to his grace in such a way that their relationship with God is renewed, and his image in them restored. As I. M. Crombie said,

> Christian worship is neither a kind of poetry nor a kind of *acesis*, neither a giving vent to feelings of awe and reverence, nor a cultivation of the soul. Fundamentally it is thought of by the Christian as an entry into a relationship with a transcendent being, whom non-Christians do not believe to be there to enter into relationship with. Christian worship, therefore, is not only something which the non-Christian *does* not do, it is something which, by virtue of the difference of his beliefs, the non-Christian *cannot* do . . .[161]

Such considerations may not be overlooked for, as H. J. Paton cautioned,

> a too exclusive concern with language may have its own pitfalls if it leads us to lose sight of what is being talked about – rather like a dog that glues its nose to the end of the walking-stick with which we are trying to point.[162]

Our discussion of some philosophical accounts of language really do suggest that if the objective reference of religious language is prohibited, the claim to truth is banished with it: 'Truth and reference are so intimately interrelated that without one we lack the other. No truth, no reference; no reference, no truth.'[163] In the absence of a truth-claim we can land in a sea of subjective relativistic ideas of the weirdest kind, with no criteria for distinguishing between them. There is no need for this, however, because Christian truth-claims can be tested in ways appropriate to their content. Such testing occurs 'in the interplay between their practical verification and their exposure to historical, literary and philosophical criticism'.[164] What, in more detail, such testing and even justification might entail, and how it might be accomplished, will concern us in Chapter 6.

So far in this chapter we have seen that both logical positivism (whose general attitude lingers on) and 'Wittgensteinianism' turn upon prescriptions which restrict what others than the faithful, and not just Christians alone, may wish to say. Positivists work with a restricted view of 'fact' and seek a method of verification which, though appropriate in some contexts, is not so in all; while Wittgenstein and his heirs, for all their concern with language use, preclude the ontological reference of religious language, and hence the claims to truth, which Christians wish to make. We have found no adequate justifications for these dogmatic principles of exclusion. But it is not merely that two varieties of analytical philosophy can exclude what Christians wish to say; the entire linguistic approach can (though it need not and should not) constitute a principle of exclusion, as the quotation from Paton indicated. For it can seek to repress or extinguish metaphysical questions altogether. Or it can simply ignore them in its preoccupation with analysis, in which case E. L. Mascall's quip concerning the 'Cartesian obsession with clarity and distinctness' applies: 'Like a diet consisting entirely of disinfectants, it may preserve you from poisoning, but only at the expense of starvation.'[165] Less provocative is Michael Foster's remark that philosophical analysis can unfortunately construe 'mystery' either as a lack of knowledge which science may make good, or as a lack of clarity of thought which philosophy can cure.[166] Ironically, though not surprisingly given the transcendent reference of which it frequently disapproves, it can also neglect a use of language prominent in the Christian tradition, namely that of analogy – a device which will occupy us in due course.

IV

First, however, we must consider one more tangle of issues which travels under the label 'postmodernism'.[167] A general caution concerning labelling as such may first be in order. To take an example from outside our immediate field of interest: in the second half of the nineteenth century in England it would not have been difficult to find an Anglo-Catholic priest who was 'conservative' – even positively medieval – liturgically, a 'liberal' higher critic *vis-à-vis* the Bible, and an out and out social 'radical'. To have used any one of these labels as a blanket description of the priest in question would have been to hide more than was revealed. Coming closer to home: I wrote *Philosophical Idealism* in Calgary, from which city the distant Rockies can be seen. They appear two-dimensional and smooth, like an opened-out Christmas cracker crown. But the nearer one goes to them the clearer it becomes that they are three-dimensional, rugged and layered with inner valleys, ravines and the like. So it is with the 'idealists'. They share a family resemblance which, at a distance, may justify the label; but the closer one's inspection of them, the greater the theoretical variety which appears. The postmodern condition (I speak advisedly, for there is no one postmodern theory) encompasses a more disparate number of writers still – so much so that one observer has wondered 'whether the label "postmodernism" really categorizes anything at all. When it is possible to call any number of heterogeneous items "postmodern" – from Madonna to Mark C. Taylor – we may reasonably ask how useful the term is.'[168] Certain it is that we are here dealing with a mood or a tendency rather than with a school or even a group. Moreover, some, notably Jacques Derrida and Michel Foucault, who are frequently regarded as high priests of postmodernism, decline the label.[169]

We may proceed gently by drawing a distinction between 'modernity' and 'modernism' and, analogously, between 'postmodernity' and 'postmodernism'. In my university Modern History began in 1485 (no day specified!) and, while the first few lectures were designed to show that matters were not as straightforward as the course title implied, the Battle of Bosworth Field and the inauguration of the Tudor dynasty were deemed a significant turning point from the medieval to the modern periods – though the 'end' of the Middle Ages is no less problematic a concept than the 'beginning' of modernity. Be that as it may, the modern period is characterized by the Renaissance, the Reformation, the rise of modern science, the epistemological elevation – whether by Cartesians or Lockians – of the self, and the expansion of trade around the world; though there is semantic evidence to suggest that it is only from the Enlightenment onwards (and when did that begin?) that the term 'modern' began to characterize an era, as distinct from marking the boundary between the ancient and the present.[170]

As for 'modernism', this term first gained currency in the realm of the arts, where it characterized a variety of anti-realist-or-representational movements which developed from about 1890 onwards, and eventually encompassed

> atonalism in music, anti-representationalism in art (i.e. abstract art), free verse in poetry, fragmentation and 'stream of consciousness' in the novel, functionalism in architecture (Bauhaus) and the general move away from linear and representational forms and towards the use of

new spatial configurations in the arts (e.g. in the technique known as 'collage').[171]

Motivating much of this activity, and of extra-artistic import too, was the sense of a society on the brink: of war, of the Marxist experiment, of new models in science – in general, of a retreat from the security of older models of rationality and religion to a brave new world in which, in extreme instances, the irrational, or at least ideological relativism, might be lauded. Thus cultural and societal 'modernism' carried the seeds of the postmodern critique of the modernity from which it had itself issued. The term 'post-modern', first used by Frederico de Onis in the context of the arts in the 1930s,[172] came to be applied to the architectural eclecticism of the 1970s, and thence to literature, philosophy and theology. Broadly, it represents a challenge to Enlightenment rationalism as manifested not only in thought, but as fuelling industrialization, technology and those self-validating 'metanarratives', whether scientific, religious, philosophical or political, which have, so it is believed, held so many in captivity. Thus, for example, Jean-François Lyotard writes, 'Simplifying in the extreme, I define *postmodern* as incredulity towards metanarratives.'[173] In contrast to such grand-scale narratives postmodernists elevate the particular, the eclectic and, in denying the distinction between the knower and the known, risk opening (and in some cases actually open) the gates to a subjective relativism which denies that there is any truth other than mine. This general remark requires qualification in respect of such a postmodernist as Lyotard, for example, who had recourse to Wittgenstein and proposed that science is a language game which is pursued not because it affords access to universal truth, but because it has useful practical benefits. There is a pragmatic emphasis here which is recapitulated in the writings of Richard Rorty.[174] It must also be noted that, because of their concern for inter-human relations, many more socially orientated postmodernists – feminists, liberationists and others among them – rightly wish to give a voice to those whom history is said to have passed by, who have been violated by abusive regimes, economic structures and cultural conventions; though the question of how far such attitudes are distinguishable from those of modernism at its best, and how far they presuppose a metanarrative concerning justice and humanity, is not easy to determine.

On the intellectual side, postmodernists make much of their critique of the Enlightenment. If one further autobiographical reference may be made, I would advert to my astonishment when I first attended the annual meeting of the American Academy of Religion. It seemed almost impossible for many of the speakers to proceed without reference to Foucault and Derrida – names scarcely discussed at that time in England and Switzerland, where I had formerly lived. I was sorely tempted to wonder whether, if I were to get into my trench with my tin hat on, the 'postmodernists' would soon go away. The ideas – dare one call it the rhetoric? – seemed to a novice to be discharged not with the precision of artillery fire, but with the wantonness of grapeshot. Moreover, some speakers employed *ad hominem* tactics designed to denigrate philosophers and theologians who were not of the 'true faith', thereby displaying a distastefully sectarian spirit. Most distressing of all were the papers which began with the confident assertion, 'Now that the Enlightenment project is over . . .' Yet no attempt was made to indicate to which Enlightenment reference was being made – the English, the Scottish and the French being significantly different from one another (and the first two much less anticlerical than the last); no Enlightenment texts were rebutted or even reviewed; no criteria were presented in accordance with which one might, *per impossible*, determine that an entire intellectual movement had run into the sand;[175] and such positive benefits of the Enlightenment as the elevation of the individual conscience over untoward authorities, whether biblicist, eccleciastical or political – something to which postmodernists in their other-regarding moments make significant appeal – went unrecorded.[176] Yet again, there seemed little recognition of the fact that during the so-called 'Age of Enlightenment' there was not only philosophical criticism of the epistemology repudiated by postmodernists – by Berkeley and William Law, for example – but also the experimentalism of Methodism and the wildness of a number of charismatic sects. Even so sober and helpful an interpreter of the period as Martin Henry exaggerates when he writes: 'Because of its avowedly anti-Christian slant, the Enlightenment is often considered to be anti-religious . . . The Enlightenment saw itself, rather, for the most part as combating only "revealed" religion.'[177] This description would exclude Locke, often called the father of the Enlightenment's English version, who was by no means hostile to revelation as such.[178] All of which increased my long-standing resolve to distinguish carefully between rationality and rationalism, science and scientism, the experiential and the empirical: matters with which Chapters 6 and 7 will be much concerned.[179]

To many postmodernists, Henri-Louis Bergson is a more remote, Friedrich Nietzsche an omnipresent, inspiration; though it would be a serious mistake to suppose that the postmodernist heirs of these thinkers are clones of them. Far from it: postmodernists tend to spill much ink over what their persuasion amounts to, and by no means all of them agree on the matter.[180] Nevertheless, a number of the earlier writers' themes hover around the offerings of their postmodernist successors. Thus, for example, it is one of the interesting coincidences (some might say ironies) of intellectual history that in 1903, the very year in which G. E. Moore published *Principia Ethica*, that early model of ordinary language analysis, Bergson published his thoughts on metaphysics in the *Revue de Métaphysique et de Morale*. He here proposes that intuition is 'the kind of *intellectual sympathy* by which one places oneself within an object in order to coincide with what is unique in it and consequently inexpressible'.[181] In apparent contradiction of this, he also said in quasi-Moore-like fashion that 'There is nothing in philosophy which could not be said in everyday language.'[182] The solution clearly is that, concerning the deepest things, philosophy can only remain silent. No more than Moore did Bergson have a principled objection to metaphysics as such, but whereas, historically, metaphysicians had concerned themselves largely with Being as rationally apprehended, Bergson fastens upon Becoming as the ultimate reality, to which intuition, as defined above, affords us access. He further explains that intuition is 'instinct that has become disinterested, self-conscious, capable of reflecting upon its object and of enlarging it indefinitely'.[183] The self which thus intuits is not the Cartesian self with its substance over against the Cartesian matter with its substance, but one which encompasses both matter and spirit. While matter and spirit are not absolutely separable, we are at our deepest level spiritual beings, whose particularities of experience and memory cannot literally be conveyed to anyone else. Implicit here is Bergson's important critique of mechanism gone totalitarian. Mechanism, in itself no enemy, must, he felt, be subordinated to the purposes of life. Because of Bergson's insistence upon this theme, one of his

English contemporaries, L. P. Jacks, declared of his writings that 'if they have not led us to the promised Land . . . they have certainly shaken the throne of the Pharaoh who holds us in bondage'.[184] Thus Bergson developed, over against Darwinism, his purposive creative evolutionism, according to which, through the good offices of memory (which has to do with the preservation of the past and not just the conscious recollection of it), the individual has a perception of change throughout life, this change being a product of the vital (but impersonal and hence not equatable with the divine) impulse – the *élan vital*. Indeed, Bergson declared that the 'intuition' of duration was the key to his thought;[185] though another of his contemporaries, the Scot, A. S. Pringle-Pattison, found in the Bergsonian exposition of time and duration 'an ultra-Heraclitean doctrine of universal flux' which would entail 'the discarding of all qualitative distinctions whatsoever', make it impossible to conceive of the past as truly past, and leave us with a doctrine with which 'An unearthly ballet of bloodless categories would be concrete in comparison'.[186] In a stimulating paper Pringle-Pattison's former student, the theologian H. R. Mackintosh, found Bergson in a class of his own where illustrations were concerned: '"Consciousness or supra-consciousness," he writes in a famous sentence, "is the name for the rocket whose extinguished fragments fall back as matter." We admire, even when we ask doubtfully what the picturesque words can mean.'[187] He noted Bergson's optimism, his favouring of intuition above intellectualism, and expressed concern at the general impression conveyed by Bergson's writings that reality is a flux, for this obscures 'the companion and supporting truth that change is significant only by contrast with the permament'.[188] For all that, Bergson's views on the inexpressible, his critique of Cartesian dualism, and his opposition to mechanism became part of the air which many postmodernists breathed.[189]

The influence of Nietzsche is even more pervasive. It emerges in connection with his trenchant critique of Enlightenment rationalism, and his conviction that classical metaphysics is barren and beyond redemption. Indeed, the only world which exists is the phenomenal world – the allegedly 'real' world has been '*lyingly added*'.[190] Consistent with this he holds that religion cannot find a basis in either traditional natural theology or in the desiccated doctrines of deism.[191] But, if he is stoutly opposed to rationalism,

Nietzsche, contrary to what some have imagined, is no enemy of reason as such. On the contrary, we must push reason to its limit – even to the realization that God is dead. Eschewing the temptation to cling to religion – a technique of evasion – or to manufacture palliatives or to install humanity in the place vacated by God as some humanists were doing, we must seek a means of dealing with nihilistic conclusions reached. Amidst the ruins of the old value and belief systems we must reinterpret and re-evaluate, and by such means contribute to the 'enhancement' of life. Such work will draw upon a variety of sources, and will be perspectival in character and naturalistic in direction.[192] If, as we saw, the positivists said that only certain things counted as facts, and we replied that all 'facts' are interpreted facts, Nietzsche declared that there are no facts, only interpretations. We are thus freed from intellectual systems inherited from our culture, and are able to create our own value system (a possibility which Heidegger, among others, eagerly grasped). This 'transvaluation of values' is undertaken on the basis of the universal will to power: that power which characterizes people of integrity, not those who desire to dominate others – which desire is, in fact, characteristic of those who are weak and frustrated by their ineptitude. Against this Nietzschean background it seems to transpire that while some who, though sympathetic to some aspects of postmodernism, are dismayed to the point of the apocalyptic by certain features of postmodernity – 'We are on the edge of an abyss'[193] – others, like Don Cupitt, are jolly to the point of ecstasy: 'Your God is only your faith in him, your values are only your commitment to them. That is liberation,' he trills: 'You're free.'[194]

There is much in the works of Nietzsche which is tantalizingly ambivalent. At times he professes a devotion to truth, at others his naturalism forbids this and, though there is hazard in the declaration, it is the latter which more accurately suggests the conclusion to which the main thrust of his position tends. This has greatly perplexed many non-postmodernist comentators on his writings. Thus from an earlier period Pringle-Pattison writes:

> there can be no conclusion, no argument at all, where there is no standard of truth. In such a case one man's word is as good as another's, and Nietzsche becomes the victim of the same dilemma which Plato pressed upon Protagoras: If we are to argue at all, he must admit that the opinion of those who think him false is just as true as the thesis he

> himself defends . . . Nietzsche's . . . theory of knowledge, with its denial of any objective standard, and its substitution of the beneficial for the true, is anticipated almost verbally in the Protagoreanism which is combated in the *Theatetus*.[195]

Similar concerns have been raised in our own time by Hugo Meynell, among others:

> There is a curious ambiguity in Nietzsche's epistemological doctrines and assumptions. Often he seems to be exhorting his readers to insist on truth, and on the human authenticity which will be content with nothing less . . . But on other occasions, he appears to be claiming that 'truth' itself is nothing but a falsifying imposition of our subjective theoretical assumptions on a recalcitrant reality, which is terrifying and chaotic rather than orderly, manageable and domesticated, and in constant flux as opposed to stable and enduring.[196]

Traces of this ambiguity may be found in a number of Nietzsche's postmodernist successors. In Meynell's own view, if we seek human authenticity we must be attentive to data presented to us in sensation and feeling; we must intelligently question those data; we must reasonably affirm provisionally the explanation best supported by the data; and having reached our value judgement in the matter we must act responsibly in the light of it. To anyone who might query the principles on which such a procedure is founded, Meynell replies (as if echoing Pringle-Pattison), 'The principles which I have sketched need no further foundation; they establish themselves by virtue of the fact that any attempt to argue against them is self-defeating.'[197]

With such remarks in mind, warning us that Christian discourse which posits a correspondence between utterance and reality will come under increasing attack, we must take a further step towards fully flowering postmodernism. A significant signpost on the way is the structuralist Ferdinand de Saussure's posthumous *Course in General Linguistics* (1916). The underlying idea is that language use presupposes abstract linguistic potentialities. To put it otherwise, language (*langue*) is a structured system designed for social use, while *parole* designates an individual's use of shared linguistic structures in particular contexts. To Saussure, the linguistic system comprises words – 'signs' – which have sound and signification; but (and this is crucial from our point of view) that which is signified by 'signs' is not an objective entity, but the concept articulated by the 'sign'. Different languages have their own ways of distinguishing between one term and another, and hence in every case meaning is determined by reference to the language system being used. It is as if linguistic structures have taken on the role of the external forces of older materialisms.

In all of this there appears to be yet another barrier imposed between the structured language and the real world to which, as has often been thought, language refers. The problem of reference is similarly raised in the writings of Jacques Lacan, for example, where it is enmeshed in a psychoanalytic theory which I am not competent to judge, but before which I am, to put it mildly, given pause by the stong reaction of Raymond Tallis, who has described Lacan in general terms as 'one of the fattest spiders at the heart of the web of muddled not-quite-thinkable-thoughts and evidence-free assertions of limitless scope, which practitioners of theorhea have woven into their version of the humanities'; and, more particularly, as a philosophical fraud and a psychoanalytical charlatan.[198] As to language, Lacan regards it as a social construct which has no literal objective reference or meaning, but which has its roots in the speaker's unconscious. The not unchallenged allegation that from Aristotle to Locke words are signs of the mental states of those who use them is problematic enough, but to regard them as signs of unconscious states invites a double impenetrability. A prominent implication of Lacan's position is that we cannot but be suspicious of the claims of scientists and others to impartiality and objectivity, for really their use of language cloaks an unworthy 'will to power' – shades of Nietzsche. But if words only refer to other words, all speech is metaphorical, and the situation is underlined that our language does not and cannot refer to reality – a circumstance which has called forth this pertinent observation from Eric Matthews: Lacan 'cannot give his account of the distinctive features of the unconscious, as a use of language to conceal what people are really feeling, without presupposing a use of language to express feelings and thoughts directly'.[199]

There followed the poststructuralists, whose general position briefly stated is that linguistic meanings are ever changing (Heraclitus and Bergson come to mind once more). These changes are owing to contextual diversity. It is impossible to put a stop to reinterpretations, and hence 'meaning' is for ever 'deferred'. There is no independent reality other than the 'text', and by this is meant that there is nothing which is not 'text'.[200] This move leads us towards the deconstructionists: indeed the point just made is almost a quotation from Derrida: 'there is nothing outside of the text' (there is no outside-text; *il n'y a pas de hors-texte*).[201] The general drift of the deconstructionists is that their structuralist forebears were misguided in positing a system of language. There is no such system. There is diversity, divergence, change, flux. We are thus led towards the view that there are many possible perspectives in our intellectually pluralist world and, in some writers, to a subjective relativist theory of truth.

Quite apart from the fact that he is still productive, it is not easy to place Derrida in all of this. He cannot be aligned with those who wish absolutely to repudiate the Enlightenment (hence his repudiation of the label 'postmodernist'), for, while he does not think that the Enlightenment's goal of clear and distinct ideas is attainable, he nevertheless works within the tradition to reform it. Indeed, he cannot do otherwise for, referring to the 'logocentricity' of the Enlightenment, he says, 'it is not a question of "rejecting" these notions; they are necessary and, at least at present, nothing is conceivable for us without them'.[202] To all intents and purposes deconstruction is a never-ending pursuit, and its practitioners cannot proceed without that which requires to be deconstructed.[203]

More particularly, Derrida takes issue with the place which Saussure accords to the signifier on the ground that this legitimates an unwarrantable transcendentalism. Further, where Saussure proposed that meanings are determined by differences between words within a given language system, Derrida coins the term *différance* which signifies both difference and deferral (of meaning), thereby correcting Saussure and opposing the tradition's metaphysics of presence – by which he means the Enlightenment quest of a sure foundation for knowledge. Thus in interpreting a text – and when thinking of literary texts Derrida draws no distinction between philosophical texts and texts of other kinds – an unlimited variety of results is possible. This does not mean, however, that the overt meaning of a text is to be overlooked as being of no consequence; rather, it is to be surpassed: 'to pass from an obvious to a latent language, one must first be rigorously sure of the obvious meaning'.[204] For all his desire to correct Saussure, however, Derrida on occasion agrees with his predecessor in thinking that language is non-externally referential, as it were. Meanings are given by the relations of words within a language; but there are so many such relations that we can never pronounce with finality that a particular expression means *this*.[205] What we can affirm, to repeat, is that language as a self-referential system of signs has no extra-linguistic reference.[206] On the other hand, Derrida has denounced those who understand his approach as entailing 'a suspicion of reference. Deconstruction is always concerned with the "other" of language'; and while the 'other' may not be 'a "referent" in the normal sense which linguists have attached to the term', it does not follow that 'there is *nothing* beyond language'.[207] One does wonder, however, how Derrida's apparently contradictory assertions are to be harmonized, not to mention the question of what, on his terms, the extra-linguistic 'other' might be.

However it may finally turn out to be with Derrida himself, the underlying epistemological presupposition of deconstruction as widely perceived and practised is that we have no means of stepping outside of the confines of our thought and language with a view to obtaining knowledge of anything allegedly existing independently of them. Hence Hugo Meynell's trenchant declaration: 'deconstruction is intrinsically and comprehensively subversive, fundamentally opposed to reason or God, destructive of any basis for objectivity outside the self, and undermining of the capacity of language to refer to anything'.[208] Elsewhere, with a little less huffing and puffing, he avers:

> It is self-destructive to deny that we are capable of coming to true or well-founded judgments; reality is nothing other than what true judgments are about and well-founded judgments tend to be about. So the language, and for that matter the writing, in which we express our judgments is after all in principle capable of describing reality.[209]

Derrida, he continues, fails to see 'the self-destructive nature of the claim that we cannot make well-grounded judgments of fact or value'.[210] As if rising to Derrida's defence, and with reference to Rorty as well, James Olthuis explains that

> Neither thinker believes that we make the world by describing it, although both thinkers believe that it is fair to say that we do not have a world apart from our descriptions. This distinction is crucial. Both thinkers mean to assess the impact that the linguistic, historical, and

> cultural contingency of our various descriptions has on our understanding of the world.[211]

But, on the terms of these authors, what is it that we describe? Of what have we an understanding? In the absence of objective reference the answer is not clear. There is at least incipient relativism here, and when relativism becomes full-blown it does, as Colin Gunton has written, imply 'an imperious claim for its own truth which is viciously intolerant because it is undiscussable in the terms of the ideology in which it is propounded'.[212]

Richard Rorty, to whom reference has already been made, is one who bestrides the postmodern–modern divide – or, perhaps, in deference to the actualities of transmission and time lags in the history of ideas, I should say that he is a debtor to trends relatively ancient and vociferously current. For while he has imbibed postmodernist notions concerning the reading of texts and the non-privileging of philosophical texts, his pragmatism reveals him as a debtor to Peirce and Dewey,[213] and his recourse to language games marks him as a qualified heir of Wittgenstein. Thus he writes that the pragmatist 'wants solidarity to be our *only* comfort, and to be seen not to require metaphysical support'.[214] But for our present purpose his most troubling claim is that 'there is no way to get outside our beliefs and our language so as to find some test other than coherence'.[215] These words will echo in our ears to the end of this section.

George Lindbeck, too, has learned from postmodernism and Wittgenstein, while from Rorty he receives the idea that language games are meaningful within particular cultural-linguistic frameworks. To Lindbeck doctrines are rules which govern the game played within a particular form of life. Christianity derives its identity from the following rules, though these are not the sum total of Christian rules:

> First, there is the monotheistic principle . . . Second, there is the principle of historical specificity: the stories of Jesus refer to a genuine human being who was born, lived and died in a particular time and place. Third, there is the principle of what may be infelicitously called Christological maximalism: every possible importance is to be ascribed to Jesus that is not inconsistent with the first rules.[216]

He denies that Christian doctrines are cognitive, that they are grounded in an experience which is then articulated, and that they are partially one and partially the other.[217] Such doctrines do not make objective truth-claims; they are second-order rules which govern religious practice: 'communally authoritative rules of discourse, attitude, and action'.[218] Christianity is meaningful as it is practised; there is no need to resort to the kind of foundation which would purportedly render the faith meaningful by showing its rootedness in a supposed fundamental meaning structure. As we steep ourselves in the authoritative texts of a community, and as they become our interpretative framework, we find that there is no more real world than the ones they create.[219]

At first glance this would seem to preclude a revelation from 'beyond', and to suggest mutually supportive psycho-pragmatism. But at this point Lindbeck is puzzling. He suggests that theology, as second-order discourse, makes no cognitive claims, but first-order religious language may well do so. He says that the cultural-linguistic approach does not entail the rejection or acceptance of 'epistemological realism and correspondence theory of truth'.[220] This is because theology and doctrine do not make true or false assertions about God and his relations to ourselves, they merely speak about such assertions.[221] But as practised, true religion, when utilized as a way corresponding to ultimate reality, is 'ontologically (and "propositionally") true'.[222] No doubt the fault is in myself, but at this point I am lost. A coherence theory of truth deemed to work within a language game is a graspable idea; to use religion as a way corresponding to ultimate reality so that propositional truth may be articulated is a confusing prospect indeed. What is the analysis of 'use'? How does one use religion so as to correspond to ultimate reality – and what is that? And what is the relation between such ontology and the articulation of true propositions? Lindbeck writes, 'Doctrines regulate truth claims by excluding some and permitting others, but the logic of their communally authoritative use hinders or prevents them from specifying positively what is affirmed.'[223] How and why does their logic thus hinder or prevent? And, since doctrines are entertained by people, how can believers exclude or permit truth-claims without presupposing that which is to be positively affirmed? But, again, I may have misunderstood Lindbeck. What seems generally clear, however, is that Lindbeck's postliberalism is anti-foundational, communitarian and structured around the historic Christ event. It does not deny that there is a revelation from 'without', but it appears to tie it exclusively to the Christian community in such a way as to prompt fears of the intellectual 'ghetto' on the part of some.[224]

My concern has been the limited one of attempting to understand the bearing of postmodernist views on the reference of language. Since the phenomenon under investigation is multifaceted, and some of its positions elusive, it is difficult to reach reliable general conclusions. The reminder that we do not have a God's eye view, and are not even Cartesian ponderers fully self-conscious,[225] or 'uncontaminated' Kantian agents, and that in interpreting any text we inevitably bring ourselves with all our perspectival advantages, limitations and baggage to the task is well taken; and, moreover, it is a point on which heirs of philosophers as various as Wittgenstein, Heidegger, MacIntyre and Derrida are in accord. But if interpersonal communication is to be achieved, and something resembling interpretative anarchy is to be avoided, Donald MacKinnon's distinction between 'the kind of invention which makes discovery possible' and 'the kind of invention which simply finds its end in the entertainment, both of the inventor, and the recipients of his invention'[226] must be heeded. The distinction is drawn upon the basis of our inability 'to dispense with concern with the factuality of any world with which we have to do'.[227] With more particular reference to Christianity he declares that, 'however complex, diverse and rich the world of Christian language, that language in the end draws its point from the belief that some things [concerning Christ] are the case'.[228]

It is this underlying consideration of truth as correspondence with reality which fundamentally challenges the drift of much postmodern thought (and we shall explore this idea further in the following chapters). Rorty denies such correspondence, despite his rejection of the relativist notion that one claim is as good as any other, and his belief that, in the absence of neutral standards of objectivity, persuading others that such and such is the best policy is the most that is potentially achievable, and that if such persuasion fails then no articulation of a metanarrative would make any difference.[229] Positively, his view is that 'true' is merely a word used to commend 'beliefs which he or she finds good to believe'.[230] But this seems to place us on a very slippery slope, and it calls to mind Lyotard's rejection of metanarratives in favour of self-accrediting particular narratives. Along this line there is no basis for choosing between the most sublime and the most degrading views of humanity – with all their respective possible practical outcomes ranging from respect, nurture and care to Nazi-like obliteration: there are no defensible moral sanctions. To put it crudely, if we all make it up as we go along, some of us will not make it – a possibility which makes the following utterance of Rorty, in which he specifies the ideological link between Dewey, Foucault, James and Nietzsche, sound utterly chilling:

> There is nothing deep down inside us except what we have put there ourselves, no criterion that we have not created in the course of creating a practice, no standard of rationality that is not an appeal to such a criterion, no rigorous argumentation that is not an obedience to our own conventions.[231]

An enormous gulf is fixed between this doctrine and that of the *imago dei*;[232] indeed, the language used undercuts the entire Christian doctrine of creation.

Against the position just described we may set that of Anthony Quinton who, however much some may misunderstand his propensity for teasing postmodernists as indicating that he is 'not serious', has nevertheless clearly set down the universally available and familiar sources of validation to which analytic philosophers (and not only they) appeal:

> They are three in number: our common capacity to understand, and to some extent to define, the meaning or meanings of our words; our common capacity to judge the validity of trains of reasoning and to acquire an understanding of the implicit principles involved as set out in logic; and our common agreement as to the obvious truth of some matters of fact. None of these need be taken as fixed or final. Our grasp of meaning is always improvable. Our intuitive judgements of logical consequence and consistency are corrigible and our logical systems often caricature or oversimplify the implicit rules of our thinking. What we all agree to be obviously true may be vulnerable to criticism. But by setting out our arguments as clearly as possible and with as much logical explicitness as possible, and by exposing them to the criticism of others and acknowledging an obligation to respond to those criticisms by something other than an indeterminate claim to have been misunderstood, we may hope to take part fruitfully in what Samuel Johnson called 'the common pursuit of true judgement'.[233]

This policy statement together with the stated qualifications seem not only eminently reasonable but necessary if intellectual activity is happily to proceed. Not a few postmodernist writers, for all their contrary presuppositions, give grounds for the suspicion that at least some of the time they endorse it themselves.

VI

In this chapter I have sought to evaluate three prominent intellectual tendencies – loosely characterized as logical positivist, Wittgensteinian and postmodernist – all of which place road blocks against Christian linguistic usage, and which if heeded would inhibit Christian confession. The logical positivists brand Christian assertions as literally nonsense; the Wittgensteinians and the postmodernists, while allowing their use, query their objective reference, and Derrida denies that language is used to make assertions which are true or false. I have brought out the way in which these challenges are posed so that it becomes clear that each has a doctrine of meaning, use or reference which rules out or reduces Christian claims. In discussing these positions I have suggested that there are other ways of construing facticity than the positivist; other usages intended by Christians than those prescribed by some of the Wittgensteinians; and that the postmodernist repudiation of epistemological realism is self-defeating. The conclusions are negative; but the first thing to do with road blocks is to remove them, or to skirt around them. Christian confessors need to be encouraged to think that their progress is not finally arrested by any of these. It is a further question whether there are any good grounds for the Christian claims, and we shall turn to this question in Chapters 6 and 7. But the priority was to address those who would rule out the Christian claims *ab initio*, or who wish to prescribe the meanings open to Christians, or deny the objective reference of Christian discourse altogether. It needs to be made clear that all such policies rest upon doctrines to which we are not obliged to subscribe, above all because where the Christian confession is concerned they are, to reiterate the homely image, all attempts to pick up soup on a fork.

Intriguingly, some postmodernist authors hint that they understand this well. Emanuel Lévinas, for example, who acknowledges the influence of Bergson upon his thought and regards Bergson as the one who prepared the soil for the reception of Heidegger's phenomenology in France,[234] articulates an ethical basis for his thought which is rooted in the fact of the Other who is over against me in such a way that 'the ethical relationship which subtends discourse is not a species of consciousness whose ray emanates from the I; it puts the I in question. This putting in question emanates from the other.'[235] While the posited otherness is in the first instance concerned with other human beings, it does seem that behind it lies an absolute Other which is beyond, or 'otherwise than Being'.[236] Lévinas has no qualms about identifying this absolute Other with the God of Judaism and Christianity, and he regards his approach as preferable to older ontological religious metaphysics, which sought to comprehend God and hence, by attempting the impossible, became 'atheistic'. Derrida likewise, influenced by Lévinas, and unflattered by suggestions that he advocates a negative theology (despite the fact that he himself drew the analogy in *Différance* in 1968), nevertheless makes many references to the Other, the sacred.[237] And Wittgenstein mused, 'It strikes me that a religious belief could only be something like a passionate commitment to a system of reference.'[238] Admittedly such glimpses of a transcendent other are not universally to be found in postmodernist writers – still less in one like Rorty, whose postmodernism is blended with a down-to-earth pragmatism, and whose recourse to language games has been challenged on the ground that

> subjects have the ability to make sense, to disclose the world in new ways, not just to play language games. Even in 'argument' there can never be certainty that playing a language game from one subject's perspective is the same as playing it from another's. The fact is that contemporary philosophy needs better conceptions of the subject, not as the mirror of a ready-made world, but as the locus of world-disclosure and meaning-transformation.[239]

But, from the point of view of Christian confession, this returns us to the idea of the *imago dei*, and of the fact of the approach of the divine, supremely in Christ. Since this approach is that of the creator who roots himself in this world, we are led next to a consideration of transcendence, immanence and history. We shall not leave issues concerning language entirely behind; on the contrary, the question of how one speaks of such a being is inextricably interwoven with the themes proposed for consideration. As I. M. Crombie wrote,

> Christ . . . is the word of God to us; both the evidence of the reality of God, and also the declaration of Him to us. Being the declaration of a mystery He is to be taken both as comprehensible (or it would not be a declaration) and as incomprehensible (or it would not be a mystery); that is, as the visible, tangible, intelligible image of what stands outside our comprehension.[240]

5

Transcendence, Immanence and History

At the heart of the Christian confession is the announcement that in Christ, and supremely in the Cross–resurrection event, God has acted once for all for the redemption of the world. As widely, though not universally construed, this claim turns upon an understanding of the eternal God as at once transcendent and immanent, and as capable of, and as actually, working in the midst of human history. It is further presupposed that there are adequate ways of speaking of this. My task in this chapter is to discuss the terms 'transcendence' and 'immanence' in relation to their history in Western thought, so that I can show how they become 'rebaptized' in Christian usage. This will entail a consideration of the further terms 'natural' and 'supernatural', and will lead us into some reflections on history.

The question of transcendence and immanence is unusually complicated both because of the way in which philosophical and theological considerations have become entwined in the course of Christian history, and because of the multifarious factors which have caused one or other of the terms to be emphasized at different times. Certainly there is no way of compartmentalizing the investigation in such a way as to allow us to say 'This is their philosophical, this their theological history'. Equally, when responding to such a claim as that during the past half-century there has been a 'loss of transcendence' in Western theology, we cannot say that the proposition is entirely clear; or that, insofar as we have an inkling of its meaning, it is wholly accurate, for time lags both complicate the history of thought and greatly add to its interest.

As we proceed we shall do well to have some cautions in mind, and these I spell out quite bluntly:

- If transcendence is not qualified by immanence, deism (as popularly conceived[1]) will loom before us.
- If immanence is not qualified by transcendence, pantheism, or at least pantheizing tendencies, will be a likely consequence.
- If transcendence is not qualified by the supernatural, the way will open to naturalism, agnosticism and atheism.
- If the supernatural is not qualified by immanence, a fantastic outcome may result.
- If we do not distinguish between epistemological and metaphysical transcendence we shall become needlessly confused.
- If we do not view transcendence and the supernatural in relation to the Incarnation, we may be tempted to rest in a philosophy of being rather than a theology of grace, thereby making it difficult to conceive of God's acting redemptively (or even at all) in history.
- In the entire discussion the Creator–creature distinction (not absolute disjunction) must be maintained: a distinction which is, at its root, ethical. We are concerned with the transcendence of immanent, holy, active love.

I

'Transcendent' and 'transcendental' are terms which, during the course of intellectual history, have had a number of homes, some of which scarcely seem to occupy the same planet, let alone the same street. There is a great gulf fixed between, for example, the being of the Schoolmen, Kant's epistemological transcendentalism, and the Romantic transcendentalism of Emerson, Theodore Parker and others. In attempting to untangle some of the threads of discussion we may profitably begin with Aristotle, though I shall in due course introduce Plato also.

As is well known, Aristotle's investigation of predicates, which he understands to be existing entities, prompts his account of the categories. There are, he says, ten 'classes of predicates', or categories: 'Essence, Quantity, Quality, Relation, Place, Time, Position,

State, Activity, Passivity', and 'the accident and genus and property and definition of anything will always be in one of these categories'.[2] Encouraged not least by the way in which Aristotle related unity and being: 'there are many senses in which a thing is said to be, but all refer to one starting-point',[3] many medieval Schoolmen elevated what they regarded as the transcendentals above all logical categories. Among the transcendentals being is supreme, and others in the (varied) lists include the one, the true and the good.[4] Philip the Chancellor argued that such realities are common to all being, and Alexander of Hales, Bonaventure, Albertus Magnus and Aquinas were all influenced by him on this point.[5] Aquinas's list of transcendentals comprises reality, being, truth, goodness, specific character and unity. Because these are shared, after their manner, by God and human beings we may attain knowledge of God by analogy. In Aquinas and other writers, however, the idea of transcendence is qualified by that of immanence. This note may also be found in Aristotle, however hard it may be to square with his teaching concerning the unmoved Mover. He writes:

> life . . . belongs to God; for the actuality of thought is life, and God is that actuality; and God's self-dependent actuality is life most good and eternal. We say therefore that God is a living being, eternal, most good, so that life and duration continuous and eternal belong to God; for this *is* God.[6]

For his part Aquinas holds that God, as absolute being, alone has independent existence; he is immanent in all creation, which is an expression of his will: 'God is in all things, not, indeed, as part of their essence, nor as an accident, but as an agent present to that upon which it acts.'[7]

With Aristotle's reference to the ethical quality of the divine we may return to the other classical root of Christian talk about transcendence: the Platonic. To a greater degree than Aristotle, Plato gives the good precedence over being as such. The idea of the good is supreme over all other ideas or forms. These ideas are real, though they do not occupy space or time, and we cannot experience them directly. We may, however, discern the presence and 'images' of such forms as 'temperance, courage, liberality, high-mindedness' – and their opposites.[8] But

> This, then, which gives to the objects of knowledge their truth and to him who knows them his power of knowing, is the Form or essential nature of Goodness . . . [The objects of knowledge] derive from the Good not only their power of being known, but their very being and reality; and Goodness is not the same thing as being, but even beyond being, surpassing it in dignity and power.[9]

As he goes on to explain, the Good reigns 'over the domain of all that is intelligible'.[10]

If these transcendent forms are integral to Plato's metaphysics, he is not without a notion of immanence. Thus, for example, certain inter-textual oscillations notwithstanding, he thinks in terms of a world soul,[11] and he rebukes Anaxagoras for understanding Mind as being remote from the world and human activity. In explaining human activity 'the man made no use of Mind, nor gave it any responsibility for the management of things, but mentioned as causes air and ether and water and many other strange things'.[12]

Like the Aristotelian, the Platonic legacy to Christian thought is extremely diverse in character. We have Plotinus, staunch opponent of Stoic materialism,[13] and pioneer of Neoplatonism, a major intellectual objective of which was to unite Plato's forms with the doctrine of God and the soul. Practically, the goal was mystical union with the One, this to be achieved by contemplation and ascetic practices leading to a joyous ecstasy from which intellectual and sensory influences were excluded. For all their pantheistic tendencies, and notwithstanding the variegated arrangements of triadic emanations in which some of them delighted, the Plotinian One is ever *in situ*, so to speak. Indeed, as Dom Placid Spearritt has said, 'The priority of the One over the many can fairly be called the keystone of Neoplatonism.'[14]

Influenced by prevailing Platonism, Augustine understood the transcendentals to reside in the divine mind, but he was equally open to immanentist doctrine. Not for him a God who, having created the world, withdrew from it. On the contrary, he presents a lengthy list of God's creative activities and declares:

> these things the one true God makes and does, but as *the same* God, – that is, as He who is wholly everywhere, included in no space, bounded by no chains, mutable in no part of His being, filling heaven and earth with omnipresent power, not with a needy nature. Therefore He

> governs all things in such a manner as to allow them to perform and exercise their own proper movements. For although they can be nothing without Him, they are not what He is.[15]

Here we see that, if Augustine eschews 'deism', he also repudiates any immanentism which would deny or attempt to obliterate the Creator–creature distinction.

By the time of Proclus, Neoplatonism's systematizer *par excellence*, Christianity had become the official religion, and those Neoplatonic ideas which were serviceable – or at least sufficiently disguisable (in which connection Proclus's elaborate mediatorial pantheon comes to mind as being a particularly bold departure from the Bible) – had been so pressed into Christian service that the school had little more to offer. It degenerated into formal scholasticism under Marinus, Isidorus, Hegian, Zenodotus and Damascius. Eventually, in 529, Justinian closed it down in the interests of orthodoxy. H. W. Clark's epitaph is chilling enough: 'The system, having begun by keeping open mind for anything and everything that could by any possibility be crammed in, had finished by turning the said mind into a rag-bag of miscellaneous scraps.'[16]

By now, however, the Pseudo-Dionysius had reworked the teaching of Proclus in such a way as to maintain that the highest knowledge we have of God is that afforded to us by mystical ignorance. God is beyond all predicates, whether negative or positive. He is the One. He is the self-contained simple essence about whom we can know nothing. (Proclus, we recall, had allowed that we might know God via contemplation and the performance of ascetic practices.) Nevertheless, God must be spoken of, and the Bible encourages us to speak of him. How can we do this? Suppose that we wish to say that God is good (affirmative theology). At once the realization strikes us that God far surpasses anything we could mean by 'good'. Accordingly, after the example of Proclus, we must deny him that name – thereby engaging in negative theology. We thus come to see that we know God best by accepting that we do not know him, and by the practice of superlative theology we are led to understand him as 'supergoodness'. Our difficulties of utterance notwithstanding, the human soul is ever united with God.

However it may be with God, the Pseudo-Dionysius is not inhibited from providing an account of the nine choirs of angels, divided into three orders to correspond with the terrestrial hierarchy of bishops, priests and deacons, whose role, like that of the sacraments, is to advance the work of humanity's deification. The ways of purgation, illumination and union are stages in this process.[17] All of which proved stimulating to mystical Germans like Eckhart and Tauler, Englishmen like Richard Rolle, and the Spaniards Theresa of Avila and John of the Cross.

The Pseudo-Dionysius speaks much of redemption, but his Christ is not so much one who atones by a historical Cross as one who, emanating as he does from the super-essential One, is competent to point others to his, and their, source. Moreover, 'the plainest article of divinity, namely the Incarnation and Birth of Jesus in Human Form, cannot be expressed by any Language or known by any Mind'.[18] This is all of a piece with the author's refusal to accept evil as properly *being* at all; so that, as we saw, even his sympathetic commentator, C. E. Rolt, whilst acknowledging the Pseudo-Dionysius's desire to yield no ground to the Manichaean dualists of his day, feels compelled to say:

> It is, however, this ugliness of things that Dionysius fails to emphasize, and herein lies the great weakness in his teaching . . . The fault of Dionysius is the natural failure of his mental type to grasp the mere facts of the actual world as mere facts.[19]

It must be emphasized that to the Pseudo-Dionysius the conviction that God far surpasses anything we can think or say is a properly rational one: not for him the uncharted sea of chance or emotion. Nor should we forget that Augustine also was properly aware of the necessity of a certain Christian agnosticism which recognizes that if we can fully comprehend something then the object of our comprehension cannot be God.[20] Even so Copleston was not wide of the mark when he pronounced this verdict: 'The Pseudo-Dionysius meant to . . . express Christian theology and Christian mysticism in a neo-Platonic philosophical framework and scheme; but it can scarcely be gainsaid that, when a clash occurred, the neo-Platonic elements tended to prevail.'[21] If a final illustration were needed, we might instance the Pseudo-Dionysius's efforts to maintain, with Augustine and Boethius, the Creator–creature distinction, while under the emanational, and generally victorious, pull of Proclus:

> Now we must proceed to the Name of 'Being' which is truly applied by the Divine Science to Him that truly Is. But this we must say, that it is not the purpose of our discourse to reveal the Super-Essential Being in its Super-Essential Nature . . . but only to celebrate the Emanation of the Absolute Divine Essence into the universe of things . . . [22]

Among those who were indebted to the Pseudo-Dionysius was Maximus the Confessor, and he in turn was the source of some of the Platonic elements which John of Damascus incorporated into his predominantly Aristotelian philosophy along with a good deal of the Pseudo-Dionysius's angelology. But by far the most significant impact of the Pseudo-Dionysius was upon John Scottus Eriugena. Seldom can an accomplished linguist have been given a more congenial task than was Eriugena, when Charles the Bald asked him to translate the work of the Pseudo-Dionysius. In addition to his translations he wrote a commentary of the same author's *Celestial Hierarchy* and, for good measure, on the *Ambigua* of Maximus and the *De hominis opifco* of Gregory of Nyssa.

Eriugena thinks in the categories of both transcendence and immanence, though the latter takes precedence. On the one hand he suggests that God is so exalted that he cannot even know himself, for if he did, he would be defined, and hence limited, which he cannot be.[23] On the other hand, he believes that God knows himself in creating. His greatest work is his *De divisione naturae*, in which he presents a fourfold categorization of nature – understanding by 'nature' all that can be thought about, including God. There is first God qua nature which created the world, but is not itself created. Secondly, there are the (Platonic) ideas which are created and which themselves create.[24] Thirdly, there are the sensible objects around us which are created, but which do not themselves create. Finally, there is nature, which neither creates nor is created; this, again, is God. In a word, God is the alpha and the omega of Eriugena's system: the One from whom all things proceed and to whom they all return. Eriugena summarized his position thus: 'When we hear that God made all things, we ought to understand by it nothing else than that God is in all things, that is, subsists as the essence of all things.'[25]

To some it appeared that Eriugena had tumbled headlong into pantheism, and for this he was condemned at Paris in 1210, and again by Honorius III at Sens in 1225. But, as in all works influenced by Neoplatonism, the One is ever there; and since Eriugena's intentions were biblicist (his highly allegorical hermeneutic notwithstanding) and honest, we may fairly speak only of pantheizing tendencies. What has not always been so readily appreciated is that, as well as being a debtor to Neoplatonism, Eriugena was a harbinger from within the Dark Ages of that Renaissance humanism which found its ultimate ground of truth where he did: in the human soul. On the other hand, there is a deterministic inevitability (which looks forwards in some respects to Spinoza) in Eriugena's plan of salvation which would not appeal to later humanists who elevated human beings as arbiters of their fate.

The changes continued to be rung throughout the Middle Ages. For all his indebtedness to the Pseudo-Dionysius, Bonaventure had recourse to Aristotle against the Neoplatonic conception of God as an abstract unity, and this protest greatly influenced the way in which he couched his doctrine of the Trinity. For his part Ulrich of Strasbourg reorganized the Aristotelian categories in such a way as to deprive being of its pre-eminent place. He promoted goodness to that position, with light, beauty and love following in succession.[26] There is also an interesting transcendence–immanence bifurcation between Eckhart and Duns Scotus, with the former at times embracing a mysticism which brings God so close to human beings that they are almost indistinguishable, and Duns, in the interests of maintaining his ethical voluntarism, placing God at an extreme remove from the world.

Thus far we have encountered a metaphysic of being, construed as ontologically distinct from ourselves and, by Christian writers, identified with God. Accompanying this, in greater or lesser degrees, is the epistemological claim that we can know nothing of God – so highly exalted is he above all our thoughts and words. We have also witnessed an immanentist tendency, veering in some writers towards pantheism; and, to a lesser degree, some appreciation of the transcendent construed in ethical terms as the good. This last theme comes into greater prominence following the Reformation, and especially in connection with the doctrine of humanity. God is perfect in holiness, and while we owe our dignity to our creation in his image we are, ethically, by reason of our sin – with acknowledgements to the Puritans and apologies to a most useful species within the created order – worms.

II

By now the potent seeds of human autonomy had been sown which in their own way threatened received ideas of transcendence. To many God became practically (if not in most writers, theoretically) redundant. It is perhaps not too great an exaggeration to say that the self-exaltation of allegedly autonomous humanity and the attack upon the transcendence of God supernaturally conceived are frequently two sides of the same coin. I say 'frequently' rather than 'universally' because there are those who have forsaken belief in a transcendent, supernatural deity, and who have also come to despair of humanity in its angst-ridden condition. The roots of the tendency go a long way back and may involve the human being's desire to be autonomous in thought, self-sufficient in life, competent to achieve salvation – or any combination of these. Thus, for example, Aquinas's view that the human will is fallen but the human intellect is not, came to be associated with the medieval dichotomy between natural and revealed knowledge, reason and faith. It was then only a matter of time before reason was exploited by some in an intellectual environment in which faith had for many become redundant. That environment was the post-Renaissance one in which those in the van of intellectual endeavour were flexing their epistemological muscles and feeling that, with scientific advance, geographical discovery and the like, the world was their oyster. Naturalists employed presuppositions which ruled God out of the natural order, and the Reformation thrust, so influential upon some scientists to this day, which saw science as explicating *God's* handiwork was never entirely victorious. In this connection it is not without significance that Galileo was more concerned with mechanics than with causal explanation: 'Teleological explanation, characteristic of earlier thought, had given way to descriptive *explanation*',[27] and all of this explaining was conducted in harmony with that Renaissance spirit which had inculcated the right of private judgement.[28]

That very judgement was called into question by Descartes, at least for methodological purposes. Whereas the scientists were investigating matter, Descartes, resting on the received dualism of matter and spirit, and pursuing the introspective path in quest of a secure epistemological base, concentrated upon spirit. Hence, again, another strand in the preparation for deism. Hume's critique of miracles and of the classical theistic arguments on the one hand disturbed the confidence of many in a transcendent God and on the other awoke Kant from his dogmatic slumber.

Kant offers a distinctly different account of the terms 'transcendent' and 'transcendental' from anything we have met so far. Indeed, he draws a sharp distinction between them. According to his epistemology, we cannot know *noumena*, things in themselves, but only phenomena. The mind orders the sometimes confused deliverances of the senses, but has no knowledge of transcendent realities. At the same time the transcendental realities of God, freedom and immortality, are postulates (that is, conditions) of practical reason. They are not objects of knowledge, but they are required to undergird morality. In addition there are certain transcendental principles such as causality. These do not originate in sense data, they are constitutive of knowledge and are presupposed by all experience:

> A transcendental principle is one by which we think the universal a priori condition under which alone things can become objects of our cognition in general; on the other hand, a principle is called metaphysical if it is one [by] which [we] think the a priori condition under which alone objects whose concept must be given empirically can be further determined a priori. Thus the principle by which we cognize bodies as substances and as changeable substances is transcendental if it says that a change in them must have a cause; but it is metaphysical if it says that a change in them must have an *external* cause.[29]

He elsewhere explains that 'transcendental' refers not to our cognition of things, but only to our faculty of cognition.[30]

Kant's ideas proved fertile in numerous directions, some of them mutually contradictory. The idea of the regulative as distinct from the speculative knowledge of God became in the hands of Hamilton and Mansel a weapon wielded against the immanentist pantheism of their day. But their peril was that of rendering the epistemological distance between God and ourselves so unbridgeable as to vitiate any notion of the *imago dei*. Others, aware of our intellectual limitations, emphasized the feelings, or our intuitions, as affording an approach to the God who is for ever beyond us. Thus, famously, Pascal:

> The heart has its own reasons which Reason does not know; a thousand things declare it . . . Tis the heart, not reason, that feels God. This is

> Faith: God felt by the heart, not by reason . . . Do not wonder to see simple folk believe without reasoning. God gives them love of Him and hatred of self. He inclines their heart to believe. We shall never believe with a belief that avails and springs from faith, unless God inclines the heart; and we believe as soon as He inclines it.[31]

Thus, equally famously, Schleiermacher, first in 1799 and then in 1821–2:

> The usual conception of God as one single being outside of the world and behind the world is not the beginning and the end of religion. It is only one manner of expressing God, seldom entirely pure and always inadequate . . . [T]he true nature of religion is . . . immediate consciousness of the Deity as He is found in ourselves and in the world.[32]

> The common element in all howsoever diverse expressions of piety, by which these are conjointly distinguished from all other feelings, or, in other words, the self-identical essence of piety, is this: the consciousness of being absolutely dependent, or, which is the same thing, of being in relation with God.[33]

So was heralded Romanticism in theology, of which Coleridge was a leading English and Emerson and the transcendentalists leading American exponents.[34] This multi-faceted movement may broadly be characterized as insisting that human beings are spiritual and not merely intellectual beings; as extolling the spirit of wonder and according a high place to the imagination; and as emphasizing the unity of humanity with the created order.[35] However varied their accents,[36] the Romantic message is that at its deepest level the human being is a spiritual being, and that the transcendent Spirit is immanent in the created order and supremely in the human heart. A similar result is achieved by post-Hegelian immanentists – not least by those who were most inclined to construe Christianity in idealistic terms. The discussion of the ways in which they did this was my preoccupation in *Philosophical Idealism and Christian Belief*, and the evidence gathered cannot be reproduced here. Suffice it to say that in all such cases the reality of the external world is put at risk, the Creator–creature distinction is threatened, pantheizing tendencies hover, history is idealized, evil becomes a stage on the way to a greater good rather than an aberrant violation of God's law and the divine–human continuity is emphasized to such a degree that, especially against a hinterland of evolutionary thought, human recovery becomes an almost automatic process scarcely needing the radical rescue of the Cross. Concomitantly, Christian doctrines are modified so that, for example, for Edward Caird the death of Jesus seems to have more to do with the dying and rising motif operative throughout the created order than with something which happened at Calvary:

> The death of Jesus was thus . . . the first clear demonstration that the idea of a Universal God which underlies all religion is not merely the abstract idea of an infinite Being in which everything finite is merged and lost, but that it is a productive principle which can restore out of itself all, and more than all, it seems to take away.[37]

Underlying all of this, and in some instances directly fuelled by it, is the repudiation of that tendency commonly called deistic, which would conceive of God as withdrawn from the world: a position viewed as opening the door to naturalism, materialism and agnosticism. But the tendency predates the deists. The Roman Catholic scholar Henri de Lubac has argued that some Renaissance theologians, in their desire to resist humanist extremes, so over-emphasized the supernatural as against the natural as to pave the way for deism.[38] This is the peril of a non-immanently grounded supernatural. In a quite different context the Mercersburg theologian, J. W. Nevin, in whom Romantic tendencies are wedded to strong convictions concerning the catholicity of the Church, its nature as an organism and the importance of the patristic heritage, strove to resist what he regarded as the abstract supernaturalism of those he branded 'sects'. Such bodies, he argued, with their distinguishing doctrinal markers, were prone to a rationalistic tendency. Indeed,

> A Rationalism that denies the supernatural altogether, and a Supernaturalism that will not allow it to enter into any concrete union with the natural, are at bottom much of the same nature; and the last needs only the force of true consecutive thinking always, to pass over peacefully into the arms of the first. Sects start usually in abstract supernaturalism, with an affectation of hyper-spiritual perfection. But the rationalistic element comes at once into view, both in their thinking and practice.[39]

The combination of Romanticism, ideas of human autonomy, evolutionary thought and post-Hegelian immanentist philosophy were ingredients, variously combined with 'advanced' views concerning biblical criticism, which constituted the soil in which liberal theology flourished in the declining years of the nineteenth century and the early decades of the twentieth. R. J. Campbell's book *The New Theology* (1907) was a popular exposition of liberalism by one who held the prominent position of minister at London's City Temple. Campbell opposed the transcendentalist tendency which causes people to 'think of God as above and apart from His world instead of expressing Himself through His world',[40] and he commended the New Theology as 'an untrammelled return to the Christian sources in the light of modern thought. Its starting-point is a re-emphasis of the Christian belief in the Divine immanence in the universe and in mankind.'[41] And what is his concept of the divine? Campbell's God is 'the one reality I cannot get away from, for, whatever else it may be, it is myself'; and when he added that 'the whole cosmic process is one long incarnation and uprising of the being of God from itself to itself'[42] he caused more than a fluttering in the theological dovecotes; he drew heavy fire from the biggest theological gun the Congregationalists had at the time, P. T. Forsyth, himself an erstwhile liberal theologian. Ever concerned to root his theology in the Cross and to honour the holy love of the transcendent yet immanent God, Forsyth concluded that the exponents of the New Theology 'become as much the doctrinaire victims of a speculative theology as our forefathers were the victims of an orthodox theology'.[43]

Unconsciously in the wake of Forsyth, and in conscious opposition to the liberal theology in which he had been reared, Karl Barth re-emphasized the divine transcendence in the years following the First World War:[44]

> The loftiness, the sovereignty, the majesty, the holiness, the glory – even what is termed the transcendence of God – what is this but this self-determination, this freedom, of the divine living and loving, the divine person? . . . The biblical witness to God sees His transcendence of all that is distinct from Himself, not only in the distinction as such, which is supremely and decisively characterised as His freedom from all conditioning by that which is distinct from Himself, but furthermore and supremely in the fact that without sacrificing His distinction and

> freedom, but in the exercise of them, He enters into and faithfully maintains communion with this reality other than Himself in His activity as Creator, Reconciler and Redeemer . . . He who can and does do this is the God of Holy Scripture, the triune God known to us in revelation.[45]

With this strong assertion that the transcendent God is known by his free revelation alone goes Barth's critique of natural theology. This will occupy us in the next chapter. But for the present we must turn to those, some of them erstwhile Barthians, who came to repudiate what they took to be Barth's extreme doctrine of transcendence.

III

The reaction was not long in coming. Two years before Barth died in 1968 Gordon Kaufman felt able to declare that 'the radical "eclipse of God" (Buber) or even the final irretrievable death of God (Nietzsche) appears to be the most momentous theological fact of our age'.[46] With the reference to Nietzsche we have a link with our earlier discussion of postmodernists, to many of whom he has been an inspiration. But the roots of death-of-God theology lie further back. J. P. F. Richter (d. 1825) suggested that God is no longer required as the cement of the universe or the explanation of things; and hence human beings may justifiably live without postulating the divine.[47] From a different direction, once Hegelian immanentism had, to the satisfaction of some, sundered the spiritual–natural dichotomy, not least by its claim that the divine realizes itself in the human, it was an easy task for Feuerbach to argue that the spiritual was but a projection of the human. Notoriously dramatic was Nietzsche's announcement that, having killed God, humanity must now, in the role of superman, assume the role of lord of history: 'God is dead! God remains dead! And we have killed him! . . . Shall we not ourselves have to become Gods, merely to seem worthy of it?'[48] By now Comte and Mill among others had extolled the Religion of Humanity, and Marx and Engels were filling the space vacated by God with their materialistic-revolutionary idealization of humanity. The death-of-God theologians (a by no means homogeneous group) of the 1960s thus inherited a tradition in which more is attempted than the adjustment of current thought to new knowledge; the attempt was to replace the old (and especially Barth's wholly other God) with the new.

In so far as we may speak of a general tendency in death-of-God theology, it consists in a denial of the transcendent which turns upon the affirmation of the natural (or secular) side of the nature–spirit dichotomy. Whereas Barth sought to respond to the Word from the other side of the gulf, so to speak, the death-of-God theologians refuse this comfort. They are with Tillich in his aversion to mythological God-talk, but they have no place for his Being-itself. They complain that Bultmann's existentialism was vitiated by its Heideggerian ontologism. But they all wish to affirm the importance of Jesus. In the words of Altizer and Hamilton,

> There was once a God to whom adoration, praise and trust were appropriate, possible, and even necessary, but that now there is no such God. This is the position of the death of God or radical theology. It is an atheist position, but with a difference. If there was a God, and if there now isn't, it should be possible to indicate why this change took place, when it took place, and who was responsible for it.[49]

On this theme many variations were played. To Gabriel Vahanian the death of God meant that God had died (for all practical purposes) in our culture. It is not that God does not exist; the fact is that as far as present Western culture is concerned, he is irrelevant. Vahanian has criticized those who have gone further than this, and they in turn have regarded him as unduly conservative in his belief that reason's failure to demonstrate God is theology's opportunity: 'God is not necessary but he is inevitable. He is wholly other and wholly present.'[50] With this William Hamilton was by no means content: 'We are not talking about the absence of the experience of God, but about the experience of the absence of God.'[51] Yet Hamilton is claimed by *Jesus*: not, indeed, because in coming to Jesus we

> meet a God hitherto unknown. We come to Jesus because the God we have found apart from him is a kind of absentee enemy who does not make it possible for us either to think or to live as the Christians we wish to be.[52]

This leads us to the note of victory which is strongly sounded by Hamilton: 'Christianity's real contribution is this: when asked what it means by God, it points to the cross. Jesus is Lord by being a servant . . . He exercises his divinity and his sovereign power from the cross.'[53] There is a methodological proposal here which I find congenial: it is difficult to see how Christians could, or would wish to, testify to their understanding of God without adverting to the Cross.

Thomas A. J. Altizer sounds the most flamboyantly daring of all the radical theologians, but in some ways, especially in his underlying Hegelianism (something he shares with Tillich), he is the most old-fashioned. Thus, he can declare that 'God has actually died in Christ . . . this death is both a historical and a cosmic event, and, as such, it is a final and irrevocable event, which cannot be reversed by a subsequent religious or cosmic movement.'[54] It follows that 'a Christian confession of the death of God is a response to the real absence of God himself . . . To speak the name of God in a time of his withdrawal is nothing less than blasphemy.'[55] The Christian is thus impelled 'to seek the presence and reality of Christ in a world that is totally estranged from Christianity's established vision of the sacred'.[56] Altizer could hardly underline his point in a more dramatic way: 'God has died in *our* time, in *our* history, in *our* experience.'[57] Transcendence has collapsed into immanence, and we now have to realize 'a new and awesome human autonomy'.[58] The twentieth century has brought home to us 'the radical immanence of modern man, an immanence dissolving even the memory or the shadow of transcendence'.[59] With Blake, to whom Altizer has frequent recourse, we must acknowledge that the transcendent God of the Old Testament is no more. But although God has died in history, it is also true that Christ is risen within history; the theatre of Christ's activity is *here*.

It would seem that if in Tillich we have Hegel clothed in existentialist terminology, so here we have him viewed through spectacles supplied by Blake and Nietzsche and fitted by process thinkers from Bergson to Hartshorne. It would also seem that far from querying the Creator–creature distinction, Altizer does away with it altogether: indeed for him God's *kenosis* does away with it.

Of all the death-of-God theologians, Paul van Buren offers the position that will sound most familiar to those who have been schooled in the English (I use the term advisedly) tradition of linguistic analysis. He brings empiricist analytical techniques to bear upon God-talk with a view to showing that the word 'God' is dead.[60] For van Buren there can be no reliable discourse about God – least of all talk of an 'experienced non-objective reality' such as Schubert Ogden, himself an anti-supernaturalist, has proposed. We are left with no God who may be said to be transcendent, but we do have commitment to Jesus of Nazareth, the truly free man who frees his followers – and that in a manner which seems to me to be uncannily reminiscent of that adopted by the erstwhile transcendent God. Ogden, by contrast, criticized (even) Bultmann for being too bound to the past events of Nazareth; and this despite the fact that Ogden could encapsulate Bultmann's reduction of 'the entire contents of the traditional confession' thus: 'I henceforth understand myself no longer in terms of my past, but solely in terms of the future that is here and now disclosed to me as grace in my encounter with the church's proclamation.'[61]

With the mention of Ogden we leave the death-of-God theologians and turn to process thought. If the emphasis of the former lay in repudiating transcendence, that of the latter is found in its immanentism, but both are disenchanted with classical theism. God, according to the classical Greek tradition, exists *a se*. The concept of temporality cannot be applied to him. This, so the process thinkers claim, fostered the unwholesomely transcendent view of God which, passing from the Aristotelian 'unmoved Mover' through the scholastic *ens realissimum*, reached its climax in deism, where God was understood as static, external, uninvolved. Needless to say, none of these ideas appealed to those who sympathized with the general trend of nineteenth-century evolutionary thought, and wished to forsake the static view of God for the dynamic, the fixed for the developing.

In approaching process thought it is necessary to keep a sense of perspective. I suspect that, if we consider Jews and Christians at large, deism (of various kinds) and its precursors were ever minority interests (though not for that reason right or wrong). Thus, for example, the Old Testament tells of a creative God who works through historical events, who addresses his people, who has a purpose for them. The New Testament is replete with teleological and eschatological motifs and, above all, it has the God-man at its heart. How could the Almighty have become more involved and closer, we might ask? In post-biblical times, to take random examples only, we find Duns Scotus correcting undue Thomist emphasis upon 'being' with his teaching concerning the primacy of the ethical; we find the best of the mystics, Puritans, pietists, Quakers, Moravians and others, experimentally persuaded of the reality of God in their midst; and we find the conviction of the presence of God inspiring phenomena as various as the ecclesiologies of Dissent and the testimonies of Christian existentialists. In all these cases the transcendence of God was regarded much more as a matter of his character as holy than as a matter of the quasi-geographical distance between him and human beings. The process theologians have not, therefore, succeeded where all others failed in bringing God near.

They have, however, made two radically new proposals.[62] First, they have revived the Greek idea, shunned in the orthodox tradition, of a developing God. Secondly, whereas Plato thought of the self-creating deity as being far removed from the world of matter, with the process thinkers immanence reigns and emergent evolution is their model. Thus Whitehead can say, 'It is as true to say that God creates the World, as that the World creates God.'[63] Furthermore, 'Neither God, nor the World, reaches static completion. Both are in the grip of the ultimate metaphysical ground, the creative advance into novelty. Either of them, God and the World, is the instrument of novelty for the other.'[64] Whitehead thus seeks to overcome the difficulty bequeathed to us by the old nature–spirit dichotomy, namely, that 'the worst of a gulf is, that it is very difficult to know what is happening on the further side'.[65] While it is true that Whitehead wishes to preserve transcendence by introducing his dipolar theism, according to which God's primordial nature is eternal and beyond human knowledge while his consequent nature is that by which he acts dynamically in the world, lovingly 'luring' it on its evolutionary way towards the goal he has appointed for it, it is the immanentist aspect which exerts the greater pull. Hence his disciple, H. N. Wieman, can assert that 'the only creative God we recognize is the creative event itself'.[66] There is some reason to suspect that at this point transcendence has become so inconsequential, or at any rate, it has ceased to be anything other than an extension of the world, that it is impotent to serve as the bulwark between process thinkers' desiderated panentheism and that full-blown pantheism which they wish to repudiate.

Undeterred, Schubert Ogden and Norman Pittenger expounded process theology, and both focus upon the Incarnation, which Pittenger calls 'the event of Jesus Christ' – an event which is not so much the 'supreme anomaly' as the 'classical instance'.[67] In Charles Hartshorne's view Christ is the supreme symbol of God's activity and meaning in his world. No 'classical' theologian need disagree with the view that Christ is not an isolated 'entrance' or 'intervention' of God in the world otherwise deprived of his presence and action; but this is by no means to agree that 'the "incarnation" of God in Jesus Christ is focally but not exclusively true of him' (shades of the 'first among equals' Jesus of some older liberal theologians). Ogden has no inhibitions at this point: God literally participates in humanity, yet at the same time (following Heidegger) God's being is infinite while ours is not. But this seems an extreme statement from one who wishes to oppose the idea of temporal infinity. As James Richmond has remarked, if the philosophical sceptic 'finds "temporal infinity" to be a stark contradiction in terms, he may find "infinite temporality" to be equally, not less, contradictory'.[68] This difficulty of reconciling the absoluteness of God with his temporality is the most serious obstacle of all. In this connection it is interesting to juxtapose William Temple's criticism of Whitehead and R. Gregor Smith's criticism of Ogden:

> About the consequent nature of God Professor Whitehead has much to say that is edifying, but it is hard to see by what right he says it. One is glad to know that he has the consolation of believing that 'the love in the world passes into the love in heaven, and floods back again into the world', so that 'in this sense God is the great companion – the fellow-sufferer who understands'. This is very near the Christian Gospel, and if only Professor Whitehead would for creativity say Father, for 'primordial nature of God' say Eternal Word, and for 'consequent nature of God' say Holy Spirit, he would perhaps be able to show ground for his gratifying conclusions. But he cannot use those terms, precisely because each of them imports the notion of Personality as distinct from Organism. The very reason which gives to the Christian scheme its philosophical superiority is that which precludes Professor Whitehead from adopting it.[69]

> Ogden is forced into a very serious inconsistency when he asks us to accept the reality of God as meaning both the abstract principle of all relatedness and the self-creative activity of God. Certainly, this variation of the process philosophies of Whitehead and Hartshorne can help us to grasp the significance of human historical becoming; but it cannot also expect to save the absoluteness of God except as a face-saving gesture, or an idle speculation.[70]

The nub of both criticisms is that the abstract conflicts with the personal, the idea of organism with that of historical event.

There can be no doubt that in declaring against the ideas of God as 'unmoved Mover', 'ruling Caesar' and 'ruthless Moralist', Whitehead was making a salutary anti-deist protest. Eugene Peters has praised process thought for its stand against an other-worldliness which, regarding God as 'wholly other', 'tends to paralyze theological curiosity and inquiry'.[71] Again, process theology facilitates Christian confession by focusing upon God's revelation in Christ in a way which would be impossible if God absolutely transcended the categories.[72] It proclaims a God who enters into the sufferings of humanity with victorious potential: 'God has nowhere to hide himself from any sorrow or joy whatever, but must share in all the wealth and all the burden of the world.'[73] It exhorts us to embrace a new vision of what it means to be God's co-workers.[74] Above all, it demands an adequate doctrine of immanence: God may not be excluded from any part of his universe, all of which is 'alive with his life',[75] while at the same time striving to give us a God who is 'both utterly absolute and totally related'.[76]

However, I cannot but feel that these positive points are purchased at too great a price. Moreover, they can be expressed equally well by a theology which does not batten itself to process thought. As with the older idealism, the question becomes: 'Is the Creator–creature distinction adequately preserved in process thought?' If it is not, we cannot do justice either to humanity's need or to God's gracious provision in Christ. David Jenkins has expressed the point admirably:

> Whatever [God's] relationship to continuing processes and developing patterns, he himself is not to be equated with those processes and patterns, and he is not dependent for his being God, or his being as God, in any way on the movements, developments, changes in materiality and history. This insight into the transcendent independence of God in his goodness is, I am convinced, a valid one . . . The true God exists because he is the true God and it is a *consequence* of his transcendentally independent existence both that man exists and that man has the hope of fulfilment as man.[77]

Alongside this affirmation I should like to place two others, which were written with post-Hegelian immanentism and evolutionary thought in mind. The first is by James Orr, the second by P. T. Forsyth:

> A God in process is of necessity an incomplete God – can never be a true, personal God.[78] His being is merged in that of the universe; sin, even, is an element of His life. I hold it to be indubitable that God, in order truly to be God, must possess Himself in the eternal fulness and completeness of His own personal life; must possess Himself for Himself, and be raised entirely above the transiency, and the contingency of the world-process. We are then enabled to think of the world and history, not as the necessary unfolding of a logical process, but as the revelation of a free and holy purpose; and inconsistency is no longer felt in the idea of an action of God along supernatural lines – above the plane of mere nature, as wisdom and love may dictate – for the benefit of His creature man.[79]

> Any theology that places us in a spiritual *process*, or native movement between the finite and the infinite, depreciates the value of spiritual *act*, and thus makes us independent of the grace of God. Its movement is processional spectacular, aesthetic, it is not historic, dramatic, tragic or ethical. If it speak of the grace of God it does not take it with moral seriousness.[80]

These quotations clearly suggest not only that there can be divine immanence (properly dear to process thought) if God's independence is posited, but that there cannot be immanence if it is not.[81] They also relieve the Almighty of the difficulty of being less than absolute, as he must almost inevitably be in process thought (and ought such a one to command our absolute allegiance?); and they preserve him from being at the mercy of the contingent, ever adapting himself as novel eventualities arise.[82] The place of the contingent is, indeed, one of the most intractable problems to arise in connection with process thought.

Summing up, we may say that whereas Barth weights the scales in the direction of transcendence, the process theologians emphasize immanence; but neither have foreclosed discussion of the problem encapsulated long ago by H. R. Mackintosh in these terms: 'It is the "living" God who says, "I the Lord change not". How these two conceptions can be true at once is an insoluble problem; it is but one of a class of problems not accidental but native to genuine thought concerning God.'[83]

IV

We have now taken a number of soundings in the history of Christian thought with a view to showing how the terms 'transcendence' and 'immanence' have been used. We saw that some writers opted for transcendence over immanence, while others gave precedence to immanence, and yet others sought to hold the two in balance. A minority dispensed altogether with transcendence as traditionally understood. Some thought more in terms of 'being', and to this philosophical concept they attempted to wed the Christian God; others emphasized the epistemological difference between ourselves and God, with all the strains upon our language which ensue. We briefly reviewed Kant's novel usage of 'transcendental', and observed the differing lines of thought which flowed in his wake. The reappraisals stimulated by Romanticism, post-Hegelian immanentism and evolutionary thought were all noted, as were the positions of those who set out from the Christian revelation as centred in the Incarnation and the Cross. Against this background I should like to state a positive position, drawing further writers into the picture for illustrative purposes – a position in which I shall resume the cautions listed at the beginning of this chapter. My running question will be: will the truly 'radical' person be the one who reasserts the often neglected truth that the fact of God's atoning intervention in Christ in face of humanity's dire need affords a number of clues as to how we may speak of the transcendent God who addresses us; of the immanent God who is alongside and within us; and of a God under whose gracious authority, and by whose present power, we are challenged to live our lives in grateful response?

Putting matters negatively, there is much to be said for A. E. Taylor's remark that 'The metaphysical denial of divine transcendence carries with it self-righteousness in morality, as well as Pelagianism in theological speculation.'[84] We come to think that we can enrol God as a supporter of our favoured socio-political causes; we can even come to believe that we are responsible for our own salvation. But at once Taylor warns in the other direction: 'exclusive insistence on transcendence has its dangers too; it leads to a "supralapsarian" theology and an antinomian "going as you please" in morality'.[85] Well, these are possibilities, no doubt. The challenge, therefore, is to steer clear of the classical matter–spirit dichotomy without obliterating the Creator–creature distinction on the one hand, or lining up behind Comte's religion of humanity on the other. Having doffed my cap in the direction of the death-of-God theologians, I almost feel inclined, with a due measure of humility and godly defiance, to propose God's resurrection! Instead, I shall summon the Puritan, Stephen Charnock, who said of God:

> He is within and above all places, though places should be infinite in number. As he was before and beyond all time, so he is above and beyond all place; being from eternity before any real time, he must also be without as well and within any real space; if God were only confined to the world, he would be no more infinite in his essence than the world is in quantity; as a moment cannot be conceived from eternity, wherein God was not in being, so a space cannot be conceived in the mind of man wherein God is not present; he is not contained in the world nor in the heavens.[86]

As we saw when pondering the language of worship, geography is not here to the point, and those who would make a meal out of Charnock's 'above' and 'beyond' are more than a little tiresome. The passage concerns God's character more than his location: he is the eternal, transcendent–immanent One. Other critics, however, may wish to question Charnock's prudence in making such claims (now understood to be about God's character). How does he know all of this? Charnock would have been the first to agree with Calvin that God's 'essence is so incomprehensible that his majesty is hidden, remote from all our senses'.[87] But although we do not know God as he is in himself, we know him as he makes himself known to us – it is a question of revelation, of God's address to humanity. Were there no revelation the believer would be unable to worship, indeed, unable to believe. For to posit the absolutely incomprehensible is to place oneself in a logically impossible situation (shades of Spencer's Unknowable).

A perfectly laudable fear of deism, as popularly understood, and a recognition of the fact of increasing secularization, coupled with the desire to uphold in some way the idea of God's activity in the world, has prompted many to think in terms of 'transcendence from below'. Of these, some fall into the category of patient analysts, others into that comprising the followers of Bonhoeffer. (The borderline is blurred, and I imply neither that analysts are precluded from following Bonhoeffer, nor that his disciples are invariably non-analytical and impatient.) Among the patient analysts we might number G. F. Woods and Gordon Kaufman. They have paid particular attention to empirical situations which prompt transcendent references and, while their interests are predominantly religious, we should be reminded by Roger Trigg that

> The transcendence of reality over our conceptual scheme is a more general problem than simply the question of our knowledge of God. Even sub-atomic particles could be considered transcendent in the sense that their nature outstrips our understanding and our ability to describe them.[88]

G. F. Woods accepts as accurate R. W. Hepburn's observation that to sacrifice language concerning transcendent personal being is to move outside of Christianity.[89] Whereas Hepburn considers such language imperilled, Woods seeks a way of rehabilitating its meaningfulness by elucidating its empirical anchorage. He grants that if the transcendent is defined as that which lies outside of human experience then it can never be experienced; but he disallows this definition, and finds no justification for the assertion that the transcendent is what we can never understand. By means of analogical explanation, based upon our experience of self-transcendence, and of being transcended by beings other than ourselves, he comes to the view that 'The problems of transcendence are the problems of being.'[90] The analogies must, however, be carefully employed, for we may not suggest that 'the divine being needs something to transcend in order to be'.[91] Nevertheless,

> In our experience of the changing, we have also a curious experience of the unchanging. I believe that we are gradually driven towards an awareness of some being, which is variously styled pure, absolute, or transcendent. The conclusion is being itself. It is difficult to say whether one experiences this pure being or whether more usually one experiences being transcended by it.[92]

Writing as he was in the heyday of the empiricist critique of religious discourse, one can understand Woods's determination to retain as much empirical anchorage as possible. But what if the transcendent comes to our aid? What if there is revelation from 'beyond'? What if God has spoken and acted supremely in Christ?

In other words, we may sympathize with Woods's pupil, Rupert Hoare, who regretted the absence in his mentor's work of a christocentric base for language concerning the 'other' with whom we have to do: 'It is the changelessness of God's love as revealed in Christ that is best described by the analogy of transcendence.'[93]

Woods's contemporary, I. T. Ramsey, was similarly concerned to root religious discourse in empirical soil. According to Ramsey the purpose of religious language is to evoke a situation which involves the discernment of something which is spatio-temporal *and more*. The final outcome will be a 'cosmic disclosure' which prompts total commitment on the part of the one who receives it. Ramsey illustrates his thesis by reference to models and qualifiers. A model is a term which grounds a theological story in empirical fact, while a qualifier both develops the model in a certain direction until 'the penny drops' or 'the ice breaks' – a disclosure takes place – and then claims an appropriate, logically odd, placing for the word 'God'. Thus in 'first cause', 'cause' is the model, 'first' the qualifier. Ramsey's work attracted a number of criticisms.[94] Some argued that the description of psychological processes were unhelpfully intertwined with epistemological claims to truth; others found him guilty of undue subjectivism. That he himself was not unaware of the pitfalls is clear:

> There is no question of a characteristically religious situation being merely 'emotional', if that word is thought to claim that the characteristic features we have been mentioning are entirely (in some way or another) 'subjective'. Let us emphasize, without any possibility of misunderstanding that all of these situations, all these characteristically different situations, when they occur, have an *objective* reference and are, as all situations, *subject–object* in structure. When situations 'come alive', or the 'ice breaks', there is objective 'depth' in these situations along with and alongside any subjective changes.[95]

Many felt, however, that while Ramsey *emphasized* this, he did not show it, and did not defend himself adequately against the charge of psychologism. When, finally, he came to concentrate upon 'I' as a model which was so appropriately odd that it could be taken as an analogue for 'God',[96] he was, in the opinion of some, bordering on a Cartesian autonomy of thought which would make it difficult to conceive of God (minus inverted commas) – that is, of God as a reality over against individuals. As Paul Helm asked, 'Since God is necessarily screened behind . . . symbolism the idea that all this [disclosure] language is *about* God is difficult to swallow. How can a language which is wholly non-cognitive and non-descriptive in character yet be referential in character?' Further, '[W]hat *are* the criteria of consistency (presumably logical consistency) for symbols? Is the symbol of a rock (say) logically consistent with the symbol of a father? How do we decide this? And what distinguished a divine disclosure from a Satanic delusion?'[97]

A similar question arises in connection with Tillich's distinction between sign and symbol. He informs us that while 'The statement that God is being-itself is a non-symbolic statement . . . nothing else can be said about God as God which is not symbolic.'[98] Such symbols are not the same as signs, for, whereas signs can be substituted arbitrarily, and bear no necessary relation to their referent, 'the symbol participates in the reality of that for which it stands'.[99] As far as I am aware, Tillich nowhere made the nature of this participation clear. But the main point here is that, if all God-language is symbolic because that to which it points is absolutely other and beyond our comprehension, how should we select or reject the symbols; how can we ever be sure that we are referring to God, and does it matter whether we can be sure or not; and is there an intelligible basis for communication between ourselves and God, assuming that he should wish to address us? One sometimes feels that some more liberal theologians are so anxious to ensure that they are not like other people, or even as those dreaded fundamentalists, that their horror of propositional truth leaves them dangling over a sea of subjectivity from which their sermons and prayers inconsistently save them.

There is a feeling when reading Woods, Ramsey and Tillich that we are like archers, shooting a variety of different arrows into a void, hoping that some of them will hit a target we cannot see.

Like Woods and Ramsey, Gordon Kaufman seeks to provide empirical anchorage for the concept of transcendence, maintaining that 'our speech about this Other arises because certain features of experience force us up against the limit(s) of all possible knowledge and experience'.[100] In terminology which, though ethical rather than ontological, is not far removed from that of Woods, Kaufman maintains that 'Talk about God appears when the ultimate Limit is understood on analogy with the experience of *personal limiting* as known in the intercourse and interaction of personal wills.'[101] His limited objective is to show the way in which the cognitive *meaningfulness* of religious language could be defended. As to its *truth*:

> Only on the ground that God had in fact revealed himself could it be claimed that he exists; only if there were and is some sort of movement from beyond the Limit to us, making known to us through the medium of the Limit the reality of that which lies beyond, could we be in a position to speak of such a reality at all; only if God actually 'spoke' to man could we know there is a God.[102]

Here once again is the question of the transcendent's self-revelation, and bound up with this is the question of authority. Kaufman takes more account than Woods of the fact that, apart from an authoritative revelation which meets us in history, we are at a loss. One recalls the observation of Ronald Gregor Smith that such Heidegger-influenced theologians as John Macquarrie tend to qualify 'Being' in some such way as 'Being understood as gracious'. Why? '[B]ecause this is what faith teaches him to do . . . We speak of God as holy, as gracious, as giving us life, because through his historical approaches to men we encounter him, in faith, as holy, as gracious and as giving us life.'[103] With this, questions of history loom before us; but we must reserve those for the next section of this chapter.

Turning now to those who have asserted an empirically grounded transcendence in the wake of Bonhoeffer (though their antecedents are very mixed and I refer to their spirit in contrast to that of the analysts, as much as to their lineage), I shall briefly revert to John Robinson, and then turn to Harvey Cox. Robinson, as we saw, was concerned in *Honest to God* to communicate the Gospel to secular people, and in this he is at one with Harvey Cox. Robinson's ploy is to encourage secular human beings to realize the Other within the depths of their being. But is the God thus conceived anything other than a projection of ourselves?[104] Would not Feuerbach applaud the reduction of theology to anthropology implicit in the words, 'A statement is "theological" not because it asks *ultimate* questions about the meaning of existence . . .'?[105] Once more we have transcendence apparently lost in immanence, whereas, traditionally, 'Transcendence means, and has always meant, *difference* . . . God's transcendence opposes pantheism, not intimacy.'[106]

A similar problem arises in *The Secular City*, where Harvey Cox writes, 'God meets us as the transcendent, at those aspects of our experience which can never be transmuted into extensions of ourselves. He meets us in the wholly other.'[107] More specifically, it is the areas of social change which are the locus of the Kingdom of God.[108] From this position it is not a long step to those bolder theologies of revolution which tend to identify the socio-political *status quo* with the devil and revolution with God. Thus the half-truth antithesis of Emilio Castro: 'The coming of Jesus Christ into the world is a secular event, not a religious one.'[109] The caution of Stanley Kane is to the point:

> making theology 'relevant' by requiring it at the outset to accept as basic principles the dominant thought-forms of one's culture does not automatically give it something worthwhile and significant to say, while it does rob it of the capacity to make fundamental criticisms.[110]

Some of the practical-religious consequences of the loss of transcendence have been spelled out in characteristically homely fashion by Rabbi Blue:

> If the transcendent is avoided then the results must be faced. Without the awareness of God Rabbis become communal executives and fund-raisers. Synagogues become community centres with or without a worship area and there is no difference between a Rabbinical diploma and a university doctorate. Concern for Jewish purpose is replaced by schemes for Jewish survival, the Halacha, the creative law becomes a matter of expertise, and the debates of the Jewish world proceed from a political and not from a religious centre.[111]

We need be under no illusion that such comments apply to Judaism only. Harvey Cox, for example, can rejoice, with a zeal of which the Stoics would have approved, that 'the previous nooks and crannies reserved for the transcendent have all been made immanent'.[112] The choices open up before us once again: pantheism, or humanism, naturalism, agnosticism, atheism?

But some, including J. A. T. Robinson who, as we saw, found spatial metaphors so troubling in the 1960s, also sought to detach 'the Christian doctrine of God from any necessary dependence on a "supranaturalist" world-view'.[113] I wish to suggest, however, that, for all its unfortunate associations with Hollywood, psychic spookery and the like, a concept of transcendence which is devoid of supernatural connotations will admit self-transcendence – as when we think about ourselves, or 'surpass ourselves' in some endeavour – and little more; and when such an approach is applied to Jesus Christ, as it was by Strauss, who famously declared that 'In the person and acts of Jesus no supernaturalism shall be suffered to remain',[114] the biblical record is vitiated and the Gospel threatened. The biblical narrative is either idealized off the stage of history, or else Jesus becomes one in whom God dwells immanently, to a greater degree, perhaps, than he dwells in others, but that is all. In his critique of Otto Pfleiderer's Gifford Lectures Robert Rainy wrote:

> In the scheme of the Lecturer it is plain that much turns on the alleged incongruity of supernatural Christanity. A system of the world which is to proceed mainly by development and growth, ought not to be interfered with by an Incarnation, and by a revealing process leading up to an Incarnation. That, Dr. Pfleiderer says, is to undo the scheme of thought from the bottom.[115]

Nothing could be at a further pole from Bonhoeffer's view that 'From God to reality, not from reality to God, goes the path of theology.'[116] For his part, James Orr, while he could understand supernaturalists on the one hand and agnostics on the other, found Pfleiderer 'plainly incompetent' in proclaiming a God of love who is not to be identified with the natural order, a supernatural which is tied to the natural order, and the impossibility of miracles.[117] Underlying all of this was an implied or actual attack upon biblical authority; and that this was something which concerned not only orthodox theologians like Rainy and Orr, but the older generation of biblicist Unitarians too, is clear from Roger Thomas's remark:

> Perhaps what stood out most in imagination was [Theodore] Parker's anti-supernaturalism, that is to say, the rejection of the evidential value of miracles, including that of the Resurrection. But there was something at bottom far more radical; it was the removal of the doctrinal authority of the Bible. In the long run what was more important was that Martineau and Parker, in removing Biblical authority, put nothing similar in its place. Martineau placed the seat of authority in conscience; Parker, meeting the question of a test of doctrine, said, 'Try it by reason, conscience and faith.'[118]

There is a welcome emphasis upon the ethical here, but however much we may believe that our noblest ideals are derived from

God, unless the transcendent God is conceived of as supernatural and not simply as our own self projected to infinity, ethics will ultimately be at risk. Hence, for example, L. P. Hickock's criticism of a variety of American Transcendentalism: 'It transcends the phenomenal in sensation, truly and philosophically, and such is its deservedly great praise; but to it the supernatural is darkness.'[119] For, as Rashdall observed,

> it needs no very elaborate demonstration to show that if all souls are equally part of God, God cannot be an object of moral reverence. A Religion that is based on such a Theology must be a Religion that frankly takes leave of Ethics.[120]

When pondering the nature of the true supernatural in Christianity R. S. Franks concurs:

> Is it the sheer supernatural or the ethical supernatural? Is it the awesome holy or the ethical holy? We say, in reply, that God's transcendence is never to be separated from its ethical quality. It may be power, but it is power ethically controlled for ethical ends. This means that God deals differently with persons and things; that, while things are subject to His simple power, in dealing with men He always respects the moral personality.[121]

That there is biblical warrant for such a view seems clear. Undeniably, images of space and distance are used of God in the Bible, but as I pointed out earlier, the scriptural notion of transcendence has more to do with God's character than with his location. The distinction is moral more than spatial. A biblical scholar writes typically:

> Yahweh is holy in two main senses . . . Firstly, Yahweh is holy in the sense that He stands utterly above the created world; He is the wholly other, the incomprehensible, the unanalysable, the unfathomable . . . But on the other hand Yahweh is holy inasmuch as He imparts Himself . . . His holiness is dynamic, exacting; it confronts man to pour out on him a new life.[122]

The God who is 'high and lifted up' (Isaiah 6: 1) is the same as he who says, 'I am with you' (Isaiah 41: 10). God the holy one stands over against us, yet he is closer than a brother; and his holy love both judges and saves. In Christ that love is active for human redemption; and in the light of this revelation of God's holy love, all notions of transcendence understood phenomenologically are inadequate.[123] Forsyth went so far as to say that 'The holy, however intimate to us, has no meaning except as the transcendent.'[124] According to this understanding, transcendence, though logically prior to immanence in the sense that God and the world are not correlative terms,[125] is properly correlative to immanence, given that God is the creator. Of transcendence and immanence thus conceived, Christ the God-man is the paradigm: 'Transcendence without immanence makes nonsense of God, immanence without transcendence makes nonsense of man. Both are quite untrue to the givenness of Jesus Christ.'[126] Colin Gunton has similarly expressed himself, albeit in more directly trinitarian terms:

> The triune God, eternally one in the richness and variety of his being, has made himself responsible for our time by taking upon himself the burden of our alienation. That is why he is to be discerned at the heart of our existence. The transcendent is not that from which we have to escape if we are to be human. It is rather that through which the immanent is enabled to bloom and flourish.[127]

It is the fact of the Word made flesh which at once reveals the transcendent as supernatural and vanquishes immanentisms of every kind, and makes the Gospel a stumbling-block to 'Greeks' of every age, clime and theological faculty; he through whom all things were made yet tabernacled with us. The Christological teaching derivable from Philippians 2 comes to mind as being among the sublimest statements of the truth I am seeking, however falteringly, to express.

It is, however, necessary to explain more fully what is meant by saying that the Gospel concerns a supernatural act. I understand the saving act to be supernatural in two respects: first, its provision is not from nature, least of all from human beings, but from the holy God of all grace. Secondly, it has to restore nature, especially ours. This second proposition implies that nature, especially ours, has gone awry; that is to say, it adverts to the Christian understanding of sin as rebellion against God. Hence, 'natural' is ambiguous when used in Christian theology of human beings. It denotes both their status as part of God's creation and their condition as imperfect, by contrast with Jesus Christ who, said Luther, is Proper Man. Richard Baxter's words may nowadays seem a little melodramatic, but they are none the worse for that:

> When Christ comes with regenerating, saving grace, he finds no man sitting still, but all posting to eternal ruin, and making haste towards hell; till, by conviction, he first brings them to a stand; and then, by conversion, turns first their hearts, and then their lives sincerely to him.[128]

The 'new' being's nature qua human remains the same; there is continuity between what was and what is: the *imago dei* was ever there, the individual's personality is not erased. As Stephen Charnock put it, 'The sponge retains the nature of a sponge, though encompassed by the sea, and moving in it, and the sea still retains its own nature.'[129] But the individual now has what Christians call new life in Christ, a life grounded in a new relationship with God to which the response can only be, 'This is the Lord's doing and it is marvellous in our eyes.'[130] It is all of grace, and it will not suffice to say that 'The supernatural is the natural seen in its spiritual significance.'[131] B. B. Warfield thundered, 'The Christian man is not the product of the regenerative forces of nature under however divine direction; he is not an "evolution" out of the natural man; he is a new creation.'[132] P. T. Forsyth was right: 'In a positive Gospel . . . everything turns on a real supernatural revelation, on a fundamental perdition, a radical evil, and a rescue from without as the one thing that makes a Christian humanity.'[133]

Nothing that has been said should be taken as implying the dualism that 'nature' is an autonomous, religious, sphere utterly distinct from another 'supernatural' realm: that way lies the eventual redundancy of the 'supernatural'. As James Denney observed, 'When we define the supernatural only in a religious way, and refuse to form a conception of it in relation to nature or history, the practical result is that we surrender it altogether.'[134] The claim rather is that the Incarnation, and supremely the Cross–resurrection event, witnesses to the immanence of the transcendent holy God, who graciously redeems in an act which the nature (including humanity) could neither have imagined nor undertaken.[135] If this is so, it is not difficult to see why H. H. Farmer argued that the 'true' supernatural is not the contranatural, but the personal.[136] But it is the personal as the gratuitously surprising – as we saw Thomas Willcox found the Gospel to be when he surmised that 'nature', that is, human nature, would have arranged humanity's fate quite differently, and in such a way that sinners would not have stood a chance. Moreover, the faith by which the gift of new life is grasped is itself, in the sense defined, a supernatural gift: for our faith is one enabled by God the Holy Spirit, so that none may boast.[137]

It therefore seems to me that those who, like John Robinson, applaud Tillich for his 'great contribution to theology',[138] namely, his divorcing of the transcendent from the supranatural, are missing something of vital importance. They are in danger of remaining on the nature side of the old nature–spirit dichotomy for, as we have seen, 'transcendence' can all too easily become self-transcendence only, and immanence can tend in a pantheizing direction until the door is opened to naturalism. Indeed, the attempt to hold together transcendence, immanence and the supernatural seems to militate against the nature–spirit dichotomy, while those who would exclude the supernatural seem to be working with precisely the old dualism. As John Oman advised, 'The Supernatural must be inquired into, like the Natural, as a world in which we live and move and have our being.'[139]

As far as Christians are concerned, that world is one which witnesses to a supernatural presence, a supernatural act of regeneration and re-creation, and a supernatural power for living. In answer to the question, 'Why should God trouble thus to intervene?' Christians may suitably join with Calvin in replying, 'Because it is to the praise and glory of his grace.' An enthusiastic evangelist might reply, 'Because that's the way it is, brothers and sisters.' And, however unsophisticated it may appear to some who inhabit senior common rooms and suppose themselves to be far from their deathbeds, many a childlike believer will gratefully reply:

> I am not skilled to understand
> What God hath willed, what God hath planned;
> I only know at his right hand
> Stands One who is my Saviour.[140]

Nothing that has been said implies the blurring of the Creator–creature distinction; on the contrary, it affirms it, but does so with special emphasis upon the ethical nature of the distinction. Although it is to Origen's credit that he denied Celsus's identification of the world and God, and although Augustine was correct in saying that 'Nothing can exist without him, yet nothing is what he is',[141] the Creator–creature distinction concerns more than cosmology. There is the moral distinction too, and to recognize ourselves before the holy as we are is to be aware of transcendent, holy love. It is not a matter of ascending the scale of being – that, said Lovell Cocks, is just 'pantheism in its Sunday best'.[142] It is to embark upon that new life in which the Creator–creature distinction becomes ever clearer, not least because 'They who fain would serve Thee best / Are conscious most of wrong within'.[143] But the distance is now a stimulus rather than a threat:

> 'It is one thing to be God', says St. Augustine 'and another to be partaker of God', and the essential character of this antithesis cannot be better or more emphatically expressed than in the well-known words of St. Thomas – 'We come as sick to the physician of life, unclean to the fountain of mercy, poor and needy to the Lord of all things . . . that we may receive the bread of angels, the King of Kings, the Lord of Lords, with a humble, lowly, and contrite heart.'[144]

In Christian theology the work of regeneration, and the work of bringing home to individuals the meaning of God's saving act in Christ, is traditionally said to be that of God the Holy Spirit. I need hardly point out that the notion of the indwelling Spirit is not to be regarded as a usurpation of the human – that would lead us to pantheism once more.[145] It is rather an account of how the sinner is prompted to seek forgiveness. The Spirit is the source of that restlessness of which Augustine spoke, which will not be stilled until we rest in God;[146] and of the realization expressed in the evangelical hymn:

> I sought the Lord and afterward I knew
> He moved my soul to seek Him, seeking me;
> It was not I that found, O Saviour true;
> No, I was found by Thee.[147]

The Spirit's work is not just to *be* 'that of God in every man' (George Fox), it is to make plain the moral gulf between God and ourselves and to prompt our desire for a remedy; it is to bring home to us Augustine's realization, 'You were with me, but I was not with you.'[148] But, if he is known to be savingly present, the Spirit has been at work in a gracious, unmerited way.[149] The Spirit is God as personally and restoratively present to us; he is not just our better selves. And just as the world and God are not to be identified, nor are the defaced *imago dei* and the Spirit: 'There is thus a real operational distinction between God's immanence as essence and as presence.'[150] The neglect of this point brings us close to pantheism yet again. Theodore Parker comes to mind, and so does W. N. Clarke, who writes: 'Salvation is not an exceptional gift from afar, but the characteristic working-out of the eternal divinity of God, and the communion of the Holy Spirit is the fulfilment of the ideal of existence.'[151] I have said enough about terms like 'afar', but what concerns me here is the suggestion that things are so inevitable that salvation is not an exceptional gift at all. To assert this is to have scuppered the Gospel.[152]

V

It remains to examine the claim that the transcendent–immanent God acts in the midst of human history, and that supremely in Christ. We shall first see how the claim has been made from the nineteenth century onwards; we shall note the positions of those who from a variety of motives have sought to oppose or minimize the claim; and I shall affirm the view that the traditional claim may not be surrendered by those who would commend the Christian faith.

We may set out from an address delivered to the Congregational Union of England and Wales by Enoch Mellor in 1863. If nothing else, his cadences of yesteryear will refresh those who have struggled with the clinical language of the philosophical analysts and the opaque deliverances of some postmodernists. Speaking two years after the publication of Colenso's commentary on Romans – a work which caused consternation in some circles for its alleged repudiation of cherished Christian beliefs – and with reference to broader questions of history which were by then becoming clamant, Mellor declared:

> Christ never taught that He was unrelated to the past. He stands upon it, He repudiates all other foundations. The facts of the Old Testament are cited by Himself and His apostles in the New. Many may deny them, and yet imagine that they can preserve the character and the mission of Christ. They can as soon smite from a building its foundation and leave the superstructure where it was, or tear the roof from a fabric in the vain fancy that its texture will be firm and compact as ever

> . . . We have to declare an eternal purpose, purposed in Christ Jesus before the world was – to narrate events that have happened once and for ever upon the theatre of the earth – to preach a redemption accomplished through suffering and blood – a resurrection, an ascension, an intercession, a judgment, a heaven, a hell! . . . In an age which has given so many indications of a tendency to undervalue the historic in Christanity, and to inculcate the belief that its reputed miracles encumber and despiritualize it, is it not incumbent on us to hold and publish the truth that there is no Gospel which is not historical? . . . If, unhappily, faith in the facts of the Gospel should in any of us begin to yield, our power as preachers will tremble as if smitten with palsy; and if that faith should desert us, we shall be as weak as Samson when shorn of his locks. The life of Christianity is in its facts, the motives of Christianity are in its facts, the impulses of Christianity are in its facts, the consolations of Christianity are in its facts, – it stands in its facts, or with its facts it falls.[153]

This is a stout assertion of the historicity of the gospels, and of the necessity of Christianity's historical rootedness. But it is more than that. It is the statement of one who is both content to regard miracles as having evidential value, and aware that the putative facts of the Gospel are interpreted – they concern 'an eternal purpose, purposed in Christ Jesus before the world was', for example – and to be apprehended by faith. Mellor thus appears as one who stands between the times. Thirty-six years on, Robert Flint judged matters thus: he argued that the Christian revelation is self-evidencing; its inherent reasonableness, not reasons extrinsic to it, 'constitute[s] the strongest proof of its truth'. This being so, the evidentialists 'certainly erred seriously when they separated, to the extent which they did, the proof of Christianity from its substance and content'; but equally at fault are those who have returned to the error of the deists (which the evidentialists for a time successfully combated), and have succumbed to 'the illusion that Christian faith is quite independent of historical facts and probable evidence'.[154]

Mellor's contemporary, the Mercersburg theologian J. W. Nevin, went so far as to say that 'Christ is the central fact, from which all other historical facts derive their significance. He is the key that unlocks its mysteries and apparent contradictions.'[155] This, undoubtedly, is a statement of faith, and an enigmatic one at that – at least to anyone with a positivistic approach to history, who might wonder how such claims could be empirically demonstrated.

But Nevin was not alone. The Presbyterian Henry Boynton Smith, of Union Theological Seminary, New York, was equally convinced that Christ is the centre of history, and that history bears 'the insignia of divine power'.[156] P. T. Forsyth understood the work of Christ as 'the supreme and compendious moral act in history', because of which 'thought places it at the creative centre of the new Humanity'. We thus have 'the turning-point of human destiny for all Eternity: we have the presence and act of God decisive for that purpose, a final salvation but not a final science of saving truth, a final faith but not a final theology'.[157] From the standpoint of biblical scholarship C. H. Dodd explained that Christianity

> takes the series of events recorded or reflected in the Bible, from the call of Abraham to the emergence of the Church, and declares that in this series the ultimate reality of all history, which is the purpose of God, is finally revealed, because the series itself is controlled by the supreme event of all – the life, death and resurrection of Jesus Christ. This valuation of the series is not imposed on it from without, but is an integral part of the history itself.[158]

The significance of Dodd's last sentence will become apparent as we proceed, but for a final illustration of the view that Jesus Christ is the centre of history, or in some sense 'final', we may turn to Lesslie Newbigin's short book, *The Finality of Christ.* He argues that 'To speak of the finality of Christ is to speak of the Gospel as the clue to history.'[159] This means that, contrary to the view of some other religions, history has meaning, that a particular understanding of God's character is entertained, that history is (against apparent counter-evidence) coherent and that the end of history is intimated to believers who are still in the midst of it. He makes it clear that while the Church is called to be the community which lives by the claim to Christ's centrality, it is nevertheless Christ and not Christianity as such who is final:

> To claim finality for Christ is to endorse the judgment of the apostles that in this life, death and resurrection God himself was uniquely present and that therefore the meaning and origin and end of all things was disclosed; it is to join with the apostles in making this judgment.[160]

To claim finality for Christ is, further, 'to imply a summons to men to forsake other claims to ultimate loyalty and to be converted to him'[161] – at which point the scandal of particularity presses acutely.

From the examples given it is clear not only that it is believed that Christianity as a religion has a history, but that history as such is particularly important to Christian faith, for the claim is that God has acted decisively within it. But as soon as this is said we face the questions of the availability and reliability of the evidence, the witnesses, the texts. What is to count as evidence? If, as was the case, we did not wish to allow the logical positivists to forget that there are no brute facts, and that all facts are interpreted, and selected according to various presuppositions and interests, we cannot now say that the historian faces specific facts 'neat'. We should take force of G. F. Woods's remark that 'no impersonal thing is a piece of evidence in itself. It becomes of evidential value only in relation to some historian conducting some historical enquiry. Its status as "evidence" is derived from the activity of persons who are acting as historians.'[162] Thus, as Anders Jeffner has said, 'The goal must be to do justice to the moral and religious life, without negating the knowledge that is based on science, or the results of scholarly research.'[163] But scholarly research can tend in directions hostile to the Christian claim, as William Temple pointed out long ago. Christianity, he wrote, is

> according to its own claim, primarily a self-revelation of God in a historical Person, and in that Person's life, death and resurrection. [At this point we recall Dodd's sentence affirming the valuation of the history as integral to it.] Because of this, it is open to attack on the historical plane as no other religion is. Because it is this, it is involved in all the difficulties that attend the treatment of the temporal and contingent as possessing the value of the eternal and absolute. These are peculiar difficulties of the Christian religion, from which others are free. But they arise from the central essence of that religion.[164]

There is considerable agreement among Christians that

> were it clearly demonstrated that Jesus Christ never existed, or that He was not the divine-human Being which the New Testament represents, the catholic faith of Christendom would be proved a great delusion, and, having lost my hope for time and for eternity, I should look round for some theosophy or 'natural religion' to be for me its little availing substitute.[165]

Hugo Meynell properly points out that 'the absolutely justified principle, that Christian faith must not be allowed to dictate the results of historical investigation, twists easily into the quite different, and in my view definitely false, assumption, that no conceivable result of historical criticism would make any difference to essential Christian faith'.[166]

To put it bluntly: if it could be shown conclusively that Christ was never raised then Christianity in any vital sense would fall, however much inertia and the weight of institutions might maintain a vestigial presence in the world. This is another way of saying that a religion which claims a historical rootedness cannot distance itself from the probabilities of history: 'it seems plain that any theology, maintaining redemption as historical fact (and not merely ideal), must attach religious importance to conclusions which are technically probable rather than proven'.[167]

In referring to the resurrection I have intentionally focused upon a major claim of Christianity which purports to be historical, but is, in the way it is generally understood, unique. By this I mean what whereas secular historians would know in principle how to corroborate such assertions as that 'Jesus was born' or 'Jesus died', they would be at a loss to apply their normal methods to the assertion 'Jesus was raised', or 'Jesus ever lives', for 'normal' comparisons would be ruled out. But this simply underlines the point that a positivistic methodology cannot accommodate the Christian claim, and this is what we should expect.[168] Further, the claim that 'Jesus was crucified', which secular historians might wish to investigate using their own methods and on the basis of their own presuppositions, is not on all fours with assertions which Christians wish to make concerning the Cross as the place where sin and death are finally vanquished. Moreover, it is not simply that Christians decide to interpret events in one way rather than another. It is that God reveals himself in the events in a way which, by the Holy Spirit, becomes clamant for believers. To repeat, none of this is to deny that, if it could be shown that Jesus had never lived, Christianity would fall.[169] It is simply to agree with C. J. Wright that 'We cannot logically or historically demonstrate that "God was in Christ"; no scientific or historical fact necessitates or involves the metaphysical conclusion which the term Incarnation presupposes.' He continues, as if echoing Flint, 'It was on the forgetfulness of this surely most obvious truth that there was erected that astonishing edifice of nineteenth-century "Evidences" apologetic.'[170] My own view is that there is a good deal of circumstantial evidence for the resurrection – the change in the disciples, the fact of the Church,[171] worship on the first day (a considerable departure from tradition for the disciples) – but such evidence does not begin to encompass the meaning to Christians of the resurrection. To believers the resurrection of Jesus Christ means not simply that he was resuscitated, but that he ever lives, that sin and the grave are vanquished, and that God's final victory is assured. Moreover, this is deemed to be a revelation from God brought home by the Spirit; it is not merely an interpretation which Christian individuals place upon ancient texts. Nevertheless, the texts in question must be held to be a sufficiently reliable basis for making christological and soteriological claims which include the elements of judgement and personal commitment, and which most Christians feel bound to make.[172] So far we may agree with Humphrey Palmer: 'It is sometimes said that we do not know Jesus, but only what early Christians said about him. It would be better to say, that what we can know about him depends on what we think of them.'[173] It also depends, of course, upon what God brings home to us through their testimony. And what is brought home is, to quote T. F. Torrance, 'a *complex fact that includes its own interpretation as part of its facticity*'.[174]

This is not to deny that Christians themselves are interpreting ancient texts. They select what they deem to be items of importance, they judge the significance of these, they tell a story. In this connection a choice remark of Austin Farrer's comes to mind:

> A naïve anachronism and an unconscious selectivity often achieve more than strenuous critical effort. Your theologian first defines himself back into the First Century by exegetical precision, and then argues himself out of it again through existential agonies. There is much to be said here as elsewhere for taking things easy, and doing what comes naturally.[175]

All history is somebody's history, and every historian's presuppositions and interpretations are open to challenge. Particular events or experiences, such as the biblical exodus, may prompt an entire genre of history-writing designed to show that God rescues and cares for his faithful people. To take an extra-biblical example, Ole Peter Grell has suggested that 'it is no coincidence that the three major martyrologies of Reformed Protestantism, those of

Jean Crespin, Adriaan van Haemstede and John Foxe, all grew out of their authors' personal experiences of persecution, flight and exile'.[176] What is more, interpretations of the same events may differ significantly. Consider the differing interpretations of history provided by Western European historians and those who lived under communist regimes who, it seems, were required to write, or rather to rewrite, history to order. Or what of the discussions in Spain concerning nationalist versus regional interpretations of that country's history – discussions which prompted the rueful comment of the Catalan writer, Sergi Pamiès: 'I know that when my children study history they will be told lies, so it doesn't make any difference if it's a nationalist lie or a Spanish lie – what hurts is that they do it with my taxes.'[177] Consider, too, how judgements of significance may differ even when no such interference is present. Imagine a person browsing in a public library. She rather aimlessly takes a book from a shelf and it falls open at a page on which the first sentence reads as follows: 'The most significant event in 1940 was the departure of Tommy McQuater, George Chisholm and six other instrumentalists from Ambrose's orchestra to the Royal Air Force, where they became the nucleus of the Squadronaires Dance Band.' The first thought to pass through the reader's mind might be 'But I should have thought that the evacuation from Dunkirk was a much more significant event in 1940'; and certainly, if the book purported to provide an account of the course of the Second World War, the judgement expressed in the sentence quoted would, to say the least, be distinctly odd, even perverse. If, however, the possible borrower then notices the title of the book, *Dance Bands of the Second World War*, she will presumably adjust her opinion in the light of the context now supplied. Of course, it would still be open to her, or to another writer on the same theme, to interpret events differently and to say, for example, that what really mattered in 1940 was Vera Lynn's departure from Ambrose – the prelude to her becoming the much travelled 'Forces' sweetheart'.[178] If she needed confirmation of the reported event the records of the RAF, the files of *Melody Maker*, a number of books and the reliable memories of such surviving stalwarts of that period as Chris Hayes, Harry Gold and Billy Amstell could all be consulted. These last could vouch for the *fact* that the reported departure of musicians occurred, but the question of the significance of the fact is a further step, and one which may elicit differences of opinion even on the part of those who agree as to the fact. Enquiries undertaken to substantiate the fact would be similar in kind to those which would in principle reveal that on such a day Jesus was crucified; but no such enquiries could encapsulate all that 'Cross' and 'resurrection' mean to Christians.

P. T. Forsyth made no bones about the interpretative nature of theology:

> Our faith begins with the historic Christ. But not with the biography of Christ (except for propaedeutic purposes). We begin, in principle if not in method, with Christ the crucified. We begin with the Church's saving faith in Christ, and not with the modern man's fair verdict on Him.[179]

The familiar accusation that Christianity turns upon the writings of biased witnesses can frequently be turned upon those who level the charge. But what is clear, as Jaspers so strongly insisted,[180] is that we cannot opt out of our own situation in order to claim an Olympian vantage point from which to view all things in an absolutely unconditioned way.[181] Happily, believers do not necessarily tell lies, and furthermore, 'The refusal to allow references to anything without alluding to the person experiencing it is in the end to give up the idea of one common, objective world to which we all can have access. Instead the "world" splits into myriad pieces.'[182] But if writing can be biased, so can 'readings'. The 'world' can split, analogously, if checks are not placed against those postmodernists whose readings of texts presuppose our inability to gain access to the author's intention, and entail simply the imaginative, individualistic, response of the present existing reader. For if I cannot in principle discern the authorial intention of a classical writer, I cannot, logically, discern the meaning intended by the bank manager from whom I received a letter concerning my overdraft this morning. The methodological obliteration of communication over time which this sceptical and relativistic doctrine of meaning entails renders all present communication impossible, as well as ruling out any understanding of history, the providence of God and the communion of saints. Faced with this dire result, many might wish to reinstate any one of a number of metanarratives if constructive human discourse once more became possible.

Ironically, some of those who adopt the criticized posture seek to mount arguments in favour of their readings of history, whether

Marxist, feminist, Tory, thereby lapsing into the modernism they profess to abhor by tacitly presupposing a standard of reference against which the readings of others may be judged. If they then take the further step of 'unchurching' those whose readings differ from their own, they have tumbled into a variety of sectarianism which makes them, psychologically at least, indistinguishable from – a mirror image of – those fundamentalists whose attitudes and beliefs they sometimes denounce – despite the fact, once more, that on their relativistic presuppositions there can be nothing to choose between the opposing views.

In taking its stand on history in the way it does, Christianity does something unusual among the religions. Plato, for example, while he hoped to refine the more objectionable myths of religion, did not contemplate the irruption of the divine into history, and, as Paul later observed, the notion of a Son of God crucified in history was 'unto the Greeks foolishness'.[183] Similar offence was caused to many Hellenistic minds by the qualification that 'the Word *became flesh, he made his home among us*'.[184] We can at least understand why Reade should declare that 'The very quintessence of Christianity is the substitution of history for myth.'[185] In so doing he reveals a divide in Anglican theology, on the other side of which is W. R. Inge, whose Platonist commitment to a mystical (yet tough-minded) spirituality prompted his running theme that perfect knowledge of the Perfect is the goal of philosophy and religion alike.[186] Aristotle likewise did not conceive of a God who had a thought or a care for the world, while the Stoic tendency to identify the world with God yielded a world soul but no possibility of an incarnation in history. Hence James Iverach's summary statement: 'the highest Greek thought about God was either an empty abstraction termed being, or a God who was occupied with himself, or a God who was the living, moving principle of the world, and who was nothing apart from the world'.[187] We saw in Chapter 2 that Justin Martyr, though more inclined to speak of Christ's becoming man than other apologists, nevertheless, like them, has much to say concerning salvation from demonic powers by embracing true doctrine, but little concerning a historic Incarnation. We noted that Irenaeus, with Gnostics in his sights, was more definite on the historic Incarnation and its redemptive significance. He refers to the prophets who,

> receiving the prophetic gift from the same Word, announced His advent according to the flesh, by which the blending and communion of God and man took place according to the good pleasure of the Father, the Word of God foretelling from the beginning that God should be seen by men, and hold converse with them upon earth, should confer with them and should be present with His own creation, saving it and becoming capable of being perceived by it, and freeing us from the hands of all that hate us, that is, from every spirit of wickedness, and causing us to serve Him in holiness and righteousness all our days, in order that man, having embraced the Spirit of God, might pass into the glory of the Father.[188]

For his part, Origen, though equally keen to challenge the Gnostics, was persuaded that the true Christian Gnostic had risen above the historical events and circumstances of the life of Jesus: the eternal truths inculcated by those events are all important.

My objective in referring with almost unforgivable brevity to the Greek philosophers, and in recalling some early theologians, was to indicate that insofar as the latter sat loose to history (and they did this, as we have seen, to varying degrees), it was partly because of the pull of their Hellenistic inheritance, and partly because they were responding in kind to their intellectual opponents. They are thus in a very different position from those to whom we now turn, who seek to safeguard the faith from post-Enlightenment historical criticism turned hostile. Though their motive was different, however, one scholar at least thought that their end result landed them back with the Greeks:

> To discard all the historical affirmations to which the Church is committed, and then to offer the world a spiritualism [whether idealistic or existentialist, one might add] beyond the reach of sceptical historians, is in effect to revert to the Platonic expedient of edifying myths.[189]

If an over-simplification may be forgiven (for, in fact, there are overlaps between the positions to be distinguished) we may say that from the Enlightenment onwards two types of difficulty have been expressed where Christianity and its historical claims are concerned. Some have raised philosophical questions concerning the relation of history to eternity; others have sought to preserve the faith by loosening their ties with historical events perceived as problematic, even as unnecessary. A principal inspiration of the former class of questions is Lessing.

As P.T. Forsyth and others of his critics have hastened to explain, Lessing, with his elevation of love above doctrinal considerations,[190] and his view that the value of religions is to be judged according to the extent to which they conduce to right living, opened the way for that moral thrust in theology which Kant, in his own way, urged further. To this extent they saved Christianity from both orthodox rationalism and introverted pietism, though at the same time they gave it an ethical escape route from the onslaughts of hostile historical criticism.[191] Thus Kant declares that a revealed faith, being historical, cannot claim universality because it 'can never be universally communicated so as to produce conviction'.[192] In this he was clearly in the line of Lessing, who famously averred: 'Accidental truths of history can never become the proof of necessary truths of reason.'[193] This is because, where historical truth is concerned, probability is ineradicable; historical truths are not susceptible to rational demonstration, and hence nothing can be demonstrated by appealing to them. This is not all, however, as David Pailin and others have emphasized: Lessing's claim is that accidental and necessary truths belong to different logical types and hence neither can be derived from the other.[194] Thus he asks: 'If on historical grounds I have no objection to the statement that this Christ himself rose from the dead, must I therefore accept it as true that this risen Christ was the Son of God?'[195] This is Lessing's 'ugly, broad ditch' over which he had frequently and earnestly tried to leap, without success.[196] For him, therefore, the most that the story of Jesus can do is to symbolize religious truths.

Pailin has fairly characterized the responses to Lessing thus: (1) John Henry Newman and John Macquarrie recognize and embrace the fact that religious faith is a matter of a commitment which goes beyond what is provable; (2) Kierkegaard pits faith, construed as a leap, against reason understood as that which affords the ground of warranted judgements; (3) most theologians hold that 'faith is a deliberate assent made on the basis of what is appreciated to be evidence that can at best support only probable conclusions'.[197] I do not wish to pursue Pailin's arguments in detail, though I suspect that he concedes too much to Lessing's rationalism, or neglects possible alternative responses to him, or both. Rather, I wish to offer my own response to Lessing.

First, Lessing writes in an intellectual climate in which much importance is attached to the sufficiency of the necessary truths of reason and the accessibility to all of natural religion. But some of the cardinal assertions of Christianity, such as that God is love, are not necessary truths of reason; and an entire race of atheists has arisen since Lessing's day to remind us that natural religion is not the universal phenomenon he thought it was. The fundamental truth of the Christian Gospel is that in Christ God has acted redemptively within human history; but this is not like a truth of arithmetic. We do not prove it is the same way; we may desire to believe it; but if we do believe it it is because it has been brought home to us by God the Holy Spirit. It must be confessed that orthodox believers themselves have not always grasped this point. Hence the telling witness of Robert Mackintosh, a self-styled 'refugee' from scholastic Calvinism:

> It cannot be denied that the *historicity* of the Christian revelation is obscured in the Westminster Confession. Its writers have in view a dogmatic system, just as Romanists have in view an ecclesiastical system . . . It needed the [Enlightenment] criticism of misbeliefs and disbeliefs to teach the dogmatists what they ought to be doing – not arguing, but bearing witness – not for a doctrine, but for a life, – for one who 'was with the Father, and was manifest to us', that we 'might have life through His name', – manifest at a definite point of time, under definite circumstances, in a definite Personality; since when He has worked unceasingly, through the Church, and without the Church, and in spite of the Church – through the Bible, and outside of the Bible, and in spite of the misinterpreted Bible. Of course the representation of Christianity as resting upon argument narrows the conception of revelation. The apologists did not simply give the historic element its due place; they turned away almost entirely from the moral element . . . One is tempted to inquire, whether the Lessing view of revelation as a republishing of moral truth is not the complementary abstraction to that of the orthodox apologists.[198]

Mackintosh's contemporary, James Denney, was in general agreement and, against Lessing, he declared:

> Christianity does not mean the recognition of necessary truths of reason, but an attitude of the soul to God, determined by Christ; and history is not to the religious man a chapter of accidents, but the stage on which a Divine purpose is achieved which could not be more ineptly described than by calling it accidental. Religion can no more be

simplified by making it independent of history than respiration would be simplified by soaring beyond the atmosphere.[199]

Secondly, historical truth, though accidental in the sense that what has happened might conceivably not have happened, is not accidental in the sense that the transcendent yet immanent God is outside of history and unconcerned with it. On the contrary he guides it providentially. Thus history could be described as accidental only on the presupposition (for it has not been shown) that God is not present as creator and sustainer within it.

Thirdly, there is an affinity between God and humanity, traditionally characterized in terms of the *imago dei*, which renders redundant Lessing's way of positing the logically distinct types of necessary truths of reason and accidental truths of history. Further, there is a personal relationship with God made known through the contingencies of history as Father, which makes Pailin's third possible response to Lessing, namely, that of faith as the giving of assent on the basis of evidence that can support only probable conclusions, seem distinctly chilly. In the words of A. E. Garvie,

> The knowledge of God as Father which is mediated by Christ is neither *intuitional*, as a native endowment of the mind of man, nor *inferential*, as the conclusion of a process of reasoning, nor yet *mystical* as an immediate contact with God without any historical mediation, but *experiential* and *practical*. Salvation is *experienced*, not only in the religious consciousness, but also in the moral character; the man who through faith in the grace of Christ has found forgiveness is renewed unto holiness.[200]

Fourthly, the mediation of which Garvie speaks is a matter of God's gracious initiative. In the matter of our faith, God does not do nothing. Rather, he enables a personal response to his grace in Christ. As Forsyth expostulated, 'As a matter of fact, rightly or wrongly, history *has* yielded to the soul a God in an historic act which is in its nature eternal.'[201] This word 'eternal' brings us face to face with the eschatological reality which, once again, Lessing's way of stating matters cannot accommodate. Yet

> everything in Christian theology turns on the real presence of One who is really God and really in history; and the form of that real presence is the coming of *ho Eschatos*, who is also *ho Protos*; and His coming is

> always and everywhere *to eschaton*, an enactment of the end where man is justified even in his ungodliness by the death and resurrection of the Son of God in the rôle of Son of man.[202]

All of which is another way of saying that the interpretation of the Christ event is given in and with the event itself – however variously we ourselves may receive and construe it.

VI

We may now turn to that aspect of the question which concerns the difficulties, felt by many, which ensued when modern historical criticism was applied to the Bible and especially to the gospels. It is a long story with an extensive literature.[203] For our present purposes it will suffice to cite D. F. Strauss as exemplifying extremely those who distinguished between mythological expressions of the Christian idea and the facts of history. His critical policy was that 'in the person and acts of Jesus no supernaturalism shall be suffered to remain'.[204] Thus the resurrection becomes not a historical occurrence, but a symbol of humanity's dying and rising, Jesus being the paradigm case of this process.

Confronted by such historical scepticism, theologians and philosophers adopted a variety of positions. Ritschl, believing that by limiting human knowledge to knowledge of phenomena Kant had opened the way to a moral foundation for Christian truth, advanced his theory that 'We know the being of God only within His value for us'.[205] Ritschl does not, of course, mean that God exists only when somebody values him, but that as believers evaluate the benefits God confers upon them they are conscious of the reality of God.[206] For their part, as I showed at some length in *Philosophical Idealism and Christian Belief*, the philosophical idealists tended to sidestep the historical difficulties by construing Christianity in terms of symbolized ideas. Thus the dying and rising motif construed with reference to humanity as a whole is strong in the writings of Edward Caird,[207] and closely related to his view of divine–human continuity; while T. H. Green declared that 'the belief in the events was derived from the ideas . . . not the ideas from the real happening of the events'.[208] He further proposed that 'Christian dogma . . . must be retained in its completeness, but it must be transformed into a philosophy'.[209] Remarks such as this drew forth James Iverach's lament that for Green 'the historical Christ has vanished, and has been succeeded by the idea'.[210] Concerning a prominent personal idealist, Robert Mackintosh's verdict was that 'If we transfer Christian evidence from the "historical" to the "philosophical" with H. Rashdall – we surely cut down Christianity to the limits of theism.'[211] And P. T. Forsyth's general verdict was that 'the very historical reality of Jesus is now denied by the untrammelled evolution of criticism . . . and a totally different religion, fitted with all modern appliances and conveniences, takes its place as the religion of Monism'.[212] Not, indeed, that theologians alone were concerned by the drift from history. Where F. H. Bradley advised, 'Enquire by all means whether and how far there is good evidence for their [that is, the events of Jesus's life] happening. But do not imagine that Christianity is vitally concerned with the result of your inquiry',[213] his philosophical colleague, R. G. Collingwood, commenting on Bradley's *The Presuppositions of Critical History* (1874), noted Bradley's indebtedness to the tradition of sceptical criticism flowing down from Strauss, and pointed out that the destructiveness of the findings of that tradition of criticism 'was due not simply to the use of critical methods, but to the positivistic spirit in which those methods were used'.[214]

Undeterred, the biblical scholar Schmiedel reassured his readers that 'My inmost religious convictions would suffer no harm even if I now felt obliged to conclude that Jesus never lived',[215] on which James Denney remarked, 'How it is to be cured I do not know, but the number of people who are on the slope that ends here, and who suppose that they are Christians while it is all the same to them if Christ never lived, is appalling.'[216] Similar displeasure was expressed by W. R. Inge against the truths of history/truths of faith dualism of the Catholic Modernists who held, with Loisy, that 'The historian does not need to remove God from history, for he never encounters Him there.' This, said Inge, 'is the desperate expedient of men who wish to remain Catholics after they have ceased to be Christians'.[217]

The problematic nature of biblical, and especially of New Testament, history seems to have made a lasting impression upon both Barth and Bultmann, despite the fact that in other respects they departed significantly from their liberal teachers, Harnack and Herrmann, though H. J. Paton was not alone in observing that 'One of the strangest tendencies of modern times is to reject or belittle the historical facts and yet to construct a dogmatic theology very similar to the old – to gather, as has been said, apologetic figs from sceptical thistles.'[218] Be that as it may, references may be cited which reveal an ambivalence in Barth's view of biblical history. There can be no doubt that his overriding desire is to have the Bible interpreted in relation to his major christological thrust. The primary objective is to interpret texts as witnessing to the Word which is Christ: the question of how far they relate to the historical Jesus is of secondary importance. Indeed, consideration of the latter question would tempt one in the direction of employing natural reason and secular historical investigative techniques, whereas the main purpose of scripture is to witness to the Word of God. On the other hand, he declares that 'The death of Jesus Christ can certainly be thought of as history in the modern sense, but not the resurrection.'[219] The resurrection happened, he says, but cannot be grasped historically. We thus seem to have one class of events which are susceptible to historical investigation, and one event which is not so susceptible, yet is deemed nevertheless to have been a historical occurrence. His problem is that the witnesses to the resurrection were not impartial (the very point made, though with different motive, by generations of sceptics and scoffers); they were believers who did not set out to adduce evidence for that in which they believed. We must therefore accept their testimony by faith, for to seek objective grounds would be once again to ground faith upon human reason.

For Bultmann's earnest desire to reach modern people for whom the thought world of the Bible is remote I have nothing but praise, though it is not to my present purpose to do more than make passing reference to his programme of demythologization. Unlike some older liberal theologians who sought to smoothe away the more angular aspects of Christian doctrine so as to make the faith more palatable to modern people, Bultmann wishes to confront his readers with the scandal, or offence, of God's unique act in history in Christ. He upholds this against Gnostics ancient and modern, declaring that through this once-for-all deed God gives new life which is not otherwise available.[220] But at once we detect a tension. For Bultmann is a Lutheran, and justification by grace through faith alone is in his blood. He cannot therefore permit us to rely on anything other than faith. Hence, although on the one hand he wishes to maintain the historicity of God's redemptive act at the Cross, he also seems to undermine the historical when describing his approach in these terms:

> de-mythologizing is the radical application of the doctrine of justification by faith to the sphere of knowledge and thought. Like the doctrine of justification, de-mythologizing destroys every longing for security. There is no difference between security based on good works and security built on objectifying knowledge.[221]

On reading this the comment of R. P. C. Hanson comes to mind:

> the strongest of all the motives for historical scepticism in the minds of New Testament scholars has been the Lutheran distrust of the search of an objective basis for faith. It should be remembered that the vast majority of early form critics were Lutherans, and the majority of leading Form Critics still are Lutherans.[222]

Similar ecclesial thoughts are engendered when considering Bultmann's indebtedness to the existentialism of Heidegger, whose colleague he had been at Marburg from 1922 to 1928. As is well known, in *Being and Time* (1927) Heidegger redirected hermeneutics away from the epistemological approaches of Schleiermacher and Dilthey, towards an ontological understanding of the matter. *Dasein*, unlike other phenomena in the world, is the being who knows himself or herself as possessed by self-concern, as not being 'at home' in the world, as fallen; we are thrown into being, and are anxious. As we perceive our existential situation we can also conceive of how things might be; and authentic existence is achieved as we make the appropriate response of decision. Bultmann's Christian (Lutheran) refinement of this is to contend that it is by faith alone that such a decision is made; apart from this authentic existence will elude us. Any existence we could achieve on our own would be inauthentic. Accordingly, we must yield ourselves to God's grace as proclaimed in the *kerygma*.

However, a further and older Lutheran is implicated in Bultmann's thought: Kierkegaard, with his emphasis upon the 'infinite qualitative distinction' between eternity and time, and his conviction that 'from history one can learn nothing about Christ'.[223] The present existential situation is thus thrown into relief. Revelation is not a matter of propositions; it is not concerned with historical events in the past; it is a matter of being confronted in the here and now by him who was dead but ever lives, and making the appropriate response of faith.[224] To fasten upon details of history would, he thinks, be to make the doomed attempt 'to express the otherworldly in terms of this world and the divine in terms of human life, the other side in terms of this side'.[225] Because the saving action is that of the eternal God it cannot be subject to historical investigation. By the same token, while we may be aware of God, we cannot know him in any sense which would objectify him – such a God would not be worth knowing. We are aware of God in the moment in which by existential decision we encounter him.[226] Thus the upshot is, in Bultmann's own words, 'I *am* trying to substitute anthropology for theology, for I am interpreting theological affirmations as assertions about human life.'[227] All of which is exemplified in his distinction between history as *historisch* and as *geschichtlich*. The former denotes the method of the secular – even the positivist – historian, and concerns events which lie in the past; the latter, the existentialist view of history's significance which Bultmann espouses; and the distinction is consistent with the disjunction Bultmann posits between God and the world.[228] As Colin Gunton has written,

> if the theologian refuses to locate the action of God in time, either because that is impossible on the modern understanding of the world, or because it is theologically forbidden to attempt to 'prove' or 'verify' what must be accepted by faith alone . . . then it is not a large step to seeing the gospel in terms of truths that are in some way independent of time and history.[229]

But with this we return to the peril which confronted Bultmann's idealist predecessors, as we have seen.[230]

From none of the foregoing should we conclude that Bultmann thinks it impossible to speak of the life and deeds of Jesus.[231] But we can never proceed from assertions concerning his life to credal claims about his true nature, for example. Thus, he continues in the line of those who radically distinguished the Jesus of history from the Christ of faith. Not, indeed, that he is able to accept everything as reported about Jesus. But the consequence of his view is that 'our knowledge of Christ the Saviour cannot claim any support from historical evidence'.[232] He separates out the resurrection from all the other events of Jesus's life. He will, for example, accept that Jesus lived on this earth,[233] while insisting that the significance of the Incarnation is eschatological.[234] Martin Kähler, with his view that 'the real Christ is the preached Christ', seems to be the fountainhead of this claim.[235] Again, Bultmann will agree that crucifixion of Jesus occurred in history, while at the same time holding that to believe in the Cross is to make the Cross 'the determining power of [one's] life';[236] but he denies the historicity of the resurrection,[237] remarking that 'The real Easter faith is faith in the word of preaching which brings illumination.'[238] Against this reductionism H. P. Owen rightly protested:

> the essence of the Resurrection is that it both occurred in time and transcended time . . . When St Paul preached the Resurrection he preached an historical event that had objectively occurred . . . At the same time he preached the risen Christ as an historic person who was present subjectively to believers through the Holy Spirit. St. Paul did not regard these two elements in his Kerygma as coexisting in a dialectical tension; he thought of them as complementary aspects of a single fact.[239]

It follows that in the New Testament 'faith', though existential, is not a Bultmannian 'leap'; rather, it 'is always grounded in a sure apprehension of the objective historical facts of apostolic testimony'.[240] We may allow D. W. Forrest, a younger contemporary of Kähler, to proclaim the moral:

> To declare to those who assail the genuineness of the Gospels, that our faith would remain substantially unchanged even if they succeeded in discrediting them, is to play into their hands. 'Precisely as we thought,' they reply. 'Your faith is founded on an inward experience of your own, corroborated by the similar experience of other people; it is a devout imagination, partly your own, partly inherited. But you may as well drop out the historical element, when you have lost all direct touch with historical proof.' *It is exactly this direct touch with the historical Jesus* which the simplest Christian knows to lie at the root of his confidence.[241]

The probabilities of history are not to be sidestepped either in the name of idealism whether rationalistically or existentially construed. On the other hand,

> If the historian as such were able to discern the Godhead within the historical Jesus, the Incarnation would be a mere theophany. But the historian as such knows Jesus only 'after the flesh,' and his reconstruction of the historical figure is always a picture on the two dimensional

plane of historical causality. Faith cannot be rescued from this embarrassment. Because God becomes man in Jesus the historian must be allowed to say his say, yet his research creates no crucial difficulties for faith so long as his Jesus of History is *not* a Jesus whom the believer cannot regard as the incarnate Word.[242]

The Cross–resurrection event is the paradigm case in history of the transcendent–immanent God's action in his Son to vanquish sin and the grave, and to open the kingdom of heaven to all believers. Positivistic historians may be expected to work with preupppositions which exclude such a claim; it is doubly disconcerting when theologians embrace a time–eternity dualism which encourages them in the same direction.[243] Among those who have, post-Bultmann, sought to maintain judicious balance is Wolfhart Pannenberg, and with his observation I shall conclude my investigation of the philosophical or historico-theological reasons (in my view untenable) why some have sat loose to the historical rootedness of the Christian faith:

> A person does not bring faith with him to the event as though faith were the basis for finding the revelation of God in the history of Israel and Jesus Christ. Rather, it is through an open appropriation of these elements that true faith is sparked. A faith that lacks a historical basis with no obligation to square them with history is impossible to distinguish from superstition and illusion.[244]

It remains briefly to note the positions of one philosopher and one theologian. The philosopher is Wittgenstein, in whose writings the philosophical and historical considerations we have been reviewing are blended in an intriguing way. I shall quote him, interspersing his remarks with my own italicized comments:

> Christianity does not *rest* in historical truth; rather it offers us a (historical) narrative and says: now believe!
> *Christianity does not originate in historical truths positivistically conceived. It rests on God's grace which, though active historically supremely in Christ (and hence accessible by us), does not originate in history – it is supernatural in the sense proposed earlier.*
> Queer as it sounds: The historical accounts in the Gospels might, historically speaking, be *demonstrably false*, and yet belief lose nothing by this: *not*, however, because it [belief] concerns 'universal truths of reason'! [Truths, that is, which any person possessing reason must *a priori* rationally accept].

> *Wittgenstein refuses the route taken by philosophical idealists.*
> Rather, because historical proof (the historical proof game) is irrelevant to belief [in Jesus Christ as God].[245]
> *This is because Wittgenstein regards the concept of the God-man as logically absurd. It would therefore be pointless to seek historical proof. Leaving on one side the fact that he here begs the Christological question, I would ask, 'While Christians do not believe only because of the history construed in secular ways, would they not be irrational if they continued to believe if that history revealed once and for all that Jesus never lived?' And did not Wittgenstein himself elsewhere say:* If we imagine the facts otherwise than as they are, certain language-games lose some of their importance.[246]
> *In the case to hand, if the crucial facts of Christianity were otherwise than they are the religion would fall. This dire outcome need not be expected, however, because Christianity's facts, though interpretable by us in diverse and even contradictory ways, are most notable for being at the same time in history yet not of it – rooted here, yet of eschatological significance and divine donation. 'God is His own interpreter, And He will make it plain'*[247] *– well, if not as plain as a pikestaff, at least not utterly opaque.*

The theologian is Maurice Wiles. In a number of books and articles he has, in a lucid and sensitive way, raised the question of God's action in the world. It is not my intention to examine his argument in detail, but simply to draw attention to his method in relation to the foregoing discussion. His strategy is to tackle the broad question of God's providential activity in the world prior to discussing the particular case of Jesus, 'because apart from that broader question the more specific claims about Christ cannot even be coherently formulated, let alone appropriately discussed'.[248] This is consistent with his earlier approach:

> The glory of the created order, the potential for good of the natural setting of our human life, the worth of human relationships – all these are implicit in the kind of theistic belief that I have been developing. They do not logically require belief in the incarnation.[249]

On reading such claims I wonder whether, by starting elsewhere than from God's act in Christ, we may not tend in a 'Greek' direction whereby undifferentiated Being is our subject, rather than the God and Father of our Lord Jesus Christ; and where the christologically unspecific idea of God as 'the living God, the course of all life and the source of that authentic life which his worshippers seek to realize in grateful awareness of his all-pervasive and sustaining presence'[250] is the last word. This Hellenizing possibility is enhanced when Wiles understands 'a God-given resurrection' as 'the answer to human finitude and death'.[251] Undeniably this Hellenistic estimate that the human problem centres in finitude flows into Patristic writers and others. But if, as I think it can fairly be claimed, the New Testament places the emphasis upon the divine–human relationship disrupted by sin – that is to say: if the emphasis is interpersonal as between God and ourselves, moral more than ontological, a gracious gift of a holy Father's forgiveness offered through the Spirit on the ground of the Son's finished work – then to start elsewhere than from the Cross may lead us to attenuate the Gospel. It will also, incidentally, deprive us of an answer to Karl Popper who, with reference to the calamities of history, contends that 'If history is the work of a merciful God, it can be so only if His will for us is inscrutable, incomprehensible, and unfathomable.'[252] For it is in the Cross–resurrection event that we discern God's will and witness his victory in principle over all the calamities that might and do smite us: 'This insistence on the ontic reality of history, despite the way in which it eludes our direct grasp, means already that we are not dealing with "cunningly devised fables" when the power and coming of our Lord Jesus Christ is made known.'[253]

Moreover, the discernment of which I speak is undertaken not in solitariness, but, to resume the ecclesiological theme, in a 'community of discernment',[254] to use Ross Bender's phrase; and the task of discernment

> is to be carried out within a cognitive frame of reference which involves first, the perception that God is acting in human history; second, a lively sense of being caught up in God's purposive activity; and third, an awareness of the eschatological character of our existence.[255]

The transcendent-yet-immanent holy God, who by a supernatural miracle of grace acts redemptively in the world, brings his truth home to us by the Holy Spirit and grants us new life. Having once spoken, supremely in the Cross–resurrection event, he does not leave us. Rather, 'by His Holy Spirit, he also assures me of eternal life, and makes me wholeheartedly willing and ready from now on to live for him'.[256] But this conjunction of cognition and experience prompts us towards Part III of this book. A paragraph by Ronald Hepburn will provide a bridge between this chapter and the next. With reference to the Christian view of history he writes:

> There are at work here two *disastrously* conflicting movements of thought. The one wants to speak of God entering into the relativities of history. According to the other, we must emphasize that God is no object among objects, no person among persons: his mode of being is so unlike that of objects or persons that it is scarcely possible to think of him as any sort of individual entity at all, however exalted. He is 'Being-Itself', or 'beyond being'.[257]

As to the first position, while it cannot be denied that, notably at Christmas-time, one hears talk of God in the manger, this is, strictly, careless talk; for, as I hope this chapter has made plain, it is God in Christ, God the Son, who is incarnate, and Jesus of Nazareth is very much bound up with the relativities of history. As to the second position, this anticipates our discussion of natural theology, one aspect of which will concern the helpfulness or otherwise to Christian confession of the legacy of Greek ontological language which, as we have just seen, flows down to our own time in the stimulating writings of Maurice Wiles, among others.

III

ALTERNATIVE APOLOGETIC STARTING POINTS

What more can be done to the Disgrace and Ruin of Christianity than to make the world believe that we have no reason for it.

(Richard Baxter, *The Saint's Everlasting Rest*, 1650)

I remain unconvinced that *my* difficulty in believing in God says very much about God . . . I cannot seriously entertain the notion that the reality of any God worthy of the name depends on how vividly I am able to conceive of him at a given moment.

(Robert McAfee Brown, *The New Christian*, 2 April 1970)

6

Reason and Revelation

It is time to take stock. In Part I of this book I sought to express as positively as I could what the generality of Christians wish to confess. I claimed that such confession is a broad, ecclesial task, one aspect of which is the intellectual commendation of the faith to enquirers or professional opponents. I then discussed the Christian idea that the confessors are, like all people, created in the image of God; and, in view of the different accents in which the faith has been confessed at different times and places, I asked how far we may legitimately speak of the one faith of the ages. I concluded that the gathering in worship of the ecclesial community and the confession of Christ as Lord and Saviour is a witness to this unity, however much doctrinal formulations and individual testimonies may vary over time.

In Part II I first tackled the views of positivists, Wittgensteinians and postmodernists, and sought to show how, in their different ways, they appear to exclude from the outset the possibility that Christian discourse genuinely refers to God; and then I turned more particularly to those for whom the ideas of transcendence, immanence and a supernatural act of God in history are from various points of view problematic. My hope was to show that the presuppositions of such critics need not be adopted, and that when they are not Christian claims have their opportunity. Clearly, the strategy in Part II was negative; it entailed showing how, if we set out from certain starting points, we shall not be able to admit Christian claims. What I must now seek to do in Part III is to ask how far good positive grounds may be offered for Christian claims. Traditionally, appeals to reason and experience have been made.

We must consider the viability of these in this chapter and the next.

In approaching these themes we are immediately confronted by two problems. The first is the breadth of connotation of the terms 'reason', 'revelation', 'faith' and 'experience'. The second is that of deciding in which order to treat them. A case can be made for several methods of approach, but I shall be guided by the main course of Christian intellectual history. I propose first to discuss reason and revelation (because of what is frequently understood as the two-stage approach of traditional natural theology, in which revelation is deemed to supplement the deliverances of reason – a more problematic interpretation of natural theology than is sometimes appreciated); and then faith and experience (faith and experience having come into their own, so to speak, in the wake of searching Enlightenment critiques of classical theism). I should emphasize, however, that my objective is to show that the proposed division of topics is artificial, since if we would commend the Christian faith we cannot rest content with strong disjunctions between reason and revelation, reason and faith, experience and reason. That is, I shall hope to end with an understanding of faithful reason and reasonable faith – with a reasonable eclecticism which is not the product of muddle, but is appropriate to the nature of what is to be commended, namely, a Gospel which appeals to the whole person.[1] My proposed division of topics is thus partly attributable to the fact that one cannot say everything at once; partly to the fact that in the history of Christian apologetics thinkers have as a matter of fact taken either reason, revelation, faith or experience as their starting points.

I

On 13 February 1852 the Reverend Thomas Weaver, for fifty-four years minister in Shrewsbury, died. The celebrated John Angell James preached the funeral oration. Conscious that 'God is gathering home His aged labourers to Himself', James called upon young ministers to devote themselves wholeheartedly to the cause of the Gospel: 'Talk they of intellectualism, of philosophy, of rationalism', he declared, 'the best intellectualism, philosophy, and rationalism, are all contained in the glorious Gospel.'[2] James did not delay over clarifying his meaning or defining his terms – and perhaps a funeral service was not the place, nor he the best person, for this. Although I do not expect complete success, I cannot be as abstemious as James. On the contrary, if I am even to approach my objective, I must pay careful attention to the changes which have been rung on such terms as those which tripped so lightly from the preacher's tongue.

According to the old faculty psychology, reason was contrasted with faith, inspiration and the like, as if these were independent yet related entities in the mind. The eighteenth-century Presbyterian divine John Taylor was not untypical in offering the following definition:

> Reason is that Faculty of Mind, by which we perceive, or understand the Truth, or the Natures of Things, and are capable of considering, distinguishing, comparing and judging of their Natures, Properties, Circumstances and Relations, and of discerning what is agreeable to, or inconsistent with them.[3]

Such hypostasizing is nowadays distinctly unfashionable, for it is understood that I do not somehow possess a mental entity, 'reason', in the way in which I possess a nose. Rather, I engage in the activity or process of reasoning; and I do this in order to construct and evaluate arguments, to devise and commend theories, to determine and justify actions, to discriminate between truth and falsehood, to offer explanations, to order my experience, to understand and evaluate the arguments, activities and products of others. It is widely agreed that the rules of deductive logic concern the relations between propositions, not the way things are in the world, and that, while they are not to be violated in argumentation, their terms of reference comprise part only of the sphere within which human reasoning occurs. Hence, 'To be "reasonable" is a much broader concept than to be a follower of a set of specifiable rules of logic.'[4] That this view is generally held is, as we shall see, all to the good where the enterprise of commending the Christian faith is concerned; and so are the challenges which have been posed to the notion that there is one 'scientific method' of establishing all claims to knowledge in the empirical sphere. It is not that Christian claims are such that they need the assistance of sloppy argumentation; it is that, as with the restrictive methodologies of the positivists, Wittgensteinians and some postmodernists, no barriers must be erected *ab initio* which would preclude the articulation of the Christian case.

That case includes the claim that, in John Wesley's words, Christianity is

> a religion evidently founded on, and in every way agreeable to, eternal reason, to the essential nature of things. Its foundation stands on the nature of God and the nature of man, together with their mutual relations. And it is every way suitable thereunto. To the nature of God, for it begins in knowing him . . . It goes on in loving him and all mankind . . . It ends in serving him, in doing his will, in obeying him whom we know and love. It is in every way suited to the nature of man, for it begins in man's knowing himself: knowing himself to be what he really is – foolish, vicious, miserable. It goes on to point out the remedy for this . . . It finishes all by restoring the due relations between God and man . . .[5]

Clearly, this is Wesley in epistemological mode: he knows quite well that Christianity is founded upon God's grace (and I have already hinted that there are dangers for Christian apologetics in thinking of God in terms of eternal reason – and of Being and the Absolute – rather than in terms of holy love supremely revealed at the Cross). But my point here is that Wesley's words underline the fact that, far from being exhaustively defined in terms of logical inference, 'reason' concerns faith, obediential living (the 'reasonable service' of the Book of Common Prayer), self-knowledge and, above all, knowledge of God. This paves the way for the argument to be made later that truth apprehended by faith is not non-rational[6] – indeed, that we intuitively grasp the reality of both God and the world. But we grasp what is presented to us; and here we verge upon the theme of revelation for, as Nathanael Emmons pointed out, by reason 'we are to understand the natural power, faculty or capacity of discerning and investigating truth, as improved by exercise, and assisted by divine revelation'.[7] Accordingly, I endorse W. G. De Burgh's view that while logical processes 'are intrinsic to the exercise of man's intellect . . . the reduction of reason to ratiocination . . . entails its vilification. Ratiocination is a means to an end; and, if this alone be the business of the intellect, reason becomes "the slave of the passions."'[8] In the even more succinct words of (presumably) Simon Patrick, 'he that will rightly make use of his Reason, must take all that is reasonable into consideration'.[9]

By means of a few soundings, I shall first exemplify the diverse attitudes adopted towards human reason in the course of Christian intellectual history. This will lead us towards a consideration of the viability of natural theology, a major apologetic tool which many Christian thinkers have utilized.

Armed with the caution that my classifications do not imply absolute disjunctions (indeed, they are little more than an attempt to find a coherent pathway through a mass of material), we may first note some who regard reason as limited because wounded by sin; others who tend in the direction of, and in some cases arrive at, the undue exaltation of human rational powers – these will raise for us the questions of revelation as propositional, the foundationalist–nonfoundationalist issue, and the degree to which, if at all, Christian claims are rationally justifiable; and still others who understand reason as limited in the sense of requiring supplementation by revelation. Among these last are often thought to be exponents of natural theology. Some of those who viewed human reason askance will introduce Chapter 7 on faith, knowledge and experience.[10]

II

Turning first to those who have regarded human reason as limited because wounded by sin, we may fittingly set out from Calvin himself.[11] It is in the first place of great importance that we grasp the notion that, for Calvin, the knowledge of God is far more than a matter of rational assent. According to his epistemology, to know God is to honour him and live piously in his sight:

> [T]he knowledge of God, as I understand it, is that by which we not only conceive that there is a God, but also grasp what befits us and is proper to his glory, in fine, what is to our advantage to know of him. Indeed, we shall not say that, properly speaking, God is known where there is no religion or piety.[12]

It is of this knowledge that human beings are deprived by sin's corruption:

> [W]e declare that man is corrupted through natural vitiation, but a vitiation that did not flow from nature. We deny that it has flowed from nature in order to indicate that it is an adventitious quality which comes

upon man rather than a substantial property which has been implanted from the beginning. Yet we call it 'natural' in order that no man may think that anyone obtains it through bad conduct, since it holds all men fast by hereditary right.[13]

However, the dire consequences of Adam's fall have not totally obliterated human reason. The *sensus divinitatis*, given in humanity's creation, is vestigially operative, the *imago dei* is not totally obliterated; and hence (following Paul in Romans 1) human beings are without excuse in their turning from God.[14] But human reason is impaired,[15] and the will, bound by sin, 'cannot move toward good, much less apply itself thereto'.[16] While there is a 'seed of religon in all men',[17] people, through blindness, obstinacy and vanity, smother and corrupt it. Not surprisingly, therefore, where knowledge of God in Calvin's broad sense is concerned, and supremely where knowledge of God as Father is concerned, 'the greatest geniuses are blinder than moles!'[18]

Nevertheless, the reason, though corrupt, is not absolutely moribund. It is, after all, 'proper to our nature',[19] and 'some vestige remains imprinted in [man's] very vices'.[20] Enough of reason remains to distinguish human beings from beasts;[21] while in 'things below' – politics, social order, the arts and science – reason is not altogether incapacitated and, since 'it is bestowed indiscriminately upon pious and impious, it is rightly counted among natural gifts'.[22]

The question arises: is the *sensus divinitatis*, the natural knowledge that all have by virtue of their creation, rightly construed in terms of general revelation? Dewey J. Hoitinga, Jr., denies that it is properly so understood. He argues that this natural knowledge of God 'originates differently that [*sic*] the knowledge of revelation'.[23] Undoubtedly Calvin would not agree with Arnulfus Provincialis, for example, that because the human being's *occulus intellectualis* has been blinded in consequence of the Fall, we must resort to philosophy to conduct us to true knowledge and reverence.[24] On the contrary,

> the Word of God is not received by faith if it flits about in the top of the brain, but when it takes root in the depth of the heart . . . It is harder for the heart to be furnished with assurance than for the mind to be endowed with thought. The Spirit accordingly served as a seal, to seal up in our hearts those very promises the certainty of which it has previously impressed upon our minds . . . [25]

In Calvin's view we shall not know God in the fullest sense apart from the inward testimony of the Holy Spirit. Nevertheless, if God is knowable only as he graciously makes himself known, whether in grace or nature, it seems precious to deny the term 'revelation' to the latter, as Hoitinga recommends.

In his vindication of the doctrine of the Trinity the seventeenth-century Congregationalist John Owen sought to answer those who objected that the doctrine was contrary to reason. In the course of his argument he clearly states his own view of reason as such. He points out that his adversaries are judging the truth by 'the carnal reason of men', and that their reason is 'weak, maimed, and imperfect'. Moreover (appealing to a long-standing claim), 'Many things are *above* reason, – that is as considered in this or that subject, as men, – which are not at all *against it*.'[26] Elsewhere, in relation to saving knowledge, he writes:

> of this introduction of Christ and grace in him into our relation unto God, there are no notions in the natural conceptions of our minds; nor are they discoverable by reason in the best and utmost of its exercise, I Cor. ii. 14. For before our understandings were darkened, and our reason debased by the fall, there were no such things revealed or proposed unto us . . . seeing they suppose the entrance of sin.[27]

In more homely language John Flavel concurs:

> The light of reason was at first the bright lamp or candle of the Lord, till sin, like a thief, melted it down to snuff; whereby (comparatively speaking) it becomes a poor glimmering light in the best of men, and almost quite extinguished in some men. Fallen man is become less than himself, and will never act like himself, till he be fully restored to himself.[28]

Using a different set of equally homely images, Richard Baxter made the same point:

> To true reason which is at liberty, and not enthralled by sensuality and error, the light of nature might have a sufficiency to lead men up to the love of God, and a life of holiness; but experience telleth us that the reason of the world is darkened, and captivated by sensuality, and that few men can well use their own faculties; and such eyes need spectacles, such cripples need crutches, yea, such diseases call for a physician. Prove once that the world is not diseased, and then we will confess that their natural food may serve the turn, without any other diet or physic.[29]

It seems clear that those, like Owen and Flavel, who stand in the line of classical Calvinism understand the Spirit's work as bringing home God's word of salvation to people in such a way that there is that 'renewal of the mind' of which Paul spoke.[30] But the Quaker Robert Barclay seems to take matters a step further, suggesting not that what is warped is renewed and refashioned, but that something alien is implanted. Writing in defence of Friends, he declares:

> It will manifestly appear by what is above said, that we understand not the divine principle to be any part of man's nature, nor yet to be any relics of any good which Adam lost by his fall, in that we make it a distinct thing from man's soul, and all the faculties of it . . .[31]

The context is Barclay's repudiation of rationalism and 'notions', but, as a latter-day Quaker wrote,

> we cannot possibly follow [Barclay] when he makes the Light of God in the soul, which is for him the only organ by which man can reach a real knowledge of Divine truth, something altogether non-rational and non-human. How can a man exercise a faculty which is not *his* at all – which is not part of his real nature?[32]

More conventional Calvinist teaching was propagated in the eighteenth century by Thomas Boston in Scotland and Jonathan Edwards in America;[33] but later in the century Joseph Bellamy drew a sharper distinction between natural and moral inability thus:

> The more unable to love God we are, the more we are to blame . . . There is not one tittle in the Old Testament or in the New, in the law or in the gospel, that gives the least intimation of any deficiency in our natural faculties . . . The gospel aims to recover us to love God only with all our hearts, but makes no provision for our having any new natural capacity: as to our natural capacities, all is well.[34]

Thus, like Barclay, Bellamy appeals to supernatural agency in the matter of salvation, but thinks of it in moral-affective terms. Moreover, he does not agree with Barclay that our natural faculties are impaired. As the nineteenth century approached, the Welsh Congregationalist Edward Williams was found reverting to the view that sin impairs the understanding, so that everyone is like a traveller lost on the way home:

> Were it perfect day, he might discern a straight plain path; but being overtaken by night, introduced by sin, he has only a faint light 'shining in a dark place' to guide him. Besides he has wandered and naturally lost his path. His will however, being set upon his home some step must be taken.[35]

Since it appears that the traveller is able to take a step, a softening of some versions of Calvinism is here detectable. No such concessions are to be found in the writings of the nineteenth-century American Henry Boyton Smith, who thought that some later New England theologians had made too much of natural ability, and whose doctrinal antennae were highly sensitive to the faintest whiff of Arminianism.[36]

On 6 November 1850 W. Hendry Stowell delivered his inaugural lecture as president of Cheshunt (theological) College. I cite him as one who, although he is not concerned to expound the noetic effects of sin in detail, clearly has them in mind in the following words to his students:

> The doctrines of Theology have, in common with all truths, to encounter the foregone conclusions of age, country, associations, habits, tastes, and interests; but, in addition to these, they have to encounter the opposition of the corrupt heart to the *manifest purpose* for which these doctrines are revealed . . . The perception of this most important difference will prevent your wondering that some men of exalted and cultured intellect have opposed the simplest and most essential truths of Christianity. Had intellectual pre-eminence been all that is required in the study of Theology, such a fact would have greatly perplexed us . . . If you would avoid the snares by which [such cultured persons] have been caught, it is imperative that you should remember the peculiarly sacred and spiritual character of Theology, which demands other and higher qualities than those in which these victims of their own presumption have excelled.[37]

These remarks of Stowell, like those of his ecclesiastical forebear John Owen, carry the seeds of an epistemological transition within Reformed thought such as is exemplified by Abraham Kuyper[38] and his intellectual successors, among whom Cornelius Van Til is not the least significant. Like Calvin and his seventeenth-century Puritan heirs, those of what one might broadly call this Dutch tradition do not in the first instance (or, in some cases, at all) adduce a set of theistic arguments designed to elicit the unbeliever's reasoned assent.[39] 'Reason' is construed broadly in relation to the *imago dei*, and the knowledge of God entails the response of love and godly living. But Kuyper and some of his heirs give the theme what can only be described as a post-Enlightenment twist when they focus in the way they do upon the antithesis between the regenerate and the unregenerate – that distinction to which Stowell loosely alludes – and make epistemological capital out of it. Moreover, their views turn upon a view of the Bible as inerrant in its original autographs, and upon revelation as propositional – on neither of which would it here be pertinent to comment.

As a result of sin, Kuyper 'fearlessly' states, '*falsehood* in every sense and form is now in the world'. It causes unintentional mistakes in observation and memory; self-delusion and self-deception; it warps the imagination; it opens us to the deceptions of others; it is the origin of 'All sorts of wrong and sickly commotions [which] bestir themselves in our body and work their effect in our spiritual dispositions; and it vitiates the relationships of life'.[40] The world is thus abnormal and, when the sovereign God's regenerating grace restores some to a right relationship with God, an antithesis is set up between the regenerate and the unregenerate which has epistemological consequences. For the unregenerate and the regenerate set out from fundamentally different presuppositions, and there can be no coalescence of starting points: they view the whole of life from utterly different perspectives, 'and they cannot desist from the constant endeavour to pull down to the ground the entire edifice of their respective controverted assertions, all the supports included, on which their assertions rest'.[41] There is thus a decisive, though not an absolute, difference between the two classes of people – not absolute, because culture manifests a legacy of Christian principles; believers and unbelievers can agree on empirical matters and utilize logic and the principles of mathematics, and the believer is renewed but not utterly remade: there is pre- and post-regeneration continuity.

In all of this Kuyper develops and narrows Calvin's somewhat fluid notion of common grace (as distinct from saving, or regenerating grace) – God's love as manifested in the world, fostering the good in all and restraining the worst sinful excesses of all.[42] Conversely, he draws out the epistemological implications of Calvin's remark that, because the unregenerate 'do not look to the goal that God's wisdom prescribes, what they do, though it seems good in the doing, yet by its perverse intention is sin'.[43] It must be said that it is not always clear how Kuyper wishes us to understand the relationship between common and special grace; and that there is an ambivalence in his teaching on common grace, which is sometimes understood as affording common ground on which believers and unbelievers may stand in the socio-political affairs of life, but which at other times is subject to the antithesis to such a degree that separated Christian organizations and institutions are deemed necessary in all spheres of life.[44] There is thus an oscillation in his thought between an absolute insistence upon the antithesis and the humanly uniting effects of God's common grace.[45]

I said that 'some of' Kuyper's followers took the epistemological route because others, including Herman Dooyeweerd, D. H. T. Vollenhoven and H. Stoker, emphasized much more the so-called orders of creation which, while not overcoming humanity's sinful alienation from God, nevertheless were held to afford a basis for life in human society. Thus Dooyeweerd argues that creation, fall and redemption must be held together (and accuses Barth of failing to allow the creation motif to permeate all his thinking), and explains that 'Sin changed not the creational decrees, but the direction of the human heart. Man's heart turned away from the Creator.'[46] The effects of the Fall are widely pervasive: human beings can no longer control natural phenomena; the institutions of Church and state were required, but

> Neither the structures of the various aspects of reality, nor the structures that determine the nature of concrete creatures, nor the principles which serve as norms for human action, were altered by the fall. A denial of this leads to the unscriptural conclusion that the fall is as broad as creation; i.e., that the fall destroyed the very nature of creation. This would mean that sin plays a self-determining, autonomous role over against God, the creator of all. Whoever maintains such a position robs God of his sovereignty and grants Satan a power equal to that of the origin of all things.[47]

Among those who faulted Dooyeweerd for elevating his philosophy of the cosmonomic idea above scripture was Van Til.[48] He drew out the implications of Kuyper's thought for epistemology and apologetics, thereby distancing himself (though not absolutely) not only from such other American Dooyeweerdians as

H. Evan Runner, David H. Freeman, Robert D. Knudsen and Calvin Seerveld, but also from that line of Christian evidentialists flowing down from Butler via the Princetonians Charles Hodge and B. B. Warfield. His complaint against the latter was their too easy assumption of common ground between believer and unbeliever, and their Arminian confidence (allegedly shared by Aquinas and his heirs) in the ability of human beings to reason their way to God. Both errors result from the failure to pay due heed to the noetic effects of sin.

From Van Til's prolific writings it is possible to extract a number of claims which, taken together, summarize his position on the matters in hand. First, self-confessedly autonomous human beings stand over against God: 'When man became a sinner he made of himself instead of God the ultimate or final reference point. And it is precisely this presupposition, as it controls without exception all forms of non-Christian philosophy, that must be brought into question.'[49] The believer and the unbeliever do not share epistemological common ground. Hence, where empirical matters are concerned, since there are no uninterpreted facts, the one is logically bound to construe facts differently from the other. Secondly, however, unbelievers have a knowledge of God which, though wilfully suppressed, suffices for them to understand the apologetic evidences which Christians present to them. Indeed, 'No man can escape knowing God. It is indelibly involved in his awareness of anything whatsoever.'[50] As he elsewhere expressed it, 'though he is dead in sins, this deadness of the natural man is an *ethical* deadness, not a metaphysical escape from God'.[51] It follows, thirdly, that there can be no natural theology in the sense of a reasoned demonstration of God's existence to a supposedly neutral natural man: there is no such person. At the same time, Van Til insists that there is an objectively valid proof of God's existence: it is not merely probable that God exists; but the proof takes the form of the claim that 'unless [the truth of the Christian claim] is presupposed there is no possibility of "proving" anything at all. The actual state of affairs as preached by Christianity is the necessary foundation of "proof" itself.'[52] What, fourthly, becomes of apologetic method? Is there a point of contact as between believer and unbeliever? There is, and it resides 'in the fact that every man is made in the image of God and has impressed upon him the law of God'.[53] On this basis supposedly autonomous human beings must be challenged to see that they view the facts of revelation through distorting spectacles. It must clearly be understood that

> Basic to all the doctrines of Christian theism is that of the self-contained God, or, if we wish, that of the ontological trinity . . . [and that] In spite of this claim to neutrality on the part of the non-Christian the Reformed apologist must point out that *every* method, the supposedly neutral no less than any other, presupposes either the truth or the falsity of Christian theism.

As to method, 'The Christian apologist must place himself upon the position of his opponent, assuming the correctness of his method merely for argument's sake, in order to show him that on such a position the "facts" are not facts and the "laws" are not laws.'[54] At this point Van Til both departs from Kuyper, to whom the attempt to reason with natural man was futile,[55] and draws closer to Warfield and the evidentialists; for Christian evidences may be adduced in support of the Christian position – but only because the presuppositions are in place, not because it is wrongly supposed that natural, allegedly neutral, man's reason will take him to God.[56]

Having presented Van Til's position as concisely and accurately as I can, I should like to make a few observations. The first concerns an ambivalence in his work. For although, as I have noted, he does grant that in the shared knowledge of God there is common ground between believer and unbeliever sufficient for the mounting of apologetic arguments, he can also declare that 'It will be quite impossible then to find a common area of knowledge between believers and unbelievers unless there is agreement between them as to the nature of man himself.'[57] Moreover, if the noetic effects of sin, and natural man's option for the wrong presupposition, are as devastating as Van Til supposes, why should he think that unbelievers will construe his arguments aright? As with Kuyper, his disciple seems to fluctuate between an epistemological dualism as between the regenerate and the unregenerate, whilst at the same time compromising the full severity of this with a commitment to common grace and the *imago dei*. The ominous thought occurs that, if pressed to its logical conclusion, the epistemological wielding of the noetic effects of sin renders it impossible for the regererate intellectually to reach the unregenerate. Quite apart from the devastating consequences this would have for mission, the believers' method would have insulated them epistemologically from the rest of humanity no less than the method of the positivists, Wittgensteinians and postmodernists queried the Christian believer's linguistic ability to refer to God.[58]

Again, while it may be true that there are no uninterpreted facts – the very point I proposed against the positivists – Van Til does not seem to draw the necessary distinction that Henry Stob, among others, has proposed between what he calls ontological reason, 'a grasping and shaping organ that must conform to and be shaped by its object – the real',[59] and that technical reason which 'is directed toward the formation and ordering of ideas, and which enables man to think'.[60] By neglecting what Stob calls scientific abstractionism (which yields particular systems – for example, number systems) in favour of the total system, Van Til sometimes goes as far as to suggest that believers and unbelievers cannot mean the same thing by 'two plus two equals four'.[61] The presuppositionalist Gordon H. Clark has, in characteristically pungent style, taken up a position similar to that of Stob in respect of logic, the principles of which believer and unbeliever alike may grasp and utilize:

> The preaching of the Gospel . . . presupposes at least the rational remnants of the image of God in man.
>
> It is strange that anyone who thinks he is a Christian should deprecate logic . . . The law of contradiction cannot be sinful. Quite the contrary, it is our violations of the law of contradiction that are sinful. Yet the strictures which some devotional writers place on 'merely human' logic are amazing. Can such pious stupidity really mean that a syllogism which is valid for us is invalid for God? If two plus two is four in our arithmetic, does God have a different arithmetic in which two and two make three or perhaps five?[62]

We may conclude that to press the regenerate–unregenerate dualism to its limits is to render human communication impossible. It may well be a distinction of eternal significance, but here below it does not preclude a good deal of epistemological common ground as between Christians and others. The foundation of this common ground is humanity's creation in the *imago dei*; it is that *sensus divinitatis* which seems non-expungeable from many an agnostic or atheist, and which some of them – the humanist Ronald Hepburn for one – are more than willing to acknowledge.[63] If a Christian presuppositionalist wishes to say that a non-believer does not see the world in the correct perspective – does not understand, for example, that the system of numbers is God-ordered – this in no way rules out the shared use of mathematical procedures by all and sundry. No doubt the wilful refusal on the part of an individual to 'think God's thoughts after him' – even to suppress the intimations of the divine, or to flout what Victorians would have called 'the nobler aspirations of the race' – may prompt the person to use his or her reasoning powers to sinful ends. Not even (perhaps especially not) the regenerate are perfect, and Paul's struggle with the 'old Adam' within was never-ending. Equally ongoing is the Spirit's work of sanctification, that renewing of the mind which is the gracious work of God the Holy Spirit, a work of which few have spoken more devotionally than the Scottish Puritan William Guthrie.[64] Another Scot, E. P. Dickie, may articulate our conclusion thus far:

> The disturbance caused in human reason by man's fallen state is seen at its maximum when reason seeks to apply itself unaided to the spiritual nature of man and his relations with God, and at its minimum when it is engaged in the sciences and in the sphere of the formal.[65]

III

That many pre-Reformation theologians set great store by reason cannot be denied. Justin Martyr, for example, argued that, but for the fact that human beings are led astray by demons, unworthy conventions and bad examples, natural reason would suffice to prompt right behaviour (no Adamic impediments here).[66] Clement of Alexandria, like Justin before him, regarded the pre-Christian Greek philosophers as sometimes having grasped and promulgated truth,[67] but he went further in seeking to present Christian truth in what to him was a philosophically respectable way – that is, he wished to apply speculative reasoning to the adumbration of a system of Christian truth (which is not to deny the intensely practical motive of encouraging godly living among Christians which inspires much of his work). More highly speculative is Denys the Pseudo-Areopagite's view of God as transcending all reason. Accordingly, while 'on the one hand he is reached by Intuition, Reason, Understanding, Perception, Conjecture, Appearance,

Name, etc., . . . on the other hand, He cannot be grasped by Intuition, Language, or Name, and He is not anything in the world nor is He known in anything'.[68] Among John Scottus Eriugena's preoccupations was that of stating the due relations between right reason and right authority, which cannot be in conflict since both originate in God.[69] Indeed, reason, part of God's creation, is, like all the rest of creation, in course of its return to God. Anselm, as is well known, had no compunction at all about applying the skills of reasoning to theological questions, and his ontological argument for God's existence is widely discussed to this day. Abelard was even more determined in the same direction, in his case not baulking at setting Father against Father in the interest of the quest for truth. Later, with the conversion of Muslims in his sights, Raymond Lull set out to show that the doctrines of Christianity were not unreasonable, and that objections to them could be countered; while Aquinas contributed his profound synthesis of reason and revelation, of which more anon.

Although, in the variety of ways thus hastily described, reason played a prominent part in the thinking of pre-Aquinas Christians, the change of intellectual atmosphere as we approach the 'modern' period cannot be gainsaid. (I place 'modern' in inverted commas because, with the time lags and throw-backs which characterize all periods of intellectual history, precise dating is impossible: general intellectual moods are rather in view.) For this reason, F. C. Copleston regularly qualified the term 'rationalism' in such a way as to clarify the truth that where Anselm, for example, was concerned,

> If by rationalism one means an attitude of mind which denies revelation and faith, St. Anselm was certainly no rationalist, since he accepted the primacy of faith and the fact of authority and only then went on to attempt to understand the data of faith . . . [I]t would show an entire misunderstanding of Anselm's attitude, were one to suppose that he was prepared to reject the doctrine of the Trinity, for example, if he was unable to find *rationes necessariae* for it . . . [I]f we insist on interpreting St. Anselm as though he lived after St. Thomas and had clearly distinguished the separate provinces of theology and philosophy, we shall only be guilty of an anachronism and of a misinterpretation.[70]

Of Aquinas himself Copleston declared that, unlike later rationalists, he 'did not believe that there are innate ideas or principles from which we can proceed to deduce a metaphysical system on a mathematical model'.[71]

Let us, then, attempt to specify the change of intellectual mood in a little more detail. First, we may note the rise of modern science, many of whose exponents understood themselves as engaged in the reverential task of studying God's handiwork. On the one hand, their activities gave impetus to empirical enquiries in many fields, while on the other hand, with the commitment of a Galileo to the view that nature in its fundamental structure is mathematically ordered, they nurtured the quest of many philosophers – supremely Descartes – for a coherent intellectual system marked by precision and clarity. Secondly, there was a perceived need to counter the scepticism of Montaigne, who, in the wake of the publication in the mid-sixteenth century of the Latin translations of Sextus Empiricus who, in turn, handed on the thoughts of the sceptic Pyrrho of Elis, argued that sense-bound human reason was incapable of metaphysical activity; and of Charron who, in face of reason's presumed impotence, opted for faith.[72] Descartes was in conscious reaction against the sceptics, as, from a very different perspective, was Pascal, whom I shall mention in the following section. Thirdly, there was a growing distrust of authoritarianisms, whether ecclesiastical or biblicist, and a concomitant concern to free people from intellectual subservience to schemes which they could not with integrity endorse. As we might expect, the theologically avant-garde made much of this principle, as when John Knowles, a seventeenth-century self-styled 'Independent Presbyterian', after diligently searching the scriptures, was suspected of heresy regarding the Trinity. In answer he explained that he had resolved 'not to trust others to try for me, or to pin my faith on another's sleeve, nor beleeve as the Church beleeves, being not desirous to try truths by whole sale, but to receive it as God discovers it'.[73] But, as Geoffrey Nuttall has reminded us, a learned Calvinist, Thomas Goodwin, was quoted as having had no difficulty in affirming the same (and in much the same language):

> I must not take up Religion by the lumps (as once Mr. Thomas Goodwin said) I must not pin my faith upon the sleeve of any person or persons upon earth, though never so holy or learned, as not knowing whither they may carry it . . . both God and man will expect from me, that I be able to render a Scripturall Reason of my faith and conscience.[74]

Fourthly, as to the manner of proceeding: there was a widespread feeling, at a time of religious wars in Europe and a genuine fear of civil disorder instigated by Commonwealth sectaries in England, that a tolerant spirit was advisable, and 'enthusiasm' potentially dangerous. People as prominent as the 'ever memorable' John Hales[75] and John Locke[76] were of this opinion, as was Lucius Cary, Lord Falkland, who gave perhaps the pithiest expression to it: 'Truth in likelyhood is, where her author God was, in the *still voice*, and not the *loud wind*.'[77]

It was at a time when the above influences were at work in varying degrees that Descartes, in opposition to the sceptics of his time, embarked upon his epistemological quest of quasi-mathematical certainty.[78] He was, he tells us, 'especially delighted with the mathematics, on account of the certitude and evidence of their reasonings'.[79] His particular agony was how to reconcile the authority of the Church, which he wished to honour ('I revered our theology'[80]), with his conviction that we may be said to have knowledge only of those things of which we have a clear and distinct idea. That is to say, Church authority notwithstanding, the reason can, by its 'natural light' attain certain truth which is then the starting point for further rational deductions. Descartes resolves not to presume to subject revealed truths to 'the impotency of my reason',[81] and leaves such matters to the sphere of faith, whilst reserving the questions of the existence of God and the soul to philosophy – but not to any kind of philosophy. He is mistrustful of the deliverances of the senses, and hence adumbrates his celebrated dualism. He shuns the idea that any deliverances of the senses could yield absolute knowledge, and drives a wedge between spirit – the concern of the intellect – and matter – the concern of the sciences.[82] In pursuit of his goal Descartes embarks upon his method of systematic doubt, eventually concluding (in however circular a fashion) that the one thing he could not doubt was the existence of the doubter and, hence, *cogito ergo sum*.[83] I shall have more to say concerning Descartes's application of his method to the question of God's existence when I come shortly to natural theology. The point at present is to see how modern rationalism was ushered on its way by 'the father of modern philosophy', and to confirm the hint given earlier that Descartes's response to the challenges of his intellectual environment, which included his disjunction of faith and reason, leads him to abstract reason as an epistemological tool from traditionally associated terms in a way that would – could – never have occurred to theologians up to and including Aquinas. There is a distinct difference of mood between 'faith seeking understanding' and Descartes's quasi-mathematical quest of rational certainty, and this notwithstanding the latter's faithfulness to his Church and his desire to place knowledge of God on a firm foundation.

I now wish to show that those who set great store by reason did not all proceed in exactly the same way. While 'rationalism' denotes those who stand more or less in the line of Descartes, it also comes to embrace those who deny the supernatural, who, like the deists of the eighteenth century, find that natural religion suffices; and those in the nineteenth century who repudiate religion altogether. The matter is further complicated by the fact that a writer may be rationalist in some respects but not in others – the fact that Locke is (for good or ill) lumped with 'the British empiricists' in philosophy courses should not obscure the fact that in ethics he is a rational intuitionist.[84] Again, as Bruce Kuklick has pointed out in connection with some American divines,

> It is important to understand that rationalism is defined in relation to other positions. A theologian or philosopher is designated a rationalist according to the thinker to whom he is compared. Edwards and the new Divinity men were rationalists within the orthodox tradition, but appear less so in contrast to the Unitarians. The early Unitarians were rationalists in the context of their debate with Andover and in comparison to the Princeton realists, and so were their Harvard Divinity School successors. Harvard philosophers of the middle of the nineteenth century – like Francis Bowen – were more rationalist than their predecessors. But in comparison to thinkers like Horace Bushnell, writing at the same time, or their successors, like William James, or academic contemporaries like Noah Porter, mid-century Harvard philosohers appeared more committed to strict observation.[85]

With these cautions in mind some further English illustrations[86] may be offered. From some points of view Richard Hooker, who died when Descartes was but four years of age, anticipates the Frenchman. The Anglican divine's mission was to justify the arrangements of the Elizabethan settlement over against the Puritans whom he regarded as turning the Bible into a rule book to be construed mechanically, and whose appeal to faith led them, he thought, in an irrational direction.[87] Not, indeed, that his own work is devoid of biblical exposition. On the contrary, a number of his remarks concerning reason occur in the context of his discussion of Paul's letter to the Romans, in the course of which he understands Paul (Romans 1: 14) as meaning that 'by the force of the light of Reason, wherewith God illuminateth every one which cometh into the world, men being enabled to know truth from falsehood, and good from evil, do thereby learn in many things what the will of God is'.[88] Moreover, 'In every kind of knowledge some such grounds there are, as that being proposed the mind doth presently embrace them as free from all possibility of error, clear and manifest without proof.'[89] Reason's importance for our moral activity is underlined: 'the natural measure whereby to judge our doings, is the sentence of Reason',[90] the laws of which 'are investigatable by Reason, without the help of Revelation supernatural and divine'.[91] These laws, as Augustine suggested, are 'principles universally agreed upon'.[92] Over and above the principles of reason are the deliverances of the Bible: 'Scripture indeed teacheth things above nature, things which our reason by itself could not reach unto.' However, 'those things also we believe, knowing by reason that the Scripture is the word of God'.[93] In other words, reason appears to have the last word.

Pace Hooker, it was quite possible for a Puritan to eschew irrationalism and enthusiasm, as witness the case of the Arminian Independent divine John Goodwin. In 1670 his book *Pleroma to Pneumatikon, or, a being filled with the Spirit*, was posthumously published. According to part of its subtitle, it is here proved 'that it is a Duty incumbent on all Men (especially Believers) that they be filled with the Spirit of God. With rules whereby to judge whether Men be filled with the Spirit of God, or a contrary spirit . . . ' In relation to alleged visitations of the Spirit Goodwin seeks to marry scripture and reason in the following way:

> Unless these discoveries, which are pretended unto and held forth with the greatest confidence, shall commend themselves for truth unto the judgments and understandings of sober and judicious men, much versed and exercised in the Scriptures, either from their own light and evidence, or else shall be made out by light of argument and demonstration, whether from the Scriptures, or clear principles in reason, to be real truths . . . they are not to be looked upon as proceeding from any fulness of the Spirit in these men, but as the exertions and puttings forth of a spirit of vanity and delusion in men.[94]

Slightly younger than Descartes were the leading Cambridge Platonists. Their dualism, whereby they identified spirit with 'an extended penetrable and active agent',[95] differed markedly from that of Descartes; and their appeal to reason as the medium of spiritual insight was different in tone from the rationalism of their contemporary, the Latitudinarian John Tillotson, Locke's friend, for whom religion's role as the promoter of morality is of particular importance. Tillotson argues that Christianity is in entire harmony with natural religion; indeed, that 'Natural religion is the foundation of all revealed religion, and revelation is designed simply to establish its duties.'[96] Reason's task is to elicit those innate ideas to which he referred in his preface to John Wilkins's *Of the Principles and Duties of Natural Religion* (1675): 'the great duties of piety and justice are written upon our hearts, and every man feels a secret obligation to them in his own conscience'.[97]

Among the many disputes which thrived from time to time during the seventeenth and eighteenth centuries was that over Socinianism. It is a long and complicated story and, as is well known, Locke was among many who were accused of the heresy. It should, however, be noted that the earlier Socinians were strongly biblicist in their approach and, furthermore, that they maintained belief in the supernatural. For their part, the eighteenth-century rational Arminians[98] (as distinct from the evangelical Arminians of the Wesleyan type), of whom the Anglican Samuel Clarke was a prominent example, followed in the line of William Laud, who had declared that 'Reason by her own light can discover how firmly the principles of Religion are true.'[99] Clarke sought a reasonable faith and tended to pursue an a priori path in theistic argument, though not without a certain eclectic recourse to cosmological considerations as deemed appropriate.[100]

As the eighteenth century progressed, cosmological and teleological arguments for God's existence assumed ever greater importance. Between Clarke at the beginning of the century and Paley's *Natural Theology* (1802) numerous divines took their apologetic cue from the Newtonian account of the order and regularities of the universe. Among many others was the American Congregationalist, Samuel Willard.[101] So popular was this mode of argumentation that it appeared not only in formal treatises, but also in the personal confessions of faith prepared by those being ordained to the ministry of the Dissenting churches – and this whether the views of the ordinands were 'progressive' or orthodox.[102]

I have elsewhere considered eighteenth-century Christian attitudes to reason in some detail,[103] but, having mentioned the rationalist Arminians, whose number included most of the General Baptists, I ought to point out that Calvinists, too, could have their rationalist moments, and their subsequent influence upon the history of Christian thought has been no less significant than that of their Arminian counterparts. Thus such a high Calvinist Baptist as John Gill, while in no way falling for that variety of rationalism which proposed that faith was a matter of intellectual assent to doctrinal propositions, nevertheless went in quest of a coherent system of biblical truth which was governed by certain axioms held a priori to be true, such as that God is the sovereign Lord, from whose Word all truth is to be deduced. Gill declared, 'I shall begin with the Being of God';[104] and off he went, his method being succinctly described in the subtitle of his major doctrinal work: *A System of Evangelical Truths deduced from the Sacred Scriptures.*[105] What is interesting here is that a number of rationalistic Arminians – Samuel Bourn and John Taylor among them – waxed vocal against what they described as 'Protestant Popery', that is, against the activities of such Calvinists as Gill, who, having devised their doctrinal schemes, were giving the impression that salvation was by assent to their efforts. Thus, for example, in the course of his ordination charge to Micaijah Towgood, the Presbyterian divine John Withers expostulated, 'What little Advantage hath the Protestant Interest gain'd by those eager first Disputes which have been set on Foot, concerning the Divine Counsels and Decrees, which some have marshall'd up with as much Exactness as if they had been Privy-Counsellors to the Almighty.'[106]

When we come to the nineteenth century we find on the one hand a more militant anti-Christian rationalism, and on the other a considerable explosion of biblical criticism, some of it conducted along rationalistic lines.[107] In this latter connection repudiations flowed from many directions, not least from the Scot William Robertson Smith who, despite 'advanced' views on bibilical criticism, for which he was deposed from his chair at the Free Church College, Aberdeen, nevertheless abhorred rationalism. To him

> Rationalism, in short, is Pelagianism of the intellect, the assertion of man's natural ability to know the things of the Spirit of God quite apart from the question whether it is by Revelation or not that these spiritual things are first set before man's reason.[108]

As the pace of the 'higher criticism' accelerated, few defended biblical inerrancy so stoutly, or on the basis of so great a weight of learning, as B. B. Warfield of Princeton Theological Seminary.[109] Like his predecessors at Old Princeton, Warfield was impressed by the common-sense realism of Reid and others, which had been transported to Princeton by the first president of the College of New Jersey, John Witherspoon, in 1764.[110] On the face of it, this was somewhat surprising, for in Scotland Witherspoon had stoutly opposed the rationalistic preaching of the Moderate party in the Church of Scotland, yet the common-sense philosophy was widely regarded as Moderate in tendency. It would seem that any qualms on this score were quelled by the belief that Reid and his colleagues had vanquished Hume's scepticism. The upshot was that, in quest of certainty, the Princetonians set about the task of adducing evidence which would substantiate the claims of faith.[111] This thrust apologetics to the fore – apologetics primarily as entailing the establishment of that knowledge of God which theology then further explicates, and, in a subsidiary sense as circumstances demand, apologetics in both its defensive and offensive guises.[112] 'Apologetics', Warfield confidently declares, 'certainly does establish the truth of Christianity as the absolute religion . . . It has for its object the laying of the foundations upon which the temple of theology is built, and by which the whole structure of theology is determined.'[113] His conviction is that no sound theology could be erected unless its foundations were secure; and by 'secure' he meant rationally demonstrable. In the absence of such a foundation the theological enterprise would be vitiated. For 'Christianity has . . . from the beginning ever come to man as the rational religion making its appeal primarily to the intellect.'[114] Thus philosophical apologetics aims to establish the existence of God; psychological apologetics establishes 'the religious nature of man and the validity of his religious sense'; and the reality of the supernatural, the divine origin of Christianity and the trustworthiness of scripture also require to be established.[115] Rationalists and mystics alike decry apologetics in the sense described, he continues, and against Ritschl's distinction between theoretical and religious knowledge Warfield contends that

> though faith be a moral act and the gift of God, it is yet formally conviction passing into confidence; and that all forms of convictions must rest on evidence as their ground, and it is not faith but reason which investigates the nature and validity of this ground.[116]

The rationalism of the above is somewhat mitigated by Warfield's admission that

> Of course mere reasoning can not make a Christian; but that is not because faith is not the result of evidence, but because a dead soul cannot respond to evidence. The action of the Holy Spirit in giving faith is not apart from evidence, but along with evidence; and in the first instance consists in preparing the soul for the reception of the evidence.

But he proceeds immediately to say that, while it is not 'by apologetics that men are made Christians . . . apologetics supplies to Christian men the systematically organized basis on which the faith of Christian men must rest'.[117]

Paul Kjoss Helseth has sought to temper the impression of Warfieldian rationalism which so many scholars have received by emphasizing the role of the Spirit's work on the individual. He grants that 'Warfield certainly affirmed that the primary mission of the Christian apologist "is no less than to reason the world into acceptance of the 'truth"',[118] but he considers that Warfield's emphasis upon the *testimonium internum Spiritus Sancti* has received insufficient attention. The Spirit restores 'a spiritual sense in the soul by which God is recognized in His Word',[119] and hence Helseth argues that Warfield's apologetic appeal is not to the reason of the natural man, but to that 'right reason' which 'presupposes the regenerating activity of the Holy Spirit on the "whole soul" of a moral agent simply because the soul is a single unit that acts in all of its functions as a single substance'.[120] Leaving on one side the problems pertaining to the concept of 'substance' in relation to 'soul', it is the overall judgement here which requires to be questioned, for it would appear to place Warfield much closer to the Dutch world-view presuppositionalists than he actually was. Taking Warfield's writings as a whole, and especially those concerning the inspiration of scripture and biblical inerrancy, there can be little doubt that the judgement of Loetscher is to be preferred. While recognizing the moral and affective work of the Spirit in Warfield's writings, he concludes that 'logically, at least, these extra-rational elements remained external additions to the system, rather than becoming organic parts of it'.[121] The matter comes to a head in a comment of Warfield's in which he contemplates the successful overthrow of the doctrine of biblical inspiration as he understands it: in such a circumstance

> we would need to give up the Biblical doctrine of inspiration; but with it we must also give up our confidence in the Biblical writers as teachers of doctrine. And if we cannot reasonably give up the latter, neither can we reasonably allow that the phenomena apparently inconsistent with the former are real, or really inconsistent with it.[122]

What is the latter sentence but a rationalist a priori appeal to the conviction that God, being a God of truth who does not lie, would not – indeed, could not – provide us with a less than inerrant scripture?[123]

For a final illustration of those who set particular store by reason I turn to the American philosopher Gordon H. Clark. An inerrantist like Warfield, a presuppositionalist like Van Til, he eschews the 'evidences' approach of the former, and faults the latter for his ambiguity over common ground as between believers and unbelievers and, as we saw, for implying on the basis of the Creator–creature distinction that a proposition may mean one thing to God and another to ourselves. Positively, Clark holds that 'no construction in philosophy is possible without some sort of presupposition or *a priori* equipment'.[124] His proposed axiom is God's self-revelation in scripture, apart from which there is no knowledge of him; and the assertion of the *imago dei* is 'an assertion of an *a priori* or innate equipment'.[125] The intelligibility of God's self-revelation in scripture presupposes logic, for 'verbal inspiration cannot be assumed prior to the law of contradiction'.[126] However, this does not make logic an axiom prior to scripture – a logical impossibility; rather, 'The law is God thinking'.[127] Thus 'Scripture, the written words of the Bible, is the mind of God. What is said in Scripture is God's thought.'[128] Conversely, '"God" as an axiom apart from Scripture, is just a name.'[129] From the axiom of Scripture 'it follows syllogistically that such and such a sentence is true because it is the Word of God'.[130] In this way Clark sets out to adumbrate a coherent, logically ordered, system, based on the conviction that knowledge is possible only on the basis of what God has seen fit to reveal in the infallible Bible, and that 'truth' applies only to propositions contained in scripture or deduced by necessary inference therefrom. We seem to be back with Descartes's dualism, which now allows only that science has some operational usefulness; it cannot deal with truth the source of which is the God of scripture alone.[131] This questionable dualism apart, and leaving on one side for the moment the matter of biblical inerrancy, it would seem that Clark has undue confidence in the human being's ability to read off God's propositions from the Bible as if these were there neat, in every case unproblematic, and requiring no interpretation (either by ourselves or by the Holy Spirit) whatsoever.[132] But this leads me to make a few stock-taking remarks on those who have emphasized – in some cases over-emphasized – reason, before turning to the two major matters arising from the discussion so far.

We have seen that the 'modern' period is characterized by a significantly different intellectual mood from that which was current in Aquinas's day, and that the rationalism flowing down from Descartes spawned rationalists of differing hues. The theologically orthodox could be as rationalist in method as their heterodox contemporaries; and many of the latter, in the eighteenth century, were as biblicist and supernaturalist as some of their nineteenth-century theologically conservative successors. From the nineteenth century onwards we found bifurcation among the orthodox, with the evidentialists tending in one direction, the presuppositionalists in another, but both by no means untinged by rationalism.

While it has not been our purpose to delve into the anti-Christian rationalism of the period 1850–1920, some of which was no less virulently polemical than some of the anti-Roman, anti-Ritualist or anti-Modernist pamphleteering of the times, a more sober, scientifically minded positivist, Ernst Mach, waxed lyrical concerning his rationalist inheritance:

> Rationalism does not seem to have gained a broad theatre of action till the literature of the eighteenth century. Humanistic, philosophical, historical, and physical science here met and gave each other mutual encouragement. All who have experienced, in part, in its literature, this wonderful emancipation of the human intellect, will feel during their whole lives a deep, elegiacal regret for the eighteenth century.[133]

With this Mach rules himself out as a fountainhead of postmodernism! He also overlooks other, more enthusiastic, features of the eighteenth century. But as far as it goes his comment has point. To repeat my earlier remark: the emancipation of the human being from untoward authorities, whether ecclesiastical or biblicist, and the concomitant quest of integrity of belief was a victory to which, in their several ways, Socinians, rationalistic Arminians, Unitarians and even deists contributed. No doubt there was some reductionist, moralistic preaching – though in the wake of a century of civic unrest, some of it in the name of religion, the exhortation to godly living did not come amiss; certainly there are examples of rationalistic theology which almost justify the element of caricature which finds its way into H. R. Mackintosh's judgement:

> Christianity came in many quarters to be represented as no more than the confirmation of truths which had long been in the possession of natural reason . . . The triumphant certainties of the Apostolic faith lapse into rational and necessary axioms, so commonplace and decent that to acquiesce in them is hardly worth a sinner's while . . . There is little to produce 'joy unspeakable and full of glory' in a form of Christianity which, with half a sheet of notepaper and a spare hour, the average man can construct for himself . . . It is by no means surprising that the clergy who proclaimed such a message frequently exhibited a keener interest in sport or agriculture than in the cure of souls.[134]

Again, the eighteenth-century ideal of scientific method could yield some rather emaciated apologetics, as Robert Mackintosh observed:

> William Paley (1743–1805) borrows from many writers; he borrows Lardner's learning and Butler's 'particular evidence for Christianity', viz. Miracles, prophecy and 'history'; and he states his points with perfect clearness. No man ever filled a typical position more exactly than Paley. Eighteenth-century ethics – Hedonism, with a theological background. Empiricist Natural Theology – the argument from Design. Christian Evidences – the strong probability of the resurrection of Christ and the consequent authority of his teaching. *Horae Paulinae* – mutual confirmation of *Acts* and Epistles; better, though one-sided. When such exclusively 'external' arguments are urged, the contents of Christianity go for next to nothing.[135]

But none of this should prompt us to downplay the significance of integrity and reasonableness for any who would profess and confess the Christian faith. This point has been well taken by Gadamer, for example: 'The Enlightenment's distinction between faith in authority and using one's own reason is, in itself, legitimate. If the prestige of authority displaces one's own judgement, then authority is in fact a source of prejudices.'[136]

It cannot, however, be denied that the temptation to intellectualism proved strong in some quarters. Thus, in the context of the need to confess the faith, John Harrison exhorted the Unitarians of Kendal in 1827 as follows: 'Every christian is to judge for himself between truth and error, and to be fully persuaded in his own mind as to the soundness of the opinions he finally adopts.'[137] There does not seem to be much room here for weak faith, the doubt of believers, the immature Christian, or for that work of God the Holy Spirit in enlightening the mind. Nor is there space for the confirmation of experience – one's own or that of the churchly fellowship now or through the Christian centuries. The caution of another Unitarian, C. B. Upton, comes to mind:

> If the revelation of the universal and the divine is recognized in the theoretical reason and in that alone, the inevitable result is a Pantheistic conception of God, man and the universe, in which both nature and humanity come to be regarded merely as transient and illusory appearances, temporary phases of the eternal thought-principle, which thought-principle, as being itself timeless and therefore by us wholly inconceivable, is the only true reality . . . [This] transforms sin from an ontological reality into an inevitable and therefore salutary phase in the evolution of finite souls, and renders unintelligible that felt personal relationship and communion between God and His rational creatures which is presupposed alike in the ethical and in the religious experience of mankind.[138]

That those absolute idealists of the period 1870–1920 who sought to propound their Christian views via the medium of, or in relation to, their philosophy tended in the direction thus described it was part of my purpose to demonstrate in *Philosophical Idealism and Christian Belief*, and I need not repeat the story here. Suffice it to say that when intellectualists become so optimistic (or presumptuous) as to imply that particular individuals, abstracted from the challenges and confusions of this mortal life, occupy a privileged Olympian rationalistic vantage point, the denial of the postmodernists comes as a welcome relief, even if their relativizing tendencies cause concern.

However, it is not the more determined intellectualists alone who cause concern. Evidentialists of the Warfield type also prompt unease. Quite apart from their adherence to biblical inerrancy, they seem to have fallen for the scientific model in too uncritical a way – as if the basic Christian claims were the sort of things that could be demonstrated by the piling up of evidence concerning the reliability of texts, the possibility of miracles, the fulfilment of prophecy and the like.[139] It is not difficult to sympathize with Coleridge's exasperation: '*Evidences* of Christianity! I am weary of the Word. Make a man feel the *want* of it; rouse him, if you can, to the self-knowledge of his *need* of it; and you may safely trust to its own Evidence. . .'[140] Further, as we saw, they, no less than the presuppositionalists, can neglect that inner witness of the Holy Spirit who, however technically competent in logic, however industrious a sifter of evidence, a person may be, is the agent of that regeneration by which God's image is set on the way to restoration, and one begins to 'see' – however limited one's logical and 'scientific' abilities – the faith being for all sorts and conditions of people.

It will thus be clear that none of my concerns about rationalism entail our tumbling into irrationalism. They do, however, go some way to endorsing my aspiration of arriving at a reasonable eclecticism which can accommodate not only human reasoning abilities, such as they are *vis-à-vis* God on the one hand and human sinfulness on the other, but also the Christian experience, individual and corporate, in the intellectual commendation of the faith (which, as we recall, is not the only way in which the faith is to be commended). But this is to anticipate, and we must proceed step by step. As a premonition of what is to come, however, the case of Charles Gore and Hastings Rashdall may be cited. Gore's biographer writes:

> The data which formed the material of Gore's thought included the facts of specifically Christian experience both individual and corporate . . . Rashdall, on the other hand, was more disposed to frame his outlook from the implications of moral and physical science and secular history, in abstraction, and to apply this construction as an adequate clue to the elucidation of religion . . . That was the cross-road from which in contrary directions they took their departure.[141]

Two others, the one an Anglican, the other a Dissenter writing from Kendal almost exactly a century before his successor,

Harrison, to whom I have already referred, may state the moral. Clement Webb writes, 'Rationalism is not really so much an excess of confidence in reason as a want of confidence in it; since it does not attempt to understand a great part of human experience.'[142] William Pendlebury has in his sights those 'infidels' who are using reason against the faith:

> From a serious perusal of [their] writings we may easily observe, that 'tis not close Thinking and impartial Reasoning, join'd with true Learning, but a Narrowness of Mind, which disposeth Men to consider a few Things, join'd with a certain hardiness and Obstinacy of Temper, which has made them Infidels.[143]

IV

I come now to the two matters arising from the foregoing discussion. First I wish to take up the question implicit in our discussion of both presuppositionalists like Van Til and Clark and evidentialists like Warfield: what are we to make of the idea of revelation in propositions, some of which are deemed to be literally true? Some remarks upon biblical inerrancy will be unavoidable, but I propose to set the discussion in a wider context, by taking up an aspect of the nature of religious language, namely, its analogical-metaphorical nature, which did not call for direct attention when the positivists and Wittgensteinians were under review at an earlier stage in this book. We shall thus be better prepared for the subsequent discussion of natural theology.

Let us set out from a mundane illustration. Imagine a mother whose son, having committed murder, is awaiting trial. She asks a Christian friend, 'What will become of him in the end?' The friend replies, 'A long term of imprisonment, I suppose.' This reply is grounded in the knowledge that if, in this country, a person commits murder, and is not insane, and provided that no crucial extenuating circumstances can be appealed to, then the person will be found guilty as charged, and the prescribed penalty is a long period in prison. The mother's friend has thus far understood the question as one which is open to an answer given in empirical terms; that is, as a question which might be deemed to be of the same order as the question 'What will become of this in the end?'

where 'this' is a vat containing a molten mass located in a sweet factory. The reply to the latter question might be, 'It will become bars of chocolate.' In each case the answer given is based upon a reasonable expectation: on the one hand, that there will be no miscarriage of justice, on the other hand, that the ingredients of the mixture are in their correct proportions, that the machine will not break down, and so forth. In each case, given the correctness of the assumptions underlying the replies, and the absence of unforeseen circumstances, simple empirical procedures will, after the lapse of time appropriate in each case, reveal a man behind bars on the one hand, and a number of bars of chocolate on the other. Such a demonstration would properly be regarded as justifying the replies given. But suppose that the murderer's mother presses her question: 'No, what I mean is, what will become of him in the *end*?' She has not been satisfied with the obvious, matter-of-fact answer, and her emphasis upon the term 'end' suggests that she is employing it in a special way. We will suppose that she is using an analogy and, from a theological point of view, it is one having eschatological import. She is asking her friend for an account of the ways of God with people which will relate her son's misdemeanour to the concepts of God's holy love and righteous mercy, and which will indicate, so far as possible, the *post-mortem* possibilities that are open to her son.

For the successful analogical functioning of 'end' there must necessarily be certain parallels of import between the two understandings of the question, and this is precisely what we find. On both interpretations of the mother's question there is a lapse of time before the 'end'. In the former case the wheels of justice have to be given time to turn, and in the latter case the son has to complete his mortal life. Further common factors are the son himself, and the notion that his future is in some way at stake. But here the similarities end, for in the second instance, where 'end' is being used analogically, the Christian's answer to the mother's question consists in the elaboration of a framework of convictions against the background of which 'end' has an appropriate analogical use. In detail the answers given by the Christian may vary considerably. A high Calvinist, for example, might say, 'If your son is predestined to salvation, not even this murder will alter the sovereign purpose of God – but it is not for me to say whether he is so predestined or not.' A Universalist might feel inclined to say,

'We must trust your son to the mercy of God, knowing that God wills the salvation of all.' But neither has any means of laying the 'end' open to empirical investigation. If they outlive the murderer they cannot see beyond his grave; if they predecease him, how could they report on his status hereafter to any living person? Even if the evidence for survival after death provided by psychical research be accepted, it is still a long logical hop from this to Christian beliefs concerning the End. For the Christian, 'I am going to stand before the judgement seat after I die' is not logically equivalent to the child's 'I'm going to have some jelly after I've eaten my spinach'. Of course, had the mother addressed her question to an atheist her emphasis upon 'end' would not have triggered an analogical reply but, presumably, 'Well, he'll just die.'

John McIntyre is among others who have demonstrated the importance for theology of analogy. Indeed, 'the problem of relevance is the problem of analogy, the problem of discovering the figure, the image, even the parable, that will say to our generation what the *kerugma* said to the first century Christians'.[144] Again, analogy is employed by biblical scholars when they interpret passages of scripture which are otherwise silent on their chosen principle, in the light of such concepts as 'covenant' or 'the *eschaton*'.[145] Yet again, analogy is employed over the whole range of Christian doctrine, so that, for example, 'G Aulén's conception of *Christus Victor*, however biblically based, becomes in his hands the analogy whereby he interprets and criticizes post-biblical soteriologies.'[146]

However, we do not justify the use of analogy merely by showing how its employment arises, and by indicating its usefulness to theologians. We need to subject the term 'analogy' itself to brief analysis, bearing in mind the important distinction to be drawn between analogy conceived of as a conceptual device, and the method of argument by analogy. In scholastic philosophy analogy has traditionally been invoked in order to meet the difficulty which mortals experience in speaking of one who is immortal, omniscient, and so on. On the one hand, it would seem that, if the statements which believers wish to make about God are of the same kind as statements they wish to make about phenomena in the material world (that is, if terms are used univocally), the term 'God' is evacuated of all those associations of otherness which most Christians wish to retain. This is the horn of the dilemma which leads to anthropomorphism. If, on the other hand, terms are used equivocally, that is, in such a way that they are entirely divorced from human experience, then it is hard to say how human beings could mean anything by them, or even that they would have any reference at all. In face of this dilemma appeal is made to analogy, a device traditionally understood in two main ways:

1. Analogies of attribution

Compare, for example, (*a*) 'I think it will be frosty tomorrow morning', with (*b*) 'It was pretty frosty in the board room this morning'. Concerning (*a*), empirical observation will in due time confirm whether or not the morning is frosty. Here is a straightforward univocal use of language. As for (*b*), it is just possible that a univocal interpretation could be given of this, for it might be that on an exceptionally cold morning the central heating system in the board room has ceased to function. But if Jones, who was in the board room on a very cold morning, utters (*b*) to Smith and Smith says, 'What went wrong with the heating system?' Jones might reply, 'No, what I mean is that Smythe wasn't speaking to ffrench on account of that lost contract, and . . . ' It is then clear that 'frosty' in (*b*) is serving as an analogy of attribution. As a linguistic device this is colourfully descriptive, and it should prompt some discernment on the part of Smith. But it does not lay bare any of the formal properties of the board room. It merely tells us that the board room's atmosphere was frosty in such a way as to make the application of the adjective 'frosty' appropriate. And when God is the subject of analogies of attribution we have to ask how much we are really told about him when we are informed that he is loving, patient and the like. And how is the analogy to be controlled? For it might be suggested that, on the principle in question, God could be said to be sweet-tasting[147] or even evil.[148] H. D. Aiken's cheeky supposition that the Almighty might be 'a perfect stinker' comes to mind.[149]

2. Analogies of proportionality

According to this understanding of the doctrine of analogy, analogates on both sides of the equation must possess the attributes in question formally, but each in the manner appropriate to, and determined by, its nature. The following is such an analogy: as this water is hard with the kind of hardness appropriate to water (it contains too much lime), so this clay model is hard with the kind of hardness appropriate to clay models (it has dried out, or been fired). But how equivalent are these kinds of hardness? How far are water and clay models really comparable? The analogy does not tell us, yet its worth depends upon these considerations. The perplexity is increased when on one side of the supposed equation we place God and his attributes. The purpose of the analogy is to provide information about God and his nature; but the very construction of the equation presupposes that we select certain characteristics which we deem to appropriate to God, and that we rule out others which we consider to be not fitting. Christians have not, with noticeable frequency, constructed analogies of proportionality in such terms as the following: as Jones is spiteful in a manner appropriate to human beings, so God is spiteful in a manner appropriate to God. It may be said that such an equation is unthinkable. But by itself the analogy of proportionality does not tell us that it is. When asked how we become aware of proportionality, Thomists (reaching back to the Greeks) employ the doctrine of universals to show that, since human beings are created by, and are dependent upon, and therefore 'participate in', eternal, uncreated Being, proportionality may legitimately be inferred. But this raises two questions at least. From the theological point of view it may be questioned whether the presupposition that God and humanity possess identical characteristics is tenable, given the infinite, holy God and finite, sinful human beings. From the philosophical side, attention may be drawn to the fact that, since we can speak of Being at all only by analogy, how can we obtain an independent foundation which would constitute a suitable basis for the drawing of further analogies?

It would thus seem that there are formidable difficulties in the path of a Christian who wishes to justify his or her descriptions of God by arguments from analogy. As a linguistic device, however, used within the context of a reasonably clearly definable framework of convictions, analogies may be the only means of avoiding otherwise uncommunicative silence. Even then we should do well to heed the distinction between positive and negative analogy; that is to say, we must note not only the ways in which A is like B, but also the ways in which they are unlike; we should hope that our readers or hearers will endeavour to contribute a certain imaginative sympathy in response to our efforts at communication; and we should select our analogies with some eye to those we are addressing, lest we land them in the predicament of the boy who, 'hearing that God was high and bright, assumed that the weathercock on the barn must be God, for it was the highest and brightest object he knew'.[150] He had not realized that he was being treated to some analogies.

Donald Bloesch explains that

> An analogy conveys conceptual content; a metaphor alludes to that which escapes conceptualization. To say that God is a Rock or Fortress is metaphorical, but to call God Father or Lord is analogical. A metaphor connotes a suggested likeness between two things that are manifestly dissimilar, whereas an analogy presupposes an underlying similarity or congruity in the midst of real difference. The language of faith contains metaphor, analogy, and concept, but what is conveyed is something much more than mystical insight or self-understanding. Faith language communicates by the power of the Spirit a real, objective disclosure of the living God in actual human history, a disclosure which can be only partially grasped by reason, but which does not entirely elude reason. While rationalism reduces mystery to meaning that is clear and distinct and mysticism dissolves meaning into mystery, biblical religion affirms that meaning shines through mystery.[151]

This paragraph nicely relates the linguistic considerations of this section to our discussion of rationalism in the previous section, and recalls our discussion of history in the preceding chapter. But it also leads us back again to the question of revelation in propositions.

The question is, although we cannot comprehend God as he is in himself, is he so transcendent, or otherwise impotent, that he cannot communicate with us through intelligible, literally true propositions? Yes, God acts in history and addresses his people thereby; undoubtedly many of the biblical passages are poetic, parabolic, apocalyptic in type; nor is there an inherently linguistic problem (though there may be historical problems) with narratives purporting to record actual events. But can God straighforwardly tell us something about himself? Am I alone in being somewhat perplexed by those theologians who shuffle through their packs of metaphors and analogies and symbols with a view to determining their appropriateness when used of God – as if God has not gone to rather considerable lengths to tell us a thing of two by his Spirit through the Word? If I am told that mine is simply the naive response of 'the person in the pew' I shall simply retort, 'But such persons comprise the bulk of confessors', adding, ever so piously, 'and "it seemed good to the Holy Spirit and to us" to see things in this way'.[152] In a word, there is an effort of communication, if one may so speak, from God's side too – and first. At this point it is possible that I am within sight of Jüngel's point on what he calls the 'analogy of advent'. If this means that God is doing something to assist our conceptualization, well and good. His context is a critique of what I might call the 'Greek' line of emphasizing God's ineffability. However, when Jüngel declares that it is 'the difference between God and man, which is constitutive of the essence of the Christian faith' I demur, because (*a*) important though the Creator–creature distinction is, this seems to be a relapse into a 'Greek' mode of thinking; and (*b*) it is the grace of God in the Gospel which is constitutive of the Christian faith. Jüngel writes:

> In that in Evangelical speech God comes close to men, he carries out his divinity's own humanity, in order to make concrete the difference between his divinity's own humanity and the humanity of man. The difference between God and man, which is constitutive of the essence of the Christian faith, is thus not the difference of a still greater dissimilarity, but rather, conversely, the difference of a still greater similarity between God and man in the midst of a great dissimilarity.[153]

Suppose, then, that we learn from scripture that God is 'the God and father of our Lord Jesus Christ', and that Jesus encourages us to pray to God as 'Our Father'. It seems to me, in the light of the foregoing discussion, that 'Father' here is an analogy; the term is not employed univocally of ourselves and God (and hence the denial that God is masculine should not need to be made); and yet there is sufficient commonality of connotation that the proposition 'God is our Father' is true.[154] I take this on the authority of Jesus himself (and I am aware that that appeal can invite a regress of questions, but I here take a stand).[155] An ontological claim, expressed analogically, is here being made. As in Exodus 3: 14, so in the New Testament, God names himself. 'Father' is not in the first place, therefore, one of a number of analogies which we think it appropriate to use of God.[156] It is encouraging to be able to call a distinguished New Testament scholar to my aid at this point:

> On *a priori* grounds there is no compelling reason why Revelation should be found in 'mighty acts' of God but not in words. Indeed, words can be a better medium of communication than events which

> need to be explained. Moreover, the explanation of events as 'mighty acts' of God is itself a historical judgment, no doubt valid, but nevertheless exposed to all the uncertainties of such judgments. The truth is that we cannot avoid some theory of Biblical inspiration if we are to find a worthy doctrine of Revelation, and we ought not to be deterred from this search by the fear of returning to a pre-critical form of the doctrine, as involving an inerrant authority to be accepted without further question.[157]

From the fact that the Bible encourages us to use metaphorical language of God with no literal equivalence of meaning intended – fortress, hen and chicks, rock – it does not follow that he may not address us via analogies intended to convey literal truth.[158] Nor is it required that in order to convey literal truth to us we need a Bible which is inerrant in the original autographs (which, as it happens, are not to hand). It would seem that some inerrantists take insufficient account of the fact that we have the biblical treasure in earthen vessels. It could hardly be otherwise, given the historicity, and hence the ambiguous context, of the revelation, and the fallibility of the original authors. To the reply that God so cared for and guided the authors that they were preserved from error in everything they wrote, it is difficult, in the light of scholarship, not simply to retort, 'No he did not.'[159] I do not accuse the more responsible conservative scholars of espousing a crude 'dictation' theory of inspiration,[160] but there is surely a caution in the fact that some are adept at detecting gradations of inerrancy, with some claiming that all biblical statements – even those purporting to be 'scientific' – are literally true, while others hold that the Bible is inerrant only in what it says concerning the Gospel and the plan of salvation.

Calvin put much of it in a nutshell: 'The word itself, whatever be the way in which it is conveyed to us, is a kind of mirror in which faith beholds God . . . it is always by his word that he manifests himself to those whom he designs to draw to himself.'[161] By the use of the term 'mirror' Calvin warns us against bibliolatry; with the phrase, 'by the word' he establishes a bulwark against unwholesome subjectivisms.[162] Hubert Cunliffe-Jones was right to warn us that 'We must be careful not to identify the witness of the Holy Spirit with every strange warming of the human heart.'[163] At this point we are helped by the sanctions of the fellowship and the tradition, as I pointed out in Chapter 2 above. These are the more necessary because, as with our understanding of history, so with our interpretation of the Bible: 'All religious readers in fact go to the Bible with some sort of presupposition. However firmly they may believe that they accept "the word of God" without question, they have certain prior beliefs which determine their interpretation.'[164] Thus, for example, even the most conservative Christians preach more sermons from Romans than from Obadiah – and that not only because the former contains more verses than the latter.

In seeking to commend the position I am adopting I face more than one obstacle. The first relates to the human condition, and was aptly expressed by P. T. Forsyth: 'We may . . . take it that the authority of a holy Gospel cannot be proved to the natural man. The offence of the Cross has not ceased. It must first capture him and make him a supernatural man.'[165] The second has to do with the sometimes unexpected manner of God's revelation – the choice of insignificant Israel, the Cross as a way to victory – and his facility for toppling our a prioris which begin, 'Surely God would not . . . ' or 'God can do no other than . . . ' Above all, 'There is absolutely no reason why God should forgive and redeem men. All the reason we know, apart from His own revelation of Himself and His purpose, is against it. There is nothing we have less natural reason to expect . . . '[166] Yet God redeems.

Equally, to return to our main point here, there can be no a prioris which would rule out the possibility of God's communication with those who are created in his image. He not only acts in history, but he addresses us by his Spirit through the Word. The Gospel is a message, not a mime; it is interpreted action, and whereas

> Blind unbelief is sure to err
> And scan his work in vain;
> God is his own interpreter,
> And he will make it plain.[167]

For this reason, however much or little we may learn of God elsewhere,[168]

> *Formally* considered our theological statements are true in so far as they are faithful responses to the self-communication of the Truth of God in the way in which He reveals Himself in and through the witness of the Holy Scripture, in the historical life of the Church, for it is there in the Holy Scripture that we actually hear God's Word.[169]

It follows that 'the human concepts which arise in faith under the creative impact of the speech of God are grounded beyond themselves in the *ratio veritatis* of the divine Being'. [170] Though never exhaustive,[171] our knowledge of God is true to the extent that it is reflective of God's knowledge of himself.

By grace we are in touch with the Father through the Son by the Spirit. We are not at a quasi-geographical distance from God, eagerly firing off analogies drawn from our little experience in the hope that they will hit the target. Apart from God's informing us of what he is about, we are left with equivocation, symbols symbolizing symbols, metaphors which may or may not be worthy. Kantian epistemology then reigns supreme and we cannot know God. But this is to anticipate our next chapter.

For the present I recall the words of William Robertson Smith who, though much maligned by some conservatives in his own day because of his 'advanced' biblical views, nevertheless had the pearl of price:

> If I am asked why I receive Scripture as the word of God, and as the only perfect rule of faith and life, I answer with all the fathers of the Protestant Church, because the Bible is the only record of the redeeming love of God, because in the Bible alone I find God drawing near to man in Christ Jesus, and declaring to us in Him His will for our salvation. And this record I know to be true by the witness of His Spirit in my heart, whereby I am assured that none other than God Himself is able to speak such words unto my soul.[172]

The transcendent–immanent holy God has, by a supernatural miracle of grace, spoken in his Son. He has not left us guessing, nor himself without a witness. For the Christian it is always the case that 'The last authority of the redeemed is the Redeemer as such',[173] but the Spirit conveys the good news of Christ to us in the pages of the Bible. From this Gospel our Christian confessing derives its motivation and, to reiterate, that confessing is by word and deed; for Christianity is not life in preference to creed, but life flowing from creed; and God, having once addressed us, does not leave us. Rather, 'by His Holy Spirit, he makes me wholeheartedly willing and ready from now on to live for him'.[174]

V

The second matter arising from our account of those who have exalted reason concerns the question of foundationalism, that is to say, the philosophical doctrine that those beliefs alone are rational which are indubitable and from which further propositions may properly be inferred. Considerable attention has been devoted to the critique of foundationalism since about 1970. It is an issue which bears upon a number of related topics, not least, natural theology (the non-necessity, if not in some cases the outright rejection, of which is asserted by Reformed epistemologists), to which I shall shortly come. I deal with it independently because the conclusions reached (however tentative, since the debate continues) on the viability or otherwise of foundationalism will have a direct bearing upon the kind of natural theology, if any, which may be deemed appropriate. It goes without saying that foundationalism has been attacked from a number of quarters. One line of adverse criticism is bound up with the general postmodernist attack upon metanarratives; but what particularly interests us here is that modified version of the critique which emanates from those commonly known as Reformed epistemologists.[175] Of these Alvin Plantinga is among the most prominent, and I shall briefly recount his position. But, in order to bring out what I mean by saying that his is a modified critique of foundationalism, I shall first recall Descartes, regarded by most as the fountainhead of foundationalism. His quest of certainty, as we saw, led him to the intuition that those propositions of which he had a clear and distinct idea were true and self-verifying. C. D. Prado makes the point thus:

> Descartes thought that there could be a relation of justification between an actuality, for instance an existent God, and an idea, and that the disparity in nature or kind did not weaken or preclude the justificatory relationship. It is fundamental for Descartes that knowledge must be grounded on the simplest, most certain truths or evidence. And the linguistic appears to be once removed from the real, so the notion is that the most basic trusts are not true sentences or propositions but actualities properly and indirectly represented or 'given' in true ideas. Later the empiricists were to hold that these given actualities were sensory data, but whether for Descartes or Locke, the notion is that what grounds or justifies belief, and so makes it knowledge is something nonlinguistic, an actuality immediately present to the mind. This notion is now almost universally rejected.[176]

The position of Plantinga and others is that according to classical foundationalism as thus described, those propositions only of which I am certain may justifiably be accepted. Such propositions, so the traditional line runs, either pertain to my mental state, or they are self-evident. Such propositions enshrine properly basic beliefs. But, says Plantinga, his belief in God is neither self-evident nor to do with his own mental life. He therefore takes a short way with the classical foundationalist's favoured starting points and declares that there are other properly basic beliefs, of which belief in God is a prominent example. It is not embraced on the basis of arguments for God's existence; indeed, the believer may not be aware of such arguments; and the believer's position would be secure even if there were no arguments. Properly nonbasic beliefs are those which one justifiably holds on the basis of properly basic beliefs.[177]

We can now see how Plantinga has modified classical foundationalism: it is not that he denies that there are properly basic beliefs; it is that he will not have such beliefs restricted to those traditionally permitted by foundationalists. As Reformed epistemologists have frequently pointed out, the guiding principle of 'strong' foundationalism is self-referentially incoherent. That is to say, the view that one is behaving rationally in believing only when the belief is self-evident or incorrigible, or is inferred from other beliefs which are of that kind, is itself neither self-evident nor derived in the specified way. (This *tu quoque* move recalls the way in which Mascall and others turned the principle of verification round upon the logical positivists.) But this is not all. Plantinga further allows an important place to the believer's aesthetic, moral and religious experience, arguing in the last case that, if a person believes in a basic way that God loves him or her, that belief is internally rational and, given the experience and properly functioning rational faculties, it would be odd if the person were to repudiate the belief. Finally, Plantinga proposes that warranted beliefs such as that God exists, while not obviously true, are those properly basic beliefs which are believed by those who hold them to be true.[178] As Nicholas Wolterstorff further explains,

> It is not the case that one is warranted in accepting some theory if and only if one is warranted in believing that it is justified by propositions knowable non-inferentially and with certitude. From this it does not follow that there is no structured reality independent of our conceivings

> and believings – though the difficulties of foundationalism have led many to this position. Nor does it follow that we must give up truth as the goal of theoretical enquiry – though the difficulties of foundationalism have made this view particularly attractive to many. Nor does it follow that we can never know the truth – though the difficulties of foundationalism have led to a wave of agnosticism. Nor does it follow that one belief is as warranted for me as another. All that follows is that theorizing is without a foundation of indubitables.[179]

Wolterstorff's work manifests some indebtedness to Reid's common-sense realism, which he regards as a species of non-classical foundationalism. He welcomes the way in which Reid understands rationality in situational terms, such that what is rational in one person's situation may not be so in another's; he approves of the psychological thrust and the non-sceptical nature of Reid's theory; but he faults Reid for not supplying a criterion of justified belief, and for not taking the noetic effects of sin with sufficient seriousness. On this latter point Calvin and Kuyper are preferred.[180] There are nevertheless echoes of Reid's down-to-earthness in Wolterstorff's claim that

> A person is rationally justified in believing a certain proposition which he does believe unless he has adequate reason to cease from believing it. Our beliefs are rational unless we have reason for refraining; they are not nonrational unless we have reason *for* believing.[181]

Such is Wolterstorff's retort to the 'evidentialists', whose position he summarizes thus:

> It was insisted, in the first place, that it would be *wrong* for a person to accept Christianity, or any other form of theism, unless it was *rational* for him to do so. And it was insisted, secondly, that it is not rational for a person to do so unless he holds his religious convictions on the basis of other beliefs of his which give to those convictions adequate evidential support. No religion is acceptable unless it is rational, and no religion is rational unless supported by evidence. That is the evidentialist challenge.[182]

Some have more than suspected that Plantinga and other Reformed epistemologists have, in their response to this challenge, capitulated to fideism, but I do not think this is the case. While finding natural theology unnecessary for the believer, Plantinga does not deny that theistic arguments may have a role to play in apologetic discussion; he thinks that they can be a useful preparation for faith; and, as is well known, he has devoted a considerable amount of time to analysing them. Accordingly, his reply to the charge of fideism is that, while, for example, the truth that God was in Christ reconciling the world to himself is not a direct deliverance of reason, belief in God's existence is a deliverance of reason.

It is now time to hazard a few tentative observations on the Reformed epistemology project – tentative because the debate continues and shows no sign of abating. First, the Reformed epistemologists have done well to show that, whether in its rationalist or empiricist form the classical foundationalists imposed an intellectual straitjacket upon apologetics. As I sought to show in *John Locke and the Eighteenth-Century Divines*, Locke's way of setting out from the epistemological question landed him in a position in which he was unable to accommodate all he wished to believe and, accordingly, he had recourse to revelation, scripture, the example of Jesus – all of these being appealed to as the occasion required, but, from a systematic point of view, all of them lying side by side in such a way that the joins show. I shall return to this point in the next chapter, and would meanwhile note that, in respect of its critique of the narrowness of classical foundationalism's epistemological criteria, the protest of the Reformed epistemologists endorses the claim which I am hoping to demonstrate in the cumulative argument of this book, namely that the nature and manner of appropriation of the Gospel which is to be commended must have some bearing upon our apologetic procedures and that, in fact, a reasoned eclecticism offers the best way forward. If positivists and others would rule out Christian discourse *ab initio*, classical foundationalists, by narrowing the scope of rationality, seem to rule out from the start the kind of reasonableness which can accommodate what has happened in Christ and to believers. As William Placher has remarked,

> If theologians try to defend their claims by starting with basic, foundational truths that any rational person would have to believe or observations independent of theory and assumption, they are trying to do something that our best philosophers tell us is impossible – not merely for religious beliefs but for any beliefs whatsoever. It makes no sense to demand that Christians undertake such a self-limiting discipline as the price of entry into intellectual conversation.[183]

May it be, however, that in their own way the Reformed epistemologists are too intellectualist? Michael Vertin reminds us of some Roman Catholic critics of Reformed epistemology who, with reference to Aquinas, Newman and Lonergan, have challenged the notion that 'a direct, unmediated awareness of God is a constitutive element of concrete human rationality'.[184] Their point is that

> even in ordinary and mundane cases a rational affirmation's grounds often include an element of affectivity, choice, commitment. One may affirm X because within one's total concrete context one assesses X not just as plausible but also as desirable; and such an affirmation can be thoroughly rational. But if ordinary and mundane affirmations can rest in part on volitional grounds without their rationality being compromised, so too can the affirmation of God.[185]

I do not see that Reformed epistemologists are required to deny this. On the contrary, it seems to me that they have gone further than most philosophers of religion to elevate the position of the 'ordinary' believer whose faith is secure and whose gifts lie in directions other than the philosophical. As Terence Penelhum has rightly said,

> The Basic Belief Apologetic argues that there is no good reason to reject the claim that many people do in fact perceive or encounter [God] and that this is the source of their basic beliefs. A critic who says at this point that this argument assumes the truth of the very beliefs it is defending can indeed be accused of an epistemic double standard.[186]

In this connection K. J. Clark invokes his grandmother, 'an ordinary woman of faith'. 'If evidentialism is true', he declares, 'then my grandmother has a noetic defect – she believes in God without sufficient propositional evidence.' This is not the case, however; and it is not because 'Rationality is not simply a relation that obtains between one's beliefs. Rather, it is the complex relation between one's cognitive equipment – divinely designed – one's experiences, and the world.'[187] This being so, religious experience, as I shall hope to show in the next chapter, can go some way towards justifying a person's religious beliefs. We do not infer the beliefs from the experiences (nor believe when we endorse the conclusion of an argument to religious experience), but rather the experiences are compatible with the belief and endorse or reinforce it. It is therefore not the case that the basic beliefs of the Reformed epistemologists are groundless.[188]

There remains, however, the nagging question of truth. There is, no doubt, a plurality of properly basic beliefs; but if kinds of justification are, as Reformed epistemologists hold them to be, appropriate to the basic beliefs in question, are we not in danger of a relativism which permits the intellectual anarchy of radically opposed beliefs which, if acted upon, could lead to practical anarchy of the most dangerous kind? The response embedded in this question has been labelled 'the Great Pumpkin Objection'. If all manner of beliefs may be deemed properly basic, why may not a believer in Halloween's Great Pumpkin be regarded as entirely reasonable? Plantinga denies that such a belief is properly basic, and is not perturbed that there are no criteria for choosing in advance between one alleged basic belief and another. Rather, the value of alleged properly basic beliefs is to be tested on the ground, so to speak, by reference to the worthiness or otherwise of the supportive examples put forward by those who espouse them.[189]

This may appear to some to be a hit-and-miss way out of the relativist trap. Indeed, it prompts a number of respondents, many of them sympathetic to some aspects of Reformed epistemology, to suggest that this type of apologetic works best defensively – that is, it gives the believer some confidence that his or her trust is not misplaced; or, at least, that it is no more misplaced than it is in connection with many other commitments we hold; but it is deficient in meeting the objection of the non-believer who is quite happy with his or her own properly basic beliefs:

> We are, it seems, to envisage a believer who has come to think that he can offer no good reasons for his belief in God and who asks himself, 'Is my belief then a rational one?' If Plantinga is right, such a man can say, 'Well, at any rate my belief in God is in no worse case than my belief that other people sometimes feel pain, and no one is going to deny that *that* is rational.' This can perhaps be made to sound quite plausible. But a nonbeliever would have to transpose Plantinga's remark into something like: 'If my belief in other minds is rational, it would be equally rational for me to *adopt* a belief in God, even though I can see no good reason for adopting such a belief.' And that does not sound so good. It does seem fair to demand reasons where what is in question is the rationality of a *change of mind*. It does not, of course, follow that the appropriate reasons must be of the kind which form the natural theologian's stock in trade.[190]

Quite so, but as a number of philosophers have pointed out, 'without natural theology there is no way beyond a situation in which adherents of opposed belief systems peer over their defenses at one another and explain one another's faith away'.[191] We are back once more to the question of epistemological common ground and the *imago dei.*

One further, related, point needs to be made. The Reformed epistemologists are exponents of Christian philosophy: Kuyper and his heirs are an important part of their inheritance.[192] In due course we shall have to consider the question of world-views, but for the present I simply note the possibility that unless genuine communication with others (members of other faiths, non-believers at large) is possible – and the hint in some of Plantinga's writing that there is one sort of justifying argument for Christians and a different one for others is disquieting[193] – the outcome may be the ghettoization of 'Christian philosophy' and the impossibility of commending the faith to others. For such commendation to occur it does seem necessary that 'As ontological truth-claims the assertions of Christian faith must be compatible with all other true propositions.'[194]

VI

Turning now to those who understand reason as requiring the supplement of revelation, we may set out from Origen:

> [W]e maintain that human nature is in no way able to seek after God, or to attain a clear knowledge of Him without the help of Him whom it seeks. He makes Himself known to those who, after doing all that their powers will allow, confess that they need help from Him, who discovers Himself to those whom He approves, in so far as it is possible for man and the soul still dwelling in the body to know God.[195]

As to the manner of this revelation,

> the works of the divine providence and the design of the whole universe are as it were rays of God's nature, in comparison with his very being. Our mind cannot behold God as he is in himself, therefore it forms its conception of the Creator of the universe from the beauty of his works and the loveliness of his creatures . . .[196]

In Augustine's opinion, everybody is to a degree illuminated by the Logos, and there is no knowledge which does not originate in communion (acknowledged or not) with the divine mind.[197] In this sense all knowledge is revealed knowledge: Augustine does not maintain a sharp dichotomy between reason and revelation. However, human intellectual capacities (though by no means to be despised after the fashion of Tertullian, because reason is integral to the *imago dei*) require the special aid of revelation, not least because of the noetic effects of sin. Revelation is given in the Bible, but the message of scripture must be brought home to the individual. This comes about by a person's faith, 'For it is written, "Unless ye believe, ye shall not understand".'[198] Through faith the mind is not only informed, it is first purified.[199] Only then can the light be received. At the same time, Augustine recognizes that we cannot have faith in one of whom we have no understanding at all; but following the commitment of faith there is an increase of understanding.[200] I shall resume this theme in the next chapter.

Echoes of Augustine's approach are heard from his day to our own. In the Middle Ages Anselm's starting point is decidedly Augustinian: 'I believe in order to understand';[201] while Abelard, though not thinking that complete understanding can be reached prior to the act of faith (or, indeed, following it – he essayed no demonstrations of the kind Anselm advanced in his meditations on the existence of the God in whom he believed) leans towards 'rationalism'[202] in requiring beliefs to be in harmony with reason. In the general line of Anselm we find Hugh of St Victor. Although he does not devote himself to the rational demonstration of Christian doctrine in the way his predecessor did, he does carefully distinguish truths which are from reason, and therefore necessary; these are received apart from faith. At the other extreme there are alleged truths which are contrary to reason and are therefore unbelievable. In between are propositions which are probably true, and those which are above reason but not irrational. These alone are the object of faith.[203] Our final representative of the Augustinian–Anselmian line is Bonaventure. Living in the wake of the contribution of Aquinas, he nevertheless for the most part follows the 'old paths'. Central to his position is the claim that the light of the created intellect does not by itself suffice.

With the foregoing we may now, at least to some extent, contrast Aquinas. I say 'to some extent', because in the first place neither

Aquinas nor his predecessors became Christian believers as a result of their competence in theistic argument. Again, the customary bracketing of Aquinas with Aristotle implies no absence of Platonism in the Angelic Doctor's thought.[204] For example, the Platonic doctrine inherited by Aquinas from the Pseudo-Areopagite and John of Damascus to the effect that God is to be reached by a process of subtraction entailing the reduction of limitations, constituted a profound stimulus to Aquinas's presentation of the *via negativa.*

It is in his epistemology, however, that Aquinas's Aristotelianism emerges most clearly, especially in his assertion that, while sense experience is the fount of knowledge, the mind, illuminated by God, is capable of drawing therefrom more-than-empirical knowledge.[205] Accordingly, he opposes both the Platonic theory that forms alone are knowable, and the sensationalist theory of Democritus. As to the truth thus acquired, it is well known that Aquinas distinguishes between truth attainable by human reason, and truth attainable only as it is revealed to human beings: 'the natural light bestowed upon the soul is God's illumination, whereby we are illumined to see what pertains to natural knowledge; and for this there is required no further illumination, but only for such things as surpass natural knowledge.'[206] It is sometimes wrongly supposed that Aquinas is insisting upon two different kinds of truth. In fact he holds to the indivisibility of truth, emphasizes the inability of a truth acquired by reason to conflict with one given in revelation and, in face of that mystery which he senses to be at the heart of things, merely holds that human limitation requires more than the exercise of human reason if truths which are above, but not contary to, reason are to be apprehended at all. Among these latter truths are that God is a holy Trinity,[207] that Jesus Christ is God incarnate, and that we shall be raised. The fact that these are known from revelation does not preclude their rational, albeit incomplete, defence. Because of their divine origin such truths are certain, for whereas 'other sciences derive their certitude from the natural light of human reason, which can err, . . . this derives its certitude from the light of the divine science, which cannot err'.[208] Divine truths are received by faith; reason may clarify such truths, but cannot prove them.[209] In the words of a prominent interpreter of Aquinas:

> As [Aquinas] himself understands it, theology must be conceived as a science of Revelation. Its source is the word of God. Its basis is faith in the trust of this word. Its 'formal' unity, to speak like St. Thomas, depends precisely upon the fact that there is a Revelation, which faith received as Revelation.[210]

On the other hand, truths concerning such matters as the existence of God can, Aquinas thinks, be demonstrated by the exercise of natural reason: 'The existence of God and other like truths about God which can be known by natural reason are not articles of faith, but are preambles to the articles.'[211] With discussions of foundationalism ringing in our ears we should at this point note that Aquinas is no foundationalist, seeking to provide rational grounds for faith. For him the authorities are the Bible and the Church, and they are secure. His objective is to show that by the exercise of natural reason we can show that there is nothing irrational in belief. By reason

> we know His relationship with creatures, that is, that He is the cause of all things; also that creatures differ from Him, inasmuch as He is not in any way part of what is caused by Him; and that His effects are removed from Him, not by reason of any defect on His part, but because He superexceeds them all.[212]

This position is reiterated down the centuries in Roman Catholic circles, notably at the First Vatican Council, echoed at the Second:

> The sacred Synod professes that 'God, the first principle and last end of all things, can be known with certainty from the created world, by the natural light of human reason' (cf. Rom. 1: 20). It teaches that it is to his Revelation that we must attribute the fact 'that those things, which in themselves are not beyond the grasp of human reason, can, in the present condition of the human race, be known by all men with ease, with firm certainty, and without the contamination of error.'[213]

It thus transpires that, while Aquinas undoubtedly accords priority to faith where the deepest truths are concerned, and while his overall motivation is by no means removed from the then traditional stance of faith seeking understanding,[214] his sharper initial distinction between the provinces of philosophy and theology suggests (to employ a currently overworked term) a less holistic intellectual approach than that of Augustine or even Anselm. (To introduce a point to which I shall return later: while Aquinas speaks of the theology which is within the sphere of sacred doctrine as differing in genus from that which belongs to philosophy,[215] it has seriously been questioned whether the God treated in the latter, Being, is the same as that treated by the former, 'The God and father of our Lord Jesus Christ' – notwithstanding that he regards the distinctively Christian claims as being of a higher order than the purely philosophical, for 'grace does not destroy nature, but perfects it'.)[216] For Anselm, reason and revelation mutually interact to yield knowledge. For Aquinas, revelation completes a task which reason is competent to begin, though with the proviso just noted that God (in different senses, so to speak) is within the purview of both philosophy and theology. In Aquinas's case, while the 'faith seeking understanding' project is not disowned, an epistemology different from that of Augustine and Anselm gives his discussion a fresh emphasis. Fundamental to the Augustine–Anselm position is the belief that Christians are guided by faith even when they think they are at their most rational. God is given in the Christian's experience, and reason has the task not so much of justifying belief as of aiding in its interpretation. For Aquinas, however, there can be no direct knowledge of God in this life. Whatever is known of God is known by causal inference and analogical predication. Aquinas's analogy in this connection is one of proportionality, and some Thomists have argued that this proportionality as between the earthly realm and the realm of Being (which is what Aquinas's natural theology concerns) obtains because earthly phenomena participate in timeless Being. But, as D. M. Emmet long ago remarked, it is difficult on this basis to avoid anthropomorphism on the one hand or agnosticism on the other in our endeavour to select suitable analogies.[217] A lever was thus given to those who, in the context of the rise of modern science and of scepticism, subsequently sought to establish a natural theology on the basis of reason alone, and to those who wondered why even that was necessary. Moreover, even those not hostile to Christianity came, because of the natural theology–revelation distinction, to think of revelation more as a matter of additional information via propositions otherwise inaccessible to the human mind, than as a mode of illumination. Among those at the fountainhead of this development was Suárez, the tendency of whose thought was to make revelation propositional and faith a matter of intellectual assent to such propositions.[218] Another straw in the wind was *De providentia numinis* by Lessius of Louvain, who, on the basis of a sharp distinction between reason and revelation, confined his Christological teaching to the latter sphere. He was thus, according to Michael Buckley, one of the culprits in that methodological shift which permitted Enlightenment thinkers to take over the theologically denuded discussion of the existence of God, with the result that 'In the absence of a rich and comprehensive Christology and a Pneumatology of religious experience, Christianity enters into the defense of the existence of the Christian God without appeal to anything Christian.'[219] The upshot is that 'The prior success of natural theology comes in modern times to be regarded as a necessary condition of the rationality of faith.'[220]

One aspect of his theological inheritance which Aquinas does not seem to have brought into close relationship with his epistemology is that concerning the noetic effects of sin.[221] We have already considered this in some detail, and now I simply note the fact that, although Aquinas is in no doubt that the will no less than the intellect is involved in the act of believing, he does not in this context emphasize human inability apart from grace. The Greek inheritance may have weighed more heavily with Aquinas at this point than the Christian. As O. C. Quick pointed out,

> from the strictly Platonic and Aristotelian point of view, no divine act of atonement is either necessary or possible as a means of salvation. To Plato and Aristotle what is required for salvation is not the forgiveness of sin, but the dissipation of error; and, even if salvation were to come from God, it must take the form, not of an atoning incarnation, but of a theophany.[222]

The Reformers, as we have seen, more than made good this deficiency.

Of the major Reformers, Calvin devoted most attention to the discussion of reason. The context of one of his more celebrated remarks on reason is his discussion of the need of regeneration if we would discern spiritual things. Spiritual insight, he declares, consists in '(1) knowing God; (2) knowing his fatherly favor in our behalf, in which our salvation consists; (3) knowing how to frame our life according to the rule of his law. In the first two points – and especially in the second – the greatest geniuses are blinder than moles!'[223] He concedes that the philosophers 'may chance to sprinkle their books with droplets of truth', but 'Human reason . . . neither approaches, nor strives toward, nor even takes a straight aim at' the truth concerning 'who the true God is or what sort of God he wishes to be toward us'.[224]

However, reason as a gift of God can do many useful things. It enables progress in politics, economics and the liberal arts, and in these fields pagans no less than Christians benefit from its deliverances. Further, reason is competent to discern the goodness and power of God from contemplation of the created order,[225] but we cannot from hence infer that God is Father. Least of all can unaided human reason acquaint us with God's essence, or with such doctrinal matters as election and reprobation and the Trinity.[226] To grasp such truths that 'renewal of the mind' of which Paul speaks[227] is required, and philosophers were ignorant of this fact,

> For they set up reason alone as the ruling principle in man, and think that it alone should be listened to; to it alone, in short, they trust the conduct of their life. But the Christian philosophy [that is, the philosophy of the person renewed in Christ] bids reason give way to, submit and subject itself to, the Holy Spirit so that the man himself may no longer live but hear Christ living and reigning within him [Gal. 2: 20].[228]

Even scripture

> will ultimately suffice for a saving knowledge of God only when its certainty is founded upon the inward persuasion of the Holy Spirit. Indeed [as if to offer advance partial justification of Warfield and the evidentialists], these human testimonies which exist to confirm it will not be in vain if, as secondary aids to our feebleness, they follow the chief and highest testimony. But those who wish to prove to unbelievers that Scripture is the Word of God are acting foolishly, for only by faith can this be known.[229]

It is striking that, despite the considerable influence of Calvin's thought, his emphasis upon the noetic effects of sin and the regenerating role of the Holy Spirit, theistic argumentation surfaced rapidly even in Reformed quarters. No doubt the theologians were no less concerned by the advance of scepticism than was Descartes; certainly they wished to counter those outbreaks of 'enthusiasm' which veered towards, and in some cases gloried in, irrationalism; and, not least in England, they frequently saw the need to propound a certain number of reasonable doctrines around which, in turbulent socio-political times, the majority of citizens could gather. At all events, in the commentary of the third-generation Reformer, Ursinus, upon the Heidelberg Catechism, of which he was the principal author, we find such a definite statement as this: 'That there is a God is proved by many arguments common to Philosophy and Theology.'[230]

Many of the seventeenth-century Puritans, not excluding those who tended in an Arminian direction,[231] were in general accord with Calvin on reason, though their context influenced their mode of expression, as my remarks in square brackets will indicate in the following extracts from Richard Baxter's *Works*:

> The Spirit is not given to make our religion reasonable, but to make sinners reasonable, in habit and act, for the believing it . . . [N]or doth [the Spirit] cause us to believe by enthusiasm [by which Baxter means the unwarranted appeal to private and hence untestable 'revelations'[232]], or without reason, but he works on man as man, and causeth him to believe nothing but what is credible . . .
>
> As reason sufficeth not without the Spirit . . . so the Spirit worketh not on the will but by the reason: he moveth not man as a beast or stone, to do a thing he knoweth not why, but by illumination [the Cambridge Platonist understanding of reason as the 'candle of the Lord' may well be in Baxter's mind at this point] giveth him the soundest reason for the doing of it.
>
> I do, therefore, neither despise evidence as unnecessary [here speaks one influenced by the new science], nor trust it alone as the sufficient total cause of my belief; for if God's grace do not open mine eyes, and come down in power upon my will, and insinuate into it a sweet acquaintance with things unseen, and a taste of their goodness to delight my soul [one recalls the frequent usage by mystics of the notions of sweetness and taste], no reasons will serve to stablish and comfort me . . . [233]

I invoke one more Puritan, John Flavel. Although he does not make direct reference to the Holy Spirit in the passage to be quoted, he covers most of the bases, emphasizes the importance of revelation and faith, adverts to the ethical implications of human reasoning and, for good measure, manages a passing swipe at the Socinians:

> Reason exalts man above all earthly beings; it is his dignity and privilege, that God hath furnished him with abilities of mind, to recollect, animadvert, compare, infer, ponder, and judge his own actions. Hereby he becomes not only capable of moral government by human laws, (which no creature beside him is) but also of spiritual government by divine laws, and the blessed fruition of God in glory, which no other species of creatures (angels only excepted) have a subjected capacity for.
>
> Right reason, by the law of nature, (as a home-born judge) arbitrates and determines all things within its proper province; which province is extended far and wide. All actions, natural, moral, and civil, are weighed at this beam and standard; none are exempted, but matters of supernatural revelation; and yet even these are not wholly and in every respect, exempt from right reason: for although there be some mysteries in religion above the sphere and flight of reason: yet nothing can be found in religion, that is unreasonable.[234]
>
> And though these mysteries be not of natural investigation, but of supernatural revelation; yet reason is convinced, nothing can be more reasonable, than that it takes its place at the feet of faith; which is but to suffer itself to become pupil to an omniscient and infallible instructor. The resolution of our reason into faith, and of faith into God's veracity, are acts highly becoming reasonable beings in such cases as these . . .
>
> But in all matters properly under the jurisdiction of reason, every man is obliged to account with himself, as well as others, for the reasonableness of his own actions; and that act which will not endure the test of sound reason, it judges not fit for the entertainment of man. If reason cannot justify it, it is beneath the rank and dignity of a man to do it.[235]

Where Baxter seems to allow greater place to empirical evidence, the Cambridge Platonists are more resolutely intuitionist in approach. Against the materialism and scepticism of Hobbes, and in quest of a *via media* between the Scylla of authoritarian prelacy and the Charybdis of Puritan confessional scholasticism, they sought to elevate reason as affording intuitions of spiritual reality – that is, as having more than a purely discursive role. They shared Whichcote's view that 'Reason *discovers* what is Natural; and Reason *receives*, what is Supernatural.'[236] Indeed, reason is 'the very voice of God'.[237] Further, they were in broad agreement with his cautionary remark, 'We are not to submit our Understandings to the belief of those things, that are *contrary* to our Understanding. We must have a Reason, for that which we believe *above* our Reason.'[238] Matters above reason are revealed to us by

God; to this extent reason is not all-sufficient, though it is a medium through which revelation is communicated to us: '*a* medium' because, as John Smith claimed,

> God is not better defined to us by our understandings than by our wills and affections: He is not only the eternal reason, that Almighty mind and wisdom which our understandings converse with; but He is also that unstained Beauty and Supreme Good to which our wills are perpetually aspiring after; and wheresoever we find true beauty, love, and goodness, we may say, here or there is God.[239]

Thus, while, as a latter-day Platonist said,

> Intellectual certainty for Platonists is a matter of directly seeing or experiencing something: the whole process of philosophical discourse is only a way of preparing the mind for that flash of intuition, that 'light kindled from a leaping fire', of which Plato speaks in the Seventh Letter (341D) . . .[240]

we may say that to the Cambridge Platonists reason, while undoubtedly 'the candle of the Lord', was but a candle, not a searchlight. Moreover, the candle is lit by God: 'The Spirit of a Man is the Candle of the Lord; Lighted by God, and Lighting us to God.'[241] The Cambridge philosophers also understood, however, that if intuitions could not be shown to exemplify coherence, and to be compatible with knowledge otherwise gained, the pitfall of enthusiasm, defined by Henry More as 'a full, but false, persuasion in a Man that he is inspir'd',[242] beckoned.

Given their Platonic starting point the Cambridge men could not but emphasize the divine–human continuity. In other connections we have seen how this may blur the Creator–creature distinction and minimize the importance of the historic Cross–resurrection event. That nothing was further from the intentions of the Cambridge Platonists is clear when John Smith writes of Christ who shares our human nature; who mediates between God and humanity; and who washes our sins away in his blood.[243] Again, Whichcote makes much in his preaching of the Incarnation, resurrection and atoning work of Christ, and proclaims his understanding of the heart of the Gospel in these terms: 'There is thus in the gospel only one great matter of faith, which God proposes us to believe; the grace of God in Christ, pardon of sin in his blood, acceptance through him, going to God by him.'[244] The experiential core in such language to some extent counterbalances More's mystical thrust, as when he calls the Gospel a 'kind of engine' the purpose of which is to elevate us to the contemplative life beyond rationality.[245] Again, Smith speaks of human participation in the divine nature, though he hastens to add that this union is 'by the Platonist's leave' exclusively the gift of Christ.[246] There is thus some justification for asserting that, in their desire to bring the Church back to 'her old loving nurse the Platonick philosophy',[247] the Cambridge Platonists had more than an inkling of the distinction to be drawn between loving and smothering.

No English philosopher of the seventeenth century was less inclined to teeter on the brink of enthusiasm than Locke. But, as I have shown elsewhere,[248] his caution in this matter by no means encouraged him along the deistic path of supposing that natural religion (ambiguous term!) sufficed. On the contrary, in the very chapter in which he is highly critical of enthusiasm, he endorses the idea of revelation, and explains it carefully:

> *Revelation* is natural *Reason* enlarged by a new set of Discoveries communicated by GOD immediately, which *Reason* vouches the Truth of, by the testimony and Proofs it gives, that they come from GOD. So that he that takes away *Reason*, to make way for *Revelation*, puts out the Light of both . . .[249]

Revelation supplements, but does not extinguish, the natural light of reason; and the supplements comprise propositional information to which we are invited to give assent, provided that reason assures us that such and such is a *bona-fide* revelation from God.[250] (I do not overlook the fact that, in addition to thinking of faith as assent, Locke elsewhere distinguishes between bare assent and justifying faith, and, in his *Paraphrases*, follows Paul in understanding faith as personal trust, *fiducia*.[251]) The truths of revelation – for example, that Christ is Saviour of the world – are above reason, but not contrary to it. Thus far he is in the line of Aquinas, but in the wake of Romans 1, the first chapter of Calvin's *Institutes*, the Westminster Confession and the Savoy Declaration of Faith and Order, he makes more of the noetic effects of sin:

> Though the works of nature, in every part of them, sufficiently evidence a Deity; yet the world made so little use of their reason, that they saw him not, where, even by the impressions of himself, he was easy to be

> found. Sense and lust blinded their minds in some, and a careless inadvertency in others . . .[252]

We breathe a different air when we turn to Butler's *Analogy*, though he, no less than the Cambridge Platonists, is persuaded of the limitations of reason. Indeed, his case against the deists turns upon this fact.[253] His strategy is to take the deists' ground as far as he can, and to show its inadequacy. This, as he admits, precludes him from adverting to significant parts of the Christian testimony. He argues, for example, that the deistic claim that revealed matters are strictly beyond our ken is no argument against revelation, since much lies beyond the range of our natural reason also:

> There is no presumption, from analogy, against the truth of [the general scheme of Christianity], upon account of its not being discoverable by reason or experience. For, suppose one who never heard of revelation, of the most improved understanding, and acquainted with our whole system of natural philosophy and natural religion – such a one could not but be sensible, that it was but a very small part of the natural and moral system of the universe which he was acquainted with . . . And, therefore, that things lie beyond the natural reach of our faculties, is no sort of presumption against the truth and reality of them; because it is certain, there are innumberable things, in the constitution and government of the universe, which are thus beyond the natural reach of our faculties.[254]

Again, because

> mankind are corrupted and depraved in their moral character . . . reason shows us nothing of the particular immediate means of obtaining either temporal or spiritual benefits. This, therefore, we must learn, either from experience or revelation. And experience the present case does not admit of.[255]

It is from scripture that we learn that 'God has, by revelation, instructed men in things concerning his government, which they could not otherwise have known, and reminded them of things which they might otherwise know; and attested the truth of the whole by miracles.'[256]

Many other illustrations could be provided, but for our final example of the limitations of reason as far as information or content are concerned, we may turn to some remarks of John Elias. As far removed in temperament from the Cambridge

Platonists as from Butler, this product of the Evangelical Revival became Wales's most popular preacher. But, just as many eighteenth-century evangelicals, when confessing their faith, adopted the then familiar cosmological-cum-teleological starting point,[257] when he writes an essay on reason Elias, for all the differences in his language and attitude to the Bible, concludes much as the Cambridge Platonists and Butler did:

> Reason could never, without Divine revelation, find out that God ever intended to forgive one transgression . . . Reason cannot, without divine revelation, comprehend evangelical principles as to their utility, glory, and great importance, nor have any apprehension of the sovereign grace and love of God towards sinners . . . But faith beholds in the Divine revelation the Gospel of Christ, the way to have the pardon of sin . . . a way to restore us to the image of God, and make us fit to be with him for ever! Let us praise God more for the revelation of his will in his holy Word. Let us submit our proud reason to God's Word, and take his will in that Word respecting all things, as a sufficient determination of them.[258]

It goes without saying that, in the wake of Kant's distinction between speculative reason and practical reason, and his view that the former yields knowledge of phenomena only, while the postulates of the latter – God, freedom and immortality – are conditions of thought, the question of the limitations of reason took a fresh turn, with some Christians rejoicing that the way had now been left open for faith, while others felt free to dispense with the postulates, restrict their attention to empirical phenomena and usher in modern agnosticism and positivism. I shall have more to say about this when discussing faith and the approach to religion through morality. For the present, as I approach my conclusion to this part of my argument, I turn to the general question of the viability of natural theology, and I shall discuss this with special reference to what is frequently perceived as the Barthian embargo against it, and with the words of Robert Mackintosh ringing in my ears: 'It is due to Kant that we have to face neither deism nor dogmatic materialism, but agnosticism; and the prevalence of agnosticism warns us that the old Natural Theology is dead.'[259]

VII

There can be no question that 'classical' (by which I mean Cartesian and post-Cartesian) natural theology suffered mightily at the hands of Hume and Kant. There is no need to rehearse the story here. It is, however, very much to my purpose to review the question of the viability of natural theology as such, with a view to arriving at a sustainable position on the relation of reason and revelation with respect to the commendation of the Christian faith. We have already seen that Calvin, though by no means averse to the idea of a general revelation of God in the created order and in the *sensus divinitatis*, nevertheless set his face against demonstrative proofs of the fundamental doctrines of Christianity. By reason of the noetic effects of sin, knowledge of these could come only by the inward testimony of the Holy Spirit. Indeed,

> If we desire to provide in the best way for our consciences – that they may not be perpetually beset by the instability of doubt or vacillation, and that they may not also boggle at the smallest quibbles – we ought to seek our conviction at a higher place than human reason, that is, in the secret testimony of the Spirit.[260]

Many have followed in Calvin's wake, and to some of these – Kuyper, Plantinga and Wolterstorff – I have already referred. But none have been so hostile to traditional natural theology as Karl Barth, of whom Plantinga declared that 'His utterances on this topic, as on others, are fascinating but Delphic in everything but length.'[261] Let us investigate further.

That the early Barth received a less than rapturous reception in some British quarters is clear from the remark of the Congregational theologian A. E. Garvie in 1925, to the effect that Barthianism is 'a minor evil product of the war'.[262] That some Anglicans, too, were disinclined to follow the Barthian banner is clear from a note taken by Nathaniel Micklem following a train journey with B. H. Streeter: 'Travelled to Cambridge with Streeter. He says Christianity is in a bad way. Karl Barth has shown that we know nothing about God, and *Formgeschichte* that we know nothing about Jesus Christ. The residuum is not satisfactory.'[263] No doubt to Barth, had he known of them, these would have been ageing voices of the liberalism in which he had been reared under Harnack and Herrmann, and against which he was now in revolt.

Anthropological optimism was barren; human beings could no longer be regarded as co-operators with a loving fatherly God. Back must come the concept of the holy God before whom sinners stand under judgement. The God–man continuity of the older immanentist idealism must be replaced by an emphasis upon God's holy transcendence. Humanity is in crisis; a spiritual malaise places human beings over against God; repentance and faith, leading to forgiveness and obedience, are the only hope for humanity. Such ideas as these come to expression in Barth's *Romans* (1919).

As is well known, the early Barth was greatly influenced by Kierkegaard's existentialism. To the Swiss pastor, who had not yet attained his thirtieth birthday when the First World War broke out, it was clear that the spectator attitude was impossible, and that the need to take a stand in which one's whole being would be involved was paramount. So, too, in relation to Christianity: the response of faith, which at this stage Barth, following Kierkegaard, described as 'a leap', is to be made to the Wholly Other God who confronts human beings with his revealed Word. But that God should confront humanity, that the eternal should break into time, is utterly paradoxical (further echoes of Kierkegaard). Hence (and here Luther's 'Yes' and 'No' comes to mind) individuals are to speak of God, but they can do so only dialectically. We cannot speak of God as he is in himself, for we do not know him thus (shades of Kant's epistemology). God is not an object of human thought, as the scholastics had erroneously supposed; nor, with the mystics, may we invoke the idea of the *via negativa*. The dialectic we may employ is not that of Hegel, which moves relentlessly on in the intellectual realm; it is that of Kierkegaard, wherein faith both grasps the Yes and the No, and finds finality in Christ. It is the dialectic which is most compatible with Kierkegaard's emphasis upon the infinite qualitative difference between human beings and God. To this dialectic the early Barth, on his own admission, subscribed.[264]

Against this background of ideas Barth began to write his *Christian Dogmatics*, the first volume of which appeared in 1927. However, under the anti-existentialist criticisms of Lutherans and Roman Catholics, and influenced by Anselm, who taught him the priority of faith, and whose ideas Barth discussed in what he regarded as his most important work, *Fides Quaerens Intellectum* (1931), Barth began afresh.[265] The first volume of *Church Dogmatics* appeared in 1932. He had learned that the theologian must begin not from the human condition, still less from Kantian epistemology, but from God's revelation in Christ.[266] Faith-knowledge rather than crisis and the leap is henceforward to be his concern; the revelation of the Word of God in Christ is to be his starting point. Among other things, this will give him the security of knowing that 'if we do not commit ourselves unreservedly and finally to any specific philosophy, we will not need totally and finally to fear any philosophy'.[267]

It is not surprising that, in view of Barth's emphasis upon the sovereignty of God, many detected in his writings a return to Calvin. As Robert Franks put it, 'Calvin seemed dead, at any rate among Congregationalists, who prided themselves on having escaped from his power. But Barth has waved his magic wand; and lo, Calvin is alive again, very much alive.'[268] But Franks perceived that Barth's return to Calvin was 'a return with a difference',[269] insofar as the orthodox doctrines of total corruption, the atonement, the Church and the sacraments, are presented by Barth 'through the idea of *Krisis*'.[270] Franks here overlooks the fact that in 1927, nearly twenty years before his own article, Barth had, as we have seen, retreated from his existentialist-crisis stance.

Barth's theology became, uncompromisingly, a theology of grace. Christ is the fount of salvation and therefore of knowledge. In him alone God has spoken. Sinners can acquire knowledge of God from nowhere else. Regeneration by the Spirit is the prerequisite of the knowledge of God, and that is God's work. Barth is not hereby committed to a denial of God's revelation in his handiwork, but unbelievers do not and cannot, as a matter of fact, see God there. The believer, on the other hand, 'will acknowledge to himself that the same Eternal Word that became flesh is audible also in creation as God's primary work, audible therefore in Nature, in History, in his own heart, conscience and understanding'.[271] To know God means to be reconciled to God through his Son.

Conversely, Barth denies that 'there does exist a knowledge of God and His connection with the world and men, apart from any special and supernatural revelation'.[272] In elaborating this position he stoutly opposes the scholastic doctrine of the analogy of being – there is no such analogy, and those who say there is are attempting 'to unite Yahweh with Baal, the triune God of Holy Scripture with the concept of being of Aristotelian and Stoic philosophy.'[273] For this allegedly false analogy Barth substitutes the analogy of faith, that is, 'the correspondence of the thing known with the knowing, the object with the thought, of the Word of God with the word of man in thought and speech, even as it distinguishes true Christian prophecy taking place in faith from all that is untrue'.[274] This correspondence is established by the miracle of grace, for God, being supremely free, is in no sense required to declare himself in response to humanity's quasi-autonomous speculations concerning him.

On the basis of the above position, Barth's celebrated debate with Emil Brunner raged. Among the issues raised were the related ones of common ground and the *imago dei*. At his most consistent the early Barth especially denies that there is any natural point of contact between God and humanity. So defaced is God's image that not even human rationality can supply an effective link between Creator and creature. Moreover, any attempted employment of reason to that end can result only in the creation of an idol. *God* is not thus known.[275] Similarly, no weight is to be accorded to the utilitarian claim that natural theology, with its utilization of human reason and its assumption of common ground as between believer and unbeliever, has apologetic value. There is no knowledge of God which all human beings, qua natural, share in common. The only knowledge of God is that given through his Word. Believers must not, therefore, for apologetic purposes, place the unbeliever in the position of being 'met by a mask'.[276] Those who are truly open to God are those who are in Jesus Christ.[277] This is not to deny that believers have to make their commitment of faith, but the very faith they exercise is first given to them by God.[278]

In Brunner's opinion this account was quite inadequate. He argued that, although human beings have lost their freedom, with the result that they can no longer will the good, they have not lost their responsibility before God. Formally, God's image in man is in no way impaired, but materially it is completely lost.[279] To all of which Barth said, *Nein!*

It seems to me that the decisive objection to both Barth and Brunner on this matter was put more concisely by John Baillie than by anyone else. Brunner, he said,

> does not see that if goodness were to cease to have *any* appeal to us, then our choice of the evil way would no longer be a *choice* at all, nor in any sense whatsoever the act of a free moral agent. The truth is that a

> totally corrupt being would be as incapable of sin as would a totally illogical being of fallacious argument.[280]

He further agrees with Barth that Brunner may not separate form from matter; he agrees with Brunner against Barth that there is knowledge of God apart from the knowledge of Christ.[281] What seems clear, now that the dust of the old dispute has long since settled, is that Brunner never intended to adopt an understanding of natural theology which would bypass the need of revelation, or make God into an object of thought.[282]

Undeterred, Barth insists that humanity has lost its capacity for God,[283] and hence 'All our activities of thinking and speaking can have only a secondary significance and, as activities of the creature, cannot possibly coincide with the truth of God that is the source of truth in the world.'[284] For this reason 'Barth refuses to give natural theology the independent status of something which must be attacked and eliminated. It exists at all only as something already defeated, as something already past.'[285] Moreover, 'Barth suggests that even to dispute directly with natural theology is to engage in it',[286] and this he resolutely declines to do. As Alan Torrance has explained, Barth's 'rejection of natural theology is purely the corollary of grace – David Hume's *Dialogues* offer, for Barth, *neither* the reason *nor* the ratification for his rejection of natural theology. It is the incarnation alone which offers both.'[287]

From the other side, R. S. Franks concluded that Barth's interpretation of Romans 1 and 2, 'the starting-point of all natural theology in the Christian Church ever since', was inadequate, and hence 'I regard Barth as a great spellbinder, but I believe that the Church will presently free itself from the spell and return to saner ways of thought'.[288] And exactly fifty years ago as I write E. L. Allen permitted himself a prophecy:

> Neo-orthodoxy is not the revelation of a long forgotten truth; it is a fashion which suits the time to which it belongs and will die out as the time changes. Let its champions reflect that in fifty years time the merest tyro in theology will be speaking of Barth and Brunner as they speak today of Troeltsch and Harnack.[289]

However, any such dismissal of Barth would be as premature as it would be insubordinate. It behoves us to weigh his thought, however briefly, as we move towards our conclusion. First, it seems clear to me that the Christian confession turns upon the fact, heavily endorsed by Barth, that the triune God graciously makes himself known to human beings supremely in Christ, and did he not do so we should not know him at all. In all of this the initiative is with God. It might therefore seem that one of the implications of this position is that the God sought, and deemed provable, by traditonal natural theology is not after all the God whom Christians confess, and hence that Barth is right to have no dealings with natural theology. That is to say, along what I earlier labelled as the 'Greek' line, undifferentiated Being is the end point of the demonstration (even assuming the competence of the demonstration). The triune God of fatherly, holy love seems far removed from Being as such. Hence Bonaventure's conviction that a philosopher who proves the unity of God, but does not know that God's unity is triune, is not referring to *God's* unity.[290] Again, in the well-known words of Pascal:

> The Christians' God is not a God who is simply author of mathematical truths and of the order of the elements; that is the lot of the heathens and of the Epicureans . . . But the God of Abraham, the God of Isaac, the God of Jacob, the Christians' God, is a God of love and consolation, a God who fills the soul and heart of those whom He hath purchased, a God who makes them conscious of their misery and of His infinite mercy; who makes His home in their heart, filling it with humility, joy, confidence and love; who renders them incapable of any other object than Himself.[291]

What the traditional arguments yield, declares Pascal, is the God of deism.[292] As Hume's Philo saw, such a God 'affords no inference that affects human life, or can be the source of any action or forbearance'[293] – on which Pringle-Pattison drily remarked, 'It is not without reason that theist and atheist so amicably shake hands over their differences, for the proposition contains nothing vital either to affirm or to deny.'[294]

In our own time, Norman Malcolm, who did more than most to rekindle discussion of the ontological argument in the 1960s,[295] observed that, while he thought a version of the argument was workable, acceptance of its validity was not equivalent to believing in God in the Christian sense of the words.[296] Emil Brunner concurs: 'The "God" of the proofs for the existence of God is not the Living God of faith, but an intellectual abstraction'.[297] The same deficiency is detectable in Aristotle's 'unmoved Mover'. We do not have here the personal God who graciously intervenes to redeem and renew creation, including humanity.[298] Yet it is such a God whom, in what I have described as the primary locus of Christian confessing, Christians worship. As De Burgh observed, 'No Platonic Form of Good or Kantian Moral Law can meet the need of personal intercourse intrinsic to religious experience. Neither can the Absolute of an immanentist metaphysic.'[299] It is not the case that where the God of Christianity is concerned we begin somewhere else and then tack on, as we deem appropriate, sundry worshipful qualities. Rather, supremely in worship,

> We become aware of One Whom Jesus persuades us to call 'God the Father', and we go on to recognise that He must be creator of all things. Then, and only then, do we *know* that God exists, and what it means to say that He is Creator. And all this we have learnt, not from the study of Nature, but from the revelation of 'God the Father'.[300]

Calvin's rueful observation, not surprisingly, was that 'if men were taught only by nature, they would hold to nothing certain or solid or clear-cut, but would be so tied to confused principles as to worship an unknown God.'[301] From the standpoint of Christian confession the problem is that 'It is impossible for us to try to eliminate all that we owe to Him, in order to get at the teachings of the "natural" reason.'[302] After all,

> The words of Jesus are the voice of God. The tears of Jesus are the pity of God. The wrath of Jesus is the judgment of God. All believers confess, with adoring praise, that in their most sacred hours God and Christ merge in each other with morally indistinguishable identity. When in secret we look into God's face, still it is the face of Christ that rises up before us. To do Christ's will and God's is one thing. When we inquire as to the precise content of the term 'God' for our minds, and ask how it has been authenticated, we discover, it may be with some surprise, that without reasoning we have transferred to God the features of Christ – holy and almighty love. We are really thinking of Jesus, with His essential features exalted to infinity.[303]

Are we really dealing in all of this with two Gods, to one of which, Being, Barth would adopt the attitude of Deutero Isaiah, namely, that it is no God at all;[304] or do we have simply two different conceptions of the one God?[305] At this point I take the risk of diverging from Barth. On the ground of the Holy Spirit's witness beyond the bounds of the Church; on the ground of God's non-excludability from any part of his created order, and especially on the ground of the *imago dei* (defaced but not obliterated) and the *sensus divinitatis*, I side with those who construe the proofs of natural theology as building upon insights and intimations derivative from God's general revelation, which need to be taken into account in any attempt to commend the faith to unbelievers. When Christian confessing takes a more intellectual turn it may be appropriate to draw analogies of attribution from Being to the Christian God, just as when treating of the post-Hegelian idealists it was suggested that the same might happen in relation to the philosophical absolute and God.[306] In both cases it would, no doubt, emerge that there are more dissimilarities than similarities between God and either Being or the absolute. More generally, however, the context will be one of attending to what has traditionally been known as God's general revelation, and to this idea I feel able to be more hospitable than Barth ever was, and this because, as argued earlier, I regard 'total' in 'total depravity' as having extensive rather than intensive significance. That is to say (crudely), no part of us is wholly right; but no part of us is all bad. Moreover, while we have been told that we know God only in Christ, I do not think it has been shown that there is no knowledge of God (that is, the same, one, God) where Christ is not known. The importance of this point for the relations between Christians and those of other faiths and of none is clear, and I shall return to it in Chapter 8.

For the present, however, we must observe that because Christians and others know God, however partially, from the intimations of conscience or the beauties of nature (I am well aware of the difficulties in supposing that conscience is, in any unproblematic sense the 'voice' of God;[307] and I know enough of Hume and Mill to see the force of the counter to the teleological argument which turns upon nature's 'red-in-tooth-and-clawness'; I am here simply describing what seems empirically to be the case) then the only alternative to a notion of general revelation is the distinctly odd supposition that human beings can know God without his desiring it.[308] It seems better to endorse Robert Flint's remark of a century ago, 'The God revealed in Christ is the God who is also revealed in physical nature, in the consciousness and conscience of men, in the providential government of individuals, in the history of nations, and in Scripture.'[309] For his part Calvin would have agreed with this comprehensive affirmation,[310] and W. P. Paterson was quite convinced that 'It is not open to Christian faith to believe that God has created and governed the world in such wise that, instead of revealing Him, it radically misrepresents Him.'[311]

Yet Barth systematically denigrates the natural knowledge of God. For this he has been rebuked by N. H. G. Robinson:

> the inevitable result of [Barth's] intransigent attitude [to human truth] is to represent truth of revelation, not as something inescapable, but as thoroughly esoteric and as quite irrelevant to all human problems and all human questions. It becomes indeed, humanly speaking, a language-game which one may or may not be called upon to play. Consequently, this theological stance involves, as Barth himself later admitted, a radical inhumanity; but what he did not see is that this inhumanity, this irrelevance, cannot be corrected by a new emphasis upon the humanity of God or upon the new humanity of what is in an absolute sense a new creature. There is no escape from these implications, and the indispensable correction can be achieved only by tracing the fault further up the line of argument to its source in the fundamental presuppositions, in the basic theological strategy of fencing off divine truth, truth of revelation, on all sides, from every possibility of alliance or conflict with human truth.[312]

If Barth is right then, as has been said in a different connection, 'belief cannot argue with unbelief: it can only preach to it',[313] and one implication of this is that Christians, trapped within a ghetto of revelation and impervious to rational assaults from without, cannot, from their side, combat alien thought forms, or even inner religious fundamentalisms; yet such activity comprises one aspect of the task of commending the faith.[314] In fact, however, Barth 'cannot show that human reason is to be decried, not least because such a move is itself made with the resources of such reason'.[315] To this logical point others have added theological and religious expressions of disquiet. John Baillie enquired whether Barth's attitude towards 'natural man' did not lead him to think of the recreation of human beings more in terms of sheer omnipotence than of grace, for 'there can only be grace where there is *free acceptance* in the absence of all coercion'.[316] Along similar lines Nels Ferré spoke of the 'evil' of the neo-orthodox position in that 'Revelation becomes arbitrary, and man's faith, capricious';[317] while E. P. Dickie feared the separation of a person's secular reason from his or her religious experience: 'Discontinuity cannot be the final word.'[318] G. C. Berkouwer feared that Barth jeopardized the human being's proper responsibility before God, for 'General revelation remains a reminder of the guilt of *closed eyes*. Precisely this doctrine, therefore, uncovers for us the absoluteness of the revelation of God in Jesus Christ.'[319] And Hubert Cunliffe-Jones, himself considerably influenced by Barth, and never one to mince words, thundered:

> If Jesus Christ is indeed Lord, there *must* be some natural theology. If man could repudiate entirely the claim of God upon him he would not be human. And, because he is thus created in the Word of God, if he thinks truly about himself and about God he can apprehend dimly some faint truth of that which is written gloriously in the face of Jesus Christ.[320]

Barth aside, what of natural theology? I have suggested that God alone can reveal himself to us, and that he does this supremely in Christ, but also throughout the created order. Further, the traditional theistic arguments from Descartes onwards do not yield the Christian God, while Aquinas's position within the broader 'faith seeking understanding' project offers the possibility of the devising of analogies of attribution as between Being and the Christian God[321] – just as similar analogies might be drawn between the idealists' philosophical absolute and God. In some circumstances such analogies may have some apologetic usefulness. As for the several arguments themselves it has for more than two centuries been seriously questioned how far they succeed as demonstrations; nor is the resort to their 'cumulative' effect so readily had now that Antony Flew and others have pointed out (to use my own analogy) that five broken signposts do not point the way any more clearly than one. Few have assessed the traditional arguments as rigorously and as positively as Richard Swinburne, yet he grants that at best they render God's existence probable only.[322] Such a conclusion is by no means to be despised and, as another distinguished philosopher has observed, from the fact that thus far natural theology has failed we may not infer that it will never succeed.[323] Even so, because of who God is and who we are, I cannot imagine that a copper-bottomed demonstration of the existence of the Christian God will ever be forthcoming: 'The familiar "proofs" either fail as proofs, or, in what they prove, conclude to something other than the God of religion.'[324] Conversely, we may say that, apart from the proofs of logic and mathematics, all our fundamental beliefs, including our religious ones, may be denied by others, and questioned or doubted by ourselves, without logical inconsistency. As A. C. Ewing put it,

> When we consider belief in memory, in an external world, in minds other than one's own, in induction, in ethics, we are driven back to something which we either cannot prove at all or at least cannot prove in a way which wins general agreement among philosophers, yet we continue unflinchingly to hold the beliefs.[325]

Despite the difficulties inherent in the theistic arguments, Paul Badham insists, in a short paper in which he starts numerous hares, that theism is central for Christianity. He regrets that not enough sermons are nowadays concerned with God as such and, while he does not believe that the traditional proofs afford coercive demonstrations such that all rational persons would endorse them, he does believe that the major Christian doctrines, 'if understood in anything like their traditional form, depend on the notion of a transcendent God who exists in reality as well as in our minds'.[326] This seems to me to be undoubtedly the case, and I have no desire to deny the reality of the God who exists in reality and in our minds. Badham proceeds to argue that natural theology can leave people open to the possibility of belief, and I have just affirmed this myself. But I do not, for the reasons given above, think it can be maintained that natural theology in the sense of the traditional arguments from Descartes onwards can be said to be central to Christianity, given that they do not yield the Christian God. If, as seems to be the case, Badham smuggles Christian content into his theism (as when he wishes to have God – presumably not undifferentiated Being – preached about more regularly) then one wonders how much *natural* theology remains to him.[327] D. Z. Phillips makes a number (in fact the divine number) of concise points in response to Badham, the main thrust of which is that in claiming that Christian doctrines depend upon a logically prior belief in God's existence, he removes belief in God from the context of the Bible, the Church and religious practice within which alone it can be judged to be a belief.[328] While agreeing with Phillips that, just as it is not necessary to establish that 'This is a writing implement' before one can affirm 'This is a pen', so it is not necessary to establish that 'There exists a God' before one confesses one's faith in the incarnate Christ, I should not wish to tie the Christian God to the particular practices of the Church in the way that Phillips, presumably with Wittgensteinian forms of life in mind, seems to wish to do.

Happily, I do not think that Badham would disagree, and Phillips certainly would not, with the assertion, 'It is utterly fantastic to imagine that the religious man must await the philosopher's decision before he can believe'.[329] It is not without significance that for all his strenuous efforts in theistic argumentation, Robert Flint nevertheless declared:

> although nature may in some degree lead us to look aright on the Gospel, the Gospel is in a far higher degree needed to enable us to look aright upon nature. Pure eyes and Christian hearts can alone apprehend the heavenly truths which the book of creation imparts.[330]

After all, 'upon a general view, "natural theology" is the laborious spelling out of God's impersonal word. It is worth spelling over: all that comes from God is sacred. But we have a personal word from God. For us *the word became flesh, and tabernacled among us, and we beheld his glory*.'[331] In the words of an old Scottish Testimony:

> if a *purpose of mercy* exist with respect to the fallen, the necessity of Revelation must . . . be still more obvious; for neither the existence of such a purpose, nor the plan of its execution, is manifested by the works of nature, or can be discovered by the unassisted efforts of man.[332]

We are back at the heart of the Christian confession once more.

It should be clear by now that to query the project of natural theology – especially in its post-Descartes mode – is not to tumble into irrationalism. It does not preclude the giving of reasons for one's hope; it does not deny the importance of the intuitions from which the traditional theistic arguments set out, and which must be taken into account in the development of any Christian worldview (a topic to be resumed in Chapter 8); but it does entail allowing due place to God's prior, gracious, revelation, for apart from this we should know nothing of him. As Clement Webb put it:

> We cannot . . . assert the possibility of a *knowledge* of God which is not in some sense *revealed*; for only through God's will and initiative can we conceive any knowledge of him to be attained; neither, on the other hand, can we with a good conscience allow an external authority to

> impose upon reason a limit of which reason itself cannot recognize the *reasonableness*.[333]

Here, as it seems to me, Webb at one and the same time rightly affirms the priority of God's gracious revelatory initiative, and the abiding lesson to be learned from the Enlightenment – not least from its English 'father', Locke. But the appropriation of this knowledge is by faith which includes experience. The further discussion of this point is our business in the next chapter.

7

Faith, Knowledge and Experience

In the previous chapter I considered those who maintain that human reason is impaired by sin; those who appear unduly to exalt human reason; and those who believe that reason's deliverances require the supplement of revelation. One further position remains to be considered: that of those who in the interests of faith minimize the importance of reason, in some cases to the point of (at least occasional) denigration. A brief sampling of views will suffice.

We may set out from Tertullian's classic statement:

> What indeed has Athens to do with Jerusalem? What concord is there between the Academy and the Church? What between heretics and Christians? Our instruction comes from 'the porch of Solomon', who had himself taught that 'the Lord should be sought in simplicity of heart.' Away with all attempts to produce a mottled Christianity of Stoic, Platonic, and dialectic composition! We want no curious disputation after possessing Christ Jesus, no inquisition after enjoying the gospel! With our faith, we desire no further belief.[1]

The wedge between philosophy and faith, faith and reason, seems here to be firmly in place; and it cannot be denied that there is much in Tertullian's writings to suggest his impatience with society at large and, in particular, with pagans, Valentinian gnosticism, the dualism of Hermogenes, and Marcion. His general complaint against philosophers is that, as compared with the venerable tradition in which Christians stand, philosophers are late in the field; indeed, Tertullian alleges '*lateness* to be the characteristic of every heresy',[2] and he brands philosophers the patriarchs of heresy.[3] He does not claim that venerability by itself is a sufficient guarantee of truth; to this Christianity adds the stamp of apostolic authority.[4] Nor does Tertullian forbid the exercise of the mind by Christians. But the 'seeking' of Christians must 'be in that which is our own, – that, and only that, which can become an object of enquiry without impairing the rule of faith'.[5] In other words, Christians may legitimately raise questions within the sphere of faith, but may not question the overall credibility and authority of the faith.

At times in his writings the influence of Stoic philosophy upon Tertullian is in evidence. Thus he can say that one may be wise in the things of God 'even from one's natural powers'. He can even concede that 'philosophers have sometimes thought the same things as as ourselves'. There is a 'common intelligence wherewith God has been pleased to endow the soul of man. This intelligence has been caught up by philosophy . . . '[6] Among things known by nature are the immortality of the soul and the knowledge of God.[7] On occasion Tertullian goes so far as to suggest, in a manner reminiscent of Justin, that Christianity is an improved philosophy, since while pagan philosophers merely affect the truth, Christians actually possess it.[8]

Such concessions are, however, few and far between. Tertullian's more customary attitude is that philosophy is the cause of division within the Church, that the objections to orthodox Christianity of Valentinus and Marcion derive from the points at which they agree with heathen Platonic and Stoic thought, and that 'Heresies are themselves instigated by philosophy.'[9] Accordingly, to take the example of one theme where Tertullian pits Paul against the philosophers,

> We should never be required to try our strength in contests about the soul with philosophers, those patriarchs of heretics, as they may fairly be called. The apostle, so far back as his own times, foresaw, indeed, that philosophy would do violent injury to the truth. This admonition he was induced to offer after he had been at Athens, had become acquainted with that *loquacious* city, and had there a taste of its huckstering wiseacres and talkers.[10]

Philosophers who say the same things as Christians have simply plundered Christian sources.[11]

It seems fair to conclude that although 'Tertullian knew how to avail himself of the philosophers when it suited him',[12] he felt no pressing need to harmonize philosophy and faith. On the contrary, against Marcion's scepticism he rejoiced in the 'absurdity' of a Son of *God* who *died*: 'The Son of God died; it is by all means to be believed, because it is absurd. And he was buried, and rose again; the fact is certain, because it is impossible.'[13] Quasten puts it mildly when he says of Tertullian that 'to dissolve apparent contradictions was not given to him'.[14]

The distinction between philosophy and faith is drawn also by Gregory of Nyssa. The supernatural mysteries of faith, he thinks, are not, and cannot be, on a par with philosophical conclusions. On the other hand, the faith (that is, the things to be believed) is not irrational and, although it is to be accepted on authority, philosophy can assist by showing that its presuppositions, for example, that a God exists, are demonstrable. Meanwhile Gregory's younger contemporary in the West, Augustine, was proceeding on the basis that the plan of salvation is delineated in the entire life and work of Christ, that faith has temporal priority over reason (except in the sense that we could not believe if we had irrational souls[15]), and that understanding follows upon faith.[16] Indeed, 'Understanding is the reward of faith. Therefore, seek not to understand that thou mayest believe, but believe that thou mayest understand.'[17] In the same place Augustine adds the rider that it is the purified soul which can see, and rest in, the light; and at this point we are reminded of his deep grasp of the fact that faith is also a matter of grateful, trustful surrender to the Saviour.[18] Much later we find Bernard of Clairvaux maintaining that, while reason yields knowledge, faith is grounded in authority.[19] The final arbiter for him, however, is experience which alone assures the believer of intimate fellowship with God.[20] Bernard hotly contests Abelard's view that faith is opinion; on the contrary, faith is certitude.[21] As Louth has observed, 'In Bernard we begin to see a disjunction between knowledge and love, thinking and feeling, that was destined to have a profound influence in the West.'[22] For his part, Richard of St Victor declares that the knowledge of eternal things, some of which seem to us to be not only above, but against, reason, is gained in part by reason, in part by responding to revelation in faith. Indeed, it is 'beyond doubt' that 'nothing is held more firmly than that which is apprehended by constant faith'.[23] It seems that here, while faith yields firm knowledge, it is faith construed in terms of one's intellectual assent (*assensus*) rather than in terms of one's trustful experience (*fiducia*), as with

Bernard. Invoking yet a further meaning of 'faith', William of Auxerre has in mind the articles of faith. These, he insists, cannot be proved by reason, and those, like Arius, who have applied their reason to them have all too often landed in heresy.[24]

From these cursory illustrations the ambiguity of 'faith' emerges clearly, and I shall have more to say about this shortly. The point to be noted at present is that in the writers mentioned faith takes varying degrees of precedence over reason, and in Tertullian's writings (his occasional concessions to philosophy notwithstanding) reason is all but repudiated in preference to faith.

Before I can proceed further in our elucidation of this important yet ambiguous concept I must advert to the position of William of Ockham. In an intellectual context of growing scepticism Ockham felt that the Thomist synthesis of faith and reason was played out, and that the mystic's experience provided an inadequate basis for the defence of the faith.[25] His remedy, as is well known, was to invoke his principle of economy (Ockham's razor) according to which entities must not needlessly be multiplied. This entailed his denial of universals – a challenge to the realists. To Ockham universals were simply names (hence 'nominalism'). The effect of Ockham's procedure was to introduce a gulf between reason and revelation: we *cannot* by the exercise of natural reason know God, and hence theological dogmas must be accepted on authority, and the Bible's teaching must be heeded – a view which had a marked impact upon Luther. Gerhard Ebeling characterized the solution proposed by Ockham thus:

> On the one hand it revealed the influence of a genuine religious feeling, emphasizing the completely different nature of the subject of theology, the antithesis between theology and reason, and the basis of theology in faith and in the authority of revelation. On the other hand, this tension was obtained by an intensified and formalist use of reason which delighted in demonstrating that Church doctrine was beyond truth and demonstration, and that its authority was of value only as a positive source of an otherwise unknowable fact. It was never clear whether it was faith or reason which was most exalted by this division.[26]

For his part, R. S. Franks pointed out that

> With this Ockhamist theology the medieval opposition to Anselm reaches its final point . . . [Ockham] emphasized the difference between God and man, until no real fellowship is possible between them. God is

> so absolutely other than man, that all that the latter can do is to bow to an authority which he does not and cannot understand.[27]

Trained in, and held by many to have been impressed by, Ockhamist ways,[28] Luther welcomed the breakdown of the faith–reason synthesis supremely advanced by Aquinas and with roots in Aristotle. In his *Disputation against the Scholastic Philosophy* (1517) he repudiated the claim that one could not become a theologian without Aristotle;[29] and it seems clear that in addition to his desire, like that of Ockham before him, to counter prevailing scepticism, the presentation of Aristotle, by Pietro Pomponazzi[30] and others in the fifteenth century, as an exponent of naturalism encouraged Luther to think that the days of the natural–revealed epistemological partnership were doomed; natural reason was getting above itself. Hence Luther's rumbustuous dismissal of natural reason as a 'harlot'.[31] This is not to say that reason is of no use whatsoever. On the contrary, Luther maintains that the powers of logical thought are valuable in their own right, and in many spheres of life, both practical and ethical, human reasoning suffices. He can even say that reason is a natural light which is kindled by divine light.[32] But reason exceeds its limits when 'it interferes with God's Word and works and tries to calculate and measure them according to its own power'.[33] Such a practice serves only to massage the individual's ego. Above all, while reason 'knows that God exists . . . who or what person it may be who is properly called God, it does not know'.[34]

It it not simply that reason falls short, is weak or requires the supplement of revelation – all of this he had learned from Ockham. But whereas for Ockham scripture comprised a collection of divine oracles to be accepted on authority and of use in challenging ecclesiastical authority, Luther's point is the more experimental one that, by the Spirit, God addresses us personally in scripture – that is where we find him. To set out from natural reason is to take a false first step. God is not reached along that route, even when revelation is superadded. There is, indeed, a general knowledge of God, an instinct which even the heathen share, but this is divinely given, it is not a human acquisition, and it is quite misconstrued by those who think it supplies the foundation on which human reason can argue its way to God.[35] For this is to suppose that God can be known otherwise than by his own Word; it is to make a God of one's own specifications; it is idolatry.[36] Worse, it entails a sinful refusal to accept God's gracious approach in Christ: 'True Christian divinity . . . commandeth us not to search out the nature of God; but to know His will set out to us in Christ, whom He would have to take our flesh upon Him, to be born and to die for our sins.'[37] After all, 'There has been given to us the Word incarnate, that is placed in the manger and hung on the wood of the Cross . . . He that leaves this Son, to follow his own thoughts and speculations, is overwhelmed by the majesty of God.'[38] As we read Luther's words we cannot forget that he spoke from experience as one who had tried other customarily prescribed routes of finding God without success. He came by the path of spiritual torment to an understanding of faith which includes *assensus*, but is above all a matter of *fiducia*, confident trust in Jesus the Saviour, by whose work at the Cross we are freely justified by grace through faith.[39]

In 1524 Balthasar Hübmaier and others published *Eighteen Dissertations* containing beliefs which were typically held by the Anabaptists of Zürich, who constituted themselves formally in the following year. They set themselves against human reasoning as traditionally employed in Christian thought in the following bold terms: 'All teachings that are not of God are in vain and shall be rooted up. Here perish the disciples of Aristotle, as well as the Thomists, the Scotists, Bonaventure and Ockham, and all teaching that does not proceed from God's word.'[40] But what is especially noteworthy is the way in which piety and discipleship – characteristic notes of Anabaptism – are to the fore, occupying as they do the first and third dissertations: (1) 'Faith alone makes us pious before God'; (3) 'Such a faith must not be idle, but must reach up toward God in thankfulness, and toward man in all good works of brotherly love'.[41] Equally characteristic is the second dissertation in which saving faith is distinguished from 'historical faith': 'This belief is recognition of the mercy of God, since He hath redeemed us by the sacrifice of his only-begotten Son, And this excludes all nominal Christians who have only an historical belief in God.'[42]

With Pascal the experiential aspect of faith is to the fore. Of his *Pensées* the theologian John Oman declared, 'No book of modern times bears so distinctly the stamp of spiritual genius',[43] while Terence Penelhum has more recently judged that, though unfinished, this work 'is still the greatest work of Christian apologetics that there is or is likely to be'.[44] Pascal's strategy, negatively, is to distance himself from Descartes's rationalism. Natural reason can land one only in atheism or deism, he declares: 'Seekers after God apart from Jesus Christ, who do not get beyond nature, either fail to find sufficient light, or else manage to find a way to know God and serve Him without a mediator; and so they fall into either atheism or deism, two things which Christianity holds in almost equal abhorrence.'[45] For one thing, 'Metaphysical proofs of God are so remote from man's range of reason and so involved that they fail to grip'[46] (here Montaigne's 'cheerful man-of-the-world scepticism is transfigured . . . to a deep distrust of human reason'[47]); for another, while it is true that Christianity teaches that 'there is a God whom men can reach', it also teaches that 'there is a corruption in their nature which renders them unworthy of Him'.[48] Both of these truths must be held together, says Pascal, and in his statement of the latter his biblical and Augustinian concern with the reality and devastation of sin emerges.

No more than Luther does Pascal despise all uses of reason. In his sights is 'geometrical', that is, abstract deductive reasoning. In a wider sense, reason is useful, for although if it were possible to submit everything to reason the supernatural would be extruded from religion, without reason religion would be absurd and ridiculous. For its part, 'Faith declares what the senses do not declare, but not the contrary of what they see. It is above them, but not contrary to them.'[49] This faith, however, is not simply an emotional response to God's grace. This point cannot be emphasized too much, especially when one of Pascal's most famous utterances is in view: 'The heart has its own reasons which Reason does not know.'[50] For Pascal uses 'heart' in a variously nuanced way, but what he generally has in view is the intuitive centre of a person's being, whereby experimental knowledge is acquired, that knowledge which the redeemed person has of God through Christ. Such knowledge is, of course, open to all humble believers, not least to those who have no philosophical skills. In short, faith, which is God's gift and quite removed from human rational proofs, is appropriated by the heart, not by the reason. It is more than a matter of assent; God presents his truths to the heart, and in loving them we are enabled to say 'I believe', not 'I know'.[51]

The experimental note recurs strongly in the Puritans. For example, Richard Sibbes argues that the Word of God is self-evidencing, and is not only heard, but felt: 'I am sure I felt it, it warmed my heart, and converted me . . . Experience is the life [of] a Christian. What is all knowledge of Christ without experience . . .?'[52] Some Puritans, indeed, so emphasized experience and faith as to exclude reason entirely: 'The best way to see day-light is to put out thy Candle' advised Francis Quarles.[53] In similar vein Morgan Llwyd declared, 'a thief within is the reasoning of man which locks the door of every mind against the waft of the Holy Spirit',[54] while the radical Commonwealth sectary Lodowick Muggleton drove a wedge between reason and faith thus: 'Reason is the seed or nature of the Devil; Faith the seed or nature of God.'[55] There is thus some justice in Richard Hooker's jibe that the Puritans 'never use reason so willingly as to disgrace reason'.[56] On the other hand the Puritans were eager not only to accord faith is due place but, even more importantly, to honour the testimony of the Holy Spirit in the believer's heart. Thus in the course of a sermon in which he argues that spiritual things are spiritually, not rationally, discerned, Peter Sterry avers:

> Some say, that all truths which come by revelation of the Spirit, may also be demonstrated by Reason. But if they be, then they are no more Divine, but humane truths . . . Spirituall truths discovered by demonstrations of Reason, are like the Mistresse in her Cook-maid's clothes.[57]

The Quaker apologist, Robert Barclay, was broadly within the Puritan epistemological tradition: 'take but away the Spirit, and Christianity remains no more Christianity, than the dead carcass of a man, when the soul and spirit is departed, remains a man'.[58] He does, however, make it clear that 'because the Spirit of God is the fountain of all truth and sound reason, therefore we have well said, That *it cannot contradict either the testimony of the scripture, or right reason*'.[59] This is not to say that divine revelations are to be subject to testing either by scripture or by reason as if these were 'more noble and certain' touchstones,

> for the divine revelation, and inward illumination, is that which is evident by itself, forcing the well-disposed understanding, and irresistibly moving it to assent by its own evidence and clearness, even as the common principles of natural truths do bend the mind to a natural assent.[60]

Even as what is not altogether justifiably called the 'Age of Reason' was getting into its stride we find the stalwart

Congregationalist Thomas Bradbury echoing Tertullian and declaring that 'The Doctrines of the Gospel are unaccountable. The Words of Scripture which set them forth are absurdities to the reason of man',[61] while his Presbyterian contemporary, William Pendlebury, as we saw earlier, lambasted those who promoted infidelity by 'their over-magnifying of humane Reason, as if it were the Standard of all Truth'. Indeed, he continues, ''tis not close Thinking and impartial Reasoning, join'd with true Learning, but a Narrowness of Mind, which disposeth Men to consider a few Things, join'd with a certain Hardness and Obstinacy of Temper, which has made them Infidels'.[62] His title-page bears the motto, *Theologia est Scientia affectiva practica.*

With John Wesley in at least one of his modes the gulf between faith and sensation is clearly asserted and, in the line of the Puritans, appeal is made to the Holy Spirit:

> What a gulf is here! By what art will reason get over the immense chasm? This cannot be, till the Almighty come in to your succour, and give you that faith you have hitherto despised. Then upborne, as it were, on eagle's wings, you shall soar away into the regions of eternity, and your enlightened reason shall explore even 'the deep things of God'; God himself 'revealing them to you by his Spirit'.[63]

One of Wesley's doctrinal opponents, the Calvinist Independent Joseph Hart, showed himself in a more radical Puritan line when, in pursuit of Wesley's 'old Arminian errors', he proclaimed, 'It is a truth of singular use and solid comfort to those whose understandings are enlightened by the Spirit of God to perceive it, that religion and reason are not only widely different, but directly contrary the one to the other.'[64]

If Hart reminds us of Tertullian *redivivus*, Kierkegaard does so even more, though the intellectual context of all three differed significantly, with Tertullian standing as the opponent of arrogant philosophy in pre-Christendom times, Hart objecting to eighteenth-century rationalism, and Kierkegaard aghast at the Hegelian system. Although Kierkegaard was indebted to Schelling, and through him to Franz von Bader, he could not rest content with Romanticism. To him it was too comfortable; it occupied the aesthetic ground, and did not adequately accommodate such realities as pain and suffering. Again, as is well known, the conventionally orthodox Danish Lutheran establishment of his day gave him no satisfaction at all. Complacency and hypocrisy were everywhere evident to Kierkegaard, and it appeared that even the transition from death to life was devoid of challenge and all too automatic. As he said, 'An objective acceptance of Christianity is (*sit venia verbo*) paganism or thoughtlessness.'[65] He thus set himself the task of showing what true Christianity is, even if nobody opted for it. From his point of view the most baneful philosophical obstacle in his path was that represented by Hegel.

Kierkegaard contends that Hegel cannot make room in his system for the individual. The Hegelian monist is in the 'comical' position of having forgotten

> in a sort of world historical absent-mindedness, what it means to be a human being. Not, indeed what it means to be a human being in general; for this is the sort of thing that one might even induce a speculative philosopher to agree to; but what it means that you and I and he are human beings, each one for himself.[66]

Further, Hegelian monism overlooks the infinite qualitative difference which separates God and humanity, and which intellectual agility can never span. The only existence open to a Hegelian is conceptual existence; owing to his emphasis upon essence, Hegel can know nothing of real existence. Hegel, in fact, abstracts from real existence, and hence his contention that the real is the rational is absurd. For Kierkegaard, 'the real subject is the ethically existing subject',[67] and God is the holy one with whom sinful I have to do. It has been well said that 'The quarrel [Kierkegaard] has with Hegel is . . . that Hegel would try to make the word God a purely public word'.[68]

Above all, Hegel's philosophy was, to Kierkegaard, aristocratic and gnostic. It was grievously ill-fitted to do justice to the paradox at the heart of Christianity, namely, the paradox that God became man. Hegelianism's resultant failure to recognize the complexity of that faith which alone was adequate came as no surprise to Kierkegaard. For Hegel's view that the terms of Christianity were symbolic of a higher metaphysic he had nothing but contempt. In his view reason's task, far from smoothing away the paradox was to exhibit it in all its stark offensiveness. By faith alone is revelation grasped, and that with passionate inwardness. The God–man alone brings the transcendent to us, and in him we have faith 'in virtue of the absurd'. What is the absurd? 'The absurd is – that the eternal truth has come into being in time, that God has come into being, has been born, has grown up . . . '[69] Christians need to know the limitations of reason, and they must believe against it. The absurd cannot be known, it can only be believed.[70] What is important is not so much what one believes, but how one believes; the crucial thing is not to believe that *x y z* are true, but to *be* in the truth. With this being in the truth chronology has nothing whatsoever to do. That is, it does not follow that, if a person had lived in Jesus's day, he or she would inevitably have recognized him for who he was. In any generation faith alone recognizes him and, moreover, faith makes him our contemporary.[71] Once we have believed, the paradox is absurd no more.[72] Faith is 'the objective uncertainty due to the repulsion of the absurd held by the passion of inwardness which in this instance is intensified to the utmost degree'.[73]

It is important that we clearly understand that for Kierkegaard there is a cognitive element in the existential encounter. It is an objective uncertainty with which we have to do. God is not to be found at the end point of a logical demonstration; he is found by a leap of faith,[74] which is 'more an act of will than of intellect, a resolution rather than a recollection'.[75] Subjectivity is truth. But this is no mystical stance. Kierkegaard's paradox is as historically rooted in the actual Jesus as it could conceivably be. When he speaks of truth as subjectivity he has in mind his view of human beings as ethical, decision-taking subjects; he does not wish to defend subjective relativism, or fall prey to the charge of psychologism. Hence T. F. Torrance's explanation that for Kierkegaard 'authentic subjectivity on the part of man . . . is only possible when he collides with the objectivity of the divine subject'.[76] Kierkegaard criticized his own age at precisely this point: faith had been made 'into something so inward that it disappears completely in the end'.[77] David E. Roberts strikes the right note:

> Unquestionably, Kierkegaard believed that God is real and that He has revealed Himself in history in Jesus Christ, apart from what any individual may think, will, or believe. But he refused to refer to the reality of God and historical revelation as 'objective' because the latter word connoted for him demonstrable, conceptual knowledge, an abstraction from passionate commitment, personal decision, and the 'I–Thou' encounter. Indeed, although he believed that God was real apart from Sören Kierkegaard, he recognised that there was no way of *his* entering into relationship with God apart from Sören Kierkegaard's faith.[78]

As Kierkegaard himself put it, 'Only the truth which edifies is truth for you.'[79] To repeat, this harmonizes well with his abhorrence of Hegelian intellectualist objectivity, and with his dismay at a careless Church sitting at ease in Zion.

Although Kierkegaard abhorred Hegel's system it would be premature to conclude that he had no place for system of any kind. He operates his dialectic method to show, against Hegel, that the sharp contrasts of eternity and time and holiness and sin cannot be smoothed away; his analysis of human existence is fundamental to this thought; and reason is the means of assuring Christians that they believe 'against the understanding'.[80]

At this point the frequently reiterated objection occurs: people may have faith convictions ranging from the sublime to the bizarre; accordingly, if justifying reasons for belief cannot be supplied, how can we know whether one belief or set of beliefs is to be preferred to another? The point has been expressed by Basil Mitchell in these terms:

> Kierkegaard seems to say that faith is meritorious precisely to the degree that it spurns the help of reason and embraces a claim that is objectively absurd. It would seem to follow that it does not ultimately matter what is the content of belief so long as it is adhered to with sufficient intensity, a conclusion that Kierkegaard does not himself draw, but that has continued to inspire a whole tradition of existentialism in philosophy and theology. It has the paradoxical consequence that the experience of faith's being tested in the fires of critical debate is one that cannot, in logic, occur.[81]

Kierkegaard would reply that the Christian who contemplates whether alternative faith stances may be preferable to his or her own has ceased to believe; for faith is not a hypothesis, and the Christian faith experience cannot be doubted. From this point of view faith is the answer to a limiting question: the faith stance adopted, the leap made, there is no logical place for further questions.[82] Insofar, however, as Kierkegaard is concerned throughout to show why this is the case over against alternative understandings of the matter (especially Hegel's) – he does not simply state that it is the case – he is explicating and justifying the faith stance, and this task is a second-order one conducted at one remove from that stance itself. To this extent, when commending Christianity to others, the Christian position is treated as a hypothesis and, once again, Kierkegaard is not the irrationalist some have taken him to be. This is not to say that faith (*fiducia*) as such is a hypothesis. This would be untrue to the psychology of the matter: the believer does not go through life fearful lest at the next turn evidence will emerge to render a different hypothesis preferable to the Christian one. Furthermore, unlike scientific hypotheses, faith in the sense of *fiducia* is understood as a matter of personal commitment, not as a hypothesis on the basis of which predictions may be tested. I shall return to this point in the final chapter.

In my opinion a more serious concern arising from an examination of Kierkegaard's writings is the wedge he drives between God as absolutely Other, hidden, and humanity. Clearly he is driven in this direction by the Hegelian religion of immanence, but there is an important difference between a distinction and a disjunction. Equally, as I sought to show in *Philosophical Idealism and Christian Belief*, there is an important difference between a distinction and a continuity largely untroubled by the moral gulf between human beings and God. The latter tends in the direction of blurring the Creator–creature distinction and making evil but a stage on the way to good; the former seems to violate biblical teaching and Christian experience. For Kierkegaard God is absolutely unknown; for traditional Christianity God, though never exhaustively known, is truly known, and is known even by sinners. The *imago dei*, though defaced, is not obliterated. To make these assertions is not to say that God can be reached at the end of a demonstrative argument; it is not to deny the importance of faith as trustful commitment. It is, however, to allow that by his Holy Spirit, who blows where he wills, God is never out of touch with those to whom he has given life, and that this relationship has epistemological import. After all, 'it is impossible to believe in the *Deus revelatus* without the aid of propositions; and only the reason can understand propositions and assent to them as true'.[83]

As a final observation for the time being upon Kierkegaard's thought I would note the importance to him of Abraham's faith-obedience before God – even to the point of readiness to sacrifice Isaac. The idea, to put it in homely language, is that my faith is mine alone; it cannot be second hand. There is a solitariness here, and Kierkegaard's model is that of the lonely knight of faith. We may well imagine that Kierkegaard's disgust with the Church of his day, his Elijah-like feeling that 'I even I only am left',[84] urged him in this direction. But, as I have been at pains to urge earlier, Christian faith, though personal is not private; it is life in community; and those who make the leap of faith (*fiducia*) find themselves in a fellowship charged with the corporate task of confessing and commending the faith (that is, the Christian testimony, the way of life).

We have seen that those who tended to play down the importance of reason did so with a view to exalting faith – 'faith' being construed in a variety of ways. Not even those most hostile to reason could fail to employ it with a view to convincing us that they were right.[85] The most significant semantic development in regard to 'faith' is the experimental dimension which comes to the fore with the Reformers and flows down, in somewhat different channels through Pascal, the Puritans and Kierkegaard. The question now to be addressed is what the relation is between Christian faith and knowledge. Let us unpack this huge question piece by piece, beginning with some further observations on 'faith'.

II

In one of his miscellaneous sayings the Scottish professor of Hebrew, John 'Rabbi' Duncan, declared:

> I am not sure that we are much the better for our attempted definitions of Faith. Baxter connects it with the doctrine of the mystical union; Lampe defines it as a willingness to be saved by Christ; Halyburton and Owen as a cordial acceptance of the offer; Sandeman as simple belief in simple testimony. Well, a man is sometimes little the better for a definition, and all these perplex as well as enighten. But 'none perish that Him trust' – none perish that Him trust.[86]

While the quotation may express a true proposition, we may not take so short a way with definitions of 'faith'. Indeed, it is not difficult to add some to Duncan's list. For example, in the Second Epistle of Clement faith is closely linked with the service of God, and the argument (or caution) is that those who do not believe God's promise will be unhappy.[87] This view reappears in the writings of Irenaeus, for example, but, as we saw in Chapter 2, he also holds that by faith a believer is united with Christ and on the way to deification. With Origen, writing amidst a plethora of views within and without the Church, we find a stronger emphasis than hitherto upon the idea of 'the faith' as a body of doctrines to be believed on the authority of the apostles: indeed, nothing is to be believed as true which runs counter to the churchly and apostolic tradition.[88] In this way, as Stephen Sykes has pointed out, 'faith came to be objectified as right doctrine or "orthodoxy"'.[89] Even after the Reformation such a Puritan as Richard Baxter, while repudiating anything smacking of popish prescriptions nevertheless, in the interests of unity among Christians, advised that

> We must learn clearly the distinction between certainties and uncertainties, between fundamental issues and speculative theories of explanation. Then we can clearly distinguish the fundamentals of the faith from those that are merely private opinions. The peace of the Church depends upon the former, not upon the latter.[90]

In the following century John Wesley ranked the faiths (that is, the doctrines believed) of several groups in ascending order thus: materialists, deists, heathens or Muslims, Jews, Roman Catholics, Protestants. Of these the last (as we might expect) hold 'only those truths as necessary to salvation, which are clearly revealed in the oracles of God'.[91]

From the examples given (which could be multiplied down to our own time) we can see the origin and persistence of the understanding of faith as *assensus*. We are in the realm of the many creeds and confessions to which I adverted in Chapter 2 and, at least from Baxter and Locke onwards, we are in the company of those who seek doctrinal consensus in the interests of church unity. Not all, however, have been happy with the way in which *assensus* has been required by churchly authorities. Indeed, George Galloway contended that

> There can be little doubt that the transformation of faith, from a spiritual insight based on experience into a holding for true on grounds of tradition and authority, has been of fateful significance. It has helped men to confuse the framework of religion with its vital spirit, and prompted them to magnify quite unduly the importance of doctrinal knowledge. It has made it possible for theologians to dignify with the name of faith an unreflecting acceptance of dogmas and traditional interpretations, while it has rendered it harder for many to believe that a man may have the spirit of faith who refuses to reverence the letter.[92]

We may add that acceptance of a person's or a group's favoured formulations of Christian truth has been invoked as grounds for withholding fellowship from others who confess Christ; in other words, this attitude has fuelled that pernicious sectarian spirit which has so devastated the Church and brought the Gospel into disrepute.[93] Faith thus becomes not a joyful, enabled, response to God's grace, but a matter of submission to authority;[94] and whether those demanding submission are openly catholic or proudly exclusive Robert Mackintosh's wry cautionary word is apposite: 'Persons who herd in corners with those who share their prejudices, are apt to take the whisperings of a coterie for the verdict of "the civilised world", or even of the Almighty.'[95] More generally, 'where saving faith is identified with the believer's assent to a body of doctrine we are at the furthest remove from anything that can be regarded as a personal encounter of the believer with his Saviour and a personal assurance of forgiveness'.[96]

But while all this may be granted (at least by some), it cannot be denied that there is an intellectual element in faith. W. R. Inge stated the obvious thus: 'Faith is a feeling of certitude or positive assurance; but this feeling cannot exist without some notion, or idea, of that about which certitude is felt.'[97] As the writer to the Hebrews less prosaically put it, 'whoever comes to God must believe that he exists and rewards those who seek him'.[98] The point was not lost on the Welsh evangelical preacher John Elias: 'Faith in *Christ* is believing the testimony of God respecting him, in his holy Word';[99] or upon the German liberal theologian, Ritschl: 'faith in Christ includes the confession of His Godhead and His dominion over us'.[100]

The question arises, however: how far is faith 'a primary condition of all reasonable life?'[101] To the Anglican theologian J. R. Illingworth it was obvious that 'Christian faith is only a particular application of what is the universal and inevitable law of human life'.[102] Much depends on what is meant by 'faith'. No doubt in daily life we frequently act on the basis of presuppositions which we cannot verify: we have 'faith' that the sun will rise tomorrow.[103] Indeed, the distinguished theologian F. R. Tennant declared that, in the sense in which it is discussed in Hebrews 12, 'religious faith is psychologically of the same nature as that which underlies inductive science, and the only difference lies in the objects to which the faith refers'.[104] He distinguishes this faith from belief and trust and designates it 'venturesome supposition'.[105] It is not confronted by data; rather, it generates ideas which may yield knowledge.[106] Thus the religious person, no less than the scientist, postulates an object – God, in the case of the former – and by living as if there were a God he or she discovers that the hypothesis is practically verified.[107] To John Hick this was 'one of the most damaging defenses [of religion] in the whole history of apologetics'.[108] In particular Hick challenged Tennant's claim that 'Spiritual efficacy, or capacity to promote pious and moral life, is one thing; Reality of the ideal Objects figuring in efficacious doctrines is another',[109] for this is tantamount to surrendering the religious claim, 'For to the believer faith is not a probability but a certainty'.[110]

Hick correctly perceives that, with his view of religious faith as a hypothesis, as a propositional attitude of the same epistemological order as scientific knowledge, Tennant echoes Aquinas.[111] What is clear is that faith is thus understood, whether by Tennant or by anyone else, in the context of an intellectualist discussion of the subject. It is significant that, as I pointed out, Tennant makes it clear that he is not concerned with faith as belief or trust. That is, the will is excluded from consideration. But while, as I have agreed, faith in the Christian sense incorporates intellectual content, such faith is, as Augustine saw,[112] at least equally a matter of the will, a voluntary engagement of the person with faith's object, namely God known in Christ. It would seem from his Nuremberg *Confession* that the Anabaptist Hans Denck had a rounded view of the matter, as Rufus Jones explains:

> His leading question in the *Confession* is 'Who gives me faith? Is it inborn, or is it *won*? Is it communicated by parents, or is it an elemental *condition of the soul*?' His answer is that it is a native condition of the soul. It is a *tendency* grounded in the very structure of the soul, which pushes man after a better, purer life, and which makes him resist the *lower* natural tendencies. This situation involves battle, struggle (*Seelenkampf*) as long as one lives in the body, but the victory is well in sight when one 'sets his will towards God's will through Christ'.[113]

If human beings are created in the *imago dei* for fellowship with God, may we not say that what may appear to be 'natural faith' is a gift of God which, when directed towards him (Aquinas's unformed faith[114]) is preferable to the denial of God, and may be that which prompts an individual's religious quest in a way analogous to the promptings which some have experienced in relation to those ontological, cosmological, teleological and moral ruminations in which theistic arguments have been grounded? Calvin did not hesitate to speak of 'implicit faith', by which he meant not subservience to ecclesial authority on the part of the ignorant (something he roundly condemned the Roman Church for encouraging), but 'reverent attention' to the claims of Christ which is the 'preparation of faith'.[115]

Undoubtedly there is a logical gap between natural faith and faith as trust (*fiducia*) just as there is a logical gap between any attempted demonstration of the existence of 'a being' and faith in God in the Christian sense. It is true, as Forsyth said, that 'the verdict *is* faith, it is not a prior condition of faith . . . We do not review God's claims and then admit Him as we are satisfied.'[116] But when, in his disjunctive way, he proceeds to say, 'We do not assent and then trust', it seems to me that he denies the experience of many, namely, that they did assent intellectually to belief in God before they came to trust him existentially. Moreover, are those created in the *imago dei* to be regarded as unpromptable by the Holy Spirit until they leap? Surely that would deny God's initiative in redemption and make a work out of a leap. This is not to say that natural faith (intellectually construed), even when it fastens upon God, is identical to saving faith, but it may be more continuous with it than Lovell Cocks, one of Forsyth's pupils, on occasion supposed: 'Let it be granted, then, that it is reasonable to believe in God; we must still maintain that this kind of belief, analogous to the "natural piety" of the scientist, is not saving faith or even its beginning.'[117] Why, in the providence of God, may natural belief in the Christian God not be the beginning of *fiducia* in the sense of being, under the Holy Spirit, the prompter towards it? Lovell Cocks himself had earlier affirmed that 'saving faith presupposes natural faith (since it presupposes man with all his power and interests)',[118] and Calvin asserted that 'it is after we have learned that our salvation rests with God that we are attracted to seek him'.[119] At the very least it would seem (having regard once more to the impaired but not obliterated *imago dei*) that there is a greater degree of intellectual continuity between a believer who once believed with the head only, so to speak, than between a believer who, prior to an instantaneous conversion, was an atheist. Retrospectively, may not a believer's saving faith, among other things, bring the encouragement that previous 'natural' faith was not misplaced? Conversely, as Basil Mitchell has observed, saving faith 'may well strengthen the obligation to believe in God when the evidence is fluctuating or uncertain. For loyalty is involved . . .'[120] In the Christian context, the loyalty of which Mitchell speaks accompanies the Christian's trustful response to God's gracious call in Christ. At the heart of this response is love: 'To use the Latin formula, *fides* is not complete until it is *fides caritate formata* – a faith shaped by our loving response to God's prior love for us.'[121]

We can now begin to see more clearly why it is that Locke's anthropocentric starting point makes it difficult to accommodate all that Christians (including Locke) wish to say concerning faith and their knowledge of God. To pose the question bluntly, if we begin where Locke begins, can we easily make some major Christian claims? The question is analogous to that posed by those philosophical idealists who were closest to Christanity: if we seek to cash Christian claims in terms of philosophical idealism will there not follow certain attentuations of the Christian message? In neither case has it been implied that Locke or the Christian idealists were intellectual hypocrites; their Christianity has not been doubted. In both cases the suggestion is made that their faith breaks the bounds of their methods. Locke, we recall, declared that his purpose was 'to enquire into the Original, Certainty, and Extent of humane Knowledge; together, with the Grounds and Degrees of Belief, Opinion and Assent'.[122] As has frequently been pointed out, psychological and epistemological questions are here posed, and in his discussion Locke occasionally oscillates between them. Locke is in no doubt that demonstrative knowledge of God's existence is possible, and in the *Essay*, IV. x, he propounds his argument to this effect.[123] But he realizes that Christians wish to say much more about God than that he exists. Hence the need of revelation and faith. Although when paraphrasing Paul's epistles Locke veers in the direction of understanding faith as *fiducia* (indeed it would be difficult not to do this, given the apostle's emphasis and experience),[124] he characteristically thinks of faith as assent to propositions which supply information not otherwise attained by the exercise of reason. Of such information the Bible is the primary source. The emphasis is thus more upon intellectual assent than upon personal commitment – still less on existential leaps of faith. Hence my earlier conclusion that

> Locke's way of setting out from epistemology and then invoking revelation, Scripture, Christ as appropriate, may not be best suited to our needs now . . . The way in which Locke reached out in the direction of divine authority, the teaching of Scripture and the example of Christ, suggests that he himself felt the strain imposed upon his deepest convictions by his epistemological stance which, while properly acknowledging the limitations of human knowledge imposed the restrictions of sensation and (ambiguously construed) reflection upon the human capacity to know, and was ignored by Locke himself at crucial points. If this is so, the problem bequeathed by Locke to modern thought is not so much that of the alleged illicit elevation of reason, as that of the illegitimate constriction of human knowledge.[125]

In short, we have the consequence of a procedure in which undue heed is paid to 'a symbolism referring to those aspects of the universe which are given to the senses, or can be measured or inferred in some other way'.[126] Thus Locke can say that 'Believing in the highest Degree of Assurance is not Knowledge. That whatever is capable of Demonstration, is not, unless it be self-evident, capable to produce Knowledge.'[127]

It is not surprising that, in view of such claims, Stillingfleet and many others should find undue scepticism in Locke's writings. While none of these opponents would have denied that we do not have comprehensive knowledge of God, they were convinced that we could know more than Locke's method allowed; and their protests were the more urgent because some of the deists were regarding Locke as one of their own.[128]

The position here proposed is that even our 'natural' knowledge of God is ours because he has made us in his image and has imparted it to us; that there is epistemological no less than ontological continuity between Paul's 'old man' and 'new man', and that, by the Holy Spirit, the promptings of 'natural' faith may lead to saving faith, just as 'natural' reason carries the seeds of saving faith. But now we need to investigate the concept of saving faith more closely.

As well as rehearsing the several types of faith to which people give intellectual assent, John Wesley had much to say concerning saving faith, above all, that it is 'a sure trust and confidence that Christ died for *my* sins, that he loved *me* and gave himself for *me*'.[129] He here echoes a prominent line of thought coming down from the Reformation, whose originator is the apostle Paul. Luther neatly contrasts *assensus* with *fiducia* thus:

> There are two kinds of believing: first, a believing about God which means that I believe that what is said of God is true . . . There is, secondly, a believing in God which means that I put my trust in Him, give myself up to thinking that I can have dealings with him, and believe without any doubt that He will be and do to me according to the things said of Him. Such faith, which throws itself upon God, whether in life or in death, alone makes a Christian man.[130]

More succinctly, in his *Larger Catechism*, in explication of the first Commandment Luther says, 'To have God is nothing else than to trust and believe in Him with all the heart.' To Luther saving faith is justifying faith; it is at the opposite pole to meritorious works: 'If faith is not without all, even the smallest works, it does not justify; it is not faith.'[131] Saving faith is a gift, so that none may boast about it. By grace through faith the penitent believer, now 'in Christ', lives a new life in the power of the Spirit. Good works follow such faith; indeed, apart from it we can do nothing pleasing to God.

Such thoughts reverberate through the Reformation and Puritan writings. Thus, in Calvin's opinion,

> we shall possess a right definition of faith if we call it a firm and certain knowledge of God's benevolence toward us, founded upon the truth of the freely given promise in Christ, both revealed to our minds and sealed upon our hearts through the Holy Spirit.[132]

Again, 'faith is a singular gift of God, both in that the mind of man is purged so as to be able to taste the truth of God and in that his heart is established therein'.[133]

Struggling to cover all the bases and enter all necessary caveats, the Belgic Confession of 1561 declares:

> We believe that, to attain the true knowledge of this great mystery [that is, salvation], the Holy Ghost kindleth in our hearts an upright faith, which embraces Jesus Christ with all his merits, appropriates him, and seeks nothing more besides him. For it must needs follow, either that all things which are requisite to our salvation are not in Jesus Christ, or if all things are in him, that then those who possess Jesus Christ through faith have complete salvation in Him. Therefore, for any to assert that Christ is not sufficient, but that something more is required besides him, would be too gross a blasphemy; for hence it would follow that Christ was but half a Saviour. Therefore we justly say with Paul, *that we are justified by faith alone*, or by *faith without works*. However, to speak

> more clearly, we do not mean that faith itself justifies us, for it is only an instrument with which we embrace Christ our Righteousness. But Jesus Christ, imputing to us all his merits, and so many holy works, which he hath done for us and in our stead, is our Righteousness. And faith is an instrument that keeps us in communion with him in all his benefits, which, when they become ours, are more than sufficient to acquit us of our sins.[134]

Two years later, the Heidelberg Catechism summarized the main points,[135] and on its teaching many generations of Reformed Christians were reared.

On the radical wing of the Reformation, Menno Simons underlined the importance of regeneration and expounded saving faith as the personal appropriation of the Gospel, the consequence of which is that 'the heart is renewed, converted, justified, becomes pious, peaceable and joyous, is born a child of God, approaches with full confidence the throne of grace, and so becomes a joint-heir of Christ and a possessor of eternal life'.[136]

In more homely language, the Puritan Philip Henry was wont to observe:

> We must take hold of Christ, as a man that is sinking in deep waters takes hold of a bough, or cord, or plank. We must see him to be the only way, and rest on him accordingly . . . [T]here are three things in believing, – The sight and sense of our sin and misery. – Assent to the testimony given in the word concerning Christ, believing that though I am a great sinner, yet he is a *great* Saviour. – Application of him to ourselves, consenting to take him to be ours, and we to be his, – to be ruled by him, and saved by him.[137]

If Henry the Presbyterian speaks as from the fireside, John Owen the Independent sounds like a lawyer:

> The nature of justifying faith, with respect unto that exercise of it whereby we are justified, consisteth in *the heart's approbation of the way of justification and salvation of sinners by Jesus Christ proposed in the gospel, as proceeding from the grace, wisdom, and love of God, with its acquiescency therein as unto its own concernment and condition.*[138]

As compared with these variously robust declarations, the report of a Theological Commission prepared under the auspices of the Faith and Order department of the World Council of Churches seems somewhat emaciated:

> By 'faith' we must understand . . . a lot more than the explicit affirmation of a conviction. Faith is the proper attitude of the person whose life is totally ordered for and open to Jesus Christ. Thus it includes hope, love, confidence, humility, and conviction. This openness is expressed in a variety of ways. It consists in remembering and recognising he who came in the flesh to live among men, who died and who rose; it is adoration and obedience towards him who reigns now; it is the joyful waiting for his return.[139]

On faith as gift, faith as justifying, and faith as enabled the statement is silent. Moreover, to live a life ordered for, and open to, Jesus Christ seems less intimate than to live one in personal relationship with Christ. This deficiency has frequently been noted in the writings of Aquinas, whose intellectualism seems so often to preclude him from seeing faith as trust in a person.[140] For all their too frequent turgidity, Calvin and the Puritans knew that such a relationship was the key to the life of faith: 'The grace of faith, which I am recommending to you today', said John Flavel, 'is not only the instrument of your justification, but it is also the bond of your union with Christ, Eph. iii. 17. "That Christ may dwell in your hearts by faith."'[141]

In Reformation literature there is widespread agreement that, while saving faith is not the reward of good works, good works should follow faith. In his Preface to *Romans* (1522) Luther declares:

> It is a living, busy, active, powerful thing, faith; it is impossible for it not to do us good continually. It never asks whether good works are to be done, but before the question is put, it has already done them, and is always doing them.

According to Calvin, it is a proof of the believer's election that 'our profession of faith should find its response in a good conscience and an upright life'.[142] The Second Helvetic Confession is more specific in teaching that saving faith 'keeps us in the service we owe to God and our neighbour, strengthens our patience in adversity, fashions and makes a true confession, and in a word, brings forth good fruit of all kinds, and good works'.[143] In a manner characteristic of his Hutterian tradition, Hans Arbeiter pondered the implications of saving faith for personal discipleship:

> I find a new heart and spirit within myself which has a true horror and revulsion from the secret and public sins and vices of the world. And my heart and soul has pleasure and joy in all that pleases God. Also I find within myself the grace needed to fight sin and roguery, and to do good. This I have not received of myself, but have received it from the Lord.[144]

The English Puritan Philip Henry summed matters up from the human side thus:

> To believe, has three things in it; – 1. Assent to what is spoken as true, either from the evidence of the thing itself, or upon the account of the veracity of him that speaketh it. 2. Application of it to myself; I must look upon myself as concerned in it, and say, 'This belongs to me.' 3. Answerable affections and actions, according as the thing is that is spoken. Without this, my believing is nothing.[145]

We may call on Lovell Cocks to place the divine and human aspects side by side:

> The believer is conformed to Christ, regenerated in His image, incorporated into His life, by receiving Christ's mind – Christ's faith, Christ's confession of holy love, Christ's judgment upon sin. All of this has been *for* the believer as the ground of his justification. And now by the Holy Spirit an answering faith, confession and judgment, are offered *in* the believer and *by* him.[146]

Implicit here is a reference to the ecclesial implication of saving faith, for those incorporated into Christ's life are not so many atoms, but limbs of the body, members of the household of faith. From the standpoint I am trying to articulate in this book, namely that while particular apologetic tasks fall to those gifted to treat them the Church as a whole has the task of confessing and commending the faith, the corporate dimension may not be overlooked. The Church is the community of those who by grace not only believe certain things, but share a common commitment which prompts their worship and shapes their life. After all,

> It is not our untutored religious experience that is confronted with the story of our redemption; rather does that story come to us as members of the Body of Christ – the Church, wherein we not only learn of God's act of redemption in the past but also live in continued experience of His redemptive and sustaining grace by the same Lord and through the same Spirit.[147]

The Church comprises those who together recall God's faithfulness in calling out a people for his praise and service, and who, on recollecting, give thanks.[148] As they do this they cannot but also recall with sorrow the disastrous errors made through the centuries in the name of the Church; and insofar as the Church is an earthen vessel, comprising saints (the called) who are also sinners, they will confess their own failures in witness and service, and pray for grace to amend their ways.[149]

III

The foregoing discussion raises two important questions. What is the relation between saving faith and knowledge? How does or should religious experience function in apologetics? I shall treat each question in turn.

We may first consider the view that faith is distinct from knowledge. This position is commonplace in general epistemology where what I have called 'natural' faith is concerned. A. D. Woozley is one among many who have explained that there are two tests of knowledge and belief:

> The first concerns what is known or believed: if that is false, it must be belief; if it is true, the test is indecisive as between knowledge and belief. The second concerns the person involved: if he is unsure, or sure on inconclusive evidence, it must be belief; if he is sure on conclusive evidence, it is knowledge. It is therefore wrong to think of knowledge and belief simply as states of mind. They are partly states of mind (or, preferably, dispositions), but the difference between them may be non-mental, as the object is true or false, or mental as the subject is sure or unsure, or partly mental and partly non-mental, as the subject's attitude is due to conclusive or inconclusive evidence.[150]

We have seen, however, that saving faith is of a different order from belief as here described, though it embraces aspects of it. For example, it falls short of absolute certainty, though it may be held (psychologically) with certitude. But it is saving faith's nature as trust in, and commitment to, a person with all that that means in terms of one's standing before God and one's way of life which is the primary distinguishing mark between it and 'natural' faith or belief. We may say that saving faith in a sense takes us beyond the scope of natural knowledge. Although it is genuinely our faith, it is more a gift than an achievement.

This, however, is a modern understanding of the matter. Clement of Alexandria, for example, teaches that knowledge takes precedence over faith, and that while faith (*assensus*) in orthodox doctrines suffices for the generality of people, the true Christian gnostic aspires to an esoteric knowledge of God not universally available. Christians are not in the position of pagan philosophers who are seeking the truth; for Christians have the truth, and their quest is of an ever clearer grasp of it: 'that investigation, which accords with faith, which builds, on the foundation of faith, their august knowledge of the truth, we know to be the best'.[151] Again, 'as we say that a man can be a believer without learning, so also we assert that it is impossible for a man without learning to comprehend the things which are declared in the faith'.[152] In Clement's account of the matter the intellectual clearly takes precedence over the personal.

This tendency to place faith lower than knowledge comes down to modern times in Tennyson's lines, so frequently denounced by bristling-bearded Victorian divines: 'We have but faith, we cannot know, / For knowledge is of things we see.'[153] It is the demoting 'but' which caused particular offence, as did the denial that saving faith includes and yields knowledge. On this point John Baillie notes that Tennyson speaks in Kantian vein, and reminds us that in the New Testament to have faith in God and to know him 'are often hardly more than two ways of saying the same thing'.[154] But the main point is that *pace* scientism, according to which knowledge is restricted to what is seen, touched, handled and experimented upon, the denotation of 'knowledge' is not to be so constricted. We do not know other people in this way, still less do we know God by scientific observation and experiment, or by theoretical proof:

> If I am certain that my mother loves me, that my wife is loyal, that my friend will not desert me at the time of misfortune, my certainty is clearly of another kind from that by which I am convinced that the opposite angles of a parallelogram are equal, or that there is a famine in India, or that the day of Luther's death was February 18th, 1546.[155]

In recognition of such variety, John Heywood Thomas, in the course of his exposition of Kierkegaard's thought, presents a careful account of the difference between '(saving) faith' and 'proof'. He indicates the ambiguity of 'proof' and shows that, in saying that faith is not proof,

> We are saying that religious faith is unlike (a) the method of the lawyer who seeks to establish something, (b) the method of the scientist who wants to discover something, (c) the method of the mathematician who seeks to construct a system that will be true.[156]

But from none of this does it follow that saving faith is devoid of knowledge. Indeed, it is purely arbitrary to define 'knowledge' in such a way as to exclude that personal knowledge of God through Jesus Christ which, however partial, is given with saving faith. Such a definition would hark back to logical positivism and beyond to the nineteenth-century materialists; it would rule out not only Christian knowledge, but historical knowledge as well – a point well understood by Collingwood, whose lament concerning the realist philosophers of his day was that 'the thing they called theory of knowledge had been devised with special reference to the methodology of natural science',[157] and that it did not fit historical knowledge at all. Again, Stephen Williams has questioned why the term 'knowledge' should be reserved to the realm of logic, mathematics, sense experience and science: 'humans are not constituted so that knowledge is restricted to these things . . . Moral apprehension is a different area where scientific proofs do not apply but where there can be knowledge all the same.'[158] As for Christian knowledge, the point was bluntly made by Geoffrey F. Nuttall when reviewing a paper by a rationalistic liberal theologian:

> To compare man's knowledge of God to his knowledge of a table seems to me a scholastic sort of mistake: it is knowledge of the personal, and that alone, which is relevant, and the only real knowledge of the personal is the knowledge taken and given in a mutual love-relationship.[159]

To require absolute demonstrative certainty in the fields of historical, aesthetic, moral and religious judgement is simply to have misunderstood those fields. Nor is it out of order to point out that, however it may be in the abstracted worlds of pure mathematics and logic, many present-day scientists, awed and humbled by the scale of the potential good or harm they can do, are less prone to claim epistemological infallibility than were some of their brasher forebears – which is precisely what one would expect of those who employ their *imagination* in devising, and pin their *hopes* to (I choose my words carefully) *revisable hypotheses*.[160]

None of this, however, legitimates infallibilist epistemological claims by Christians, for, to repeat, the knowledge of God which comes by faith is partial. Indeed, as has often been pointed out,[161] in the Bible the contrast is not so much between faith and knowledge, as between faith and sight. The classic biblical verse in this connection is 1 Corinthians 13: 12, 'At present we see only puzzling reflections in a mirror, but one day we shall see face to face. My knowledge now is partial; then it will be whole, like God's knowledge of me.' This sentiment recurs in various modes of expression down through the Christian centuries. Irenaeus, for example, grants that while 'We cannot know God in his greatness, for the Father cannot be measured . . . Through his love and infinite kindness God comes within the grasp of man's knowledge.'[162] Again, we have both the *via negativa*, according to which our language is circumscribed by the greatness and majesty of God – what can we say of him?[163] – and the distinction we have already met, beloved of the Puritans and others, between a true apprehension of God and a full comprehension of him. As Tillich put it, 'Looking at God, we see that we do not have Him as an object of our knowledge, but that he has us as the subject of our existence . . . *We* may not comprehend, but we *are* comprehended.'[164]

All of this underlines once more the fact that 'natural' knowledge as ordinarily acquired will not suffice to bring us to saving faith:

> Knowledge *about* God can no doubt be mediated to us in many ways, through nature, or history, or the Bible, or the Church. But knowledge of God himself is a different matter altogether. It comes only of personal intercourse between the soul and its maker, and it rests on love, sympathy, faith, obedience, and the like.[165]

To the extent that we know, we do so because we have first been known. God has graciously taken the initiative and revealed himself to us: 'That is not the best and truest knowledge of God which is wrought out by the labour and sweat of the brain', wrote John Smith the Cambridge Platonist, 'but that which is kindled within us by a heavenly warmth in our hearts'.[166]

We are now in a position to see that, whereas all faith incorporates an intellectual element, saving faith as Christians understand it is the appropriation by grace of a revelation which is supremely personal, and at the heart of which is an experienced relationship in which believers commit themselves trustingly to the God who makes himself known in Jesus Christ. The point was made by A. E. Garvie thus: 'What God does for us and is in us is what God is for our religious knowledge. That the knowledge of God is thus conditioned by personal experience, character, purpose, is surely a truth very plainly and often taught in the Holy Scriptures.'[167] It is not that we first have saving faith and then acquire a particular kind of religious experience. Rather, experience is inherent in the commitment of faith.[168] For a classic statement of the matter we may turn to Calvin:

> Faith rests not on ignorance, but on knowledge. And this, indeed, knowledge not only of God but of the divine will. We do not obtain salvation either because we are prepared to embrace as true whatever the church has prescribed, or because we turn over to it the task of inquiring and knowing. But we do so when we know that God is our merciful Father, because of reconciliation effected through Christ [2 Cor. 5: 18–19], and that Christ has been given to us as righteousness, sanctification, and life. By this knowledge, I say, not by submission of our feeling, do we obtain entry into the Kingdom of Heaven . . . Now therefore we hold faith to be a knowledge of God's will toward us, perceived from his Word . . . [Faith is] a firm and certain knowledge of God's benevolence toward us, founded upon the truth of the freely given promise in Christ, both revealed to our minds and sealed upon our hearts through the Holy Spirit.[169]

Calvin here makes it clear that the knowledge which is saving faith encompasses knowing about God and what he has done in Christ; knowing his will; and embracing God's truth as revealed by the Word to the mind and sealed upon the heart by the Holy Spirit. It is no accident that the whole is couched in trinitarian language, for all the persons are active in the Godhead's saving work. Saving faith, therefore, does not originate in our feelings; it is a gift received at the initiative of God and its object is that same giver who has revealed himself in Christ:

> Q.21. *What is true faith?*
> A. It is not only a certain knowledge whereby I hold for truth all that God has revealed to us in His Word, but also a hearty trust which the Holy Ghost works in me through the Gospel, that not only to others,

> but to me also, forgiveness of sins, everlasting righteousness and blessedness, are given by God, out of pure grace, for the sake of Christ's merits alone.[170]

Such is one classical statement of the Christian experience.

Since the Father has revealed himself supremely in the Son, 'the degree of our knowledge of God is the degree of our knowledge of Christ. Thus our theology must have a Christological principle.'[171] On this principle, and by the sanctifying work of God the Holy Spirit, the believer's knowledge grows and deepens, for this knowing

> is one in which the knower tends to become like what he contemplates: it is a kind of knowing in which subject and object interpenetrate, where, as it were, the knower reaches out to grasp the object, or the object reaches out to grasp the subject [I should prefer to say, *because* the object has first reached out to grasp the subject].[172]

I shall return to this point at the end of this chapter. But first it is necessary to clarify the relationship between Christian experience and aesthetic and moral experience in general.

IV

I fear it will be necessary to cut a path through the vast amount of literature in aesthetics. Even the innocent-sounding question 'What is a work of art?'[173] has provoked an enormous literature, while discussions of the nature of beauty, and in particular whether it is 'in' the artefact or in the eye of the beholder, are legion. Having pondered a good deal of this literature, I presume to offer some bald affirmations and I begin, more narrowly, with art.

It seems quite clear that artists are makers of varying degrees of skill and insight. But exponents of the several crafts are, in their own way, makers too. However the line is to be drawn between the painter or composer and the wood-turner or embroiderer, it cannot be in relation to the claim that the former are somehow producers of 'the beautiful' while the latter are not; for objects in wood[174] and embroideries can be beautiful and, conversely, while some art may be beautiful, not all of it is. Painting suggests obvious examples: in addition to sunsets and hay wains, there are harrowing paintings of the Crucifixion, of the Day of Judgement, and of concentration camps.[175] Sublimity is not identical with beauty, as Kant and many others have pointed out: 'not all aesthetic judgments are judgments of taste, which as such refer to the beautiful; but some of them arise from an intellectual feeling and as such refer to the *sublime*'.[176] Architecture introduces a further consideration for, while the architect conceives of and executes the design and superintends the construction, he or she does not normally do the actual building. Yet a building may be called beautiful or ugly; but so may the work of an engineering designer, who may not personally construct machinery, but whose product may be said to have a certain beauty by reason of its lines and the action of its moveable parts. Not for nothing are there various magazines for devotees of 'vintage steam', classic motorcycles and the like.[177]

Again, both works of art and of the several crafts may be judged by people with greater or lesser degrees of sensitivity. The Harvard moral philosophers of antebellum America assumed the right to legislate on the worth of artists' endeavours, for they were the self-styled experts on such matters.[178] In most quarters nowadays such elitism is distinctly unfashionable if not abominated. But this does not make the justification of aesthetic judgements any easier. Collingwood, for example, distinguished between artists and craftsmen from the point of view of the manner of their work. The craftsman works to the design of another, the artist does not. But from the point of view of aesthetic judgement the question of the process of making is redundant, for it is the end result which is being judged.[179] Of course, where judgement is concerned, fine arts and crafts are not altogether on all fours. For, while in the case of a craft item it may be appropriate to take into consideration its usefulness, in the case of a work of art – the conviction of some schoolteachers that the display of 'noble' paintings will somehow 'improve' unruly youngsters notwithstanding – 'Whatever intellectual enlightenment or moral elevation is to be gained from works of imagination, to communicate such benefits cannot be the conscious aim of the artist; nor is the merit of his work to be measured by its didactic excellencies.'[180]

Many factors go into the making of an aesthetic judgement,[181] not least the presuppositions or prejudices of the viewer or listener. When John Wesley saw *The Raising of Lazarus* in Winchester Cathedral in October 1781 he was disappointed:

> I observed – (1) there was such a huddle of figures, that, had I not been told, I should not ever have guessed what they meant; (2) The colours in general were far too glaring, such as neither Christ not His followers ever wore. When will painters have common sense?[182]

Though it would be anachronistic to expect Wesley to have drawn the distinction between a work of art and a non-artistic snapshot, the general point that, even when painting the mundane, an artist is contributing something over and above the likeness is pertinent. Carritt recalls a story told of both Turner and Whistler. Somebody said to the artist, '"I never saw a sunset like that", and he replied, "Don't you wish you could?"'[183] Even more obvious than Wesley's are the motivations of the Vatican judges:

> the Church has, with good reason, always claimed the right to pass judgment on the arts, deciding which of the works of artists are in accordance with faith, piety, and the laws religiously handed down, and are to be considered suitable for sacred use.[184]

Calvin has sometimes been presented as a censor of all things artistic. But this is just one of many ways in which he has been grossly misrepresented. Certainly he and those in his wake were concerned lest the commandment against making graven images was broken. Accordingly, visual representations in worship, above all of God, were not permitted.[185] On the other hand Calvin declared:

> I am not gripped by the superstition of thinking absolutely no images permissible. But because sculpture and painting are gifts of God, I seek a pure and legitimate use of each, lest those things which the Lord has conferred upon us for his glory and our good be not only polluted by perverse misuse but also turned to our destruction.[186]

As for the Puritans, often perceived as iconoclasts *par excellence*, Leland Ryken has reminded us that, although they removed organs and paintings from churches, they purchased them for use in their homes; and while in prison 'John Bunyan secretly made a flute out of a chair leg'.[187]

The post-Romantic age has sometimes witnessed a variety of aestheticism which some Christians have found damaging. The following observations of John 'Rabbi' Duncan are notable in this connection, not least because they elevate the holy above the aesthetic:

> A merely aesthetic religion – such as that of Goethe and all worshippers of the Beautiful – is a miserable substitute for piety, and it never stands the tear and wear of time, *especially in the midst of great sorrows*. It is the offspring of sentiment divorced from law, and that is an illegal divorce. The want of the legal is a great blot in theology, and a practical danger in religion . . . But the aesthetic must not be eradicated, it must be supplemented. And it is the realization of the *moral* in God, and the sense of sin in man – the sinner feeling that he is in the presence of a holy God – that is the only cure for its exaggerations.[188]

Two things are suggested so far by our brief discussion of art. First, that religion is not art.[189] This is the clear conviction of Duncan, whose emphasis upon the holy serves to underline the point. It is a point, however, which seems to be lost upon G. E. Moore, for example, who regards religion as 'merely a subdivision of Art', and holds that 'Every valuable purpose which Religion serves is also served by Art . . . They are only distinguished in that the religious man thinks it necessary to assert his belief in the existence of the objects that he contemplates.'[190] The idea that the Christian confession concerns the redemption of the sinful by the holy seems here to have escaped him. Again, while Moore is right in saying that a good work of art has intrinsic value, and is not any less a good work of art because it encourages gross immorality, his view that beauty is the only quality which is good in itself falls short of the Christian claim unless (which Moore would deny) beauty, the holy and God are somehow identified.[191]

Secondly, aesthetic experience encompasses far more than the fine arts. It is not only that on the one hand there are the craftsmen and the engineers, and on the other the holy, concerning which, in view of the beauty and the demand of the holy, aesthetic and moral experience seem to be inextricably interwoven. It is that the concept of beauty extends to the natural world itself: 'we may say that *because* there is natural beauty, the aesthetic experience of humanity cannot be the same thing as human art'.[192] In this connection the following statement seems open to question, and I shall place my interpolations within square brackets:

> the aesthetic experience of works of art usually is very different from the aesthetic experience of non-artistic artefacts and natural objects. [How does the author know this? How are such experiences gauged? And have we not seen that the line between arts and crafts is not easy to draw, and that both may yield aesthetic experience?] In the latter cases,

> there is usually spectator enjoyment without insight, especially for those of us who are not artists. In the case of the aesthetic experience of works of art, however, there is much more likely to be participative enjoyment with insight. Spectator enjoyment, however refreshing, is but of passing moment . . . [But (a) far from being innocent of insight, the aesthetic experience of the natural world has inspired an entire industry of teleological argumentation down the centuries; (b) to some people works of fine art yield little insight – indeed, they cannot make head nor tail of them, whereas (c) the experienced beauties of the natural world may remain ever fresh in the memory.][193]

Although it is impossible to speak accurately of quantities in this realm, I believe that Carritt was correct in arguing that the beautiful, however defined, 'addresses' both the emotions and the intellect: 'Mere feelings are not beautiful, mere arrangement of sound, shape, colour would not be so. But when an arrangement of sound, shape, or colour seems the natural and not artificial embodiment of an experience that can be recognized in it it is beautiful.'[194] In the aesthetic response we have the elision of sensory perception, emotional response and meaning (even if, as in some modern art, the 'meaning' is that there is no meaning).[195] As William Temple said, 'Beauty, strictly speaking, concerns what is apprehended by means of the senses, though what is so apprehended may be far more than sensuous.'[196]

Returning to natural beauty: there must be few people who have not at some time undergone an aesthetic experience prompted by the beauty of the natural order. For his part De Burgh testified that 'Beauty is, I venture to suggest, most evidently displayed in nature, rather than in art.'[197] On the other hand, Richard Wollheim has argued that we bring to the appreciation of natural beauty an aesthetic attitude acquired from our contemplation of works of art (though surely many can appreciate natural beauty who seldom if ever contemplate the fine arts).[198] Our principal concern here, however, is with possibility that beauty may in some way afford a ground of Christian testimony, and a basis for commending the faith. This leads us directly to the question of the origin of beauty.

There appear to be three principal accounts of the genesis of the aesthetic experience, each of which has a long history. Thomas Reid summarizes the first two thus:

> All the objects we call beautiful agree in two things, which seem to concur in our sense of beauty. *First,* When they are perceived, or even imagined, they produce a certain agreeable emotion or feeling in the mind; and, secondly, This agreeable emotion is accompanied with an opinion or belief of their having some perfection or excellence belonging to them.[199]

Some, like Carritt, have emphasized the affective element,[200] others, like Thomas Aquinas, the idea that beauty inheres in the beautiful object. Convictions on this matter clearly influence the type of aesthetic judgements which are made. Do such judgements simply refer to the emotional response of the person making them? If this were so, 'That's beautiful' might mean simply, 'I like that!' or, if one were an emotivist, 'Wow!' An objectivist, on the other hand, might, when pronouncing a work of art or a natural panorama beautiful, mean not simply that the object being appraised exists in its own right, but that beauty is inherent in it, and would be so even if there were no witnesses or auditors of it. Objectivists might go further and claim that God is the bestower of the beauty present and experienced; that he is somehow 'in' the object or, at least, that he can be apprehended 'through' it.[201] Some, like Plotinus and Marsilius Ficinus, and supremely Augustine,[202] have identified God with beauty. The fact that it is possible to hold any of these positions without landing in logical contradiction underlines the point that it is a matter of faith to perceive God in, or as, the beautiful. We are not here dealing with the basis upon which a conclusive logical demonstration of God's existence could be constructed, any more than we are when we are in the realm of those intuitions of 'that than which no greater (or more perfect) can be conceived' which many people claim to be genuine intuitions of God.

It does not, however, follow that God is not revealed in the beautiful and, not to mention psalmists and other biblical writers, it is easy to produce a long list of testimonies from all branches of Christianity to the effect that the aesthetic experience prompts, or includes, the vision of the divine. Boethius speaks for many when he writes, 'You who are most beautiful produce the beautiful world from your divine mind and, forming it in your image, You order the perfect parts in a perfect whole.'[203] Of God Calvin asks, 'Did he not . . . render many things attractive to us, apart from their necessary use?'[204] He was no stranger either to aesthetic judgements of the most highly impassioned kind: 'You cannot in one glance survey this most vast and beautiful system of the universe, in its wide expanse, without being completely overwhelmed by the boundless force of its brightness.'[205] Elsewhere Calvin speaks of the Holy Spirit as the artist who bestows beauty on the created order.[206] In the opinion of the American Transcendentalist, John Sullivan Dwight,

> The greatest blessing which could be bestowed on the weary multitude would be to give them the sense of beauty, to open their eyes for them, and let them see how richly we are here surrounded, what a glorious temple we inhabit, how every part of it is eloquent of God.[207]

The Romantic immanentism clearly expressed here filters down into such a very different thinker as Robert Mackintosh, in many ways critical of the idealism of his teacher, Edward Caird: 'here or there, behind the veil of nature, there is a spiritual presence . . . the presence is deeply however dimly felt'.[208] The strains of idealism, though of the personal kind, linger also in William Temple's verdict: 'The whole aesthetic experience is unintelligible unless there comes through it a revelation from spirit to spirit. *There is more in Beauty than Beauty alone. There is communication from, and communion with, personal Spirit.*'[209] Of course, everything turns upon the nature of the revelation and, as with natural theology in general, it must be said that the experience of beauty as such does not yield the Christian God; indeed, unless transcendence and immanence are held in balance, beautiful objects and sounds may tend towards the 'deistic' conclusion of a God 'beyond' them all.[210] This point seems to have been taken by the early Methodist Elizabeth Ritchie (later Mortimer), who wrote of a journey to north Wales in 1786, 'Rural scenery always does me good; and though this has been, upon the whole, a day of trial, yet *I have seen God in all things*, and have ascended from earth to heaven.'[211] Those who believe in the God Christ makes known may well come to understand creation as the theatre of God's saving work; indeed, they may begin to grasp the idea of the involvement of all the persons of the Trinity in the work of creation as of redemption. It is a primary task of systematic theologians to spell out the relations of creation, re-creation and Trinity.[212] In making this point I do not intend to deny that, as with the intimations of 'natural' theology, so here: by virtue of the impaired though not obliterated *imago dei*, God may address people through the beautiful, and people may pronounce the judgement, 'This beautiful sound, object, or scene is of God' prior to their commitment of faith; the latter may be prompted by the former if, indeed, as Calvin said, the Spirit is the artist of creation.

One final consideration will lead us to the next section of this chapter. If a work of art, a human artefact, a natural scene – even a mathematical proof – may be beautiful, so may a human character. Here, as it seems to me, we approach closely the theme of moral experience. This is not to deny Thomas Chalmers's repeated insistence that people may bask in a sea of beauty without feeling 'a movement of obedience to the will of God, under the impression of his rightful authority over all the creatures whom he has formed'.[213] But it is to say that it is the pure in heart who see God.[214] To moral experience, therefore, we must now turn.

V

It does not seem possible reasonably to deny that human beings whose capacities are not impaired by disability or drugs are conscious of themselves as having moral experience. If they do not habitually seek some abstract 'good', they are aware from time to time of being under moral obligation to do, or to refrain from doing, something. Again, it cannot easily be denied that

> there is, as a matter of fact, for vast numbers of people, and possibly for all at least potentially, a very close correspondence between the idea of God and the idea of an unconditional demand upon the will . . . To the religious person, whosoever says God says absolute demand upon the will.[215]

This, I believe, is a correct assessment of the matter, though Christians must resist the temptation to turn Farmer's sentence around and to say, 'whosoever says absolute demand upon the will says God'. Unbelievers and adherents of other faiths are neither to be deprived of morality nor to be annexed as 'anonymous Christians'. This is not to deny the possibility that, to use the language of yesteryear, there are 'intimations of the divine' in moral experience. There is not, however, the basis of a coercive demonstration of God there. Moreover, those who have by grace become at one with God through Christ have an ethical motive of gratitude, a spiritual resource, an ecclesial context and an eschatological dimension to their moral reflection which, while by no means obliterating 'natural' morality, sharpen its claims and aid their fulfilment. I shall attempt to justify these bald claims, taking Kant as my starting point.

As is well known, Kant thinks in terms of the critical and the practical reason. Critical reason is brought to bear upon phenomena, it is powerless to deal with things-in-themselves, the noumenal realm. Having set out to undermine the scepticism of Hume, who had awakened him from his 'dogmatic slumber' and propelled him towards an epistemology according to which experience results from the combination of sense data with the forms of space and time and such categories as substance, which the mind supplies, Kant here verges upon scepticism again; and it is not surprising that, if some of his successors deemed his denial of knowledge of the noumena to leave room for faith, others regarded him as the fountainhead of their agnosticism. But this is not all that Kant says. By the practical reason, of which the postulates are God, freedom and immortality, we do gain some insight into reality, and this is summed up in the variously formulated categorical imperative, the burden of which is that as human beings we are conscious of being under unconditional obligation. Furthermore, 'in order that an action should be morally good, it is not enough that it *conform* to the moral law, but it must also be done *for the sake of the law*'.[216] But, Kant argues, since we ought to do only what we can do, we must postulate the freedom of the will;[217] since happiness should follow virtue but does not, in this life, always do so we must postulate immortality; and since there is the need for a righteous superintendent who will correctly apportion eschatological rewards and punishments hereafter we must postulate God.[218] From none of this, however, does it follow that the moral law derives its existence or power from God, or that a person who cannot believe in God is no longer under the obligation of the moral law.[219] Pringle-Pattison was not without justification in declaring that, 'owing to the extraordinary hold which the individualism and external deism of his century had over him, God seems to be introduced in Kant's moral theory almost as an afterthought, and He is connected with the law, not as its inspirer or author, but in the merely administrative capacity of Paymaster.'[220]

In other words, in Kant's writings the moral law seems to take precedence over God, about whom, on Kant's own epistemological principles, we can know nothing. It also takes precedence over 'the frame of nature' – Hume's starting point – notwithstanding Kant's testimony that the cosmological argument 'always deserves to be mentioned with respect. It is the oldest, clearest and most in accord with the common reason of mankind.'[221] The autonomous human will is the 'universal legislator'; it 'is not subject simply to the law, but so subject that it must be regarded *as itself giving the law*, and on this ground only, subject to the law (of which it can regard itself as the author)'.[222] Far from being immanent in morality, it would appear that God has withdrawn from it altogether. This is consistent with Kant's concern that 'To base morals on the command of God would be to make ethics heteronomous, which Kant regards as the crucial mistake of the moral philosophers who preceded him'[223] (though he does not seem to baulk at grounding his postulates on the heteronomous consideration that happiness and virtue must be properly adjusted to one another).

Let it at once be granted that, in upholding the obligatory nature of the moral law, and in seeking to stem the tide of Humean scepticism as widely perceived, Kant performed a signal service. But his epistemological concession to empiricism (we can know only the phemonenal), coupled with his reluctance (perhaps engendered by extremer examples of pietism known to him from his youth[224]) to think of God as genuinely immanent prevented him from giving due weight to factors integral to the Christian understanding of morality. He would not, for example, have been able consistently to agree with H. P. Owen that

> The Word who commands us from without is also the Word who enlightens us within. Hence God calls us to obey his law by our own insight and by the exercise of our free will. Hence too he calls us to recognize his law as the law of our being – as the principle determining our self-fulfilment.[225]

On the contrary, it is difficult to see how, on Kant's view of the moral law's independence of God and our obligation to keep it, any divine moral commandments can be other than redundant. Clement Webb's conclusion is just:

> We must acknowledge . . . in obligation not only, as Kant insisted, an aspect of autonomy, of self-imposed law, but also of a *heteronomy*, of a law imposed by another, a law imposed by God. Such a heteronomy, however, is not a heteronomy in Kant's sense, in which he felt that it was inconsistent with the genuine notion of moral obligation or duty; for a law given by God is not a law given by one who is another, since it is involved in our notion of God that he is immanent in our reason and will, which notwithstanding he transcends.[226]

With reference to Kant, Thomas McPherson pointed out that a person may without contradiction deny the existence of a universal, absolutely binding, moral law, and that such a person will remain unconvinced by Kant.[227] Nevertheless, the idea of a moral law has a long history, and it will take us forward if we review a different understanding of it, the Roman Catholic natural law tradition.

I believe that this tradition, no less than Kant's position, enshrines certain indispensable insights into human nature. But the superstructure sometimes erected upon the principle has been productive of puzzlement. The two main Protestant criticisms of the traditional Roman view were succinctly stated long ago by Daniel Day Williams. The first is that 'the Church not only puts its authority behind the ultimate principles, but it treats very complicated and debatable deductions from those principles as if they had the same authority'.[228] The second criticism is that the natural law principle 'puts a legalistic restriction upon the freedom of the Christian conscience in dealing with the unpredictable and always problematical stuff of actual social existence'.[229] This latter point is reinforced by Ronald Preston: 'the very theology whose *raison d'être* was to deal with specific problems proceeded by a deductive method of reasoning from the alleged self-evident deliverances of natural laws in a way which prevented it from dealing adequately with empirical data'.[230] In recalling these judgements from the past I in no way overlook yet another: that of the Roman Catholic James Scull who wrote, 'There is perhaps no area within contemporary Catholic life and theology undergoing renewal and reform to a greater degree than Catholic moral theology.'[231] This seems undeniable, but I cannot pursue that hare here.

Rather, my point is that, notwithstanding the way in which the natural law concept has sometimes been abused, Paul Ramsey was right to say that 'any conception of the nature of man is so far a conception of the natural law'.[232] In this sense 'natural law' stands for that capacity of moral awareness and that sense of obligation which, as Kant saw, belong to human beings as such. Herein lies the basis for cooperation between Christians, humanists, members of other religious faiths.[233] Furthermore, it does seem that any type of Christian ethical theory which denies the existence of or the worth of this common moral experience, whether on grounds of total depravity or any other, is courting difficulty not only within the field of practical ethics, but also with respect to the doctrines of the our creation in the *imago dei* and the work of the Holy Spirit, who blows where he will.[234]

Despite this, Karl Barth, who asserted the inextricably interwoven nature of ethics and dogmatics, tended by undue emphasis upon the revealed Word, to isolate both from 'unbelieving' thought to the extent that 'there must be no armistice with the peoples of Canaan and their culture and their cultus'.[235] Thus Barth was content to leave his readers in a cleft stick, uncomfortably held fast by two irreconcilable theses, that man is from the outset exposed to the moral question and yet that 'ethics . . . has its basis in the knowledge of Jesus Christ', and nowhere else, that 'it is within this circle, within the doctrine of God, that the question arises'.[236] This tendency to encapsulate ethics within the circle of revelation is manifest too in the writings of Emil Brunner, who, although he issued a needed corrective to a liberalism which was anthropologically over-optimistic, does short-circuit ethical discussion by failing to conceive of natural morality as anything other than the human being's sinful quest of independence of God.[237]

Happily, none of this is a necessary and inescapable concluson of Reformed theology; indeed, it is hard to find sanction for it in the magisterial Reformers, not to mention the New Testament, to which they paid great heed. In 1 Peter 2: 12 we find the injunction, 'Let your conduct among believers be so good that, although they now malign you as wrongdoers, reflection on your good deeds will lead them to give glory to God on the day when he comes in judgement.' It is difficult to see what this can mean if it is not an endorsement of the doctrine of natural law as I have defined it. Again, Paul reminds the Romans that Gentiles who do not possess God's law can nevertheless 'carry out its precepts by the light of nature . . . they show that what the law requires is inscribed on their hearts, and to this their conscience gives supporting witness'.[238] Yet again, in Romans 1: 19 Paul emphasized human accountability, claiming that there is no defence for those who wickedly stifle the truth of God which they know because it 'lies plain before their eyes'. Not even grievous sin removes moral responsibility, and as for total depravity:

> the assertor of the 'total depravity' of human nature, of its absolute moral blindness and incapacity, presupposes in himself and others the presence of a criterion or principle of good, in virtue of which he discerns himself to be wholly evil; yet the very proposition that human nature is wholly evil, would be unintelligible unless it were false.[239]

No doubt 'The Christian is certainly in some sense a new creation, but that clearly means not another species altogether, but a creature, a man transformed or renewed, whose transformation and renewal cannot be articulated apart from some understanding of his existence as a creature independently of that renewal.'[240] Indeed, it is hard to see how people could ever become new creatures apart from something of worth in them to which God's love could appeal. After all, 'nothing except a serious and unreserved acknowledgement of moral obligation can prepare men either to seek or to appreciate forgiveness'.[241]

However, to elaborate upon a hint already dropped, from the fact that most people have some understanding of the natural law it does not follow that they may be regarded as 'crypto' or anonymous Christians. It is one thing for a Christian to believe that everyone is a child of God; it is quite another to try to annex unbelievers to the Christian faith or even to theism. Not surprisingly this is perceived as patronizing, even offensive, because it suggests that if they did but realize it they would see that they are believers after all. To reproduce an earlier comment of mine on this matter:

> In referring to 'anonymous Christians' the Roman Catholic theologian Karl Rahner was seeking to modify the teaching of the Council of Florence (1438–1445) to the effect that those who die outside of the Catholic church 'go to the everlasting fire prepared for the devil and his angels.'[242] A motive surely to be applauded! Again, when the Presbyterian theologian John Baillie spoke of those who believe in the bottom of their hearts while denying with the top of their heads,[243] he had the humanists and agnostic of the present-day West primarily in mind. But Professor H. D. Lewis rightly pointed out that Baillie's stance permits the believer's opponent to return the charge of self-

> deception, and that the evidence that, for example, Bertrand Russell was a secret believer is notoriously difficult to find.[244] Furthermore, how can we with integrity deny the right and ability of others to express *their* deepest convictions with integrity? To deny that all are believers at heart is not to deny the Christian doctrine of our creation in the divine image . . . It is simply to allow others to speak the truth as they see it.[245]

In a word, there is a distinction to be drawn between God as in fact the fount of morality and God as known or believed to be such.[246]

It should be noted in passing that considerable advantages accrue to Christianity from the maintenance of the relative autonomy of morals. For example, the ethical critique of theology is facilitated if there is an independent criterion against which the deliverances of theologians may be measured. It is too easily overlooked by some who utter blanket condemnations of the Enlightenment that in encouraging the individual to pit his or her conscience against untoward authorities, whether biblicist or ecclesial, the route was opened for that moralizing of theology from which some of the critics themselves have so greatly benefited. It is to the credit of some of the eighteenth-century 'Arians',[247] so routinely viewed askance by the orthodox, that they struck out in this direction. Thus, for example, against double predestination, John Taylor of Norwich cautions, 'pray consider seriously what a God He must be who can be displeased with and curse His innocent creatures even before they have a being. Is this thy God, O Christian?' How can young people remember their Creator 'without the utmost Horror, who, it is supposed, hath given them Life under such deplorable Circumstances?'[248] In similar vein, and in opposition to the suggestion that the Father had to be cajoled into being merciful by the Son's sacrifice, Taylor's contemporary, Micaijah Towgood, insisted that 'Antecedent to the death of Christ he was gracious and merciful, and ready to forgive.'[249] Edwards A. Park was appealing to morality when he told a gathering of Congregational ministers in Boston in 1850 that when our words

> make an abiding impression that the divine government is harsh, pitiless, insincere, oppressive, devoid of sympathy with our most refined sentiments, reckless of even the most delicate emotion of the tenderest nature, then we may infer that we have left out of our theology some

element which should have been inserted, or have brought into it some element which we should have discarded. *Somewhere it must be wrong.*[250]

Again, such a Presbyterian philosopher as James McCosh was able, on the ground of the relative automomy of morals, and recognizing the moral fact of sin and the need of a Redeemer, to mount a moral 'proof' of the divine origin of Christianity.[251] While it is true that only on the basis of the autonomy of morals can a non-circular moral argument for God's existence be mounted, McCosh was over-optimistic that 'proof' in the demonstrative sense would result. Kant was more circumspect at this point.

To return from this brief digression: to say that not all acknowledge God is not, of course, to deny that moral experience is, like the appreciation of beauty, an avenue of God's approach to those to whom he has given life. Indeed, one of the main difficulties in the path of those who would attempt to construct an argument from morality to God is that God is too easily reduced to an 'external' guarantor of morality, rather than as one who personally approaches and addresses people in their moral experience.[252] Against this possibility John Hick suggests in one of his earlier works that 'anyone seriously committed to respect moral values as exercising a sovereign claim upon his life, must thereby implicitly believe in the reality of a trans-human source and basis for these values, which religion calls God'. He proceeds to speak of belief in 'a reality, other than the natural world, which is superior to oneself and entitled to one's obedience'.[253] Three points call for comment here. First, an unfortunately *ad hominem* flavour is imparted to the claim by the use of the word 'seriously', as if to say that naturalists, for example, are not serious in their thinking. The question of the origin of the respected moral values is distinct from that of the seriousness with which they are taken. Secondly, if we are to speak of 'implicit belief' we shall, in view of what has been said about the annexation of 'anonymous Christians', do well to recall the distinction between the order of being and the order of knowing. Thirdly, I underline the importance of the words concerning a reality 'other than the natural world'. On the one hand this implies a proper counter to naturalism, on the other, from the theological standpoint, it coheres with the idea that the Creator is distinct from the creation, as not only the doctrine of creation, but also those of transcendence and immanence insist. On these last I have written at some length; but since from one point of view this entire book is an implicit protest against naturalism on the ground that its devotees savagely delimit the territory within which rational claims can be made, or, to put it otherwise, devise the rules of the game in such a way that Christians cannot play, I should like to quote A. E. Taylor with approval:

> there is much in human life, including all the thoughts and feelings which have inspired religion in all its forms, which must be dismissed unexamined as mere illusion if our interior life is to be made part of the natural order pure and simple. I do most earnestly protest that it is intolerable presumption in a moralist to assume *ab initio* that there are not influences at work in man's soul (the free grace of God, grace given in response to the prayer of faith, or mediated by the great Christian sacraments, or, for the matter of that, by many another channel) of which, from the nature of the case, scientific determinism can take no account.

To which Taylor adds a footnote: 'For "He giveth not the spirit by *measure*."'[254]

Over the centuries much has been made of conscience as that which somehow receives or processes 'intimations of the divine will'. To Butler, for example, conscience is a 'moral and disapproving faculty' which, 'whether called conscience, moral reason, moral sense, or divine reason; whether considered as a sentiment of the understanding, or as a perception of the heart, or, which seems the truth, as including both',[255] is universally recognized. It is not so common nowadays to think of conscience as a faculty, but the term is still used (after Aquinas) to denote the activity of the mind in making a moral judgement, though frequently with an 'existential overlay'. That is to say, when thinking of conscience we think not simply in the 'coldly' intellectualist terms of moral calculation, but in terms of a personal response to a moral claim which, if we allow it to go unheeded, yields the 'bad conscience' of guilt.[256]

A complete history of the way in which conscience has been regarded would reveal an interesting variety of emphases. For example, to Henry More the Cambridge Platonist there was no question that conscience, as a source of knowledge of what was to be done and as the voice of God, could and did deliver differing answers to Jews, Turks and Christians. He seems quite unperturbed by this, though he makes it clear that reason is to be the final arbiter, and that he is not endorsing the claims to insight of 'mad-men and Fanaticks'.[257] For his part, Locke, ever eager to distance himself from the 'enthusiasts', is more mundane. To him conscience is simply 'our own Opinion or Judgment of the Moral Rectitude or Pravity of our own Actions'.[258] But it was with the inward thrust of the Romantic movement and the development of modern psychology that discussion of conscience burgeoned, with writers on all sides of the theological spectrum, as well as humanists, making their contributions. In John Henry Newman's opinion, for example, conscience is 'a messenger from above';[259] it is 'a connecting principle between the creature and his Creator'.[260] In all of which there is a link between Newman and one at the opposite theological and ecclesiastical pole, James Martineau, than whom few rated conscience more highly. To Martineau conscience is the seat of authority in religion.[261] Whereas 'In the act of Perception we are immediately introduced to an *other than ourselves that gives us what we feel*; in the act of Conscience we are immediately introduced to a *Higher than ourselves that gives us what we feel*.'[262] Thus, 'In the very constitution of the human soul there is provision for an immediate apprehension of God.'[263] Accordingly, 'We *cannot allow* the Conscience to resign for an instant its native right of immediate contact and audience with God: to delegate the privilege is treason, and to quit his eye is death.'[264]

Martineau's position was criticized from a number of points of view, and I have discussed these elsewhere.[265] Suffice it here to say that on the technical point Forsyth, for all that he held Martineau in high esteem, joined those who argued that

> Martineau had never really escaped from the old psychology which set one part or faculty of the soul to judge another. He had never really grasped the truer theory of conscience as the moral consciousness; *i.e.* as the self judging itself instead of one side or section of it judging another.[266]

Henry Sidgwick, himself teleologically inclined, repudiated Martineau's way of reaching moral decisions by recourse to the appraisal of inner springs of interest.[267] But to many the primary difficulty was the practical one that conscience is too easily tamed by ourselves, and that the simple identification of conscience with the voice of God is untenable. To them Martineau himself was 'too easily good'. He did not measure the full horror of sin, and allowed too much to native human goodness. Against him some set the apostle Paul, whose despairing cry was 'the good which I would I do not: but the evil which I would not, that I practise'.[268] In such a plight the last thing one welcomes is further moral guidance, and gratuitous advice from an ethical guru is simply a thorn in the flesh. Paul's way through was to understand that God had given a Saviour who could rescue him.

We here approach the difference which saving faith makes to Christian ethical decision-making. But in order to make the distinction clear let us recapitulate by invoking three writers who will clarify the steps in the progression. First, Robert Mackintosh writes of 'man':

> Whether he hears the voice of conscience distinctly or indistinctly, – whether he obeys it or disobeys it, – whether he interprets it wisely, or misinterprets it, – man knows that he is subject to a law which he did not make, which he can indeed violate, but which he cannot alter.[269]

This, it seems to me, is undeniable. From the Christian point of view it is also undeniable that this experience may be the environment within which the voice of God is heard by those created in the image of God. However, there is no absolute guarantee that the connection will be made and, however it may be regarding the order of being, in the order of knowing many will proceed unaware of, or in denial of, any approach of God and, to repeat, they are not to be annexed as crypto-Christians. John Tulloch, our second witness, therefore, goes too far in saying, 'Does not the very fact of a law within us directly testify to a Lawgiver without and above us? . . . The argument seems irresistible.'[270] But it is quite easily resistible, and many do resist it; for it is not so much an argument as a declaration of faith. It is none the worse for that, but it must not be confused with copper-bottomed demonstration. Thirdly, therefore, the first word in the following statement of H. D. Lewis is the operative one: 'When the voice of God is heard within the voice of conscience it is not the voice of easy accommodation but that of a deepening of all that we readily associate with conscience and with the accumulation of ethical wisdom in the past.'[271]

With this reference to 'deepening' we return to the difference which saving faith makes. Without in any way denying the importance of conscientious moral reflection as, no less than 'natural' reason and aesthetic appreciation, a theatre of operations in which

God the Holy Spirit may work, there is, as in the other cases, a logical gap between the intellectual, aesthetic or ethical contemplation of God and the response in trusting personal commitment to God's prevenient grace. This is why, with the experience of Paul and many others behind him, Forsyth declared, 'The truth of Christianity must rest on a view of life which starts with the primacy and finality of the moral, recognises the wreck of the moral, and presents the grand problem as the restitution of the moral.'[272] As to the solution of the problem: 'the historic revelation in Christ is that the real is what we know as the transcendently moral, the holy. That is the meaning of the Incarnation.'[273] But not the Incarnation in the sense only of the birth of Jesus, for 'The coming of perfect holiness is in the cross of Christ, which at once confounds, crowns, and recreates our moral world.'[274]

It is the response to the claim of holy love, together with the regenerating power of the Spirit, which puts the 'Christian' into Christian ethics. What is granted is not ethical omniscience, for the saints are always sinners, but a fresh motivation and a revived power. For all that we may allow to 'natural' morality, which is not beyond the immanence of God, the Christian ethic requires the acknowledgement of God's holy *agape*, in the light of which our best efforts are imperfect, and our need of atonement plain. Thus, on the one hand, we need to maintain that the person who has made an obediential response to God's grace is differently placed from one who has made no such response. But, on the other hand, this difference must not be advocated in such a way as to suggest either that Christianity supplements the content of natural morality or that Christians seek to prise morality away from everyone else. It seems to me that what happens when natural morality is illuminated by the Christian framework of convictions is that the context, rather than the content, of natural morality is altered. To put it bluntly, the moral is the moral whoever is looking at it. Nor does morality depend upon the confession of religious faith for its existence. But Christian faith sharpens, deepens, personalizes and revises the context of what is already there in the moral: 'Christian morality reaffirms *and* redeems the natural morality of men.'[275]

It goes without saying – or it should do – that such a claim may be made only in the utmost humility, for all is of grace. Nevertheless, as Clement Webb remarked,

> I could not be a Christian if I did not regard Christianity as providing, so to say, a focus from which objects which meet the eye of the explorer of the field of ethics may be seen in their right proportions; yet I neither suppose that all ethical knowledge is historically derived from Christianity, nor yet that historical Christianity has done equal justice to all the ethical principles which it has acknowledged; nor yet that Christianity has nothing to learn in this and other fields from other religions, which have served to convey to the souls which have devoutly practised them a genuine revelation of that divine love and goodness whereof Christ is to me . . . the highest manifestation.[276]

If, finally, we ask what is the context of Christian ethical thought and activity, we find that we have come full circle to the starting point of this study. For the context within which Christians live is one defined by the paradigm of that redeeming, victorious *agape* which finds its fullest expression in the Cross. Those who have by grace responded to what was done there have been called into a community, the Church, for, 'As a matter of fact, the historic effect of Christ's holy work was social at once. It was to create a Society. It crystallized in a Church.'[277] From within this fellowship, Christians, by the Holy Spirit, derive those sanctions and spurs, and receive that encouragement from others, which both support their moral life and give it direction, and prevent the deliverances of natural law from appearing purely theoretical.[278]

Furthermore, that same holy *agape* is what empowers Christians, equipping them with moral insight and providing them with moral courage. From many testimonies to the power of redeeming love I select one from my revered teacher, T. W. Manson:

> The living Christ still has two hands, one to point the way, and the other held out to help us along. So the Christian ideal lies before us, not as a remote and austere mountain peak, an ethical Everest which we must scale by our own skill and endurance; but as a road on which we may walk with Christ as guide and friend. And we are assured, as we set out on the journey, that he is with us always, 'even unto the end of the world'.[279]

In those last few words we have the eschatological note which can never be erased from Christian ethical theory. The Christian's moral actions have more than temporal significance, and to the extent that they are a reflection, however pale, of that *agape* which is their inspiration, it could not be otherwise. For *agape* is the hallmark of that kingdom of which there is no end. Thus, if anyone asks whether Christian ethics are teleological or deontological, the only possible reply is that they are both. There is an objective law, the law of holy love. This is not less, but more demanding than all other codes, which it fulfils. The practical living by this law entails the closest possible examination of such teleological considerations as means and ends – and all in the context of the Christian's framework of convictions. But over and above the temporally teleological there is the claim of my neighbour's and my own *telos*. No doubt a crude religious ethic of rewards and punishments is offensive, not least to non-believing-naturally-morally-aware people. Nevertheless, *the* Christian end of unimpeded eternal fellowship with and service of God, though not a bribe, still less a *quid pro quo*, is a result of that fellowship with God which even now Christians partially enjoy and which, being grounded in holy, victorious *agape*, can be broken by nothing – least of all by death. Small wonder that Richard Baxter put his finger on *the* Christian ethical motive, gratitude: 'Let Thankfulness to God thy Creator, Redeemer and Regenerator, be the very temperament of thy soul, and faithfully expressed by thy tongue and life.'[280] Or, in the stately words of the Second Helvetic Confession which underline Baxter's point and also exclude any idea of quasi-commercial transactions with God where good works are concerned:

> *The End of Good Works.* These same works ought not to be done in order that we may earn eternal life by them, for, as the apostle says, eternal life is the gift of God. Nor are they to be done for ostentation which the Lord rejects in Matt., Ch. 6, nor for gain which he also rejects in Matt., ch. 23, but for the glory of God, to adorn our calling, to show gratitude to God, and for the profit of the neighbour.[281]

Many of the claims made in this chapter are neatly summed up by Robert Mackintosh thus:

> In nature we find suggestions of God; in conscience the postulate of God; in Christ, the affirmation of God. The lower elements of revelation are all but lost apart from Christ; but Christ restores them to their true meaning; and, in having Christ, we have God and His forgiveness.[282]

What is also clear is that by an almost imperceptible progression we have found ourselves thinking in terms of distinctively

Christian religious experience. This chapter must conclude with some further reflections upon this.

VI

Let it be granted at the outset that by treating first of faith and now of experience I may have encouraged the unfortunate impression that these are two entirely discrete phenomena. Such an impression would simply be a function of one's inability to say everything at once. For while it was convenient and appropriate to discuss faith in relation to reason, I did note that when we came to faith as trust, *fiducia*, we were within the orbit of religious experience; indeed, we were actually dealing with it. For the Christian, faith-as-trust is both a personal commitment and belief in One who is supremely trustworthy.[283] As Calvin wrote,

> It is not enough then to have some vague knowledge of Christ, or to engage in airy speculations, as they say, and to be able to talk a lot about him, but he must have his seat in our hearts within, so that we are unfeignedly joined to him, and with true affection.[284]

For the Arminians, John Wesley agrees that faith 'is not barely a speculative, rational thing, a cold lifeless assent, a train of ideas in the head; but also a disposition of the heart'.[285] Trusting in the God whom Christ makes known is at the heart of Christian experience. The individual's response to God's revelation is involved, and this revelation we have already sufficiently discussed. From that discussion it is clear that Christian beliefs are neither derived from Christian religious experiences (though they may be confirmed by them), nor are such beliefs simply ways of speaking of the Christian's personal experiences.[286] There is a historical rootedness about the revelation in Christ which precludes such possibilities.

Bold though the foregoing statements sound, it is by no means suggested that where the term 'religious experience' is concerned all is plain sailing. Its range of meaning is wide and although, since I am concerned with commending the Christian faith my emphasis will be upon Christian experience, I by no means make the utterly false claims that all religious experience is Christian, or that there is no religious experience which is not Christian. Such claims would betoken either genuine ignorance of the existence of other faiths (which in today's world is surely rare) or, what is worse (and sometimes ugly), sectarian partisanship. Nor, in view of what I have said concerning those 'intimations of the divine' on which arguments for God's existence were normally built, need we deny the use of the description 'religious' to those who seek to account for their being moved by the sublime in art or nature. Again, 'religious experiences' have frequently been described – whether by Jonathan Edwards or William James – as in some way 'surprising'. But here we are concerned not so much with such particularly striking manifestations – conversion experiences, mystical experiences, 'voices' – but with continuously lived experience which, often through many viscissitudes and periods of doubt, develops and grows – as one might expect in a relationship deemed to be personal.[287] Further, the experience with which we are concerned is, though personal, not private. It concerns relations with God and with other human beings, and especially with those who comprise the Church. The experience is one of communion with God and with others – a fact which recalls the way in which, in Eastern Christianity, theology is a matter of communion before it is a matter of conceptual formulation.[288] There is an ecclesial dimension to Christian experience which may not be overlooked, and of which more shall be said shortly.

It is already clear that a broad definition of 'experience' is here in view. That is to say, we are not confining our attention to the experimental testing of hypotheses which lend themselves to such scrutiny; nor are we having exclusive recourse to sense data, or to the believer's feelings, though both of these are germane to our topic. Our concern is not with an alleged special religious 'sense' or mode of cognition which yields information of a divine order which would otherwise be unavailable to us. Rather, while acknowledging that there may be, and frequently are, heightened 'moments' in a Christian's experience in which the presence of God is keenly felt in judgement or mercy, in times of joy or sorrow, on occasions of particular challenge, we are concerned with the Christian's experience of life in its manifold relations, and this means openness both to the individual's articulated understanding of what is there to be experienced, and to the question whether or not what is said to be experienced is really 'available' in the way claimed by the believer. To put it otherwise, the question concerns the status of the Christian's claim to experience God as revealed in Christ; or again, it concerns the subject–object relationship inherent in the claim made. After all, 'if we are to have an experience, we must be conscious . . . An unconscious experience is a contradiction in terms . . . To be conscious we must be conscious of something.'[289] It will not, therefore, do to say with the psychologist J. B. Pratt that 'Personal inner experience is the only source from which religion in these days of naturalism and agnosticism, of indifference and hostility, can draw its life';[290] for this might be read as suggesting the obliterating of the objective pole. Far from it: 'The Object of Religious Experience is always God revealing himself, since it is inconceivable that God should be known or experienced except through his own act.'[291] What is more,

> The Gospel is not something which is there for our assent in the degree in which we can verify it by our previous experience either in the way of need or of rationality. Our very response to it is created in us before it is confessed by us . . . Christian experience is the experience of the authority of the Gospel; it is not an experience which becomes the authority for the Gospel . . .[292]

Yet again, we may not overlook the ethical dimension of religious experience, for it is the pure in heart who see God.[293] Small wonder that George Fox, who had more than many to say about religious experience, was moved to exhort Friends in these terms: 'We must not have Christ Jesus, the Lord of Life, put any more in the stable amongst the horses and asses, but he must now have the best chamber, the heart, and the rude, debauched spirit must be turned out.'[294] Our interest, in short, is in the Christian's way of interpreting his or her experience. For an example of this we may turn to the nineteenth-century apologist, Gilbert Wardlaw:

> that man has the experience of a Christian, who, convinced of his condition of spiritual ruin under guilt and power of sin, renounces all dependence upon merit of his own, and trusts for acceptance with God to his sovereign mercy, dispensed through the medium of the great Intercessor; and who, at the same time, depending on the inward aids of Almighty grace, consecrates himself to the service of God in all holy obedience.[295]

Lest any should rejoice that we have just used what is, from their sceptical point of view, a 'weasel word', 'interpreting', we should simply recall our earlier discussion of facticity, and point out with H. P. Owen that 'We could not [even] cognize a congeries of sense-data as a unitary "thing" without an interpretative act of the intellect.'[296]

Underlying my remarks on Christian experience will be the conviction, addressed in Chapter 4 and resumed in the last chapter, that the restriction of 'experience' to 'sense experience' – a hostage to fortune let loose by Locke[297] with consequences, via Hume and the positivists that Locke did not foresee and would almost certainly have abominated – may not be permitted to rule out of account either the aesthetic and moral experience with which this chapter was earlier concerned, or religious experience which occupies us now. There is nothing original in this appeal for a holistic approach to experience; it was, as we saw, advocated by C. B. Upton in his Hibbert Lectures of 1893.[298] Again, the eminent Methodist John Scott Lidgett declared that 'The Christian consciousness stands for the apprehension of a relationship, which answers the question of the reason, satisfies the needs of the heart, and indefinitely raises the moral stature of character and life.'[299]

In what, more precisely, does the Christian experience consist? Since Christianity is not unique among religions in yielding a subjective experience of something taken as objective, in having historical rootedness, in being in some sense communal, we are led to the basic claim that Christian experience is of God known through the Christ of the Bible[300] by the illumination of the Holy Spirit. It is an experience of the God confessed as graciously active in the Cross–resurrection event, and ever present with the believer. It is, in fact, the experience engendered by the Gospel of God's grace. With that Gospel Chapter 2 of this book was concerned, and I repeat words quoted there:

> The early Christians were sure of two things, that through Christ they had found God, and that Christ was living: I believe it was fundamentally for those two things that the affirmation 'Jesus is Lord (*kurios*)' stood, the tense as well as the predicate being stressed. As their conviction, those two things were interpreted facts of their experience, and I think that to be a Christian means that one interprets one's own experience similarly.[301]

In thus expressing himself, Geoffrey Nuttall admitted that his might appear as an unfashionable individualism at a time when 'community' was in the air. But I do not see why the Church may not be conceived of as a fellowship of those, claimed by grace, who interpret their experience along the lines he suggests. There need be no disjunction here. Unquestionably, it is on the basis of the twin conviction spelled out by Nuttall that Christians view their life and, indeed, the course of history. They may elaborate upon their conviction in a variety of ways, of which only the briefest indication can be given. With Paul, the erstwhile persecutor of Christians, they may, for example, speak of their having been adopted as sons or daughters of God, of having Christ living in them; in Johannine terms they may refer to their abiding in Christ, to their life as, consequently, eternal; with the author of Hebrews they may think in terms of their place within a succession of saints of all ages. In Christ they find their moral ideal; in his life and teaching their example; in his death and resurrection their abiding hope and their confidence over against the 'problem of evil' that if an intellectual solution is frequently unavailable to the question 'Why [in the sense of, for what purpose?] do the righteous suffer?' the practical answer supplied by the Cross, 'because Christ is raised we shall be raised', suffices. All of this, they believe, is brought home to them by the Spirit through the Word, and, in company with others likewise called, they confess their faith, testify to God's love and mercy, and encourage one another in Christian living, witness and service. As they go forward they find that guilt and fear are dealt with, and the resources for the fulfilment of their calling are made available. In more technical language: justified by grace through faith, they are on the path of sanctification, and Christ, their great high priest, intercedes for them. Christian experience is thus something given in Christ, and something into which we grow; and as we grow, the genuineness of the initial experience is remarkably confirmed.[302]

I am well aware that the language I have just used and the claims I have just made may not be expected to command the assent of naturalists, materialists, positivists and others. The things of which the Christian speaks *ex hypothesi* do not fall within their experience, and their epistemological parameters are designed to exclude such testimony, as we have seen. But this does not license Christians to make claims about, or on the basis of, Christian experience which are unhelpful, misguided, impossible to substantiate. A hasty review of a miscellany of matters will make the point.

First, to return to a suggestion already made in passing: Christian theology entails reflection upon Christian experience: 'redemption comes before theology',[303] but Christian doctrine is not derived from human experience. It is a matter of God's revelation. Moreover, while, as has just been pointed out, some of Christianity's doctrines may be confirmed in Christian experience – the doctrine of forgiveness, for example – others, among them the creation of the world and the pre-existence of Christ, are beyond verification by such experience.[304] On the other hand, received teachings are interpreted in the light of current experience and in relation to diverse contexts – hence the difference of confessional emphases through time and from place to place discussed in Chapter 3. Our current experience does not always endorse the terms in which our forebears confessed the faith and hence we cannot always feel comfortable when reciting their confessions, singing their hymns or using their prayers. At this point we have to call to mind the continuities supplied by the continuous confession through the ages of Christ as Saviour and Lord, the continuous practice of worship and sacramental life and, above all, the eternal reality of the One of whom, in Christ, we have our experience. If these matters are forgotten we may well find the fulfilment of Forsyth's cautionary words: 'A faith merely experimental becomes merely empirical, and at last dies of secularity.'[305]

Secondly, while all Christians confess that Christ is Saviour and Lord, they do not all enjoy precisely the same particular experiences, nor do they experience life in exactly the same way. Christians are therefore ill advised to require very specific experiences as mandatory for fellowship, or as indications of the genuineness of faith – yet such impositions have been made, and the result has sometimes been an unfortunately stereotyped expression of Christian experience. This is not to deny the truth of H. P. Owen's observation that 'the only *saving* form of experience is one which issues in a transformed character (or at least in the beginnings of such a transformation)'.[306] From this point of view, and on grounds of ecclesiastical integrity, David Jones of Pen-Rhiw, a pioneer missionary to Madagascar, was quite in order to write to David Bogue concerning King Radama in these terms: 'I would not even admit *him* as a Christian convert unless I should find clear evidence of his true conversion & that he was really sensible of what I teach him from the Bible.'[307] The difficulties arise when very specific requirements are made – whether by Dutch pietists of the eighteenth century who denounced F. van Leenhof to the point of excommunication for denying that gloominess is a sign of true piety,[308] to present-day charismatics, some of whom elevate *glossolalia* into a test of the genuineness of others' faith. The eighteenth-century Welsh evangelist Howell Harris expected certain specific experiences of his budding preachers: 'Was cutting to the young students that go forth to preach without knowing their own misery, or Christ.'[309] But few carried matters to such introspective lengths as William Huntington and William Gadsby. To the former specific experiences were required as indicating that one was 'safe' – a policy which led in a number of cases to depression and lack of assurance; while in a sermon on 'The wrestlings of Naphtali' the latter laid it down that 'every quickened soul must be brought to feel that he is lost, helpless, and ruined, and desperately ruined too; and that there is no more ground for hope in self than there is for Beelzebub!'[310] When such a view is coupled with the Gadsbyite conviction that the Gospel is for 'sensible' sinners only, and that 'sensible' sinners meet the experiential requirements, we can see how easily neurotic introspection and personal distress might follow. Not indeed that such outcomes are confined to those of the Gospel Standard Baptist tradition. Wherever there are exaggerated experimental expectations, similar results may occur. Thus, for example, during his teenage years Joseph Parker, later to become minister of London's City Temple, read Bunyan's autobiography, *Grace Abounding to the Chief of Sinners*, and was for a period in great distress because he felt that he ought to be passing through similar spiritual crises, and was not doing so: 'So I stood outside the gate, crying bitter tears, because I had not sinned according to the magnitude and quality of another man's transgression.' Eventually he came to see that such patterning was not required. The general cautionary word to any who may suppose that favoured specific experiences are badges of Christian 'soundness' was uttered in his characteristically blunt way by P. T. Forsyth: 'Look to the Gospel and it will see to the experiences.'[311]

Thirdly, there can be such an over-emphasis upon experience as originating in, and in some authors almost confined to, feeling, that an unfortunate imbalance is introduced into both general witnessing and the apologetic commendation of the faith. In this connection Schleiermacher has sometimes been presented as the culprit. As is well known, Schleiermacher seeks to counter that rationalism which he feels has completely undermined the ontological, cosmological and teleological arguments for the existence of God, and to do so by showing religion's cultured despisers that what rationalism has demolished was not true religion at all: 'belief must be something different from a mixture of opinions about God and the world, and of precepts for one life or for two. Piety cannot be an instinct craving for a mess of metaphysical and ethical crumbs.'[312] He shortly underlines the point: 'Quantity of knowledge is not quantity of piety.'[313] At the same time, he does not wish to be misunderstood as separating knowledge and action from piety,[314] and we shall soon see the importance of this policy statement that perception, feeling and action, though not identical, are nevertheless inseparable.[315]

In 1821 Schleiermacher's *The Christian Faith* was published, and a second edition of it appeared ten years later. He here builds upon his earlier work and, in particular, proclaims his celebrated account of the essence of piety, namely, that it is 'the consciousness of being absolutely dependent, or, which is the same thing, of being in relation with God'.[316] He later speaks of a 'feeling of absolute dependence'.[317] Whatever may be said about the place which Schleiermacher accords to feeling, the point I wish to underline at present is that it is relational; there is an objective God; we are not submerged in a sea of subjectivity. This confirms the position he reached in his earlier work. He exhorts the cultured despisers of religion to

> Remember in the first place that any feeling is not an emotion of piety because in it a single object as such affects us, but only in so far as in it and along with it, it affects us as revelation of God. It is, therefore, not an individual or finite thing, but God, in whom alone the particular thing is one and all, that enters our life . . . [T]he true nature of religion is neither in this idea [that is, the 'deistic' idea of 'God as one single being outside of the world and behind the world'] nor any other, but immediate consciousness of the Deity as he is found in ourselves and in the world.[318]

Consistently with this, and from a distance of twenty-two years, he explains that

> in the first instance God signifies for us simply that which is the co-determinant of this feeling, and to which we trace our being in such a state; and any further content of the idea must be evolved out of this fundamental import assigned to it.[319]

There is a God who is known, though not from without, but from within. When an individual is conscious of God, revelation has occurred – though, again, not in the sense in which God intervenes from without. Here is the heart of Schleiermacher's Romanticism and the crux of his anti-deist protest.

It would be a grave injustice to Schleiermacher were we to suppose that his 'feeling' lands him in individualism. On the contrary, he is a faithful churchman, and his ecclesiology and his understanding of the new humanity in Christ entail the fellowship of Christians one with another.[320] Moreover, Schleiermacher's intention is to maintain that the historic Christ possessed 'an absolutely powerful God-consciousness',[321] and that our consciousness of grace is bound up with 'the peculiar redemptive activity of Christ'.[322] I should like to advance three considerations in opposition to those who consider that Schleiermacher is an unmitigated subjectivist.

(*a*) There is the semantic consideration. In the eighteenth century 'feeling' connoted more than 'having an emotion'. Thus, Schleiermacher

> defined the sense of utter dependence not as though it were an abstract proposition, but as an existential awareness that the whole of one's spontaneous activity came from a source outside oneself . . . this is best understood as Schleiermacher's paraphrase of the statement that in God we live and move and have our being.[323]

Similarly, Rupert Davies has explained that 'When Charles Wesley wrote "My God, I know, I feel Thee mine", he meant by the second verb that he was aware of the nearness and fatherly love of God in the whole of his being, not in his emotions alone', and, moreover, that the important thing was not that he and others had the experience, but that God had wrought it in them.[324] In the light of this semantic discussion, G. D. Hicks is wide of the mark when he writes, 'In speaking of a "feeling of *dependence*" Schleiermacher had, in fact given his case away. Mere feeling could not proclaim its own nature'.[325] Schleiermacher is not concerned with 'mere feeling' in Hicks's sense.

(*b*) Schleiermacher is by no means as metaphysically 'innocent' as has sometimes been supposed. This case was argued long ago by Robert Franks, who utilized italics to add strength to his words: '*Schleiermacher's psychology of religion had a metaphysical basis.*'[326] He justifies his claim by reference to Schleiermacher's *Dialektik* and *Entwurf eines Systems der Sittenlehre*, which were published in 1839 and 1835 respectively. In the former our knowledge of the world and our action in it are discussed in detail and are shown to depend upon our oneness with the universe, while in the latter the way in which our entire experience is determined by that unity is explained to Schleiermacher's own satisfaction. Franks sees these matters as consistent with Schleiermacher's earlier remarks on intuition and the feeling of absolute dependence, of which I cite the following as examples:

> At length your consciousness is finally determined as one or the other, as intuition or feeling. Then, even though you have not quite surrendered to this division and lost consciousness of your life as a unity, there remains nothing but the knowledge that they were originally one, that they issued simultaneously from the fundamental relation of your nature. Wherefore it is in this sense true what an ancient sage has taught you, that all knowledge is recollection.[327]

Again, Schleiermacher speaks of piety as 'a submission to be moved by the Whole that stands over against man',[328] and declares that 'If man is not one with the Eternal in the unity of intuition and feeling which is immediate, he remains, in the unity of consciousness which is derived, for ever apart.'[329]

(*c*) It is worth emphasizing that Schleiermacher thinks that there is much more to religion than the cultivation of pious feeling, and the strain of activism which accompanies his teleological understanding of the Kingdom of God implies a stern rebuke to any who would simply bask in godly feelings:

> With faith the will for the Kingdom of God has come into existence. This creates for every believer, in view of his individual situation in the world, challenges to activity in the Kingdom of God, answering to the powers at his command and his knowledge of the conditions by which he is surrounded.[330]

There is more than a little resemblance here to the position advanced by Jonathan Edwards: '[A]s true religion is practical, and

God hath so constituted the human nature, that the affections are very much the springs of men's actions, this also shows, that true religion must consist very much in the affections.'[331]

So much for an attempt to qualify some of the criticisms which have been made of Schleiermacher's understanding of religious experience.[332] A nagging feeling persists, however, that although, as H. R. Mackintosh put it, Schleiermacher's over-all intention was to regard feeling as 'a mode of objective apprehension, a species of emotional perception or awareness of spiritual things', and to understand God 'as confronting the soul in His real and infinite causality',[333] his statements are frequently made in psychological terms from which the knowledge component is all but excluded. He thus makes much more of the work of Christ within us than of the work of Christ for us;[334] and as for the means by which we acquire religious beliefs:

> He speaks as if all religious beliefs, or at least all doctrines, were got by *reflection upon* our religious experiences. They are 'utterances concerning religious states of mind'. But that is an absurd description. Religious doctrines are not primarily about states of the human mind, but about objective divine realities, God and His ways and His works. Schleiermacher knew that well, and in the actual working out of his system of theology he is better than his theory.[335]

If Schleiermacher thus leaves us with certain ambiguities, there can be no question that some of his successors, departing from the eighteenth-century connotation of 'feeling', determinedly made personal religious experience the sole ground of religious conviction. What Dilthey wrote of Schleiermacher applies with even greater force to such successors:

> Schleiermacher's type of piety removes from religion all will to grasp the essence of God in a relation of obedient direct knowledge. It fails to provide an explanation of the objective certainty which we find in the ethical religions that they have understood the Will of God and therefrom received an impulse to subdue the world to this divine Will.[336]

Paterson aptly contrasts Schleiermacher with Calvin in this respect:

> What Schleiermacher was impressed by in Christian experience was in truth an important fact – it was the same fact which impressed Calvin when he studied the content of the believing mind and heart, and was

> aware of a joyful feeling of assurance that a divine work of reconciliation and regeneration had been wrought, and that it had been wrought by the instrument of the Word of God. The difference was that while Calvin rightly interpreted the feeling as a finger-post pointing to the mine of revealed truth, the subjective school in its typical representatives had looked upon it as being itself the spiritual mine.[337]

A hostage to fortune was thus presented to all those critics who wished to dismiss claims to the knowledge and experience of God as mere psychologism, and to point to bizarre experiences as having a warrant on a par with those claimed by Christians if the mere having of an experience is the guarantee of the claim it is alleged to justify. For a popular example of the problem consider the Primitive Methodist minister Mr Hancox who, according to Peter Dean, minister of the Unitarian church in Walsall, advised his audience that

> if anyone puzzled them with questions as to the inspiration of the Bible, they were to act as some man who said, 'I cannot answer, but (placing his hand on his heart) the secret lies here.' Acting in this way, what superstitions may not be held? The believer in Papal infallibility, transubstantiation, witchcraft – anything, might say – 'I cannot answer it, but I feel it here.'[338]

This leads us directly to our next point.

Fourthly, the so-called argument from religious experience does not demonstrate the existence of God, for it falls at the hurdle of psychologism: the charge that the Christian is merely reporting his experience, not proving that God exists. I do not at all deny that, as in the case of the other theistic arguments, contemplation of the argument from religious experience may prompt an individual's religious quest, and many stimulating discussions of the argument are available.[339] Nevertheless, of the religious believer John Hick rightly said that 'He lives in the presence of God, though he is unable to prove by any dialectical process that God exists.'[340] For this reason Forsyth said that 'Our proof of Him is little more than setting forth in an orderly or impressive way the situation or experiences in which He is borne home on us. It is not a case of syllogism but of observation and experience.'[341] If this be granted the sting is drawn from a number of anti-theistic challenges. Thus when A. G. N. Flew asks, 'How and when would we be justified in making inferences from the facts of the occurrence of religious experience, considered as a purely psychological phenomenon, to conclusions about the supposed objective religious truths?'[342] we may reply that to the Christian God is not an inference drawn from experience; rather, he is encountered in all our human experience.[343] But from the fact that God is known 'inwardly' we need not conclude with the sceptic that religious experience is thereby suspect; for since everything that we know is inwardly experienced, the denial of any aspect of our experience is to that extent a denial of an objective order as such. And those who wish to deny such an order usually seem happier if there is someone else around with whom they can argue the point! Similarly, if the complaint of circularity be made, namely, that our religious experiences are interpreted in the light of beliefs already acquired, and therefore we cannot invoke our experiences in justification of our beliefs, we can reply only that all thought is thus circular, and that not all circularity is vicious. Thus, for example, 'The "laws" of science are generalisations from particular observed events, but the events are explained and understood scientifically in the light of the "laws".'[344]

I have just uttered 'encounter' language, and thereby hangs a tale. It is a tale which is commonly thought to have begun with Martin Buber's celebrated distinction between 'I–Thou' and 'I–it' encounters, though among trains of thought which lie behind Buber's writings is Franz Rosenzweig's theory that dialogue with God is a possibility for people.[345] Prominent among British theologians who propounded encounter theology were D. M. Baillie and his brother John, and H. H. Farmer, who owed an intellectual debt to John Oman.[346] It was not until the 1950s that analytical philosophers trained their sights upon such theologians. Thus, for example, C. B. Martin rebukes Farmer for his view that 'All the basic elements in our experience are incommunicable' on the ground that 'Just in so far as the experience of God is unique and incommunicable in this way, then just so far it is not to the point in supporting the existential claim "God exists".'[347] A similar conclusion is reached by Ronald Hepburn, who fastens upon the point that if we are liable to be mistaken when we think we are experiencing other persons as they really are, how much more so when we claim to be experiencing God.[348] However, it should be pointed out that Farmer, like other encounter theologians, is not intending to demonstrate God's existence on the basis of religious experience. On the contrary, as John Hick explained in defence of his teacher, Hepburn has 'considerably simplified and overstated the position which he opposes', for Farmer holds that theistic proofs are 'as religiously improper as they are philosophically inadequate'. Accordingly, he seeks

> to present Christian theism as a coherent possibility, which gains the believer's allegiance through the compelling quality of his own religious experience, and which finds confirmation both in the pragmatic outworking of his faith and in rational reflection upon human experience as a whole. This is not a way of thinking which eschews logic and relies solely upon a unique, incommunicable, self-certifying experience of encounter with God.[349]

The concept of a self-authenticating experience is a further red rag to the analytical bull. Peter Donovan has responded to Hepburn's and Flew's charges in this connection. The latter writes:

> If Farmer were right in thinking that Christian experience of God must be self-authenticating then the proper conclusions would be that there could not be such an experience: for, in so far as it is experience of God in the sense which involves the actual existence of the object, it cannot be self-authenticating; whereas, if it really is to be self-authenticating, it cannot demand a reference to an actual God.[350]

Donovan replies that Farmer uses the phrase 'self-authenticating' once only, adding that 'Farmer's point is that if what Christians believe is *true* then experience of God, being *ex hypothesi* interpersonal experience, can logically (i.e. "in the nature of the case") be expected to have the distinctive features of interpersonal awareness.'[351]

Flew would retort that no matter how real Farmer's and Baillie's experiences may be to themselves, is it not the case that 'to the outside observer it must seem that they are just imagining things? For there is nothing there which he can discern for them to be having their personal relations with.'[352] Clearly, however, Flew's 'outside observer' is one whose constricted epistemology, like that of others we have earlier considered, excludes from the outset the kind of experiences which the Christian actually has. Philosophers who cannot accommodate both the sensory and the spiritual are, with some justification, labelled 'single-environment' philosophers by Bernard Ramm.[353] Long before Flew (though in full awareness of agnostic, positivist and naturalistic criticism) Scott Lidgett bluntly averred that the Christian 'cannot even in consideration of an unbeliever ignore the experience upon which his whole case must rest'.[354] With an equal measure of godly defiance H. R. Mackintosh spelled out the nature of the Christian's experience of being 'in Christ':

> This is an experimental truth, against which the argument of this or that man that he does not have any such experience has no cogency. Men do pass out of themselves to make the will of Christ theirs and their will His; having died with Him they also live with Him. In him they share the relationship of sons [and, as we should nowadays add, daughters] of God, and are supported in the struggle with self and evil by His sympathy and communion. They share, they really share, His conflict and His triumph . . . As members of His body they are His hands and His feet, doing His will for men.[355]

Two very important points follow. First, to repeat, the Christian's experience is not of an undifferentiated deity or a Greek or deist 'Being'; it is of the God made known in Christ, with all that that entails concerning the witness of the life and ministry of Jesus on the stage of human history – the subject of Chapter 5 above. This means among other things that although in using 'encounter' or 'meeting' language with reference to God the Christian is employing an analogy, the human pillar of the linguistic bridge, so to speak, is not as weak as has sometimes been supposed by those who demand independent 'external tests' of religious experience. Secondly, with the last of Mackintosh's sentences just quoted we come to the ecclesial dimension of Christian experience, and this we may relate to a final challenge sometimes posed to Christians (or other religious believers): if the experience which you claim to enjoy is as important as you say it is, show us how others can acquire it.

As already explained, Christianity, though personal, is not private; it is life in a community of faith. Indeed, 'You cannot have for ever or for long the Christian experience of God without the Divine Society that is the result, the assurance, and the vehicle of that experience.'[356] The challenge that Christians show others how they may come by religious experience is often voiced by those who think in terms of specific (even odd) experiences, and think of them in an individualistic way.[357] But it is not nonsensical to think in terms of shared experience mutually communicated by one to another by means of language (spoken or visual) in an interpersonal social act. It is a philosopher's abstraction to worry over much about the analysis of 'same' in the question 'Is A having the same experience as B?' Empirically (a word which may appeal to many such analysts) it would seem that when a goal is scored at a football match both elation and despair are experiences shared according to which team the persons experiencing the emotions support. The fact that I cannot experience my neighbour's experience directly is not significant because we *judge* the nature of a person's experience not by somehow commandeering his or her experience, but by the attendant evidence – by the jumping up and down in glee when the goal is scored, or the sitting morosely, head in hands, for the same reason.[358] The moral is that 'part of the world of common experience for each of us is the rest of us'.[359] But, of course, from the fact that a number of people claim to be sharing an experience of God's grace in Christ it does not follow that they are so doing: fifty million Frenchmen can be wrong. No doubt if there are sufficient numbers of such witnesses, if they are trustworthy and if there testimony is consistent, the difficulty is somewhat mitigated and, as Trueblood says, 'It is possible that they are all deluded, but it is important that we know how many men and what sort of men we are accusing when we say this.'[360] The problem is, however, that there are numerous, genuine and internally consistent persons who subscribe to faiths other than the Christian, and thus the question of the truth of the content of the confession is clamantly raised. To this last point I shall return in the next chapter.

Again, it is possible to seek certain experiences, for example, that of being healthy. In this quest many thousands, having gorged themselves over Christmas and having guiltily made New Year resolutions, sign on at gymnasia. In the past, perhaps some were impressed by that 'triumph of medicine', Scott's Emulsion, which, according to page 1 of *The [Charlottetown, PEI] Daily Examiner* for 25 April 1895 had been proved by experience 'not only to stop the progress of Pulmonary Consumption, but by its continued use, health and vigour could be fully restored'. On page 4, however, we learn that Mrs R. S. Bowness died aged forty-four: 'Consumption was the cause of death.' Did she seek health and vigour by taking Scott's Emulsion? Did she take it and it failed to live up to the advertisement's promise? We shall never know. But experiences can be sought, with or without success. Where Christian experience is concerned the placing of oneself within earshot of the Gospel in the context of an encouraging Christian fellowship may be a first step towards receiving the experience which (if only for the sake of argument) some sceptics say they wonder how to obtain.[361] Of course, grace is ever a free gift, not an acquisition; placing oneself, in the right spirit, within the worshipping community is a necessary, but not a sufficient condition of success; however, according to Augustine and countless others, the sincere seeker has already been prompted to seek, and the promise remains intact: those who seek find:[362] 'Hence the witness-bearing of a Christian before the world is an appeal to latent powers and sources of perception in every human breast.'[363] This I take to be one more way of adverting to the *imago dei*. Where the seeker is concerned the first experience may be as described by Forsyth:

> It is only when we set about repenting or loving with all our heart, soul, strength and mind that we discover our impotence to do either, and therefore realise the prime necessity of what most sharply differentiates the best Theism from evangelical faith. We can neither repent nor love with our might till we have come to terms with that holiness in God which assumed in the Cross its own complete satisfaction and power.[364]

But this implies that 'We cannot have Christian experience except by appropriation of Christian truth',[365] and once again the cognitive import of experience is to the fore. But so also is that further challenge I posed in connection with ecclesially shared experience: do not all religions claim truth? Why should one of them be more trustworthy than any of the others? What are we to say about this, given our earlier reservations concerning properly basic beliefs? I shall return to these questions in the conclusion, but I wish to sum up much of what I have been saying concerning Christian experience by referring to a particular concept (sometimes misunderstood by Christians themselves): assurance.

VII

According to a prominent line of pre-Reformation theologians, assurance, or certitude, in matters of faith was not to be sought, and could be dangerous. Hence Augustine's caution: '[T]hat which the apostle says, checks many from mischievous elation: "Wherefore let him who seems to stand take heed lest he fall."'[366] Hence also Bernard of Clairvaux's much later explanation that 'God denies us assurance, but only that he may prevent us from growing careless.'[367] The heirs of the Reformation, on the other hand, have generally endorsed the position implied in H. R. Mackintosh's rhetorical question, 'When we look believingly at God in Christ, where is the presumption in being quite sure of His compassion to the sinful?'[368] At the fountainhead of this departure from the older line of thought stands Luther who was convinced that, although it would indeed be presumptuous to indulge in the prideful boast that one is of the elect, and although sin ever seeks to drag Christians down, God's promise is sure, that by grace through faith people are put right with God and are eternally secure. The ground of their assurance, therefore, is not in themselves or their feelings or actions, but in Christ their righteousness. Calvin underlines the point:

> no one, except he be blinded by presumption, and fascinated by self-love, can feel assured that God will be a rewarder of his merits. Hence this confidence of which we speak recumbs not on works, nor on man's worthiness, but on the grace of God alone; and as grace is nowhere found but in Christ, it is on Him alone that faith ought to be fixed.[369]

Consistently with this the Genevan Catechism of 1541 characterizes true faith as 'a sure and steadfast knowledge of the love of God toward us, according as He declares in His gospel that He is our Father and Saviour (through the mediation of Jesus Christ)'.[370]

To this point we see that the objectivity of assurance is emphasized: the focus is upon that of which Christians are sure. It has, however, been shown that from Beza to the Heidelberg theologians there was a turn from Calvin's Christological grounding of assurance to a more introspective understanding of the matter, coupled with a concern on the part of Christians to 'establish that God has called and chosen you'[371] by the utilization of spiritual gifts.[372] Thus in what is probably the most experimental and pastorally sensitive of all the Reformed catechisms, the last part of the answer to the Heidelberg Catechism's first question reads: 'by His Holy Spirit [God] also assures me of everlasting life, and makes me willing and ready in heart henceforth to live for him'. The subjectivist strain flows down through the years, greatly influencing the Gospel Standard Baptists, as we have seen. But there have always been cautions uttered against undue subjectivism. Thus, for example, Craig's Catechism of 1581 asks 'What are the grounds of our assurance?' and concisely answers, objectively, 'God's promise, His Spirit in us, and our Mediator'. More fully, the Westminster Larger Catechism teaches that

> Those who truly believe in Christ, and endeavour to walk in all good conscience before Him, may, without extraordinary revelation, by faith grounded upon the truth of God's promises, and by the Spirit enabling them to discern in themselves those graces to which the promises of life are made, and bearing witness with their spirits that they are the children of God, be infallibly assured that they are in the state of grace, and will persevere unto salvation.[373]

The denial of the necessity of 'extraordinary revelation' is significant given that the Catechism was produced at a time when sectaries of many kinds were claiming to have received precisely this; but the main point to note is the careful balancing of objective with subjective considerations.

Against any who might lean too far towards subjectivism, the Puritan Thomas Brooks declares that

> To make sense and feeling the judges of our spiritual conditions, what is it but to make ourselves happy and miserable, righteous and unrighteous, saved and damned in one day, ay, in one hour, when sense and reason sit as judges upon the bench?[374]

For his part Thomas Watson, taking a cue from others before him, constructs a syllogism in answering the question 'What is assurance?'

> It is not any vocal or audible voice, or brought to us by the help of an angel or revelation. Assurance consists of a practical syllogism, in which the word of God makes the major, conscience the minor, and the Spirit of God, the conclusion. The Word says, 'He that fears and loves God is loved of God;' there is the major proposition; then conscience makes the minor, 'But I fear and love God;' then the Spirit makes the conclu-

> sion, 'Therefore thou are loved of God;' and this is what the apostle calls 'The witnessing of the Spirit with our spirits, that we are his children.' Rom. 8: 16.[375]

Enough has been said to show the balance which many sought to strike between that of which we are assured (the objective) and our personal certitude (the subjective).[376] As Forsyth put it,

> All certainty is necessarily subjective so far as concerns the area where it emerges and the terms in which it comes home. The court is subjective, but the bench is not. Reality must, of course, be real for me. It must speak the language of my consciousness. But it makes much difference whether it have its *source* in my consciousness as well as its *sphere* . . .[377]

More pithily he declared, 'The seat of revelation is in the Cross and not in the heart.'[378] In the last resort, 'when the faith of the New Testament is victorious in us, we know that it is not our *experience* of Christ that matters but our experience of *Christ*'.[379]

However, as every Christian knows, the New Testament faith is not always completely victorious; there are degrees of assurance, and Christians are not immune from doubt. This point has been addressed on numerous occasions. Thus Calvin insists that weak faith is real faith, and that 'however much we are shadowed on every side with great darkness, we are nevertheless illumined as much as need be for firm assurance when, to show forth his mercy, the light of God sheds even a little of its radiance'.[380] 'There will be sometimes a trepidation', writes Thomas Watson, 'but [the Christian] is safe amidst fears and doubts; as a ship lies safe at anchor, though shaken by the wind.'[381] For his part, Baxter offered practical advice:

> Are you willing to have Christ to pardon, sanctify, guide and save you, or not? If you are, then you are a true believer and did not know it. If you are not, if you will but wait on God's word in hearing, and reading, and consider frequently and seriously of the necessity and excellency of Christ and glory, and the evil of sin, and the vanity of the world, and will but beg earnestly of God to make you willing, you shall find that God hath not appointed you this means in vain, and that this way will be more profitable to you than all your complainings.[382]

The possibility that religious doubt may accompany undue subjectivism was not lost on Samuel Walker, bishop of Truro, who has this to say about the Methodists, who define faith, prior to evidence of sanctification, as 'a *sure confidence* of God's love to *me*': this definition

> hath had this effect with most of the Methodists I have conversed with, that they have thought believing to be feeling, and faith by them hath been placed in the affections instead of the heart; the consequence of which hath been doubting, when the stir of the affections hath been less.

In other cases, 'this account of faith hath produced hard judgments; for, if a sure confidence of God's love to me be the essence of faith, then whoever want it are unbelievers'.[383] We are back once again to specific feelings and experiences as (sectarian) terms of fellowship. The injunction of Thomas Watson, that wisest and pithiest of Puritans, stands: 'The jewel of assurance is best kept in the cabinet of a humble heart.'[384]

Whatever the individual Christian's feelings or circumstances – happy or sad – Christian assurance derives from the heart of the Gospel, namely, that in the life, death and resurrection of Christ God has made himself savingly known: which returns us to the starting point of this enquiry, and urges us to its conclusion.[385]

IV

CONCLUSION AND EPILOGUE

Few of us have been trained in ways of distinctively Christian thinking about God and ourselves and the world in which we are set.

(Daniel T. Jenkins, *Prayer and the Service of God*, 1941)

For one's own part, one would thankfully spend one's whole life till one was spent out, for the privilege of removing a single obstacle from the path of hearts seeking God.

(Robert Mackintosh, *Albrecht Ritschl and his School*, 1915)

8

Conclusion: World-view, Context and Truth

In this book I have been concerned with the prolegomena to Christian apologetics. I set out from the idea that apologetics, the intellectual commendation of the Christian faith, is but one aspect of that confession by word and deed of Christ as Lord and Saviour which is the task and privilege of the whole Church. It further seemed to me that we should do well to enquire at the outset what it is that Christians wish to commend. Hence the discussion of the heart of the Gospel. This in turn raised the important question of the socio-political-intellectual context in which the confession is made, with all that that implies concerning the variety of verbal formulation through the Christian centuries. I then asked, 'Who are the confessors?', and proposed that they, and those whom they address, are created in the *imago dei*, one consequence of which is that they share epistemological common ground, apart from which the apologetic task would be ruled out from the start. It became clear, however, that, like the basic Christian confession, Christian anthropology has been discussed in different accents in different times and places. Variations in formulae and practice notwithstanding, I argued that it was legitimate to speak of the same faith through the ages.

It was next necessary to investigate some of the presuppositions of Christian confessing. I selected two for consideration: that it is possible and permissible (*pace* positivists, 'Wittgensteinians' and postmodernists) to understand Christian discourse – supremely that employed in worship – as referring to God; and that God, though transcendent, is both immanent and active in human history.

The long-standing apologetic starting points of reason and aesthetic, moral and religious experience were next reviewed, and the proposal was that while God's revelation in Christ must be the starting point if what is commended is to be Christian, we need not, in view of the *imago dei* and the extra-ecclesial work of the Holy Spirit, be sceptical regarding the place of natural theology and the several varieties of experience as media through which God may address honest seekers, notwithstanding the fact that neither the traditional theistic arguments nor claims to particular kinds of experience will by themselves yield copper-bottomed demonstrations adequate to convince the unbeliever, or even arrive at the Christian God. The relations of reason, revelation, faith, knowledge and experience all fell within our purview.

Throughout I have sought to illuminate the discussion by reference to the heritage of Christian testimony on the several points at issue. But I have also made every effort to hear and to take account of what intellectual opponents (within and without the Church) have had to say, often permitting them to speak in their own words. Insofar as I have succeeded in my project, I have shown that a reasoned eclecticism, which takes its starting point from the assurance that Jesus Christ is Lord and Saviour, or, perhaps more informatively, from the Cross–resurrection event, and then, having regard to the witnessing context, draws in appropriate ways upon the deliverances of human reasoning and experience, offers a viable method of commending the faith in an intellectual environment.

This is the most, perhaps, that can be expected of a book concerned with the prolegomena to Christian apologetics. I am well aware that I have mentioned the problem of evil only in passing, and that I have not discussed such specific questions as providence, immortality and the like at all. But I hope that I have shown the basis upon which such work may proceed, and that I have drawn the sting of some of those who say that the project is doomed from the outset.

I should like in conclusion to suggest (*a*) that the proposed method renders the articulation of a Christian world-and-life-view possible; (*b*) that such an undertaking must, in the present environment, take with full seriousness the presence of religions other than the Christian, and face up to the scandal of particularity; and (*c*) that since all religions and many non-religious systems of thought claim internal coherence, the question of truth cannot with integrity be evaded.

I

In a chapter entitled 'World Views' W. F. Zuurdeeg utters a cautionary word.[1] He points out that in 'The sentiment of rationality'[2] William James speaks of a conception of the frame of things, modes of conceiving the cosmos, a conception of the universe, ultimate explanations of the universe, and a philosophy; and that in his *Science and the Modern World*[3] Whitehead utilizes the following expressions: view of the world, scheme, cosmologies, effective outlook, intuitions as to the nature of things, ultimate ideas and cosmological scheme. However, 'Neither of these authors seems to have taken the trouble to define any of these concepts, each taking it for granted that his meaning was well understood.' Zuurdeeg further observes that the German dictionaries of the time, not least the dictionaries of philosophy, deprive their readers of a clear definition of *Weltanschauung*. A more recent publication defines the term as 'a general view of the universe and of man's place in it which affects one's conduct'.[4]

There is widespread agreement that, although the use of the term did not originate with him, Dilthey did much to popularize its use. In his opinion world-views, derived as they are from our experience of life, and hence historically conditioned, provide interpretative pictures in the light of which we may order our thinking and set out practical objectives. The most prominent world-views, he claims, travel under one of three headings: naturalism, vitalism and idealism. They are subjective, they do not admit of rational demonstration, and they are relative to the individual in his or her situation.[5] It was precisely the relativism of world-views as thus described which prompted Husserl to repudiate Dilthey's position. Where Dilthey drew a distinction between world-views and *Philosophie* – the latter being the rationally grounded exposition of objective truth – Husserl sought a comprehensive account of things which would embrace the individual's knowledge, affections and actions – the individual being not, so to speak, a prisoner of fluctuating history, but an (idealistic) observer of the world of human existence.[6] In different accents Reformed thinkers in the line of Kuyper have had much to say on the subject of world-views, understanding by the term 'some overarching, guiding and directing vision of life' in terms of which 'we experience the world'.[7]

It would seem that there is ambiguity in much of the discussion of world-views. Sometimes the emphasis is upon the starting point of reflection, or what N. H. G. Robinson called 'a basic apprehension of the universe and of our place in it, which provides the context of every action and the presupposition of every investigation'.[8] This basic apprehension is given in our experience, and in the light of it we may develop an articulated view of the world. This objective does not seem very far removed from that sought by R. F. A. Hoernlé, who declared that 'To philosophise is to *seek* an attitude towards the universe as a whole, or, in so far as the search at all succeeds, to have such an attitude.'[9] In other writers the term 'world-view' is used of a person's account of 'what it all comes to' – his or her 'philosophy of life'. Let us examine the situation a little more closely.

At a time when some analytical philosophers were tending to rejoice that their discipline had no practical usefulness, H. H. Price reassured the 'plain man' that he was not out of order in asking the philosopher to help him in his quest of a synoptic view of things. There is, said Price, a synoptic as well as an analytic clarity.[10] C. D. Broad likewise argued for the value of speculative philosophy, albeit not at the expense of critical philosophy: indeed, he did not think that the time was ripe for over-much speculation. Nevertheless, speculative philosophy encouraged thinkers to take a synoptic view of the world, and 'anyone who does not do this at some time in his life is bound to hold a very narrow and inadequate idea of Reality'.[11] Elsewhere he cautioned would-be speculators that it is not their function qua philosophers to produce a *Weltanschauung* on demand in an attempt to stop the leak in the ship of civilization; nor should they suppose that any speculative view they did adumbrate would necessarily be to the liking of Western Europeans and Americans. Finally, he noted the dire consequences which can follow the embracing of certain world-views.[12] Few did more in the middle of the last century to reflect upon the nature of world-views than Dorothy Emmet and H. A. Hodges, and to them I briefly turn.

In Emmet's opinion, we are well advised to understand a world-view as being an interpretation of life rather than an explanation or hypothesis. She grants that her definition implies a concession to relativism, but she regards it as true to the facts to hold that there is a particular kind of spiritual or intellectual experience which excites a philosopher, and from the standpoint of which a *Weltanschauung* is constructed.[13] The metaphysician, she continues, must make as careful an analysis as possible of forms of thought and experience, and then convey an account of what it all amounts to in the form of a 'total assertion'. She explains that

> A partial assertion is either a proposition stating matter of fact or a logical proposition which can be brought into a coherent system with other propositions of the same type. A total assertion cannot be verified; it expresses a judgment concerning the nature of something as a whole.[14]

Professor Emmet elsewhere amplifies her position by suggesting that a metaphysical system is a *Weltanschauung* based on analogy with something that has seemed significant to the metaphysician. We are thus not surprised to note her emphasis upon the fact that 'world' in 'world-view' is not used merely cosmologically. It includes an attitude towards life which is related to an intellectual scheme. A total assertion will serve so long as light is thrown upon the partial assertions which are accumulated empirically, and so long as further thought is stimulated:

> When [total assertions] cease to do this they will not be disproved but abandoned as irrelevant. But perhaps in the end the point at which we can say with most confidence that positive ground has been gained is in our better understanding, through its conscious articulation, of the experience from which the analogy has been drawn.[15]

For his part, Hodges understands human beings as purposeful and responsible. They take up an attitude towards life and to the world around them: 'The basic assumption, the resulting aims and methods, and the way of seeing things to which these in turn give rise – all this together is what I mean to designate by the word *standpoint*.'[16] He further explains that a standpoint need not be wholly expressible in cognitive statements; it may include elements of value judgement or volitional determination. Thus, 'Every philosophical or religious system, every intellectual or aesthetic tradition, every civilization or culture, may . . . be seen as the embodiment of a distinctive standpoint.'[17] Standpoints may be characterized by the language used to articulate them, and by words which are peculiarly their own. We may provide supporting arguments to justify the choices of standpoint we make, but such arguments are persuasive only, they do not logically demonstrate the rightness of our choices.[18] This is not to open the door to irrationalism, it is simply to recognize the fact that 'will, in the form of interest, attention, and acceptance, goes before *ratio*, and determines its possibility'.[19] As R. M. Hare remarked, 'there is no distinction between fact and illusion for a person who does not take up a certain attitude to the world'.[20]

It would seem in the light of the foregoing discussion that there is advantage in distinguishing between the basic insight in the light of which all else is viewed, and which everyone has whether it is recognized or not; and the articulated synoptic, integrative, interpretative account of 'what it all comes to' which fewer are called upon to offer. This is consistent with my view expressed at the outset that there are 'varieties of gifts', and that no adverse judgement is called for upon those whose gifts take them in other directions – and this despite what persons as eminent as McTaggart and Hocking have said.[21] Much more congenial are the views of William Wallace, who recognized that God, 'if He come at all, comes altogether, in the lowest as in the highest, sooner perhaps to the day labourer than to the speculative thinker';[22] and O. C. Quick, who lamented that 'The metaphysician fails to sympathise with the grocer'.[23] Day labourers and grocers have nothing to fear from the account here being presented. The implication of this is that the basic assumption or insight is a great leveller, and where Christianity is concerned there is much to be said for referring more specifically to the fundamental assurance which the believer has – construing assurance along the lines discussed in the preceding chapter. There is a psychological certitude (if not absolute epistemological certainty) in the believer's stance; there is confidence in owning Christ as Lord and Saviour; there is the recognition of God's grace active and victorious at the Cross; there is the challenge to walk in a particular way. These are ingredients of the basic apprehension at whose root is assurance. Launching out from this confidence, some will attempt an articulated account of how the world looks from this particular perspective. To resume Dorothy Emmet's point, 'world' will be construed in a more than cosmological way, for account will have to be taken of the several ranges of experience we have discussed, the specific points at which the Christian faith is challenged, and the dimension of the supernatural which cannot be excluded if the Gospel is to stand. In addition, the implications of the world-view for ethics, politics and the like will have to be shown in any statement which claims any degree of comprehensiveness. In the course of this work it may well be wise to relate to alternative world-views. There is common epistemological ground with those who embrace them, and it may often be possible to draw analogies between the deliverances of one world-view and another. But that this is analogical work, and not simply the one-for-one adoption of terms, must ever be remembered, because as, for example, became clear in *Philosophical Idealism and Christian Belief*, the absolute of the idealist is both like and unlike the God of Christianity. The basic apprehension is justified insofar as the scheme erected upon it is adequate to account for what happens in the world and in believers, is internally coherent and, in view of the *imago dei* and general revelation, is communicable (analogically where necessary) to others. It is no small part of commending the faith to present such a scheme to others. Not, indeed, that the scheme as such will convert anybody. The other person has his or her basic assumption, and to exchange one such assumption for another is more than simply a matter of changing one's mind on this or that ingredient in the scheme. Christians themselves may do that as their experience of Christian living develops. We do not choose our basic assumptions in the way we choose our socks: there is no Olympian vantage point from which we review all conceivable basic assumptions and then pick one. How, then is the Christian's basic assumption obtained? We are back to revelation, and response,[24] as a long list of witnesses testify. Forsyth declared that 'A philosophy can bring us to no security of a revelation; but a revelation develops a philosophy, or a view of the world'.[25] James Orr specified some of the details of such a view:

> He who with his whole heart believes in Jesus as the Son of God is thereby committed to much else besides. He is committed to a view of God, to a view of man, to a view of sin, to a view of Redemption, to a view of the purpose of God in creation and history, to a view of human destiny, found only in Christianity. This forms a 'Weltanschauung', or 'Christian view of the world' which stands in contrast with theories wrought out from a purely philosopical or scientific standpoint.[26]

A few words of caution are in order at this point. A Christian's articulated world-view will always be incomplete. This is partly because we are human and God is God, and we are in no position fully to comprehend him; partly because we are to varying degrees incompetent in what we actually manage to do; partly because none of us can intellectually encompass all of the empirical phenomena and issues of all kinds which an absolutely comprehensive world-view would accommodate – 'An intelligence before which the whole plan lay bare would be the intelligence not of a metaphysician, but of God'[27]; partly because our own ever-changing life situation causes us to review and modify our opinions on many things; and partly because of temperamental differences between the commenders of the faith which incline some, like the Polish Brethren of the sixteenth century, to adopt the posture of seekers open to further truth, while the Hutterites sought to preserve the truth which they were convinced they had received.[28] These considerations also explain why Christians may produce articulated world-views which, while they flow from the same basic assurance, take so many forms and reach conclusions which are in places contradictory. To take two examples: writing in the tradition of Christian Platonism, W. R. Inge declares that

> The truest view of the world is that which sees in it a system of law – not, however, in the limited sense in which naturalists talk of natural law, but as a system of harmonious values, which may be classified under three heads – the Good, the True, and the Beautiful.[29]

Alternatively, while

> Christian Platonism interprets Christianity primarily in terms of Truth; Forysth interpreted it primarily in terms of Grace; the one inclines to a theology of evolution, the other to a theology of crisis; the one to a gospel of Incarnation, the other to a Gospel of Redemption and Atonement.[30]

All the more important, therefore, that those called to commend the faith by articulating a Christian world-view should ever humbly recall that people are not saved or damned in accordance with their acceptance or rejection of particular accounts of the Christian *Weltanschauung*. It nevertheless remains the case that, while it is true that

> a personal relationship to God and to other human beings lies at the heart of Christianity . . . it by no means follows that any attempt to work out a synthesis in the light of Christian faith is to embark on a project contrary to the spirit of the Christian religion.[31]

One final important point remains to be added. I have spoken of the basic assurance on which Christians build the superstructure of their world-view. I would point out, however, that on the one hand Christians proceed on the basis of an underlying certitude (however unsure they may from time to time feel themselves to be). They do not regard their faith as a hypothesis which may at any moment require revision or even rejection in the light of fresh evidence. An exception to this general rule would be a believer's consciously standing back and reflecting upon his or her world-view in relation to those of others.[32] On the other hand, from the point of view of those to whom they are seeking to commend the faith, their exposition will appear as a hypothesis which they are being invited to consider as a way of accounting for things and life as they are. It is therefore in the best interests of both parties that the commendation should be as sincere, humble and generous-spirited as possible.[33] As for the believers themselves, they do well to remember that their shared basic assurance is of primary importance, and the superstructures they erect upon it should not be elevated into fortresses of sectarianism.[34] However secure the basic assurance, the superstructures are provisional and subject to modification, as suggested above.

II

An important aspect of the present-day context in which the Christian faith has to be commended is that Christians are not the only religious persons in the world. The presence of people of many religions challenges Christians to review their attitudes and to find a way of reckoning with this fact in their view of the world. This is a subject on which a vast amount has been written during the last thirty years, and I shall not add significantly to it here. I feel, however, that it is better to acknowledge the importance of the matter in this book than to pass it by altogether. I shall therefore set down a few bald theses before coming to the crucial question which the presence of those of other faiths poses to those who would commend the Christian faith.

First, the Christian doctrines of creation, of humans as created in the *imago dei*, of the extra-ecclesial work of the Holy Spirit, of the cosmic implications of the Cross, positively require Christians to treat those of other faiths with dignity (which includes not patronizing them by suggesting that they are 'anonymous Christians'), to approach them in friendship, to regard them as neighbours. All of this involves facing up to the challenge that 'It is difficult to believe in a thing passionately and to want others to believe it too, but still to respect their personality and spiritual autonomy and seek only to persuade them, and to win their willing mind.'[35] It also properly implies a cordial openness to those of other traditions, some of whom may have an equally passionate desire that Christians come to see things from their standpoint. But all of this sharing turns upon the fact that there is epistemological common ground, and, in some contexts, that there are common socio-ethical objectives, however much the accounts of their motivations may differ between a Christian, say, and a Buddhist. It should no longer be necessary to remind people that, as Vivekananda said with reference to the first Parliament of Religions in 1893, 'holiness, purity, and charity are not the exclusive possessions of any church in the world and that every system has produced men and women of the most exalted character'.[36] This is precisely what, on Christian grounds, we should expect, the possibility notwithstanding that all faiths have produced a crop of hypocrites too. Thus the Quaker Josiah Coale said that the (Native American) Indians amongst whom he found himself were 'more sober and Christ-like toward us than the Christians so-called'.[37]

Secondly, it will not do, and can appear to be insulting, to regard all religions as spokes of a wheel, all of them leading to the hub. From the side of Buddhism D. T. Suzuki has been criticized for being so keen to build intellectual bridges between East and West that he overlooked the fact that the respective intellectual traditions are not only different but mutually contradictory at many points.[38] Within the West John Hick has similarly been criticized for positing the Eternal One beyond all particular religious expressions to which all faiths witness in their equally valid ways. In the course of a concise statement of his position he writes, 'God is neither a person nor a thing, but is the transcendent reality which is conceived and experienced by different human mentalities in both personal and non-personal ways.'[39] Some critics have replied to the effect that this position is unacceptably relativist, pointing out that it obscures the fact of significant differences between what the several religions actually believe.[40] I cannot here pursue this matter further.

My main concern is with the issue announced earlier regarding the way in which Christianity's neighbours of other faiths (including humanism, New Age and many others) raise clamantly the question of truth. For although I have said that the articulation of a Christian world-view will ideally be internally coherent, other faiths can make the same claim. As Howard Root said long ago, 'If there are no grounds for believing that a Christian scheme is preferable to some non-Christian one, the choice between Christianity and some other religion (or none) becomes arbitrary, irrational, even trivial.'[41] I have already commented on the question of how far we choose a world-view. My point now is that Christians (and many others) wish to say not only that their scheme is coherent, but that its principal claims are true. What are we to make of this?

III

First, we must reaffirm the view that, while internal coherence of a world-view is a feature devoutly to be sought, there can be many coherent world-views developed from a variety of basic assumptions, some of them mutually exclusive. Thus in the Christian case we have to say that if what I have called the basic assurance – an apprehension concerning who Christ is, what God has accomplished in him and my affective response to this – could be shown to be ill-founded then the articulated world-view derived from it, however internally coherent, would be worthless. The entire edifice would, for example, be demolished if it could be conclusively shown that Jesus never lived, and hence did not do at the Cross what Christians claim he did. The Christian world-view depends upon certain things having been done in the midst of human history. In this respect Christianity differs from some other world-views which are more exhaustively intellectualist in content. But it is precisely this 'scandal of particularity' which has proved so offensive to some. It is a running theme of John Hick, for example, that it is preposterous to suppose that salvation turns upon allegiance to the founder of a religion which, in numerical terms, is a minority in the world.[42] But this leads me to my next point.

We shall not make much headway unless we distinguish clearly between the epistemological and the soteriological questions. These are often mingled in unhelpful ways. My question is not, 'Is there no salvation outside of commitment to Jesus Christ?' It is, 'What are we to make of the multiplicity of claims to truth which the several world-views currently adumbrated advance?' Several replies have been offered to this question. H. A. Hodges, for example, fully recognizing that inner consistency cannot be the criterion of a world-view's acceptability, proposed the existential test, namely, that the standpoint 'should open up possibilities of life, experience, and activity'.[43] While one might hope that a world-view would have this effect, the fact is that any number of world-views might have it, and relativism looms once more. Moreover, Hodges's existential test, unqualified in any other way, might appear to countenance the most perverse and cruel ideologies which, to some people, have afforded what they have construed as possibilities of life, experience and activity. We might then find ourselves justifying the demonic along the sentimental lines 'It does not matter what you believe or do, so long as you are sincere.' I do not see how we can responsibly skirt the question of truth. After all,

> Religious faith is not merely a way of looking at the world; it claims in some sense to be an insight into or discernment of the way things are [in the case of Christianity, I should say 'a discernment of what has been done in Christ'], and the truth of beliefs about the way things are cannot be read immediately from the experience itself.[44]

Even if a person becomes committed to a particular religion for the best of reasons (that is, the person is not behaving irrationally) it does not follow that the claims of the religion are true.[45]

Recognizing the drawbacks of coherence as a justifying principle, many, at least from Aristotle's hints onwards, have set great store by truth understood as the correspondence of our ideas and claims with things as they are in 'reality'. The pursuit of this policy is by no means unproblematic, not least because, as we have seen, if there is no such thing as an uninterpreted fact, we are already presupposing a criterion of truth in determining that *x* is a fact.

But where correspondence with the ideas of a transcendent yet immanent God is proposed, the case might seem doubly complicated. Let us try to grope towards a possible way forward.

If it is the case that God reveals, whether by action or proposition or both, there must be recipients of the revelation. But the recipients, because of perversity, the noetic effects of sin, intellectual incompetence or bias may, so to speak, only partially hear what is being 'said' or see what is being 'shown'. This is why what is believed to have been revealed at some time in the past is subject to later correction, as when Jesus drives to the heart of the old law – 'You have heard that what our forefathers were told . . . but what I tell you is this . . . '[46] – or when he tells stories to the same effect: doubtless the priest, the levite and the Good Samaritan would all have assented to the proposition that one ought to love one's neighbours, but they differed as to who qualified as 'neighbour'.[47] The upshot is that, while in principle there will be correspondence between God's ideas and the believer's, and since God is the God of truth the believer's convictions will be true insofar as they accord with God's ideas, in practice the correspondence will be less than perfect for the reasons given. To put it otherwise, if, in Christ, God has revealed something of his nature, mind and purposes to ourselves and to others – a possibility which already reintroduces what I have said concerning religious experience – then we may be assured that there is correspondence between the basic Christian claims concerning the Gospel and things as they are. Furthermore the idea of correspondence in the sense described is not only compatible with the main thrust of Chapter 4 above – namely, that Christian discourse refers to One over against us – but it entails the maintenance of the Creator–creature distinction: something that the Christian idealists found so hard to do.[48]

Precisely because individual acts of judgement and interpretation are involved in receiving God's revelation, and because these acts are subject to error and revision, we are returned to the ecclesial dimension of confessing and commending the faith; for it is within the fellowship that we adjust our imperfect grasp of God's revelation to others' accounts of it, have our more wayward interpretations corrected, and, by reflecting prayerfully on the Gospel, the heritage of Christian testimony and the context in which we are placed, come to a point where we can say with some confidence, 'It seemed good to the Holy Spirit and to us . . .' As David

Burrell has written, 'We might say, mimicking Wittgenstein, if truth is to be had, it will only be had in a tradition, within a community, in the company of friends.'[49]

Another way of expressing the point is to say that the assertions which comprise the Christian confession are articulated responses to the God of truth, and in one of its biblical senses, 'truth' refers to God's integrity, faithfulness, reliability.[50] It is a presupposition of the Christian revelation that God does not wilfully mislead us. None of this is to deny that some Christian claims are impossible to corroborate. The assertion of the eternity of the Son, 'There never was a time when the Son of God was not', comes to mind. But from the fact that we cannot corroborate a claim it does not follow that it is not true as an implicate of the faith.[51]

Positively, the point is that

> Truth is centrally related to salvation, rather than to a metaphysical system. Truth is evaluated not simply in its relationship to a reality conceived in a metaphysical sense and clearly graspable by the human mind, but also in its relationship to the mystery of Christ now living through his Spirit and, as such, not identifiable with any metaphysical system.[52]

In other words, for the Christian 'truth' ultimately concerns the heart of the Gospel, and at the heart of that is Christ, who called himself the truth:[53] 'Jesus is not the truth because His teachings are true. But His teachings are true because they express the truth which He Himself is.'[54] In him the God of truth (faithfulness) is most clearly seen and is savingly active – that is the Christian conviction, which must be articulated with sincerity, grace and joy, but also with respect to one's readers or hearers, and to the context in which one is working (the dialogue consultation is not an evangelistic rally). The importance of respect to one's hearers and readers – especially those of other faiths or of none – cannot be over-estimated, for it would be quite wrong, and in contradiction of the Christian understanding of the *imago dei*, general revelation and the work of the Holy Spirit to suppose that they know nothing of the truth, albeit what they have received has come to them along other channels. As Calvin wisely remarked, 'If we regard the Spirit of God as the sole fountain of truth, we shall neither reject the truth itself, nor despise it wherever it shall appear, unless we wish to dishonour the Spirit of God.'[55] At the same time – and here we are back to the scandal of particularity – Christians are making a claim not simply of an intellectual kind, but about things which have been done once for all in the midst of human history, and what has been done is said to have cosmic significance. More particularly, they are making a claim on the basis of a lived experience of personal relationship with the One about whom the claim is made: 'The believer is incorporated into this truth, when he transcends (without betraying) the scientific attitude in the act of faith.'[56]

However, is not an apparently privileged relationship with a person as incipiently imperialistic as an apparently absolute claim to truth? David O'Toole has gone so far as to say that the claim that one possesses the truth is inherently violent, and he cites the experience of the Sioux nation vis-à-vis the Christians whom they encountered.[57] We may allow a scholar of North American frontier missions to explain:

> The difference between Christianity and civilization did not exist in the minds of nineteenth-century Protestant missionaries and their white audiences . . . As the missionaries entered the frontiers, they planned to convert the natives *and* to help them adopt Canadian and American societies' dress. Habitation, manners, and customs . . . After all, 'as far as the temporal welfare of man is concerned, the history of the past demonstrates that even the worst form of Christianity is preferable to the best form which heathens ever know.'[58]

On this I should like to make a number of comments. First, there can be no question that on many occasions in their history Christians have been shockingly ill behaved, and have acted in such a way as to deny the Gospel they claim to profess. Secondly, there have ever been Christians who, sometimes at personal risk, have sought to counter the excesses of their co-religionists. Thirdly, we are all children of our time – a platitude which should engender a certain humility when we judge our forebears in the faith, if only because we do not know in connection with which of our own ideas and practices our successors will think, 'How could they have been so stupid not to have seen that?' The Church is ever catching up with the Gospel. Fourthly, we must try to understand that if our forebears believed, as many of them did, that unless people repented and were converted they would go to eternal torments, an urgent – even a 'violent' – attempt to rescue them from such a fate might be construed as a loving action, on analogy with saving a person unwittingly about to plunge over a precipice. Fifthly, we should note that some of those who on some occasions are quick to denounce earlier missionaries for their violence are the same ones who urge the Church to take a stand – even a revolutionary (and so far violent) one – against injustice, presumably believing that the end justifies the means (which is just what the earlier missionaries thought in relation to hellfire). Finally, and above all, we must draw a distinction between Christianity and Christ. Clearly we should not have the former without the latter, but Christians by no means make perfect witnesses, and Christ, who is the prince of peace and a Lord who stoops to do servants' work,[59] adversely judges a Church which proceeds by any other than the way of love.

But this leads us directly to the last point concerning 'truth', and here a biblical scholar may help us:

> Truth in the intellectual sense is far from being all that man needs; the primary thing is not to understand and make sense of the universe, but to know God and live a good life, and Christ's work is directed towards this end (John 17: 3) . . . Truth so understood is a stimulant to conduct rather than a matter for contemplation; something which we do, to be obeyed or disobeyed (John 3: 21; I John 1: 6; cf. also Gal. 5: 7, I Pet. 1: 22). It makes men fit not only for good living in fellowship with one another, but fit also for divine life in fellowship with God . . .[60]

The truth is something to be done in the sense that our actions accord with, exemplify and can withstand the scrutiny of it.

From many quarters the point is underlined. Thus, according to the Cambridge Platonist John Smith,

> There is a knowing of 'the truth as it is in Jesus' – as it is in a Christlike nature, as it is in that sweet, mild, humble, and loving spirit of Jesus, which spreads itself, like a morning sun, upon the souls of good men, full of light and life . . . There is an inward beauty, life, and loveliness in Divine truth, which cannot be known but when it is digested into life and practice.[61]

Tillich explains that the Johannine 'doing the truth' is not a matter of obeying the commandments. Rather, it means 'living out of the reality which is *He* who is the truth, making His being the being of ourselves and of our world . . . If the real, the ultimate, the divine reality which is His being becomes our being we are in the truth that matters.'[62] Indeed, it was precisely because his fellow Seekers had converted Christian living into an external legalism that Francis Howgill of Grayrigg exhorted them thus:

> Why trim you yourselves with the saints' words, when you are ignorant of the life? . . . Return home to within . . . and here you will see your Teacher not removed into a corner, but present when you are upon your beds and about your labour, convincing, instructing, leading, correcting, judging, and giving peace to all that love and follow Him.[63]

In different accents the moderate Calvinist Baptist Andrew Fuller reminded his contemporaries that there was 'a strong presumption' in favour of a system which promoted love, holiness and faith, and against any system which did not. And when, in his *Strictures on Sandemanianism*, he expounds the biblical idea of the 'heart' as presupposing the intellectual faculty but focusing upon the will and the affections rather than upon the understanding, he seems to anticipate Kierkegaard's later talk of a person's existing either in the truth or in sin – the latter constituting inauthentic existence.[64] All of which brings us back to the human condition, the need of grace, and the Gospel from which we set out.

Fuller's point also reminds us that the articulation of a Christian view of the world, however coherent, and however devoutly believed to be at least to some degree grounded upon claims which are in correspondence with the mind of God, will not and cannot function as a coercive demonstration of the truth of those claims. But there is more to 'truth' than logical demonstration; more to faith than intellectual assent; and those who by grace have heard God's call know that 'Where reason fails with all her powers / There faith prevails and love adores.'[65] They also take up the challenge of living in the truth, ever hoping that their lives will not altogether give the lie to their words.

IV

My method in this book has been to set out from the Gospel which Christians actually confess, and to take with full seriousness that assurance, the product of sovereign grace, in which their lives and their view of the world are rooted. At the same time, I have sought to avoid that sectarian exclusiveness which would inhibit if not altogether prevent the commendation of the faith to others. Indeed, I would claim that on occasion I have sought to keep doors open when others would have placed methodological obstacles in front of them, whether from within (Barth and others) or without (some positivists, Wittgensteinians and postmodernists) the Christian fold. No doubt the closing of doors prevents draughts, but the resulting atmosphere can become very stuffy. On the other hand, the attempt to keep doors open, albeit on good theological grounds concerning the *imago dei*, general revelation and the extra-ecclesial work of the Holy Spirit, may be taken by some Christians as an effective way of admitting intellectual tendencies which will result in the attenuation, if not the complete undermining, of the Gospel. But it need not be so, and for those who would commend the faith intellectually (which, to repeat, is neither the task of every confessor nor all there is to commending the faith) it need not be so. It is not irreverent to suppose that the Spirit of truth, who blows where he will, and is competent to 'guide us into all the truth',[66] is more than capable of nudging us towards a reasoned eclecticism which takes account of the transcendent yet immanent God who, on the basis of his self-revelation in history and in our rational, aesthetic, moral and religious experience, we rightly address as Father. Our scheme will be as coherent as we can make it, and we may hope that it will not be too foreign to the truth of him who is Lord and Saviour. While maintaining a reverent agnosticism before ultimate mystery, we know enough, and a reasoned eclecticism need not be a haphazard muddle. Rather, we may hope that its content and manner will not utterly disgrace that holy, redeeming love, supremely active at the Cross, which is its mainspring.

As for the trilogy, of which this volume is the final part: it has been to a considerable extent a tale of alternative apologetic starting points. In attempting to adjudicate upon these I have on many occasions felt myself to be walking a tightrope. I welcome Locke's endeavour to show the reasonableness of Christianity even though I feel constrained to set out from the Gospel rather than from a psycho-epistemological enquiry. If we set out from the question 'What do, or can, human beings know?' we may well find that scepticism is the unavoidable undertow, and that any revelation (sometimes inadequately construed as propositions requiring assent) will somehow have to be wedded to our otherwise anthropocentric epistemology. While greatly valuing the Enlightenment protest in favour of the importance of the individual conscience in matters of faith, over against untoward authorities whether biblicist or ecclesiastical, I stop short of rational*ism*, and consider that the individual's conscience is most happily exercised and schooled within the ecclesial fellowship. Again, I applaud the way in which the Christian idealists engaged with the thought of their day, friendly and hostile, though the tendency of their philosophy (if not of their actual religion) inclined them to blur the Creator–creature distinction, and to draw the sting of sin by making evil but a stage on the way to a greater good. Among the lessons to be learned from them is that the 'absolute' of philosophy is not the God of Christianity, and that when utilizing terms from other thought systems or world-views we must ever heed the fact that we are engaged in an analogical task, that there are disanalogies too, and that where loan terms are concerned we are not so much poachers as anabaptists.

For all that may be learned from them, it seemed to me that in their different ways both Locke and the Christian idealists of the period 1870–1954 (the latter year being that of the long-lived Clement Webb's death) confessed more than could comfortably be accommodated within their chosen philosophical methods. It therefore occurred to me that the question from which a Christian apologetic ought to set out is, 'What, in history and in the life of believers, has God done in Christ?' More succinctly, 'What is the Gospel?' It is on the basis of what has happened that the primary Christian confession, 'Jesus Christ is Lord and Saviour', is made, and it is this confession which is to be commended to others. As we saw, the posing of the question led directly to a consideration of the status of the confessors as members of an ecclesial fellowship, and of their nature, shared with all others, as created in the image of God – with all that doctrine implies regarding epistemological common ground.

To welcome the stringency applied to discourse – not least Christian discourse – by the analytical philosophers is not necessarily to share their presuppositions, whether positivist or 'Wittgensteinian', concerning what, if anything, may properly be said of God; and the salutary reminder from many postmodernists that none of us has a 'God's eye view', that we are neither fully self-conscious Cartesian ponderers nor 'uncontaminated' Kantian agents, need not prompt us to slide into a relativism which should (but, oddly does not always) preclude attempts to use language with referential intent and mount arguments in the hope of persuading others. The queried methodologies would exclude from the outset the confession which most Christians wish to make, and deny their enabled response to, and experience of, God's grace actively revealed at the Cross, as well as their new life of faith-union with their risen and present Lord, who is the truth, who challenges his followers to be in, and do, the truth. While in accord with Barth that, unless God make himself known, we have no knowledge of him at all, I am unable to be as negative as he concerning the traditional starting points of apologetics in reason and moral, aesthetic and religious experience. Not, indeed, that I think that those starting points lead to logical demonstrations of God's existence; but they do witness to factors which must be taken into account (often analogically) in any Christian view of the world, and in any attempt intellectually to commend the faith to others. They also facilitate those dialogues with members of other faiths and of none in which it is incumbent upon at least some suitably equipped Christians to participate if the Christian faith is not to be regarded as that of a ghetto, and if common action on behalf of just causes – those matters which bear upon our shared humanity – is to be stimulated.

I hope that I have made it clear that walking a tightrope is not equivalent to sitting on the fence. While it is my personal view that a fully articulated Christian world-view will be trinitarian in content and pattern – not least because the Father, with whose mind the believer's thoughts are in partial correspondence, is known through the Son by the illumination of the Spirit – my task here has been to recognize that the starting point of the apologist may properly differ from that of the systematician. In other words, if, as has often been said, apologetics leads a person only to the gateway of the faith, my concern is to ensure that believers (not least theologians) understand that the gateway permits both the ingress of new Christians and the egress of believers into the 'world'. Analogously, as we saw at the outset, P. T. Forsyth distinguished between the fundamental truths of the faith which are 'the deep motive of the Church' and 'the first method of the missionary'.[67]

I suppose, somewhat more technically, I have advocated a rooted yet mediating style of commending the faith. While I have found few who have driven so decisively to the heart of the Gospel as P. T. Forsyth, I am unable to be as disjunctive as he quite frequently is. Where he says, 'It is this, it is not that', I sometimes wish to say, 'It is partly this, and partly that'. My impression is that mediators, appearing less bold (or belligerent), have a harder time recruiting disciples. This, however, in no way concerns me. I also suspect that mediators are quite likely to be sniped at from all sides. This, certainly, was the experience of Richard Baxter: 'I will sometimes go on both sides the Hedge, though by so doing I be scratcht.'[68] If I suffer a like fate I shall be honoured to be in the company of the seventeenth century's Reformed pastor *par excellence*. In any case, there is comfort in the thought that if one's reasoned eclecticism should be shown to be faulty, no one's salvation (not even mine) is at stake; and, as another of my guides said,

> Often it is when we do badly, when we ourselves are crushed, when the laugh goes against us – then it is that our witness-bearing is accepted by God, and that some honest heart among our antagonists, looking for truth, perceives in us and in our witness bearing that which cannot be put aside. Christianity is moral and supernatural from first to last, and the apologist constitutes no exception to that great law of the kingdom of God, 'When I am weak, then am I strong' (II Cor. 12: 10).[69]

9

Epilogue

Unusually in a work of this kind, I append an Epilogue in the form of a small anthology of verse. I have constantly reiterated the importance of the ecclesial fellowship, and while the poems I have selected concern death – Paul's 'last enemy', now vanquished – they also call to mind that larger Church of which, even now, Christians believe themselves to be, by grace, a part:

> In the communion of Thy saints
> Is wisdom, safety, and delight;
> And when my heart declines and faints,
> 'Tis raisèd by their heat and light.[1]

In what must surely be one of the most poignant poems in the English language, John Clare (1793–1864), the self-taught poet,[2] who was confined to an asylum for the last twenty-seven years of his life, hopes against hope. Arnold Francis Mee (1901–66), Hebrew scholar deprived of sight, gentle wit, and minister to rural Congregational churches including the historic High Chapel, Ravenstonedale, writes as one whose hope is sure. His forebear in the faith, Philip Doddridge (1702–51), pastor, hymn-writer and Dissenting academy tutor at Northampton, died in such a manner that his widow, Mercy, recalled the quoted verse, which appears in one of his hymns.

The older divines used to urge the necessity of 'making a good death', believing as they did that for most Christians dying constitutes the final apologetic challenge, and affords the last earthly opportunity of confessing and commending the faith. The following verses will thus put a large part of the discussion of my trilogy in perspective, and I leave them to speak for themselves.[3]

I am! Yet what I am none cares or knows,
My friends forsake me like a memory lost;
I am the self-consumer of my woes,
They rise and vanish in oblivious host,
Like shades in love and death's oblivion lost;
And yet I am! And live with shadows tost.

Into the nothingness of scorn and noise,
Into the living sea of waking dreams,
Where there is neither sense of life nor joys,
But the vast shipwreck of my life's esteems;
And e'en the dearest – that I loved the best –
Are strange – nay, rather stranger than the rest.

I long for scenes where man has never trod;
A place where woman never smil'd or wept;
There to abide with my creator, GOD,
And sleep as I in childhood sweetly slept:
Untroubling and untroubled where I lie;
The grass below – above the vaulted sky.

(John Clare, 'I am!')

As one gone blind grows sensitive to hear
And finds new wonder in the power of touch;
So too at night perception grows more keen
And learns new ways of finding out our path:
So, likewise in the soul's dark hour of gloom
We learn to walk alone, by faith, not sight,
Through that strange country where the spirit dwells
Where God comes near as never in the day.
For be the pathway bright, or be it dim,
The dark and light are both alike to Him.

(Arnold Francis Mee, 'Night' (last verse))

Some day the quiet latch will lift,
  And I shall know that he is there;
And greet the long-awaited friend
  Whose coming is the end of care.
So gently will he steal within
  (As soft and silent as the snow)
I shall but raise my eyes and smile,
  And set my hand in his, and go.

(Arnold Francis Mee, 'Death')

When death o'er nature shall prevail,
And all its pow'rs of language fail,
Joy thro' my swimming eyes shall break,
And mean the thanks I cannot speak.

(Philip Doddridge, 'From a Hymn')

Notes

Chapter 1: Introduction

1 Samuel Bourn, *A Charge Delivered at the Ordination of the Reverend Mr. Job Orton; at Shrewsbury, September 18. 1745*, Birmingham: T. Warren, 1745, 44–5. For Bourn (1689–1754) and Orton (1717–83) see *The Dictionary of National Biography*; for an account of Bourn and two contemporary Presbyterian divines, see Alan P. F. Sell, *Dissenting Thought and the Life of the Churches: Studies in an English Tradition*, Lewiston, NY: Edwin Mellen Press, 1990, ch. 7.

2 C. S. Rodd, reviewing Frances Young, ed., *Dare We Speak of God in Public?*, London: Mowbray, 1995, in *The Expository Times,* CVI no. 12, September 1995, 356.

3 Of course, only that can be forgotten which was once known. Because of the expansion (especially in a professional direction) of the theological curriculum during the second half of the twentieth century, and because the total length of the course is generally as it ever was, or is shorter, hard choices have to be made, and it cannot be assumed that traditional core courses – biblical, doctrinal, historical and systematic – receive the attention which once they did. I state a fact, I do not imply a judgement. But this state of affairs does explain a certain gappiness in students' theological experience. I do not nostalgically imply that there were no gaps in the knowledge of past generations of theological students; but, because of the explosion of knowledge, the multiplication of disciplines and the shortage of time, the problem is exacerbated today. See further Alan P. F. Sell, *Conservation and Exploration in Christian Theology,* Caernarfon: Gwasg Pantycelyn, 1993, 11–12.

4 John S. Mbiti, 'Christianity and traditional religions in Africa', *International Review of Mission,* LIX, no. 236, October 1970, 438.

5 P. T. Forsyth, reviewing Robert Mackintosh, *A First Primer of*

Apologetics, in *The Examiner,* 10 January 1901, 222. I owe this reference to Leslie McCurdy. In Forsyth's sights were those liberal theologians who were, as he thought, tailoring the Gospel to suit the predilections of modern people.

6 Not that things antiquarian are to be despised. Whether in biblical studies, church history or theology we need those who patiently deal with the 'bones' – and may their tribe increase. The worth of scholarly findings is not to be judged by the criterion of immediate relevance; but the apologetic task is, by its nature, so to be judged.

7 I sought to show how much intellectual variety there was between some of these who were at one in their Presbyterian allegiance in *Defending and Declaring the Faith: Some Scottish Examples 1860–1920,* Exeter: Paternoster Press, and Colorado Springs: Helmers & Howard, 1987. My present title echoes the earlier one, but is also intended to suggest that an apologetic at the beginning of Christianity's third millennium needs to focus upon that which is positively to be confessed, and to arise from the general commendation of the faith by speech and act which is the calling of the Christian community, from the midst of whom the individual apologist commends the faith as a specific intellectual vocation. I place 'liberal' and 'conservative' within inverted commas in order to signal the fact that these are among theology's most slippery terms, which have often been turned into badges of sectarianism. In what follows the inverted commas will be omitted, but their presence should be understood. See further Alan P. F. Sell, *Theology in Turmoil: The Roots, Course and Significance of the Conservative-Liberal Debate in Modern Theology* (1986), reprinted Eugene, OR: Wipf & Stock, 1998, chs. 5 and 6. For some analogous concerns see Gilbert Ryle, 'Taking sides in philosophy', *Philosophy,* XII no. 47, July 1937, 317–32.

8 See further, on the decline of the evidences, Dale A. Johnson, 'The end of the "evidences" : a study in Nonconformist theological transition', *Journal of the United Reformed Church History Society,* II no. 3, 1979, 62–72; idem, *The Changing Shape of English Nonconformity, 1825–1925*, New York: OUP, 1999. Some apologists down to our own time emphasize the classical arguments of natural theology, while others advance the 'evidences' – miracle, prophecy, the character of Christ. For an example of the former see Cornelius Van Til, *Defense of the Faith,* Philadelphia: Presbyterian and Reformed Publishing Company, 1955; for an example of the latter see Bernard Ramm, *Protestant Christian Evidences,* Chicago: Moody Press, 1953.

9 R. Flint, 'Present-day Christian apologetics', in his *Sermons and Addresses,* Edinburgh: William Blackwood, 1899, 306.

10 William Knight, ed., *Colloquia Peripatetica: Deep-sea Soundings, being Notes of Conversations with the late John Duncan, LL. D.*, Edinburgh:

Oliphant, Anderson & Ferrier, 6th edn. 1907, 170. That such a 'liberal' theologian as Harnack could reveal a certain sympathy with this 'conservative' high Calvinist is clear from his remark that theologians 'only half discharge their duties if they think it enough to treat of the Gospel in the recondite language of learning and bury it in scholarly folios'. See his *What is Christianity?*, London: Ernest Benn, 1958, p. v.

11 W. G. Blaikie, *William Garden Blaikie: An Autobiography*, London: Hodder & Stoughton, 1901, 201.

12 P. T. Forsyth, 'Veracity, reality and regeneration', *London Quarterly Review*, 123, April 1915, 204. As T. F. Torrance has reminded us, a similar position was taken by Hilary of Poitiers, and the Scots Robert Boyd and Robert Leighton. See his *Scottish Theology from John Knox to John McLeod Campbell*, Edinburgh: T. & T. Clark, 1996, 159.

13 Robert Mackintosh, *A First Primer of Apologetics*, London: Andrew Melrose, 2nd edn. 1904, 23.

14 Alan P. F. Sell, *John Locke and the Eighteenth-Century Divines*, Cardiff: University of Wales Press, 1997, 12; cf. 274.

15 A. Campbell Fraser, 'John Locke as a factor in modern thought', *Proceedings of the British Academy*, I, 1903–4, 235.

16 Alan P. F. Sell, *John Locke and the Eighteenth-Century Divines*, 57. This book is, chronologically, the second of the three, though its subject matter is earliest in time. The order of publication is explained by the fact that it took me more years to gather the widely scattered responses to Locke than it did to locate the resources I needed to write *Philosophical Idealism and Christian Belief*. Since the first two volumes can be read as studies in their own right, the order of their appearance is not disruptive: the trilogy is a series, not a serial.

17 W. H. V. Reade, *The Christian Challenge to Philosophy*, London: SPCK, 1951, 117.

18 Perrin J. Spooner, 'Beyond apologetic', *The Congregational Quarterly*, XXXIV no. 4, October 1956, 335.

19 In seeking an apologetic which may be described as a reasonable eclecticism, I may be taken by some as following in the line of Joseph Butler, who wrote in *The Analogy of Religion* [1736], London: Ward, Lock, n.d., 186, 'the truth of our religion, like the truth of common matters, is to be judged by all the evidence taken together. And unless the whole series of things which may be alleged in this argument, and every particular thing in it, can reasonably be supposed to have been by accident (for here the stress of the argument for Christianity lies), then is the truth of it proved . . .' Butler's objective, however, was to meet the deists as far as possible on their own ground, and on the basis of commonly shared convictions, such as that the world was created by God. He fully recognized (p. 192) that 'I have argued upon the prin-

ciples of others, not my own; and have omitted what I think true, and of the utmost importance, because by others thought unintelligible, or not true'. While seeking to understand the standpoints of others, the Christian apologist need not trim on their account lest it become impossible thereafter to introduce distinctively Christian claims. Furthermore, in this post-Christendom age apologists cannot assume that the common ground Butler shared with his deistic contemporaries will be shared by theirs.

20 Cf. Henri de Lubac's essay of 1930, 'Apologetics and theology', reprinted in his *Theological Fragments*, San Francisco: Ignatius Press, 1980.

21 R. Flint, *Theism*, Edinburgh: William Blackwood, 9th edn., 1895, 354 n. ix.

22 Sell, *John Locke*, 277.

23 Idem, *Philosophical Idealism and Christian Belief*, Cardiff: University of Wales Press and New York: St Martin's Press, 1995, 235.

24 Robert Barclay, *An Apology for the True Christian Divinity* (1675), Glasgow: R. Barclay Murdoch, 14th edn. 1886, 9.

25 M. Blondel, 'The letter on apologetics', in Alexander Dru and Illtyd Trethowan, eds., *Maurice Blondel: Letter on Apologetics and History of Dogma*, London: Harvill Press, 1964, 129.

26 Sell, *Philosophical Idealism*, 234.

27 Ibid., 223, and *John Locke*, 274.

28 W. H. V. Reade, *Christian Challenge*, 116.

29 Augustine, *Confessions*, VII. 9.

30 See further Sell, *Philosophical Idealism*, 122–4, 229–30. Some have argued that Augustine did not rebaptize enough neoplatonic concepts – evil as a privation of good, for example. For one such writer see Bernard Ramm, *Varieties of Christian Apologetics*, Grand Rapids: Baker Book House, 1963, 154. On the other hand, Alan of Lille (d. 1203) branded as arrogant those who sought to dress the terms of natural science in theological clothes. See P. Glorieux, 'La Somme "Quoniam homines" d'Alain de Lille', *Archives d'histoire doctrinale et littéraire du Moyen Age*, 1952, 119.

31 *Philosophical Idealism*, p. ix.

32 Although I here express the problem from the point of view of Christian confessing, pre-Christian literature contains examples of those who realized that the erection of certain epistemological boundaries to knowledge would preclude what they knew, or desired to know. The example *par excellence* is Socrates, who tells us that 'When I was a young man I was wonderfully keen on that wisdom which they call natural science, for I thought it splendid to know the causes of everything, why it comes to be, why it perishes and why it exists.' He came

to see, however, that the naturalistic account of causes fell far short of the reasons he sought, and in his quest for intellectual satisfaction he was pressed towards the beautiful and the good. See Plato's *Phaedo,* trans. G. M. A. Grube, Indianapolis: Hackett, 1977, 96, 100. The theme is resumed in the allegory of the cave, *Republic,* VII.

33 M. Sheehan, *Apologetics and Christian Doctrine: A Course of Religious Instruction for Schools and Colleges,* Dublin: M. H. Gill, 1955, 1.

34 See Austin Flannery, *Vatican Council II: The Conciliar and Post-Conciliar Documents,* Collegeville, MN: Liturgical Press, 5th printing, 1980.

35 William C. Placher, *Unapologetic Theology: A Christian Voice in a Pluralistic Conversation,* Louisville: Westminster/John Knox, 1989, 11.

36 Alan Richardson, *Christian Apologetics,* London: SCM Press, 1947, 20, 21.

37 Here, as in the Bible, the term 'saint' is synonymous with 'believer', 'Christian'.

38 Robert Flint, 'Present-day Christian apologetics', in *Sermons and Addresses,* Edinburgh: Blackwood, 1899, 299. For Flint see Sell, *Defending and Declaring,* ch. 3.

39 Ibid., 301.

40 A. B. Bruce, *Apologetics; or, Christianity Defensively Stated,* Edinburgh: T. & T. Clark, 1927, 37. Cf. idem, *The Chief End of Revelation,* London: Hodder & Stoughton [1881], preface to 2nd edn, 1890, p. vii, where, however, Bruce throws the net slightly wider, hoping 'to help men of an ingenuous spirit, troubled with doubts bred of philosophy or science, while morally in sympathy with believers'. For Bruce see Sell, *Defending and Declaring,* ch. 5.

41 P. T. Forsyth, *The Person and Place of Jesus Christ* (1909), London: Independent Press, 1961, 84. See further Sell, 'P. T. Forsyth as unsystematic systematician', in Trevor Hart, ed., *Justice the True and Only Mercy,* Edinburgh: T. & T. Clark, 1995, esp. 126–34. Of course, the liberals thought that they were making Christianity more intelligible to 'modern man', and demonstrating its compatibility with the best thought of the age. A glance at Abelard's *De unitate et trinitate divina* will swiftly dispel any thought that this is a modern motive only.

42 John Sutherland Black and George Chrystal, eds., *Lectures and Essays of William Robertson Smith,* London: Adam & Charles Black, 1912, 313–14.

43 A. Richardson, *Christian Apologetics,* 19. The inverted commas around 'secular' are Richardson's.

44 Robert Mackintosh, 'Apologetics', *Encyclopedia Britannica,* 11th edn. 1910–11, 189.

45 J. V. L. Casserley, *The Christian in Philosophy,* London: Faber & Faber, 1949, 111; cf. 253.

46 Ibid., 254.

47 Ibid., 262.

48 P. T. Forsyth, *Positive Preaching and the Modern Mind* (1907), London: Independent Press, 1964, 59.

49 A. J. Grieve's address, reprinted in Charles E. Surman, *Alexander James Grieve, MA, DD, 1874–1952*, Manchester: Lancashire Independent College, 1953, 95. Grieve quotes (not quite accurately) from R. Mackintosh, *Historic Theories of Atonement*, London: Hodder & Stoughton, 1920, 195.

50 See Irenaeus, *Adversus omnes Haereses, passim.*

51 C. S. Lewis, *Beyond Personality: The Christian Idea of God*, London: Geoffrey Bles, 1944, 27.

52 Augustine, *On Christian Doctrine*, I. i. 1.

53 P. T. Forsyth, *Missions in State and Church*, London: Hodder and Stoughton, 1908, 19.

54 W. P. Paterson, *The Rule of Faith*, London: Hodder & Stoughton, 1912, 9.

55 Aquinas, *In Met.* 12. 9.

56 See H. R. Fox Bourne, *The Life of John Locke*, London: Henry S. King, 1876, II, 557. This is not to deny that the apologist is sometimes sorely tried, as when Robert Mackintosh expostulated, 'There is hardly now one wretched little freethinking undergraduate who will not tell you just where Jesus went wrong, and why'. See his 'Recent philosophy and Christian doctrine', *Proceedings of the International Congregational Council*, III, London: Congregational Union of England and Wales, 1908, 77.

57 Charles E. Raven, *Jesus and the Gospel of Love*, London: Hodder & Stoughton, 1931, 22.

Chapter 2: Confession and Church

1 P. T. Forsyth, *The Person and Place of Jesus Christ* (1909), London: Independent Press, 1961, 25.

2 H. Küng, *Theology for the Third Millennium: An Ecumenical View* (1988), London: Harper Collins, 1991, 122.

3 H. R. Mackintosh, *The Originality of the Christian Message*, London: Duckworth, 1920, 5.

4 C. C. J. Webb, *A Study of Religious Thought in England from 1850*, Oxford: Clarendon Press, 1933, 88.

5 P. T. Forsyth, *The Principle of Authority* (1913), London: Independent Press, 1952, 219.

6 J. Jewel, *An Apology of the Church of England*, ed. J. E. Booty, Ithaca, NY: Cornell University Press, 1963, 123.

7 G. H. Clark, *What Do Presbyterians Believe?*, Philadelphia: Presbyterian and Reformed, 1965, 47, 172.

8 P. T. Forsyth, *Principle of Authority*, 93. See further on Forsyth's method, Alan P. F. Sell, 'P. T. Forsyth as unsystematic systematician', in Trevor Hart, ed., *Justice the True and Only Mercy: Essays on the Life and Theology of Peter Taylor Forsyth*, Edinburgh: T. & T. Clark, 1995, 110–45.

9 Cf. Leonard Hodgson's remark in *Christian Faith and Practice*, Oxford: Blackwell, 1952, 5: 'The question is not whether we *should* have a creedless religion; it is whether or not we *can* have a creedless life.'

10 Erasmus, Preface to the *Works* of Hilary, 1523, London edn. 1642.

11 J. Denney, *Jesus and the Gospel*, London: Hodder & Stoughton, 2nd edn. 1909, 403.

12 P. Carnegie Simpson, *The Fact of Christ*, London: Hodder & Stoughton, 1924, 20, 21.

13 J. Orr, *The Progress of Dogma*, London: James Clarke, 1901, 8–9.

14 J. Butler's advertisement to his *Analogy*, 1st edn. 1736.

15 J. Taylor, *A Further Defence of the Common Rights of Christians, and of the Sufficiency of Scripture, without the Aid of Human Schemes, Creeds, Confessions &c.*, 1733, 78. See further Alan P. F. Sell, *Dissenting Thought and the Life of the Churches: Studies in an English Tradition*, Lewiston, NY: Edwin Mellen Press, 1990, ch. 7.

16 B. B. Warfield, 'What is Calvinism?', in *Selected Shorter Writings of Benjamin B. Warfield*, ed. J. E. Meeter, Nutley, NJ: Presbyterian and Reformed, 2 vols. 1970, 1973, I, 389.

17 Anon., *The Inquirer*, 9 March 1878, 157 (a).

18 See further Alan P. F. Sell, 'Friends and philosophy', *The Friends' Quarterly*, XVII, 1973, 72–82 and 111–22. For Barclay and the inward, universal saving light see idem, *Commemorations. Studies in Christian Thought and History* (1993), Eugene, OR: Wipf & Stock, 1998, ch. 6. For distrust of 'notions' emanating from a quite different quarter note the comment of Thomas Erskine of Linlathen in a letter of November 1833 to Lady Elgin: 'I believe all *notions* of Religion, however true, to be absolutely useless or worse than useless . . . [Christ] is the truth. A doctrine that can be separated from Himself is a vanity and deception.' Quoted by John Tulloch, *Movements of Religious Thought in Britain during the Nineteenth Century* (1885), Leicester: Leicester University Press, 1971, 141 n.

19 P. T. Forsyth, *Person and Place of Jesus Christ*, 264. A further motive in specifying a form of words has been that of establishing a common platform on which diverse 'tribes' of Christians could stand together. In politically and religiously volatile times this was Locke's motive in proposing 'Jesus is the Messiah' as the indispensable minimum of Christian belief. See further Alan P. F. Sell, *John Locke and the*

Eighteenth-Century Divines, Cardiff: University of Wales Press, 1997, 186–201.

20 W. M. Clow, *The Cross in Christian Experience*, London: Hodder & Stoughton, 1908, 321.

21 J. Macpherson, *The Confession of Faith* (1881), Edinburgh: T. & T. Clark, 1958, 6.

22 *To the Christian Reader, especially Heads of Families* - the Preface to the Westminster Confession of Faith.

23 R. Mackintosh, *The Obsoleteness of the Westminster Confession of Faith*, 53, bound with idem, *Essays Towards a New Theology*, Glasgow: Maclehose, 1889. Mackintosh was a self-styled 'refugee' from Free Church Presbyterianism to Congregationalism. See further Alan P. F. Sell, *Robert Mackintosh: Theologian of Integrity*, Berne: Peter Lang, 1977.

24 T. F. Torrance, *Scottish Theology from John Knox to John McLeod Campbell*, Edinburgh: T. & T. Clark, 1996, 133. See further Alasdair I. C. Heron, ed., *The Westminster Confession in the Church Today*, Edinburgh: Saint Andrew Press, 1982.

25 See Alan P. F. Sell, *Aspects of Christian Integrity* (1990), Eugene, OR: Wipf & Stock, 1998, 88–92. This is not to deny that some of the teaching concerning the papacy may constitute something of an ecumenical nuisance.

26 G. Wainwright, *Methodists in Dialog*, Nashville: Kingswood Books, 1995, 134.

27 Bernard Lord Manning, *Essays in Orthodox Dissent* (1939), London: Independent Press, 1953, 168.

28 P. T. Forsyth, *Positive Preaching and the Modern Mind* (1907), London: Independent Press, 1967, 141.

29 See Geoffrey F. Nuttall's insufficiently well-known pamphlet, *Congregationalists and Creeds*, London: Epworth Press, 1966.

30 *The English Hymnal*, Oxford: OUP, n.d., 390.

31 R. Mackintosh, *Obsoleteness*, 29.

32 J. Calvin, *Institutes*, II. ix. 2.

33 T. Watson, *A Body of Divinity* (from *A Body of Practical Divinity*, 1692), London: The Banner of Truth Trust, 1975, 161.

34 H. R. Mackintosh, *Originality of the Christian Message*, 76.

35 P. T. Forsyth, *The Church, the Gospel and Society*, London: Independent Press, 1962, 99.

36 S. Sykes, 'The essence of Christianity', *Religious Studies*, VI, 1971, 296.

37 Ibid., 300.

38 P. T. Forsyth, 'The distinctive thing in Christian experience', *Hibbert Journal*, VI, 1908, 486.

39 P. T. Forsyth, *The Church and the Sacraments* (1917), London: Independent Press, 1947, 83.

40 P. T. Forsyth, *Person and Place of Jesus Christ*, 168.

41 R. Mackintosh, *Historic Theories of Atonement*, 199.

42 I do not imply that Anglicans alone pursue the strongly incarnational path. There were, for example, skirmishes within the German Reformed Church between the strongly Pauline J. H. A. Bomberger and the strongly incarnational J. W. Nevin and the Mercersburg theologians. See Alan P. F. Sell, *Commemorations*, ch. 11.

43 J. R. Illingworth, 'The Incarnation in relation to development', in *Lux Mundi*, London: John Murray, 1889, 155. See further Alan P. F. Sell, *Philosophical Idealism and Christian Belief*, especially 196–7.

44 A. M. Ramsey, *From Gore to Temple*, London: Longmans, 1960, 4.

45 Ibid., 40.

46 J. Denney, *The Christian Doctrine of Reconciliation*, London: Hodder & Stoughton, 1917, 65.

47 P. T. Forsyth, *The Divine Self-Emptying*, bound with *The Taste of Death and the Life of Grace*, London: James Clarke, 1901, 116.

48 J. A. Baker, 'The essence of Christianity', *Expository Times*, LXXXVII, 1975, 36.

49 Ibid., 37.

50 Ibid., 38.

51 Geoffrey F. Nuttall, 'The Congregational theological conference, 1937', *Congregational Quarterly*, XV, 1937, 505.

52 John Milbank, Graham Ward and Catherine Pickstock, *Radical Orthodoxy: A New Theology*, London: Routledge, 1999, 2. It should not be supposed that all Cambridge theologians have signed up to radical orthodoxy. On the contrary, one might say that lashings of criticism have been brought to bear upon it from some Cambridge theological quarters. See, for example, Nicholas Lash, 'Where does holy teaching leave philosophy? Questions on Milbank's Aquinas', *Modern Theology*, XV no. 4, October 1999, 433–44; Douglas Hedley, review of *Radical Orthodoxy* in *Journal of Theological Studies*, LI pt. 1, April 2000, 405–8. See also Don Cupitt, 'My postmodern witch', *Modern Believing*, NS XXXIX no. 4, October, 1998, 5–10. An appended note informs us that Cupitt 'has recently retired from academic work in order to think'. Some may feel strangely disquieted by the negative implication lurking here.

53 See further Sell, *Philosophical Idealism and Christian Belief*, ch. 5.

54 Idem, '*Agape*, atonement and Christian ethics', *Downside Review*, XCI, 1973, 86. This conviction lay at the heart of the gentle criticism I presumed to offer of some of the contributors to John Hick, ed., *The Myth of God Incarnate*, London: SCM Press, 1977. See *Aspects of Christian Integrity* (1990), Eugene, OR: Wipf & Stock, 1998, 43–5.

55 James Orr, *The Christian View of God and the World*, Edinburgh: Elliot, 1897, 22.

[56] James Iverach, *The Truth of Christianity*, Edinburgh: T. & T. Clark, n.d., 16.

[57] See further Stephen Sykes, 'The strange persistence of kenotic christology', in Alistair Kee and Eugene T. Long, eds., *Being and Truth: Essays in Honour of John Macquarrie*, London: SCM Press, 1986, 368.

[58] B. Jowett, 'On atonement and satisfaction', quoted by B. M. G. Reardon, *Religious Thought in the Victorian Age*, London: Longmans, 1971, 334.

[59] It is quite possible that the extreme atonement doctrine here rebuked motivated some towards an equally one-sided view of the Incarnation.

[60] P. T. Forsyth, *The Work of Christ* (1910), London: Independent Press, 1958, 15.

[61] G. Ebeling quoting Luther's *Works* (Weimar edn. 1883–) in his *Luther*, London: Collins Fontana, 1975, 267.

[62] P. T. Forsyth, *Work of Christ*, 85.

[63] George Redford and John Angell James, eds., *The Autobiography of William Jay* (1854), Edinburgh: The Banner of Truth Trust, 1974, 85. Jay was ordained at Argyle Independent Church, Bath in 1791, and remained there until his death in 1853.

[64] T. Willcox, *Honey out of the Rock* (Psalm 81: 16), reprinted by Zoar Publications, Sheffield, *c.*1975, 9.

[65] H. F. Lovell Cocks, *By Faith Alone*, London: James Clarke, 1943, 144–5.

[66] S. Sykes, 'Strange persistence', 295.

[67] P. T. Forsyth, *Person and Place of Jesus Christ*, 214.

[68] W. Manson, *The Way of the Cross*, London: Hodder & Stoughton, 1958, 25.

[69] J. Calvin, *Institutes*, IV. i. 3.

[70] Lewis Benson, *Friends and the Truth*, privately published, 1965, 12.

[71] H. R. Mackintosh, *Originality of the Christian Message*, 5.

[72] P. T. Forsyth, *Work of Christ*, 119.

[73] J. Owen, Sermon XXI, 'Gospel charity', in his *Works*, ed. William H. Goold (1850–3), London: The Banner of Truth Trust, 1968, IX, 262. For a witty update of such sentiments see B. L. Manning, *Why Not Abandon the Church?* (1939), London: Independent Press, 1958, 37–8.

[74] See his *Catholicism: A Study of Dogma in Relation to the Corporate Destiny of Mankind*, London: Burns, Oates & Washbourne, 1950.

[75] J. Stoughton, *Reminiscences of Congregationalism Fifty Years Ago*, London: Hodder & Stoughton, 1881, 87.

[76] Robert S. Paul, *The Atonement and the Sacraments: The Relation of the Atonement to the Sacraments of Baptism and the Lord's Supper*, London: Hodder & Stoughton, 1961, 268.

[77] In contrast with the foregoing we may note Kwasi Wiredu's argument

that 'religion in Africa is predominantly of a personal rather than an institutional character'. See Philip L. Quinn and Charles Taliaferro, eds., *A Companion to Philosophy of Religion*, Oxford: Blackwell, 1997, 35.

78 *Epistle of Ignatius to the Ephesians*, I, 55.

79 R. Traill, *Works*, Edinburgh: The Banner of Truth Trust, 1975, I, 14.

80 J. S. Whale, *Christian Doctrine*, London: Collins Fontana, 1958, 146.

81 A. S. Pringle-Pattison, *The Duty of Candour in Religious Teaching*, London: Hodder & Stoughton, [1920], 9–10. The fleeting thought occurs that Pringle-Pattison, a lay professor of philosophy, did not have to rely upon the goodwill of the saints for his next crust.

82 W. R. Inge, *Outspoken Essays*, 2nd ser., London: Longmans, 1922, 58.

83 See J. Neil Henderson, 'Spa in the Dust Bowl: Oklahoma's hidden paradise', in Howard F. Stein and Robert F. Hill, eds., *The Culture of Oklahoma*, Norman: Oklahoma University Press, 1993, ch. 7; cf. the editors' paper, 'The culture of Oklahoma', 205–8.

84 Daniel T. Jenkins, *Prayer and the Service of God* (1944), London: Religious Book Club, 1946, 78.

85 B. L. Manning, *Essays in Orthodox Dissent* (1939), London: Independent Press, 1953, 83–4.

86 T. George, 'The Baptist tradition', in D. G. Hart and R. Albert Mohler, jun., eds., *Theological Education in the Evangelical Tradition*, Grand Rapids: Baker Books, 1996, 42.

87 Ibid., quoting Winthrop S. Hudson, ed., *Baptist Concepts of the Church*, Valley Forge, PA: Judson Press, 1959, 216.

88 J. Denny Weaver, *Becoming Anabaptist: The Origin and Significance of Sixteenth-Century Anabaptism*, Scottdale, PA: Herald Press, 1987, 132. Cf. idem, 'Perspectives on a Mennonite theology', *Conrad Grebel Review*, II, 1984, 189–210.

89 A. E. Taylor, *The Philosophical Review*, XV, 1906, 416.

90 Ion Bria, 'Christians and Europe: (9) An Orthodox reflection', *Epworth Review*, XXV no. 1, January 1998, 63.

91 *Observer*, 7 January 1900, 4(c).

92 H. Butterfield, *Christianity and History*, London: G. Bell, 1950, 136.

93 J. Kent, *The Unacceptable Face: The Modern Church in the Eyes of the Historian*, London: SCM Press, 1987, 6.

94 Cf. L. P. Jacks, *Religious Perplexities*, London: Hodder & Stoughton, 1923, 84–6.

95 Ron Crocombe and Marjorie Tuainekore Crocombe, 'Polynesia in Review: Issues and events, 1 July 1995 to 30 June 1996. The Cook Islands', *The Contemporary Pacific: A Journal of Island Affairs*, IX, Spring 1997, 224.

96 Larry Rasmussen, 'The right direction, but a longer journey', in Thomas F. Best and Martin Robra, eds., *Ecclesiology and Ethics:*

Ecumenical Engagement, Moral Formation and the Nature of the Church, Geneva: WCC Publications, 1997, 106.

97 *The Backwoods Preacher: Being the Autobiography of Peter Cartwright, An American Methodist Travelling Preacher*, London: Wesleyan-Methodist Book-room, n.d., 30–1.

98 *Primitive Methodist Magazine*, May 1894, 359–60.

99 *Letter to Diognetus*, V, 4–5.

100 Tertullian, *Apologeticum*, ch. 38.

101 Ross T. Bender, *Education for Peoplehood*, Elkhart, IN: Institute of Mennonite Studies, 1997, 63.

102 Stanley Hauerwas and William Willimon, *Resident Aliens: Life in the Christian Colony*, Nashville: Abingdon, 1989, 48, 49.

103 See, for example, James Gustafson, 'The sectarian temptation: reflections on theology, the Church and the university', *Proceedings of the Catholic Theological Society*, XL, 1985, 83–94. Hauerwas has replied in his *Christian Existence Today: Essays on Church, World, and Living in Between*, Durham, NC: Labyrinth Press, 1988, 1–21.

104 J. W. Nevin, 'The spirit of prophecy', *Mercersburg Review*, April 1877, 181.

105 D. Bonhoeffer, *Ethics*, ed. Eberhard Bethge, London: SCM Press, 1955, 320–1.

106 W. Brueggemann, *Cadences of Home*, Louisville: Westminster/John Knox, 1997, 13.

107 Ibid.

108 David F. Wells, *God in the Wasteland: The Reality of Truth in a World of Fading Dreams*, Grand Rapids: Eerdmans, 1995, 151. Of course, there is 'other-worldliness' and 'other-worldliness'! For a moving plea that Christian Platonism properly conceived is not other-worldly in a pejorative sense of the term see Hilary Armstrong, 'Platonism', in Ian Ramsey, ed., *Prospect for Metaphysics*, London: Allen & Unwin, 1961, 108–9.

109 A. B. Bruce, *Apologetics; or, Christianity Defensively Stated*, Edinburgh: T. & T. Clark, 3rd edn. 1927, 21.

110 For further reflections upon 'the broadest sense' see John G. Stackhouse, jun., 'From architecture to argument: historic resources for Christian apologetics', in Timothy R. Phillips and Dennis L. Okholm, eds., *Christian Apologetics in the Postmodern World*, Downers Grove, IL: InterVarsity Press, 1995, ch. 3 – a work which came to my attention after the present section was written.

111 J. Taylor, *A Discourse of the Liberty of Prophesying: Shewing the Unreasonableness of prescribing to other mens Faith, and the Iniquity of persecuting differing opinions*, London: R. Royston, 1647, Epistle Dedicatory.

112 E. F. Scott, *The Varieties of New Testament Religion*, New York: Charles Scribner's, 1943, p. vi. Scott goes so far as to say (p. 2) that, in view of the variety, 'No book . . . could be less fitted to serve as a touch-stone for orthodox belief'.

113 It is not implied that Christianity alone has been influenced by changing intellectual and social environments. It is well known that Judaism has come down to us in diverse modes of expression and, to cite an example from the non-Judaeo-Christian world, the teaching of Zarathustra is patient of more than one interpretation. See Mary Boyce, *Zoroastrians: Their Religious Beliefs and Practices*, London: Routledge & Kegan Paul, 3rd revised edn. 1987.

114 H. G. Meecham, *The Epistle to Diognetus*, Manchester: Manchester University Press, 1949, 87.

115 Ignatius of Antioch, *Ad Eph.*, IX. See further I. A. Saliba, 'The Bishop of Antioch and the heretics: a study of a primitive christology', *Evangelical Quarterly*, LIV, 1982, 65–76; Cullen I. K. Story, 'The christology of Ignatius of Antioch', *Evangelical Quarterly*, LVI, 1984, 173–82.

116 E. F. Osborn, *Justin Martyr*, Tübingen: J. C. B. Mohr, 1973, 156. He cites Ignatius, *Eph.* XX.1.

117 L. W. Barnard, *Justin Martyr: His Life and Thought*, Cambridge: CUP, 1967, 81. Cf. Peter Widdicombe, 'Justin Martyr and the Fatherhood of God', *Laval Théologique et Philosophique*, LIV no. 1, 1998, 113: 'Justin's doctrine of God bears the hallmarks of Middle Platonist speculation about the nature of the divine.' M. J. Edwards, 'On the Platonic schooling of Justin Martyr', *Journal of Theological Studies*, XLII pt. 1, 1991, 17–34. See further Craig M. Watts, 'The humanity of Jesus in Justin Martyr's soteriology', *Evangelical Quarterly*, LVI, 1984, 21–33. Watts leaves it an open question 'whether the cross is important to Justin because it is essential to his soteriology, or whether it is essential only because of the central place it holds in the Christian tradition which he adopts, and, therefore, must be appended to his thought though it plays no integral part to its actual structure' (30). For a useful analysis of the options presented by scholars, namely, that Justin totally assimilated/ totally rejected/partially and critically assimilated Platonism, see Charles Nahm, 'The debate on the "Platonism" of Justin Martyr', *The Second Century*, IX no. 3, 1992, 129–51.

118 Justin Martyr, *Dialogue with Trypho*, CXXVII.

119 Ibid., CXXIX. Hence the conclusion of some scholars that Justin stands at the fountainhead of Arianism. See, for example, Henry Chadwick, *Early Christian Thought and the Classical Tradition*, London: OUP, 1966, 16.

120 For the suggestion that Justin is removed from Paul in a further respect,

namely, that owing to changed circumstances surrounding the Bar Kochba revolt of 132–5, and to the increasingly Gentile composition of Christianity, Justin makes Abraham the father of Gentiles, the true Israel, only, whereas to Paul Abraham was the spiritual father of both Jews and Gentiles, see Rodney Werline, 'The transformation of Pauline arguments in Justin Martyr's *Dialogue with Trypho*', *Harvard Theological Review*, XCII no. 1, January 1999, 79–93. For the 'frankly speculative' view that 'Justin was what he claimed to be: a Christian philosopher whose teachings are based on the Scriptures', see Walter H. Wagner, 'Toward understanding Justin Martyr', *Cithara: Studies in the Judeo-Christian Tradition*, XXXIV no. 2, 1995, 3–26.

121 *Dialogue with Trypho*, C.

122 Ibid., LXXIV.

123 Ibid., LXXXVI.

124 See Cullen I. K. Story, 'The Cross as ultimate in the writings of Justin Martyr', *Ultimate Reality and Meaning*, XXI no. 1, 1998, 18–34.

125 P. J. Widdicombe, 'Justin Martyr', 122.

126 A. Harnack, *History of Dogma*, London: Williams & Norgate, 1896, II, 171. Cf. E. F. Osborn, *Justin Martyr*, Tübingen: Mohr, 1973, 84. While finding Justin more adequate than other Apologists, J. K. Mozley judged that 'taking the group as a whole, one would describe them as implying that men are redeemed by being given and by following the true doctrine whereby they can gain freedom from the errors intrroduced by evil, demonic powers'. See *The Beginnings of Christian Theology*, Cambridge: CUP, 1931, 54.

127 See, for example, *Against Heresies*, V. xviii. 2. See further R. M. Grant, *Irenaeus of Lyons*, London: Routledge, 1997.

128 *Against Heresies*, V. xxi. 1–2. For a full discussion of this see J. Daniélou, *Gospel Message and Hellenistic Culture*, London: Darton, Longman & Todd, 1973, 166–83.

129 *Against Heresies*, III. xviii. 1. See further J. Fantino, 'Le Passage du premier Adam au Second Adam comme expression du salut chez Irénée de Lyon', *Vigiliae Christianae*, LII no. 4, 1998, 418–29; Manfred Hauke, *Heilsverlust in Adam*, Paderborn: Bonifatius Druck, Buchverlag, [1993].

130 *Against Heresies*, V, preface.

131 R. A. Norris, *God and the World in Early Christian Theology*, London: Black, 1966, 72.

132 *Against Heresies*, II. xiv. 7.

133 Ibid., V. i. 1.

134 M. Wiles, *The Christian Fathers*, London: SCM Press, 1966, 134. See further T. D. Barnes, *Tertullian: A Historical and Literary Study* (1971), Oxford: Clarendon Press, 1985.

135 Tertullian, *Adversus Marcionem*, II. xxvii.

136 Idem, *De Resurrectione Carnis*, lxiii.

137 Idem, *Adv. Marc.*, III. viii; cf. *De Baptismo*, xi.

138 See S. R. C. Lilla, *Clement of Alexandria: A Study in Christian Platonism and Gnosticism*, London: OUP, 1971, ch. 3; E. F. Osborn, *The Philosophy of Clement of Alexandria*, Cambridge: CUP, 1957; A. Van den Hoek, *Clement of Alexandria and his Use of Philo in the Stromateis*, Leiden: E. J. Brill, 1988.

139 Clement of Alexandria, *Paedogogus*, I. i.

140 Idem, *Stromateis*, VI. ix.

141 Ibid., I. vii; cf. II. xv and VII. xvi; *Paed.* I. xiii.

142 S. R. C. Lilla, *Clement*, 159.

143 Clement of Alexandria, *Stromateis*, II. xlviii. 1.

144 Clement of Alexandria, *Protreptikos*, xi.

145 T. R. Glover, *The Conflict of Religions in the Early Roman Empire*, London: Methuen, 1909, 303. For Walter H. Wagner's view of 'Clement of Alexandria's self-understanding', see *Cithara: Studies in the Judeo-Christian Tradition*, XXXVI no. 1, 1996, 5–21.

146 Origen, *De Principiis*, I, I. iii. Cf. Plotinus, *Enneads*, III. viii. 8, where the One is said to be prior to existing things, and is not itself an existing thing.

147 See, for example, idem, *Contra Celsum*, II, 66, 69; III, 61; IV, 15, 18; VI, 68, etc.

148 Idem, *Discourse with Heraclides*, in J. E. L. Oulton and H. Chadwick, eds., *Alexandrian Christianity*, London: SCM Press, 1954, 454.

149 J. Locke, *A Second Vindication of the Reasonableness of Christianity*, in his *Works*, 1812, VII, 229.

150 Idem, *The Reasonableness of Christianity*, *Works*, VII, 357–8.

151 Idem, *A Letter Concerning Toleration*, *Works*, VI, 57.

152 Idem, *The Reasonableness of Christianity*, ibid., 97, cf. 100. See further Sell, *John Locke*, 185–201.

153 Dr Williams's Library, London, MS. 1: 11.

154 R. Baxter, *Reliquiae Baxterianae*, ed. M. Sylvester, 1696, II. xxviii. 148.

155 Ibid., III. cxli. 61.

156 Ibid., I. ii. 52.

157 Idem, *The Reformed Pastor*, London: SCM Press, 1956, 101.

158 Idem, *Rel.Bax.*, I. xl. 27.

159 Quoted in *Memorable Unitarians, being a Series of Brief Biographical Sketches*, London: British and Foreign Unitarian Association, 1906, 294–5. This work is based upon, and expands, Robert Spears's *A Record of Unitarian Worthies*, 1877.

160 *Howell Harris's Visits to Pembrokeshire*, transcribed from his diaries by Tom Beynon, Aberystwyth: Cambrian News Press, 1966, 207.

[161] See B. R. White, 'John Gill in London', *Baptist Quarterly*, XXII, 1967, 82; George M. Ella, *John Gill and the Cause of God and Truth*, Egglestone, Co. Durham: Go Publications, 1995, *passim*; Robert W. Oliver, 'John Gill (1697–1771): his life and ministry', in Michael A. G. Haykin, ed., *The Life and Thought of John Gill (1697–1771): A Tercentennial Appreciation*, Leiden: Brill, 1997, 12–18.

[162] T. Crosby, *The History of the English Baptists*, London, 1740, IV, 15, 16 (spelling modernized). See further Alan P. F. Sell, *The Great Debate. Calvinism, Arminianism and Salvation* (1982), Eugene, OR: Wipf & Stock, 1998, ch. 3.

[163] Philip Schaff, *The Creeds of Christendom*, Grand Rapids: Baker Book House, 1985, I, 815.

[164] *Proceedings* of the Second General Council of the World Presbyterian Alliance, 1880, 24.

[165] *Proceedings* of the Third General Council of the World Presbyterian Alliance, 1884, 161. See further Hubert W. Morrow, 'Admission of the Cumberland Presbyterian Church to the World Alliance of Reformed Churches', *Journal of Presbyterian History*, LV, 1977, 58–73; Alan P. F. Sell, *A Reformed, Evangelical, Catholic Theology: The Contribution of the World Alliance of Reformed Churches 1875–1982* (1991), Eugene, OR: Wipf & Stock, 1998, 20, 260, 267.

[166] Minutes of the 1832 assembly, quoted by Williston Walker, *The Creeds and Platforms of Congregationalism* (1893), Boston: The Pilgrim Press, 1960, 546. See further Sell, *Dissenting Thought and the Life of the Churches*, ch. 1.

[167] Ibid., 549.

[168] See further Alan P. F. Sell, 'Approaches to moral philosophy among the eighteenth-century Dissenters of England and Wales', *Jahrbuch für Recht und Ethik*, VIII, 2000, 263–313.

[169] Quoted by John Stoughton, *Reminiscences of Congregationalism Fifty Years Ago*, 53–4.

[170] J. H. Godwin, *Christian Faith: Its Nature, Object, Causes and Effects*, London: Jackson, Walford & Hodder, 1862, 73.

[171] B. Grant, *The Rescue of Faith; Or a Vindication of the Cross of Christ: Being an Analysis and Refutation of the Rationalism of the Age, as embodied in the Congregational Lecture on Christian Faith, by the Rev. J. H. Godwin, Professor in New College, St. John's Wood, London*, London: Ward, 1862, p. viii.

[172] Ibid., 61.

[173] E. R. Conder, 'The decay of theology', *Congregational Year Book*, 1874, 72.

[174] Ibid., 75, 76.

175 R. V. Pryce, 'The redemptive work of the Lord Jesus Christ', in *The Ancient Faith in Modern Light*, Edinburgh: T. & T. Clark, 1897, 224.

176 Ibid., 216.

177 W. F. Adeney, *A Century's Progress in Religious Life and Thought*, London: James Clarke, 1901, 116.

178 Ibid., 120. Payne's Congregational Lecture is *The Doctrine of Original Sin, or the Natural State and Character of Man Unfolded*, London, 1845.

179 Ibid., 122.

180 Ibid., 123.

181 Ibid., 142. Few in England did more to promote the idea of God's Fatherhood than the Methodist theologian John Scott Lidgett. See, for example, *The Fatherhood of God in Christian Truth and Life*, Edinburgh: T. & T. Clark, 1902, and his general account of *The Victorian Transformation of Theology*, London: Epworth Press, 1934.

182 R. Mackintosh, *Essays Towards a New Theology*, 475.

183 Quoted from a paper on 'Christian individualism' by John Waddington, *Congregational History 1850–1880*, London: Longmans, Green, 1880, 407.

184 For more on this complicated story see Alan P. F. Sell, *Theology in Turmoil: The Roots, Course and Significance of the Conservative–Liberal Debate in Modern Theology* (1986), Eugene, OR: Wipf & Stock, 1998.

185 P. T. Forsyth, *Principle of Authority*, 261.

186 C. H. Dodd, *The Apostolic Preaching and its Developments*, London: Hodder & Stoughton, 1970, 91–2.

187 Laurence Soper, 'An English liberal', *Downside Review*, LXXXVIII, 1970, 34.

188 J. Calvin, *Institutes*, IV. viii. 5.

Chapter 3: Confessors and Continuity

1 Clement of Alexandria, *Exhortation to the Heathen*, XII, my italics.

2 Idem, *Miscellanies*, V. xiv.

3 Origen, *De Principiis*, III. vi. 1.

4 See Gregory of Nyssa, *On Perfection*.

5 John of Damascus, *An Exact Exposition of the Orthodox Faith*, II. xii.

6 Peter Lombard, *Sentences*, Lib. II, Dist. 16.D.

7 Cyril of Alexandria, *De Dogm. Solutione*, III.

8 J. Calvin, *Institutes*, I. xiv. 3, cf. II. xii. 6. See further T. F. Torrance, *Calvin's Doctrine of Man*, London: Lutterworth, 1949; idem, *Theology in Reconstruction*, London: SCM Press, 1965, ch. 6.

9 Ibid., III. ii. 6.

10 Idem, *Commentary* on Colossians 3: 20.

11 A. Fuller, *The Complete Works of the Rev. Andrew Fuller*, London:

Holdsworth & Ball, V, 1832, 349. The grounds on which A. H. Kirkby, who refers to this passage, claims that Fuller distinguishes between image and likeness are not specified. See his unpublished doctoral dissertation, 'The Theology of Andrew Fuller and its Relation to Calvinism', University of Edinburgh, 1956, 146.

12 H. F. Lovell Cocks, *By Faith Alone*, London: James Clarke, 1943, 61.

13 W. H. Bennett, *Genesis*, in *The Century Bible*, London: Caxton Publishing Co., n.d., *ad. loc.* This is not the place for an exhaustive discussion of the biblical evidence. See, however, D. J. A. Clines, 'The image of God in man', *Tyndale Bulletin*, XIX, 1968, 53–103.

14 T. C. Vriezen, 'La Création de l'homme d'apres l'image de Dieu', *OTS*, II, 1943, 99. However, this view has subsequently been queried and qualified by some scholars. Such qualifications do not, however, affect the main point concerning the parallelism rather than the distinction between 'image' and 'likeness'.

15 Claus Westermann, *Genesis I–XI*, Minneapolis: Augsburg Publishing House, 1974, 148.

16 Ibid., 155.

17 Ibid.

18 Ibid., 158. I am grateful to my former colleague, Michael DeRoche, for a reassuring discussion of the Genesis text. On the day before writing this paragraph I read an article by Robin McKie, the science editor of the *Observer*, in which he quotes Carl Swisher, of the Berkeley Geochronology Centre in California, thus: 'Even atheists and agnostics have become inculcated with the idea that there is only one God, and that we – *Homo sapiens* – are made in his image, not a lot of other hominids, like the Neanderthals, as well'. 'In other words', McKie comments, 'we may have to think again about what it means to be made in His image.' *Observer*, 13 February 2000, 22(f).

19 See Irenaeus, *Demonstratio*, 12, 14, 16; *Against Heresies*, III. xxiii. 5, IV. xxxviii. 3. Among prominent Western theologians who, in the twentieth century, pursued what they understood as the Irenaean line were F. R. Tennant, in *The Origin and Propagation of Sin*, Cambridge: CUP, 2nd edn. 1906, and John Hick, in *Evil and the God of Love*, London: Collins Fontana, 1968.

20 Clement of Alexandria, *Protrep.* XI.

21 Gregory of Nyssa, *De virginitate* XII.

22 Irenaeus, *Against Heresies*, II. xxxv. 5. See the discussion in David Cairns, *The Image of God in Man* (1953), rev. edn. London: Collins Fontana, 1973, ch. 5.

23 Ibid., V. xvi. 2.

24 Augustine, *The City of God*, III. xxii, XIII, XIV.

25 *Heidelberg Catechism*, Q and A 6–8.

26 J. Owen, *Works* (1850–3), London: The Banner of Truth Trust, 1966, III, 418. The Calvinist divine, Thomas Boston, was even blunter. Of post-Fall humanity he asks: 'What that stock is now. Ah! Most unlike to what it was when planted by the Author of all good. A blast from hell, and a bite from the venomous teeth of the old serpent, have made it a degenerate stock, nay, a killing stock.' See his *Human Nature in its Fourfold State* (1720), London: The Banner of Truth Trust, 1964, 259.

27 J. Calvin, *Sermon* on Job 15: 8–16.

28 Idem, *Sermon* on Ephesians 2: 1–2; 44: 17–18. Cf. *Sermon* on Galatians 5: 19–23; *Institutes*, III. iii. 9.

29 Idem, *Sermon* on Deuteronomy 24: 19–20.

30 See T. Ware, *The Orthodox Church*, Harmondsworth: Penguin, rev. edn. 1984, 228.

31 That it is not only the doctrine of humanity which can be vitiated by an untoward understanding of original sin is clear from some remarks of the historian, Geoffrey F. Nuttall, in the Preface to his study of *The Holy Spirit in Puritan Faith and Experience*, Oxford: Blackwell, 1943, p. vii, where Otto and Barth are especially in view: 'Neo-Thomists and Neo-Calvinists agree in laying emphasis upon dogmas and confessions, and tend to treat faith as assent to a static deposit, to a closed system, of doctrine, rather than as an *energeia* springing directly from living, personal experience. In the reaction against an optimistic humanism which seemed hardly to need any doctrine of the Holy Spirit, human incapacity through Original Sin has been so exaggerated latterly as virtually to deny the doctrine.'

32 T. Chalmers, *The Works of Thomas Chalmers*, 25 vols. Glasgow: Collins, 1836–42, VI, 15.

33 J. Whale, *Christian Doctrine* (1941), London: Collins Fontana, 1957, 40.

34 T. Watson, *A Body of Divinity* (from *A Body of Practical Divinity*, 1692), London: The Banner of Truth Trust, 1965, 119.

35 H. F. Lovell Cocks, *By Faith Alone*, 61, 63.

36 See P. Tillich, *Systematic Theology*, Chicago: University of Chicago Press, 1957, II, 51.

37 Rupert of Deutz, *De Glorif. Trin.*, III. xxx; IV. ii. *Migne*, CLXIX. The reference is to Romans 5: 20. For an earlier hint in the same direction see Tertullian, *De resurrectione carnis*, VI.

38 *Summa Theologiae*, III. Q ii. 13.

39 Duns Scotus, *Sent.* III, dist. vii. Q 3.

40 Thomas Aquinas, *Summa Theologiae*, III. i., arts. 1–3.

41 Irenaeus, *Against Heresies*, V. xvi. 2.

42 Athanasius, *Second Oration against the Arians*, LXX.

43 Colossians 1: 15; cf. 2 Corinthians 4: 4.

44 Colossians 3: 10; cf. Romans 8: 29; 1 Corinthians 15: 49; 2 Corinthians 3: 18. Note that there is no echo of Hebrew parallelism here: no reference to a supposedly distinct 'likeness'.

45 Colossians 3: 11. In Galatians 3: 28 the same point is made with reference to the union of believers in Christ.

46 See especially Irenaeus, *Against Heresies*, V. Preface.

47 But see G. W. Butterworth, 'The Deification of man in Clement of Alexandria', *Journal of Theological Studies*, XVII, 1916, 157–69.

48 Clement of Alexandria, *Miscellanies*, II. xviii. My italics.

49 John of Damascus, *Orthodox Faith*, II. xii. This is consistent with his view of the Incarnation – hence of the material (not least icons) – in the human knowledge of God. See James R. Payton, jun., 'John of Damascus on human cognition: an element in his apologetic for icons', *Church History*, LXV, 1996, 173–83.

50 Benjamin Drewery, *Origen and the Doctrine of Grace*, London: Epworth Press, 1960, 200–1. See further idem, 'Deification', in Peter Brooke, ed., *Christian Spirituality: Essays in Honour of Gordon Rupp*, London: SCM Press, 1975, 35–62. The more sympathetic W. R. Inge, however, points out 'how much more stiff and personal our word God is than the Greek *Theos* as used in antiquity', where it meant 'particularly an immortal, and the gift of immortality conferred deification'. See his *Mysticism in Religion* (1947), London: Rider, 1969, 57; cf. idem, *Christian Mysticism*, London: Methuen, 1899, 356–68.

51 See H. R. Mackintosh's important article, 'The unio mystica as a theological conception', *The Expositor*, February 1909, reprinted in his *Some Aspects of Christian Belief*, London: Hodder & Stoughton, [1923], ch. 6.

52 2 Corinthians 5: 17.

53 John 15: 4.

54 1 John 3: 2.

55 John 17: 23.

56 G. Farel, *Le Sommaire*, ed. J. G. Baum, Geneva: Jules-Guillaume Fick, 1867, 31.

57 J. Calvin, *Commentary* on 1 Corinthians 11: 24. See further Charles Partee, *Calvin and Classical Philosophy*, Leiden: E. J. Brill, 1977.

58 J. W. Nevin, *The Mystical Presence and Other Writings on the Eucharist* (1846), Philadelphia: United Church Press, 1968, 173. Nevin's original subtitle is significant: *A Vindication of the Reformed or Calvinistic Doctrine of the Holy Eucharist* – this in the context of increasing individualism in North American religious life, 'new measures' revivalism, and the turning of many New England Congregationalists (pejoratively denominated 'Puritans' by Nevin) to Unitarianism.

59 Athanasius, *De Incarnatione*, LIV.

60 Archimandrite Sofrony, *The Undistorted Image*, London: Faith Press, 1958, 101.

61 R. G. Stephanopulos, in John Meyendorff and Joseph McLelland, eds., *The New Man: An Orthodox and Reformed Dialogue*, [no place given] Agora Books, 1973, 150, 152, 159.

62 V. Lossky, *The Mystical Theology of the Eastern Church*, Cambridge: James Clarke, 1957, 87. My italics.

63 Ibid., 126.

64 Georgios I. Mantzaridis, *The Deification of Man: St Gregory Palamas and the Orthodox Tradition*, Crestwood, NY: St Vladimir's Seminary Press, 1984, 109. Palamas's distinction between the essence and energies of God has prompted considerable discussion. See, for example, John Cheng, 'The distinction between God's essence and energy: Gregory Palamas' idea of ultimate reality and meaning', *Ultimate Reality and Meaning*, XXI no. 1, 1998, 56–75. For the argument that there is a harbinger of Palamas's distinction in Maximus see Vasilios Karayiannis, *Maxime le Confesseur. Essence et énergies de Dieu*, Paris: Beauchesne, 1993. See also Gregory of Nyssa, *In Eccl. Sermo*, 7, in W. Jaeger, ed., *Works*, Leiden: E. J. Brill, 1962, V, 415–16: 'In speaking of God, when there is question of his essence, then is the time to keep silence. When, however, it is a question of his operation (*energeia*), a knowledge of which can come down even to us, that is the time to speak of his omnipotence . . . and to use words to this extent.'

65 See *Anglican-Orthodox Dialogue: The Moscow Agreed Statement*, London: SPCK, 1977, 45–8.

66 John Meyendorff, 'Unity of the Church – unity of mankind', in Constantin G. Patelos, ed., *The Orthodox Church in the Ecumenical Movement: Documents and Statements 1902–1975*, Geneva: World Council of Churches, 1978, 312–13.

67 D. S. Cairns, *The Image of God in Man*, 109.

68 Antonio de Godoy Sobrinho, 'Commentary on the agreed statement on christology', in *Agreed Statements from the Orthodox-Reformed Dialogue*, Geneva: World Alliance of Reformed Churches, 1998, 59.

69 Ibid., 60. Though it is misleading to say that Christ's 'humiliation made him human, his exaltation made him divine'. Rather, we have the condescension of the divine, the exaltation of the human. Cf. Donald MacKinnon, *Themes in Theology: The Threefold Cord*, Edinburgh: T. & T. Clark, 1987, 139.

70 H. R. Mackintosh, *Some Aspects of Christian Belief*, 115–16. He quoted Maurice's *Life and Letters*, I, 156.

71 Ibid., 116.

72 Ephesians 2: 9.

73 J. W. Nevin, 'The mystical union', *Weekly Messenger*, 8 October 1845,

2091. See further Alan P. F. Sell, *Aspects of Christian Integrity* (1991), Eugene, OR: Wipf & Stock, 1998, 40–2. For similar tendencies among the British idealists see idem, *Philosophical Idealism and Christian Belief,* Cardiff: University of Wales Press, and New York: St Martin's Press, 1995, ch. 5.

74 R. V. Pryce, 'The redemptive work of the Lord Jesus Christ', 211, 212.

75 *The Orthodox Church in the Ecumenical Movement*, 110.

76 *Go Forth in Peace: Orthodox Perspectives on Mission*, compiled and edited by Ion Bria, Geneva: World Council of Churches, 1986, 5.

77 John of Damascus, *Orthodox Faith*, IV. ix. My italics.

78 Ibid., IV. xiii.

79 See G. I. Mantzaridis, *The Deification of Man*, 26–7, 61.

80 Pseudo-Dionysius, *The Divine Names and the Mystical Theology*, trans. C. E. Rolt, London: SPCK, 1975, 21.

81 J. H. A. Bomberger, 'Regeneration', *Proceedings* of the World Presbyterian Alliance, II, 1880, 552.

82 N. Lossky, 'Orthodoxy', in N. Lossky et al., eds., *Dictionary of the Ecumenical Movement,* Geneva: WCC Publications, 1991, 765–6.

83 Origen, *De Principiis*, VI.

84 1 Corinthians 3: 9.

85 Irenaeus, *Against Heresies*, IV. xxxvii. 7.

86 R. S. Franks, *A History of the Doctrine of the Work of Christ*, London: Hodder & Stoughton, n.d., I, 48.

87 Maximus the Confessor, *Cap.* I. 42.

88 Athanasius, *V. Antonii*, XX.

89 Pseudo-Dionysius, *The Divine Names*, I. See further Placid Spearritt, 'The soul's participation in God according to Pseudo-Dionysius', *Downside Review*, LXXXVIII, 1970, 378–92.

90 T. Ware, *The Orthodox Church*, 241, 242. My italics.

91 M. Luther, *Werke*, ed. J. F. K. Knaake et al., Weimar, 1883– , VII, 361.

92 F. D. E. Schleiermacher, *The Christian Faith*, trans. and ed. H. R. Mackintosh and J. S. Stewart, Edinburgh: T. & T. Clark, 1960, 314.

93 1 Peter 5: 1.

94 Vincent of Lérins, *Commonitorium*, XXX. xxviii.

95 Ibid., II. iii.

96 P. T. Forsyth, *Positive Preaching and the Modern Mind* (1907), London: Independent Press, 1964, 141; *The Principle of Authority* (1913), London: Independent Press, 1952, 219.

97 *The Theological and Miscellaneous Works of Joseph Priestley*, ed. J. T. Rutt (1817–1831), reprinted with a new Introduction by John Stephens, Bristol: Thoemmes Press, 1999, XXII, 125–6.

98 George Chryssides, *The Elements of Unitarianism*, Shaftesbury: Element Books, 1998, 106. It is intriguing that, according to the author (p.

61–2), in the few Unitarian churches where Holy Communion is still celebrated it is a 'low key' affair. One church does not hold communion on Sundays 'lest it intrude on the sensitivities of worshippers who might feel uncomfortable with the rite' (p. 62). The communicants thus seem more sensitive to others than their presumably free and liberal co-religionists. We may further surmise that at least one modern Unitarian has not altogether given up on miracles, for Chryssides informs us (p. 20) that the Unitarian Thomas 'Belsham was one of the first members of the clergy [*sic* – for the benefit of American readers?] to reject the biblical account of the six-day creation, believing it to be irreconcilable with Darwin's evolutionary theory'. Belsham died in 1829 – thirty years before *The Origin of Species* was published, and probably ten years before Darwin began to develop his theory.

99 Charles W. Wendtè, 'The story of "Robert Elsmere"', in *Reasonable Religion: A Series of Twelve Tracts for the Times*, London: British and Foreign Unitarian Association, 1893, 58.

100 James Freeman Clarke, 'How does a man become one with God?', ibid., 198.

101 See Jim Herrick, *Vision and Realism: A Hundred Years of The Freethinker*, London: G.W. Foote, 1982, 24.

102 *Unitarian Christian Herald*, no. 34, August 1999, 7, quoting Simon Hoggart's article in the *Guardian*, 10 April 1999.

103 In some ways analogous to non-Christian Unitarians are those who describe themselves as post-Christian feminists. Janet Soskice describes them as holding that, since 'In Christian (and other) religious texts we have a language and a symbolic system which privileges fathers and sons, and not mothers and daughters', those who immerse themselves in this 'are drinking an ideologically poisoned draft'. Such feminists pose to the generality of Christians the question, 'What do we change if we change fundamental metaphors within a faith?' See her 'Religious language', in Philip L. Quinn and Charles Taliaferro, eds., *A Companion to Philosophy of Religion*, Oxford: Blackwell, 1997, 202.

104 Alan Wykes, *The Royal Hampshire Regiment*, London: Hamish Hamilton, 1968, 115.

105 Ibid., 120.

106 J. Laird, *Recent Philosophy*, London: Thornton Butterworth, 1936, 11.

107 Ibid., 13.

108 1 Corinthians 6: 20; 7: 23.

109 Robert Mackintosh, *The Insufficiency of Revivalism as a Religious System*, bound with his *Essays Towards a New Theology*, Glasgow: MacLehose, 1889, 8.

110 B. L. Manning, *Essays in Orthodox Dissent* (1939), London:

Independent Press, 1953, 117. The 'earthen vessel' to which Manning refers is the local Congregational church, but his words also describe the empirical Church in its entirety.

111 See J. McLeod Campbell, *The Nature of the Atonement*, Cambridge: Macmillan, 1856. See further George M. Tuttle, *So Rich a Soil: John McLeod Campbell on Christian Atonement*, Edinburgh: Handsel Press, 1986; Michael Jinkins, *Love is of the Essence: An Introduction to the Theology of John McLeod Campbell*, Edinburgh: Saint Andrew Press, 1993.

112 See James N. McGuire, 'A kinder, gentler Calvinism', *The A[ssociate] R[eformed] P[resbyterian]*, XXV no. 10, October 2000, 10–11. To this Dean Turbeville replied in the January 2001 issue, and the editor, Ben Johnston, summed up in the following month, awarding points all round.

113 A. B. Bruce, *The Training of the Twelve*, Edinburgh: T. & T. Clark, 1871, 172. Cf. idem, *The Kingdom of God: Christ's Teaching according to the Synoptic Gospels*, Edinburgh: T. & T. Clark, 4th edn. 1891, ch. 8.

114 B. L. Manning, *Essays in Orthodox Dissent*, 113–14.

115 Cf. Hugo A. Meynell, *The Theology of Bernard Lonergan*, Atlanta, GA: Scholars Press, 1986, 19: 'The person in the pew probably cannot understand just what it is for Christ to be consubstantial with the Father, but if one is an orthodox Christian one will have a degree of devotion to Christ which would be blasphemous if he were not. To reproach *doctrines* and *systematics* for not being *communications* . . . is like reproaching cancer-research for not applying itself directly to the cure of patients.'

116 See Lewis S. Mudge, 'Towards a hermeneutic of the household: "Ecclesiology and Ethics" after Harare', *Ecumenical Review*, LI no. 3, July 1999, 252.

117 A. Raleigh, 'Christianity and modern progress' (Chairman's Inaugural Address, 12 May 1868), *Congregational Year Book 1869*, London: Hodder & Stoughton, 1869, 21.

118 R. Barclay, *An Apology for the True Christian Divinity* (1678), Glasgow: R. Barclay Murdoch, 1886, 25.

119 A. E. Taylor, *The Faith of a Moralist*, Series II, London: Macmillan, 1931, 390.

120 J. W. Nevin, *Human Freedom and a Plea for Philosophy*, Mercersburg: P. A. Rice, 1850, 42.

121 C. B. Upton, *Lectures on the Bases of Religious Belief*, London: Williams & Norgate, 1894, 50.

122 Hans-Georg Gadamer, *Truth and Method*, London: Sheed & Ward, 2nd. English edn. 1989, 279.

123 Jürgen Moltmann, *Theology of Hope*, London: SCM Press, 1967, 64.

124 R. Mackintosh, 'Recent philosophy and Christian doctrine', *Proceedings of the Third International Congregational Council*, London: Congregational Union of England and Wales, 1908, 84.

Chapter 4: The Meaning, Use and Reference of Religious Language

1 H. Kohl, *The Age of Complexity*, New York: Mentor, 1965, 271.
2 The series began in *Mind* in 1940.
3 H. J. Paton, 'Faith and logic' (a review of the 1957 volume edited by Basil Mitchell), *Philosophy*, XXXIII, October 1958, 357.
4 See my attempt at an account of the course of the philosophy of religion, *The Philosophy of Religion 1875–1980* (1988), Bristol: Thoemmes Press, 1996. See also Eugene Thomas Long, *Twentieth-Century Western Philosophy of Religion 1900–2000*, Dordrecht: Kluwer Academic Press, 2000.
5 For the most substantial outworking of Moore's policy see his *Principia Ethica*, Cambridge: CUP, 1903. Opinions differ as to whether Moore's interest in common sense took predecence over his concern with ordinary language. Opting for the former, A. R. White claimed that 'Malcolm and those who agree with him have reversed the correct relative positions of the two'. See his *G. E. Moore: A Critical Appraisal*, Oxford: Blackwell, 1958, 7.
6 See his celebrated paper, 'The refutation of idealism', *Mind*, NS XII, 1903, 433–53.
7 See B. Russell, *On Scientific Method in Philosophy*, Oxford: Clarendon Press, 1914, 19.
8 R. G. Collingwood, *An Essay on Philosophical Method*, Oxford: Clarendon Press, 1933, 121.
9 Ibid., 146.
10 C. D. Broad, *The Mind and its Place in Nature*, London: Kegan Paul, 1925, preface.
11 W. G. De Burgh, 'Logic and faith', *Philosophy*, I, 1926, 424.
12 Ibid., 425.
13 R. B. Braithwaite, 'Philosophy', in H. Wright, ed., *University Studies*, London: Ivor Nicholson & Watson, 1933.
14 L. S. Stebbing, 'The method of analysis in metaphysics', *Proceedings of the Aristotelian Society*, XXXIII, 1933, 65. Cf. her 'Logical positivism and analysis', *Proceedings of the British Academy*, 1933, 53–87. For further contemporary reflections upon analytical approaches in philosophy see A. Duncan-Jones and A. J. Ayer, 'Does philosophy analyse

common sense?', *Proceedings of the Aristotelian Society, supplementary volume*, XVI, 1937, 139–76; J. H. Muirhead, 'Where is philosophy going?', *Philosophy*, XII, 1937, 387–94; G. Ryle, 'Taking sides in philosophy', *Philosophy*, XII, 1937, 317–32; B. Russell, 'On verification', *Proceedings of the Aristotelian Society*, XXXVIII, 1938, 1–20; R. E. Steadman, 'A defence of speculative philosophy', *Proceedings of the Aristotelian Society*, XXXVIII, 1938, 112–42; J. Wisdom, 'Metaphysics and verification', *Mind*, XLVII, 1938, 452–98; M. Black, 'The "paradox of analysis"', *Mind*, LIII, 1944, 263–7; and idem, 'The "paradox of analysis" again', *Mind*, LIV, 1945, 272–3.

15 See her review of Whitehead's *Religion in the Making*, *Mind*, NS XXXIX, 1930, 475.

16 L. S. Stebbing, 'Some puzzles about analysis', *Proceedings of the Aristotelian Society*, XXXIX, 1939, 84.

17 J. Wisdom, 'Is analysis a useful method in philosophy?', *Proceedings of the Aristotelian Society, supplementary volume* XIII, 1934, 65–89.

18 Idem, *Mind*, 1931–3.

19 I much regret that I have mislaid the source of this quotation. A possible retort comes to mind: If people cannot think straight about cooking cakes, they are unlikely to make much headway with angst.

20 See G. Ryle, 'Systematically misleading expressions', *Proceedings of the Aristotelian Society*, XXXII, 1932, reprinted in his *Collected Papers*, London: Hutchinson, 1971, II, 39–62. Ryle, of Oxford, was influenced by Moore and the later writings of Wittgenstein, of Cambridge. See G. E. Moore, 'The justification of analysis', notes of a lecture given by Moore, taken by Margaret Masterman and corrected by Moore, *Analysis*, I, 1934, 28–30.

21 H. H. Price, 'Logical positivism and theology', *Philosophy*, X, 1935, 331.

22 K. Britton, 'The truth of religious propositions', *Analysis*, III, 1935, 27.

23 A. C. Ewing, 'Religious assertions in the light of contemporary philosophy', *Philosophy*, XXXII, 1957, 206.

24 R. M. Hare, 'Religion and morals', in B. Mitchell, ed., *Faith and Logic*, London: Allen & Unwin, 1957, 180.

25 R. W. Hepburn, *Christianity and Paradox*, London: Watts, 1957, ch. 11.

26 H. J. Paton, *In Defence of Reason*, London: Hutchinson, 1951, 13.

27 T. M. Knox, 'Two conceptions of philosophy', *Philosophy*, XXXVI, 1961, 289–308.

28 A. C. Ewing, 'The necessity of metaphysics', in H. D. Lewis, ed., *Contemporary British Philosophy*, London: Allen & Unwin, 1956, 145–9.

29 H. H. Price, 'Clarity is not enough', *Proceedings of the Aristotelian Society, supplementary volume*, XIX, 1945, reprinted in H. D. Lewis, ed., *Clarity is Not Enough: Essays in Criticism of Linguistic Philosophy*, London: Allen & Unwin, 1963, 15–41. Cf. C. D. Broad, 'Some meth-

ods in speculative philosophy', *Proceedings of the Aristotelian Society, supplementary volume*, XXI, 1947, 1–32. Other contemporary stock-taking contributions include B. A. Farrell, 'An appraisal of therapeutic positivism', *Mind*, LV, 1946, 24–48, 133–50; R. B. Braithwaite, 'Belief and Action', *Proceedings of the Aristotelian Society, supplementary volume*, XX, 1946, 1–19; K. R. Popper, W. C. Kneale and A. J. Ayer, 'What can logic do for philosophy?', *Proceedings of the Aristotelian Society, supplementary volume*, XXII, 1948, 141–78; A. C. Ewing, 'Philosophical analysis', in *Philosophical Studies: Essays in Memory of L. Susan Stebbing*, London: Allen & Unwin, 1948; Max Black, *Language and Philosophy*, Ithaca, NY: Cornell University Press, 1949; idem, ed., *Philosophical Analysis*, Ithaca, NY: Cornell University Press, 1950.

30 In Lewis, ed., *Clarity is Not Enough*, 39.

31 S. Hampshire, 'In Memoriam J. L. Austin', *Proceedings of the Aristotelian Society*, LX, 1960, III.

32 Ibid., VI.

33 S. Hampshire, 'Are all philosophical questions questions of language?', *Proceedings of the Aristotelian Society, supplementary volume*, XXII, 1948, 46–7.

34 See, for example, A. G. N. Flew and A. MacIntyre, eds., *New Essays in Philosophical Theology*, London: SCM Press, 1955; B. Mitchell, ed., *Faith and Logic*, London: Allen & Unwin, 1957; I. T. Ramsey, ed., *Prospect for Metaphysics*, London: Allen and Unwin, 1961; H. D. Lewis, ed., *Clarity is Not Enough*; John Hick, ed., *Faith and the Philosophers*, London: Macmillan, 1964; G. N. Vesey, *Talk of God*, London: Macmillan, 1969.

35 I place the term within inverted commas on this occasion only by way of signalling my awareness that some thus labelled feel uncomfortable about it. On the other hand, Anthony Quinton is utterly persuaded that there is a 'true church' of Wittgensteinians, the wings of whose guru he proceeds, with some relish, to clip. See A. Quinton, *From Wodehouse to Wittgenstein*, Manchester: Carcanet, 1998, 335–56.

36 The description 'amorphous collocation' is not intended pejoratively, still less patronizingly. It is intended literally: those in question are too diverse to constitute a school, too dispersed to constitute a group and, in some cases, too individualistic to have much to do (intellectually at least) with anyone else. In any case, I am always wary of labelling philosophers and theologians too precisely. For example, Locke was not an empiricist in ethics; the idealists by no means spoke with one voice; 'analysis', as we have just seen, encompasses a variety of attitudes and pursuits; and it is possible for one and the same person to be a 'liberal' biblical critic and a 'conservative' liturgist.

37 A. N. Prior, review of H. D. Lewis, ed., *Contemporary British Philosophy*, 3rd ser. *Philosophy*, XXXIII, 1958, 361.

38 I am not sufficiently superstitious to read anything into the fact that both Ayer and Irving Berlin, the song's writer, died in 1989.

39 *Contemporary Critiques of Religion*, New York: Herder & Herder, 1971, and *An Introduction to the Philosophy of Religion*, New York: St Martin's Press, 1982, exemplify this prolific author's approach.

40 A. J. Ayer, 'Demonstration of the impossibility of metaphysics', *Mind*, XLIII, 1934, 335–6.

41 Idem, *Language, Truth and Logic*, London: Victor Gollancz, 2nd edn. 1946, 115.

42 Ibid., 116.

43 Ibid., 9.

44 Ibid., 9–10.

45 Ibid., 10.

46 R. G. Collingwood, *An Essay on Metaphysics*, Oxford: Clarendon Press, 1940, 197.

47 W. V. O. Quine, *From a Logical Point of View*, Cambridge, MA: Harvard University Press, 1953, 42.

48 D. Papineau, review of Ben Rogers, *A. J. Ayer: A Life*, in *Times Higher Education Supplement*, 19 November 1999, 28.

49 E. L. Mascall, *Words and Images: A Study in Theological Discourse*, London: Longmans, Green, 1957, 6–13.

50 H. H. Price, 'Logical positivism and theology', *Philosophy*, X, 1935, 320.

51 I. M. Crombie, 'The possibility of theological statements', in B. Mitchell, ed., *Faith and Logic*, 83. It will be clear that in this discussion 'meaningless' is not used in the sense of 'irrelevant to life' – as it is, for example, by Langdon Gilkey in *Naming the Whirlwind: The Renewal of God Language*, Indianapolis: Bobbs-Merrill, 1969. For a critique of Gilkey's usage see Frederick Ferré, 'A renewal of God-language?', *Journal of Religion*, LII no. 3, 1972, 286–304.

52 See A. C. Ewing, 'Religious assertions in the light of contemporary philosophy', *Philosophy*, XXXII, 1957, 207. H. H. Price's appraisal was more generous; see his paper, 'Logical positivism and theology', 321–5.

53 E. E. Harris, *Revelation through Reason*, London: Allen & Unwin, 1959, 47–8; cf. ibid., 42.

54 A. G. N. Flew, *New Essays in Philosophical Theology*, 97.

55 Ibid., 99.

56 Ibid. See also Frederick Ferré, *Language, Logic and God*, London: Eyre & Spottiswoode, 1962, 50–2; Alan P. F. Sell, *The Philosophy of Religion 1875–1980*, 151–3. See also the thoughtful article by N. H. G. Robinson, 'Is providence credible today?', *Scottish Journal of Theology*,

XXX, 1977, 215–31. He holds that 'Flew's argument about the two explorers in the jungle does not establish a non-religious outlook, it simply *expresses* it and already presupposes the rejection of religion' (221).

57 Flew's refinement of his position is noted by W. D. Hudson in *Wittgenstein and Religious Belief*, London: Macmillan, 1975, 145, where he refers to Flew's unpublished paper, 'Theology and falsification in retrospect'.

58 H. P. Owen, review of A. G. N. Flew, *God and Philosophy*, in *Religious Studies*, II, 1966–7, 282–5. For evidence that twenty years later Flew's challenge was still under review see Donald Wiebe, 'The cognitive status of religious belief', *Sophia*, XXIII no. 3, October 1984, 4–21. He finds that Flew errs in showing 'a poor understanding of the nature of religious assertions', and 'fails to see that scientific statements or assertions cannot be restricted simply to . . . assertions of "normal science"', 16. For the view that the theologian Paul van Buren allows too much to falsificationism see D. M. MacKay, 'Language, meaning and God', *Philosophy*, XLVII, 1972, 1–17.

59 P. R. Clifford, 'The factual reference of theological statements', *Religious Studies*, III, 1967, 340.

60 Ibid., 345. He refers to his paper, 'Omnipotence and the problem of evil', *Journal of Religion*, XLI, 1961, 118–28.

61 See Jerry H. Gill, 'J. L. Austin and the religious use of language', *Sophia*, VIII no. 2, 1969, 29–37.

62 F. Ferré, *Language, Logic and God*, 43–4.

63 B. Mitchell, 'The grace of God', in idem, ed., *Faith and Logic*, 155, 160.

64 T. M. Knox, 'Two conceptions of philosophy', 306–7.

65 H. J. Paton, *The Modern Predicament*, London: Allen & Unwin, 1955, 42.

66 A. J. Ayer, *Language, Truth and Logic*, 15.

67 Idem, *Philosophy and Language*, Oxford: Clarendon Press, 1960, 18.

68 Idem, 'Metaphysics and common sense', reprinted in idem, *Metaphysics and Common Sense*, London: Macmillan, 1967, 81. In a review of G. Ryle, ed., *The Revolution in Philosophy*, James Bastable draws attention to what he calls Ayer's 'obituary notice on the Vienna Circle'. However, he claims that many of the ideas of logical positivism live on – 'in particular', reports Bastable, 'its partial claim to a new spirit in philosophy "of logical rigour and intellectual responsibility" (p. 86), which seems oddly forgetful of his compatriots, Duns Scotus, William Ockham *et alibi aliorum*'. See *Philosophical Studies* (Ireland), VI, 1956, 198.

69 A. Quinton, *From Wodehouse to Wittgenstein*, 343.

70 L. Wittgenstein, *Tractatus Logico-Philosophicus* (1922), London: Routledge & Kegan Paul, 1981, 6.53.

71 Ibid., 6.522. Rush Rhees construes this proposition thus: the mystical '*shows* itself precisely *in* the rigorous use of language, in saying what can be expressed'. See his *Discussions of Wittgenstein* (1970), Bristol: Thoemmes Press, 1996, 42. See further on Wittgenstein's relations with the positivists, W. Donald Hudson, *Wittgenstein and Religious Belief*, ch. 4.

72 P. A. Schlipp, ed., *The Philosophy of Rudolf Carnap*, La Salle, IL: Open Court, 1963, 27.

73 For a case along these lines see A. Boyce Gibson, *Theism and Empiricism*, London: SCM Press, 1970. My words, 'a prominent aspect of', carry the caution that although Locke (in the wake of Bacon, Hobbes and Gassendi) advocated an empiricist epistemology, he also accorded a place to reflection and to revelation. In these latter respects he has not been followed by all of those otherwise indebted to him.

74 D. F. Pears, *Wittgenstein*, London: Collins Fontana, 1971, 46; cf. idem, *The False Prison: A Study of the Development of Wittgenstein's Philosophy*, Oxford: Clarendon Press, 1987, ch. 1.

75 L. Wittgenstein, *Tractatus*, 6.53.

76 Ibid., 2.063, 2.1, 2.11, 2.12, 2.1512.

77 Ibid., 4.022.

78 See David G. Stern, *Wittgenstein on Mind and Language*, London: OUP, 1995.

79 These have been conveniently spelled out by Anthony Kenny, *Wittgenstein*, Harmondsworth: Penguin, 1973, ch. 12; cf. idem, *The Legacy of Wittgenstein*, Oxford: Blackwell, 1984, pp. viii–x.

80 He did not forsake it altogether. See his *Lectures and Conversations on Aesthetics, Psychology and Religious Belief*, ed. Cyril Barrett, Oxford: Blackwell, 1966, 65–72. See further John Churchill, 'Wittgenstein's lectures on religious belief', *Sophia*, XX no. 3, October 1981, 33–9.

81 L. Wittgenstein, *Tractatus*, 3.311.

82 Ibid., 7.

83 Ibid., 4.116.

84 Ibid., *Philosophical Investigations*, Oxford: Blackwell, 2nd edn. 1958, I, 43.

85 Idem, *Lectures and Conversations*, 2.

86 Idem, *Philosophical Investigations*, 124. For an exposition of this remark by one generally sympathetic to Wittgenstein see D. Z. Phillips, *Wittgenstein and Religion*, London: Macmillan, 1993, ch. 15.

87 L. Wittgenstein, *Culture and Value*, trans. Peter Winch, Oxford: Blackwell, 1980, 2.

88 Idem, *Lectures and Conversations*, 57–8.

89 G. Berkeley, *Principles of Human Knowledge*, author's introduction, §20; *Alciphron*, VII.14, in Alexander Campbell Fraser, *The Works of George Berkeley D.D., Formerly Bishop of Cloyne*, Oxford: Clarendon Press, 1901, I, 251 and II, 344 respectively.

90 For something of the context for these assertions see Alan P. F. Sell, *John Locke and the Eighteenth-Century Divines*, ch. 2.

91 N. Malcolm, *Ludwig Wittgenstein: A Memoir* (1958), Oxford: OUP, 1984, 60. See further idem, with a response by Peter Winch, *Wittgenstein: A Religious Point of View?*, Ithaca, NY: Cornell University Press, 1993. Malcolm here considers what it could mean to say that there is something analogous to a religious point of view in Wittgenstein's later work. See also William James DeAngelis, 'Ludwig Wittgenstein – A religious point of view? Thoughts on Norman Malcolm's last philosophical project', *Dialogue*, XXXVI, 1997, 819–42. In 'Ludwig Wittgenstein: a Christian in philosophy', *Scottish Journal of Theology*, 1998 no. 2, 131–61, James Wm. McClendon, jun., and Brad J. Kellenberg present Wittgenstein as 'a quiet Christian'. Certainly he was not a noisy one. A more generous verdict than the following could hardly have been pronounced by a Thomist: 'Wittgenstein was passionately convinced that beyond the desecrated world of exact language was what could not be said but showed itself, and his overt scepticism was always on the point of becoming that very different and eventually quite positive thing, a cloud of unknowing.' So D. J. B. Hawkins, *Wittgenstein and the Cult of Language*, London: Blackfriars Publications, 1957, 9.

92 F. Waismann, 'Notes on talks with Wittgenstein', trans. Max Black, *Philosophical Review* LXXIV, 1965, 16.

93 L. Wittgenstein, *Lectures and Conversations*, 57.

94 Idem, *Zettel* (1967), ed. G. E. M. Anscombe and G. H. Von Wright, Oxford: Blackwell, 1981, §545.

95 Idem, *Culture and Value*, 85.

96 Idem, *Tractatus*, 5.641.

97 Idem, *Culture and Value*, 50. See further Douglas Huff, 'Wittgenstein, solipsism, and religious belief', *Sophia*, XXXI no. 1 and 2, 1992, 37–52; Jens Glebe-Møller, 'Two views of religion in Wittgenstein', in Richard H. Bell, ed., *The Grammar of the Heart: Thinking with Kierkegaard and Wittgenstein. New Essays in Moral Philosophy and Theology*, New York: Harper & Row, 1998. In 'After Wittgenstein', *Religious Studies*, XII, 1976, 494, N. H. G. Robinson claimed that, with his suggestion that the language game is played, Wittgenstein was 'setting aside his own earlier – in a sense, non-cognitive – affirmation of the mystical, and his warning that whereof one cannot speak thereof one must be silent'. It seems more accurate to say that, however inconsistently, Wittgenstein continued to endorse both social language

games and the idea of the solitary individual to whom, as language is used, the mystical may show itself.

98 Idem, *Philosophical Investigations*, I, 23.

99 D. Z. Phillips chides Terence Penelhum for overlooking this point. See his review of Philip L. Quinn and Charles Taliaferro, eds., *A Companion to Philosophy of Religion*, Oxford: Blackwell, 1997, in *International Journal for Philosophy of Religion*, XLIV, 1998, 59.

100 Ibid.

101 Ibid., I, 66–7. Though Rush Rhees felt that the family resemblance analogy does not suffice to show how language hangs together. See his *Wittgenstein and the Possibility of Discourse*, ed. D. Z. Phillips, Cambridge: CUP, 1998, 142.

102 In connection with religious language games Keith Ward once asked, 'Do we have to agree on definitions before we can play the game? If so, it's not much like religion; if not, it's not much like a game.' See his review of W. Donald Hudson, *A Philosophical Approach to Religion*, in *Mind*, LXXXV, 1976, 474.

103 L. Wittgenstein, *Philosophical Investigations*, I, 664.

104 Idem, *On Certainty*, New York: J. & J. Harper, 1969, §403.

105 Idem, *Tractatus*, 3.26.

106 Idem, *Philosophical Investigations*, I, 1. Cf. Robert J. Fogelin, *Wittgenstein*, London: Routledge & Kegan Paul, 1976, 206: '[W]ith all the reservations needed, we can notice that one simple theme has surprising domination in the text [of *Philosophical Investigations*]: Wittgenstein continually attempts to dislodge the preconception that words gain their meaning through standing for things.'

107 Ibid., I, 109.

108 For a trenchant critique of Wittgenstein's language games to the effect that they are laden with untoward theory see John W. Cook, 'Wittgenstein and religious belief', *Philosophy*, LXIII, 1988, 427–52. Cf. Helen Hervey, 'The problem of the model language-game', *Philosophy*, XXXVI, 1961, 349–51.

109 R. G. Collingwood, *The Principles of Art*, Oxford: Clarendon Press, 1938, 7. See T. J. Diffey, 'Aesthetics and philosophical method', in David Boucher, James Connelly and Tariq Modood, eds., *Philosophy, History and Civilization: Interdisciplinary Perspectives on R. G. Collingwood*, Cardiff: University of Wales Press, 1995, 63–78. To notice this distinction between Collingwood and Wittgenstein is not to deny that, as David Boucher has said, 'There are remarkable similarities between Wittgenstein's description of the foundations of a language game as logically ultimate, unverifiable and not analytically true, and Collingwood's doctrine of Absolute Presuppositions.' Ibid., 28 n. 49.

110 L. Wittgenstein, *Lectures and Conversations*, 59.

111 Ibid., 71.

112 D. Z. Phillips, *The Concept of Prayer*, London: Macmillan, 1965, 10.

113 Ibid., 121.

114 Alan P. F. Sell, *The Philosophy of Religion 1875–1980*, 209. Phillips – his content and his gusto – have provoked numerous responses over the years. The following are among earlier examples: W. D. Hudson, John Hick, Humphrey Palmer and D. Z. Phillips, 'The philosophical discussion of religious discourse', *Theology*, LXXI, 1968, 98–122; Wayne Grennan, 'Wittgenstein on religious utterances', *Sophia*, XV no. 3, 1976, 13–18; and others to be mentioned below. For Phillips on prayer see R. T. Allen, 'On not understanding prayer', *Sophia*, X no. 3, 1971, 1–7.

115 I do not overlook the fact that Wittgenstein allowed the possibility that there were many different concepts of God (and presumably also of prayer?). Phillips's concept of prayer may on this basis be in order; but we may still query whether it is the concept of most Christian believers.

116 See, for example, Kai Nielsen, 'Wittgensteinian fideism', *Philosophy*, XLII, July 1967, 191–209; idem, 'The coherence of Wittgensteinian fideism', *Sophia*, XI no. 3, 1972, 4–12.

117 D. Z. Phillips, *Faith and Philosophical Enquiry*, 132.

118 Idem, *Wittgenstein and Religion*, ch. 5, where he addresses the kind of challenge posed by John Hick in *God and the Universe of Faiths*, London: Macmillan, 1973, 49, to the effect that along Phillips's line 'Religious language would become a protected discourse, no longer under obligation to show its compatibility with established conclusions in other spheres, because it makes no claims which could agree or conflict with scientific knowledge or philosophical reflection'. See also Mary Hesse's reference to a Wittgensteinian 'ghetto mentality' in her 'Criteria of truth in science and theology', *Religious Studies*, XI, 1975, 387. Because he falls too readily for the alleged 'monadic isolation' of language games, quoting Linge with approval that they are 'a multitude of hermetically sealed usages and corresponding life forms', David West is able to contrast Gadamer favourably with Wittgenstein, because for the former 'the fact that understanding always presupposes the standpoint of particular historical contexts or horizons need not imply that genuine critique and mutal understanding between them is impossible'. See D. West, *An Introduction to Continental Philosophy*, London: Polity Press, 1996, 116, 115. He quotes D. E. Linge, Introduction to H.-G. Gadamer, *Philosophical Hermeneutics*, Berkeley: University of California Press, 1976, pp. xxxvi–xxxvii. Overall, West's book is among the better introductions to its somewhat muddy field.

119 D. Z. Phillips, *Wittgenstein and Religion*, 56.

[120] Ibid., 67.

[121] Ibid., 69.

[122] Ibid., 72.

[123] See A. Olding, 'D. Z. Phillips and religious language', *Sophia*, XVI no. 1, 1977, 23–8.

[124] Cf. William L. Power, 'Analysis and theology', *Sophia*, XVII no. 2, 1978, 17: '[T]hose who argue that theists in general have not intended to assert or deny certain things about God and his relation to his creatures are historically incorrect.' He quotes the theologian Schubert M. Ogen to similar effect. See the latter's 'God and philosophy: a discussion with Anthony Flew', *Journal of Religion*, XLVIII no. 2, 1968, 162.

[125] N. H. G. Robinson, 'The logical placing of the name "God"', *Scottish Journal of Theology*, XXIV, 1971, 133.

[126] D. Z. Phillips, *Faith and Philosophical Enquiry*, 17.

[127] Ibid., 60; cf. *Wittgenstein and Religion*, 62.

[128] For an example of such a view see E. S. Brightman, *The Philosophy of Religion*, London: Skeffington, 1947.

[129] For a fuller statement along similar lines see John King-Farlow and William N. Christensen, *Faith and the Life of Reason*, Dordrecht: Reidel Publishing Co., 1972, 94–9. It is, however, marred by its disparaging tone and its *ad hominem* flavour. See also Michael Scott and Andrew Moore, 'Can theological realism be refuted?', *Religious Studies*, XXXIII, 1997, 401–18.

[130] J. Hick, 'The philosophical discussion of religious discourse', 101.

[131] Ibid., 102.

[132] Ibid., 119.

[133] Ibid., 120.

[134] D. Z. Phillips, *Death and Immortality*, London: Macmillan, 1970, 55.

[135] S. Hampshire, 'The interpretation of language: words and concepts', in C. A. Mace, ed., *British Philosophy in the Mid-Century*, 271.

[136] T. McPherson, 'Religion as the inexpressible', in *New Essays in Philosophical Theology*, 132–3.

[137] F. Ferré, *Language, Logic and God*, 37.

[138] D. Z. Phillips, *Wittgenstein and Religion*, 66, quoting J. A. Passmore, 'Christianity and positivism', *Australasian Journal of Philosophy*, XXXV, 1957, 128.

[139] See, for example, P. Ricoeur, *The Rule of Metaphor: Multi-Disciplinary Studies of the Creation of Meaning in Language* (Fr. edn. 1975), Toronto: University of Toronto Press, 1978; idem, 'Philosophy and religious language', *Journal of Religion*, LIV no. 1, 1974, 71–85.

[140] W. P. Alston, 'Religious language', in P. Edwards, ed., *Encyclopedia of Philosophy*, London: Collier-Macmillan, 1967.

[141] Christopher Insole, 'A Wittgensteinian philosophy of religion – or a

philosophy of Wittgensteinian religion?', *Heythrop Journal*, XXXIX no. 2, 1998, 155.

[142] David F. Pears, *The New Republic*, 19 May 1986, 39, quoted by Huston Smith, 'Postmodernism's impact on the study of religion', *Journal of the American Academy of Religion*, LVIII no. 4, Winter 1990, 662.

[143] John Webster, for example, finds Eberhard Jüngel deficient in this respect. See David F. Ford, ed., *The Modern Theologians*, Oxford: Blackwell, 2nd edn. 1997, 63. Again, W. Donald Hudson has queried the way in which both W. Pannenberg and T. F. Torrance respectively speak of language which 'leaps over the frontiers of logic' and which 'breaks through all our linguistic and logical forms'. In each case his point is that 'what it is self-stultifying to say does not cease to be self-stultifying simply because it is said about God'. See his 'God revealed in creation', *Expository Times*, CIV no. 2, 1992, 48(a); no. 5, 1996, 133(b). I have myself noted the way in which, during the latter decades of the twentieth century, many professional philosophers – Penelhum, Gale, Swinburne and Meynell among them – have brought their skills to bear upon substantive theological questions with a degree of sophistication which theologians too frequently fail to emulate. See Alan P. F. Sell, *Conservation and Exploration in Christian Theology*, Caernarfon: Gwasg Pantycelyn, [1993], 20–1.

[144] Consistent with the main thrust of this book I have Christian discourse primarily in mind, but I do not at all wish to deny that other religions have their own concerns with religious language. Consider, for example, Madhyamaka thought within Buddhism, which, suspicious of substantive claims, concentrates upon exposing weaknesses in the assertions of others; or that type of Buddhist thought which distinguishes between mundane and transcendental truths. For these see respectively K. Bhattacharya, *The Dialectical Method of Nagarjuna*, Delhi: Banarsidass, 1986; R. P. Hayes, *Dignaga on the Interpretation of Signs*, Dordrecht: Kluwer, 1988.

[145] Isaiah 6: 5.

[146] See J. O. Urmson, *Philosophical Analysis: Its Development between the Two World Wars*, Oxford: Clarendon Press, 1956, 197.

[147] S. Vere Benson, *The Observer's Book of British Birds*, London: Frederick Warne, 1952, 106.

[148] This, it should be noted, is a different type of jumbling up from the uni-level efforts of the rapidly spoken comedian, Max Bacon, who, in a heavy East End of London Jewish accent, would wonderfully mangle fairy stories: 'Den de Fader Bear said, "Who's been sleeping in my porridge?. . ."'

[149] MFP 2041.

[150] *Sudan Witness*, XIII, 1966, 54.

151 D. A. Pailin, *Probing the Foundations: A Study in Theistic Reconstruction*, Kampen: Kok Pharos, 1994, 13.

152 Erik Routley, *Music, Sacred and Profane*, London: Independent Press, 1960, 125.

153 J. A. T. Robinson, *Honest to God*, London: SCM Press, 1963, ch. 1.

154 Matthew 6: 22; Luke 11: 34.

155 J. J. Müller, *When Christ Comes Again*, 1956, 35.

156 See T. R. Miles, *Religion and the Scientific Outlook*, London: Allen & Unwin, 1959.

157 J. A. T. Robinson, *Jesus and his Coming*, London: SCM Press, 1957, 180–1.

158 N. H. G. Robinson, 'The logical placing of the name "God"', *Scottish Journal of Theology*, XXIV, 1971, 139.

159 Galatians 2: 20. For illuminating discussions of paradox see F. Ferré, *Language, Logic and God*, 46–8; D. M. Baillie, *God was in Christ*, London: Faber, 1961, ch. 5; George B. Hall, 'D. M. Baillie: a theology of paradox', in David A. S. Fergusson, ed., *Christ, Church and Society: Essays on John Baillie and Donald Baillie*, Edinburgh: T. & T. Clark, 1993, 65–85; J. Heywood Thomas, *Subjectivity and Paradox*, Oxford: Blackwell, 1957, ch. 5. In a number of works Austin Farrer propounded a theory of double agency, according to which believers are most free when they are responding to God's grace.

160 Though it is from an empirical point of view contradictory to assert that the eternal God was fully revealed in a human life. But this, again, takes us to the heart of the paradox of the Incarnation, namely, that what does not from one standpoint appear to be a fact at all, is *the* fact – to the positivists a stumbling-block and to the Wittgensteinians foolishness, but to traditional believers the power of God and the wisdom of God.

161 I. M. Crombie, 'The possibility of theological statements', 32. In societies where the state requires religious worship in its schools, have not numerous teachers discovered that while pupils may be herded into a hall, they cannot be made to worship?

162 H. J. Paton, *The Modern Predicament*, 34. Cf. F. Ferré, *Language, Logic and God*, 159.

163 Richard M. Martin, *Logic, Language and Metaphysics*, New York: New York University Press, 1971, 5. Cf. N. H. G. Robinson, 'The logic of religious language', in *Talk of God*, 6; idem, 'The problem of natural theology', *Religious Studies*, VIII, 1972, 322.

164 Nicholas Lash, 'Ideology, metaphor and analogy', in Brian Hebblethwaite and Stewart Sutherland, eds., *The Philosophical Frontiers of Christian Theology: Essays Presented to D. M. MacKinnon*, Cambridge: CUP, 1982, 87.

[165] E. L. Mascall, *Words and Images*, 75.

[166] M. B. Foster, *Mystery and Philosophy*, London: SCM Press, 1957, ch. 1.

[167] The inverted commas specify the term to be considered; they have no ironic postmodern overtones. If the analysts have taught us to mind our words, the postmodernists teach us how much can be said by utilizing the lowly comma. As Linda Hutcheon explains, postmodernist discourse 'is rather like saying something while at the same time putting inverted commas around what is being said. The effect is to highlight, or "highlight", and to subvert, or "subvert", and the mode is therefore a "knowing" and an ironic – even an "ironic" – one.' So now we know – or 'know'. See her *The Politics of Postmodernism*, London: Routledge, 1989, 1.

[168] Hugh Rayment-Pickard, review of Terrence W. Tilley et al., *Postmodern Theologies*, in *Modern Believing*, NS XXXVII no. 3, July 1996, 68.

[169] Just as Dewi Phillips protests that he is not a Wittgensteinian fideist, despite what Kai Nielsen and others say about him.

[170] See further Martin Henry, 'God in postmodernity', *Irish Theological Quarterly*, LXIII no. 1, 1998, 4.

[171] Ibid., 5. Other prominent modernists are the literary figures Proust and Joyce, the composer, Schoenberg, and the architect Le Corbusier.

[172] So M. Calinescu, *Faces of Modernity*, London: Indiana University Press, 1977, 133; cited by Barry Smart, *Postmodernity*, London: Routledge, 1993, 19.

[173] J.-F. Lyotard, *The Postmodern Condition*, trans. G. Bennington and B. Massumi, Manchester: Manchester University Press, 1984, p. xxiv.

[174] See, for example, R. Rorty, *Consequences of Pragmatism*, Brighton: Harvester Press, 1982, ch. 9. Cf. the judgement of Charles Taylor: 'Rorty offers a great leap into non-realism: where there have hitherto been thought to be facts- or truths-of-the-matter, there turn out to be only rival languages, between which we end up plumping, if we do, because in some way one works better for us than the others.' See his 'Rorty in the epistemological tradition', in Alan Malachowski, ed., *Reading Rorty*, Oxford: Blackwell, 1990, 258.

[175] For evidence to support the contention that Enlightenment motifs not only linger, but are enthusiastically championed by some to this day see Margaret Canovan, 'Reason recycled: the Enlightenment today', *Enlightenment and Dissent*, IX, 1990, 3–13.

[176] Interestingly, three self-styled 'radically orthodox' theologians can admit, in their 'damning with faint praise' way, that 'since the Enlightenment was in effect a critique of decadent early modern Christianity, it *is* sometimes possible to learn from it'. It is not altogether clear, however, whether their italicized word betokens arrogance, a patronizing attitude, or genuine surprise that one may

'sometimes' learn from the Enlightenment. Perhaps the last, for they immediately add, 'though in the end the Enlightenment itself massively repeated the decadence'. This is proclaimed with a confidence which only a fool would challenge, though one cannot stifle the queries: how does a general climate of thought such as the Enlightenment 'massively repeat' the decadence of an earlier age? And where is the evidence that it did? See John Milbank, Graham Ward and Catherine Pickstock, 'Introduction. Suspending the material: the turn of radical orthodoxy', in their edited volume, *Radical Orthodoxy*, London: Routledge, 1999, 2–3.

177 M. Henry, 'The Enlightenment and Romanticism', *Irish Theological Quarterly*, LXIII no. 3, 1998, 252–3.

178 See Alan P. F. Sell, *John Locke and the Eighteenth-Century Divines*, Cardiff: University of Wales Press, 1977, ch. 3.

179 I am not concerned to investigate in detail the reading of history proposed by postmodernists and their near relatives (especially Foucault).

180 See, for example, Ingeborg Hoesterey, ed., *Zeitgeist in Babel: The Postmodernist Controversy*, Bloomington, IN: Indiana University Press, 1991.

181 Republished as *An Introduction to Metaphysics*, trans. T. E. Hulme, London: Macmillan, 1913, 6. For lucid accounts of Bergson see A. R. Lacey, *Bergson*, London: Routledge, 1989; Eric Matthews, *Twentieth-Century French Philosophy*, Oxford: OUP, 1996, ch. 2.

182 H. Bergson, *Mélanges*, Paris: PUF, 1972, 939. On this matter postmodernists of the 'windier', jargon-laden kind appear studiously to have ignored Bergson.

183 Idem, *Creative Evolution* (1907), trans. A. Mitchell, London: Macmillan, 1911, 186.

184 L. P. Jacks, *The Revolt Against Mechanism*, London: Allen & Unwin, 1933, 49.

185 H. Bergson, *Mélanges*, 1148.

186 A. S. Pringle-Pattison, *The Idea of God in the Light of Recent Philosophy*, New York: OUP, 1920, 385. The entire chapter, 19, constitutes a telling critique of Bergson and others, which is the more significant as coming not from a mechanist or materialist, but from a leading personal idealist, for whom see further Alan P. F. Sell, *Philosophical Idealism and Christian Belief.*

187 H. R. Mackintosh, *Some Aspects of Christian Thought*, London: Hodder & Stoughton, [1923], 239.

188 Ibid., 254.

189 Not, indeed, that Bergson's influence is restricted to postmodernists. His theme of creative evolution, for example, was among the inspira-

tions of Teilhard de Chardin. Bergson was aware of the undoubted similarities between his position and the 'stream of consciousness' views of William James; but whereas James set out from introspective psychology, Bergson turned to it in the wake of his reflections upon scientific and mathematical accounts of time.

190 F. Nietzsche, *Twilight of the Idols and the Anti-Christ*, trans. R. J. Hollingdale, Harmondsworth: Penguin, 1968, 36.

191 We should note in passing that the deists are, like others we have noted, subjected to blanket descriptions and denunciations. In fact, they, no less than philosophical analysts and postmodernists, display considerable variety; and the question of who should count as a deist is not one capable of a glib answer. See Alan P. F. Sell, ' "The Gospel its own witness": Deism, Thomas Paine and Andrew Fuller', in a *festschrift* for Allison A. Trites, Macon, GA: Mercer University Press, forthcoming.

192 It is interesting to compare Nietzsche with his German contemporary Rudolf Eucken at this point. They were in considerable accord concerning the Enlightenment, Eucken holding that 'At the beginning of the Modern Age, especially in the transition to the Enlightenment, apparently established truths became problematic . . . the present is in a similar situation. The threads that we have hitherto followed break; all external help is rejected, as is also the authority of history; nothing else remains to us than our own capacity, and the hope to find in it a new support and the basis for a new construction.' But Eucken's response to this situation was to adumbrate a spiritual evolutionism, not to have recourse to naturalism, as Nietzsche did. See R. Eucken, *Life's Basis and Life's Ideal*, London: A. & C. Black, rev. edn. 1918, 304. Eucken's lamp burned brightly and briefly, and little attention has been paid to him of late – as I discovered when invited to write the short article on him in the *Biographical Dictionary of Twentieth-Century Philosophers*, London: Routledge, 1996.

193 J. Richard Middleton and Brian J. Walsh, *Truth is Stranger than it Used to Be: Biblical Faith in a Postmodern Age*, London: SPCK, 1995, 26. For a searching review of this book see John W. Cooper, *Calvin Theological Journal*, XXXI no. 1, April 1995, 287–93.

194 D. Cupitt, *The Time Being*, London: SCM Press, 1992, 66. At one point I contemplated more detailed reference to Don Cupitt. The problem is that like the universally loved heavyweight boxer, Henry Cooper, Cupitt is for ever 'bobbin' an' weavin', and a moving target is notoriously difficult to hit. Or, if a more classical allusion be preferred, Cupitt is the Heraclitus of contemporary theology: in his own words, 'we love mobility. We don't want creeds.' See his *Radicals and the Future of the Church*, London: SCM Press, 1989, 112. Others have

been less inhibited than I. See, for example, Stephen Ross White, *Don Cupitt and the Future of Doctrine*, London: SCM Press, 1994.

195 A. S. Pringle-Pattison, *Man's Place in the Cosmos and Other Essays*, Edinburgh: Blackwood, 1902, 319.

196 H. Meynell, 'On Nietzsche, postmodernism and the new Enlightenment', *New Blackfriars*, LXXVI, January 1995, 6.

197 Ibid., 7–8. Here, as elsewhere, Meynell reveals his indebtedness to Bernard Lonergan, especially to the latter's view that we come to know so far as we are attentive, intelligent and reasonable. We act aright when we are responsible. In an admirably concise article Meynell writes, 'Suppose someone denies that these are the foundations of knowledge. Either she has grounds for this denial, or she has not. If she has no grounds, what is the point of attending to what she says? But if she has such grounds, what can these be other than that she has attended to the relevant evidence, envisaged the possibilities that these are (and that these are not) the foundations of knowledge, and judged that the evidence supports the view that they are not? But in that case she will be implicitly appealing to those very grounds of knowledge – the same grounds of knowledge she is explicitly denying.' See his 'Lonergan's search for knowledge', *Literary Review of Canada*, February 1993, 15a. See further idem, 'Lonergan's method: its nature and uses', *Scottish Journal of Theology*, XXVII no. 2, May 1974, 162–80.

198 R. Tallis, 'The shrink from hell', a review of Elizabeth Roudinesco, *Jacques Lacan*, in *The Times Higher Education Supplement*, 31 October 1997, 20.

199 E. Matthews, *Twentieth-Century French Philosophy*, 155.

200 See, for further explanation, Dan R. Stiver, *The Philosophy of Religious Language: Sign, Symbol and Story*, Oxford: Blackwell, 1996.

201 J. Derrida, *Of Grammatology*, trans. G. Spivak, Baltimore: Johns Hopkins University Press, 1974, 158.

202 Ibid., 13.

203 See idem, *Limited Inc.*, trans. Samuel Weber, Evanston, IL: Northwestern University Press, 1988, 116.

204 Idem, *Writing and Difference*, trans. A. Bass, London: Routledge & Kegan Paul, 1978, 32.

205 Catherine Pickstock's remark is not, in view of this, surprising: 'It seems, therefore, that Derrida et al. have not offered an exhaustive phenomenology of the "nothing",' See *Radical Orthodoxy*, 272. Is it too fanciful to imagine certain analytical philosophers devoutly thanking God for small mercies?

206 See J. Derrida, *Of Grammatology*, 7. Derrida, prompted not least by his passionate concern for justice (will this lead him towards a meta-

narrative?), has recently been making more favourable remarks concerning religion – though it is a non-religious religion having no transcendent reference. See his paper in J. Derrida and Gianni Vattimo, *Religion*, Stanford, CA: Stanford University Press, 1998.

207 See Richard Kearney, *Dialogues with Contemporary Continental Thinkers: The Phenomenological Heritage*, Manchester: Manchester University Press, 1984, 123–4.

208 H. Meynell, 'Archdeconstruction and postmodernism', *Heythrop Journal*, XXXVI, 1995, 128.

209 Idem, *Reconstructing Philosophy*, Toronto: University of Toronto Press, 1998, 202.

210 Ibid., 208.

211 J. H. Olthuis, ed., *Knowing Other-wise: Philosophy at the Threshold of Spirituality*, New York: Fordham University Press, 1998, 109.

212 Colin Gunton, *The One, the Three and the Many*, Cambridge: CUP, 1993, 106.

213 Which calls to mind Roy Harris's cheeky assertion, 'Nowadays there is not much to choose intellectually between the cult of Peirce and the cult of Presley. The chief difference is that most of Elvis's cult members do not hold posts in American universities . . . Peirce was probably the most prolific purveyor of half-baked ideas in western philosophy since Jeremy Bentham, and he supplied a whole hideous vocabulary of neologisms in which to enshrine them for posterity.' See his 'Put that in your pipe and smoke it', a review of Floyd Merrell, *Semiosis in the Postmodern Age*, in *The Times Higher Education Supplement*, 22 September 1995, 21.

214 R. Rorty, *Objectivity, Relativism and Truth*, Cambridge: CUP, 1991, 32.

215 Idem, *Philosophy and the Mirror of Nature*, Oxford: Blackwell, 1980, 178.

216 G. Lindbeck, *The Nature of Doctrine: Religion and Theology in a Postliberal Age*, London: SPCK, 1984, 94.

217 Ibid., 16.

218 Ibid., 18.

219 Ibid., 117. It would seem, therefore, that Albert Outler's use of the phrase 'to the human family' in the following sentence should be replaced by 'to the Christian community': 'The aim of a postliberal hermeneutics is to reposition Holy Scripture as a unique linguistic medium of God's self-communication to the human family.' See his 'Toward a post-liberal hermeneutics', *Theology Today*, XLII no. 3, October 1985, 286.

220 Ibid., 69.

221 Ibid.

222 Ibid., 52.

[223] Ibid., 19.

[224] See, for example, David A. Pailin, *Probing the Foundations: A Study in Theistic Reconstruction*, Kampen: Kok Pharos, 1994, 55. See further Terrence W. Tilley et al., *Postmodern Theologies: The Challenge of Religious Diversity*, Maryknoll, NY: Orbis Books, 1966, ch. 7, especially p. 106.

[225] See, for example, the editor in Robert P. Scharlemann, ed., *Theology at the End of the Century: A Dialogue on the Postmodern*, Richmond: University Press of Virginia, 1990, 2.

[226] Donald MacKinnon, *The Problem of Metaphysics*, Cambridge: CUP, 1974, 76.

[227] Ibid., 44.

[228] Idem in George W. Roberts and Donovan E. Smucker, eds., *Borderlands of Theology and Other Essays*, London: Lutterworth Press, 1968, 74.

[229] See his interview with Sean Sayers, *The Times Higher Education Supplement*, 6 June 1997, 18.

[230] R. Rorty, 'Science as solidarity', in H. Lawson and L. Appignanesi, eds., *Dismantling Truth: Reality in the Postmodern World*, New York: St Martin's Press, 1989, 11.

[231] R. Rorty, *Consequences of Pragmatism*, p. xlii. Cf. idem, *Contingency, Irony and Solidarity*, Cambridge: CUP, 1989, 5.

[232] It goes without saying that this doctrine should not be construed in such a way as to suggest that infants and those whose mental capacities do not, so far as we can tell, permit them voluntarily to respond to the approach of God, are any the less made in his image, with all the dignity that that entails. On the contrary, we have every reason to believe from the gospels that they have a special place in the heart of God, as they should have in ours. 'In as much . . .' Matthew 25: 31–46. It is not easy to see how the genuine advocacy of some postmodernists for justice is consistent with the basic philosophical position of some of them, according to which there is nothing to choose between justice and injustice. Neither is it easy to see how the following statement is anything other than a metanarrative of a kind doleful to the point of morbid – and, for good measure, based on the fallacy of incomplete enumeration: 'When convinced of the truth or right of a given world view, a culture has only two significant options: totalitarian control of the opposition, or annihilation of it.' So Kenneth J. Gergen, *The Saturated Self: Dilemmas of Identity in Contemporary Life*, New York: Basic Books, 1991, 252.

[233] A. Quinton, *From Wodehouse to Wittgenstein*, 65–6.

[234] See Richard Kearney, *Dialogue with Contemporary Continental Thinkers*, 49.

[235] E. Lévinas, *Totality and Infinity: An Essay on Exteriority*, trans. Alphonso Lingis, Pittsburgh: Duquesne University Press, 1969, 195. Indebtedness to Martin Buber is clear. Interesting parallels are to be found in the writings of such other Jewish thinkers as Hermann Cohen and Franz Rosenzweig. Lévinas became increasingly critical of Heidegger who, he thought, paid insufficient attention to the Other.

[236] See idem, *Otherwise than Being*, trans. Alphonso Lingis, The Hague: Martinus Nijhoff, 1981. Cf. the Roman Catholic writer Jean-Luc Marion, *God without Being*, trans. Thomas A. Carlson, Chicago: University of Chicago Press, 1991.

[237] John D. Caputo is among those who find in (or draw from) Derrida's writings parallels between deconstruction and negative theology. See his book *The Prayers and Tears of Jacques Derrida: Religion without Religion*, Bloomington, IN: Indiana Unviersity Press, 1997.

[238] L. Wittgenstein, journal entry of 1947, in E. T. Oakes, ed., *German Essays on Religion*, New York: Continuum, 1994, 227. Well, passionate commitment to a person lies at the heart of Christianity, such commitment undoubtedly entailing a system of reference. Still, Wittgenstein is not far from the kingdom at this point.

[239] Andrew Bowie, 'Sense and significant nonsense', an extract from his Inaugural Lecture as professor of European Philosophy at Anglia Polytechnic University, 17 March 1993. In *The Times Higher Education Supplement*, 27 August 1993, 15.

[240] I. M. Crombie, in *Faith and Logic*, 68. We seem here to hear an echo of John 1: 18: 'No one has ever seen God; God's only Son, he who is nearest to the Father's heart, has made him known.'

Chapter 5: Transcendence, Immanence and History

[1] I thus signal my concern that 'deism' employed to denote a transcendently remote God does not accurately describe the position of some of those commonly designated 'deist', and that such labelling is in any case problematic. See further Alan P. F. Sell, '"The Gospel its own Witness": deism, Thomas Paine and Andrew Fuller', forthcoming in a *festschrift* for Allison A. Trites, Macon, GA: Mercer University Press.

[2] Aristotle, *Topica*, 9, trans. W. A. Pickard-Cambridge, in *The Works of Aristotle Translated into English*, ed. W. D. Ross, Oxford: Clarendon Press, 1928, I. This is not the place to discuss Aristotle's categories in detail. They have prompted an extensive literature, amongst which George Grote's *Aristotle*, London: John Murray, 1880, ch. 3, is not the least interesting.

[3] Aristotle, *Metaphysica*, 1003^{b}, in *Works*, VIII, 2nd edn., 1928.

[4] See further J. A. Aertsen, 'The medieval doctrine of the transcenden-

tals: the current state of research', *Bulletin de philosophie médiévale*, XXXIII, 1991, 130–47.

5 Philip's work is *Summa de bono*, *c.*1225–8. See the edn. by N. Wicki, Berne, 1985.

6 Aristotle, *Metaphysica*, 1072^{b}, 26–9.

7 Aquinas, *Summa Theologiae*, I, q. 8.

8 Plato, *Republic*, ed. F. M. Cornford, Oxford: Clarendon Press, 1951, 89.

9 Ibid., 215.

10 Ibid., 219.

11 Idem, *Laws*, 896a5–b1.

12 Idem, *Phaedo*, 98cd.

13 See, for example, *Enneads*, 5. 9. 13, trans. Stephen MacKenna, London: Faber & Faber, 4th edn. rev. B. S. Page, 1969.

14 P. Spearritt, 'Neoplatonism', in A. Richardson, ed., *A Dictionary of Christian Theology*, London: SCM Press, 1969, 227.

15 Augustine, *The City of God*, VII.xxx.

16 H. W. Clark, *Liberal Orthodoxy*, London: Chapman & Hall, 1914, 42.

17 See further Placid Spearritt, 'The soul's participation in God according to Pseudo-Dionysius', *Downside Review*, LXXXVIII, 1970, 378–92.

18 Pseudo-Dionysius, *The Divine Names and the Mystical Theology*, London: SPCK, 1975, II, 9.

19 Ibid., 21.

20 See, for example, *De Trinitate* 5. 1. 1, 7. 4. 7.

21 F. C. Copleston, *A History of Philosophy*, Westminster, MD: Image Books, 1962, II. i, 115.

22 Pseudo-Dionysius, *The Divine Names*, V, 1.

23 John Scottus Eriugena, *De divisione naturae*, III, 20, IV, 5.

24 Unlike Augustine, for whom the ideas are eternally present in God, Eriugena holds that they have a beginning, though not one in time.

25 John Scottus Eriugena, *De divisione naturae*, I, 72.

26 Ulrich of Strasbourg, *De summo bono*, II, 3, ed. A. de Libera, Hamburg: Meiner, 1987.

27 Ian G. Barbour, *Issues in Science and Religion*, London: SCM Press, 1966, 26.

28 P. T. Forsyth was among those who argued that this right was not, contrary to popular belief, a product of the Reformation: 'The Reformation certainly made religion personal, but it did not make it individualistic . . . What the Reformation said was that the layman with his Bible in his hand had at his side the same Holy Spirit as the minister.' See his *The Principle of Authority* (1913), London: Independent Press, 1952, 283. Moreover, the Reformers, though profoundly influenced by humanism, were not as sanguine as some humanists

concerning the competence of human reason and conscience when unaided by the Spirit.

29 I. Kant, *Critique of Judgment*, trans. Werner S. Pluhar, Indianapolis: Hackett, 1987, 20.

30 Idem, *Prolegomena to any Future Metaphysics*, trans. of Paul Carus revised by James W. Ellington, Indianapolis: Hackett, 1985, 37.

31 *Pascal's Pensées*, ed. H. F. Stewart, London: Routledge & Kegan Paul, 1950, nos. 626, 627, 631.

32 F. D. E. Schleiermacher, *On Religion: Speeches to its Cultured Despisers*, trans. John Oman, New York: Harper & Row, 1958, 101.

33 Idem, *The Christian Faith*, trans. H. R. Mackintosh and J. S. Stewart, Edinburgh: T. & T. Clark, 1960, 13.

34 The literature on these is vast. For Coleridge see C. R. Sanders, *Coleridge and the Broad Church Movement*, Durham NC: Duke University Press, 1942; Douglas Hedley, *Coleridge, Philosophy and Religion*, Cambridge: CUP, 2000. A. B. Bruce's discussion of Frances Power Cobbe, Theodore Parker and Martineau among others remains of interest. See his *Apologetics; or, Christianity Defensively Stated*, Edinburgh: T. & T. Clark, 1927, bk. I, ch. 6.

35 I here draw on the description offered by V. F. Storr, *The Development of English Theology in the Nineteenth Century*, London: Longmans, 1913, 127–30.

36 For example, the transcendentalists' definitions of 'reason' varied: 'Those who recognised such a faculty sometimes called it by different names, such as "Spirit", "Mind", "Soul", and they also differed in the claims they made for it. For some Transcendentalists it was simply an inner light or conscience; for others it was the voice of God; for still others it was literally God himself immanent in man. Some regarded the informing spirit primarily as an impersonal cosmic force; others continued to think of it in traditional anthropomorphic terms.' So Lawrence Buell, *Literary Transcendentalism*, Ithaca, NY: Cornell University Press, 1973, 5.

37 E. Caird, *The Evolution of Religion*, Glasgow: Maclehose, 1893, II, 193. See further Alan P. F. Sell, *Philosophical Idealism and Christian Belief*, ch. 5. For similar tendencies in the thought of Caird's older brother, John, and for Edward's concern that John was too much under Hegel's spell, see idem, *Defending and Declaring the Faith: Some Scottish Examples 1860–1920*, Exeter: Paternoster Press, and Colorado Springs: Helmers & Howard, 1987, ch. 4.

38 Karl Rahner has suggested that the reaction against the dualism of nature and grace has been so strong in some twentieth-century Roman Catholic theology that the two spheres have been well nigh merged into one. See his *Theological Investigations*, London: Darton, Longman & Todd, 1961, I, 287–346.

39 J. W. Nevin, 'The sect system'. Nevin contributed this article to the first volume of his *Mercersburg Review*, September and November, 1849. It was occasioned by the publication in 1848 of John Winebrenner's *History of all the Religious Denominations in the United States*, Harrisburg, PA – just seventy miles from Mercersburg.

40 R. J. Campbell, *The New Theology*, London: Chapman & Hall, 1907, 4.

41 Ibid.

42 Donald G. Bloesch quotes Campbell thus when arguing that William Blake, T. J. Altizer, Michel Quoist, J. A. T. Robinson, R. Gregor Smith and Campbell himself have embraced a 'pan-sacramentalist or pantheistic orientation', thereby losing the distinction between 'the holy and the profane, the spiritual and the secular'. See 'The missing dimension', *Reformed Review*, XXVI no. 3, Spring 1973, 164. See further Alan P. F. Sell, *Theology in Turmoil: The Roots, Course and Significance of the Conservative–Liberal Debate in Modern Theology* (1986), Eugene, OR: Wipf & Stock, 1998. Campbell subsequently recanted, returned to the Church of England and became canon and chancellor of the diocese of Chichester. His autobiography is entitled *A Spiritual Pilgrimage*, London: Williams & Norgate, 1916.

43 P. T. Forsyth, 'The distinctive thing in Christian experience', *The Hibbert Journal*, VI, April 1908, 485.

44 Forsyth has been called 'a Barthian before Barth'. John Thompson has asked, in a helpful paper, 'Was Forsyth really a Barthian before Barth?' He finds that they shared roots in liberal theology, and, for all their stylistic differences, articulated a number of common themes. See Trevor Hart, ed., *Justice the True and Only Mercy: Essays on the Life and Theology of Peter Taylor Forsyth*, Edinburgh: T. & T. Clark, 1996, 237–55. My own view is that, for all the commonalities, while both shared a strong christological emphasis, Barth's dogmatics were structured in a more clearly trinitarian way than Forsyth's writings (many of which were occasional); Forsyth never loosened his grasp on the sacraments as the later Barth did; and Forsyth had more time for apologetics than did Barth (on which point see my paper in the Hart collection).

45 K. Barth, *Church Dogmatics*, II, i, Edinburgh: T. & T. Clark, 1957, 302–3.

46 Gordon D. Kaufman, 'On the meaning of "God": transcendence without mythology', *Harvard Theological Review*, LIX, 1966, 105.

47 See his 'Speech of the dead Christ', in *Flower, Fruit and Thorn Pieces*, 2 vols. Leipzig, 1871, I, 278–85.

48 F. Nietzsche, *The Joyful Wisdom*, in *The Complete Works of Friedrich Nietzsche*, ed. Oscar Levy, Edinburgh: T. N. Foulis, 1910, X, 168. For a study of Nietzsche which takes seriously his professed atheism and construes it as more than blindly antagonistic defiance see Alistair Kee, *Nietzsche Against the Crucified*, London: SCM Press, 1999.

[49] T. J. J. Altizer and W. Hamilton, *Radical Theology and the Death of God*, Harmondsworth: Penguin, 1968, 14. How different this 'radical' theology is from the current brand of radical orthodoxy emanating from those associated with Cambridge. I do not deny that in the wake of the 'classical' death-of-God theologians have come many others, among them Mark C. Taylor, according to whose a/theology we no longer have a transcendent point of reference or guarantor of truth, and are left with our perceptions and interpretations and constructions of reality which in fact constitute us. We are left with self-engendered pragmatism. In his earlier writings Taylor left a place for immanent flux, but more recently, as in 'The politics of Theo–ry', *Journal of the American Academy of Religion*, LIX, 1991, 1–37, he seems to have become wary of this, presumably lest it encourage the reintroduction of ideas of a personal immanent presence: 'To pursue the trace of the "god" of nonidentity who is never present is to pursue a trace other than the One left by the god of identity' (ibid., 34).

[50] G. Vahanian, *Wait without Idols*, New York: Braziller, 1964, 46.

[51] W. Hamilton, *Radical Theology*, 40.

[52] Idem, *The New Essence of Christianity*, London: Darton, Longman & Todd, 1966, 68.

[53] Ibid., 82.

[54] T. J. J. Altizer, *Christian Atheism*, London: Collins, 1966, 103.

[55] Idem, 'Creative negation in theology', *Christian Century*, 7 July 1965, quoted by Richard Wolff, *Is God Dead?*, Wheaton, IL: Tyndale House Publishers, 1966, 19.

[56] Idem, *The Gospel of Christian Atheism*, 103.

[57] Idem, *Radical Theology*, 102.

[58] Ibid., 30.

[59] Idem, *Christian Atheism*, 22.

[60] Paul M. van Buren, *The Secular Meaning of the Gospel*, Harmondsworth: Penguin, 1968, 108.

[61] Schubert M. Ogden, *Christ without Myth*, London: Collins, 1962, 133.

[62] For a concise statement of the main thrust of process theology from one broadly sympathetic with it see David A. Pailin, *Probing the Foundations: A Study in Theistic Reconstruction*, Kampen: Kok Pharos, 1994, ch. 5.

[63] A. N. Whitehead, *Process and Reality* (1929), New York: Harper, 1960, 528.

[64] Ibid., 529. I confess to finding it difficult to assign meaning to some of Whitehead's remarks. In this I am not alone. See L. Susan Stebbing's review of *Process and Reality* in *Mind*, XXXIX, 1930, 475.

[65] Idem, *Adventures of Ideas*, Cambridge: CUP, 1935, 217.

[66] H. N. Wieman, *The Source of Human Good*, Chicago: Chicago University Press, 1946, 7.

[67] N. Pittenger, 'The doctrine of Christ in process theology', *Expository Times*, LXXXII, October 1970, 9.

[68] J. Richmond, 'God, time and process philosophy', *Theology*, LXVIII, 1965, 241.

[69] W. Temple, *Nature, Man and God*, London: Macmillan, 1934, 259. E. S. Brightman's finite God comes to mind at this point; and E. L. Mascall's view that Whitehead's 'God' is really the principle of creativity. See E. S. Brightman, *The Philosophy of Religion*, London: Skeffington, 1947; E. L. Mascall, *He who is* (1943), London: Darton, Longman & Todd, 1966; idem, *The Openness of Being*, London: Darton, Longman & Todd, 1971.

[70] R. G. Smith, *The Doctrine of God*, London: Collins, 1970, 157.

[71] Eugene H. Peters, 'A framework for Christian thought', *Journal of Religion*, LVI, 1966, 375.

[72] Ibid., 379.

[73] C. Hartshorne, *Man's Vision of God*, Hamden, CT: Archon Books, 1964, 198.

[74] Though I suppose that a process or a theology of hope future-fixation could inspire an avoidance of mission of Thessalonican proportions. Hence Rubem Alves once labelled the idea of the coming God of the future a new docetism, and welcomed revolutionary thought as a defence against it: the revolutionary cannot overlook the brutality of the present on the ground that the future alone matters. See his *A Theology of Human Hope*, St Meinrad, IN: Abbey Press, 1972.

[75] John 1: 4.

[76] D. A. Pailin, *Probing the Foundations*, 162. Cf. idem, 'The utterly absolute and the totally related', *New Blackfriars*, LXVIII, May 1987, 243–55.

[77] D. E. Jenkins, *The Glory of Man*, London: SCM Press, 1967, 108.

[78] Cf. Diogenes Allen, *The Path of Perfect Love*, Cambridge, MA: Cowley Publications, 1992, 44.

[79] James Orr, *The Progress of Dogma*, London: James Clarke, 1901, 323–4 n. For Orr see further Alan P. F. Sell, *Defending and Declaring the Faith*, ch. 7; G. G. Scorgie, *A Call for Continuity: The Theological Contribution of James Orr*, Macon, GA: Mercer University Press, 1989.

[80] P. T. Forsyth, *Positive Preaching and the Modern Mind* (1907), London: Independent Press, 1964, 146.

[81] In his article 'Advantages and disadvantages in the process approach to God', *Irish Theological Quarterly*, XLIV, 1977, 31–8, E. R. Baltazar expresses a preference for process thought over alleged Thomist substance-staticism. In a reply (ibid., 232–42) Maurice Curtin employs a homely illustration: 'Parents can exercise a certain concern for their children which in a certain sense is total. And the reason is

that they are independent of their children. But the concern of children for their parents can be never more than partial. God can dominate the whole span of time and history and exercise an absolutely total concern for everything in its individuality. A dependent God, a God affected by the process of creation, is really a contradiction', 238.

82 Hugo Meynell makes the point in 'The theology of Hartshorne', *Journal of Theological Studies*, XXIV, 1973, 153.

83 H. R. Mackintosh, *Some Aspects of Christian Belief*, London: Hodder & Stoughton, n.d. (preface, 1923), 153.

84 A. E. Taylor, *The Faith of a Moralist*, London: Macmillan, 1930, I, 229.

85 Ibid.

86 S. Charnock, *The Existence and Attributes of God* (1683), Grand Rapids: Sovereign Grace Publishers, 1971, 155.

87 J. Calvin, *Institute of the Christian Religion*, I. v. 1.

88 Roger Trigg, *Rationality and Religion*, Oxford: Blackwell, 1998, 205.

89 G. F. Woods, 'The idea of the transcendent', in A. R. Vidler, ed., *Soundings*, Cambridge: CUP, 1963, 45; cf. R. W. Hepburn, *Christianity and Paradox*, London: Watts, 1958, 193–4. See further G. F. Woods, *Theological Explanation*, London: Nisbet, 1958. I should still claim that this lucid work merits close attention even if Woods, as external examiner, had not approved of my MA thesis!

90 G. F. Woods, 'The idea of the transcendent', 61.

91 Ibid., 64.

92 Ibid., 63.

93 Rupert Hoare, 'The idea of the transcendent: G. F. Woods as a theological teacher', *Theology*, LXVIII, 1967, 402.

94 See further Alan P. F. Sell, *Philosophy of Religion 1875–1980*, 182–4, and in addition to critical papers there specified see W. D. Hudson, 'Discernment situations: some philosophical difficulties', *Scottish Journal of Theology*, XIX no. 4, 1966, 434–45; H. P. Owen, 'The philosophical theology of I. T. Ramsey', *Theology*, LXXIV, 1971, 67–74, and Ramsey's response, ibid., 125–7; Brian Hebblethwaite, 'The philosophical theology of I. T. Ramsey: some further reflections', *Theology*, LXXVI, 1973, 638–45.

95 I. T. Ramsey, *Religious Language*, London: SCM Press, 1957, 27–8.

96 Idem, 'On the possibility and purpose of a metaphysical theology', in I. T. Ramsey, ed., *Prospect for Metaphysics*, London: Allen & Unwin, 1961, 194.

97 Paul Helm, review of Ramsey's *Christian Empiricism* (1974) in *Religious Studies*, X, 1974, 505.

98 Paul Tillich, *Systematic Theology*, Chicago: University of Chicago Press, 1951, I, 238–9.

99 Ibid., 239. See further John Heywood Thomas, 'Religious language as

symbolism', *Religious Studies*, I, October 1965, 89–93; idem, *Paul Tillich: An Appraisal*, London: SCM Press, 1963, 56, 136.

100 G. D. Kaufman, 'On the meaning of "God": transcendence without mythology', *Harvard Theological Review*, LIX, 1966, 112.

101 Ibid., 122.

102 Ibid., 132.

103 R. Gregor Smith, *The Doctrine of God*, London: Collins, 1970, 107; cf. idem, *The Free Man*, London: Collins, 1969, 119: 'we are only involved in speculation, unanchored to historical experience, when we speak of God either as being or a Being'.

104 Cf. T. F. Torrance, *God and Rationality*, London: OUP, 1971, 80–1.

105 J. A. T. Robinson, *Honest to God*, 49.

106 A. A. Vogel, *The Next Christian Epoch*, New York: Harper & Row, 1966, 78.

107 H. Cox, *The Secular City*, London: SCM Press, 1965, 262.

108 Ibid., ch. 5.

109 Quoted by Peter Wagner, *Latin American Theology*, Grand Rapids: Eerdmans, 1971, 52.

110 G. Stanley Kane, 'God-language and secular experience', *International Journal for Philosophy of Religion*, II, 1971, 91.

111 Lionel Blue, 'In search of the transcendent, 2', *The Month*, July 1974, 643. The first sentence calls to mind P. T. Forsyth's words concerning the Christian minister. See *The Church and the Sacraments* (1917), London: Independent Press, 1953, 132–3.

112 H. Cox, 'Afterword', in D. Callahan, ed., *The Secular City Debate*, New York: Macmillan, 1966, 196.

113 J. A. T. Robinson, 'The debate continues', in David L. Edwards, ed., *The Honest to God Debate*, London: SCM Press, 1963, 236.

114 D. F. Strauss, *A New Life of Jesus for the German People*, English trans., 1865, I, xii.

115 R. Rainy et al., *The Supernatural in Christianity*, Edinburgh: T. & T. Clark, 1894, 15. Pfleiderer's lectures were entitled *Philosophy and the Development of Religion*.

116 D. Bonhoeffer, *Act and Being*, New York: Harper, 1961, 89.

117 In *The Supernatural in Christianity*, 46. See further Alan P. F. Sell, *Defending and Declaring the Faith*, ch. 7.

118 Roger Thomas, 'When is a Unitarian not a Unitarian?', *Transactions of the Unitarian Historical Society*, XIV no. 3, October 1969, 111, quoting Albert Réville, *The Life and Writings of Theodore Parker*, 1865, 168. For Martineau on the seat of authority see Alan P. F. Sell, *Commemorations: Studies in Christian Thought and History*, ch. 1.

119 Laurens P. Hickock, *Rational Psychology; or, the Subjective Idea and the Objective Law of all Intelligence*, Auburn: Derby, Miller, 1849, 75.

120 Hastings Rashdall, *Ideas and Ideals*, Oxford: Blackwell, 1928, 196.

121 R. S. Franks, *The Atonement*, London: OUP, 1934, 142.

122 P. Bonnard, 'Holy', in J.-J. Von Allmen, ed., *Vocabulary of the Bible*, London: Lutterworth, 1958, 166. Cf. T. Rees, *The Holy Spirit*, London: Duckworth, 1915, 23–5.

123 Cf. H. D. Lewis, *Our Experience of God*, London: Allen & Unwin, 1959, ch. 3; J. Heywood Thomas, 'The transcendence of God', *London Quarterly and Holborn Review*, July 1964, 184–9.

124 P. T. Forsyth, *The Principle of Authority*, 1913, London: Independent Press, 1952, 181.

125 See J. R. Illingworth, *Divine Transcendence*, London: Macmillan, 1911, 14–15; W. Temple, *Nature, Man and God*, 269–70.

126 D. Jenkins, *The Glory of Man*, 104, cf. 53.

127 C. E. Gunton, *Enlightenment and Alienation: An Essay towards a Trinitarian Theology*, Basingstoke: Marshall, Morgan & Scott, 1985, 155.

128 R. Baxter, *The Saint's Everlasting Rest*, in *The Practical Works of The Rev. Richard Baxter*, London: James Duncan, 1830, XXII, 37–8. Cf. A. S. Pringle-Pattison, 'God in action', in B. H. Streeter, ed., *The Spirit*, London: Macmillan, 1928, 30–2.

129 S. Charnock, *The Existence and Attributes of God*, 153; cf. *Westminster Confession*, II. ii.

130 Psalm 108: 23.

131 W. Adams Brown, *Christian Theology in Outline*, Edinburgh: T. & T. Clark, 1923, 229.

132 B. B. Warfield, 'Christian supernaturalism', in his *Biblical and Theological Studies*, ed. Samuel G. Craig, Philadelphia: Presbyterian and Reformed Publishing Co., 1952, 20.

133 P. T. Forsyth, *Positive Preaching and the Modern Mind* (1907), London: Independent Press, 1964, 161.

134 J. Denney, *Studies in Theology*, London: Hodder & Stoughton, 1902, 13.

135 For the argument that causal agencies may not be classified as either 'natural' or 'supernatural' see T. R. Miles, 'On excluding the supernatural', *Religious Studies*, I, 1965, 141–50.

136 H. H. Farmer, *The World and God*, London: Nisbet, 1935, 6; cf. 59, 65.

137 Ephesians 2: 9.

138 J. A. T. Robinson, *Honest to God*, 56.

139 J. Oman, *The Natural and the Supernatural*, Cambridge: CUP, 1931, 72.

140 Dora Greenwell (1821–82).

141 Augustine, *The City of God*, VII. xxx.

142 H. F. Lovell Cocks, *By Faith Alone*, London: James Clarke, 1943, 151.

143 From Henry Twells's hymn, 'At even, when the sun was set'.

[144] J. R. Illingworth, *Divine Transcendence and its Reflection in Religious Authority*, London: Macmillan, 1911, 17.

[145] As, for example, W. R. Inge properly warned. See *Christian Mysticism*, London: Methuen, 1899, 121.

[146] Augustine, *Confessions*, I. i.

[147] Anon., *The Pilgrim Hymnal*, 1904. Concerning the manner of the Spirit's working, it is no doubt generally the case that he does not 'cause you to speak as a clock that striketh it knoweth not what', but rather 'supposeth nature, and worketh on man as man'. However, G. F. Nuttall, who quotes these words of Richard Baxter, cautions us against ruling out the extraordinary type of experience, however unusual it may be. See his *The Holy Spirit in Puritan Faith and Experience*, Oxford: Blackwell, 1946, 169–72.

[148] Augustine, *Confessions*, X. xxvii.

[149] See the exposition by N. H. Snaith, 'God: transcendent and immanent', *Expository Times*, LXVIII, 1956, 68–71.

[150] N. F. S. Ferré, *The Christian Understanding of God*, London: SCM Press, 1951, 61. Richard Baxter criticized the Quakers for identifying 'the Spirit of God as creator' with 'the Spirit of Christ the Redeemer'. See G. F. Nuttall, *The Holy Spirit in Puritan Faith and Experience*, Oxford: Blackwell, 1946, 174.

[151] W. N. Clarke, *The Christian Doctrine of God*, Edinburgh: T. & T. Clark, 1909, 342–3.

[152] For an older discussion of the transcendent God's saving work which remains instructive, see J. Scott Lidgett, *The Christian Religion, its Meaning and Proof*, London: Robert Culley, [1907], 446–79.

[153] Quoted by John Waddington, *Congregational History 1850–1880*, London: Longmans, 1850, 399, 401, 402.

[154] Robert Flint, 'Some requirements of a present-day Christian apologetics', a lecture delivered on 22 March 1899, reprinted in his *Sermons and Addresses*, Edinburgh: Blackwood, 1899, 306–7.

[155] J. W. Nevin, 'Lectures on history', in Theodore Appel, *The Life and Work of John Williamson Nevin, D.D., LL.D.*, Philadelphia: Reformed Church Publication House, 1889, 598.

[156] H. B. Smith, *System of Christian Theology*, ed. William S. Karr, New York, 3rd edn., 1886, 487.

[157] P. T. Forsyth, 'Christ and the Christian principle', in *London Theological Studies*, London: University of London Press, 1911, 142 n., 166.

[158] C. H. Dodd, *History and the Gospels*, London: Nisbet, 1938, 30.

[159] L. Newbigin, *The Finality of Christ*, London: SCM Press, 1969, 65.

[160] Ibid., 76.

[161] Ibid., 87.

[162] G. F. Woods, *Theological Explanation*, London: Nisbet, 1958, 99.

[163] A. Jeffner, *Theology and Integration: Four Essays in Philosophical Theology*, Uppsala, 1987, 71.

[164] W. Temple, *Nature, Man and God*, London: Macmillan, 1934, 436.

[165] N. Micklem, *What is the Faith?*, London: Hodder & Stoughton, 1936, 16. To each his own: I should probably seek out a secluded cottage with a very small garden. 'Very small', because, not having green fingers, the withering of my plantings and the rampaging of weeds would serve only to remind me of the question, 'Why do the righteous suffer?' – to which, in the circumstances then prevailing, I should have no answer. I should go for long walks, play my records, watch television and deliver meals on wheels to the elderly until such time as some kind soul started delivering them to me.

[166] H. Meynell, *Is Christianity True?*, London: Geoffrey Chapman, 1994, 92 n. 4.

[167] Robert Mackintosh, 'Apologetics', *Encyclopedia Britannica*, 11th edn. 1910–11, 192(b).

[168] Cf. Michael Ramsey, *The Resurrection of Christ*, London: G. Bles, 1945, 53, where we are warned against presuppositions which would seek to fit Jesus Christ 'into certain naturalistic beliefs about the world, man and religion'.

[169] For a full discussion of the issues here briefly announced see T. A. Roberts, *History and Christian Apologetic*, London: SPCK, 1960.

[170] C. J. Wright, *Modern Issues in Religious Thought*, London: Epworth Press, 1937, 163.

[171] Cf. the following comment of the New Testament scholar, C. F. D. Moule, in a review of C. F. Evans, *Is 'Holy Scripture' Christian?*, *Theology*, LXXIV, 1971, 420: 'Would it not be more objective to start from the *coming into existence of the Christian movement*? To do that immediately confronts the historian with the Easter-belief and demands that he account for it. But to start from "Christianity", as "a form of salvation or of saving truth" diverts the quest to something more subjective and more easily dissoluble.'

[172] See further T. A. Roberts, 'Fact and value in historical theology', *The Modern Churchman*, NS XVIII nos. 1 and 2, Winter 1975, 13–21.

[173] H. Palmer, *The Logic of Gospel Criticism*, London: Macmillan, 1968, 183.

[174] T. F. Torrance, *Theological Science*, London: OUP, 1969, 326 (his italics).

[175] A. Farrer, *Faith and Speculation*, London: Adam & Charles Black, 1967, 102.

[176] O. P. Grell, 'Merchants and ministers', in Andrew Pettegree et al., eds., *Calvinism in Europe, 1540–1620*, Cambridge: CUP, 1994, 267.

[177] Quoted by Emma Daly, *Observer*, 2 July 2000, 25.

178 I devise this illustration by way of doffing my cap to the currently fashionable (in some circles) discipline of cultural studies, and in order to amuse Richard M. Gale, through whose rigorously logical book, *The Existence of God*, there shines an evident delight in the songs of which it is sometimes said, 'They don't write them that way any more'. I also recall with affection the waggish student who, during a discussion of Ambrose (of Milan), declared, 'I *do* like his signature tune, "When day is done"!'

179 P. T. Forsyth, *The Cruciality of the Cross* (1909), London: Independent Press, 1957, 17.

180 This is a prominent theme in his *The Perennial Scope of Philosophy*, trans. R. Mannheim, New York: Philosophical Library, 1949.

181 Gadamer is among those who have stoutly insisted upon this point. See, for example, his *Truth and Method*, London: Sheed & Ward, 2nd edn. 1989, 301.

182 Roger Trigg, *Rationality and Religion: Does Faith need Reason?*, Oxford: Blackwell, 1998, 101.

183 1 Corinthians 1: 23 (AV). More recent translations substitute 'Gentiles' for 'Greeks'.

184 John 1: 14. My italics.

185 W. H. V. Reade, *The Christian Challenge to Philosophy*, London: SPCK, 1951, 58.

186 See, for example, W. R. Inge, *Christian Mysticism*, London: Methuen, 1899; idem, *The Philosophy of Plotinus*, London: Longmans, Green, 1918. Elsewhere, in a lucid and succinct paper, Inge records the view with which he sympathizes thus: 'The three truths which Plotinus is most anxious to establish are (1) the spiritual nature of reality, as aginst the materialism of the Epicureans and Stoics; (2) the possibility of gaining a real knowledge of ultimate truth, as against the scepticism of the new Academy and the pragmatism of the eclectics; and (3) as against the Gnostics, the unity, goodness, and sacredness of the universe. There is no sense in which the charge of "extreme dualism" can be fastened on Neoplatonism.' See his *Mysticism in Religion* (1947), London: Rider, 1969, 143. Another Anglican, Leonard Hodgson, leans in the direction of Reade. See his *The Doctrine of the Atonement*, London: Nisbet, 1951, 122.

187 J. Iverach, *The Truth of Christianity*, Edinburgh: T. & T. Clark, n.d., 20.

188 Irenaeus, *Generatio inenarrabilis*, IV. xx. 4.

189 W. H. V. Reade, *The Christian Challenge to Philosophy*, 57.

190 See G. E. Lessing, *The Testament of John*, in H. Chadwick, trans. and ed., *Lessing's Theological Writings*, London: Adam & Charles Black, 1956.

191 See P. T. Forsyth, 'Christ and the Christian principle', 141–2 n.

192 I. Kant, *Religion within the Limits of Reason Alone*, New York: Harper, 1996, 100.

193 G. E. Lessing, 'On the proof of the Spirit and of power', in *Theological Writings*, 53.

194 See D. A. Pailin, *Probing the Foundations: A Study in Theistic Reconstruction*, Kampen: Kok Pharos, 1994, 150–1. Cf. idem, 'History and faith: (2) Is it a mistake to hold that the Christian faith rests on history?', *Epworth Review*, XIX no. 3, September 1992, 39–50; 'The supposedly historical basis of theological understanding', in Sarah Coakley and David Pailin, eds., *The Making and Remaking of Christian Doctrine: Essays in honour of Maurice Wiles*, Oxford: Clarendon Press, 1993, 213–37.

195 G. E. Lessing, *Theological Writings*, 54.

196 Ibid., 55.

197 D. A. Pailin, *Probing the Foundations*, 149.

198 R. Mackintosh, *Essays Towards a New Theology*, Glasgow: MacLehose, 1889, 354.

199 J. Denney, *Jesus and the Gospel*, London: Hodder & Stoughton, 2nd edn. 1909, 375–6.

200 A. E. Garvie, *The Christian Doctrine of the Godhead, or The Apostolic Benediction as the Christian Creed*, London: Hodder & Stoughton, [1925], 20–1.

201 P. T. Forsyth, 'Christ and the Christian principle', 141.

202 W. A. Whitehouse, 'The modern discussion of eschatology', in *Eschatology: Four Papers read to the Society for the Study of Theology*, (Scottish Journal of Theology Occasional Papers, no. 2), Edinburgh: Oliver & Boyd, 1953, 72.

203 For references to some of this, and for a brief account of the matter, see Alan P. F. Sell, *Theology in Turmoil*, ch. 2.

204 D. F. Strauss, *A New Life of Jesus for the German People*, English trans., 1865, I, xii.

205 A. Ritschl, *The Christian Doctrine of Justification and Reconciliation*, III, trans. H. R. Mackintosh and A. B. Macaulay, Edinburgh: T. & T. Clark, 1900, 212. See further Alan P. F. Sell, *Theology in Turmoil*, ch. 4.

206 Ritschl's move did not, of course, go uncriticized. For example, while giving the Ritschlians credit for 'insisting on the reality, importance, and self-evidencing power of what is specifically Christian in theology', Robert Flint faulted them because 'they pretend to possess or demand from others a Christian faith so exclusively drawn from the revelation of God in Christ . . . as to be independent of all objections to it which natural reason, ordinary knowledge, science, or philosophy can suggest'. See his *Sermons and Addresses*, Edinburgh: Blackwood, 1899, 312.

207 See, for example, E. Caird, *Hegel*, Edinburgh: Blackwood, 1891, 218; idem, 'St. Paul and evolution', *Hibbert Journal*, II no. 1, October 1903, 13.

208 T. H. Green, letter to Henry Scott Holland in Stephen Paget, ed., *Henry Scott Holland: Memoir and Letters*, London: John Murray, 1921, 66. Cf. *Works of Thomas Hill Green*, ed. R. L. Nettleship, London: Longmans, Green, 3 vols., 1885–8, III, 260, 266. For the general position see Alan P. F. Sell, *Philosophical Idealism and Christian Belief*, 188–206, 234.

209 T. H. Green, *Works*, III, 182.

210 J. Iverach, 'Professor Thomas Hill Green', *Expository Times*, IV, 1892–3, 167.

211 R. Mackintosh, 'Apologetics', 192(b).

212 P. T. Forsyth, 'Christ and the Christian principle', 137.

213 F. H. Bradley, *Principles of Logic*, London: OUP, 2nd edn. 1922, 689.

214 R. G. Collingwood, *The Idea of History*, ed. T. M. Knox, Oxford: Clarendon Press, 1946, 135. See further T. A. Roberts, 'The historian and the believer' (a review article of Van A. Harvey's book of that title), *Religious Studies*, VII no. 3, 1971, 251–7. See further Leon Pompa, 'Collingwood's theory of historical knowledge', in David Boucher et al., eds., *Philosophy History and Civilization: Interdisciplinary Perspectives on R. G. Collingwood*, Cardiff: University of Wales Press, 1995, especially 170–1.

215 P. W. Schmiedel, *Jesus in Modern Criticism*, London: A. & C. Black, 1907, 85.

216 J. Denney, *Letters of Principal James Denney to W. Robertson Nicoll, 1893–1917*, London: Hodder & Stoughton, 1920, 99–100; letter of 7 November 1907. Schmiedel did not in fact think it could be shown that Jesus never lived.

217 W. R. Inge, *The Religious Philosophy of Plotinus and Some Modern Philosophies of Religion*, London: The Lindsey Press [1914], 24 (where Loisy is quoted), 25.

218 H. J. Paton, *The Modern Predicament: A Study in the Philosophy of Religion*, London: Allen & Unwin, 1955, 235.

219 K. Barth, *Church Dogmatics*, Edinburgh: T. & T. Clark, 1956, IV, 1, 336. For a fuller discussion of these points see Roger Trigg, *Rationality and Religion*, ch. 5.

220 R. Bultmann, *Kerygma and Myth*, ed. H. W. Bartsch, trans. R. H. Fuller, London: SCM Press, 1953, 209.

221 Idem, *Jesus Christ and Mythology*, London: SCM Press, 1958, 84.

222 R. P. C. Hanson, 'The enterprise of emancipating Christian belief from history', in Anthony Hanson, ed., *Vindications: Essays in the Historical Basis of Christianity*, London: SCM Press, 1961, 64–5.

[223] S. Kierkegaard, *Training in Christianity*, Princeton: Princeton University Press, 1941, 28.

[224] See R. Bultmann, *Existence and Faith: Shorter Writings of Rudolf Bultmann*, London: Hodder & Stoughton, 1961, 101–2.

[225] H.W. Bartsch, ed., *Kerygma and Myth*, London: SPCK, 1953, 10 n. 2. While it would be anachronistic, and otherwise preposterous, to cast John Bunyan as a Bultmannite, his words nevertheless come to mind: 'I will venture my eternal soul upon His word, sink or swim, come Heaven, come Hell. Lord Jesus, if Thou wilt catch me, do; if not, I will venture for Thy name.' Quoted by Geoffrey F. Nuttall, *Christian Pacifism in History* (1958), 2nd edn. Berkeley, CA: World Without War Council, 1971, 75.

[226] The literature on Bultmann is vast, and no extended critique of him is possible here. My sole objective is to show a further route via which theologians may sit loose to the historical events of Jesus's life. However, one cannot help wondering with David Jenkins whether the implication of Bultmann's position is that if people stopped deciding for God, theism would be no more. See his *Guide to the Debate about God*, London: Lutterworth, 1966, 69–70. I shall have more to say concerning the language of encounter in the penultimate chapter. Cf. H. P. Owen, *Revelation and Existence*, 117: 'The New Testament speaks of a unique movement in past history whereby God took time into his own Being and eternalized it. Bultmann knows only a Kierkegaardian dialiectic according to which eternity crosses time whenever God meets man in an encounter.'

[227] R. Bultmann, *Kerygma and Myth*, 107. For a discussion of some of the responses to this proposal see James Richmond, *Faith and Philosophy*, London: Hodder & Stoughton, 1966, ch. 5.

[228] On this last point T. F. Torrance and Maurice Wiles are in accord. See *Theological Science*, London: OUP, 1969, 329, and *God's Action in the World*, London: SCM Press, 1986, 32.

[229] C. Gunton, 'Rudolf Bultmann and the location of language about God', *Theology*, LXXV, 1972, 538.

[230] Cf. J. C. O'Neill, 'Bultmann and Hegel', *Journal of Theological Studies*, XXI, 1970, 400.

[231] See, for example, *Kerygma and Myth*, 34–7. For the respects in which Bultmann both echoes and differs from the position of Troeltsch see A. O. Dyson, *The Immortality of the Past*, London: SCM Press, 1974, 88–9.

[232] H. P. Owen, *Revelation and Existence*, 48. This remains one of the most concise, and lucid, accounts of Bultmann's thought on key issues.

[233] For evidence that the puzzles surrounding historicity are not necessarily eased by theologians significantly different from Bultmann,

consider this remark by the editors of *Radical Orthodoxy*, 13, made as they rehearse the views of one of their number, Graham Ward: 'The body of Jesus "is both individual and historically particular, and collective and historically extended through time".' Is this intended as an incarnational-cum-ecclesiological assertion, in which case there is a play on 'body' – unless these radicals literally identify the Church with Christ's body? Or is the reference to the ubiquity of Christ's body – in which case the hoary question of the relation of this to the ascension rears its head once more. Or are they simply as confused as they are confusing? Whatever the answer, there are clearer (if less shorthand) ways of writing.

234 One sometimes wonders whether Bultmann means that Christ is incarnate only when the Word is preached, just as one wondered whether God exists only in the moment of existential encounter. On the former point see Norman Young, 'Bultmann's view of history', *Church Quarterly Review*, 165, 1964, 426.

235 See Kähler's work of 1886, *The So-called Historical Jesus and the Historic Biblical Christ*, English trans., Philadelphia: Fortress Press, 1964, 66. The *historisch/geschichtlich* distinction likewise originates with him.

236 R. Bultmann, *Kerygma and Myth*, 36.

237 Idem, *Theology of the New Testament*, London: SCM Press, 1952, I, 303.

238 Idem, *Kerygma and Myth*, 42. Can it be that only a degree of existential emotion distinguishes faith in the Word of preaching from the simple assent to the apostolic testimony of the eighteenth-century Sandemanians, whose way of construing *sola fide* prompted the charge of antinomianism which was levelled against them? See further Alan P. F. Sell, *Dissenting Thought and the Life of the Churches*, 407–17.

239 H. P. Owen, *Revelation and Existence*, 115. For a view of the resurrection at the opposite pole to that of Bultmann, see William Lane Craig, *Assessing the New Testament Evidence for the Historicity of the Resurrection of Jesus*, Lewiston, NY: Edwin Mellen Press, 1987.

240 Ibid., 49. We may here recall earlier disputes not altogether dissimilar to those occasioned by the existentialists' tendency to neglect historical events. Many Puritans levelled the ahistorical charge against the Quakers' insistence on the fundamental importance of the spirit of Christ within. For example, on the title-page of his anti-Quaker tract, *The Great Mysteries of Godlinesse and Ungodlinesse*, Ralph Farmer described himself as 'a servant of that Jesus Christ that was crucified at Jerusalem above sixteen hundred years ago'.

241 D. W. Forrest, *The Christ of History and of Experience* (1897), Edinburgh: T. & T. Clark, 7th edn. 1914, 330.

[242] H. F. Lovell Cocks, *By Faith Alone*, London: James Clarke, 1943, 106. See Alan P. F. Sell, *Commemorations*, ch. 13, for my attempt to reintroduce this gracious, modest and undeservedly neglected theologian.

[243] Cf. Hugo Meynell's remark in *Sense, Nonsense and Christianity*, London: Sheed & Ward, 1964, 265: 'It is remarkable that the criterion of true faith stated by Bultmann – that its content should not be subject to verification – is the same as the criterion of meaninglessness advanced by the logical positivists.'

[244] W. Pannenberg in *Revelation as History*, New York: Macmillan, 1969, 120.

[245] L. Wittgenstein, *Culture and Value*, ed. G. H. Von Wright, trans. Peter Winch, Oxford: Blackwell, 1980, 32.

[246] Idem, *On Certainty*, para. 63.

[247] From the hymn of William Cowper (1731–1800), 'God moves in a mysterious way'.

[248] M. Wiles, *God's Action in the World*, 6.

[249] Idem, *The Remaking of Christian Doctrine*, London: SCM Press, 1974, 119.

[250] Idem, *God's Action in the World*, 108 – the last sentence.

[251] Ibid., 76. In an earlier work, however, he did introduce a reference to sin: the resurrection is not an event, but 'a conviction that by the grace sin and death have been and can be overcome in human life'. See M. Wiles, *Christian Believing: The Nature of the Christian Faith and its Expression in Holy Scripture and Creeds*, London: SPCK, 1976, 129. This begs the question of whether the atonement does anything for God.

[252] K. Popper, 'Emancipation through knowledge', in Paul Kurtz and Timothy J. Madigan, eds., *Challenges to the Enlightenment*, Buffalo, NY: Prometheus Books, 1994, 63.

[253] W. A. Whitehouse, *Eschatology*, 82–3. I am well aware that Christian confessors who would commend the faith today cannot bypass the practically clamant question: how does Christianity's particularist claim fare in a world generally deemed to be pluralist? (I say 'generally' because there are those who point to particular geographical areas of England, Wales, India and elsewhere, and say that they are ethnically and religiously homogeneous). But apart from the fact that many other areas are not so, the simple acknowledgement of the fact of other religions implicitly poses the question. It is a question which has engendered a large literature and an ongoing debate, and I shall briefly return to it in the concluding chapter of this book. My present purpose is served if I have shown that the claim that the transcendent-immanent God acts in history cannot be surrendered by Christians without undermining their proclamation, and that some of

the objections to the idea fall when the presuppositions of those who advance them are exposed and examined.

254 Cf. R. C. Moberly, *Reason and Religion: Some Aspects of their Mutual Interdependence*, London: Longmans, Green, 1896, 132: 'If on the one hand it is true . . . that theological insight . . . comes to the corporate body through the inspired mind and life of individuals, it is none the less true that the individual mind or conscience apprehends, and acquires apprehensiveness, in and through both the moral discipline of gregarious life, and the intellectual dutifulness of lowly Church membership.'

255 Ross T. Bender, *Education for Peoplehood: Essays on the Teaching Ministry of the Church*, Elkhart, IN: Institute of Mennonite Studies, 1997, 187.

256 *Heidelberg Catechism*, Answer to Q. 1, in A. C. Cochrane, *Reformed Confessions of the Sixteenth Century*, Philadelphia: Westminster Press, 1966, 305.

257 R. W. Hepburn, 'The Gospel and the claims of logic', in *Religion and Humanism*, London: British Broadcasting Corporation, 1964, 15.

Chapter 6: Reason and Revelation

1 Cf. J. R. Lucas, 'Reason restored', in William J. Abraham and Steven W. Holtzer, eds., *The Rationality of Religious Belief: Essays in Honour of Basil Mitchell*, Oxford: Clarendon Press, 1987, 72: 'Once we recognize that there are many different forms of reasoning, and many different types of cogent argument, we shall turn a less than sympathetic ear to the sceptic who complains that moral, or philosophical, or theological, or metaphysical argument is not some other form of argument.'

2 Quoted by John Waddington, *Congregational History 1850–1880*, London: Longmans, Green, 1880, 64.

3 J. Taylor, *A Sketch of Moral Philosophy*, 1760, 32.

4 Maurice Wiles, 'The reasonableness of Christianity', in W. J. Abraham and S. Holtzer, eds., *The Rationality of Religious Belief*, Oxford: Clarendon Press, 1987, 41.

5 J. Wesley, *The Works of John Wesley*, Oxford and (later) Nashville, TN, 1975– , XI, 55. See further Geoffrey Wainwright (who quotes the above passage more fully), *Methodists in Dialog*, Nashville, TN: Kingswood Books, 1995, ch. 7.

6 G. K. Chesterton's epigram comes to mind: 'Reason is itself a matter of faith. It is an act of faith to assert that our thoughts have any relation to reality at all.' See his *Orthodoxy*, London: John Lane, 1909, 56.

7 N. Emmons, *The Works of Nathanael Emmons*, ed. Jacob Ide, Boston: Crocker & Brewster, 1842, IV, 93.

8 W. G. De Burgh, *Towards a Religious Philosophy*, London: Macdonald & Evans, 1937, 3. There is a considerable amount of wisdom to be mined in what some might disparagingly refer to as this 'older work'. What a change of gear when the chair of philosophy at Reading passed from De Burgh and his successor, H. A. Hodges, to A. G. N. Flew!

9 *A Brief Account of the new Sect of Latitude-Men Together with some reflections on the new Philosophy: By S: P: of Cambridge: In answer to a Letter from his Friend at Oxford* (1662), reprinted Los Angeles: William Andrews Clark Memorial Library, University of California, 1963, 10.

10 The above classification is not exhaustive. For present purposes I leave on one side those who, by taking the mystical path, understood human reason as that which may be surpassed, in which connection utterances of, for example, John of the Cross and Richard and Hugh of St Victor come to mind; as does the quip quoted by Samuel G. Craig in his *Christianity Rightly So Called*, Presbyterian and Reformed Publishing Company, 1956, 248: 'the rationalist blows cold, the mystic hot; warm up a rationalist and you get a mystic; cool down a mystic and you get a rationalist'. The context concerns the tendency of rationalists and mystics alike to sit loose to historic facts.

11 From the mass of studies on this theme the following may be selected as being, in different respects, helpful: T. F. Torrance, *Calvin's Doctrine of Man*, London: Lutterworth, 1949, chs. 7, 8; Charles Partee, *Calvin and Classical Philosophy*, Leiden: E. J. Brill, 1977; Paul Helm, 'John Calvin, the *sensus divinitatis*, and the noetic effects of sin', *International Journal for Philosophy of Religion*, XLIII, 1998, 87–107.

12 J. Calvin, *Institutes*, I. ii. 1.

13 Ibid., II. i. 11.

14 Ibid., I. v. 15.

15 See Calvin's *Commentary* on Psalm 119: 73.

16 Idem, *Institutes*, II. iii. 5.

17 Ibid., I. iv. 1.

18 Ibid., II. ii. 18. Cf., for example, Calvin's *Commentary* on Romans 1: 20, 26, 28.

19 Ibid., II. ii. 17.

20 Ibid., I. xv. 6.

21 Ibid., II. ii. 12.

22 Ibid., II. ii. 13, 14.

23 D. J. Hoitinga, jun., 'Faith and reason in Calvin's doctrine', in Hendrik Hart et al., eds., *Rationality in the Calvinian Tradition*, Lanham, MD: University Press of America, 1983, 20.

24 See Claude Lafleur, ed., *Quatre introductions à la philosophie au xiiie siècle: Textes critiques et études historiques*, Montreal: L'Institut d'études médiévales, Université de Montréal, 1988, 303 ff.

[25] J. Calvin, *Institutes*, III. ii. 36.

[26] J. Owen, *Works*, II, 411–12.

[27] Ibid., V, 45.

[28] J. Flavel, *Works*, VI, 473.

[29] R. Baxter, *The Reasons of the Christian Religion*, in *The Practical Works of the Rev. Richard Baxter*, ed. William Orme, London: James Duncan, 1830, XXI, 135.

[30] Ephesians 4: 23.

[31] R. Barclay, *An Apology of the True Christian Divinity as the same is held forth and preached by the people, in scorn, called Quakers* (1678), Glasgow: R. Barclay Murdoch, 1886, proposition V. VI. 16.

[32] Edward Grubb, *Quaker Thought and History: A Volume of Essays*, London: Swarthmore Press, 1925, 30.

[33] See T. Boston, *Human Nature in its Fourfold State* (1720), London: Banner of Truth Trust, 1964, 79–96; Jonathan Edwards, *Works* (1834), Edinburgh: Banner of Truth Trust, 1974, II, 817.

[34] J. Bellamy, *The Works of Joseph Bellamy, D.D.*, 2 vols. 1850, I, 100–1.

[35] E. Williams, *The Works of the Reverend Edward Williams, D.D.*, ed. Evan Davies, 4 vols., 1862, I, 86. See further W. T. Owen, *Edward Williams, D.D. 1750–1813: His Life, Thought and Influence*, Cardiff: University of Wales Press, 1963, ch. 8.

[36] See H. B. Smith, *System of Christian Theology*, ed. William S. Karr, 4th rev. edn., New York: A. and C. Armstrong, 1891, 328.

[37] *An Address to the Students of Cheshunt College, delivered by The Rev. W. Hendry Stowell, D.D., at his Public Recognition as the President of that Institution*, London: John Snow, 1850, 16–18.

[38] For a brief, general, introduction to Kuyper see Rex Ambler, 'The Christian mind of Abraham Kuyper', in *Profitable for Doctrine and Reproof*, papers of the Puritan and Reformed Studies Conference, 1960, 5–14.

[39] Cf. Paul Helm, 'John Calvin, the *sensus divinitatis*, and the noetic effects of sin', 87: 'Calvin shows little or no interest in the rationality of religious beliefs as such; he shows much more interest in establishing the fact that all men know God, or at least have the capacity for knowing God.' It is not at all suggested that all Christian presuppositionalist heirs of Kuyper are Dutch. By general consent the outstanding theologian who is not is Carl H. F. Henry. See his *God, Revelation and Authority*, 6 vols., Waco, TX: Word Books, 1976–83.

[40] A. Kuyper, *Sacred Theology* (1898), Wilmington, DE: Associated Publishers and Authors, n.d., 29–30.

[41] Idem, *Lectures on Calvinism* (1898), Grand Rapids, MI: Eerdmans, 1961, 133.

[42] See, for example, J. Calvin, *Institutes*, II. ii. 17.

[43] Ibid., III. xiv. 3.

[44] See J. Klapwijk, 'Rationality in the Dutch Neo-Calvinist tradition', in H. Hart et al., *Rationality in the Calvinian Tradition*, 101.

[45] Cf. James D. Bratt, 'The Dutch schools', in David F. Wells, ed., *Reformed Theology in America: A History of its Modern Development*, Grand Rapids, MI: Eerdmans, 1985, 146.

[46] H. Dooyeweerd, *Roots of Western Culture: Pagan, Secular and Christian Options*, Toronto: Wedge Publishing Corporation, 1979, 59.

[47] Ibid., 60. For the debate within the Free University of Amsterdam between Dooyeweerd and C. H. Van Peursen see Jacob Klapwijk, 'Rationality in the Dutch Neo-Calvinist tradition', 93–111; Albert Wolters, 'Dutch neo-Calvinism: worldview, philosophy and rationality', in H. Hart et al., *Rationality in the Calvinian Tradition*, Lanham, MD: University Press of America, 1983, 113–31. Those trained in quite other philosophical ways may find the following expositions of Dooyeweerd's thought reasonably accessible: A. L. Conradie, *The Neo-Calvinist Concept of Philosophy*, Pietermaritzburg: University of Natal Press, 1960; L. Kalsbeek, *Contours of a Christian Philosophy*, Toronto: Wedge Publishing Corporation, 1975. See also the collection of papers ed. C. T. McIntire, *The Legacy of Hermann Dooyeweerd*, Lanham, MD: University Press of America, 1985; and John Bolt's review of this work in *Calvin Theological Journal*, XXI no. 2, November 1986, 296–9. For an illuminating account of 'Dutch philosophical influences in America', see Richard J. Mouw's paper, *Calvin Theological Journal*, XXIV no. 1, April 1989, 93–120.

[48] See also John M. Frame and Leonard J. Coppes, *The Amsterdam Philosophy: A Preliminary Critique*, Phillipsburg, NJ: Harmony Press, n.d.

[49] C. Van Til, *The Defense of the Faith*, Philadelphia: Presbyterian and Reformed Publishing Co., 1955, 94.

[50] Ibid., 109; cf. 171–5; idem, *A Christian Theory of Knowledge*, Grand Rapids, MI: Baker Book House, 1969, 18–19.

[51] Idem, *A Christian Theory of Knowledge*, 245.

[52] Idem, 'My credo', in *Jerusalem and Athens: Critical Discussions on the Philosophy and Apologetics of Cornelius Van Til*, ed. E. R. Geehan, Grand Rapids, MI: Baker Book House, 1971, 21.

[53] Idem, *The Defense of the Faith*, 111.

[54] Ibid., 117.

[55] Ibid., 363.

[56] For an interesting argument to the effect that Van Til and the evidentialists are not absolutely opposed, as is sometimes more than hinted, see Greg L. Bahnsen, 'The apologetical tradition of the O[rthodox] P[resbyterian] C[hurch]', in Charles G. Dennison and Richard C.

Gamble, eds., *Pressing Toward the Mark: Essays Commemorating Fifty Years of the Orthodox Presbyterian Church*, Philadelphia: Committee for the Historian of the OPC, 1986, 259–94. See also the same author's paper, 'Induction, inerrancy and presuppositionalism', *Journal of the Evangelical Theological Society*, XX no. 4, December 1977, 292–5; Thom Notaro, *Van Til and the Use of Evidence*, Phillipsburg, NJ: Presbyterian and Reformed Publishing Co., 1980. It would therefore seem that Kenneth C. Harper's blunt assertion that 'Van Til's presuppositionalism assumes that empirical knowledge is useless, since the non-Christian is operating with *a priori* commitments that exclude God' requires qualification. See his paper, 'Edward John Carnell: an evaluation of his apologetics', *Journal of the Evangelical Theological Society*, XX no. 2, June 1977, 138.

57 C. Van Til, *The Defense of the Faith*, 84.

58 It may be thought in general that the 'Dutch' thinkers make too much of sin. In emphasizing the importance of sin they are in good company (some of whom were more graphic than they, among them C. H. Spurgeon who, in his tract *Free Will, A Slave!* rebuked those preachers who gave the impression 'that when Adam fell down he only broke his little finger and not his neck'). I neither wish to defend nor repudiate them at this point (though none who take the holiness of God's love seriously can sit light to sin), but simply to remark that there have not been lacking brands of theology which have done the reverse with unfortunate results. Thus, some thought that the Unitarian James Martineau was 'too easily good', and of him A. B. Bruce remarked, 'He has not sufficiently borne in mind the veil that is on the face of the human soul, preventing it from seeing the light of God.' A. B. Bruce, *Apologetics; or, Christianity Defensively Stated*, Edinburgh: T. & T. Clark, 1903, 173. Cf. Alan P. F. Sell, *Commemorations: Studies in Christian Thought and History*, 24.

59 H. Stob, 'The concept of antithesis', in Peter De Klerk and Richard R. De Ridder, eds., *Perspectives on the Christian Reformed Church: Studies in its History, Theology and Ecumenicity*, Grand Rapids, MI: Baker Book House, 1983, 249.

60 Ibid., 250.

61 See the criticism of him by Gordon H. Clark, himself a Christian presuppositionalist, in 'Apologetics', in *Contemporary Evangelical Thought*, ed. Carl F. H. Henry, Grand Rapids, MI: Baker Book House, 1968, 159.

62 G. H. Clark, 'The Wheaton Lectures', in Ronald H. Nash, ed., *The Philosophy of Gordon H. Clark: A Festschrift*, Philadelphia: Presbyterian and Reformed Publishing Co., 1968, 76.

63 'What we should be doing above all', he writes, 'is keeping alive the

religious imagination and simultaneously confronting its products with a searching, uninhibited rational critique: setting partial vision against vision, as it were chord against chord in an unresting, taut progression.' See R. W. Hepburn, 'A critique of humanist theology', in H. J. Blackham, ed., *Objections to Humanism*, Harmondsworth: Penguin, 1963, 53. Cf. idem, 'Poetry and religious belief', in *Metaphysical Beliefs*, London: SCM Press (1957), 1970, 75–156.

64 See W. Guthic, *The Christian's Great Interest* (1658), Publication Committee of the Free Presbyterian Church of Scotland, [1951], ch. 4.

65 E. P. Dickie, *God is Light*, London: Hodder & Stoughton, 1953, 144.

66 Justin Martyr, *Apology*, I. v.

67 See, for example, *Exhortation to the Heathen*, VI; *The Miscellanies*, XVII.

68 Dionysius the Areopagite, *The Divine Names*, trans. C. E. Rolt, London: SPCK, 1923; 1975, 152. Edwin Hatch's verdict upon Neoplatonism comes to mind: 'that splendid vision of incomparable and irrecoverable cloudland in which the sun of Greek philosophy set'. See his *The Influence of Greek Ideas and Usages upon the Christian Church*, London: Williams & Norgate, 1907, 133.

69 John Scottus Eriugena, *De divisione naturae*, I. 66.

70 F. C. Copleston, *A History of Philosophy* (1950), Garden City, NY: Image Books, 1962, II pt. I, 179.

71 Idem, *Aquinas*, Harmondsworth: Penguin, 1955, 23.

72 A vast literature may be consulted on the rise of modern science; for the scepticism of the period see Richard H. Popkin, *The History of Scepticism from Erasmus to Spinoza*, Berkeley and Los Angeles: University of California Press, 1979; Richard Watson and James Force, eds., *The High Road to Pyrrhonism*, San Diego: Austin Hill Press, 1980; R. H Popkin, 'The role of scepticism in modern philosophy reconsidered', *Journal of the History of Philosophy*, XXXI, 1993, 501–17. For a lucid philosophical discussion see Terence Penelhum, *God and Skepticism*, Dordrecht: Reidel, 1983.

73 Knowles's Letter is in S. Eaton, *The Mystery of God Incarnate*, 1650, 233–5.

74 Anon., *Independency Accused . . . and Acquitted*, 1645, 1, quoted by G. F. Nuttall in his review of H. John McLachlan, *Socinianism in Seventeenth-Century England*, London: OUP, 1951, in *The Journal of Theological Studies*, NS II, pt. 2, October 1951, 222.

75 See the quotation with which I have prefaced my Introduction.

76 See the references to enthusiasm, toleration and the indispensable minimum of belief in Alan P. F. Sell, *John Locke and the Eighteenth-Century Divines*. When Lefferts A. Loetscher writes that 'willingness to see truth dismembered and reduced to "essentials" was more congenial to the eighteenth century – to rationalism, seeking the lightest load of

faith that reason must bear' he is adverting to a motive at odds with that of Locke, whose quest of the indispensable minimum of belief was motivated by his desire to find a platform on which Christians could stand together in dangerous times. See L. A. Loetscher, *The Broadening Church: A Study of Theological Issues in the Presbyterian Church since 1869*, Philadelphia: University of Pennsylvania Press, 1954, 98.

77 L. Cary, *Discourse of the Infallibility of the Church of Rome*, 1651, 25.

78 For Descartes's motivation see further Graeme Hunter, 'Descartes' apology', *Studies in Religion*, XXVII no. 2, 1988, 179–91. Not, indeed, that Descartes was the first to take mathematics as his exemplar. W. H. V. Reade has properly reminded us, with reference to the age of Plato and Aristotle, that 'Philosophy has never quite recovered from its infant malady of mathematics'. See his *The Christian Challenge to Philosophy*, London: SPCK, 1951, 105–6.

79 R. Descartes, *Discourse on Method*, London: J. M. Dent (1912), 1934, 7.

80 Ibid.

81 Ibid., 8.

82 It is not our purpose to enter into debate with Descartes and others, but simply to observe the course they are charting. For some puckish, elegantly expressed, comments of yesteryear upon Descartes see Henry Rogers, *Essays Selected from Contributions to the Edinburgh Review*, III, 1855. For example, Rogers observes, p. 73, that both the more inductive Bacon and the more deductive Descartes 'thought that a system of rules might be devised which would do much more than any such system can; which, in fact, would wonderfully diminish that interval which must ever subsist between a great genius and a great blockhead'. See further Alan P. F. Sell, *Dissenting Thought and the Life of the Churches*, ch. 18; and, for Rogers himself, ibid., ch. 17.

83 We should recall that, for Descartes, 'thought' included 'all that which so takes place in us that we of ourselves are immediately conscious of it', thereby eliding understanding, will, imagination and perception. See *The Principles of Philosophy*, I. ix, in Descartes, *A Discourse on Method*; cf. Elizabeth Anscombe and Peter Thomas Geach, *Descartes: Philosophical Writings*, London: Nelson, 1954, pp. xlvii–xlviii, 183.

84 It is only by disregarding such important qualifications as these that Alister McGrath can so easily place 'Christianity' and 'Enlightenment rationalism' in separate, mutually opposed camps. For this he deserves to be haunted by John Gill! See his *The Genesis of Doctrine*, Oxford: Blackwell, 1990, 199. Elsewhere McGrath characterizes postmodernists as holding that a line may be drawn from the Enlightenment, 'an intellectually dubious movement', to 'the Nazi holocaust and the Stalinist purge'. If we were to accept this account we should have to say that, notwithstanding Locke's gradual move in the direction of ever

wider toleration, postmodernists border upon the hysterical. See his *The Renewal of Anglicanism*, London: SPCK, 1993, 17. That some Anglicans are more discriminating is clear from Mark D. Chapman, 'Why the Enlightenment project does not have to fail', *Heythrop Journal*, XXXIX, 1998, 379–93.

85 Bruce Kuklick, *Churchmen and Philosophers from Jonathan Edwards to John Dewey*, New Haven: Yale University Press, 1985, 88 n.

86 The foregoing citation tempts me to cast the net much wider, as does the fascinating story of rationalism in Holland, where the minister at Franeker, Balthasar Bekker, defended Descartes and then, at the Provincial Synod, defended himself successfully against a complaint from the Classis of Leeuwarden. In 1691 he countered superstition, but did it along Cartesian lines: in view of the dichotomoy between the spiritual and material realms, neither angels nor demons could help or harm human bodies. Insofar as this contradicted scripture, he was deposed from the ministry and then excommunicated from the Church. Meanwhile the Cartesian Herman Alexander Roell was appointed to teach philosophy and theology in 1685. He and others accorded a prominent place to reason apart from revelation, and against this his colleague, Ulrich Huber, protested vigorously. But sufficient variations upon the theme will become apparent if, on grounds of space, I confine my attention to England.

87 See further Peter Munz, *The Place of Hooker in the History of Thought*, London: Routledge & Kegan Paul, 1952, 40–1.

88 R. Hooker, *The Works of that Learned and Judicious Divine, Mr Richard Hooker: with an account of his Life and Death by Isaac Walton*, Oxford: OUP, 3rd edn., 1845, I, 227.

89 Ibid., 228.

90 Ibid., 232.

91 Ibid., 233.

92 Ibid., 235.

93 Ibid., 374–5.

94 J. Goodwin, *Pleroma to Pneumatikon*, 308. Quoted by Geoffrey F. Nuttall, *The Holy Spirit in Puritan Faith and Experience*, Oxford: Blackwell, 1946, 43. It is a familiar charge against rationalizing divines that they were 'cold' and 'dry' in the pulpit. No doubt some were (though for dryness some high Calvinists could run them close), but see Alan P. F. Sell, *Dissenting Thought and the Life of the Churches*, 155–6; and consider Benjamin Coleman of the Arminian Brattle Street Church, Boston, 'a rationalist who luxuriated in emotion'. See Daniel Walker Howe, *The Unitarian Conscience: Harvard Moral Philosophy, 1805–1861*, Middletown, CT: Wesleyan University Press (1970), 1988, 152–3. In one of his more one-sided remarks W. R. Inge

declared of his own period, 'Our extreme dislike of the eighteenth century, and our tendency to vilify this period and all its works, are very symptomatic. The eighteenth century believed in reason, and disliked moods of excitement.' See *The Religious Philosophy of Plotinus and some Modern Philosophies of Religion*, London: Lidsey Press, [1914], 16. No doubt some of the hearers of this Essex Hall Lecture would have agreed, but others would have recognized this for the half-truth it was – in the age of evangelical religious excitements from one end of the land to the other.

95 The description is that of G. A. J. Rogers, *Locke's Enlightenment*, Hildesheim: Georg Olms, 1998, 177, cf. 118–25.

96 J. Tillotson, *The Works of Dr. John Tillotson*, ed. Thomas Birch, 10 vols., 1820, II, 333.

97 For an excellent characterization of latitudinarianism see Martin Fitzpatrick, 'Latitudinarianism at the parting of the ways', in John Walsh et al., *The Church of England c.1689–c.1833: From Toleration to Tractarianism*, Cambridge: CUP, 1993. He points out (pp. 211–12) that Latitudinarianism 'could be easily threatened by too great an emphasis on any one component at the expense of the others: too great an emphasis upon rationality could lead away from Christian orthodoxy to natural religion; too great an emphasis upon individul conscience could lead to a religious individualism which was incompatible with any formal ecclesiastical organization. Yet, in a sense, Latitudinarianism was an attempt to cope with these very problems.' I shall return to the Cambridge Platonists later in this chapter.

98 For a brief account see Alan P. F. Sell, *Dissenting Thought and the Life of the Churches*, ch. 2.

99 W. Laud, *A Relation of the Conference between W. Laud and Mr Fisher the Jesuit*, 3rd edn. 1673, 165.

100 See further Alan P. F. Sell, *Dissenting Thought and the Life of the Churches*, ch. 4.

101 See E. Benson Lowrie, *The Shape of the Puritan Mind: The Theology of Samuel Willard*, New Haven, CT: Yale University Press, 1974.

102 For some examples see Alan P. F. Sell, *Dissenting Thought and the Life of the Churches*, ch. 1.

103 See *John Locke and the Eighteenth-Century Divines*, ch. 3.

104 J. Gill, *Complete Body of Doctrinal and Practical Divinity* (1767, 1770), reprinted (from the 1839 edn.) Grand Rapids, MI: Baker Book House, 1978, I, 1. On the general point see Raymond Brown, *The English Baptists of the Eighteenth Century*, London: Baptist Historical Society, 1986, 5–6; Frank Louis Maudlin, 'Truth, heritage, and eighteenth-century English Baptists', *Baptist Quarterly*, XXXV no. 5, January 1994, 211–28.

[105] This is not to deny the force of Gregory A. Wills's claim that 'Rationalism gave [Gill's] defense its form, but its controlling idea had less to do with reason than with the affections . . . Gill was not trying to reach the heart through the head. He did not believe that the will followed the dictates of reason. Rather the dictates of the heart determined the will. Gill sought to reach the heart through his rationalistic method of preaching.' See 'The spirituality of John Gill', in Michael A. G. Haykin, ed., *The Life and Thought of John Gill (1697–1771): A Tercentennial Appreciation*, Leiden: Brill, 1997, 191, 203–4.

[106] J. Withers, *A Charge given to Mr. Micaijah Towgood, at his Ordination in Moreton Hampstead, Devon, August 21, 1722*, 1723, 20. See further Alan P. F. Sell, *Dissenting Thought and the Life of the Churches*, ch. 7.

[107] On both there exists an enormous literature. For a sketch, with references, of the biblical criticism, see Alan P. F. Sell, *Theology in Turmoil: The Roots, Course and Significance of the Conservative–Liberal Debate in Modern Theology* (1986), Eugene, OR: Wipf & Stock, 1998, ch. 2.

[108] W. R. Smith, *Lectures and Essays*, ed. J. S. Black and G. Crystal, London: Adam & Charles Black, 1912, 151–2. See further Richard Allan Riesen, *Criticism and Faith in Late Victorian Scotland*, Lanham, MD: University Press of America, 1985. Interestingly, the nineteenth-century American theologian Henry Boynton Smith was of the opinion that, in view of its tendency to absorb religion in philosophy, German philosophical idealism was 'more blasting to piety, and fatal to simple experimental religion than all the biblical criticism of the Rationalists'. See Mrs H. B. Smith, *Henry Boynton Smith: His Life and Work*, New York: A. C. Armstrong, 1881, 59.

[109] The degree to which Virginia stands behind Old Princeton should not be overlooked. See, for example, Morton Smith, 'The Southern tradition', in David F. Wells, ed., *Reformed Theology in America: A History of its Modern Development*, Grand Rapids, MI: Eerdmans, 1985, 189–207.

[110] See further Sydney E. Ahlstrom, 'The Scottish philosophy and American theology', *Church History*, XXIV, 1955, 257–72.

[111] In contrast to the presuppositionalist debtors to Holland, as we shall see in section V. For an interesting study by one who was schooled in Princetonian evidentialism but subsequently reverted to his Dutch inheritance see M. Eugene Osterhaven, 'Faith, reason and theology', *Reformed Review*, LI no. 3,Spring 1998, 183–201.

[112] For the apologetics of Old Princeton see David B. Calhoun, *Princeton Seminary: The Majestic Testimony 1869–1929*, Edinburgh: Banner of Truth Trust, 1996, 179–82, 415–521.

[113] B. B. Warfield, 'Apologetics', in *The New Schaff-Herzog Encyclopedia of Religious Knowledge*, New York: Funk & Wagnells, 1908, I, 234, 235.

114 Idem, 'The right of systematic theology', *Presbyterian and Reformed Review*, VII, July 1896, 459. We seem here to hear an echo of Moise Amyraut's remark, quoted in Jack B. Rogers and Donald K. McKim, *The Authority and Interpretation of the Bible*, San Francisco: Harper & Row, 1979, 197 n. 247: 'Belief in scriptural truths must be founded on reason and be consistent with proper logic' – yet Amyraut was no favourite of Reformed theologians. See Alan P. F. Sell, *The Great Debate: Calvinism, Arminianism and Salvation* (1982), Eugene, OR: Wipf & Stock, 1998, ch. 1.

115 B. B. Warfield, 'Apologetics', 236.

116 Ibid., 236. He quotes Aquinas in support of this view.

117 Ibid., 237.

118 P. K. Helseth, 'B. B. Warfield's apologetical appeal to "right reason": evidence of "a rather bald rationalism"?', *Scottish Bulletin of Evangelical Theology*, XVI no. 2, Autumn 1998, 159, quoting *Selected Shorter Writings of Benjamin B. Warfield*, Nutley, NJ: Presbyterian and Reformed Publishing Co., II, 1973, 213.

119 Ibid., 169, quoting B. B. Warfield, 'Calvin's doctrine of the knowledge of God', in *Augustine*, Philadelphia: Presbyterian and Reformed Publishing Co., 1956, 33.

120 Ibid., 174.

121 L. A. Loetscher, *The Broadening Church*, 22. It is instructive to read Mike Parsons, 'Warfield and scripture', *Churchman*, XCI no. 3, July 1977, 198–220, alongside Helseth's paper.

122 B. B. Warfield, *Inspiration and Authority*, Philadelphia: Presbyterian and Reformed Publishing Co., 1948, 220.

123 Cf. M. Parsons, 'Warfield and scripture', 216.

124 G. H. Clark, 'The Wheaton Lectures', 57.

125 Ibid., 62.

126 Ibid., 64.

127 Ibid., 67.

128 Ibid., 69.

129 Ibid., 72.

130 Ibid., 88. I cannot resist the feeling that Clark echoes Glanvill, whose position Peter Harrison has described thus: 'The fundamentals of religion fall into the same category as those *a priori* rational truths which constitute the basis of our reasoning faculty. "God exists" is thus of the order of the principle of contradiction. We can no more reasonably deny the former than the latter . . .' See his *'Religion' and the Religions in the English Enlightenment*, Cambridge: CUP, 1990, 36. The influence upon Clark of Descartes and the Cambridge Platonists is also apparent, though the matter cannot be pursued further here.

131 See further Robert D. Knudsen, 'Tendencies in Christian apologetics',

in *Jerusalem and Athens*, 287; Gilbert B. Weaver, 'Gordon Clark: Christian apologist', in *The Philosophy of Gordon H. Clark*, ch. 9. For Clark's response see ibid., ch. 22. These sources give the flavour of the tangled web of debate between Clark, Van Til and others. For the view that Clark's difficulty in securing ordination in the Orthodox Presbyterian Church and his eventual resignation from its ministry had to do not only with his opinions but with tensions within the Church as to whether it should continue stoutly Reformed or (as Clark recommended against modernism) associate itself with the broader evangelical movement, see Michael A. Hakkenberg, 'The battle over the ordination of Gordon H. Clark', in *Pressing Toward the Mark*, ch. 19.

132 Clark's position has descended to a number of thinkers to whom he was mentor, in particular Carl F. H. Henry and E. J. Carnell. For representative criticisms of Henry see I. John Hesselink, *On Being Reformed: Distinctive Characteristics and Common Misunderstandings*, Ann Arbor, MI: Servant Books, 1983, ch. 5; Ray S. Anderson, 'Evangelical theology', in David F. Ford, ed., *The Modern Theologians*, Oxford: Blackwell, 2nd edn. 1997, 489–92; R. Albert Mohler, jun., 'Carl F. H. Henry', in Timothy George and David S. Dockery, eds., *Baptist Theologians*, Nashville: Broadman Press, 1990, ch. 27. For Carnell see Gordon R. Lewis, 'Van Til and Carnell – Part I', and Charles M. Horne, 'Van Til and Carnell – Part II' – each with a response by Van Til, in *Jerusalem and Athens*, chs. 19, 20; L. Joseph Rosas III, 'Edward John Carnell', in *Baptist Theologians*, ch. 31. The papers in *Baptist Theologians* have bibliographies.

133 E. Mach, *The Science of Mechanics*, trans. T. J. McCormack, Chicago: Open Court Publishing Co., 1893, 45.

134 H. R. Mackintosh, *Types of Modern Theology*, London: Nisbet, 1937, 10, 11, 15.

135 R. Mackintosh, 'Apologetics', in *Encyclopedia Britannica*, 11th edn., 1910–11, 192(a). W. R. Inge's quip comes to mind, concerning Paley's *Evidences*, 'on which a Cambridge don pronounced a suitable epitaph when he said that Paley had the merit of reducing Christianity to a form eminently fitted for examination purposes'. See W. R. Inge, *The Church in the World*, London: Longmans, Green, 1927, 251.

136 H.-G. Gadamer, *Truth and Method*, trans. J. Weinsheimer and D. G. Marshall, New York: Continuum, 2nd revised edn., 1989, 279.

137 J. Harrison, *The duty of confessing Christ before men: A Sermon delivered before the Society of Unitarian Christians in Kendal*, Kendal: Richard Lough, 1827, quoted by Francis Nicholson and Ernest Axon, *The Older Nonconformity in Kendal*, Kendal: Titus Wilson, 1915, 385.

138 C. B. Upton, *Lectures on the Bases of Religious Belief*, London: Williams & Norgate, 1894, 30–1.

139 See further Kelly James Clark, *Return to Reason*, Grand Rapids, MI: Eerdmans, 1990, ch. 4.

140 S. T. Coleridge, *Aids to Reflection*, in *The Collected Works of Samuel Taylor Coleridge*, London: Routledge, IX, 1993, 405–6. See Douglas Hedley, *Coleridge, Philosophy and Religion*, Cambridge: CUP, 2000. The quest of evidences continues unabated in some conservative evangelical circles to this day. See, for example, Kelly James Clark's discussion of Norman Geisler and others in *Return to Reason*, 46–53. In a review of Norman L. Geisler and Paul D. Feinberg, *Introduction to Philosophy: A Christian Perspective* (1980), John W. Cooper detects a significant contradiction. On the one hand the authors declare (p. 379) that 'it is necessary for us to have good evidence or reason to believe *that* God is, and *that* the Bible is His Word before we place unconditional faith in God and in His Word'. On the other hand they confess (p. 131), 'The depth of our commitment clearly exceeds the evidence that we possess.' Accordingly, they resort to the authority of God himself, while maintaining that 'the believer does find reasonable *support* for his faith in experiential and historical evidences and miracles'. This is a considerable modification of the first position stated. See Cooper's review in *Calvin Theological Journal*, XVI no. 1, April 1981, 87–91.

141 G. L. Prestige, *The Life of Charles Gore, A Great Englishman*, London: William Heinemann, 1935, 197.

142 C. C. J. Webb, *Studies in the History of Natural Theology*, Oxford: Clarendon Press, 1915, 358.

143 W. Pendlebury, *The Practical Influences of the Speculative Doctrine of Christianity Demonstrated: In a Discourse upon I Tim: vi: 3 Last Clause*, London: Eman. Matthews, 1726, preface. It would appear that 'infidels' are ever with us, as witness Peter Atkins, 'O come on all ye faithful, away with the manger', *The Times Higher Education Supplement*, 25 December 1998, 12. An apparent exponent of scientism and a self-confessed apostle of innatism, he writes, 'Thank goodness it is Christmas. For those of us who regard Christianity (like all religions) as puerile nonsense, a dangerously misleading corruption of the intellect and an intrinsic evil of society, it is a great pleasure to see the religious trappings of this ancient festival dissolving in the vitriol of commercialism . . . [W]hen one stands on the good side of the fence that divides innate truth (that is, science) from wishful-thinking (that is, religion) and sees the gush of sugary balm poured on young minds at this time of year, one can only regret the incipient perversion taking place in the name of pleasure and fun.' It is, of course, perfectly possible for Christians to regret some aspects of the commercialization of Christmas; and it is not clear how far, if at all, Atkins's tongue is in his cheek. But if he is sincere he has made a

sublime parade of ignorance, which might be tolerable in a street preacher's heckler, but which, coming as it does from the professor of chemistry at the University of Oxford, reveals an illiberality which one does not expect in higher education, and an arrogance which, in all probability, he would not tolerate from 'outsiders' who presumed to rubbish his own discipline. One year on, Atkins produces an Advent treat in which, reviewing Ian Barbour, *When Science meets Religion: Enemies, Strangers or Partners?*, he declares in his *ad hominem* way (though without the wit of the best of the nineteenth-century secularist press), 'This book is a testament to the delusion of theologians that they are contributing something useful to our understanding of the world . . . How much easier it is to accept the stark, clear-sighted view of right-thinking individuals who see that there is neither evidence nor need for God and that all the suggested answers in this book are but vacuous musings.' *THES*, 8 December, 2000, 32.

144 J. McIntyre, 'Analogy', *Scottish Journal of Theology*, XII, March 1959, 3.

145 Ibid., 4.

146 Ibid., 5.

147 Frederick Ferré, *Language, Logic and God*, London: Eyre & Spottiswoode, 1962, 74.

148 H. D. Lewis, *Philosophy of Religion*, London: English Universities Press, 1965, 216.

149 H. D. Aiken, 'God and evil: a study of some relations between faith and morals', *Ethics*, LXVIII, 1958, 82.

150 G. W. Allport, *The Individual and his Religion*, London: Constable, 1951, 33.

151 D. G. Bloesch, *The Battle for the Trinity: The Debate over Inclusive God-Language*, Ann Arbor, MI: Vine Books, 1985, 21.

152 The allusion is to Acts 15: 28 (AV).

153 E. Jüngel, *God as the Mystery of the World: On the Foundation of the Theology of the Crucified One in the Dispute between Theism and Atheism*, Edinburgh: T. & T. Clark, 1983, 288. I find it hard to construe the latter half of the second sentence, but I expect it is very important.

154 Cf. E. J. Carnell, *A Philosophy of the Christian Religion*, Grand Rapids, MI: Eerdmans, 1952, 306: 'Revelation would be sheer gibberish if there were not a univocal, rational element uniting the meaning of propositions entertained by both man and God.'

155 Cf. the following remark of Stewart R. Sutherland, 'The concept of revelation', in *Religion, Reason and the Self: Essays in Honour of Hywel D. Lewis*, ed. Sutherland and T. A. Roberts, Cardiff: University of Wales Press, 1989, 40: 'I do not think that one can separate questions about authoritative sources of revelation from questions about the truth of the content of revelation.'

[156] I am well aware that at this point I am on the brink of a major current discussion with a huge literature. The comments I have just made clearly bear upon the doctrine of the Trinity, the language of worship, the experience and place in the Church of women. I can here only assert, without substantiating, my opinions: we should do well to testify to the interpersonal relations of the Trinity, being cautious of liturgical linguistic substitutions which obscure this; a much wider use of biblical metaphors (masculine and feminine) should be used of God in worship; and, in Christ's one family, in which the old barriers between male and female, bond and free (and black and white, sick and well, young and elderly) have been done away, we should redouble our efforts to ensure that love and justice prevail, and that each is able to bring his or her gifts to the service of God. On the question of liturgical language, one of the most pastorally sensitive and theologically balanced statements I have seen is that of the Committee on Church Doctrine of the Presbyterian Church of Canada. See *The Acts and Proceedings of the One Hundred and Fourteenth General Assembly of the Presbyterian Church in Canada*, 1988, 256–61.

[157] Vincent Taylor, 'Religious certainty, II', *Expository Times*, LXXII, 1960, 51.

[158] David Brown has accused Paul Avis of undue reluctance to concede a role to literal language in theology. See his review of the latter's *God and the Creative Imagination*, London: Routledge, 1999, in *Expository Times*, CXI, no. 6, March 2000, 212–13.

[159] The phrase 'in the light of scholarship' will, no doubt, discredit me in the eyes of some. But when conservative scholars, attempting to marry ostensibly conflicting narrative accounts, resort to such ploys as, 'Well, the scribe was copying an inaccurate ms. – but he copied it accurately!' we may be forgiven for preferring the surmises of the 'ungodly'. Even E. J. Carnell contemplated the validity of such a ploy; see his *The Case for Orthodox Theology*, London: Marshall, Morgan & Scott, 1961, ch. 8. We may note that as soon as an inerrantist asks, 'Is writer A using an inaccurate document here?', he is using his reasoning powers to 'judge' the scriptures no less than a 'liberal'. He may even be suggesting that correct copying is more important than truth. A similar situation arises when inerrantists agree that there is poetry, parable, symbol in the Bible. How do they distinguish between these and the literal except by reasoning and making judgements? Both sides can access the same type of argument: to the inerrantist complaint, 'If you pick and choose among the "reliable" and the "unreliable" history, where do you stop?', the liberal can retort, 'If you allow parable, poetry and the like, why not admit that Adam and Eve are mythological characters?'

160 Accusations and denials have flowed freely on this issue during the last fifty years, and interwoven with them are the questions (a) is fundamentalism ancient or modern – for a summary consideration with references see Alan P. F. Sell, *Theology in Turmoil*, 101–2; and (b) what precisely was the Reformers' view of scripture? As to this, whereas J. K. S. Reid affirms that 'for Luther, Scripture is not the Word, but only the witness to the Word' (*The Authority of Scripture*, London: Methuen, 1957, 72; cf. Philip S. Watson, *Let God Be God*, London: Epworth Press, 1947, 179 n. 30), John Warwick Montgomery vigorously contests this view (*God's Inerrant Word*, ed. J. W. Montgomery, Minneapolis: Bethany Fellowship, 1974, 66 ff.). My own summary judgement is that there is ambiguity on the matter in the Reformers' writings at a time when inerrancy versus non-inerrancy was not the technical issue it has subsequently become; that Calvin especially, with his doctrine of the inner witness of the Holy Spirit, adopted a predominantly spiritual stance, and that when he or others employed the term 'dictation' – as they did (for example, Calvin's *Commentary* on II Timothy 3: 16) – they were adverting metaphorically to the accuracy of the testimony rather than to the process of its achievement. Cf. H. R. Mackintosh in C. Gore, ed., *The Doctrine of the Infallible Book*, London: SCM Press, 1924. The Puritan Richard Sibbes spoke for many when he said that 'The Scripture is but the *mode*, the manner of conveying the Word of God'. See his *Divine Meditations*, reprinted Sheffield: Zoar Publications, *c.*1975, no. 180. Or Richard Baxter: 'Words are but the body of scripture, and the sense the soul', *Practical Works*, ed. William Orme, 1830, XXI, 530. Yet another debate concerns the question of the fidelity or otherwise of latter-day Reformed theologians to the older Calvinism. Thus, for example, Thomas M. Lindsay queried whether Warfield and other Old Princetonians were faithful to the (non-scholastic) Reformers in 'The doctrine of scripture: the Reformers and the Princeton School', *The Expositor*, 5th ser. I, 1895, 278–93. More recently Jack B. Rogers has found neither Warfield nor Van Til true to the experimentalism of the Westminster Confession. See 'Van Til and Warfield on scripture', in E. R. Geehan, ed., *Jerusalem and Athens*, 154–65; and Van Til's response, ibid., 165–71.

161 J. Calvin, *Institutes*, III. ii. 6.

162 Many scholars have expressed themselves on the question of whether Calvin was an inerrantist. Roger Nicole not only conveniently placed them in two 'teams', but also offered a reward of $100 to 'the first person who would present an authentic text of Calvin in which Calvin rejects the truthfulness of the autographic text of any statement of Scripture'. He further explains, 'I did not designate a higher figure,

not because of a lack of assurance but because my financial limitations might make a larger offer incredible.' Not all scholars have been as self-sacrificial, or as sporting, as this. See Roger Nicole, 'John Calvin and inerrancy', *Journal of the Evangelical Theological Society*, XXV no. 4, December 1982, 425–42.

163 H. Cunliffe-Jones, *The Authority of the Biblical Revelation*, London: James Clarke, 1945, 95.

164 C. H. Dodd, *The Authority of the Bible* (1929), London: Collins Fontana, 1960, 21.

165 P. T. Forsyth, *Positive Preaching and the Modern Mind* (1907), London: Independent Press, 1964, 34. There is here an echo of the Puritan Thomas Willcox, whom I quoted in Chapter 2 above.

166 Idem, 'Authority and theology', *Hibbert Journal*, IV, 1905, 72.

167 From William Cowper's hymn, 'God moves in a mysterious way . . .'

168 I refer, of course, to nature, conscience, tradition. Even John Bunyan, somewhat to his own surprise, recognized that God could speak outside of the canonical scriptures: when the words 'Look at the generations of old and see: did ever any trust in God, and were confounded?' released him from a mood of depression, Bunyan sought them in vain in his Bible, but found them in extra-canonical Ecclesiasticus. 'This at first', he tells us, 'did somewhat daunt me . . . [however] though it was not in those Texts that we call Holy and Canonical, yet forasmuch as this sentence was the sum and substance of many of the promises, it was my duty to take the comfort of it.' See his autobiography, *Grace Abounding to the Chief of Sinners*, paras. 62–5. For some reflections upon authority see Alan P. F. Sell, *Commemorations: Studies in Christian Thought and History*, ch. 1.

169 T. F. Torrance, *Theological Science*, London: OUP, 1969, 191.

170 Idem, *Transformation and Convergence in the Frame of Knowledge*, Grand Rapids, MI: Eerdmans, 1984, 317.

171 I readily take the point expressed by Paul, Augustine, the Pseudo-Dionysius, Calvin and many others, including Richard Hooker: 'our soundest knowledge is to know that we know him not indeed as he is, neither can know him; and our safest eloquence concerning him is our silence, when we confess without confession that his glory is inexplicable, his greatness above our capacity and reach'. See *The Laws of Ecclesiastical Polity*, II. ii. 2. There is a religious agnosticism which is ever appropriate; there is an epistemological agnosticism which is finally destructive of all knowledge.

172 W. R. Smith, quoted by James Denney, *Studies in Theology*, London: Hodder & Stoughton, 1902, 204–5.

173 P. T. Forsyth, *The Principle of Authority* (1913), London: Independent Press, 1952, 250.

174 *Heidelberg Catechism*, Q1.

175 The term 'Reformed epistemology', coined by Alvin Plantinga, is not unproblematic. The term 'Reformed' is generally understood to refer to that Christian communion which descends from Zwingli, Calvin and many others. Ecclesiastically the Reformed communion embraces philosophers of many different stripes – process thinkers, pluralists, existentialists and others, as well as the Reformed epistemologists. From this point of view I have elsewhere made bold to suggest that the men of Grand Rapids have hijacked the term 'Reformed'. Conversely, William Alston, though an Anglican, is in considerable accord with the Reformed epistemologists. In explication of the term, Plantinga has said that the originators at Calvin College 'to some extent looked for inspiration to John Calvin'. See 'Reformed epistemology', in Philip L. Quinn and Charles Taliaferro, eds., *A Companion to Philosophy of Religion*, Oxford: Blackwell, 1997, 383. This begs the question of the extent, and raises that of the interpretation of Calvin. How far was he a Reformed epistemologist? Paul Helm has suggested that, with respect to those of Calvin's writings to which Plantinga adverts, 'there is no evidence from the passages cited (or from any similar passages) that Calvin has in mind the rationality of religious belief'. Rather, Calvin is concerned with human responsibility; in particular with that culpability which accompanies the refusal to live in accordance with what is known via the *sensus divinitatis*. See P. Helm, *Faith and Understanding*, Edinburgh: Edinburgh University Press, 1997, 197–201. For a full-length study of the approaches of Plantinga and Alston see Mark S. McLeod, *Rationality and Theistic Belief*, Ithaca, NY: Cornell University Press, 1993.

176 C. G. Prado, *Descartes and Foucault: A Contrastive Introduction to Philosophy*, Ottawa: University of Ottawa Press, 1992, 52. For brief comment on Hume's empiricist foundationalism see Joel C. Weinsheimer, *Eighteenth-Century Hermeneutics: Philosophy of Interpretation in England from Locke to Burke*, New Haven: Yale University Press, 1993, 107–8.

177 It is interesting to speculate how far an analogy may be drawn between the Reformed epistemologists' 'properly basic beliefs' and R. G. Collingwood's 'absolute presuppositions'. Cf. Adrian Oldfield, 'Metaphysics and history in Collingwood's thought', in David Boucher, James Connelly and Tariq Modood, eds., *Philosophy, History and Civilization: Interdisciplinary Perspectives on R. G. Collingwood*, Cardiff: University of Wales Press, 1995, esp. 191–200.

178 This bald attempt to summarize a vast expository literature has in part been guided by Pantinga's own summary in Quinn and Taliaferro, eds., *Companion*, ch. 49.

179 N. Wolterstorff, *Reason within the Bounds of Religion*, Grand Rapids, MI: Eerdmans, 1976, 52–3.

180 See idem, 'Thomas Reid on rationality', in H. Hart et al., *Rationality in the Calvinian Tradition*, 43–69. See further Kelly James Clark, *Return to Reason: A Critique of Enlightenment Evidentialism and a Defense of Reason and Belief in God*, Grand Rapids, MI: Eerdmans, 1990, 143–51.

181 Idem, 'Can belief in God be rational if it has no foundations?', in A. Plantinga and N. Wolterstorff, eds., *Faith and Rationality*, Notre Dame, IN: University of Notre Dame Press, 1983, 163.

182 Idem, *Faith and Rationality*, 6. The Reformed epistemologists thus set their faces against a considerable amount of conservative evangelical apologetics which continues in the line of Warfield and Old Princeton. See, for example, Richard R. Topping, 'The anti-foundational challenge to evangelical apologetics', *Evangelical Quarterly*, LXIII no. 1, 1991, 45–60, where the contributions of Carl F. H. Henry and Stuart C. Hackett are under review.

183 William C. Placher, *Unapologetic Theology: A Christian Voice in a Pluralistic Conversation*, Louisville, KY: Westminster/John Knox, 1989, 34–5.

184 M. Vertin, review of Linda Zagzebski, ed., *Rational Faith: Catholic Responses to Reformed Epistemology*, Notre Dame, IN: University of Notre Dame Press, 1993, in *Studies in Religion*, XXIV no. 3, 1995, 370.

185 Ibid., 371.

186 T. Penelhum, *Reason and Religious Faith*, 101.

187 K. J. Clark, *Return to Reason*, 157–8.

188 See further A. Plantinga, 'The Reformed objection to natural theology', in H. Hart et al., *Rationality in the Calvinian Tradition*, 376–80. For the theological application (and perhaps a few misapplications) of the position described in this paragraph see John E. Thiel, *Nonfoundationalism*, Minneapolis: Fortress Press, 1994.

189 See A. Plantinga in *Rationality in the Calvinian Tradition*, 373–6. Among a number of writers who are troubled at this point we find Christoph Schwöbel, *God: Action and Revelation*, Kampen: Kok Pharos, 1992, 144; Stephen T. Davis, *God, Reason and Theistic Proofs*, Edinburgh: Edinburgh University Press, 1997, 87–8.

190 G. E. Hughes, 'Plantinga on God's existence', *Philosophical Review*, LXXIX no. 2, April 1970, 252.

191 T. Penelhum, *Reason and Religious Faith*, 136.

192 See, for example, N. Wolterstorff in Quinn and Taliaferro, eds., *Companion to Philosophy of Religion*, 167–9.

193 See A. Plantinga, 'Advice to Christian philosophers', *Faith and*

Philosophy, I no. 3, July 1984, 256. This point is developed by D. Z. Phillips, *Wittgenstein and Religion*, Basingstoke: Macmillan, 1993, 225 ff. As we might expect, Phillips is more than happy to agree with Plantinga that 'It has indeed been a scandal in the philosophy of religion that it has been assumed, for so long, that foundationalism and evidentialism are the appropriate philosphical modes for discussing religious belief'; ibid., 226.

194 Christoph Schwöbel, *God: Action and Revelation*, 16. Cf. Dirk-Martin Grube, 'Religious experience after foundationalism', *Religious Studies*, XXXI no. 1, March 1995, 37–52.

195 Origen, *Contra Celsum*, VII. 42. See further Henri Crouzel, *Origen*, Edinburgh: T. & T. Clark, 1989.

196 Idem, *De Principiis*, I. i. 6.

197 Here is an aspect of Augustine's debt to Stoic thought. For a classic study see E. Gilson, *Reason and Revelation in the Middle Ages*, New York: Charles Scribner's Sons, 1938.

198 Augustine, *On Faith and the Creed*, I.

199 Idem, *City of God*, XI. 2; cf. idem, *On Christian Doctrine*, I. 10.

200 Cf. Paul Helm's exposition in *Faith and Understanding*, 27–8. I speak of 'the commitment of faith', but we should remember that, for Augustine, as well as a willed commitment, 'faith' denotes, *inter alia*, assent and the acceptance of authority; and it can be assured or tentative.

201 Anselm, *Proslogion*, I.

202 I place 'rationalism' in inverted commas by way of cautioning that with Abelard we are far removed from the intellectual environment of Descartes and later rationalists. In Abelard's case his 'rationalist' protest was in part an expression of an independent spirit who could not bend his mind to dogmatic pronouncements for which he could see no rational grounds. In latter-day ecclesiastical assemblies he would be the one raising points of order; in certain political circles he would be the one suspected of being 'off message'. Of the authority of scripture he was in no doubt whatsoever.

203 Hugh of St Victor, *De sacramentis*, I. 3. 30.

204 Cf. A. E. Taylor, *Philosophical Studies*, London: Macmillan, 1934, 247: 'The Thomist philosophy is no mere Aristotelianism revised but a masterly synthesis of both Plato and Aristotle with one another and with Augustine, effected by original insight of the first order.'

205 In this paragraph and the next I expand some remarks in *The Philosophy of Religion 1875–1980* (1988), Bristol: Thoemmes Press, 1996, 85.

206 Aquinas, *Summa Theologica*, Q109, art. 2, reply obj. 2.

207 See Aquinas, *Summa Theologica*, I. Q32, art. 1. Quotations are from

Anton C. Pegis, ed., *Basic Writings of Saint Thomas Aquinas*, New York: Random House, 1945.

208 Aquinas, *Summa Theologica*, I, Q1, 5th art.; cf. 6th art., reply obj. 2.

209 Ibid., I, Q1, 8th art., reply obj. 2.

210 Etienne Gilson, *The Christian Philosophy of St. Thomas Aquinas*, New York: Random House, 1956, 10.

211 Aquinas, *Summa Theologica*, I. Q2, 2nd art., reply obj. 1.

212 Ibid., I. Q12, 12th art.

213 Austin Flannery, ed., *Vatican Council II: The Conciliar and Post Conciliar Documents*, Collegeville, MN: Liturgical Press, 1975, 752–3. It is in no way denied that Vatican II went further than its predecessor in affirming revelation as God's personal self-comunication: 'Revelation no longer appears simply as a body of supernatural truths contained in Scripture and taught by the Church. There is a clear movement in *Dei Verbum* away from revelation as simply *revelata* (truths disclosed) to *revelatio* (personal disclosure).' So Dermot A. Lane, *The Experience of God: An Invitation to Do Theology*, Dublin: Veritas Publications, 1981, 46.

214 Hence N. Wolterstorff's distinction between Aquinas and Locke in A. Plantinga and N. Wolterstorff, eds., *Rationality and Religious Belief*, 141. Cf. the qualifications proposed by Paul Helm, *Faith and Understanding*, 30–2.

215 Aquinas, *Summa Theologica*, I, Q1 9th art., reply obj. 2; I, Q1 1st art., reply obj. 2. Cf. E. Gilson, *The Elements of Christian Philosophy*, New York: New American Library of World Literature, 1963, ch. 2.

216 See Arvin Vos, *Aquinas, Calvin, and Contemporary Protestant Thought: A Critique of Protestant Views on the Thought of Thomas Aquinas*, Washington: Christian College Consortium, 1985, 104.

217 Dorothy M. Emmet, 'The use of analogy in metaphysics', *Proceedings of the Aristotelian Society*, XLI, 1941, 1–26; idem, *The Nature of Metaphysical Thinking*, London: Macmillan, 1946, ch. 8.

218 See further John Montag, 'Revelation: the false legacy of Suárez', in John Milbank et al., eds., *Radical Orthodoxy*, London: Routledge, 1999, ch. 2.

219 Michael J. Buckley, *At the Origins of Modern Atheism*, New Haven: Yale University Press, 1987, 67. Buckley is, of course, well aware that, from classical Greece onwards, 'atheism' has appeared in various guises and that, accordingly, Christian responses to it have been couched in a variety of terms.

220 T. Penelhum, *Reason and Religious Faith*, 26. Cf. G. de Broglie, 'La Vrai Notion thomiste des *perambua fidei*', *Gregorianum*, XXXIV, 1953, 341–89.

221 Cf. Henry Stob, *Theological Reflections*, Grand Rapids, MI: Eerdmans, 1981, 130.

222 O. C. Quick, *Doctrines of the Creed*, London: Collins Fontana, 1963, 201.

223 J. Calvin, *Institutes of the Christian Religion*, ed. John T. McNeill, trans. and indexed by Ford Lewis Battles, Philadelphia: Westminster Press, 1960, II.18.

224 Ibid.

225 See, for example, ibid., I. v. 2. Leonard Hodgson thus goes too far in saying that 'Whereas for St. Thomas reason can discover certain truths, including certain truths about God in nature, for Calvin human reason apart from faith can have no such certain knowledge at all'. The distortions of human knowledge which Calvin later specifies, and which Hodgson cites in support, result from the sinful suppression of the natural knowledge of God. See L. Hodgson, *The Doctrine of the Trinity*, London: Nisbet (1943), 1960, 204.

226 For a compendium see Leroy Nixon, *John Calvin's Teachings on Human Reason*, New York: Exposition Press, 1963.

227 Ephesians 4: 23

228 J. Calvin, *Institutes*, III. vii. 1. However, the Calvinist systematician Turretin was convinced that human reason could pronounce upon which doctrines – notably the Roman Catholic transubstantiation and the Lutheran ubiquity – were *not* tenable. See his *Inst. Theol.* I. ix. 9. See further Richard A. Muller, *Post-Reformation Reformed Dogmatics*, Grand Rapids, MI: Baker Book House, 1987, I, ch. 7.

229 Ibid., I. viii. 13.

230 Z. Ursinus, *Corpus Doctrinae Christianae*, Frankfurt, 1621, 117. For a full examination of this point see John Platt, *Reformed Thought and Scholasticism: The Arguments for the Existence of God in Dutch Theology, 1575–1650*, Leiden: E. J. Brill, 1982, 54–60; cf. John Patrick Donnelly, 'Immortality and method in Ursinus's theological ambience', in Dirk Visser, ed., *Controversy and Conciliation: The Reformation and the Palatinate 1559–1583*, Allison Park, PA: Pickwick Publications, 1986, 182–95.

231 Among these was John Goodwin. William J. Wainwright's characterization of the Puritans as 'good Calvinists' thus requires qualification. See Quinn and Taliaferro, eds., *Companion*, Oxford: Blackwell, 1977, 61.

232 Cf. J. Locke's chapter 'Of enthusiasm', which he added to the 4th edn (1700) of *An Essay concerning Human Understanding*.

233 R. Baxter, *The Practical Works of the Rev. Richard Baxter*, London: James Duncan, 1830, XXII, xxxii; IV, 295; XVIII, 297. Baxter's methodological eclecticism emerges in the fact that, while he knew More and Whichcote, and quoted Plato, Plotinus and Ficinus frequently, he also testifies, 'next Practical Divinity, no Books so suited

with my Disposition as Aquinas, Scotus, Durandus, Ockham and their Disciples; because I thought they narrowly searched after Truth'. See *Reliquiae Baxterianae*, ed. M. Sylvester 1669, I, 6.

234 This familiar point is echoed, for example, by John Owen. See *The Works of John Owen*, ed. William Goold (1850–3), London: Banner of Truth Trust, 16 vols. 1968, IV, 54.

235 J. Flavel, *Works*, 6 vols. (1820), London: Banner of Truth Trust, 1968, VI, 472–3.

236 B. Whichcote, *Moral and Religious Aphorisms: Collected from the manuscript papers of the Reverend and Learned Doctor Whichcote*, London: Samuel Salter, 1753, no. 13.

237 Ibid., no. 76.

238 Ibid., no. 771.

239 J. Smith, 'Of the existence and nature of God', in *Select Discourses*, Cambridge: CUP, 1859, 141.

240 Hilary Armstrong, 'Platonism', in Ian Ramsey, ed., *Prospect for Metaphysics*, London: Allen & Unwin, 1961, 95.

241 B. Whichcote, *Moral and Religious Aphorisms*, no. 916.

242 H. More, *A Collection of Several Philosophical Writings of Dr. Henry More, Fellow of Christ's College, Cambridge*, London, 4th edn., 1712, 2.

243 J. Smith, *Select Discourses*, London: Rivingtons & Cochran, 1821, 358.

244 B. Whichcote, *Works*, Aberdeen, 1751, III, 113.

245 H. More, *An Explanation of the Grand Mystery of Godliness*, 1660, 361.

246 J. Smith, *Select Discourses*, 1821, 24.

247 In *A Brief Account of the New Sect of Latitude-men: Together with some Reflections upon the new Philosophy*, by S.P. (possibly Simon Patrick), 1662.

248 See Alan P. F. Sell, *John Locke and the Eighteenth-Century Divines*, ch. 3.

249 J. Locke, *An Essay concerning Human Understanding*, ed. Peter H. Nidditch, Oxford: Clarendon Press, 1975, IV. xix. 4.

250 See ibid., IV. xix. 14.

251 Idem, *The Reasonableness of Christianity as delivered in the Scriptures*, in *The Works of John Locke in Ten Volumes*, 11th edn., London: W. Otridge et al., 1812, VII, 129ff.; *A Second Vindication*, ibid., 285–6, 414; idem, *A Paraphrase and Notes on the Epistles of St. Paul*, ed. Arthur W. Wainwright, Oxford: Clarendon Press, 2 vols. 1987, I, 136, on Galatians 3: 7.

252 Idem, *The Reasonableness of Christianity*, 135. This is not to deny that elsewhere, as Paul Helm has pointed out in *Faith and Understanding*, 21, Locke mounts a pragmatic argument for the necessity of revelation. But this is not his only argument for it.

253 For a fuller account of the English deists and their opponents see Alan

P. F. Sell, '"The Gospel its own Witness": deism, Thomas Paine and Andrew Fuller', forthcoming in a *festschrift* for Allison A. Trites, Macon, GA: Mercer University Press.

254 J. Butler, *The Analogy of Religion to the Constitution and Course of Nature* (1736), London: Ward, Lock, n.d., 121.

255 Ibid., 116. Cf. idem, *Fifteen Sermons preached at the Rolls Chapel* (1726), London: G. Bell (1914), 1953, 88.

256 Ibid., 127.

257 See Alan P. F. Sell, *Dissenting Thought and the Life of the Churches*, 37–40.

258 Edward Morgan, *John Elias: Life, Letters and Essays* (1844, 1847), Edinburgh: Banner of Truth Trust, 1973, 348.

259 R. Mackintosh, *Essays Towards a New Theology*, Glasgow: Maclehose, 1889, 367.

260 Calvin, *Institutes*, I. vii. 4.

261 A. Plantinga, 'The Reformed objection to natural thology', 367. He introduces this paper with an exposition of Herman Bavinck and Calvin on natural theology, before proceeding to a discussion of properly basic beliefs, which I have noted earlier. It should not be supposed that the Dutch alone have perpetuated the Reformed anti-natural theology stance. For example, Robert Leighton, archbishop of Glasgow in the seventeenth century, asked 'why should we use the pitiful light of a candle to discover the sun, and eagerly go about to prove the Being of Him who gave being to every thing else?' See his *Works*, ed. J. F. Pearson, London, 1825, IV, 223. Again, in the eighteenth century the vicar of St Catharine's, Dublin, John Ellis, argued against Locke's position concerning revelation, asserting that 'The deep things of God, and all notices we have of spiritual and immaterial objects of divine knowledge "God hath revealed them unto us by his divine spirit."' See [John Ellis], *The Knowledge of Divine Things from Revelation, not from Reason or Nature* (1743), London: Thomas Tegg, 1837, 142. Cf. Alan P. F. Sell, *John Locke and the Eighteenth-Century Divines*, 80, 23, 33, 72.

262 A. E. Garvie, 'Fifty years' retrospect', *Congregational Quarterly*, VII, 1929, 21.

263 N. Micklem, *The Box and the Puppets*, London: Geoffrey Bles, 1957, 52–3.

264 See K. Barth, Preface to the 2nd edn. of *The Epistle to the Romans*, London: OUP, 1968, 10.

265 See Gordon Watson, 'Karl Barth and St. Anselm's theological programme', *Scottish Journal of Theology*, XXX no. 1, 1977, 31–45.

266 He confesses his earlier Kantian adhesions in his *Credo*, London: Hodder & Stoughton, 1964, 185.

267 K. Barth, *Church Dogmatics*, Edinburgh: T. & T. Clark, 1963, I. ii. 275.

268 R. S. Franks, 'Trends in recent theology', *Congregational Quarterly*, XXIII, 1945, 29.

269 Ibid., 19.

270 Ibid., 25.

271 Quoted by H. R. Mackintosh, *Types of Modern Theology*, London: Nisbet, 1937, 277.

272 K. Barth, *The Knowledge of God and the Service of God in the Teaching of the Reformation*, London: Hodder & Stoughton, 1938, 4. These are Barth's Gifford Lectures, and he adds, 'I certainly see – with astonishment – that such a science as Lord Gifford has in mind [that is, natural theology] does exist, but I do not see how it is possible for it to exist' (p. 5).

273 Idem, *Church Dogmatics*, II. i. 84.

274 Idem, *The Doctrine of the Word of God* (CD I, pt. 1), Edinburgh: T. & T. Clark, 1936, 279. We may note that Barth's sympathetic commentator, Herbert Hartwell, agrees with those Roman Catholic scholars who hold that Barth has misunderstood the Thomist analogy of being to be concerned with two levels of being, rather than with the proportionality of intrinsically analogical being. See his *The Theology of Karl Barth: An Introduction*, London: Duckworth, 1964, 184–5. See further Stephanus Du Toit, 'Revelation or reveilaton? Barth and postmodernism', *Heythrop Journal*, XL no. 1, January 1999, 10–11.

275 See *Church Dogmatics*, II. i. 86–7.

276 Ibid., 92.

277 Ibid., 150–1.

278 Ibid., I. ii. 266.

279 E. Brunner, *Nature and Grace*, reprinted in *Natural Theology*, London: Geoffrey Bles, 1946, 22–4. Barth's reply, *Nein!*, is reprinted here also.

280 J. Baillie, *Our Knowledge of God*, London: OUP, 1952, 33.

281 Ibid., 30.

282 See further Joan E. O'Donovan, 'Man in the image of God: the disagreement between Barth and Brunner reconsidered', *Scottish Journal of Theology*, XXXIX no. 4, 1986, 433–59.

283 See K. Barth, *Church Dogmatics*, I. i. 273.

284 Idem, *Credo*, 186.

285 Ned Wisnefske, *Our Natural Knowledge of God*, New York: Peter Lang, 1990, 72.

286 Geoffrey W. Bromiley, 'Karl Barth and Anglicanism', *The Churchman*, LXXXVIII no. 1, January–March 1974, 12.

287 Alan Torrance, 'Does God suffer? Incarnation and impassibility', in Trevor Hart and Daniel Thimell, eds., *Christ in Our Place: The Humanity of God in Christ for the Reconciliation of the World: Essays presented to James*

Torrance, Exeter: Paternoster Publications, 1989, 355 n. 23. In this paragraph, and on this sensitive issue, I have taken care to quote some who may be trusted to get Barth right. Ninian Smart, however, writes with reference to Barth, 'a rationally coherent presentation of an exclusively revelationist position forms a kind of natural theology, even when natural theology in the traditional sense is repudiated'. See his *The Science of Religion and the Sociology of Knowledge: Some Methodological Questions*, Princeton: Princeton University Press, 1973.

288 R. S. Franks, 'Trends in recent theology', 29.

289 E. L. Allen, 'The new orthodoxy and the contemporary mood', *Congregational Quarterly*, XXVIII no. 2, April 1950, 142.

290 See Bonaventure, *Sent.* 3. 4.

291 B. Pascal, *Pascal's Pensées*, ed. H. F. Stewart, London: Routledge & Kegal Paul, 1950, 7–8.

292 See the illuminating study by Terence Penelhum, 'Human nature and truth: Hume and Pascal', *Lumen*, XII, 1993, 45–64.

293 D. Hume, *Dialogues Concerning Natural Religion*, pt. XII (1779), Harmondsworth: Penguin, 1990, 138.

294 A. S. Pringle-Pattison, *The Idea of God in the Light of Recent Philosophy*, 2nd rev. edn., New York: OUP, 1920, 23.

295 For a brief account of the flow of discussion of the theistic proofs between 1960 and 1980 see Alan P. F. Sell, *The Philosophy of Religion 1875–1980*, 215–27.

296 N. Malcolm, 'Anselm's ontological arguments', *Philosophical Review*, 1960; reprinted in John Hick, ed., *The Existence of God*, New York: Macmillan, 1964, 67.

297 E. Brunner, *Revelation and Reason: The Christian Doctrine of Faith and Knowledge* (1941), London: SCM Press, [1946], 340–1; cf. 45. Cf. D. Elton Trueblood, *The Trustworthiness of Religious Experience*, London: Allen & Unwin, 1939, 14: 'The chief weakness of the traditional proofs lies in the fact that the God to whom they point is an *inference* and it is not as an inference that God has been or can be worshipped.' See also the reference to Newman Smyth and Samuel Harris in Daniel Day Williams, *The Andover Liberals*, New York: Octagon Books, 1970, 42; and Cook Wilson's famous remark, 'We don't want merely inferred friends. Could we possibly be satisfied with an inferred God?' See his paper on 'Rational grounds for belief in God', in *Statement and Inference*, Oxford: Clarendon Press, 1926, II, 853.

298 See Norbert Samuelson, 'That the God of the philosophers is not the God of Abraham, Isaac, and Jacob', *Harvard Theological Review*, LXV no. 1, January 1972, 2–27.

299 W. G. De Burgh, *Towards a Religious Philosophy*, London: MacDonald & Evans, 1937, 39. Cf. E. P. Dickie, *God is Light*, 154.

[300] W. A. Whitehouse, *Christian Faith and the Scientific Attitude*, Edinburgh: Oliver & Boyd, 1952, 56.

[301] J. Calvin, *Institutes*, I. v. 12.

[302] J. H. Leckie, ed., *David W. Forrest, D.D.*, London: Hodder & Stoughton, 1919, 279.

[303] H. R. Mackintosh, *The Doctrine of the Person of Christ* (1912), Edinburgh: T. & T. Clark, 1956, 340.

[304] See Isaiah 44.

[305] Cf. the distinction of Gustav Weigel and Arthur J. Madden, *Religion and the Knowledge of God*, Englewood Cliffs, NJ: Prentice Hall, 1961, 159.

[306] See Alan P. F. Sell, *Philosophical Idealism and Christian Belief*, ch. 3.

[307] See the discussion of James Martineau in Alan P. F. Sell, *Commemorations*, ch. 1.

[308] Cf. H. R. Mackintosh, *The Christian Apprehension of God*, London: SCM Press, 1929, 65.

[309] R. Flint, *Sermons and Addresses*, 322.

[310] See J. Calvin, *Institutes*, I. iii. 1, I. v. 9, etc.

[311] W. P. Paterson, *The Rule of Faith*, 133–4.

[312] N. H. G. Robinson, 'The problem of natural theology', *Religious Studies*, VIII no. 4, December 1972, 325. The reference here is to Barth's later work, *The Humanity of God*, London: Collins, 1961, in which he had much to say concerning God's quest for human beings. See further James Richmond, *Faith and Philosophy*, London: Hodder & Stroughton, 1966, 151. It must also be granted that Barth can say that the Gentiles have always 'objectively' known God. See his *A Shorter Commentary on Romans*, London: SCM Press, 1959, 28. This uncharacteristic remark is, however, qualified in *Church Dogmatics*, IV. iii. 135ff., where Barth speaks (somewhat confusingly) of the 'luminosity' of, but not the revelation in, nature; this because faith is not required to sense the 'luminosity'. In the paper quoted Robinson responds to T. F. Torrance, 'The problem of natural theology in the thought of Karl Barth', *Religious Studies*, VI no. 2, June 1970, 121–35. Among other things Robinson notes (p. 329) Torrance's claim that Barth affirmed natural theology 'within the understanding of faith'. Robinson retorts that 'this is no longer *natural* theology . . . it goes no way towards meeting the criticism that on Barth's representation of it the truth of revelation remains esoteric and irrelevant'. G. W. H. Lampe has suggested that, with his narrative of the magi, Matthew indicates 'that he was prepared to acknowledge gentile sources of revelation, not only, like Luke in Paul's speech at Athens, as testimonies to monotheism against idolatry, but even, in parallel with the Prophets, as witnesses to Christ'. See his 'Athens and Jerusalem: joint witnesses

to Christ?', in Brian Hebblethwaite and Stewart Sutherland, eds., *The Philosophical Frontiers of Christian Theology: Essays presented to D. M. MacKinnon*, Cambridge: CUP, 1982, 36.

313 Alasdair MacIntyre, 'The logical status of religious beliefs', in S. E. Toulmin et al., *Metaphysical Beliefs*, London: SCM Press, 1957, 201.

314 Cf. Howard Root, 'Beginning all over again', *Soundings: Essays Concerning Christian Understanding*, ed. A. R. Vidler, Cambridge: CUP, 1963, 14–15.

315 Roger Trigg, *Rationality and Religion*, 178.

316 J. Baillie, *Our Knowledge of God*, 24.

317 N. F. S. Ferré, *Searchlight on Contemporary Theology*, New York: Harper, 1961, 104; cf. 151–2. I have sometimes been tempted to think that an analogy may be drawn between Barth and the Puritan John Cotton, whose pneumatology all but obliterated the human person, and prompted Thomas Shepard's rebuke that, according to Cotton, 'there is seeing in a Christian without an eye, and hearing without an ear, and knowing Christ without an understanding'. See William B. K. Stoever, 'Nature, grace, and John Cotton', *Church History*, XLIV, 1975, 29.

318 E. P. Dickie, *God is Light*, 127. Of course, the Barthians feared a dualism from the other direction. Thus, for example, Daniel Jenkins writes, 'The Reformed attack on Natural Theology is due to an anxiety to preserve the catholicity of the Church because a preoccupation with Natural Theology involves a turning away from Jesus Christ Who is the life of the Church. Natural Theology attempts to set up another source of knowledge of God alongside Jesus Christ and thus threatens His Lordship.' See his *The Nature of Catholicity*, London: Faber & Faber, 1942, 69. This complaint may apply to the Cartesian and post-Cartesian natural theologies which set out from human reason to argue to God, but it does not hold against the broader understanding of God's general revelation, according to which all knowledge of God is from God.

319 G. C. Berkouwer, 'General and special divine revelation', in C. F. H. Henry, ed., *Revelation and the Bible*, London: Tyndale, 1959, 19.

320 H. Cunliffe-Jones, *The Authority of Biblical Revelation*, London: James Clarke, 1945, 88.

321 Though for a concise account of the Franciscan opposition to the Thomist natural theology on the ground that from an argument grounded in physical bodies one may infer only physical causes, and hence the 'god' arrived at would not be transcendent, see David Luscombe, *Medieval Thought*, Oxford: OUP, 1997, 94–5.

322 See, for example, R. Swinburne, 'Intellectual biography', in Alan G. Padgett, ed., *Reason and the Christian Religion*, Oxford: OUP, 1994, 10.

323 T. Penelhum, *Problems of Religious Knowledge*, London: Macmillan, 1971, ch. 3.

324 W. G. De Burgh, *Towards a Religious Philosophy*, 40.

325 A. C. Ewing, *The Fundamental Questions of Philosophy*, London: Routledge & Kegan Paul, 1951, 241.

326 P. Badham, 'The centrality of theism for Christianity', in Stephen T. Davis, ed., *Philosophy and Theological Discourse*, Basingstoke: Macmillan, 1997, 8.

327 R. W. Dale's cautionary word is worth pondering: 'Theism may be as serious an obstacle to the reception of the Christian Gospel as Atheism; for the God of many theists is a God so remote from man that it is inconceivable to them that He should have become "flesh" at the impulse of an infinite love for our race, and should have lived a life of conflict and of suffering, and died a death of shame and sorrow for our salvation.' See his *Christian Doctrine: A Series of Discourses* (1894), London: Hodder & Stoughton, 1903, 40–1.

328 See D. Z. Phillips, 'Notes on a "monstrous illusion",' in Davis, ed., *Philosophy and Theological Discourse*, 15–21. While granting that no one 'has ever been led to a living faith in God simply by a chain of syllogisms', A. E. Taylor observes that 'a man cannot be expected to receive anything as . . . a communication from God until he is at least satisfied that it is reasonable to believe that there is some One to make the communication'. See his *Does God Exist?* (1945), London: Collins Fontana, 1961, 17. While in no way denying that some may puzzle things out in the way implied, I suspect that many more Christians would wish to say that the assurance of God is given in and with the revelation of God.

329 John Heywood Thomas, *Subjectivity and Paradox: A Study of Kierkegaard*, Oxford: Blackwell, 1957, 143.

330 R. Flint, *Sermons and Addresses*, 60. See further Alan P. F. Sell, *Defending and Declaring the Faith*, 52–3, where the quotation given from an earlier version of the sermon is modified in the book now quoted.

331 Robert Mackintosh, 'Professor Gwatkin on revelation', *Expository Times*, XVIII, 1906–7, 223.

332 *Testimony of the United Associate Synod of the Secession Church*, Edinburgh [1834], 4th edn., 27.

333 C. C. J. Webb, *Religious Experience*, London: OUP, [1945], 32. Cf. idem, *Problems in the Relations of God and Man*, 1911, London: Nisbet, 124; 43; cf. 26, 38–9. Leonard Hodgson adds the thought that to suppose we could attain to knowledge of God apart from God's revelatory initiative would betoken 'a view of reason which is comparable in the intellectual sphere to Pelagianism in the moral'. See his *The Place of Reason in Christian Apologetic*, Oxford: Blackwell, 1925, 45–6.

Chapter 7: Faith, Knowledge and Experience

1 Tertullian, *De Praescriptione Haereticorum* VII.
2 Idem, *Adversus Marcionem* V. xix.
3 Idem, *Adversus Hermogenem* 8.
4 Idem, *Praes.Haer.* XIII.
5 Ibid., XII.
6 Idem, *De Anima* II.
7 Idem, *De Resurrectione Carnis* III.
8 See idem, *Ad Nat.* II. iv.
9 Idem, *Praes. Haer.* VII.
10 Idem, *De Anima* III.
11 Idem, *Apologeticum* XLVII.
12 James Orr, *The Progress of Dogma*, London: James Clarke, 1901, 46 n.
13 Tertullian, *De Carne Christi* V.
14 J. Quasten, *Patrology*, II, Utrecht: Spectrum, 1935, 320.
15 Augustine, *Ep.* CXX. 3.
16 Idem, *Sermons* CXVIII, 1.
17 Idem, *Sermons* XLIII. iii. 4; *In Joan. Evang.* XXIX 6.
18 See further John Burnaby, *Amor Dei: A Study of the Religion of St. Augustine*, London: Hodder & Stoughton, 1938, 78–9.
19 Bernard of Clairvaux, *De Consideratione* V. iii. 5.
20 Idem, *Sermo in cantica canticorum* XXII. 2. cf. VI. 9.
21 Idem, *Ep.* CXC. 9.
22 Andrew Louth, 'Mysticism', in Gordon S. Wakefield, ed., *A Dictionary of Christian Spirituality*, London: SCM Press, 1983, 273. He properly notes the twelfth-century turn to subjectivism in mysticism, which reflected a broader societal concern with the individual – an important corrective of any who may be tempted to suppose that the Romantics were the first to stumble across the individual. For a stimulating paper which poses many relevant questions see Martin Henry, 'How Christian is Christian mysticism?', *Irish Theological Quarterly*, LXIV no. 1, Spring 1999, 29–54.
23 Richard of St Victor, *On the Trinity*, 2, in Eugene R. Fairweather, trans. and ed., *A Scholastic Miscellany: Anselm to Ockham*, London: SCM Press, 1966, 325. Interestingly, Kierkegaard was later to find support in a similar remark of Hugh of St Victor. See *Papirer* X 2 A 354, quoted by J. Heywood Thomas, *Subjectivity and Paradox*, Oxford: Blackwell, 1957, 120.
24 William of Auxerre, *Summa Aurea*, ed. J. Ribaillier, Paris, 1980, 16ff.
25 See further Warren A. Quanbeck, 'Luther's early exegesis', in Roland H. Bainton et al., *Luther Today: Martin Luther Lectures*, Decorah, IA: Luther College Press, 1957.

[26] G. Ebeling, *Luther: An Introduction to his Thought* (1964), London: Collins Fontana, 1975, 85–6.

[27] R. S. Franks, *The Atonement*, Oxford: OUP, 1934, 18. T. F. Torrance argues that Calvin's epistemology represents a counter to that of Ockham in *Theology in Reconstruction*, ch. 5, esp. 78–81.

[28] I express myself with caution because the extent of Luther's indebtedness to Ockham is still a matter of debate. See Brian A. Gerrish, *Grace and Reason: A Study of the Theology of Luther*, Oxford: Clarendon Press, 1962, 5.

[29] Luther, *Disputation against the Scholastic Philosophy*, 1517, Art. 41.

[30] For whom see C. C. J. Webb, *Studies in the History of Natural Theology* (1915), Oxford: Clarendon Press, 1970, ch. 6.

[31] Luther, *Works*, Weimar, 1883– , XLV, 39.

[32] Ibid., X, i, 203. 4.

[33] Idem, *Works*, ed. Jaroslav J. Pelikan and Helmut T. Lehmann, Philadelphia: Westminster Press, 1955, XXXII, 27.

[34] Idem, *Kritische Gesamtausgabe* (*Tischreden*), Weimar edn., XIX, 206, 31.

[35] See idem, *Werke*, XXXVII, 388. 16.

[36] Ibid., I, 425. 2.

[37] Idem, *A Commentary on St. Paul's Epistle to the Galatians*, ed. Erasmus Middleton, London, 1807, 11. Of the vast literature on Luther, Philip S. Watson, *Let God Be God: An Interpretation of the Theology of Martin Luther*, London: Epworth, 1947, remains among the soundest expositions of his thought.

[38] Idem, *Werke*, XXXIX, I, 389. 10.

[39] See the exposition by John Whale, *The Protestant Tradition: An Essay in Interpretation*, Cambridge: CUP, 1960, ch. 4.

[40] *Eighteen Dissertations concerning the Entire Christian Life and of what it Consists. Propositions upheld at Walshut by Dr. Balthasar Friedberger* [that is, Hübmaier – he often called himself after the place of his birth], *and Others*, 1524, in William L. Lumpkin, *Baptist Confessions of Faith*, Valley Forge, PA: Judson Press (1969), rev. edn. reprinted 1983, 21.

[41] Ibid., 20.

[42] Ibid. It is thus difficult to agree with P. T. Forsyth that 'Inspiration took the place of faith with these Spiritualists [i.e. the Anabaptists], as happened also in the case of their legatees, the Quakers, with a supernatural inner light, and the Rationalists, with a natural.' See his *Faith, Freedom and the Future* (1912), London: Independent Press, 1955, 58. Cf. Alan P. F. Sell, *Dissenting Thought and the Life of the Churches*, 582–3. Of course, there were various tendencies within Anabaptism, but Forsyth's statement is too sweeping to be entirely just.

[43] John Oman, *The Problem of Faith and Freedom in the Last Two Centuries*, London: Hodder & Stoughton, 1906, 62.

44 T. Penelhum, *Reason and Religious Faith*, Boulder, CO: Westview Press, 1995, 29. Can it be that Penelhum throws his customary caution to the winds in the last phrase here? Although Clement Webb declared in his Preface that 'Pascal is not to me especially sympathetic, nor is he a teacher to whom I feel myself under a peculiar obligation', his account of *Pascal's Philosophy of Religion*, Oxford: Clarendon Press, 1929, continues to illuminate its subject. Not all modern philosophers have been as generous. See the replies to some of them by Michael Martin, 'Four critiques of Pascal's wager', *Sophia*, XIV no. 1, March 1975, 1–11. See also James Cargile, 'Pascal's wager', *Philosophy*, XLI, July 1966, 250–7.

45 B. Pascal, *Pensées*, trans. H. F. Stewart, London: Routledge & Kegan Paul, 1950, 9.

46 Ibid., 5.

47 So Robert Mackintosh, 'Apologetics', *Encyclopedia Britannica*, 11th edn, 1910–11, 191(a).

48 B. Pascal, *Pensées*, 7.

49 Ibid., 127.

50 Ibid., 343.

51 Ibid., 127.

52 R. Sibbes, *Works*, ed. A. B. Grosart, 1862, IV, 363, 412.

53 Francis Quarles, *Enchyridion*, 1640, III, 91, quoted by A. Patrides, ed., *The Cambridge Platonists*, Cambridge, MA: Harvard University Press, 1970, 9.

54 M. Llwyd, *Gweithiau Morgan Llwyd*, ed. T. E. Ellis, Bangor: Jarvis and Foster, 1899, 190; M. Llwyd, *Gweithiau Morgan Llwyd*, ed. J. H. Davies, London: Dent, 1908.

55 Quoted by Alexander Gordon, 'The origin of the Muggletonians', *Proceedings of the Literary and Philosophical Society of Liverpool*, 1869, 275.

56 R. Hooker, *Of the Laws of Ecclesiastical Polity*, III, viii. 4.

57 P. Sterry, *The Spirits Conviction of Sinne*, 1645. The standard account of the place of the Holy Spirit in Puritan epistemology is Geoffrey F. Nuttall's *The Holy Spirit in Puritan Faith and Experience*, Oxford: Blackwell, 1946.

58 R. Barclay, *An Apology for the True Christian Divinity, as the same is held forth and preached by the People, in scorn, called Quakers* (1678), Glasgow: R. Barclay Murdoch, 1886, 28–9. See further Alan P. F. Sell, *Commemorations: Studies in Christian Thought and History*, ch. 6.

59 R. Barclay, *An Apology*, 42.

60 Ibid. With a painful history of Quaker and other suffering behind him, Barclay also laments the way in which reason has been used in Christian history to justify persecution, ibid., 39–40.

61 Quoted by F. J. Powicke in Albert Peel, ed., *Essays Congregational and*

Catholic, London: Congregational Union of England and Wales (1931), 306.

62 W. Pendlebury, *The Practical Influences of the Speculative Doctrine of Christianity Demonstrated*, London: Eman. Matthews, 1726, quoted by Francis Nicholson and Ernest Axon, *The Older Nonconformity of Kendal*, Kendal: Titus Wilson, 1915, 243, 244. However, the account within which the sermon extracts fall reveals that Pendlebury could, in other connections, be more than a little obstinate and tetchy.

63 J. Wesley, *Works*, 3rd edn., ed. T. Jackson, 1829–31, VIII, 14.

64 J. Hart, *The Unreasonableness of Religion: Being Remarks and Animadversions on Mr J. Wesley's Sermon on Romans viii. 32*, 1741.

65 S. Kierkegaard, *Concluding Unscientific Postscript*, Princeton: Princeton University Press, 1968, 116.

66 Ibid., 109.

67 Ibid., 281.

68 J. Heywood Thomas, *Subjectivity and Paradox*, 71.

69 Kierkegaard, *Concluding Unscientific Postscript*, 188.

70 Ibid., 189.

71 Idem, *Philosophical Fragments*, Princeton: Princeton University Press, 1964, 84–5.

72 Cf. *The Sonnets of Kierkegaard*, London: OUP, 1951, 1084, and *Papirer* X 6 A 79; cf. J. H. Thomas, *Subjectivity and Paradox*, 132–3.

73 Kierkegaard, *Concluding Unscientific Postscript*, 540.

74 When discussing Pascal on faith I deliberately omitted any reference to his celebrated wager. It seems to me that some writers have been too eager to lump Pascal and Kierkegaard together as fideists of similar kinds. However, whereas Kierkegaard's leap is a matter of casting all upon God, Pascal's wager is a prudential calculation which, if things turn out one way rather than the other, will justify faith. Among many discussions of the wager see James Cargile, 'Pascal's wager', *Philosophy*, XLI, July 1966, 250–7; Robert Holyer, 'Pascal on belief and the religious life', *Scottish Journal of Theology*, XXXV, 1982, 431–45; Terence Penelhum, *Religion and Rationality*, New York: Random House, 1971; a reply to Penelhum in George N. Schlesinger, *New Perspectives on Old-Time Religion*, Oxford: Clarendon Press, 1988, ch. 6; and Penelhum's illuminating paper, 'Human nature and truth: Hume and Pascal', *Lumen*, XII, 1993, 45–64. For a concise account of many of the issues surrounding fideism see T. Penelhum, 'Fideism', in Philip L. Quinn and Charles Taliaferro, eds., *A Companion to Philosophy of Religion*, Oxford: Blackwell, 1997, ch. 48.

75 So Merold Westphal, *Kierkegaard's Critique of Religion and Society* (1987), University Park, PA: Pennsylvania State University Press, 1991, 92.

76 T. F. Torrance, *Theological Science*, London: OUP, 1969, 5.

77 Words of Kierkegaard written in 1849, quoted by J. H. Thomas from *Papirer* X 2 A 207, in *Subjectivity and Paradox*, Oxford: Blackwell, 1957, 147. Cf. *Concluding Unscientific Postscript*, 23–4; *Philosophical Fragments*, *passim*. H. J. Blackham relegates his sensitive account of Kierkegaard's subjectivism to a footnote in his *Six Existentialist Thinkers*, London: Routledge & Kegan Paul, 1961, 18–19.

78 D. E. Roberts, *Existentialism and Religious Belief*, ed. Roger Hazelton, New York: OUP, 1959, 84–5.

79 Kierkegaard, *Either–Or*, Garden City, NY: Doubleday Anchor Books, 1959, II, 356.

80 Ibid., 504.

81 B. Mitchell, 'Faith and the limitations of open-mindedness', in J. J. Macintosh and H. A. Meynell, eds., *Faith, Scepticism and Personal Identity: A Festschrift for Terence Penelhum*, Calgary: University of Calgary Press, 1994, 41.

82 See further J. H. Thomas, *Subjectivity and Paradox*, 151–8; cf. Stephen Toulmin, *An Examination of the Place of Reason in Ethics*, Cambridge: CUP, 1960, ch.14.

83 H. P. Owen, *The Christian Knowledge of God*, London: Athlone Press, 1969, 41–2.

84 1 Kings 19: 10, 14.

85 The judgement of the Unitarian divine, Robert Aspland, in a sermon addressed to the young on Philippians 4: 8 comes to mind: 'The pretence of excluding reason from religion is the idlest of all follies; they that set it up, expose its vanity by their own conduct, for they always reason as well as they can, and allege what they think reason for discarding reason altogether.' See *The Beauty and Excellence of Christian Morality*, London: Smallfield, 1838, 10–11. The sermon was delivered at the New Gravel-Pit Meeting-house, Hackney, on 6 May 1838.

86 David Brown, *The Life of Rabbi Duncan* (1872), Glasgow: Free Presbyterian Publications, 1986, 414–15. Duncan quotes the last line of Psalm 34 in the Scottish metrical version.

87 II Clement, XI.

88 See Origen, *De Principiis*, pref. 2.

89 S. Sykes, 'Faith', in Geoffrey Wainwright, ed., *Keeping the Faith: Essays to Mark the Centenary of Lux Mundi*, Philadelphia: Fortress Press, and Allison Park, PA: Pickwick Publications, 1988, 3. There is much of value still to be found in W. P. Paterson's Baird Lecture for 1905, *The Rule of Faith*, London: Hodder & Stoughton, 1912.

90 R. Baxter, *The Reformed Pastor* (1656), abridged edn., ed. James M. Houston, Portland, OR: Multnomah Press, 1982, 25.

91 J. Wesley, *The Works of the Rev. John Wesley, A.M.*, London: Wesleyan Conference Office, 1872, VII, 198.

92 G. Galloway, *The Philosophy of Religion*, Edinburgh: T. & T. Clark, 1914, 305–6.

93 See further Alan P. F. Sell, *Aspects of Christian Integrity* (1990), Eugene, OR: Wipf & Stock, 1998, ch. 3; idem, *Commemorations* (1993), Eugene, OR: Wipf & Stock, 1998, ch. 2; idem, 'Reformed identity: a non-issue of catholic significance', *Reformed Review*, LIV no. 1, Autumn 2000, 17–27.

94 Cf. Sydney Cave, *The Doctrines of the Christian Faith* (1931), London: Independent Press, 1952, 48–9; H. A. Hodges, *The Pattern of Atonement*, London: SCM Press, 1955, 85.

95 R. Mackintosh, *The Obsoleteness of the Westminster Confession of Faith*, bound with *Essays Towards a New Theology*, Glasgow: Maclehose, 1889, 52.

96 H. F. Lovell Cocks, *By Faith Alone*, London: James Clark, 1943, 144–5.

97 W. R. Inge, *Faith*, London: Duckworth, 1909, 198.

98 Hebrews 11: 6.

99 Edward Morgan, *John Elias, Life, Letters and Essays* (1844, 1847), Edinburgh: Banner of Truth Trust, 1973, 370.

100 A. Ritschl, *The Christian Doctrine of Justification and Reconciliation*, Edinburgh: T. & T. Clark, 2nd edn., 1900, 593.

101 The phrase is that of W. G. de Burgh, *Towards a Religious Philosophy*, London: MacDonald & Evans, 1937, 30.

102 J. R. Illingworth, *Reason and Revelation: An Essay in Christian Apology*, London: Macmillan, 1902, 206.

103 As J. H. Gill has pointed out, we should not 'infer from this that no approach is more probable than the alternatives. Indeed, if this were true it would be impossible to say that the Christian frame of reference is "better" than others in any meaningful sense whatsoever. This, of course, would render witnessing quite impossible.' See 'The possibility of apologetics', *Scottish Journal of Theology*, XVI no. 2, June 1963, 145. I shall return to this point in my final chapter.

104 F. R. Tennant, *The Nature of Belief*, London: Centenary Press, 1943, 71.

105 Ibid., 78.

106 Ibid., 62.

107 For a more detailed discussion see Tennant's *Philosophical Theology*, Cambridge: CUP, 1928, I ch. 11.

108 J. Hick, *Faith and Knowledge*, London: Macmillan (1957), 2nd edn. 1966, 51.

109 F. R. Tennant, *Philosophical Theology*, I, 302.

110 Ibid., 53.

111 Cf. Arvin Vos, *Aquinas, Calvin, and Contemporary Protestant Thought: A*

Critique of Protestant Views on the Thought of Thomas Aquinas, Washington, DC: Christian University Press, 1985, ch. 2.

112 See, for example, Augustine, *De spiritu et littera* XXXVI.

113 Rufus M. Jones, *Studies in Mystical Religion*, London: Macmillan, 1909, 384.

114 See Aquinas, *Summa Theologica*, Q2 art. 2.

115 J. Calvin, *Institutes*, III. ii. 5, contrast 3.

116 P. T. Forsyth, *The Principle of Authority* (1912), London: Independent Press, 1952, 146.

117 H. F. Lovell Cocks, *By Faith Alone*, London: James Clarke, 1943, 32. I never feel closer to heresy than when I presume to query Forsyth and Cocks!

118 Ibid., 9.

119 J. Calvin, *Institutes*, III. ii. 7.

120 B. Mitchell, 'Faith and the limitations of open-mindedness', in J. J. Macintosh and H. A. Meynell, eds., *Faith, Scepticism and Personal Identity*, 42.

121 H. P. Owen, *Christian Knowledge of God*, 315.

122 J. Locke, *An Essay Concerning Human Understanding*, ed. Peter H. Nidditch, Oxford: Clarendon Press, 1975, I. i. 2.

123 See Alan P. F. Sell, *John Locke and the Eighteenth-Century Divines*, 64.

124 Ibid, 87–8, 218, 272. For an illuminating account of Locke's religious thought which appeared just after my book was published see G. A. J. Rogers, *Locke's Enlightenment: Aspects of the Origin, Nature, and Impact of his Philosophy*, Hildesheim: Georg Olms Verlag, 1998, ch. 11. For my review of this work see *The European Legacy*, IV no. 4, 1999, 102–5.

125 Ibid., 275–6.

126 Isaiah Berlin, *The Age of Enlightenment*, New York: Mentor Books, 1956, 18.

127 J. Locke, *A Fourth Letter for Toleration*, in *The Works of John Locke*, 12th edn., London, 1823, VI, 558.

128 See further Alan P. F. Sell, *John Locke and the Eighteenth-Century Divines*, chs. 2, 3.

129 J. Wesley, *Standard Sermons*, I, 125.

130 M. Luther, *Works* (Erlangen edn.), XXII, 15.

131 Ibid. (Weimar edn.) VII, 231.

132 J. Calvin, *Institutes*, III. ii. 7.

133 Ibid., III. ii. 33.

134 Belgic Confession, art. XXII. Cf. the Gallican Confession, arts. XX, XXI; the Second Helvetic Confession, XV, XVI, the Westminster Confession, XI, XIV etc. Frank Hugh Foster points out that in stating that by saving faith 'a Christian believeth to be true whatsoever is revealed in the Word' (XIV. 2), it confounds saving faith with historical

faith. See his *A Genetic History of the New England Theology* (1907), New York: Garland, 1987, 27.

135 See QQ59–64.

136 *The Complete Writings of Menno Simons*, ed. John C. Wenger, Scottdale: Herald Press, 1956, 115.

137 Matthew Henry, *The Life of the Rev. Philip Henry, A.M.* (1698), corrected and enlarged by J. B. Williams (1828), Edinburgh: Banner of Truth Trust, 1974, 141.

138 J. Owen, *Works*, V, 93. Among the clearest of all Puritan expositors is Thomas Watson. See *A Body of Divinity* (from *A Body of Practical Divinity*, 1692), London: Banner of Truth Trust, 1965, ch. 5.

139 *Une seul Seigneur, un seul baptême*, trans. J.-P. Gabus, Geneva: World Council of Churches, 1960, 53; quoted by Gerard Kelly, *Recognition: Advancing Ecumenical Thinking*, New York: Peter Lang, 1996, 94.

140 So, for example, W. G. De Burgh, *Towards a Religious Philosophy*, 18.

141 J. Flavel, *Works*, IV, 207.

142 J. Calvin, *Comm.* II Peter, 1: 10.

143 Second Helvetic Confession, 1566, XVI.

144 Quoted by Leonard Gross, *The Golden Years of the Hutterites: The Witness and Thought of the Communal Moravian Anabaptists during the Walpot Era, 1565–1578*, Scottdale: Herald Press, 1980, 76.

145 *The Life of Mr. Philip Henry*, 175. Cf. the characterization of faith by the latter-day Presbyterian, H. P. Owen in *The Christian Knowledge of God*, 153: 'Faith has three main aspects: apprehension, assent, and trust. To believe in God is to apprehend him as an objective reality, to assent to propositions concerning his existence and nature, and to trust him as the source of salvation.'

146 H. F. Lovell Cocks, *By Faith Alone*, 183.

147 John Marsh, 'The Congregational theological conference, 1937', *Congregational Quarterly*, XV no. 4, October 1937, 501. Marsh here reports on a paper given by Hubert Cunliffe-Jones.

148 Cf. Stephen Sykes, 'Faith', in Geoffrey Wainwright, ed., *Keeping the Faith*, 20–2.

149 Cf. Maurice Wiles, 'Belief, openness and religious commitment', *Theology*, CI, May–June 1998, 171.

150 A. D. Woozley, *Theory of Knowledge: An Introduction*, London: Hutchinson's University Library, 1949, 193.

151 Clement of Alexandria, *Stromateis* V. i.

152 Ibid., I. vi.

153 Alfred Lord Tennyson, 'In Memoriam', prologue.

154 J. Baillie, *The Sense of the Presence of God*, London: OUP, 1962, 5. He invokes the support of Bultmann, *Theology of the New Testament*, London: SCM Press, 1955, II, 128.

[155] Karl Heim, *Glaubensgewissheit*, II, 3, quoted by Sydney Cave, *The Doctrines of the Christian Faith*, 37.

[156] J. H. Thomas, *Subjectivity and Paradox*, 139. Cf. Maurice Blondel, *The Letter on Apologetics*, trans. Alexander Dru and Illtyd Trethowan, London: Harvill Press, 1964, 134: 'Since, by hypothesis, faith is a gratuitous gift, no apologetic, however demonstrative we may suppose it to be, can communicate it or produce it.' According to Kierkegaard, says J. H. Thomas, 'Since religious faith is a matter of subjectivity belief cannot be identified simply with knowledge; and if what we know cannot be proved then it is not knowledge at all' (p. 90).

[157] R. G. Collingwood, *An Autobiography* (1939), Harmondsworth: Penguin Books, 1944, 60. Among other contemporary philosophers who queried the stranglehold of scientific method upon philosophy was R. F. A. Hoernlé. See the chapter, 'The idol of scientific method', in his *Studies in Contemporary Metaphysics*, London: Kegan Paul Trench Trubner, 1920, 24–49; cf. Alan P. F. Sell, *The Philosophy of Religion 1875–1980* (1988), Bristol: Thoemmes Press, 1986, 80–1.

[158] Stephen N. Williams, *Faith and Certainty*, Leicester: Religious and Theological Studies Fellowship, 1994, 36.

[159] G. F. Nuttall, 'The Congregational theological conference, 1937', *Congregational Quarterly*, XV no. 4, October 1937, 503.

[160] John Hick's discussion in *Faith and Knowledge*, ch. 9, to which I am indebted in this paragraph, is relevant here. Cf. also W. H. V. Reade, *The Christian Challenge to Philosophy*, London: SPCK, 1951, 5: 'To maintain that any one kind of knowledge is the very sum of wisdom, is to argue that all others are not, and this means that the expert will have to pronounce many judgements beyond the scope of his proper authority.'

[161] For example, by R. C. Moberly, *Reason and Religion: Some Aspects of their Mutual Interdependence*, London: Longmans, Green, 1896, 85.

[162] Irenaeus, *Adversus Haereses* IV. xx. 1., III. xxiv. 1.

[163] It would take us too far afield to argue the point here, but I endorse Hilary Armstrong's view that those Christians who followed the apophatic way did not intend to assert our absolute ignorance of God, and that their negative language was balanced by positive ways of speaking of God. See his 'Platonism', in I. T. Ramsey, ed., *The Prospect for Metaphysics: Essays of Metaphysical Exploration*, London: Allen & Unwin, 1961, 104.

[164] P. Tillich, *The New Being*, 77. Cf. Thomas Torrance's exposition of John Knox's thought, in his *Scottish Theology from John Knox to John McLeod Campbell*, Edinburgh: T. & T. Clark, 1996, 6: 'This God whom we know cannot be fitted into *our* knowledge. God cannot be commanded by our reasons – cannot be comprehended by our minds.'

165 W. B. Selbie, *The Validity of Christian Belief*, London: Nicholson & Watson, 1939, 39.

166 J. Smith, 'A Prefatory Discourse concerning the True Way or Method of attaining Divine Knowledge', in his *Select Discourses*, Cambridge: CUP, 1859, 3.

167 A. E. Garvie, 'The nature of religious knowledge and the certainty of Christian faith', in *Mansfield College Essays*, London: Hodder & Stoughton, 1909, 174. Garvie cites a number of biblical verses in support, among them John 7: 17, 'If any man willeth to do His will, he shall know of the teaching whether it be of God, or whether I speak from myself.'

168 Cf. W. G. De Burgh, *Towards a Religious Philosophy*, 15–16; H. F. Lovell Cocks, *By Faith Alone*, 30; Donald M. Baillie, *Faith in God and its Christian Consummation* (1927), London: Faber & Faber, 1964, 113, 117. For interestingly different slants on Baillie's thesis see John McIntyre's Foreword to the 1964 edn., and Ray S. Anderson, 'Faith, doubt and moral commitment: an analysis of D. M. Baillie's *Faith in God*', in David A. S. Fergusson, ed., *Christ, Church and Society: Essays on John Baillie and Donald Baillie*, Edinburgh: T. & T. Clark, 1993, esp. 44.

169 J. Calvin, *Institutes*, III. ii. 2, 6, 7. For a succinct account see further Cornelis van der Kooi, 'Within proper limits: basic features of John Calvin's theological epistemology', *Calvin Theological Journal*, XXIX no. 2, November 1994, 364–87. For the intellectual hinterland see William J. Bouwsma, 'Calvin and the Renaissance crisis of knowing', *Calvin Theological Journal*, XVII no. 2, November 1982, 190–211.

170 *Heidelberg Catechism*, 1563.

171 Henry Harbaugh, quoted by George W. Richards, *The Theology of Rev. Prof. Henry Harbaugh, D.D.*, Philadelphia, PA: Publication, and Sunday School Board of the Reformed Church in the United States, 1918, 62. See further Merle Upton Fox, 'An Annotated Bibliography of the Works of Rev. Henry Harbaugh, D.D.', a Masters thesis, Lutheran Theological Seminary, Gettysburg, PA., 1990, published by the author, 1997. Harbaugh (1817–67) is the author of the Mercersburg Academy hymn, 'Jesus, I live to Thee'. See further the chapter, 'Christ the object of faith', in H. R. Mackintosh, *The Doctrine of the Person of Jesus Christ* (1912), Edinburgh: T. & T. Clark, 1956, 345–62.

172 W. R. Matthews, 'The problem of religious knowledge', *Modern Churchman*, XLIV no. 4, December 1954, 279.

173 This question was posed and concisely addressed by Ruth Saw in *Philosophy*, XXXVI, January 1961, 18–29.

174 Within hours of writing this sentence I noticed the journal,

Revolutions, in my dentist's waiting room. Thinking it distinctly odd that she would have anything to do with a subversive political movement, I was reassured to discover that it is the organ of the British Wood Turners' Association.

175 H. H. Farmer wrote, 'over large areas of his life man can create beauty if he intends it, and if he does not intend it, it just does not happen, as, for example, in a modern industrial monstrosity like Wigan or Stoke'. See his *Towards Belief in God*, London: SCM Press, 1942, part II, 189. While, as we now know only too well, human beings can wreak havoc upon the environment to the extent of devastating parts of it with dire results, Farmer's uncharacteristic 'sounding off' concerning Wigan and Stoke prompts the knee-jerk reaction that a town like Wigan, which has been producing Uncle Joe's Mint Balls (no additives) for more than a century has something to be said for it, as does a city like Stoke which inspired the novels of Arnold Bennett. More seriously, Farmer's comment requires to be qualified by the realization that people did not set out to create any ugliness there may have been in those towns; on the contrary, the ugliness (much of which has subsequently been attended to) was a (no doubt unfortunate) by-product of industry, the main objectives of which were to hew coal for the benefit of human beings (Wigan) and to produce ceramics, some of them exquisite in their beauty, and others of great utility to all who do not care for earth closets (Stoke). Nor can it be denied that there is a certain beauty overall, and in particular in terms of mechanical movement or intricate brickwork, in at least selected examples of machines, pitheads, mills and factories, some of which are now prized as part of our industrial heritage.

176 I. Kant, *Critique of Judgment*, trans. and introd. Werner S. Pluhar, Indianapolis: Hackett, 1987, 32.

177 I note that one of these last carries a column, 'Where are they now?', in which enthusiasts seek the whereabouts of their long-since-sold-on bikes in the way that some seek long-lost members of their families. There is a devotion here which some might regard as idolatrous; but I for one, though never presuming to belong to the oily rag and leathers brigade, can understand it. (I wonder where my old Matchless 350 is?)

178 See Daniel Walker Howe, *The Unitarian Conscience: Harvard Moral Philosophy, 1805–1861* (1970), Middletown, CT: Wesleyan University Press, 1988, 185. Cf. the aristocratic assertion of A. J. Balfour, 'We cannot . . . assume that there is a great body of aesthetic experience which all normal persons possess in common . . . Many normal persons have no such feelings, or none worth talking about.' See his *Theism and Humanism*, London: Hodder & Stoughton, 1915, 73.

179 See further John Hospers, 'The Croce–Collingwood theory of art', *Philosophy*, XXXI, October 1956, 308.

180 John Caird, *University Addresses*, Glasgow: MacLehose, 1899, 292.

181 I do not overlook the growing literature in support of the view that aesthetic judgments are not necessary to art appreciation. See further Richard H. Bell, 'The aesthetic factor in art and religion', *Religious Studies*, XXII no. 2, June 1986, 181–92. The objective of an artist might, on this view, be to make a statement of some kind – perhaps of a protesting kind. Such artists would not meet, and would not wish to meet, John Caird's definition of 'the best and highest art' which lies close to religion: 'They disclose to us – the one by imaginative representation, the other by spiritual insight and aspiration – the ideal of a fairer, nobler, more complete and harmonious life than the common eye can discern in the world of our ordinary experience.' See his *University Sermons*, Glasgow: Maclehose, 1898, 327, cf. 336. H. D. Lewis was saying something similar as late as 1951: 'The artist is . . . a seer, and his essential function, in his relation to others, is to make them see something to which they are normally blind.' See *Morals and Revelation*, London: Allen and Unwin, 1951, 209. I am likewise unsure whether artists of the more iconoclastic sort would agree that 'the participative experience of art . . . always includes the presence and articulation of Being'. So F. David Martin, 'The aesthetic in religious experience', *Religious Studies*, IV no. 1, October 1968, 23. I confess I am not altogether sure what Martin means. Again, W. G. De Burgh, *Knowledge of the Individual*, London: OUP, 1939, 40, quotes Whitehead as saying that art is 'a message from the unseen', which 'unlooses depths of feeling from behind the frontier where precision of conscousness fails'. Not all critics have been able to see Tracey Emin's unmade bed in this light – and, of course, Whitehead himself was spared the vision.

182 *The Journal of the Rev. John Wesley, A.M.*, ed. Nehemiah Curnock, London: Charles Kelly, [1909], VI, 337, entry for 9 October 1781.

183 E. F. Carritt, *What Is Beauty? A First Introduction to the Subject and to Modern Theories*, Oxford: Clarendon Press, 1932, 22.

184 *The Constitution on the Sacred Liturgy*, 1963, in Austin Flannery, ed., *Vatican II: The Consiliar and Post-Conciliar Documents*, Collegeville, MN: Liturgical Press, 1975, 34.

185 See, for example, J. Calvin, *Institute*, I. xi. 4.

186 Ibid., I. xi. 12. Abraham Kuyper's hindsight explanation (or selective memory) is as follows: 'Only under the auspices of its religious principle could Calvinism have created a general art-style, and just because it had reached a so much higher stage of religious development, its very principle forbade it the symbolical expression of its religion in

visible and sensual forms.' See his *Lectures on Calvinism*, Grand Rapids, MI: Associated Publishers and Authors, n.d., 92.

187 L. Ryken, *Worldly Saints: The Puritans as they Really were*, Grand Rapids, MI: Zondervan, 1986, 4. See further Horton Davies, 'Art and music in Puritan worship', appendix B of his *The Worship of the English Puritans*, London: Dacre Press, 1948.

188 David Brown, *The Life of Rabbi Duncan*, 66. Cf. Thomas Chalmers, *A Series of Discourses on the Christian Revelation, Viewed in Connection with the Modern Astronomy*, Glasgow: John Smith, 1817, 217–19.

189 For a defence of this view in characteristically homiletic style see H. D. Lewis, *Morals and Revelation*, ch. 9.

190 G. E. Moore, quoted from the Moore Papers at Cambridge University Library by Tom Regan, *Bloomsbury's Prophet: G. E. Moore and the Development of his Moral Philosophy*, Philadelphia: Temple University Press, 1986, 168.

191 Ibid., 163–4, 170. Hans Urs von Balthasar is prominent among theologians who have set out to produce a theological aesthetics. That is, one which is not dependent upon the concepts of 'natural' aesthetics, but one which takes God's revelation in the incarnate Christ as its starting point. This appears to be a quasi-Barthian stance. However, there is also what one might call a 'classical natural theology undertow' in his work which enables him to suggest that inferences may be drawn from the world's beauty to God, its source. See his *The Glory of the Lord: A Theological Aesthetics*, ed. Joseph Fessio and John Riches, Edinburgh: T. & T. Clark, 1982, I, 38. See further Noel Dermot O'Donoghue, 'A theology of beauty', *Irish Theological Quarterly*, L nos. 2–4, 1983–4, 250–6; Roland Chia, 'Theological aesthetics or aesthetic theology? Some reflections on the theology of Hans Urs von Balthasar', *Scottish Journal of Theology*, XLIX no. 1, 1996, 75–95.

192 John Laird, *The Idea of Value*, Cambridge: CUP, 1929, 151.

193 F. David Martin, 'The aesthetic in religious experience', *Religious Studies*, IV no. 1, October 1968, 19.

194 E. F. Carritt, *What is Beauty?*, 84.

195 See further Diané Collinson, 'Aesthetic meaning', in Oswald Hanfling, ed., *Philosophical Aesthetics: An Introduction*, Oxford: Blackwell, 1992, 113.

196 W. Temple, *Christus Veritas: An Essay*, London: Macmillan, 1930, 28.

197 W. G. De Burgh, *Knowledge of the Individual*, 23.

198 See R. Wollheim, *Art and its Objects*, Harmondsworth: Penguin Books, 1970, 119. For further examples of the differences of opinion on this matter see David Best, 'The aesthetic and the artistic', *Philosophy*, LVII, July 1982, 358–9.

199 T. Reid, *Essays on the Intellectual Powers of Man*, in *The Works of Thomas*

Reid, D.D., ed. W. Hamilton, Edinburgh: MacLachlan and Stewart, 1863, I, 498b.

200 In this respect Carritt is in a long line coming down from Kant.

201 See further W. D. Glasgow, 'Knowledge of God', *Philosophy*, XXXII, July 1957, 229–40; Constance I. Smith's comment on the foregoing, *Philosophy*, XXXIII, January 1958, 56; and Glasgow's reply, ibid., 57. See also Hugh Bredin, 'The theory of beauty', in J. McEvoy, *Philosophy and Totality*, Belfast: The Queen's University, 1977, 33–48, esp. 35–40.

202 Augustine, *Ep.* 120. 20. See further J. Burnaby, *Amor Dei*, 157–8.

203 Boethius, *The Consolation of Philosophy*, trans. Richard Green, Indianapolis: Bobbs-Merrill, 1962, 60.

204 J. Calvin, *Institute*, III. x. 2.

205 Ibid., I. v. 1.

206 Idem, *Corpus Reformatorum*, ed. C. G. Bretschneider and H. E. Bindseil, Halle-Salle, 1834–60, XXXIV, 441.

207 J. S. Dwight, 'The religion of beauty', 1840, in *Selected Writings of the American Transcendentalists*, Toronto: New American Library of Canada, 1966, 304.

208 Robert Mackintosh, *Values: A Bird's Eye Survey*, London: Independent Press, n.d., 93.

209 W. Temple, *Nature, Man and God*, London: Macmillan, 1934, 253, his italics. These Gifford Lectures are dedicated to Edward Caird.

210 See further Jeremy Begbie, 'The Gospel, the arts and our culture', in Hugh Montefiore, ed., *The Gospel and Contemporary Culture*, London: Mowbray, 1992, 70.

211 Agnes Bulmer, *Memoirs of Mrs. Elizabeth Mortimer*, London: Mason, 1859, 104; my italics. For relevant reflections of the Roman Catholic philosopher Bernard Lonergan, see *Topics in Education*, ch. 9, in his *Works*, Toronto: University of Toronto Press, X, 1993, 222. See further Hilary Anne-Marie Mooney, 'Bernard Lonergan and the role of the aesthetic in theology', *Irish Theological Quarterly*, LXIII no. 4, 1988, 362–78.

212 I have attempted this task for ministers and church members in Alan P. F. Sell, *God Our Father* (1980), Shippensburg, PA: Ragged Edge Press, 2000, chs. 5–7.

213 T. Chalmers, *A Series of Discourses*, 234.

214 Matthew 5: 8.

215 H. H. Farmer, *Towards Belief in God*, II, 196.

216 I. Kant, *Fundamental Principles of the Metaphysic of Ethics*, trans. T. K. Abbott, London: Longmans, Green, 10th edn., 1926, 5.

217 Of the three postulates, freedom is 'the only concept of the supersensible which (by means of the causality that we think in it) proves in

nature that it has objective reality, by the effects it can produce in it'. So Kant, *Critique of Judgment*, 368, cf. 362.

218 Idem, *Critique of Judgment*, 366–8. To Robert Mackintosh 'such an argument is more hedonist than moral'. See his *Essays Towards a New Theology*, 1889, 369.

219 Ibid., 340.

220 A. S. Pringle-Pattison, *The Idea of God in the Light of Recent Philosophy*, New York: OUP, 2nd rev. edn. 1920, 35; cf. 34, where the oddity is noted that, while human beings are not to be treated as ends in themselves, God here seems to have instrumental value only – as a *deus ex machina*. Donald M. MacKinnon has reminded us that 'To understand Kant's ethics, and especially his view of the relations of ethics to religion, it is most important to realize that he develops his often curiously elusive ethical ideas in part at least as a protest against the morally destructive effects wrought on human life by competing religious authoritarianisms.' See his *Themes in Theology: The Three-Fold Cord*, Edinburgh: T. & T. Clark, 1987, 25.

221 I. Kant, *Critique of Pure Reason* (1781), 'Transcendental Dialectic', II. iii. sect. 6. Hume's remark concerning the teleological argument comes to mind: 'A purpose, an intention, a design strikes everywhere the most careless, the most stupid thinker'. See his *Dialogues Concerning Natural Religion*, pt. XII (1779), Harmondsworth: Penguin, 1990, 125.

222 Idem, *Fundamental Principles*, 58.

223 S. Körner, *Kant*, Harmondsworth: Penguin Books, 1955, 169.

224 So W. G. De Burgh, *From Morality to Religion*, London: MacDonald & Evans, 1938, 156.

225 H. P. Owen, *W. R. Matthews: Philosopher and Theologian*, London: Athlone Press, 1976, 41. Though Kant did sometimes speak of the moral law as divinely commanded – on which point see C. C. J. Webb, *Divine Personality and Human Life*, London: Allen & Unwin, 1920, 119.

226 C. C. J. Webb, *A Century of Anglican Theology*, Oxford: Blackwell, 1923, 101. Cf. idem, *Divine Personality*, 132.

227 T. McPherson, *The Philosophy of Religion*, London: D. Van Nostrand, 1965, 94.

228 D. D. Williams, *Interpreting Theology 1918–1952*, London: SCM Press, 1953, 74.

229 Ibid.

230 R. H. Preston, 'The study of Christian ethics', *Theology*, LXVII, 1964, 146.

231 J. P. Scull, 'Roman Catholic moral theology (contemporary)', in J. Macquarrie, ed., *The Dictionary of Christian Ethics*, London: SCM Press, 1967, 302.

232 P. Ramsey, *Nine Modern Moralists*, Englewood Cliffs, NJ: Prentice Hall, 1962, 112.

233 For some of my earlier thoughts on this question, with some of which I still agree, see Alan P. F. Sell, 'Christians, humanists and common ground', *Journal of Moral Education*, I, 1972, 177–85.

234 This point is developed by John Macquarrie, *Three Issues in Ethics*, London: SCM Press, 1970.

235 K. Barth, *Church Dogmatics*, II. 2, 524.

236 N. H. G. Robinson, *The Groundwork of Christian Ethics*, London: Collins, 1971, 132. I think of Robinson as one of the more unjustly neglected theologians, whose pertinent observations in many writings on Christian ethical *theory* would greatly benefit those who are tempted to dive headlong into the *issues*. For an alternative reading of Barth on ethics see John B. Webster, *Barth's Ethics of Revelation*, Cambridge: CUP, 1995; idem, *Barth's Moral Theology: Human Action in Barth's Thought*, Grand Rapids, MI: Eerdmans, 1998.

237 See further idem, 130ff.

238 Romans 2: 14–15.

239 John Caird, *The Fundamental Ideas of Christianity*, Glasgow: MacLehose, 1899, II, 75.

240 N. H. G. Robinson, *The Groundwork of Christian Ethics*, 16.

241 H. R. Mackintosh, *The Christian Experience of Forgiveness* (1927), London: Collins Fontana, 1961, 223.

242 See, for example, K. Rahner, *Theological Investigations*, London: Darton, Longman & Todd, 1969, ch. 6.

243 See, for example, J. Baillie, *The Sense of the Presence of God*, London: OUP, 1962, 76–87.

244 H. D. Lewis, *Philosophy of Religion*, London: English Universities Press, 1965, 119–20. For his part, H. P. Owen declares that 'Baillie gives his case away in his *Our Knowledge of God* (Oxford 1939, p. 64). There he supports his view by quoting the words of Jacob in Genesis 28: 16–17: "Surely the Lord is in this place, and I knew it not; this is none other but the house of God, and this is the gate of heaven". Yet the whole point of these verses is that while God was present Jacob did *not* know him.' See *The Moral Argument for Christian Theism*, London: Allen & Unwin, 1965, 36–7.

245 Alan P. F. Sell, *Aspects of Christian Integrity* (1990), Eugene, OR: Wipf & Stock, 1998, 120.

246 See further H. P. Owen, *The Moral Argument for Christian Theism*, 36. This work is among the most lucid treatments of its subject.

247 The inverted commas remind us that a number of those thus designated protested that they had derived their ideas from the Bible, and were quite unacquainted with the views of Arius himself.

248 J. Taylor, *The Scripture-Doctrine of Original Sin*, 1740, 151.

249 M. Towgood, *The Grounds of Faith in Jesus Christ*, 1784, 31. For Taylor and Towgood (and Samuel Bourn) see further Alan P. F. Sell, *Dissenting Thought and the Life of the Churches*, ch. 7. So slow were some to learn this lesson (the intervening contributions of Erskine of Linlathen, McLeod Campbell and others notwithstanding) that one hundred years later the erstwhile Christian, W. K. Clifford, found it necessary to reiterate the point: 'If God holds all mankind guilty for the sin of Adam, if he has visited upon the innocent the punishment of the guilty, . . . then it is wrong to worship him.' See his *Lectures and Essays*, London: Macmillan, 2nd edn., 1886, 373.

250 E. A. Park, *The Theology of the Intellect and of the Feelings: A discourse delivered before the convention of the Congregational ministers of Massachusetts, in Brattle Street Meeting House, Boston, May 30, 1850*, Andover: W. F. Draper. Many other illustrations of the moral critique of theology might be offered. For some of these which bear particularly on theological method see Alan P. F. Sell, 'Approaches to moral philosophy among the eighteenth-century Dissenters of England and Wales', *Jahrbuch fürRecht und Ethik*, VII, 2000, 1–50, especially 35–42.

251 See J. McCosh, *The Intuitions of the Mind, Inductively Investigated*, London: Macmillan, 2nd revised edn., 1865.

252 See further H. D. Lewis, *Our Experience of God*, London: Allen & Unwin, 1959, 267–8.

253 J. Hick, *Philosophy of Religion*, Englewood Cliffs, NJ: Prentice Hall, 1963, 27–8.

254 A. E. Taylor, 'The freedom of man', in J. H. Muirhead, ed., *Contemporary British Philosophy*, 2nd ser., London: Allen and Unwin (1925), 2nd impression, 1953, 303. The reference is to John 3: 34 (AV). See further Alan P. F. Sell, *Philosophical Idealism and Christian Belief*, 102.

255 J. Butler, *Dissertation II: Of the Nature of Virtue*, in his *The Analogy of Religion*, London: Ward Lock, n.d. 209–10. Among discussions of Butler on conscience see Austin Duncan-Jones, *Butler's Moral Philosophy*, Harmondsworth: Penguin Books, 1952, ch. 3; Terence Penelhum, *Butler*, London: Routledge & Kegan Paul, 1985, ch. 3; Stephen Darwall, 'Conscience as self-authorizing in Butler's ethics', in Christopher Cunliffe, ed., *Joseph Butler's Moral and Religious Thought: Tercentenary Essays*, Oxford: Clarendon Press, 1992, ch. 11.

256 Near the beginning of my publishing life there appeared '"Conscience" in recent discussion', *Theology*, LXVI, December 1963, 498–504. I am somewhat surprised to find that as a snapshot of the situation at that time it is fairly acceptable, though I have since learned how risky it is to use words like 'recent' in titles.

257 H. More, *An Explanation of the Grand Mystery of Godliness*, London: J. Flesher, 1660, X, 517.

258 J. Locke, *An Essay Concerning Human Understanding*, I. iii. 8. For More and Locke on conscience see further G. A. J. Rogers, *Locke's Enlightenment*, ch. 8.

259 J. H. Newman, *An Essay on the Development of Christian Doctrine*, London: Toovey, 1845, 348.

260 Idem, *An Essay in Aid of a Grammar of Assent*, ed. I. T. Ker, Oxford: Clarendon Press, 1985, 81. For a comparison of Newman with Martineau – and also with C. H. Spurgeon – on the locus of authority in religion see Alan P. F. Sell, *Commemorations*, ch. 1.

261 See J. Martineau, *The Seat of Authority in Religion*, London: Longmans, 1890.

262 J. Martineau, *A Study of Religion*, Oxford: Clarendon Press, 2nd rev. edn., 1900, 27. Cf. idem, *Types of Ethical Theory*, Oxford: Clarendon Press, 1891, II, 104.

263 Idem, *The Seat of Authority in Religion*, 651.

264 Idem, 'The watch-night lamps', a sermon quoted by James Drummond and C. B. Upton, *The Life and Letters of James Martineau*, London: James Nisbet, 1902, I, 200. It would seem that N. H. G. Robinson goes too far in placing Martineau in the company of those, including Mill and Sidgwick, who discussed morality 'in total independence of religion'. See his *The Groundwork of Christian Ethics*, 22.

265 See Alan P. F. Sell, *Commemorations*, ch. 1; and for a comparison of Martineau's response to the Enlightenment with that of A. Campbell Fraser see ibid., ch. 10.

266 P. T. Forsyth, 'Dr. Martineau', *London Quarterly Review*, XCIII, NS III, 1900, 228.

267 See H. Sidgwick, *Lectures on the Ethics of T. H. Green, Mr. Herbert Spencer, and J. Martineau*, London: Macmillan, 1902.

268 Romans 7: 15. Paul is no Kantian! To him 'ought' does not imply 'can' – he is not in the realm of logical inference, but of moral plight: 'I ought, but, by reason of my sinful will, I cannot.'

269 R. Mackintosh, *Essays Towards a New Theology*, 372.

270 J. Tulloch, *Theism: The Witness of Reason and Nature to an All-Wise and Beneficent Creator*, Edinburgh: Blackwood, 1855, 270.

271 H. D. Lewis, 'The voice of conscience and the voice of God', in I. T. Ramsey, ed., *Christian Ethics and Contemporary Philosophy*, London: SCM Press, 1966, 179. Because of this it is strange that Lewis should elsewhere write 'moral excellence, in the strict sense, is attained when we do right on the occasions when our formed characters, subject as they may be to the refining influence of grace, are not of the strength to ensure that we do right or find our firmest inclinations in accord

with our consciences. Grace is not at work here, for this is the point *par excellence* where God leaves it to us to co-operate with Him and respond in a way that is wholly our own.' See *Our Experience of God*, 271. But if our characters are subject to 'the refining influence of grace', and if grace is enabling grace, as I believe it to be, then we cannot be 'subject to it' and left on our own. On the contrary, there is 'grace to give us timely help' (Hebrews 4: 16). Of any response to God's grace it must be said that it is our own. But, retrospectively, the Christian's attitude will always be, 'I – yet not I, but Christ' (cf. Galatians 2: 20). With Lewis's remark may be contrasted that of Donald MacKinnon: 'What I want to suggest is that we have to see the work of God in Christ as that which secures against the ever-present menace of their dissolution, our frail, but genuine, human perceptions and affirmations (in action) of the morally excellent.' See William Purcell, ed., *The Resurrection: A Dialogue Arising from Broadcasts by G. W. H. Lampe and D. M. MacKinnon*, London: Mowbray, 1966, 108–9.

272 P. T. Forsyth, 'A rallying ground for the Free Churches: the reality of grace', *Hibbert Journal*, IV no. 4, July 1906, 834–5. In this connection the observation of John 'Rabbi' Duncan is interesting: 'I do not wonder that there are infidels, because the two greatest facts in our religion seem to be a denial of all moral government whatever. 1st, That the guilty, and the fearfully guilty, should be freely pardoned; and 2d, That the only perfect innocent in the universe should be the greatest sufferer in the universe.' See William Knight, *Colloquia Peripatetica. Deep-Sea Soundings. Being Notes of Conversations with the Late John Duncan, LL.D.*, Edinburgh: Oliphant, Anderson & Ferrier, 6th edn., 1907, 16.

273 Idem, 'Christ and the Christian principle', in *London Theological Studies*, by members of the Faculty of Theology in the University of London, London: University of London Press, 1911, 153.

274 Idem, 'Revelation, old and new' (1911), reprinted in *Revelation Old and New*, ed. John Huxtable, London: Independent Press, 1962, 22. It was because he missed the idea of regeneration in connection with Christian ethics that Forsyth faulted Hastings Rashdall's book, *Christ and the Conscience*, notwithstanding that 'No book on Christian ethic so good has appeared among us'. See his *This Life and the Next* (1918), London: Independent Press, 1953, 74.

275 N. H. G. Robinson, *The Groundwork of Christian Ethics*, 305. In expressing myself as I have done in the present paragraph my indebtedness to Robinson is clear. Cf. also Alan P. F. Sell, '*Agape*, atonement and Christian ethics', *Downside Review*, XCI, April 1973, 83–100, with much of which I am still in sympathy; idem, *Aspects of Christian Integrity*, 75.

[276] C. C. J. Webb, *The Contribution of Christianity to Ethics*, Calcutta: University of Calcutta Press, 1932, 4.

[277] P. T. Forsyth, 'A holy Church the moral guide of society' (1905), reprinted in *The Church, The Gospel and Society*, London: Independent Press, 1962, 31.

[278] It is by no means implied that Christians and non-Christians may not frequently decide that they ought to do X, where X is, for example, making a monetary contribution to a good cause. Their motives will to some extent overlap: they both wish to help the needy, they both feel under a moral obligation; but the full accounts of why they do what they do will differ. For example, the Christian may regard his or her act theologically in terms of the stewardship of gifts given by God. The measure of common ground is, however, of vital importance in circumstances in which people of goodwill need to stand together on socio-ethical issues. See further Alan P. F. Sell, *Aspects of Christian Integrity* (1990), Eugene, OR: Wipf & Stock, 1998, 72–5.

[279] T. W. Manson, *Ethics and the Gospel*, London: SCM Press, 1960, 68.

[280] R. Baxter, *A Christian Directory*, 1673, I. iii, quoted by Sydney Cave, *The Christian Way*, London: Independent Press, 1949, 157. Against this, Hastings Rashdall's account of the Christian ethical motivation in face of the problem of evil seems anaemic indeed: 'Enough for us to know two things: (1) that enough good will be realised to justify its being willed by a righteous and all-wise Mind, (2) that our co-operation is required in realising it. And this is all that is necessary to justify religious faith and to inspire moral effort.' See his *Ideas and Ideals*, Oxford: Blackwell, 1928, 239. For his part, Richard Baxter is clearly in the line of Calvin on this matter, for to Calvin, gratitude, obedience and faithful living were integrally related. See, for example, his *Commentary* on Philippians 4: 6.

[281] *The Second Helvetic Confession*, 1566, XVI.

[282] R. Mackintosh, *Essays Towards a New Theology*, 389.

[283] The point was elaborated by Donald M. Baillie, *Faith in God and its Christian Consummation* (1927), London: Faber & Faber, 1964, ch. 3, especially 113–17. Cf. John Baillie, *The Sense of the Presence of God*, London: OUP, 1962, 65.

[284] J. Calvin, *Sermons on Ephesians*, Edinburgh: Banner of Truth Trust, 1973, 291.

[285] J. Wesley, *Works*, ed. W. Reginald Ward and Richard P. Heitzenrater, Nashville: Abingdon, XVIII, 1984, 250.

[286] It is thus significant that when Calvin argues that our experience of misery spurs us to look to God for salvation, the beliefs that God is and that humanity is ruined by the Fall are presupposed, for the experience of misery is interpreted in the light of them. See *Institutes*, I. i.

[287] Cf. H. D. Lewis, *Our Experience of God*, 125: '[W]hile the distinctiveness of the "live" religious experience, as I have called it, must not be overlooked or underestimated, we must not regard it as the intrusion of a wholly unusual factor into the normal occasions of life, or something peculiar which happens to us oddly now and again, but, normally at least, as the renewal of a formative influence by which the remainder is deeply affected and which, in consequence, the latter is more and more predisposed to receive.' It is reported that the Church of England theologian O. C. Quick sometimes said that he had never had a religious experience. '[A]nd', remarked the Archbishop of Canterbury, 'in the misleading sense of that phrase popularized by William James this is probably true. But of course his whole experience was religious, because it was his apprehension of the world as God has made it and therein also of the God who made it. For him, to think at all was to theologize, for God was in all his thought.' See 'Memoir' prefixed to O. C. Quick, *The Gospel of the New World: A Study in the Christian Doctrine of Atonement*, London: Nisbet, 1944, xiii. The last six words quoted constitute a fitting epitaph to Quick, and one to be coveted.

[288] See John Meyendorff, 'Byzantium as center of theological thought in the Christian East', in Patrick Henry, ed., *Schools of Thought in the Christian Tradition*, Philadelphia: Fortress Press, 1984, 68.

[289] Leonard Hodgson, 'Experience, religious experience, and Christian experience', in his *The Place of Reason in Christian Apologetic*, Oxford: Blackwell, 1925, 71.

[290] Quoted by W. R. Inge, *Mysticism and Religion* (1947), London: Rider, 1969, 28.

[291] C. C. J. Webb, *Religious Experience*, London: OUP, [1945], 39.

[292] P. T. Forsyth, *The Principle of Authority* (1913), London: Independent Press, 1952, 333–4. Cf. Bernard Ramm, *Protestant Christian Evidences* (1953), Chicago: Moody Press, 1972, 211: 'We do not have certain imaginative, emotional, and intellectual elements we fuse into something we call "religious experience." God, Christ, salvation, forgiveness appear to the Christian consciousness as objective and real. They no more appear to be the creation of our minds than do the bird or automobile of sensory perception.'

[293] Matthew 5: 8.

[294] *The Journal of George Fox*, revised edn. by John L. Nickalls, London: Religious Society of Friends, 1975, 312. See further for example, Howard H. Brinton, *Friends for 300 Years* (1952), Wallingford, PA: Pendle Hill Publications, 1965, ch. 2; Douglas Gwyn, *Apocalypse of the Word: The Life and Message of George Fox*, Richmond, IN: Friends United Press, 1986, ch. 3.

[295] G. Wardlaw, *Experimental Evidence a Ground for Assurance that Christianity is Divine*, Glasgow: Maclehose, 1849, 36.

[296] H. P. Owen, *The Christian Knowledge of God*, London: Athlone Press, 1969, 179.

[297] See Alan P. F. Sell, *John Locke and the Eighteenth-Century Divines*, ch. 2.

[298] The reference is to C. B. Upton, *Lectures on the Bases of Religious Belief*, London: Williams & Norgate, 1894, 50.

[299] J. Scott Lidgett, 'Spiritual discernment, its place in Christian evidences', in *Studies in Christian Evidences*, 2nd ser., London: Charles H. Kelly, n.d. but late nineteenth century, 293.

[300] Cf. Calvin: 'Christ has no commerce with us, nor we with him, apart from Scripture.' *Institutes*, III. ii. 6; L. Hodgson, *The Place of Reason in Christian Apologetic*, 82: 'Christian experience, then, is controlled by being related to the historic Christ of the Gospels.'

[301] G. F. Nuttall, 'The Congregational theological conference, 1937', *Congregational Quarterly*, XV no. 4, October 1937, 505.

[302] Cf. N. S. F. Ferré, *Searchlights on Contemporary Theology*, New York: Harper, 1961, 195: 'Only as the power of forgiveness through God's grace and our faith becomes the power of Christ for new lives and for a leavened world shall we grasp in grateful confirmation the nature and the power of Christian experience.'

[303] L. W. Grensted, *The Atonement in History and Life* (1929), London: SPCK, 1936, 285.

[304] Cf. P. T. Forsyth, *Positive Preaching and the Modern Mind* (1907), London: Independent Press, 1964, 86.

[305] P. T. Forsyth, *Revelation Old and New: Sermons and Addresses*, ed. John Huxtable, London: Independent Press, 1962, 76. Not surprisingly Forsyth opposed those within his own ecclesiastical tradition who divorced experience from creed in the manner exemplified by J. S. Griffiths: 'The position of our Congregational churches, that experience of Christ, not creed, is the basis of fellowship, commends itself to commonsense as well as to conscience.' See 'Congregationalism and creeds', *Congregational Quarterly*, XVII no. 2, April 1939, 190. We may not be saved by credal subscription, but nor are we saved by subjective feelings. Cf. the remark of Richard E. Wentz concerning a prominent strand of American theology: 'From Nathaniel Taylor to Horace Bushnell, the theological paths showed evidence of the footfalls of human confidence in the near self-sufficiency of individual experience and practical reason.' See his *John Williamson Nevin, American Theologian*, New York: OUP, 1997, 33.

[306] H. P. Owen, *The Christian Knowledge of God*, 195.

[307] David Jones to David Bogue, Antananarivo, 3 November 1820;

London Missionary Society Archives, School of Oriental and African Studies Library, London, Box 1, Folder 1, Jacket B.

308 See D. H. Kromminga, *The Christian Reformed Tradition from the Reformation to the Present*, Grand Rapids, MI: Eerdmans, 1943, 61.

309 *Howell Harris's Visits to Pembrokeshire*, trans. Tom Beynon, Aberystwyth: Cambrian News Press, 1966, 126; diary entry for 29 December 1746, Glancothi.

310 *Sermons of William Gadsby, 1773–1844*, Harpenden, Herts.: Gospel Standard Trust, 1991, 161. See further Kenneth Dix's most informative doctoral thesis, Keele University, 1997, which is shortly to be published by the Baptist Historical Society: *English Strict and Particular Baptists in the Nineteenth Century*, 26, 39. See also Alan P. F. Sell, *The Great Debate: Calvinism, Arminianism and Salvation* (1982), Eugene, OR: 1998, *passim*. Among other things Huntington is remembered for his pride in not having an Oxford or Cambridge DD. He claimed only the letters SS – Sinner Saved – and appended them to his name on his many writings.

311 P. T. Forsyth, *Revelation Old and New*, 71.

312 F. D. E. Schleiermacher, *On Religion: Speeches to its Cultured Despisers* (1799), trans. John Oman, New York: Harper 1958, 31.

313 Ibid., 35.

314 Ibid., 38.

315 Ibid., 45.

316 Idem, *The Christian Faith*, trans. H. R. Mackintosh and J. S. Stewart, Edinburgh: T. & T. Clark, 1928, 12.

317 Ibid., 17.

318 Idem, *Speeches on Religion*, 101.

319 Idem, *The Christian Faith*, 17.

320 See, for example, ibid., 26–31.

321 Ibid., 387.

322 Ibid., 431.

323 John Kent, *The End of the Line*, London: SCM Press, 1978, 43. Though, in view of Schleiermacher's anti-deist protest the word 'outside' is problematic – 'other than', certainly.

324 Rupert Davies, 'The people called Methodists. 1. Our doctrines', in Rupert Davies and Gordon Rupp, eds., *A History of the Methodist Church in Great Britain*, London: Epworth Press, 1965, 149.

325 G. Dawes Hicks, *The Philosophical Bases of Theism*, London: Allen & Unwin, 1937. In an early work John Baillie accused Schleiermacher of making 'feeling' too vague and subjective without reference to the semantic point I have proposed for consideration. See his *The Interpretation of Religion: An Introductory Study of Theological Principles*, Edinburgh: T. & T. Clark, 1929, 212–14.

[326] R. S. Franks, *The Metaphysical Justification of Religion*, London: University of London Press, 1929, 46.

[327] F. D. E. Schleiermacher, *Speeches on Religion*, 44.

[328] Ibid., 37.

[329] Ibid., 40. See in a related connection Douglas Hedley, 'Was Schleiermacher a Christian Platonist?', *Dionysius*, December 1999.

[330] Idem, *The Christian Faith*, 521–2.

[331] J. Edwards, *Works* (1834), Edinburgh: Banner of Truth Trust, 1974, I, 238a.

[332] Schleiermacher has also been accused of attenuating certain Christian doctrines – not least those of the Trinity and eternal life. See James Richmond, *Faith and Philosophy*, London: Hodder & Stoughton, 1966, 69–70. However, this charge is not germane to our present enquiry.

[333] H. R. Mackintosh, *Types of Modern Theology*, London: Nisbet, 1937, 48.

[334] Cf. W. P. Paterson, *The Rule of Faith*, London: Hodder & Stoughton, 1912, 363.

[335] D. M. Baillie, *Faith in God and its Christian Consummation*, 114.

[336] W. Dilthey, *Leben Schleiermachers*, 2nd edn., Berlin, 1922, I, 460, quoted by J. M. Creed, *The Divinity of Christ* (1938), London: Collins Fontana, 1964, 35. See further H. A. Hodges, *The Philosophy of Wilhelm Dilthey*, London: Routledge & Kegan Paul, 1952.

[337] W. P. Paterson, *The Rule of Faith*, 168–9. Hence a prominent theme in Wolfhart Pannenberg's writings, namely, that the post-Enlightenment retreat into subjectivism fostered irrationalism in theology and at best minimized the place of history construed eschatologically.

[338] P. Dean in his monthly magazine, *The Religious Reformer*, November 1883. An incomplete set is held in the Local History Room of Walsall Public Library. For more of Dean's escapades and prejudices see Alan P. F. Sell, *Dissenting Thought and the Life of the Churches*, ch. 16. Wanton appeals to experience in part explain the attempt of late nineteenth-century liberal theologians to redress the balance. Thus, for example, Wilhelm Herrmann, Barth's teacher, declared that 'in the human Jesus we have met with a fact whose content is incomparably richer than any feelings which arise within ourselves'. See his *The Communion of the Christian with God* (1896), New York: Putnam, 1906.

[339] See, for example, Richard Swinburne, *The Existence of God*, Oxford: Clarendon Press, 1979, ch. 13; William P. Alston, *Perceiving God: The Epistemology of Religious Experience*, Ithaca, NY: Cornell University Press, 1991; Richard Gale, *On the Nature and Existence of God*, Cambridge: CUP, 1991, ch. 8; Stephen T. Davis, *God, Reason and Theistic Proofs*, Edinburgh: Edinburgh University Press, 1997, ch. 7.

340 J. Hick, *Faith and Knowledge*, Ithaca, NY: Cornell University Press, 1957, 132.

341 P. T. Forsyth, *The Principle of Authority*, 109.

342 A. G. N. Flew, *God and Philosophy*, London: Hutchinson, 1966, 129.

343 Cf. Illtyd Trethowan, 'On Professor Antony Flew's *God and Philosophy*', *Downside Review*, LXXXVII, January 1970, 13.

344 L. Hodgson, *The Place of Reason in Christian Apologetic*, 76.

345 See F. Rosenzweig, *The Star of Redemption*, trans. William Hallo, Boston: Beacon Press, 1964. Brief discussions of Buber by philosophers include H. J. Paton, *The Modern Predicament*, London: Allen & Unwin, 3rd impression, 1962, ch. 11; H. D. Lewis, 'The elusive self and the I–thou relation', in G. N. A. Vesey, ed., *Talk of God*, 168–84. See also H. D. Lewis, *The Elusive Self*, London: Macmillan, 1982.

346 The trend is set in their early works: D. M. Baillie, *Faith in God and its Christian Consummation*, 1927, London: Faber & Faber, 1964; John Baillie, *The Interpretation of Religion*, Edinburgh: T. & T. Clark, 1929; H. H. Farmer, *Experience of God*, London: SCM Press, 1929.

347 C. B. Martin, 'A religious way of knowing', in A. G. N. Flew and A. MacIntyre, *New Essays in Philosophical Theology*, London: SCM Press, 1955, 82. He refers to Farmer's *Towards Belief in God*, 41.

348 R. W. Hepburn, *Christianity and Paradox* (1958), London: Watts, 1966, ch. 3.

349 J. Hick, 'A philosopher criticizes theology', *London Quarterly and Holborn Review*, April 1962, 105.

350 A. G. N. Flew, *God and Philosophy*, 133. Cf. R. W. Hepburn, *Christianity and Paradox*, 28–9, 44.

351 P. Donovan, 'Phenomenology as apologetics', *Scottish Journal of Theology*, XXVII no. 4, November 1974, 404. Cf. Robert A. Oakes's argument to the effect that from the fact that we may be deluded concerning experiences it does not follow that no experiences are self-authenticating. See his 'Religious experience and rational certainty', *Religious Studies*, XII no. 3, September 1976, 311–18.

352 A. G. N. Flew, *God and Philosophy*, 136.

353 B. Ramm, *Protestant Christian Evidences*, 210.

354 J. Scott Lidgett, 'Spiritual discernment', 283.

355 H. R. Mackintosh, *Some Aspects of Christian Belief*, London: Hodder & Stoughton, [1923], 119.

356 Bernard Lord Manning, *Essays in Orthodox Dissent* (1939), London: Independent Press, 1953, 26.

357 From his characterization of the comprehensiveness of 'religious experience' Flew omits the social dimension entirely. See *God and Philosophy*, 125.

358 Cf Hugo Meynell, *Redirecting Philosophy: Reflections of the Nature of*

Knowledge from Plato to Lonergan, Toronto: University of Toronto Press, 1998, 184.

359 John Macmurray, *The Structure of Religious Experience*, London: Faber & Faber, 1936, 39.

360 D. E. Trueblood, *The Trustworthiness of Religious Experience*, 38; cf. 32.

361 Cf. Thomas McPherson, *The Philosophy of Religion*, 124.

362 Matthew 7: 7; Luke 11: 9. The Quaker philosopher D. Elton Trueblood has memorably written, 'The communion of saints is another name for "The Fellowship of Verification."' See his *The Trustworthiness of Religious Experience*, London: Allen & Unwin, 1939, 93. From a different ecclesiastical tradition W. G. De Burgh speaks of 'The experiences of individuals [which] are moulded into a living unity of corporate faith and action, which in turn directs and enriches personal devotion.' See his *Towards a Religious Philosophy*, 51. Thus the mutual edification of the saints.

363 Robert Mackintosh, *Essays Towards a New Theology*, 352.

364 P. T. Forsyth, *The Principle of Authority*, 89.

365 Robert Flint, *Sermons and Addresses*, 332.

366 Augustine, *On the gift of perseverance*, XIX.

367 Bernard of Clairvaux, *Sept.* s. I. 1, quoted by J. S. Whale, *The Protestant Tradition* (1955), Cambridge: CUP, 1960, 85.

368 H. R. Mackintosh, *The Christian Experience of Forgiveness* (1927), London: Collins Fontana, 1961, 214.

369 J. Calvin, *Commentary on Hebrews*, 11: 6.

370 Answer to Question 111. For this and other catechisms to which I shall refer see Thomas F. Torrance, trans. and ed., *The School of Faith: The Catechisms of the Reformed Church*, London: James Clarke, 1959.

371 1 Peter 2: 10.

372 See Stephen Brachlow, *The Communion of Saints: Radical Puritan and Separatist Ecclesiology 1570–1625*, Oxford: OUP, 1988, 31. Brachlow refers to the fuller discussion of R. T. Kendall, *Calvin and English Calvinism to 1649*, Oxford: OUP, 1979, 9–41.

373 *Westminster Larger Catechism*, Answer to Question 80. The doctrine of assurance is receiving renewed attention at the present time. See, for example, Joel R. Beeke, *Assurance of Faith: Calvin, English Puritanism, and the Dutch Second Reformation*, New York: Peter Lang, 1991; A. T. B. McGowan, *The Federal Theology of Thomas Boston*, Carlisle: Paternoster Publishing for Rutherford House, Edinburgh, 1997, ch. 9.

374 T. Brooks, *Heaven on Earth: A Treatise on Christian Assurance* (1654), London: Banner of Truth Trust, 1961, 109.

375 T. Watson, *A Body of Divinity*, London: Banner of Truth Trust, 1965, 251.

376 Though it is not necessary for our present purpose, it would easily

have been possible to multiply examples from later periods, in which connection John Wesley's wrestlings with the concept of assurance are especially interesting. For these see Geoffrey Wainwright, *Methodists in Dialog*, Nashville, TN: Kingswood Books, 1995, 59–64. Not indeed that all Calvinists thought that Arminians were entitled to assurance. For example, Thomas Brooks, to whom assurance is 'the suburbs of paradise', has a provocative subheading, 'Assurance not for Arminians'. His point is that since Arminians, not subscribing to the doctrine of the perseverence of the saints, believe that a Christian may finally fall from grace they 'are not ashamed to say, that God may crown a man one hour, and uncrown him in the next; they blush not to say that a man may be happy and miserable, under love and under wrath, an heir of heaven and a firebrand of hell, a child of light and a child of darkness, and all in an hour. Oh what miserable comforters are these!' See his *Heaven on Earth*, 30–2. Happily, we need not at this time venture further into this doctrinal thicket.

377 P. T. Forsyth, *The Principle of Authority*, 75.

378 Idem, 'The distinctive thing in Christian experience', *Hibbert Journal* VI, 1908, 486.

379 N. F. S. Ferré, *Christ and the Christian*, London: Collins, 1958, 26. It is interesting to note the way in which discussions of assurance seem to parallel Quaker discussion of the Light. See, for example, Richenda Scott, *Tradition and Experience*, London: Allen & Unwin, 1964, 11–12.

380 J. Calvin, *Institutes*, III. ii. 19.

381 T. Watson, *A Body of Divinity*, 251.

382 R. Baxter, *Works*, IX, 264. For Baxter's own doubts, and for his view that 'Certainty cannot go beyond the objective Evidence: for it is caused thereby as the print on the Wax is caused by that on the Seal', see N. H. Keeble, *The Literary Culture of Nonconformity*, Leicester: Leicester University Press, 1987, 160, 162.

383 E. Sidney, *The Life and Ministry of the Rev. Samuel Walker, B.A.*, 2nd edn., 1838, 154–5, quoted by G. C. B. Davies, *The Early Cornish Evangelicals 1735–1760*, London: SPCK, 1951. I do not imply that Methodists necessarily think and behave as here described. For a Methodist account of the matter see Arthur S. Yates, *The Doctrine of Assurance with Special Reference to John Wesley*, London: Epworth Press, 1952.

384 T. Watson, *A Body of Divinity*, 260.

385 For some among many testimonies along this line see Alfred Cave, in *The Atonement in Modern Religious Thought*, London: James Clarke, 1900, 243; H. R. Mackintosh, *Some Aspects of Christian Belief*, 33.

Chapter 8: Conclusion: World-view, Context and Truth

1 W. F. Zuurdeeg, *An Analytical Philosophy of Religion*, London: Allen & Unwin, 1959, 96.

2 In Albury Castell, ed., *Essays in Pragmatism*, New York: Hafner, 1952.

3 Alfred N. Whitehead, *Science and the Modern World*, Cambridge: CUP, 1936.

4 M. J. Inwood in Ted Honderich, ed., *The Oxford Companion to Philosophy*, Oxford: OUP, 1995, 909a.

5 See further W. Dilthey, *Introducton to the Human Sciences*, trans. R. J. Betanzos, Detroit: Wayne State University Press, 1988; H. A. Hodges, *The Philosophy of Wilhelm Dilthey*, London: Routledge & Kegan Paul, 1952.

6 See E. Husserl, 'Philosophy as rigorous science', in *Phenomenology and the Crisis of Philosophy*, trans. Q. Lauer, New York: Harper Torchbooks, 1965.

7 J. Richard Middleton and Brian J. Walsh, 'Facing the postmodern scalpel: can the Christian faith withstand deconstruction?', in Timothy R. Phillips and Dennis L. Okholm, *Christian Apologetics in the Postmodern World*, Downer's Grove, IL: InterVarsity Press, 1995, 134; see further Brian J. Walsh and J. Richard Middleton, *The Transforming Vision: Shaping a Christian World View*, Downer's Grove, IL: InterVarsity Press, 1984.

8 N. H. G. Robinson, 'After Wittgenstein', *Religious Studies*, XII no. 4, December 1976, 506.

9 R. F. A. Hoernlé, *Studies in Contemporary Metaphysics*, London: Kegan Paul, Trench, Trubner 1920, 11 (my italics).

10 See H. H. Price, 'Clarity is not enough', *Proceedings of the Aristotelian Society, Supplementary Volume*, 19, 1945; reprinted in H. D. Lewis, ed., *Clarity is Not Enough*, London: Allen & Unwin, 1963, 15–41.

11 C. D. Broad, 'Critical and speculative philosophy', in J. H. Muirhead, ed., *Contemporary British Philosophy*, 1st ser., London: Allen & Unwin, 1924, 98.

12 C. D. Broad, 'Two lectures on the nature of philosophy', in H. D. Lewis, ed., *Clarity is Not Enough*, 46.

13 See D. M. Emmet, 'The use of analogy in metaphysics', *Proceedings of the Aristotelian Society*, 41, 1941, 27–46. I should like to say how much I gained, as a raw undergraduate, from Professor Emmet's lectures on Berkeley.

14 Ibid., 39. Cf. idem, 'Can philosophical theories transcend experience?', *Proceedings of the Aristotelian Society*, XX, 1946, 202–3. See also her

book, *The Nature of Metaphysical Thinking*, London: Macmillan, 1945, 196–201.

15 Idem, 'The choice of a world outlook', *Philosophy*, XXIII, 1948, 45–6.

16 H. A. Hodges, *Languages, Standpoints and Attitudes*, London: OUP, 1953, 15.

17 Ibid., 16.

18 Ibid., 61.

19 Ibid., 61–2.

20 R. M. Hare, 'Religion and morals', in Basil Mitchell, ed., *Faith and Logic*, London: Allen & Unwin, 1957, 190.

21 McTaggart said that no one had a right to religion who had not studied metaphysics, and that since most people lacked the disposition, education and leisure required for such a pursuit, 'most people have no right to accept any religion as true'. See his *Some Dogmas of Religion* (1906), London: Edward Arnold, 1930, 292–3; and Hocking agreed: see R. B. Perry, 'Contemporary philosophy of religion', *Harvard Theological Review*, July 1914, 378–95.

22 W. Wallace, *Lectures and Essays on Natural Theology and Ethics*, Oxford: Clarendon Press, 1898, 163.

23 O. C. Quick, *Modern Philosophy and the Incarnation*, London: SPCK, 1915, 7.

24 That, logically and in fact, is the order, for God in Christ takes the initiative. Hence I cannot agree with Merold Westphal who, following Kierkegaard says that 'theological affirmation is grounded in presuppositions that are chosen, not proven'. See *Kierkegaard's Critique of Reason and Society* (1987), University Park, PA: Pennsylvania State University Press, 1991, 94. They are indeed not proven, but they are first given, and our response is enabled by the Giver.

25 P. T. Forsyth, *Positive Preaching and the Modern Mind* (1907), London: Independent Press, 1970, 190.

26 J. Orr, *The Christian View of God and the World*, Edinburgh: Elliot, 1893 edn., 4.

27 A. E. Taylor, *The Faith of a Moralist*, London: Macmillan, 1931, II, 389. In view of this H. Cunliffe-Jones's call for 'a Christian philosophy of the universe' sounds over-ambitious. See his paper, 'Theology', in the volume he edited, *The Congregational Ministry in the Modern World*, London: Independent Press, 1955, 89. He was, however, in good company: 'The human mind will not permanently renounce the attempt to find a theory of the universe which shall include all being, even the highest.' So William Sanday, *Christologies Ancient and Modern*, Oxford: Clarendon Press, 1910, 96. J. K. Mozley was more realistic: 'What has not been done, and is so vast an undertaking that it is difficult to conceive of its ever being done, is a description of life which

would relate it in its whole character and in detail to the fact of the incarnation of God in Christ. Any such work would be a new kind of *summa theologica.*' See his *The Doctrine of the Incarnation*, London: Unicorn Press, 1936, 29. A partial analogy may be drawn from a different field. George Gershwin declared, 'True music must repeat the thought and aspirations of the people and the time. My people are American. My time is today.' On this the music critic, Richard Morrison, comments, 'What messianic presumption! What all-embracing ambition! It takes chutzpah to say such things, especially if your parents emigrated to the country (with "plenty o' nothin") only 30 years earlier.' See *The Times*, 4 September 1998, 35. But, despite his synthesizing abilities, and the fact that he struck a chord with many (as a particular articulation of a Christian world-view might do), there were others, equally American and equally musical, to whom Gershwin did not speak so directly in his time: the respective, sometimes squabbling, devotees of New Orleans versus Chicago-style jazz; the aficionados of 'Hawaiian' music (so much of it by Harry Owens from O'Neil in land-locked Nebraska); the folklorists intent upon recalling the musical traditions of the African-Americans, American Indians and Anglo-Celts; the Western swing of such groups as Bob Wills and his Texas Playboys; and the continuing classical tradition.

28 See Leonard Gross, *The Golden Years of the Hutterites*, Scottdale, PA: Herald Press, 1980, 163.

29 W. R. Inge, *The Religious Philosophy of Plotinus and some Modern Philosophies of Religion*, London: Lindsey Press, [1914], 37.

30 Gwilym O. Griffith, *The Theology of P. T. Forsyth*, London: Lutterworth Press, 1948, 94. However, Forsyth did not overlook the fact that while 'Revelation is not statement . . . it must be capable of statement'. See his *Faith, Freedom and the Future* (1912), London: Independent Press, 1955, 239. The remark of Robert J. Palmer is to the point: 'In theology we can expect distortion when, e.g. existential truth (truth as encounter or truth as subjectivity) and logical truth (proposition, statement) are set forth as though they were mutually exclusive options.' See his 'The rehabilitation of truth in theology', *Scottish Journal of Theology*, XXVIII no. 3, 1975, 207.

31 Frederick C. Copleston, 'Faith and philosophy', in Stewart R. Sutherland and T. A. Roberts, eds., *Religion, Reason and the Self: Essays in Honour of Hywel D. Lewis*, Cardiff: University of Wales Press, 1989, 57.

32 Cf. W. R. Matthews, *Essays in Construction*, London: Nisbet, 1934, 48–9: 'When we worship God He is to us certainly not a mere hypothesis. But we must sometimes, as Bishop Butler says, "sit down in a cool hour" and reflect upon the logical basis of our faith and worship. When we do this, we cannot avoid recognizing that our belief in God is one

possible way of thinking of the universe and can be compared with other ways.'

33 See the remarks made in the preceding chapter when discussing Kierkegaard.

34 Jack Rogers pursues this theme in detail with special reference to the Presbyterian Church USA. See *Claiming the Center: Churches and Conflicting Worldviews*, Louisville: Westminster/John Knox, 1995. It is easy to see that what he says has a wider application.

35 Geoffrey F. Nuttall, *Christian Pacifism in History*, Oxford: Blackwell, 1958, 61.

36 See Haridas Bhattacharya, ed., *The Cultural Heritage of India*, Calcutta: Ramakrishna Mission Institute of Culture, 1956, IV, 709.

37 Quoted by Howard Brinton, *Friends for 300 Years*, Philadelphia: Pendle Hill Publications, 1952, 38.

38 Torataro Shimamura, 'D. T. Suzuki's place in the history of human thought', in Masao Abe, ed., *A Zen Life: D. T. Suzuki Remembered*, New York: Weatherhill, 1986, 66.

39 J. Hick, 'Towards a philosophy of religious pluralism', *Faith and Freedom*, XXXIV pt. 3, Summer 1981, 141.

40 See, for example, Hugo A. Meynell, *Is Christianity True?*, London: Geoffrey Chapman, 1994, 47–9. As long ago as 1931 O. C. Quick noted with pleasure that 'There is much evidence that men's minds are already in revolt against the gospel of mere tolerance and relativism, which has for a time deceived them with the name of liberty.' See *The Ground of Faith and the Chaos of Thought*, London: Nisbet, 1931, 25. This is just one more exemplification of the fact that ideas tend to go out of fashion rather than to suffer final disproof. However, they sometimes return with a difference: 'The new relativism is . . . more subtle. Instead of attacking, it trivializes. Instead of rejecting Christianity as false, it grants relative truth. The faith is true for Christians but not necessarily for anyone else.' So John W. Cooper, 'Reformed apologetics and the challenge of post-modern relativism', *Calvin Theological Journal*, XXVIII no. 1, April 1993, 110. He further argues that relativism claims to affirm the validity of all systems, whilst at the same time implying the falsehood of those, like Christianity, Islam, Marxism and others, which hold that there is a universal standard of truth (115). Cf. Ian Barnes, 'Christianity in a pluralist society: a dialogue with Lesslie Newbigin', *St. Mark's Review*, 158, Winter 1994, 28; Klaas Runia, 'Why Christianity of all religions?', *European Journal of Theology*, VI no. 1, 1977, 57–72.

41 H. Root, 'Beginning all over again', in A. Vidler, ed., *Soundings: Essays Concerning Christian Understanding*, Cambridge: CUP, 1963, 13.

42 Cf. Paul Badham (Hick's former student), 'The influence of religious

pluralism on the contemporary understanding of Christian salvation', *Dialogue and Alliance*, II no. 2, Summer 1988, 38.

43 H. A. Hodges, *Languages, Standpoints and Attitudes*, 63.

44 Eugene Thomas Long, 'Experience and the justification of religious belief', *Religious Studies*, XVII no. 4, December 1981, 500.

45 Cf. Terence Penelhum, *Reason and Religious Faith*, Boulder, CO: Westview Press, 1995, 83.

46 Matthew 5.

47 Luke 10: 25–37.

48 See Alan P. F. Sell, *Philosophical Idealism and Christian Belief*, Cardiff: University of Wales Press, and New York: St. Martin's Press, 1995, 131–5 and *passim*.

49 D. Burrell, 'Religious experience and religious truth', *Irish Theological Quarterly*, LXII nos. 2–3, 1996–7, 186.

50 See, for example, Hosea 2: 20; Deut. 32: 4. Writing this paragraph as I am on Valentine's day, I am reminded of the way in which this Old Testament usage flows down to our own time when greetings cards and the songs of Tin Pan Alley capitalize upon 'true' love. See further the interesting paper by J. R. Lucas, 'True', *Philosophy*, XLIV, July 1969, 175–86.

51 See further Hugo A. Meynell's illuminating discussion in *Redirecting Philosophy: Reflections on the Nature of Knowledge from Plato to Lonergan*, Toronto: University of Toronto Press, 1998, ch. 2. I shall not delay over the self-defeating claim of some postmodernists that 'There is no truth' is the only true proposition.

52 Thomas Corbett, 'Criteria for theological truth', *Irish Theological Quarterly*, L nos. 2–4, 1983/4, 139.

53 John 14: 6.

54 Paul Tillich, *The New Being*, New York: Charles Scribner's, 1955, 69–70.

55 J. Calvin, *Institutes*, II. xi. 15.

56 W. A. Whitehouse, *Christian Faith and the Scientific Attitude*, Edinburgh: Oliver & Boyd, 1952, 90.

57 In an appendix to Stanley Hauerwas, *After Christendom*, Nashville, TN: Abingdon, 1991.

58 C. L. Higham, *Noble, Wretched, and Redeemable: Protestant Missionaries to the Indians in Canada and the United States, 1820–1900*, Albuquerque: University of New Mexico Press, and Calgary: University of Calgary Press, 2000, 11. The quoted words are those of John Harns, *The Great Commission; or the Christian Church Constituted and Charged to Convey the Gospel to the World*, Boston: Gould, Kendall & Lincoln, 1842, 196.

59 John 13: 5.

[60] E. C. Blackman, 'Truth', in Alan Richardson, ed., *A Theological Word Book of the Bible*, London: SCM Press, 1950, 270b.

[61] J. Smith, 'A prefatory discourse concerning the true way or method of attaining divine knowledge', *Select Discourses*, Cambridge: CUP, 1859, 8.

[62] P. Tillich, *The New Being*, 71.

[63] F. Howgill, *A Lamentation for the Scattered Tribes*, 1656.

[64] See *The Complete Works of the Rev. Andrew Fuller*, London: Holdsworth & Ball, 1831, II, 387; S. Kierkegaard, *Philosophical Fragments or a Fragment of Philosophy*, Princeton: Princeton University Press, 1944, 9–10, 47, 50; idem, *Concluding Unscientific Postscript*, London: OUP, 1941, ch. 2.

[65] So Isaac Watts in his hymn 'We give immortal praise'. Watts would have been the last person to wish to have his words invoked as an excuse for intellectual laziness.

[66] John 16: 13.

[67] P. T. Forsyth, *Missions in State and Church*, 1908, 250–1.

[68] R. Baxter, *A Third Defence of the Cause of Peace*, 1681, II, 85.

[69] R. Mackintosh, *A First Primer of Apologetics* (1900), London: Andrew Melrose, 2nd edn., 1904, 25.

Chapter 9: Epilogue

[1] From Richard Baxter's hymn, 'He wants not friends that hath Thy love'.

[2] Current literary scholars do not favour the designation 'peasant poet' which has traditionally been applied to Clare and others like him. See, for example, John Goodridge, ed., *The Independent Spirit: John Clare and the Self-taught Tradition*, Helpston: The John Clare Society and The Margaret Grainger Memorial Trust, 1994.

[3] For John Clare's poem see his *Works*, Ware, Herts.: Wordsworth Editions, 1995, 176. Arnold Mee's verses are in the memorial volume, *Arnold Francis Mee 1901–1966*, privately printed, 41. I am most grateful to the author, Joan W. Moody – the late Mr Mee's daughter – for permission to reproduce them here.

Select Bibliography

Note: The names of all authors discussed or cited in the foregoing text and/or notes will be found in the Index of Persons.

Alston, William P., *Perceiving God: The Epistemology of Religious Experience*, Ithaca, NY: Cornell University Press, 1991.

Altizer, T. J. J., *The Gospel of Christian Atheism*, London: Collins, 1966.

—— and Hamilton, William, *Radical Theology and the Death of God*, Harmondsworth: Penguin, 1968.

Anglican–Orthodox Dialogue: The Moscow Agreed Statement, London: SPCK, 1977.

Aristotle, *Works*, ed. W. D. Ross, Oxford: Clarendon Press, 1928.

Armstrong, Hilary, 'Platonism', in Ian Ramsey, ed., *Prospect for Metaphysics*, London: Allen & Unwin, 1961.

Austin, J. L., 'Other minds', *Proceedings of the Aristotelian Society, Supplementary Volume*, XX, 1946, 148–67.

Ayer, A. J., 'Demonstration of the impossibility of metaphysics', *Mind*, XLIII, 1934, 335–45.

—— *Language, Truth and Logic*, London: Victor Gollancz, 1936; 2nd edn. 1946.

—— *Philosophy and Language*, Oxford: Clarendon Press, 1960.

—— *Metaphysics and Common Sense*, London: Macmillan, 1967.

Badham, Paul, 'The influence of religious pluralism on the contemporary understanding of Christian salvation', *Dialogue and Alliance*, II no. 2, Summer 1988, 33–9.

—— 'The centrality of theism for Christianity', in Stephen T. Davis, ed., *Philosophy and Theological Discourse*, Basingstoke: Macmillan, 1997.

Bahnsen, Greg L., 'Induction, inerrancy and presuppositionalism', *Journal of the Evangelical Theological Society*, XX no. 4, December 1977, 292–5.

—— 'The apologetical tradition of the O[rthodox] P[resbyterian] C[hurch]', in Charles G. Dennison and Richard C. Gamble, eds., *Pressing Toward the Mark: Essays Commemorating Fifty Years of the Orthodox Presbyterian Church*, Philadelphia: Committee for the Historian of the OPC, 1986, 259–94.

Baillie, Donald M., *Faith in God and its Christian Consummation* (1927), London: Faber & Faber, 1964.

God was in Christ, London: Faber & Faber, 1961.

Baillie, John, *The Interpretation of Religion: An Introductory Study of Theological Principles*, Edinburgh: T. & T. Clark, 1929.

—— *Our Knowledge of God*, London: OUP, 1952.

—— *The Sense of the Presence of God*, London: OUP, 1962.

Baker, J. A., 'The essence of Christianity', *Expository Times*, LXXXVII, 1975, 36–9.

Balthasar, Hans Urs von, *The Glory of the Lord: A Theological Aesthetics*, ed. Joseph Fessio and John Riches, Edinburgh: T. & T. Clark, 1982.

Barclay, Robert, *An Apology for the True Christian Divinity* (1675), Glasgow: R. Barclay Murdoch, 14th edn. 1886.

Barnard, L. W., *Justin Martyr: His Life and Thought*, Cambridge: CUP, 1967.

Barnes, T. D., *Tertullian: A Historical and Literary Study* (1971), Oxford: Clarendon Press, 1985.

Barth, Karl, *Church Dogmatics*, Edinburgh: T. & T. Clark, 1936–69.

—— *The Knowledge of God and the Service of God in the Teaching of the Reformation*, London: Hodder & Stoughton, 1938.

—— *Nein!* Reprinted in *Natural Theology*, London: G. Bles, 1946.

—— *A Shorter Commentary on Romans*, London: SCM Press, 1959.

—— *The Humanity of God*, London: Collins, 1961.

—— *Credo*, London: Hodder & Stoughton, 1964.

—— *The Epistle to the Romans*, London: OUP, 2nd edn. 1968.

Baxter, Richard, *Reliquiae Baxterianae*, ed. M. Sylvester, 1696.

—— *The Practical Works of the Rev. Richard Baxter*, London: James Duncan, 1830.

Beeke, Joel R., *Assurance of Faith: Calvin, English Puritanism, and the Dutch Second Reformation*, New York: Peter Lang, 1991.

Begbie, Jeremy, 'The Gospel, the arts and our culture', in Hugh Montefiore, ed., *The Gospel and Contemporary Culture*, London: Mowbray, 1992.

Bell, Richard H., 'The aesthetic factor in art and religion', *Religious Studies*, XXII no. 2, June 1986, 181–92.

Benson, Lewis, *Friends and the Truth*, privately published, 1965.

Bergson, Henri, *Creative Evolution*, trans. A. Mitchell, London: Macmillan, 1911.

—— *An Introduction to Metaphysics*, trans. T. E. Hulme, London: Macmillan, 1913.

—— *Mélanges*, Paris: PUF, 1972.

Berkeley, George, *Works*, ed. A. Campbell Fraser, Oxford: Clarendon Press, 1901.

Berkouwer, G. C., 'General and special divine revelation', in C. F. H. Henry, ed., *Revelation and the Bible*, London: Tyndale, 1959.

Best, David, 'The aesthetic and the artistic', *Philosophy*, LVII, July 1982, 357–72.

Black, Max, 'The "paradox of analysis"', *Mind*, LIII, 1944, 263–7.

—— 'The "paradox of analysis" again', *Mind*, LIV, 1945, 272–3.

—— *Language and Philosophy*, Ithaca, NY: Cornell University Press, 1949.

—— ed., *Philosophical Analysis*, Ithaca, NY: Cornell University Press, 1950.

Bloesch, Donald G., 'The missing dimension', *Reformed Review*, XXVI no. 3, Spring 1973, 162–8, 179–88.

Blondel, M., 'The letter on apologetics', in Alexander Dru and Illtyd Trethowan, eds., *Maurice Blondel: Letter on Apologetics and History of Dogma*, London: Harvill Press, 1964.

Boston, Thomas, *Human Nature in its Fourfold State* (1720), London: The Banner of Truth Trust, 1966.

Boucher, David, Connelly, James and Modood, Tariq, eds., *Philosophy, History and Civilization: Interdisciplinary Perspectives on R. G. Collingwood*, Cardiff: University of Wales Press, 1995.

Braithwaite, R. B., 'Philosophy', in H. Wright, ed., *University Studies*, London: Ivor Nicholson & Watson, 1933.

—— 'Belief and action', *Proceedings of the Aristotelian Society, Supplementary Volume*, XX, 1946, 1–19.

—— *An Empiricist's View of the Nature of Religious Belief*, Cambridge: CUP, 1955.

Bratt, James D., 'The Dutch schools', in David F. Wells, ed., *Reformed Theology in America*, Grand Rapids: Eerdmans, 1985.

Bredin, Hugh, 'The theory of beauty', in J. McEvoy, ed., *Philosophy and Totality*, Belfast: Queen's University, 1977, 33–48.

Bria, Ion, ed., *Go Forth in Peace: Orthodox Perspectives on Mission*, Geneva: World Council of Churches, 1986, 62–7.

—— 'Christians and Europe: (9) An Orthodox reflection', *Epworth Review*, CCV no. 1, January 1998, 62–78.

Britton, Karl, 'The truth of religious propositions', *Analysis*, III, 1935, 21–7.

Broad, C. D., 'Critical and speculative philosophy', in J. H. Muirhead, ed., *Contemporary British Philosophy*, 1st ser., London: Allen & Unwin, 1924.

—— *The Mind and its Place in Nature*, London: Kegan Paul, 1925.
—— 'Some methods in speculative philosophy', *Proceedings of the Aristotelian Society, Supplementary Volume*, XXI, 1947, 1–32.
—— 'Two lectures on the nature of philosophy', in H. D. Lewis, ed., *Clarity is Not Enough*, London: Allen & Unwin, 1963.
Bromiley, Geoffrey W., 'Karl Barth and Anglicanism', *The Churchman*, LXXXVIII no. 1, January–March 1974, 9–24.
Brooks, Thomas, *Heaven on Earth: A Treatise on Christian Assurance* (1654), London: The Banner of Truth Trust, 1961.
Bruce, A. B., *The Training of the Twelve*, Edinburgh: T. & T. Clark, 1871.
—— *The Chief End of Revelation*, London: Hodder & Stoughton, [1881].
—— *The Kingdom of God: Christ's Teaching According to the Synoptic Gospels*, Edinburgh: T. & T. Clark, 4th edn. 1891.
—— *Apologetics; or, Christianity Defensively Stated* (1892), Edinburgh: T. & T. Clark, 1927.
Brunner, Emil, *Revelation and Reason: The Christian Doctrine of Faith and Knowledge* (1941), London: SCM Press, [1946].
——*Nature and Grace*, reprinted in *Natural Theology*, London: G. Bles, 1946.
Buckley, Michael J., *At the Origins of Modern Atheism*, New Haven, CT: Yale University Press, 1987.
Bultmann, Rudolf, *Theology of the New Testament*, London: SCM Press, 1952.
—— *Kerygma and Myth*, ed. H. W. Bartsch, trans. R. H. Fuller, London: SCM Press, 1953.
—— *Jesus Christ and Mythology*, London: SCM Press, 1958.
—— *Existence and Faith: Shorter Writings of Rudolf Bultmann*, London: Hodder & Stoughton, 1961.
Burgh, W. G. de, 'Logic and faith', *Philosophy*, I, 1926, 419–35.
—— *Towards a Religious Philosophy*, London: Macdonald & Evans, 1937.
—— *From Morality to Religion*, London: Macdonald & Evans, 1938.
—— *Knowledge of the Individual*, London: OUP, 1939.
Burnaby, John, *Amor Dei: A Study of the Religion of St. Augustine*, London: Hodder & Stoughton, 1938.
Burrell, D., 'Religious experience and religious truth', *Irish Theological Quarterly*, LXII nos. 20–3, 1996–7, 185–99.
Butler, Joseph, *Fifteen Sermons preached at the Rolls Chapel* (1726), London: G. Bell, 1953.
—— *The Analogy of Religion to the Constitution and Course of Nature* (1736), London: Ward, Lock, n.d.
Butterfield, Herbert, *Christianity and History*, London: G. Bell, 1950.
Butterworth, G. W., 'The deification of man in Clement of Alexandria', *Journal of Theological Studies*, XVII, 1916, 157–69.

Caird, Edward, *Hegel*, Edinburgh: Blackwood, 1891.

—— *The Evolution of Religion*, Glasgow: Maclehose, 2 vols. 1893.

—— 'St. Paul and evolution', *Hibbert Journal*, II no. 1, October 1903, 1–19.

Caird, John, *University Sermons*, Glasgow: Maclehose, 1898.

—— *The Fundamental Ideas of Christianity*, Glasgow: Maclehose, 1899.

—— *University Addresses*, Glasgow: Maclehose, 1899.

Cairns, David, *The Image of God in Man*, London: Collins Fontana, 1973.

Callahan, D., ed., *The Secular City Debate*, New York: Macmillan, 1966.

Calvin, J., *Institutes*, trans. Ford Lewis Battles, ed. J. T. McNeil, Philadelphia: Westminster Press, 2 vols. 1961.

Campbell, John McLeod, *The Nature of the Atonement*, Cambridge: Macmillan, 1856.

Campbell, R. J., *The New Theology*, London: Chapman & Hall, 1907.

—— *A Spiritual Pilgrimage*, London: Williams & Norgate, 1916.

Caputo, John D., *The Prayers and Tears of Jacques Derrida: Religion without Religion*, Bloomington, IN: Indiana University Press, 1997.

Carnell, E. J., *A Philosophy of the Christian Religion*, Grand Rapids: Eerdmans, 1952.

—— *The Case for Orthodox Theology*, London: Marshall, Morgan & Scott, 1961.

Carritt, E. F., *What is Beauty? A First Introduction to the Subject and to Modern Theories*, Oxford: Clarendon Press, 1932.

Casserley, J. V. L., *The Christian in Philosophy*, London: Faber & Faber, 1949.

Chadwick, Henry, trans. and ed., *Lessing's Theological Writings*, London: Adam & Charles Black, 1956.

Chapman, Mark D., 'Why the Enlightenment does not have to fail', *Heythrop Journal*, XXXIX, 1998, 379–93.

Charnock, Stephen, *The Existence and Attributes of God*, Grand Rapids: Sovereign Grace, 1971.

Cheng, John, 'The distinction between God's essence and energy: Gregory Palamas' idea of ultimate reality and meaning', *Ultimate Reality and Meaning*, XXI no. 1, 1998, 56–75.

Chia, Roland, 'Theological aesthetics or aesthetic theology? Some reflections on the theology of Hans Urs von Balthasar', *Scottish Journal of Theology*, XLIX no. 1, 1996, 75–95.

Clark, Gordon H., *What do Presbyterians Believe?* Philadelphia: Presbyterian and Reformed Publishing Co., 1965.

—— 'Apologetics', in Henry, C. F. H., ed., *Contemporary Evangelical Thought*, Grand Rapids: Baker Book House, 1968.

—— 'The Wheaton Lectures', in Ronald H. Nash, ed., *The Philosophy of Gordon H. Clark: A Festschrift*, Philadelphia: Presbyterian and Reformed Publishing Co., 1968.

Clark, Kelly James, *Return to Reason: A Critique of Enlightenment Evidentialism and a Defense of Reason and Belief in God*, Grand Rapids: Eerdmans, 1990.

Clifford, P. R., 'The factual reference of theological statements', *Religious Studies*, III, 1967, 339–46.

Clines, D. J. A., 'The image of God in man', *Tyndale Bulletin*, XIX, 1968, 53–103.

Clow, W. M., *The Cross in Christian Experience*, London: Hodder & Stoughton, 1908.

Cochrane, A. C., *Reformed Confessions of the Sixteenth Century*, Philadelphia: Westminster Press, 1966.

Cocks, H. F. Lovell, *By Faith Alone*, London: James Clarke, 1943.

Collingwood, R. G., *An Essay on Philosophical Method*, Oxford: Clarendon Press, 1933.

—— *The Principles of Art*, Oxford: Clarendon Press, 1938.

—— *An Autobiography* (1939), Harmondsworth: Penguin, 1944.

—— *An Essay on Metaphysics*, Oxford: Clarendon Press, 1940.

—— *The Idea of History*, ed. T. M. Knox, Oxford: Clarendon Press, 1946.

Collinson, Diané, 'Aesthetic meaning', in Hanfling, Oswald, ed., *Philosophical Aesthetics. An Introduction*, Oxford: Blackwell, 1992.

Conder, Eustace R., 'The decay of theology', *Congregational Year Book*, 1874, 64–80.

Conradie, A. L., *The Neo-Calvinist Concept of Philosophy*, Pietermaritzburg: Natal University Press, 1960.

Cooper, John W., 'Reformed apologetics and the challenge of post-modern relativism', *Calvin Theological Journal*, XXVIII no. 1, April 1993, 108–20.

Copleston, F. C., *Aquinas*, Harmondsworth: Penguin, 1955.

—— 'Faith and philosophy', in S. R. Sutherland and T. A. Roberts, eds., *Religion, Reason and the Self*, Cardiff: University of Wales Press, 1989.

Corbett, Thomas, 'Criteria for theological truth', *Irish Theological Quarterly*, L nos. 2–4, 1983–4, 134–50.

Crombie, I. M., 'The possibility of theological statements', in B. Mitchell, ed., *Faith and Logic*, London: Allen & Unwin, 1957.

Crousel, Henri, *Origen*, Edinburgh: T. & T. Clark, 1989.

Cullen, I. K. Story, 'The Christology of Ignatius of Antioch', *Evangelical Quarterly*, LVI, 1984, 173–82.

—— 'The Cross as ultimate in the writings of Justin Martyr', *Ultimate Reality and Meaning*, XXI no. 1, 1998, 18–34.

Cunliffe-Jones, Hubert, *The Authority of the Biblical Revelation*, London: James Clarke, 1945.

Cupitt, Don, *Radicals and the Future of the Church*, London: SCM Press, 1989.

—— *The Time Being*, London: SCM Press, 1992.

—— 'My postmodern witch', *Modern Believing*, NS XXXIX no. 4, October 1998, 5–10.

Dale, R. W., *Christian Doctrine: A Series of Discourses*, [1894], London: Hodder & Stoughton, 1903.

Daniélou, J., *Gospel Message and Hellenistic Culture*, London: Darton, Longman & Todd, 1973.

Darwall, Stephen, 'Conscience as self-authorizing in Butler's ethics', in Christopher Cunliffe, ed., *Joseph Butler's Moral and Religious Thought. Tercentenary Essays*, Oxford: Clarendon Press, 1992.

Davis, Stephen T., *God, Reason and Theistic Proofs*, Edinburgh: Edinburgh University Press, 1997.

—— ed., *Philosophy and Theological Discourse*, Basingstoke: Macmillan, 1997.

DeKlerk, Peter, and De Ridder, Richard R., *Perspectives on the Christian Reformed Church: Studies in History, Theology and Ecumenicity*, Grand Rapids: Eerdmans, 1983.

Denney, James, *Studies in Theology*, London: Hodder & Stoughton, 1902.

—— *Jesus and the Gospel*, London: Hodder and Stoughton, 2nd edn. 1909.

—— *The Christian Doctrine of Reconciliation*, London: Hodder & Stoughton, 1917.

—— *Letters of Principal James Denney to W. Robertson Nicoll, 1893–1917*, London: Hodder & Stoughton, 1920.

Dennison, Charles G., and Gamble, Richard C., eds., *Pressing Toward the Mark: Essays commemorating Fifty Years of the Orthodox Presbyterian Church*, Philadelphia: Committee for the Historian of the OPC, 1986.

Derrida, Jacques, *Of Grammatology*, trans. G. Spivak, Baltimore: Johns Hopkins University Press, 1974.

—— *Writing and Difference*, trans. A. Bass, London: Routledge & Kegan Paul, 1978.

—— *Limited Inc.*, trans. Samuel Weber, Evanston, IL: Northwestern University Press, 1988.

—— and Vattimo, Gianni, *Religion*, Stanford, CA: Stanford University Press, 1998.

Descartes, R., *Discourse on Method* (1637), London: J. M. Dent, 1912, 1934.

Dickie, E. P., *God is Light*, London: Hodder & Stoughton, 1953.

Diffey, T. J., 'Aesthetics and philosophical method', in David Boucher et al., eds., *Philosophy, History and Civilization*, Cardiff: University of Wales Press, 1995, 63–78.

Dilthey, W., *Introduction to the Human Sciences*, trans. R. J. Betanzos, Detroit: Wayne State University Press, 1988.

Dionysius the Pseudo-Areopagite, *The Divine Names and the Mystical Theology*, trans. C. E. Rolt, London: SPCK, 1975.

Dodd, C. H., *The Authority of the Bible* (1929), London: Collins Fontana, 1960.
—— *The Apostolic Preaching and its Developments* (1936), London: Hodder & Stoughton, 1970.
—— *History and the Gospels*, London: Nisbet, 1938.
Dooyeweerd, Herman, *Roots of Western Culture: Pagan, Secular and Christian Options*, Toronto: Wedge Publishing Corporation, 1979.
Drewery, Benjamin, *Origen and the Doctrine of Grace*, London: Epworth Press, 1960.
—— 'Deification', in Peter Brooke, ed., *Christian Spirituality: Essays in Honour of Gordon Rupp*, London: SCM Press, 1975.
Duncan-Jones, A. and Ayer, A. J., 'Does philosophy analyse common sense?', *Proceedings of the Aristotelian Society, Supplementary Volume*, XVI, 1937, 139–76.
—— *Butler's Moral Philosophy*, Harmondsworth: Penguin, 1952.
Du Toit, Stephanus, 'Revelation or reveilaton? Barth and postmodernism', *Heythrop Journal*, XL no. 1, January 1999, 1–18.
Dwight, J. S., 'The religion of beauty', in *Selected Writings of American Transcendentalists*, Toronto: The New American Library of Canada, 1966.
Ebeling, G., *Luther*, London: Collins Fontana, 1975.
Edwards, David L., *The Honest to God Debate*, London: SCM Press, 1963.
Edwards, M. J., 'On the Platonic schooling of Justin Martyr', *Journal of Theological Studies*, XLII pt. 1, 1991, 17–34.
[Ellis, John], *The Knowledge of Divine Things from Revelation, not from Reason or Nature* (1743), London: Thomas Tegg, 1837.
Emmet, Dorothy M., 'The use of analogy in metaphysics', *Proceedings of the Aristotelian Society*, XLI, 1941, 1–26.
—— 'Can philosophical theories transcend experience?', *Proceedings of the Aristotelian Society*, XX, 1946, 198–209.
—— *The Nature of Metaphysical Thinking*, London: Macmillan, 1946.
—— 'The choice of a world outlook', *Philosophy*, XXIII, 1948, 208–26.
Eriugena, John Scottus, *De divisione naturae*, I–III, trans. I. P. Sheldon-Williams and L. Bieler, *Scriptores Latini Hiberniae*, 7, 9, 11, Dublin, 1968–81.
Eucken, Rudolf, *Life's Basis and Life's Ideal*, London: A. & C. Black, rev. edn. 1918.
Ewing, A. C., 'Philosophical analysis', in *Philosophical Studies: Essays in Memory of L. Susan Stebbing*, London: Allen & Unwin, 1948.
—— *The Fundamental Questions of Philosophy*, London: Routledge & Kegan Paul, 1951.
—— 'The necessity of metaphysics', in H. D. Lewis, ed., *Contemporary British Philosophy*, London: Allen & Unwin, 1956.

—— 'Religious assertions in the light of contemporary philosophy', *Philosophy*, XXXII, 1957, 206–18.

Fantino, J., 'Le Passage du premier Adam au Second Adam comme expression du salut chez Irénée de Lyon', *Vigilae Christianae*, LII no. 4, 1998, 418–29.

Farmer, H. H., *Experience of God*, London: SCM Press, 1929.

—— *The World and God*, London: Nisbet, 1935.

—— *Towards Belief in God*, London: SCM Press, pt. II, 1942.

Farrer, Austin, *Faith and Speculation*, London: Adam & Charles Black, 1967.

Fergusson, David A. S., *Christ, Church and Society: Essays on John Baillie and Donald Baillie*, Edinburgh: T. & T. Clark, 1993.

Ferré, Frederick, *Language, Logic and God*, London: Eyre & Spottiswoode, 1962.

—— 'A renewal of God-language?', *Journal of Religion*, LII no. 3, 1972, 286–304.

Ferré, Nels F. S., *The Christian Understanding of God*, London: SCM Press, 1951.

—— *Christ and the Christian*, London: Collins, 1958.

—— *Searchlight on Contemporary Theology*, New York: Harper, 1961.

Fitzpatrick, Martin, 'Latitudinarianism at the parting of the ways', in John Walsh, Colin Hayden and Stephen Taylor, eds., *The Church of England c.1689–c.1833. From Toleration to Tractarianism*, Cambridge: CUP, 1993.

Flannery, Austin, *Vatican Council II. The Conciliar and Post-Conciliar Documents*, Collegeville, MN: Liturgical Press, 5th printing, 1980.

Flavel, John, *Works* (1820), London: Banner of Truth Trust, 1968.

Flew, A. G. N., *God and Philosophy*, London: Hutchinson, 1966.

—— and MacIntyre, A., *New Essays in Philosophical Theology*, London: SCM Press, 1955.

Flint, Robert, *Sermons and Addresses*, Edinburgh: William Blackwood, 1899.

—— *Theism*, Edinburgh: William Blackwood, 9th edn. 1895.

Fogelin, Robert J., *Wittgenstein*, London: Routledge & Kegan Paul, 1976.

Forrest, D. W., *The Christ of History and of Experience* (1897), Edinburgh: T & T. Clark, 7th edn. 1914.

Forsyth, P. T., 'A rallying ground for the Free Churches: the reality of grace', *Hibbert Journal*, IV no. 4, July 1906, 824–44.

—— *Positive Preaching and the Modern Mind* (1907), London: Independent Press, 1964.

—— *Missions in State and Church*, London: Hodder & Stoughton, 1908.

—— 'The distinctive thing in Christian experience', *Hibbert Journal*, VI, 1908, 481–99.

—— *The Cruciality of the Cross* (1909), London: Independent Press, 1957.

—— *The Person and Place of Jesus Christ* (1909), London: Independent Press, 1961.
—— *The Work of Christ* (1910), London: Independent Press, 1958.
—— *The Principle of Authority* (1913), London: Independent Press, 1952.
—— 'Veracity, reality and regeneration', *London Quarterly Review.*, 123, April 1915, 193–216.
—— *The Church and the Sacraments* (1917), London: Independent Press, 1947.
—— *The Justification of God* (1917), London: Independent Press, 1957.
—— *This Life and the Next* (1918), London: Independent Press, 1953.
—— *The Church, the Gospel and Society*, London: Independent Press, 1962.
—— *Revelation Old and New*, ed. J. Huxtable, London: Independent Press, 1962.
Foster, M. B., *Mystery and Philosophy*, London: SCM Press, 1957.
Frame, John M., and Coppes, Leonard J., *The Amsterdam Philosophy: A Preliminary Critique*, Phillipsburg, NJ: Harmony Press, n.d.
Franks, R. S., *A History of the Doctrine of the Work of Christ*, London: Hodder & Stoughton, n.d.
—— *The Metaphysical Justification of Religion*, London: University of London Press, 1929.
—— *The Atonement*, London: OUP, 1934.
—— 'Trends in recent theology', *Congregational Quarterly*, XXIII, 1945, 19–29.
Fraser, A. Campbell, 'John Locke as a factor in modern thought', *Proceedings of the British Academy*, I, 1903–4, 221–35.
Gadamer, Hans-Georg, *Philosophical Hermeneutics*, Berkeley: University of California Press, 1976.
—— *Truth and Method*, London: Sheed & Ward, 2nd English edn. 1989.
Gale, Richard, *On the Nature and Existence of God*, Cambridge: CUP, 1991.
Garvie, A. E., 'The nature of religious knowledge and the certainty of Christian faith', in *Mansfield College Essays*, London: Hodder & Stoughton, 1909.
—— The *Christian Doctrine of the Godhead, or The Apostolic Benediction as the Christian Creed*, London: Hodder & Stoughton, [1925].
—— 'Fifty years' retrospect', *Congregational Quarterly*, VII, 1929, 18–25.
Geehan, E. R., ed., *Jerusalem and Athens. Critical Discussion on the Philosophy and Apologetics of Cornelius Van Til*, Grand Rapids: Baker Book House, 1971.
Gilkey, Langdon, *Naming the Whirlwind: The Renewal of God Language*, Indianapolis: Bobbs-Merrill, 1969.

Gill, Jerry H., 'The possibility of apologetics', *Scottish Journal of Theology*, XVI no. 2, June 1963, 136–50.

—— 'J. L. Austin and the religious use of language', *Sophia*, VIII no. 2, 1969, 29–37.

Gilson, E., *Reason and Revelation in the Middle Ages*, New York: Charles Scribner's Sons, 1938.

—— *The Christian Philosophy of St. Thomas Aquinas*, New York: Random House, 1956.

—— *The Elements of Christian Philosophy*, New York: American Library of World Literature, 1963.

Gore, C., ed., *The Doctrine of the Infallible Book*, London: SCM Press, 1924.

Grant, R. M., *Irenaeus of Lyons*, London: Routledge, 1997.

Grensted, L. W., *The Atonement in History and Life* (1929), London: SPCK, 1936.

Griffith, Gwilym O., *The Theology of P. T. Forsyth*, London: Lutterworth Press, 1948.

Grube, Dirk-Martin, 'Religious experience after foundationalism', *Religious Studies*, XXXI no. 1, March 1995, 37–52.

Gunton, Colin E., 'Rudolf Bultmann and the location of language about God', *Theology*, LXXV, 1972, 535–9.

—— *Enlightenment and Alienation: An Essay towards a Trinitarian Theology*, Basingstoke: Marshall, Morgan & Scott, 1985.

—— *The One, The Three and the Many*, Cambridge: CUP, 1993.

Hales, John, *Golden Remains of the Ever Memorable Mr. John Hales*, 1659.

Hall, George B., 'D. M. Baillie: a theology of paradox', in David A. S. Fergusson, ed., *Christ, Church and Society*, Edinburgh: T. & T. Clark, 1993.

Hamilton, William, *The New Essence of Christianity*, London: Darton, Longman & Todd, 1966.

Hampshire, Stuart, 'Are all philosophical questions questions of language?' *Proceedings of the Aristotelian Society, Supplementary Volume*, XXII, 1948, 31–48.

—— 'The interpretation of religious language: words and concepts', in C. A. Mace, ed., *British Philosophy in the Mid-Century*, London: Allen & Unwin, 1957.

—— 'In Memoriam J. L. Austin', *Proceedings of the Aristotelian Society*, LX, 1960, I-XIV.

Hanson, R. P. C., 'The enterprise of emancipating Christian belief from history', in Anthony Hanson, ed., *Vindications: Essays in the Historical Basis of Christianity*, London: SCM Press, 1961.

Hare, R. M., 'Religion and morals', in Basil Mitchell, ed., *Faith and Logic*, London: Allen & Unwin, 1957.

Harnack, Adolf von, *History of Dogma*, London: Williams & Norgate, 1896.

—— *What is Christianity?*, London: Ernest Benn, 1958.

Harper, Kenneth C., 'Edward J. Carnell: an evaluation of his apologetics', *Journal of the Evangelical Theological Society*, XX no. 2, June 1977, 133–45.

Hart, Hendrik, Johan van der Hoeven and Nicholas Wolterstorff, eds., *Rationality in the Calvinian Tradition*, Lanham, MD: University Press of America, 1983.

Hart, Trevor, ed., *Justice the True and Only Mercy: Essays on the Life and Theology of Peter Taylor Forsyth*, Edinburgh: T. & T. Clark, 1995.

Hartshorne, Charles, *Man's Vision of God*, Hamden, CT: Archon Books, 1964.

Hatch, Edwin, *The Influence of Greek Ideas and Usages upon the Christian Church*, London: Williams & Norgate, 1907.

Hauerwas, Stanley, *Christian Existence Today: Essays on Church, World, and Living in Between*, Durham, NC: Labyrinth Press, 1988.

—— and Willimon, William, *Resident Aliens: A Life in the Christian Colony*, Nashville: Abingdon, 1989.

—— *After Christendom*, Nashville: Abingdon, 1991.

Hawkins, D. J. B., *Wittgenstein and the Cult of Language*, London: Blackfriars Publications, 1957.

Hebblethwaite, Brian, 'The philosophical theology of I. T. Ramsey: some further reflections', *Theology*, LXXVI, 1973, 638–45.

—— and Sutherland, Stewart, *The Philosophical Frontiers of Christian Theology: Essays presented to D. M. MacKinnon*, Cambridge: CUP, 1982.

Hedley, Douglas, 'Was Schleiermacher a Christian Platonist?', *Dionysius*, December 1999.

—— *Coleridge, Philosophy and Religion*, Cambridge: CUP, 2000.

Helm, Paul, *Faith and Understanding*, Edinburgh: Edinburgh University Press, 1997.

—— 'John Calvin, the *sensus divinitatis*, and the noetic effects of sin', *International Journal for Philosophy of Religion*, XLIII, 1998, 87–107.

Helseth, Paul K., 'B. B. Warfield's apologetical appeal to "right reason": evidence of "a rather bald rationalism"?', *Scottish Bulletin of Evangelical Theology*, XVI no. 2, Autumn 1998, 156–77.

Henry, Carl H. F., *God, Revelation and Authority*, Waco, TX: Word Books, 6 vols. 1976–83.

Henry, Martin, 'God in postmodernity', *Irish Theological Quarterly*, LXIII no. 1, 1998, 3–21.

—— 'The Enlightenment and Romanticism', *Irish Theological Quarterly*, LXIII no. 3, 1998, 250–62.

Hepburn, R. W., *Christianity and Paradox*, London: Watts, 1958.

—— 'Poetry and religious belief', in *Metaphysical Beliefs*, London: SCM Press, 1957.
—— 'A critique of humanist theology', in H. J. Blackham, ed., *Objections to Humanism*, Harmondsworth: Penguin, 1963.
—— 'The Gospel and the claims of logic', in *Religion and Humanism*, London: British Broadcasting Corporation, 1964.
Hesse, Mary, 'Criteria of truth in science and theology', *Religious Studies*, XI, 1975, 385–400.
Hesselink, I. John, *On Being Reformed: Distinctive Characteristics and Common Misunderstandings*, Ann Arbor, MI: Servant Books, 1983.
Hick, John, *Faith and Knowledge* (1957), London: Macmillan, 2nd edn. 1966.
—— 'A philosopher criticizes theology', *London Quarterly and Holborn Review*, April 1962, 103–10.
—— *Philosophy of Religion*, Englewood Cliffs, NJ: Prentice-Hall, 1963.
—— ed., *The Existence of God*, New York: Macmillan, 1964.
—— ed., *Faith and the Philosophers*, London: Macmillan, 1964.
—— *Evil and the God of Love*, London: Collins Fontana, 1968.
—— *God and the Universe of Faiths*, London: Macmillan, 1973.
—— 'Towards a philosophy of religious pluralism', *Faith and Freedom*, XXXIV pt. 3, Summer 1981, 139–56.
Hoare, Rupert, 'The idea of the transcendent: G. F. Woods as a theological teacher', *Theology*, LXVIII, 1967, 397–402.
Hodges, H. A., *The Philosophy of Wilhelm Dilthey*, London: Routledge & Kegan Paul, 1952.
—— *Languages, Standpoints and Attitudes*, London: OUP, 1953.
Hodgson, Leonard, *The Place of Reason in Christian Apologetic*, Oxford: Blackwell, 1925.
—— *The Doctrine of the Trinity* (1943), London: Nisbet, 1960.
—— *The Doctrine of the Atonement*, London: Nisbet, 1951.
—— *Christian Faith and Practice*, Oxford: Blackwell, 1952.
Hoernlé, R. F. A., *Studies in Contemporary Metaphysics*, London: Kegan Paul Trench Trubner, 1920.
Hoitinga, D. J., jun., 'Faith and reason in Calvin's doctrine', in H. Hart et al., eds., *Rationality in the Calvinian Tradition*, Lanham, MD: University Press of America, 1985.
Horne, Charles M., 'Van Til and Carnell – Part II', in E. R. Geehan, ed., *Jerusalem and Athens*, Grand Rapids: Baker Book House, 1971.
Hospers, John, 'The Croce-Collingwood theory of art', *Philosophy*, XXXI, October 1956, 291–308.
Hudson, W. D., 'Discernment situations: some philosophical difficulties', *Scottish Journal of Theology*, XIX no. 4, 1966, 434–45.
—— *Wittgenstein and Religious Belief*, London: Macmillan, 1975.

—— 'God revealed in creation', *Expository Times*, CIV no. 2, 1992, 47–8.
—— 'Questions people ask, 7. An updated philosophy of theism', *Expository Times*, CVII no. 5, 1996, 132–7.
—— Hick, J., Palmer, Humphrey and Phillips, D. Z., 'The philosophical discussion of religious discourse', *Theology*, LXXI, 1968, 98–122.
Hughes, G. E., 'Plantinga on God's existence', *The Philosophical Review*, LXXIX no. 2, April 1970, 246–52.
Hume, David, *Dialogues Concerning Natural Religion* (1779), Harmondsworth: Penguin, 1990.
Husserl, E., 'Philosophy as rigorous science', in *Phenomenology and the Crisis of Philosophy*, trans. Q. Lauer, New York: Harper Torchbooks, 1965.
Huxtable, John, *The Bible Says*, London: SCM Press, 1962.
Illingworth, J. R., 'The Incarnation in relation to development', in *Lux Mundi*, London: John Murray, 1889.
—— *Reason and Revelation: An Essay in Christian Apology*, London: Macmillan, 1902.
—— *Divine Transcendence*, London: Macmillan, 1911.
Inge, W. R., *Christian Mysticism*, London: Methuen, 1899.
—— *The Philosophy of Plotinus*, London: Longmans, Green, 1918.
—— *Mysticism in Religion* (1947), London: Rider, 1969.
Iverach, James, *The Truth of Christianity*, Edinburgh: T. & T. Clark, n.d.
Jacks, L. P., *Religious Perplexities*, London: Hodder & Stoughton, 1923.
—— *The Revolt Against Mechanism*, London: Allen & Unwin, 1933.
Jaspers, Karl, *The Perennial Scope of Philosophy*, trans. R. Mannheim, New York: Philosophical Library, 1949.
Jeffner, Anders, *Theology and Integration. Four Essays in Philosophical Theology*, Uppsala: Acta Universitatis Upsaliensis, 1987.
Jenkins, David E., *Guide to the Debate about God*, London: Lutterworth, 1966.
—— *The Glory of Man*, London: SCM Press, 1967.
Johnson, Dale A., 'The end of the "evidences": a study in Nonconformist theological transition', *Journal of the United Reformed Church History Society*, II no. 3, 1979, 62–72.
—— *The Changing Shape of English Nonconformity, 1825–1925*, New York: OUP, 1999.
Jüngel, E., *God as the Mystery of the World. On the Foundation of the Theology of the Crucified One in the Dispute between Theism and Atheism*, Edinburgh: T. & T. Clark, 1983.
Kalsbeek, L., *Contours of a Christian Philosophy*, Toronto: Wedge Publishing Corporation, 1975.
Kane, G. Stanley, 'God-language and secular experience', *International Journal for Philosophy of Religion*, II, 1971, 78–98.

Kant, I., *Critique of Pure Reason*, trans. J. M. D. Meiklejohn, London: Bell, 1884.

—— *Fundamental Principles of the Metaphysic of Ethics*, trans. T. K. Abbott, London: Longmans, Green, 10th edn. 1926.

—— *Prolegomena to any Future Metaphysics*, trans. Paul Carus, rev. James W. Ellington, Indianapolis: Hackett, 1985.

—— *Critique of Judgment*, trans. Werner S. Pluhar, Indianapolis: Hackett, 1987.

—— *Religion within the Limits of Reason Alone*, New York: Harper, 1996.

Karayiannis, Vasilios, *Maxime le Confesseur: Essence et énergies de Dieu*, Paris: Beauchesne, 1993.

Kaufman, Gordon D., 'On the meaning of "God": transcendence without mythology', *Harvard Theological Review*, LIX, 1966.

Kearney, Richard, *Dialogues with Contemporary Continental Thinkers: The Phenomenological Heritage*, Manchester: Manchester University Press, 1984.

Kenny, Anthony, *Wittgenstein*, Harmondsworth: Penguin Books, 1973.

—— *The Legacy of Wittgenstein*, Oxford: Blackwell, 1984.

Kierkegaard, S. A., *Training in Christianity*, Princeton: Princeton University Press, 1941.

—— *The Sonnets of Kierkegaard*, London: OUP, 1951.

—— *Either-Or*, Garden City, NY: Doubleday Anchor Books, 1959.

—— *Philosophical Fragments*, Princeton: Princeton University Press, 1964.

—— *Concluding Unscientific Postscript*, Princeton: Princeton University Press, 1968.

King-Farlow, John and Christensen, William N., *Faith and the Life of Reason*, Dordrecht: Reidel Publishing Co., 1972.

Klapwijk, J., 'Rationality in the Dutch Neo-Calvinist tradition', in H. Hart et al., eds., *Rationality in the Calvinian Tradition*, Lanham, MD: University Press of America, 1983.

Knox, T. M., 'Two conceptions of philosophy', *Philosophy*, XXXVI, 1961, 289–308.

Knudsen, Robert D., 'Tendencies in Christian apologetics', in E. R. Geehan, ed., *Jerusalem and Athens*, Grand Rapids: Baker Book House, 1971.

Kooi, Cornelis van der, 'Within proper limits: basic features of John Calvin's theological epistemology', *Calvin Theological Journal*, XVII no. 2, November 1982, 190–211.

Körner, S., *Kant*, Harmondsworth: Penguin, 1955.

Kuyper, Abraham, *Sacred Theology* (1898), Wilmington, DE: Associated Publishers and Authors, n.d.

—— *Lectures on Calvinism*, Grand Rapids: Eerdmans, 1961.

Lacey, A. R., *Bergson*, London: Routledge, 1989.

Lafleur, Charles, ed., *Quatre introductions à la philosophie au xiiie siècle: Textes critiques et études historique*, Montreal: L'Institut d'études médiévales, Université de Montréal, 1988.

Laird, John, *The Idea of Value*, Cambridge: CUP, 1929.

—— *Recent Philosophy*, London: Thornton Butterworth, 1936.

Lampe, G. W. H., 'Athens and Jerusalem: joint witnesses to Christ?', in B. Hebblethwaite and S. Sutherland, eds., *The Philosophical Frontiers of Christian Theology*, Cambridge: CUP, 1982.

Lane, Dermot A., *The Experience of God. An Invitation to do Theology*, Dublin: Veritas Publications, 1981.

Lash, Nicholas, 'Ideology, metaphor and analogy', in B. Hebblethwaite and S. Sutherland, eds., *The Philosophical Frontiers of Christian Theology*, Cambridge: CUP, 1982.

—— 'Where does holy teaching leave philosophy? Questions on Milbank's Aquinas', *Modern Theology*, XV no. 4, October 1999, 433–44.

Lévinas, Emmanuel, *Totality and Infinity: An Essay on Exteriority*, trans. Alphonso Lingis, Pittsburgh: Duquesne University Press, 1969.

—— *Otherwise than Being*, trans. A. Lingis, The Hague: Martinus Nijhof, 1981.

Lewis, Gordon R., 'Van Til and Carnell - Part I', in Geehan, E. R., ed., *Jerusalem and Athens*, Grand Rapids: Baker Book House, 1971.

Lewis, H. D., *Morals and Revelation*, London: Allen & Unwin, 1951.

—— *Our Experience of God*, London: Allen & Unwin, 1959.

—— ed., *Clarity is Not Enough: Essays in Criticism of Linguistic Philosophy*, London: Allen & Unwin, 1963.

—— *Philosophy of Religion*, London: English Universities Press, 1965.

—— 'The voice of conscience and the voice of God', in I. T. Ramsey, ed., *Christian Ethics and Contemporary Philosophy*, London: SCM Press, 1966.

—— 'The elusive self and the I-Thou relation', in G. N. A. Vesey, ed., *Talk of God*, London: Macmillan, 1969.

—— *The Elusive Self*, London: Macmillan, 1982.

Lilla, S. R. C., *Clement of Alexandria: A Study in Christian Platonism and Gnosticism*, London: OUP, 1971.

Lindbeck, George, *The Nature of Doctrine: Religion and Theology in a Postliberal Age*, London: SPCK, 1984.

Lindsay, Thomas M., 'The doctrine of Scripture: the Reformers and the Princeton School', *The Expositor*, 5th ser. I, 1895, 278–93.

Locke, John, *The Works of John Locke in Ten Volumes*, 11th edn. London: W. Otridge et al., 1812.

—— *An Essay Concerning Human Understanding*, ed. Peter H. Nidditch, Oxford: Clarendon Press, 1975.

—— *A Paraphrase and Notes on the Epistles of St. Paul*, ed. Arthur W. Wainwright, Oxford: Clarendon Press, 1987.

Loescher, Lefferts A., *The Broadening Church: A Study of Theological Issues in the Presbyterian Church since 1869*, Philadelphia: University of Pennsylvania Press, 1954.

Lonergan, Bernard, *Works*, Toronto: University of Toronto Press, 1988–.

Long, Eugene Thomas, 'Experience and the justification of religious belief', *Religious Studies*, XVII no. 4, December 1981, 499–510.

—— *Twentieth-century Western Philosophy of Religion 1900–2000*, Dordrecht: Kluwer Academic Press, 2000.

Lossky, V., *The Mystical Theology of the Eastern Church*, Cambridge: James Clarke, 1957.

Lubac, Henri de, *Catholicism: A Study of Dogma in Relation to the Corporate Destiny of Mankind*, London: Burns, Oates & Washbourne, 1950.

—— *Theological Fragments*, San Francisco: Ignatius Press, 1980.

Lucas, J. R., 'True', *Philosophy*, XLIV, July 1969, 175–86.

—— 'Reason restored', in William J. Abraham and Steven W. Holtzer, eds., *The Rationality of Religious Belief: Essays in Honour of Basil Mitchell*, Oxford: Clarendon Press, 1987.

Luscombe, David, *Medieval Thought*, Oxford: OUP, 1997.

Lyotard, J.-F., *The Postmodern Condition*, trans. G. Bennington and B. Massumi, Manchester: Manchester University Press, 1984.

Mace, C. A., ed., *British Philosophy in the Mid-Century*, London: Allen & Unwin, 1957.

McIntire, C. T., ed., *The Legacy of Hermann Dooyeweerd*, Lanham, MD: University Press of America, 1985.

Macintosh, J. J., and Meynell, H. A., eds., *Faith, Scepticism and Personal Identity: A Festschrift for Terence Penelhum*, Calgary: University of Calgary Press, 1994.

MacIntyre, Alasdair, 'The logical status of religious beliefs', in *Metaphysical Beliefs*, London: SCM Press, 1957.

McIntyre, John, 'Analogy', *Scottish Journal of Theology*, XII, March 1959, 1–20.

MacKinnon, Donald M., *The Problem of Metaphysics*, Cambridge: CUP, 1974.

—— *Explorations in Theology, 5*, London: SCM Press, 1979.

—— *Themes in Theology: The Threefold Cord*, Edinburgh: T. & T. Clark, 1987.

Mackintosh, H. R., *The Doctrine of the Person of Christ* (1912), Edinburgh: T. & T. Clark, 1956.

—— *The Originality of the Christian Message*, London: Duckworth, 1920.

—— *Some Aspects of Christian Belief*, London: Hodder & Stoughton, [1923].

—— *The Christian Experience of Forgiveness* (1927), London: Collins Fontana, 1966.

—— *The Christian Apprehension of God*, London: SCM Press, 1929.
—— *Types of Modern Theology*, London: Nisbet, 1937.
Mackintosh, Robert, *Essays Towards a New Theology*, Glasgow: Maclehose, 1889.
—— *A First Primer of Apologetics*, London: Andrew Melrose, 2nd edn. 1904.
—— 'Recent philosophy and Christian doctrine', *Proceedings of the Third International Congregational Council*, London: Congregational Union of England and Wales, 1908, 76–84.
—— 'Apologetics', *Encyclopedia Britannica*, 11th edn. 1910–11.
—— *Albrecht Ritschl and his School*, London: Chapman & Hall, 1915.
—— *Historic Theories of Atonement*, London: Hodder & Stoughton, 1920.
—— *Values: A Bird's Eye Survey*, London: Independent Press, 1928.
McLeod, S., *Rationality and Theistic Belief*, Ithaca, NY: Cornell University Press, 1993.
Macmurray, John, *The Structure of Religious Experience*, London: Faber & Faber, 1936.
McPherson, Thomas, 'Religion as the inexpressible', in A. G. N. Flew and A. MacIntyre, eds., *New Essays in Philosophical Theology*, London: SCM Press, 1955.
—— *The Philosophy of Religion*, London: D. Van Nostrand, 1965.
McTaggart, J. McT. E., *Some Dogmas of Religion* (1906), London: Edward Arnold, 1930.
Malcolm, Norman, 'Anselm's ontological arguments', *Philosophical Review*, 1960; reprinted in J. Hick, ed., *The Existence of God*, New York: Macmillan, 1964, 48–70.
—— *Ludwig Wittgenstein: A Memoir* (1958), Oxford: OUP, 1984.
—— *Wittgenstein: A Religious Point of View?*, Ithaca, NY: Cornell University Press, 1993.
Manning, Bernard Lord, *Essays in Orthodox Dissent* (1939), London: Independent Press, 1953.
Manson, T. W., *Ethics and the Gospel*, London: SCM Press, 1960.
Manson, William, *The Way of the Cross*, London: Hodder & Stoughton, 1958.
Mantzaridis, Georgios I., *The Deification of Man: St. Gregory Palamas and the Orthodox Tradition*, Crestwood, NY: St. Vladimir's Seminary Press, 1984.
Marion, Jean-Luc, *God without Being*, trans. Thomas A. Carlson, Chicago: University of Chicago Press, 1991.
Martin, C. B., 'A religious way of knowing', in A. G. N. Flew and A. MacIntyre, eds., *New Essays in Philosophical Theology*, London: SCM Press, 1955.
Martin, F. David, 'The aesthetic in religious experience', *Religious Studies*, IV no. 1, October 1968, 1–24.

Martineau, James, *The Seat of Authority in Religion*, London: Longmans, 1890.

—— *Types of Ethical Theory*, Oxford: Clarendon Press, 1891.

—— *A Study of Religion*, Oxford: Clarendon Press, 2nd rev. edn. 1900.

Mascall, E. L., *He who is* (1943), London: Darton, Longman & Todd, 1966.

—— *Words and Images: A Study in Theological Discourse*, London: Longmans, Green, 1957.

—— *The Openness of Being*, London: Darton, Longman & Todd, 1971.

Matthews, Eric, *Twentieth-Century French Philosophy*, Oxford: OUP, 1996.

Matthews, W. R., *Essays in Construction*, London: Nisbet, 1934.

—— 'The problem of religious knowledge', *The Modern Churchman*, XLIV no. 4, December 1954, 271–80.

Meyendorff, John, 'Unity of the Church – unity of mankind', in Constantin G. Patelos, *The Orthodox Church in the Ecumenical Movement. Documents and Statements 1902–1975*, Geneva: World Council of Churches, 1978.

—— and McLelland, Joseph, *The New Man: An Orthodox and Reformed Dialogue*, [no place given]: Agora Books, 1973.

—— 'Byzantium as center of theological thought in the Christian East', in Patrick Henry, ed., *Schools of Thought in the Christian Tradition*, Philadelphia: Fortress Press, 1984.

Meynell, Hugo A., *Sense, Nonsense and Christianity*, London: Sheed & Ward, 1964.

—— 'The theology of Hartshorne', *Journal of Theological Studies*, XXIV, 1973, 143–57.

—— 'Lonergan's method: its nature and uses', *Scottish Journal of Theology*, XXVII no. 2, May 1974, 162–80.

—— *The Theology of Bernard Lonergan*, Atlanta, GA: Scholars Press, 1986.

—— 'Lonergan's search for knowledge', *Literary Review of Canada*, February 1993, 15.

—— *Is Christianity True?*, London: Geoffrey Chapman, 1994.

—— 'On Nietzsche, postmodernisn and the new Enlightenment', *New Blackfriars*, LXXVI, January 1995, 4–18.

—— 'Archdeconstruction and postmodernism', *Heythrop Journal*, XXXVI, 1995, 128–39.

—— *Redirecting Philosophy: Reflections on the Nature of Knowledge from Plato to Lonergan*, Toronto: University of Toronto Press, 1998.

Micklem, Nathaniel, *What is the Faith?*, London: Hodder & Stoughton, 1936.

—— *The Box and the Puppets*, London: G. Bles, 1957.

Middleton, J. Richard, and Walsh, Brian J., *The Transforming Vision: Shaping a Christian World View*, Downer's Grove, IL: InterVarsity Press, 1984.

——'Facing the postmodern scalpel: can the Christian faith withstand deconstruction?' in Timothy R. Phillips and Dennis L. Okholm, eds., *Christian Apologetics in the Postmodern World*, Downer's Grove, IL: Inter-Varsity Press, 1995.

—— *Truth is Stranger than it Used to be: Biblical Faith in a Postmodern Age*, London: SPCK, 1995.

Milbank, John, Ward, Graham, and Pickstock, Catherine, *Radical Orthodoxy: A New Theology*, London: Routledge, 1999.

Miles, T. R., *Religion and the Scientific Outlook*, London: Allen & Unwin, 1959.

—— 'On excluding the supernatural', *Religious Studies*, I, 1965, 141–50.

Mitchell, Basil, 'The grace of God', in idem, ed., *Faith and Logic*, London: Allen and Unwin, 1957.

—— 'Faith and the limitations of open-mindedness', in J. J. Macintosh and H. A. Meynell, eds., *Faith, Scepticism and Personal Identity*, Calgary: University of Calgary Press, 1994.

Moberly, R. C., *Reason and Religion: Some Aspects of their Mutual Interdependence*, London: Longmans, Green, 1896.

Montgomery, John Warwick, *God's Inerrant Word*, Minneapolis: Bethany Fellowship, 1974.

Mooney, Hilary Anne-Marie, 'Bernard Lonergan and the role of the aesthetic in theology', *Irish Theological Quarterly*, LXIII no. 4, 1988, 362–78.

Moore, G. E., *Principia Ethica*, Cambridge: CUP, 1903.

—— 'The refutation of idealism', *Mind*, NS XII, 1903, 433–53.

—— 'The justification of analysis', *Analysis*, I, 1934, 28–30.

More, Henry, *An Explanation of the Grand Mystery of Godliness*, 1660.

—— *A Collection of Several Philosophical Writings of Dr. Henry More, Fellow of Christ's College, Cambridge*, London, 4th edn. 1712.

Mouw, Richard J., 'Dutch philosophical influences in America', *Calvin Theological Journal*, XXIV no. 1, April 1989, 93–120.

Mozley, J. K., *The Beginnings of Christian Theology*, Cambridge: CUP, 1931.

—— *The Doctrine of the Incarnation*, London: Unicorn Press, 1936.

Muirhead, J. H., 'Where is philosophy going?', *Philosophy*, XII, 1937, 387–94.

Nahm, Charles, 'The debate on the "Platonism" of Justin Martyr', *The Second Century*, IX no. 3, 1992, 129–51.

Nash, Ronald H., ed., *The Philosophy of Gordon H. Clark: A Festschrift*, Philadelphia: Presbyterian and Reformed Publishing Co., 1968.

Nevin, J. W., *The Mystical Presence and Other Writings on the Eucharist* (1846), Philadelphia: United Church Press, 1968.

Newbigin, J. E. Lesslie, *The Finality of Christ*, London: SCM Press, 1969.

Newman, J. H., *An Essay on the Development of Christian Doctrine*, London: Toovey, 1845.

—— *An Essay in Aid of a Grammar of Assent*, ed. I. T. Ker, Oxford: Clarendon Press, 1985.

Nicole, Roger, 'John Calvin and inerrancy', *Journal of the Evangelical Theological Society*, XXV no. 4, December 1982, 425–42.

Nielsen, Kai, 'Wittgensteinian fideism', *Philosophy*, XLII, July 1967, 191–209.

—— *Contemporary Critiques of Religion*, New York: Herder & Herder, 1971.

—— 'The coherence of Wittgensteinian fideism', *Sophia*, XI no. 3, 1972, 4–12.

—— *An Introduction to the Philosophy of Religion*, New York: St. Martin's Press, 1982.

Nietzsche, F., *Works*, ed. Oscar Levy, Edinburgh: T. N. Foulis, 1910.

—— *Twilight of the Idols and The Anti-Christ*, trans. R. J. Hollingdale, Harmondsworth: Penguin, 1968.

Norris, R. A., *God and the World in Early Christian Theology*, London: Black, 1966.

Notaro, Thom, *Van Til and the Use of Evidence*, Phillipsburg, NJ: Presbyterian and Reformed Publishing Co., 1980.

Nuttall, Geoffrey F., *The Holy Spirit in Puritan Faith and Experience*, Oxford: Blackwell, 1943.

Oakes, Robert A., 'Religious experience and rational certainty', *Religious Studies*, XII no. 3, September 1976, 311–18.

O'Donoghue, Noel D., 'A theology of beauty', *Irish Theological Quarterly*, L nos. 2–4, 1983–4, 250–6.

O'Donovan, Joan E., 'Man in the image of God: the disagreement between Barth and Brunner reconsidered', *Scottish Journal of Theology*, XXXIX no. 4, 1986, 433–59.

Ogden, Schubert M., *Christ without Myth*, London: Collins, 1962.

—— 'God and philosophy: a discussion with Anthony Flew', *Journal of Religion*, XLVIII no. 2, 1968.

Olding, A., 'D. Z. Phillips and religious language', *Sophia*, XVII no. 1, 1977, 23–8.

Oldfield, Adrian, 'Metaphysics and history in Collingwood's thought', in D. Boucher et al., eds., *Philosophy, History and Civilization*, Cardiff: University of Wales Press, 1995.

Olthuis, James H., ed., *Knowing Other-wise. Philosophy at the Threshold of Spirituality*, New York: Fordham University Press, 1998.

Oman, John, *The Problem of Faith and Freedom in the Last Two Centuries*, London: Hodder & Stoughton, 1906.

—— *The Natural and the Supernatural*, Cambridge: CUP, 1931.

O'Neill, J. C., 'Bultmann and Hegel', *Journal of Theological Studies*, XXI, 1970, 388–400.

Orr, James, *The Christian View of God and the World*, Edinburgh: Elliot, 1897.

—— *The Progress of Dogma*, London: James Clarke, 1901.

Osborn, E. F., *The Philosophy of Clement of Alexandria*, Cambridge: CUP, 1957.

—— *Justin Martyr*, Tübingen: J. C. B. Mohr, 1973.

Osterhaven, M. Eugene, 'Faith, reason and theology', *Reformed Review*, LI no. 3, Spring 1998, 183–201.

Owen, H. P., *Revelation and Existence: A Study in the Theology of Rudolf Bultmann*, Cardiff: University of Wales Press, 1957.

—— *The Moral Argument for Christian Theism*, London: Allen & Unwin, 1965.

—— Review of Flew, A. G. N., *God and Philosophy*, in *Religious Studies*, II, 1966–7, 282–5.

—— *The Christian Knowledge of God*, London: Athlone Press, 1969.

—— 'The philosophical theology of I. T. Ramsey', *Theology*, LXXIV, 1971, 67–74.

—— *W. R. Matthews: Philosopher and Theologian*, London: Athlone Press, 1976.

Owen, John, *Works*, ed. William H. Goold (1850–1853), London: Banner of Truth Trust, 1968.

Padgett, Alan G., ed., *Reason and the Christian Religion*, Oxford: OUP, 1994.

Pailin, David A., 'The utterly absolute and the totally related', *New Blackfriars*, LXVIII, May 1987, 243–55.

—— 'History and faith. (2) Is it a mistake to hold that the Christian faith rests on history?', *Epworth Review*, XIX no. 3, September 1992, 39–50.

—— 'The supposedly historical basis of theological understanding', in Sarah Coakley and David Pailin, eds., *The Making and Remaking of Christian Doctrine. Essays in Honour of Maurice Wiles*, Oxford: Clarendon Press, 1993.

—— *Probing the Foundations: A Study in Theistic Reconstruction*, Kampen: Kok Pharos, 1994.

Palmer, Robert J., 'The rehabilitation of truth in theology', *Scottish Journal of Theology*, XXVIII no. 3, 1975.

Pannenberg, W., *Revelation as History*, New York: Macmillan, 1969.

Parsons, Mike, 'Warfield and Scripture', *Churchman*, XCI no. 3, July 1977, 198–220.

Partee, Charles, *Calvin and Classical Philosophy*, Leiden: E. J. Brill, 1977.

Pascal, B., *Pascal's Pensées*, ed. H. F. Stewart, London: Routledge & Kegan Paul, 1950.

Passmore, John, 'Christianity and positivism', *Australasian Journal of Philosophy*, XXXV, 1957, 125–36.

Paterson, W. P., *The Rule of Faith*, London: Hodder & Stoughton, 1912.

Paton, H. J., *In Defence of Reason*, London: Hutchinson, 1951.

—— *The Modern Predicament*, London: Allen & Unwin, 1955.

Patrides, A., ed., *The Cambridge Platonists*, Cambridge, MA: Harvard University Press, 1970.

Payton, James R., jun., 'John of Damascus on human cognition: an element in his apologetic for icons', *Church History*, LXV, 1996, 173–83.

Pears, D. F., *Wittgenstein*, London: Collins Fontana, 1971.

—— *The False Prison: A Study of the Development of Wittgenstein's Philosophy*, Oxford: Clarendon Press, 1987.

Penelhum, Terence, *Problems of Religious Knowledge*, London: Macmillan, 1971.

—— *Religion and Rationality*, New York: Random House, 1971.

—— *God and Skepticism*, Dordrecht: Reidel, 1983.

—— *Butler*, London: Routledge & Kegan Paul, 1985.

—— 'Human nature and truth: Hume and Pascal', *Lumen*, XII, 1993, 45–64.

—— *Reason and Religious Faith*, Boulder, CO: Westview Press, 1995.

—— 'Fideism', in P. L. Quinn and C. Taliaferro, eds., *A Companion to Philosophy of Religion*, Oxford, Blackwell, 1997.

Perry, R. B., 'Contemporary philosophy of religion', *Harvard Theological Review*, July 1914, 378–95.

Phillips, D. Z., *The Concept of Prayer*, London: Macmillan, 1965.

—— *Death and Immortality*, London: Macmillan, 1970.

—— *Faith and Philosophical Enquiry*, London: Routledge, 1970.

—— *Wittgenstein and Religion*, Basingstoke: Macmillan, 1993.

—— 'Notes on a "monstrous illusion"', in S. T. Davis, ed., *Philosophy and Theological Discourse*, Basingstoke: Macmillan, 1997.

—— Review of Quinn and Taliaferro, in *International Journal for Philosophy of Religion*, XLIV, 1998, 53–63.

Placher, William C., *Unapologetic Theology: A Christian Voice in a Pluralistic Conversation*, Louisville: Westminster/John Knox, 1989.

Plantinga, Alvin, 'The Reformed objection to natural theology', in H. Hart et al., eds., *Rationality in the Calvinian Tradition*, Lanham, MD: University Press of America, 1983.

—— 'Advice to Christian philosophers', *Faith and Philosophy*, I no. 3, July 1984, 253–71.

—— 'Reformed epistemology', in P. L. Quinn and C. Taliaferro, eds., *A Companion to Philosophy of Religion*, Oxford: Blackwell, 1997.

—— and Wolterstorff, N., eds., *Faith and Rationality*, Notre Dame, IN: University of Notre Dame Press, 1983.

Platt, John, *Reformed Thought and Scholasticism: The Arguments for the Existence of God in Dutch Theology, 1575–1650*, Leiden: E. J. Brill, 1982.

Plotinus, *Enneads*, trans. Stephen MacKenna, London: Faber & Faber, 4th edn. revised by B. S. Page, 1969.

Pompa, Leon, 'Collingwood's theory of historical knowledge', in D. Boucher et al., eds., *Philosophy, History and Civilization*, Cardiff: University of Wales Press, 1995.

Popkin, Richard H., *The History of Scepticism from Erasmus to Spinoza*, Berkeley and Los Angeles: University of California Press, 1979.

—— 'The role of scepticism in modern philosophy reconsidered', *Journal of the History of Philosophy*, XXXI, 1993, 501–17.

Popper, K. R., 'Emancipation through knowledge', in Paul Kurtz and Timothy J. Madigan, eds., *Challenges to the Enlightenment*, Buffalo: Prometheus Books, 1994.

——, Kneale, W. C., and Ayer, A. J., 'What can logic do for philosophy?', *Proceedings of the Aristotelian Society, Supplementary Volume*, XXII, 1948, 141–78.

Power, William L., 'Analysis and theology', *Sophia*, XVII no. 2, 1978, 16–26.

Prado, C. G., *Descartes and Foucault: A Contrastive Introduction to Philosophy*, Ottawa: University of Ottawa Press, 1992.

Price, H. H., 'Logical positivism and theology', *Philosophy*, X, 1935, 313–31.

—— 'Clarity is not enough', *Proceedings of the Aristotelian Society, Supplementary Volume*, XIX, 1945, reprinted in H. D. Lewis, *Clarity is Not Enough*, London: Allen & Unwin, 1963.

Pringle-Pattison, A. S., *Man's Place in the Cosmos and Other Essays*, Edinburgh: Blackwood, 1902.

—— *The Duty of Candour in Religious Teaching*, London: Hodder & Stoughton, [1920].

—— *The Idea of God in the Light of Recent Philosophy*, New York: OUP, 1920.

—— 'God in action', in B. H. Streeter, ed., *The Spirit*, London: Macmillan, 1928.

Pryce, R. Vaughan, 'The redemptive work of the Lord Jesus Christ', in *The Ancient Faith in Modern Light*, Edinburgh: T. & T. Clark, 1897.

Purcell, William, ed., *The Resurrection: A Dialogue arising from Broadcasts by G. W. H. Lampe and D. M. MacKinnon*, London: Mowbray, 1966.

Quasten, J., *Patrology*, II, Utrecht: Spectrum, 1935.

Quick, O. C., *Modern Philosophy and the Incarnation*, London: SPCK, 1915.

—— *The Ground of Faith and the Chaos of Thought*, London: Nisbet, 1931.

—— *The Gospel of the New World: A Study in the Christian Doctrine of Atonement*, London: Nisbet, 1944.

—— *Doctrines of the Creed*, London: Collins Fontana, 1963.

Quinn, Philip L., and Taliaferro, Charles, eds., *A Companion to Philosophy of Religion*, Oxford: Blackwell, 1997.

Quinton, Anthony, *From Wodehouse to Wittgenstein*, Manchester: Carcanet, 1998.

Rahner, Karl, *Theological Investigations*, London: Darton, Longman & Todd, 1961–.

Rainy, Robert, Orr, James and Dods, Marcus, *The Supernatural in Christianity*, Edinburgh: T. & T. Clark, 1894.

Ramm, Bernard, *Protestant Christian Evidences*, Chicago: Moody Press, 1953.

—— *Varieties of Christian Apologetics*, Grand Rapids: Baker Book House, 1963.

Ramsey, A. M., *The Resurrection of Christ*, London: G. Bles, 1945.

—— *From Gore to Temple*, London: Longmans, 1960.

Ramsey, I. T., *Religious Language*, London: SCM Press, 1957.

—— ed., *Prospect for Metaphysics*, London: Allen & Unwin, 1961.

Rashdall, Hastings, *Ideas and Ideals*, Oxford: Blackwell, 1928.

Reade, W. H. V., *The Christian Challenge to Philosophy*, London: SPCK, 1951.

Reid, J. K. S., *The Authority of Scripture*, London: Methuen, 1957.

Reid, Thomas, *Works*, ed. William Hamilton, Edinburgh: MacLachlan & Stewart, 1863.

Rhees, Rush, *Discussions of Wittgenstein* (1970), Bristol: Thoemmes Press, 1996.

—— *Wittgenstein and the Possibility of Discourse*, ed. D. Z. Phillips, Cambridge: CUP, 1998.

Richardson, Alan, *Christian Apologetics*, London: SCM Press, 1947.

Richmond, James, 'God, time and process theology', *Theology*, LXVIII, 1965, 234–41.

—— *Faith and Philosophy*, London: Hodder & Stoughton, 1966.

Ricoeur, Paul, *The Rule of Metaphor: Multi-Disciplinary Studies of the Creation of Meaning in Language* (Fr. edn. 1975), Toronto: University of Toronto Press, 1978.

—— 'Philosophy and religious language', *Journal of Religion*, LIV no. 1, 1974, 71–85.

Riesen, Richard Allan, *Criticism and Faith in Late Victorian Scotland*, Lanham, MD: University Press of America, 1985.

Ritschl, Albrecht, *The Christian Doctrine of Justification and Reconciliation*, trans. H. R. Mackintosh and A. B. Macaulay, Edinburgh: T. & T. Clark, 1900.

Roberts, George W., and Smucker, Donovan E., eds., *Borderlands of Theology and Other Essays*, London: Lutterworth, 1968.

Roberts, T. A., *History and Christian Apologetic*, London: SPCK, 1960.
—— 'The historian and the believer', *Religious Studies*, VII no. 3, 1971, 251–7.
—— 'Fact and value in historical theology', *The Modern Churchman*, NS XVIII nos. 1 and 2, Winter 1975, 13–21.
Robinson, J. A. T., *Jesus and his Coming*, London: SCM Press, 1957.
—— *Honest to God*, London: SCM Press, 1963.
Robinson, N. H. G., *The Groundwork of Christian Ethics*, London: Collins, 1971.
—— 'The logic of religious language', in G. N. Vesey, ed., *Talk of God*, London: Macmillan, 1969.
—— 'The logical placing of the name "God"', *Scottish Journal of Theology*, XXIV, 1971, 129–48.
—— 'The problem of natural theology', *Religious Studies*, VIII, 1972, 319–33.
—— 'After Wittgenstein', *Religious Studies*, XII, 1976, 493–507.
—— 'Is providence credible today?', *Scottish Journal of Theology*, XXX, 1977, 215–31.
Rogers, G. A. J., *Locke's Enlightenment*, Hildesheim: Georg Olms, 1998.
Rogers, Jack, 'Van Til and Warfield on Scripture', in E. R. Geehan, ed., *Jerusalem and Athens*, Grand Rapids: Baker House Books, 1971.
—— *Claiming the Center: Churches and Conflicting Worldviews*, Louisville: Westminster/John Knox, 1995.
Rogers, Jack B., and McKim, Donald K., *The Authority and Interpretation of the Bible*, San Francisco: Harper & Row, 1979.
Root, Howard, 'Beginning all over again', in A. R. Vidler, ed., *Soundings*, Cambridge: CUP, 1963.
Rorty, Richard, *Philosophy and the Mirror of Nature*, Oxford: Blackwell, 1980.
—— *Consequences of Pragmatism*, Brighton: Harvester Press, 1982.
—— *Contingency, Irony and Solidarity*, Cambridge: CUP, 1989.
—— 'Science as solidarity', in H. Lawson and L. Appignanesi, eds., *Dismantling Truth: Reality in the Postmodern World*, New York: St Martin's Press, 1989.
—— *Objectivity, Relativism and Truth*, Cambridge: CUP, 1991.
—— Interview with Sean Sayers, *Times Higher Education Supplement*, 6 June 1997, 18.
Runia, Klaas, 'Why Christianity of all religions?', *European Journal of Theology*, VI no. 1, 1977, 57–72.
Russell, Bertrand, *On Scientific Method in Philosophy*, Oxford: Clarendon Press, 1914.
—— 'On verification', *Proceedings of the Aristotelian Society*, XXXVIII, 1938, 1–20.

Ryle, Gilbert, 'Systematically misleading expressions', *Proceedings of the Aristotelian Society*, XXXII, 1932, reprinted in Ryle's *Collected Papers*, London: Hutchinson, 1971, II, 39–62.

—— 'Taking sides in philosophy', *Philosophy*, XII no. 47, July 1937, 317–22.

—— *The Concept of Mind*, London: Hutchinson, 1949.

—— ed., *The Revolution in Philosophy*, London: Macmillan, 1956.

Saliba, I. A., 'The Bishop of Antioch and the heretics: a study of a primitive Christology', *Evangelical Quarterly*, LIV, 1982, 65–76.

Samuelson, Norbert, 'That the God of the philosophers is not the God of Abraham, Isaac, and Jacob', *Harvard Theological Review*, LXV no. 1, January 1972, 2–27.

Saw, Ruth, 'What is a work of art?', *Philosophy*, XXXVI, January 1961, 18–29.

Scharlemann, Robert P., ed., *Theology at the End of the Century: A Dialogue on the Postmodern*, Richmond: University Press of Virginia, 1990.

Schleiermacher, F. D. E., *On Religion. Speeches to its Cultured Despisers*, trans. John Oman, New York: Harper & Row, 1958.

—— *The Christian Faith*, trans. and ed. H. R. Mackintosh and J. S. Stewart, Edinburgh: T. & T. Clark, 1960.

Schlipp, P. A., *The Philosophy of Rudolf Carnap*, La Salle, IL: Open Court, 1963.

Schwöbel, Christoph, *God: Action and Revelation*, Kampen: Kok Pharos, 1992.

Scott, Richenda, *Tradition and Experience*, London: Allen & Unwin, 1964.

Sell, Alan P. F., 'Friends and philosophy', *The Friends' Quarterly*, XVII, 1973, 72–82, 111–22.

—— *Robert Mackintosh, Theologian of Integrity*, Berne: Peter Lang, 1977.

—— *Theology in Turmoil. The Roots, Course and Significance of the Conservative–Liberal Debate in Modern theology* (1986), Eugene, OR: Wipf & Stock, 1998.

—— *Defending and Declaring the Faith: Some Scottish Examples 1860–1920*, Exeter: Paternoster Press, and Colorado Springs: Helmers & Howard, 1987.

—— *The Philosophy of Religion 1875–1980* (1988), Bristol: Thoemmes Press, 1996.

—— *Aspects of Christian Integrity* (1990), Eugene, OR: Wipf & Stock, 1998.

—— *Dissenting Thought and the Life of the Churches: Studies in an English Tradition*, Lewiston, NY: Edwin Mellen Press, 1990.

—— *A Reformed, Evangelical, Catholic Theology: The Contribution of the World Alliance of Reformed Churches 1875–1982* (1991), Eugene, OR: Wipf & Stock, 1998.

—— *Commemorations: Studies in Christian Thought and History* (1993), Eugene, OR: Wipf & Stock, 1998.

—— *Conservation and Exploration in Christian Theology*, Caernarfon: Gwasg Pantycelyn, 1993.

—— *Philosophical Idealism and Christian Belief*, Cardiff: University of Wales Press, and New York: St Martin's Press, 1995.

—— 'P. T. Forsyth as unsystematic systematician', in Trevor Hart, ed., *Justice the True and Only Mercy*, Edinburgh: T. & T. Clark, 1995.

—— *John Locke and the Eighteenth-Century Divines*, Cardiff: University of Wales Press, 1997.

—— 'Approaches to moral philosophy among the eighteenth-century Dissenters of England and Wales', *Jahrbuch für Recht und Ethik*, VIII, 2000, 263–313.

—— 'Reformed identity – a non-issue of catholic significance', *Reformed Review*, LIV no. 1, Autumn 2000, 17–27.

—— '"The Gospel its own Witness": Deism, Thomas Paine and Andrew Fuller', forthcoming in a *festschrift* for Allison A. Trites, Macon, GA: Mercer University Press.

Sidgwick, Henry, *Lectures on the Ethics of T. H. Green, Mr. Herbert Spencer, and J. Martineau*, London: Macmillan, 1902.

Smart, Barry, *Postmodernity*, London: Routledge, 1993.

Smart, Ninian, *The Science of Religion and the Sociology of Knowledge: Some Methodological Questions*, Princeton: Princeton University Press, 1973.

Smith, Huston, 'Postmodernism's impact on the study of religion', *Journal of the American Academy of Religion*, LVIII no. 4, Winter 1990, 653–70.

Smith, John, *Select Discourses*, Cambridge: CUP, 1859.

Smith, R. Gregor, *The Free Man*, London: Collins, 1969.

—— *The Doctrine of God*, London: Collins, 1970.

Smith, William Robertson, *Lectures and Essays*, ed. J. S. Black and G. Crystal, London: Adam & Charles Black, 1912.

Snaith, Norman H., 'God: transcendent and immanent', *The Expository Times*, LXVIII, 1956, 68–71.

Sophrony, Archimandrite, *The Undistorted Image*, London: Faith Press, 1958.

Soskice, Janet, 'Religious language', in P. L. Quinn and C. Taliaferro, eds., *A Companion to Philosophy of Religion*, Oxford: Blackwell, 1997, 197–203.

Spearritt, Placid, 'Neoplatonism', in Alan Richardson, ed., *A Dictionary of Christian Theology*, London: SCM Press, 1969.

—— 'The soul's participation in God according to Pseudo-Dionysius', *Downside Review*, 1970, 378–92.

Steadman, R. E., 'A defence of speculative philosophy', *Proceedings of the Aristotelian Society*, XXXVIII, 1938, 112–42.

Stebbing, L. Susan, Review of A. N. Whitehead, *Religion in the Making*, in *Mind*, NS XXXIX, 1930, 466–75.
—— 'The method of analysis in metaphysics', *Proceedings of the Aristotelian Society*, XXXIII, 1933, 178–97.
—— 'Logical positivism and analysis', *Proceedings of the British Academy*, 1933, 53–87.
—— 'Some puzzles about analysis', *Proceedings of the Aristotelian Society*, XXXIX, 1939, 68–84.
Sterry, P., *The Spirits Conviction of Sinne*, 1645.
Stob, Henry, *Theological Reflections*, Grand Rapids: Eerdmans, 1981.
—— 'The concept of antithesis', in P. DeKlerk and R. R. De Ridder, eds., *Perspectives on the Christian Reformed Church*, Grand Rapids: Eerdmans, 1983.
Storr, Vernon F., *The Development of English Theology in the Nineteenth Century*, London: Longmans, 1913.
Strauss, D. F., *A New Life of Jesus for the German People*, English trans., 1865.
Sutherland, Stewart R., and Roberts, T. A., *Religion, Reason and the Self: Essays in Honour of Hywel D. Lewis*, Cardiff: University of Wales Press, 1989.
Swinburne, Richard, *The Existence of God*, Oxford: Clarendon Press, 1979.
—— 'Intellectual biography', in A. G. Padgett, ed., *Reason and the Christian Religion*, Oxford: OUP, 1994.
Sykes, Stephen, 'The essence of Christianity', *Religious Studies*, VI, 1971, 291–305.
—— 'The strange persistence of kenotic christology', in A. Kee and E. T. Long, eds., *Being and Truth: Essays in Honour of John Macquarrie*, London: SCM Press, 1986.
—— 'Faith', in G. Wainwright, ed., *Keeping the Faith*, Philadelphia: Fortress Press, and Allison Park, PA: Pickwick Publications, 1988.
Taylor, A. E., Review of J. M. E. McTaggart, *Some Dogmas of Religion*, in *Philosophical Review*, XV, 1906, 414–24.
—— 'The freedom of man', in J. H. Muirhead, ed., *Contemporary British Philosophy*, 2nd ser. (1925), London: Allen & Unwin, 2nd impression, 1953.
—— *The Faith of a Moralist*, Series II, London: Macmillan, 1930.
—— *Philosophical Studies*, London: Macmillan, 1934.
—— *Does God Exist?* (1945), London: Collins Fontana, 1961.
Taylor, Charles, 'Rorty in the epistemological tradition', in Alan Malachowski, ed., *Reading Rorty*, Oxford: Blackwell, 1990.
Taylor, Mark C., 'The politics of Theo–ry', *Journal of the American Academy of Religion*, LIX, 1991, 1–37.
Taylor, Vincent, 'Religious certainty', *Expository Times*, LXXII, 1960, 15–18, 49–52.

Temple, William, *Christus Veritas: An Essay*, London: Macmillan, 1930.
—— *Nature, Man and God*, London: Macmillan, 1934.
Tennant, F. R., *The Origin and Propagation of Sin*, Cambridge: CUP, 2nd edn. 1906.
—— *Philosophical Theology*, Cambridge: CUP, 1928.
—— *The Nature of Belief*, London: Centenary Press, 1943.
Thomas, J. Heywood, *Subjectivity and Paradox*, Oxford: Blackwell, 1957.
—— *Paul Tillich: An Appraisal*, London: SCM Press, 1963.
—— 'The transcendence of God', *London Quarterly and Holborn Review*, July 1964, 184–9.
—— 'Religious language as symbolism', *Religious Studies*, I, October 1965, 89–93.
Tilley, Terrence W. et al., *Postmodern Theologies: The Challenge of Religious Diversity*, Maryknoll, NY: Orbis Books, 1996.
Tillich, Paul, *The New Being*, New York: Charles Scribner's, 1955.
—— *Systematic Theology*, Chicago: University of Chicago Press, 1957.
Torrance, Thomas F., *Calvin's Doctrine of Man*, London: Lutterworth, 1949.
—— *Theology in Reconstruction*, London: SCM Press, 1965.
—— *Theological Science*, London: OUP, 1969.
—— 'The problem of natural theology in the thought of Karl Barth', *Religious Studies*, VI no. 2, June 1970, 121–35.
—— *God and Rationality*, London: OUP, 1971.
—— *Transformation and Convergence in the Frame of Knowledge*, Grand Rapids: Eerdmans, 1984.
—— *Scottish Theology from John Knox to John McLeod Campbell*, Edinburgh: T. & T. Clark, 1996.
Torrance, T. F., trans. and ed., *The School of Faith: The Catechisms of the Reformed Church*, London: James Clarke, 1959.
Toulmin, Stephen, *An Examination of the Place of Reason in Ethics*, Cambridge: CUP, 1960.
Trethowan, Illtyd, 'On Professor Antony Flew's *God and Philosophy*', *Downside Review*, LXXXVII, January 1970, 1–13.
Trigg, Roger, *Rationality and Religion, Does Faith Need Reason?*, Oxford: Blackwell, 1998.
Trueblood, D. Elton, *The Trustworthiness of Religious Experience*, London: Allen & Unwin, 1939.
Urmson, J. O., *Philosophical Analysis: Its Development between the Two World Wars*, Oxford: Clarendon Press, 1956.
Vahanian, Gabriel, *Wait without Idols*, New York: Braziller, 1964.
Van Buren, Paul, *The Secular Meaning of the Gospel*, Harmondsworth: Penguin, 1968.
Van den Hoek, A., *Clement of Alexandria and his Use of Philo in the Stromateis*, Leiden: E. J. Brill, 1988.

Van Til, Cornelius, *The Defense of the Faith*, Philadelphia: Presbyterian and Reformed Publishing Co., 1955.

—— *A Christian Theory of Knowledge*, Grand Rapids: Baker Book House, 1969.

—— 'My credo', in E. R. Geehan, ed., *Jerusalem and Athens*, Grand Rapids: Baker Book House, 1971.

Vesey, G. N., *Talk of God*, London: Macmillan, 1969.

Vidler, A. R., ed., *Soundings: Essays concerning Christian Understanding*, Cambridge: CUP, 1963.

Vos, Arvin, *Aquinas, Calvin, and Contemporary Protestant Thought: A Critique of Protestant Views on the Thought of Thomas Aquinas*, Washington, DC: Christian College Consortium, 1985.

Vriezen, T. C., 'La Création de l'homme d'apres l'image de Dieu', *OTS*, II, 1943.

Wagner, Walter H., 'Toward understanding Justin Martyr', *Cithara: Studies in the Judeo-Christian Tradition*, XXXIV no. 2, 1995, 3–26.

—— 'Clement of Alexandria's self-understanding', *Cithara*, XXXVI no. 1, January 1996, 5–21.

Wainwright, Geoffrey, ed., *Keeping the Faith: Essays to Mark the Centenary of Lux Mundi*, Philadelphia: Fortress Press, and Allison Park, PA: Pickwick Publications, 1988.

—— *Methodists in Dialog*, Nashville: Kingswood Books, 1995.

Wainwright, William J., 'Christianity', in P. L. Quinn and C. Taliaferro, eds., *A Companion to Philosophy of Religion*, Oxford: Blackwell, 1997.

Waismann, F., 'Notes on talks with Wittgenstein', trans. Max Black, *Philosophical Review*, LXXIV, 1965, 12–16.

Ware, Timothy, *The Orthodox Church*, Harmondsworth: Penguin, rev. edn. 1984.

Warfield, B. B., 'Apologetics', in *The New Schaff–Herzog Encyclopedia of Religious Knowledge*, New York: Funk & Wagnells, 1908.

—— *Calvin and Augustine*, Philadelphia: Presbyterian and Reformed Publishing Co., 1956.

—— *Inspiration and Authority*, Philadelphia: Presbyterian and Reformed Publishing Co., 1948.

—— *Biblical and Theological Studies*, ed. Samuel G. Craig, Philadelphia: Presbyterian and Reformed Publishing Co., 1952.

—— 'What is Calvinism?', in John E. Meeter, ed., *Selected Shorter Writings of Benjamin B. Warfield*, Nutley, NJ: Presbyterian and Reformed Publishing Company, 2 vols. 1970.

Watson, Gordon, 'Karl Barth and St. Anselm's theological programme', *Scottish Journal of Theology*, XXX no. 1, 1977, 31–45.

Watson, Philip S., *Let God be God: An Interpretation of the Theology of Martin Luther*, London: Epworth Press, 1947.

Watson, Thomas, *A Body of Divinity* (1692), London: The Banner of Truth Trust, 1975.

Watts, Craig M., 'The humanity of Jesus in Justin Martyr's soteriology', *Evangelical Quarterly*, LVI, 1984, 21–33.

Weaver, Gilbert B., 'Gordon Clark: Christian apologist', in Ronald H. Nash, ed., *The Philosophy of Gordon H. Clark*, Philadelphia: Presbyterian and Reformed Publishing Co., 1968.

Webb, C. C. J., *Problems in the Relations of God and Man*, London: Nisbet, 1911.

—— *Studies in the History of Natural Theology*, Oxford: Clarendon Press, 1915.

—— *Divine Personality and Human Life*, London: Allen & Unwin, 1920.

—— *A Century of Anglican Theology and Other Lectures*, Oxford: Blackwell, 1923.

—— *Pascal's Philosophy of Religion*, Oxford: Clarendon Press, 1929.

—— *The Contribution of Christianity to Ethics*, Calcutta: University of Calcutta Press, 1932.

—— *A Study of Religious Thought in England from 1850*, Oxford: Clarendon Press, 1933.

—— *Religious Experience*, London: OUP, [1945].

Wells, David F., ed., *Reformed Theology in America: A History of its Modern Development*, Grand Rapids: Eerdmans, 1985.

Werline, Rodney, 'The transformation of Pauline arguments in Justin Martyr's *Dialogue with Trypho*', *Harvard Theological Review*, XCII no. 1, January 1999, 79–93.

West, David, *An Introduction to Continental Philosophy*, London: Polity Press, 1996.

Westphal, Merold, *Kierkegaard's Critique of Religion and Society* (1987), University Park, PA: Pennsylvania State University Press, 1991.

Whale, John S., *Christian Doctrine*, London: Collins Fontana, 1958.

—— *The Protestant Tradition: An Essay in Interpretation*, Cambridge: CUP, 1960.

Whichcote, Benjamin, *Moral and Religious Aphorisms: Collected from the Manuscript papers of the Reverend and Learned Doctor Whichcote*, London: Samuel Salter, 1753.

White, A. R., *G. E. Moore: A Critical Appraisal*, Oxford: Blackwell, 1958.

Whitehead, A. N., *Process and Reality* (1929), New York: Harper, 1960.

—— *Adventures of Ideas*, Cambridge: CUP, 1935.

—— *Science and the Modern World*, Cambridge: CUP, 1936.

Whitehouse, W. A., *Christian Faith and the Scientific Attitude*, Edinburgh: Oliver & Boyd, 1952.

—— 'The modern discussion of eschatology', in *Eschatology: Four Papers read to the Society for the Study of Theology*, Edinburgh: Oliver and Boyd, 1953.

Widdicombe, Peter, 'Justin Martyr and the Fatherhood of God', *Laval Théologique et Philosophique*, LIV no. 1, 1998, 109–26.
Wiles, Maurice, *The Christian Fathers*, London: SCM Press, 1966.
—— *The Remaking of Christian Doctrine*, London: SCM Press, 1974.
—— *Christian Believing: The Nature of the Christian Faith and its Expression in Holy Scripture and Creeds*, London: SPCK, 1976.
—— *God's Action in the World*, London: SCM Press, 1986.
—— 'The reasonableness of Christianity', in W. J. Abraham and S. Holtzer, eds., *The Rationality of Religious Belief: Essays in Honour of Basil Mitchell*, Oxford: Clarendon Press, 1987.
—— 'Belief, openness and religious commitment', *Theology*, CI, May–June 1998, 163–71.
Wilson, J. Cook, *Statement and Inference*, Oxford: Clarendon Press, 1926.
Wisdom, John, 'Logical constructions', a series, *Mind*, 1931–3.
—— 'Is analysis a useful method in philosophy?', *Proceedings of the Aristotelian Society, Supplementary Volume*, XIII, 1934, 65–89.
—— 'Metaphysics and verification', *Mind*, XLVII, 1938, 452–98.
—— 'Gods', reprinted in A. G. N. Flew and A. MacIntyre, eds., *New Essays in Philosophical Theology*, London: SCM Press, 1955.
Wittgenstein, Ludwig, *Tractatus Logico-Philosophicus* (1922), London: Routledge & Kegan Paul, 1981.
—— *Philosophical Investigations*, Oxford: Blackwell, 2nd edn. 1958.
—— *Lectures and Conversations on Aesthetics, Psychology and Religious Belief*, ed. Cyril Barrett, Oxford: Blackwell, 1966.
—— *On Certainty*, eds. G. E. M. Anscombe and G. H. Von Wright; trans. Anscombe and D. Paul, Oxford: Blackwell, 1969.
—— *Zettel* (1967), ed. G. E. M. Anscombe and G. H. Von Wright, Oxford: Blackwell, 1981.
—— *Culture and Value*, ed. Von Wright; trans Peter Winch, Oxford: Blackwell, 1980.
Wollheim, Richard, *Art and its Objects*, Harmondsworth: Penguin, 1970.
Wolters, Albert, 'Dutch neo-Calvinism: worldview, philosophy and rationality', in H. Hart et al., eds., *Rationality in the Calvinian Tradition*, Lanham, MD: University Press of America, 1983.
Wolterstorff, Nicholas, *Reason within the Bounds of Religion*, Grand Rapids: Eerdmans, 1976.
—— 'Thomas Reid on rationality', in H. Hart et al., eds., *Rationality in the Calvinian Tradition*, Lanham, MD: University Press of America, 1983.
—— 'The Reformed tradition', in P. L. Quinn and C. Taliaferro, eds., *A Companion to Philosophy of Religion*, Oxford: Blackwell, 1997.
Woods, G. F., *Theological Explanation*, London: Nisbet, 1958.
—— 'The idea of the transcendent', in A. R. Vidler, ed., *Soundings*, Cambridge: CUP, 1963.

Yates, Arthur S., *The Doctrine of Assurance with Special Reference to John Wesley*, London: Epworth Press, 1952.
Young, Norman, 'Bultmann's view of history', *Church Quarterly Review*, 165, 1964, 413–28.
Zuurdeeg, W. F., *An Analytical Philosophy of Religion*, London: Allen & Unwin, 1959.

Index of Persons

Select Index of Subjects